BANKING MARKETS
and
FINANCIAL INSTITUTIONS

THE IRWIN SERIES IN FINANCE

EDITORS

Myron J. Gordon
University of Toronto

Robert W. Johnson
Purdue University

BANKING MARKETS
and
FINANCIAL INSTITUTIONS

Edited by

THOMAS G. GIES, Ph.D.
Professor of Finance
Graduate School of Business Administration
University of Michigan

and

VINCENT P. APILADO, Ph.D.
Assistant Professor of Finance
College of Business Administration
Arizona State University

1971

Richard D. Irwin, Inc. HOMEWOOD, ILLINOIS 60430
IRWIN-DORSEY LIMITED, GEORGETOWN, ONTARIO

First Printing, March, 1971
Second Printing, January, 1972

Library of Congress Catalog Card No. 76–149901

Printed in the United States of America

To Thelma and Anne

PREFACE

Several circumstances point to the need for this collection of essays in monetary management. The first is the evolutionary process of economic and business education. The teaching of banking and monetary finance is becoming more micro-oriented, following 30 years of almost exclusively Keynesian macro-orientation. Second, derivation and implementation of national economic policy has placed increased emphasis on sophisticated monetary goals. Third, nonbank financial institutions, such as savings associations and insurance companies, have pressed for and received new powers which are aimed explicitly at strengthening their competitive position vis-à-vis that of banks. This has implications for both public and private policymaking. Fourth, the greater concern among bankers for profit has led to recasting of their stodgy, conservative posture of prior years. Fifth, cyclical "disintermediation" (i.e., funds bypassing both banks and nonbanks) has focused attention on competition among financial intermediaries by revealing their differential ability to accommodate to shifting interest rate levels and credit conditions.

The editors have chosen material appropriate to both academic and managerial audiences. The volume's organization and coverage should make it a useful supplement in courses in the management of financial institutions, money and banking, and financial economics. Further, our choice of readings has been influenced by the urgent need of practicing professionals for a systematic analysis of the operating areas where managerial decisions must be made.

February, 1971

THOMAS G. GIES
VINCENT P. APILADO

TABLE OF CONTENTS

SECTION ONE
Structure and Competition in Banking

Chapter I
DIMENSIONS IN BANKING STRUCTURE

I. A Conceptual Optimal Banking Structure for the United States[*]

Larry R. Mote

What is the "optimal" banking structure? What objectives should it fulfill? This article seeks to answer these questions. Further, the combination of this article with the following two by Mitchell and Greenbaum provide a compact summary of the most significant changes which have occurred in the banking system over the past twenty-five years and a critique of related empirical research.

Both efficiency and market power have received a great deal of attention in the burgeoning literature on banking structure. Unfortunately, knowledge of the manner in which costs vary with size or the number of banking offices or of the effect of numbers and size inequality on the degree of independence shown by banks in their pricing policies will be of little practical use in the formulation of regulatory policy until it can be brought into relationship with a more specific

statement of what it is that we are after, namely, an optimal banking structure. Among those who have kept this question on the agenda, none has been more insistent and original than Professor Stuart Greenbaum. Emphasizing structure as a means to performance, rather than an end in itself, Greenbaum has called for a re-examination of the facile assumption that stimulation of competition should be the primary goal of public policy toward the banking structure.[1] More recently, he has posed the interesting question of the manner in which bank structure policy and monetary policy are interrelated and has examined the conditions under which the goals of each might simultaneously be realized.[2] In fact, so clearly and thor-

[*]From Proceedings of a *Conference on Bank Structure and Competition*, 1969. Reprinted by permission of the publisher, the Federal Reserve Bank of Chicago.

[1]Stuart I. Greenbaum, "Competition and Efficiency in the Banking System—Empirical Research and its Policy Implications," *Journal of Political Economy*, LXXV (August, 1967, Pt. 2), pp. 461–79. (Article is included in this text.)

[2]Stuart I. Greenbaum, "On Making Banking Structure Policy and Monetary Policy Jointly," unpublished paper, October 24, 1968.

oughly has Professor Greenbaum discussed the problems involved in the concept of an optimal banking structure that no new treatment can fairly omit a dozen or so citations of his two seminal papers on the subject.

EARLIER STUDIES

On the other hand, the field is not the virgin territory that the paucity of clearly documented conclusions regarding the nature of an optimal banking structure would suggest. Clearly, such vigorous proponents of branch banking as Chapman and Westerfield in their important book of 1942 had some fairly definite ideas as to the broad outlines of a desirable banking structure.[3] Similarly, officials of the several associations of independent bankers have not been reticent in their advocacy of an atomized banking structure in which local banking markets are treated as the private preserves of those fortunate enough to have won a franchise in the form of a charter to do business.

Professor Benjamin Beckhart, still writing under the influence of the Great Depression, several years ago outlined an ideal financial system whose hallmarks were stability and solvency, in contrast to the recent emphasis on competition, risktaking, and performance.[4] Perhaps a reading of Professor Beckhart's basically conservative proposals would serve as a useful counterweight, in this period of heady adventures in expanding the scope of the banking business, to the most recent manifestations of the recurrent notion that the stock market always goes up.

As Hall and Phillips indicated in their study of the administration of the Bank Merger Act of 1960,[5] judgments regarding at least the broad characteristics of some concept of what the optimal banking structure would be are concealed in the decisions of the regulatory agencies. Though finding more agreement than disagreement among the agencies—a judgment that some would say calls for revision in the light of recent developments —Hall and Phillips were nevertheless able to discern three somewhat distinct, if vague and overlapping, philosophies. That of the Comptroller of the Currency they identified as the "balanced banking structure doctrine," that of the FDIC as the "strengthening of competition doctrine," and that of the Board of Governors as the "variety of banking services doctrine." What the three philosophies have in common is their emphasis on "the service advantages of large banks." Their differences may be stated, in somewhat simplified and exaggerated form, as follows: the Comptroller has favored increasing the variation in bank size, the FDIC decreasing it, while the Board has placed more emphasis on the "types of services offered" and less on "bank size *per se.*"[6] Since Hall and Phillips' study was completed, of course, additional details of the agencies' conceptions of the optimal banking structure have been made public.[7]

However, so far as I am aware, the first use of the term "optimum banking structure" as such, as opposed to discussions of its content, was in Roland Robinson's 1963 paper on unit banking in the

---

[3]John M. Chapman and Ray B. Westerfield, *Branch Banking* (New York: Harper and Brothers, 1942).

[4]Benjamin Haggot Beckhart, "Criteria of a Well-functioning Financial System," in *Readings in Financial Institutions,* ed. by Marshall D. Ketchum and Leon T. Kendall (Boston: Houghton Mifflin Co., 1965), pp. 79–103.

[5]George R. Hall and Charles F. Phillips, Jr., *Bank Mergers and the Regulatory Agencies: Application of the Bank Merger Act of 1960* (Washington: U. S. Board of Governors of the Federal Reserve System, 1964).

[6]*Ibid.,* p. 63.

[7]See, for example, George W. Mitchell, "Our Changing Banking Structure," remarks at the Annual Convention of the Maine Bankers Association, Bretton Woods, New Hampshire, June 14, 1968; and "A Statement of Policy," Comptroller of the Currency, *Annual Report, 1964,* (Washington: U. S. Government Printing Office, 1965), pp. 1–6.

United States.[8] But whether the terminology is new or old is unimportant; the point is that at least some vague conception of an optimal banking structure has been around for a long time.

To be sure, most of the references to it have been incidental to the investigation of a particular problem of public policy. For example, the logic of Professor Jacobs' 1964 article on the framework of commercial bank regulation inevitably led to the consideration of the properties of various alternative banking structures and the criteria for choosing between them.[9] The same logical imperative, albeit leading to quite different conclusions, is evident in Professor Clifton H. Kreps' 1966 critique of current banking regulation.[10] Even studies that have been addressed to narrower questions, such as the relationship of some aspects of bank structure to banking performance, have often yielded judgments regarding the nature of the optimal banking structure. Thus, Shull and Horvitz, in evaluating the relationship between branch banking, on the one hand, and the structure of local banking markets and banking performance, on the other, could hardly avoid rendering some verdict regarding a very fundamental aspect of banking structure.[11]

What is perhaps most disappointing is that the very bodies that have been given the broad charge of looking at the banking structure as an organic whole and coming up with an improved design have construed their assignments quite narrowly. For example, it has been a frequent occurrence in recent years for state legislatures, state banking commissions, or private banking associations to appoint study groups to examine the structure and functioning of state banking systems and make recommendations for their improvement. The final reports of many of these study groups have been made available to the public.[12] In those states in which the actual investigations have been delegated to disinterested scholars, the recommendations have almost invariably been stronger and more thoroughgoing than in those in which bankers and businessmen have played the major role.[13] Where the task of investigation has been separated from the formulation of final recommendations, the conclusions of the professional staff members have often been discarded in favor of proposals less disruptive of existing institutions. Even when study commissions have been given the more comprehensive charge of investigating the entire financial system of the United States, as was true in the case of the privately supported Commission on Money and Credit, the resulting staff

[8]Roland I. Robinson, "Unit Banking Evaluated," in *Banking and Monetary Studies*, ed. by Deane Carson (Homewood, Illinois: Richard D. Irwin, Inc., 1963), pp. 291–303.

[9]Donald Jacobs, "The Framework of Commercial Bank Regulation: An Appraisal," *National Banking Review*, I (March, 1964), pp. 343-57.

[10]Clifton H. Kreps, Jr., "Modernizing Banking Regulation," *Law and Contemporary Problems*, XXXI (Autumn, 1966), pp. 648–72.

[11]Bernard Shull and Paul Horvitz, "Branch Banking and the Structure of Competition," *National Banking Review*, I (March, 1964), 301–41, and "The Impact of Branch Banking on Bank Performance," *National Banking Review*, II (December, 1964), pp. 143-88.

[12]The following list is anything but exhaustive, but is suggestive of the large number of studies that have been commissioned: Edward E. Edwards and Gerald C. Fischer, *Banking Structure in Indiana with Recommendations for Change* (Bloomington: Foundation for Economic and Business Studies, 1968); Carter H. Golembe Associates, Inc., *Report on the Michigan Banking Structure*, Prepared for the Joint Senate-House Bank Study Committee of the Michigan Legislature (Washington, 1969); Robert F. Lanzillotti, *Banking Structure in Michigan*, 1945–1963 (East Lansing: Bureau of Business and Economic Research, Michigan State University, 1966)—a study financed by the Bank Structure Committee of the Michigan Bankers Association; and Marcus Nadler, *et al.*, *The Banking Situation in New York State* (New York: New York State Bankers Association, 1956).

[13]An exception would be the recommendation of Edwards and Fischer that some geographic restrictions on branching be retained in Indiana "[i]n order to maintain local ownership of Indiana banks and to encourage evolutionary rather than drastic change in banking structure . . .", (*Banking Structure*, p. 7).

studies and recommendations have generally been much less sweeping and innovative than one might expect or hope.[14] The narrowness typical of the individual studies is perhaps an unavoidable accompaniment of the division of labor required to fulfill the Commission's assigned task within the period of a relatively few years. But this does not explain the basic timidity of the Commission's conclusions and recommendations, which left unchallenged the system of dual chartering, the time-honored and apparently unassailable prohibition of interest on demand deposits, and, with one rather mild exception, the deference of federal banking policy to state legislation in the area of branch banking.[15] One obvious explanation is the private sponsorship of the CMC and the consequent heavy representation of the various financial industries on the Commission, which essentially excluded the possibility of making recommendations that seriously affected the interests of those industries. One is reminded to some extent of the 1955 *Report of the Attorney General's National Committee to Study the Antitrust Laws,* which, despite the distinguished credentials of the Committee's members, is a much less useful document that it might have been. The quest for unanimity resulted in a relatively innocuous report whose most pregnant passages are confined to footnotes recording the views of dissident committee members unwilling to endorse the text approved by the majority.[16]

CRITERIA OF OPTIMALITY

And yet, for one not predisposed toward "devil theories" of retardation in the field of economic theory and policy, it is difficult to accept the notion that some sort of conspiracy of vested interests has precluded the development of a coherent outline of an optimal banking structure. One plausible alternative explanation is the widespread disagreement that still exists, among agency economists and academic economists alike, concerning the ultimate ends of public policy toward the banking structure. Although the very expression "optimal banking structure" suggests the prior specification of that which is to be optimized, an explicit statement of what it is is difficult to find. Presumably, some sort of social welfare function is implied. The major problem is that this welfare function—which may be likened to an enormous jigsaw puzzle—has never been put together. Every researcher in the area of public policy toward the banking structure and every official charged with the implementation of that policy carries several pieces of the puzzle around with him in the course of his duties. Occasionally a few of them are exposed to public view; but not only does no one seem to have all the pieces of the puzzle, the pieces carried around by different people would not fit together even if one were to assemble them at one time and place.

The difficulty of assembling the puzzle is compounded by the presence of certain circumlocutions in the public discussion of issues related to the banking structure. It often happens that value judgments which are perfectly legitimate to make, but which enjoy less than uni-

---

[14]For an interesting critique of the Report of the Commission on Money and Credit and a comparison of the studies produced under its auspices with those written under the sponsorship of the 1910 National Monetary Commission, see Milton Friedman, "The Report of the Commission on Money and Credit: An Essay in Petitio Principii," *American Economic Review,* LII (May, 1962), pp. 291–302.

[15]See *Money and Credit,* Report of the Commission on Money and Credit (Englewood Cliffs, N. J.: Prentice-Hall, Inc., 1961), pp. 160, 167, and 196.

[16]See Edward S. Mason's fair but unflinching

assessment of what the committee did and did not accomplish, "Market Power and Business Conduct: Some Comments on the Report of the Attorney General's Committee on Antitrust Policy," *American Economic Review,* XLVI (May, 1956), pp. 471–81.

versal acceptance, are deliberately buried under arguments of a quite different character. This has most frequently been true of arguments directed toward the maintenance of regulatory provisions that protect small banks from the rigors of competition. By identifying the maintenance of large numbers with the existence of effective competition, the proponents of such measures have obtained the sympathy of many who might be quite hostile toward such measures if they were presented in a more straightforward manner. In practice, of course, it is often difficult to distinguish between the protection of competitors and the preservation of competition; this problem is often present in merger cases. But there are many other cases in which the distinction between competition and protection is clearcut and in which, nevertheless, one may opt for protection. For example, it might be desired, because of a distrust of bigness for its own sake, or a fear of the possible political dangers of excessive concentrations of wealth, to impose progressively stricter restraints on external growth—i.e., growth by acquisitions —beyond some critical minimum level. Whether this would best be accomplished through the application of existing laws, as seems to have been the case on certain occasions in the past under Section 7 of the Clayton Act, or whether, as Sam Peltzman argued recently in a letter to the *Wall Street Journal*,[17] it should be the subject of separate legislation is a matter best made clear at the outset. Certainly, as M. A. Adelman,[18] Robert Bork,[19] and Yale Brozen,[20] and other critics of the Justice Department have

long stressed, there is much to be said for keeping separate public policies aimed at preserving competition from those whose major purpose is to protect small business.

But even if, for the sake of argument, one were to ignore the fact that some may consider the means in terms of a continuing competitive process to be of as much importance as the ends in terms of banking performance,[21] there would still remain the problem of specifying just what these desired ends are. Professor Greenbaum has taken us part of the way, in that he has provided a list of desirable performance characteristics which should win fairly broad acceptance.[22] They can be described, very briefly, as:

1. Productive efficiency
2. Allocative neutrality
3. Absence of exploitation of consumers or suppliers of inputs
4. Responsivity to changes in technol-

[17]April 14, 1969.

[18]"The Antimerger Act: 1950–1960," *American Economic Review*, LI (May, 1961), pp. 236–44.

[19]R. H. Bork and W. S. Bowman, "The Crisis in Antitrust," *Columbia Law Review*, LXV (March, 1965), pp. 363–76.

[20]"Competition, Efficiency, and Antitrust" (paper delivered at the Business Economists' Conference, University of Chicago, May 1, 1969).

[21]This possibility is simply denied by many students of competition. Thus, Paul Horvitz has claimed that "competition is not an end in itself. Competition is desirable because of what it leads to; an efficient allocation of resources with production being carried on at minimum cost with minimum prices charged to consumers." (*Concentration and Competition in New England Banking*, Research Report No. 2 [Boston: Federal Reserve Bank of Boston, 1958], p. 165). More recently, William Paul Smith has stated: ". . . , I do not now think that competition *as such* matters at all in bank merger cases . . . . the principal concern in bank merger cases, and others involving structural change, should be the effect on performance." ("Measures of Competition and Convenience: Measures of What?" Federal Reserve Bank of Chicago, *Proceedings of a Conference on Bank Structure and Competition, 1967* [Chicago, 1967], pp. 4, 10). Essentially the same idea was repeated by Professor Stuart Greenbaum the following year: "I submit that what we want from the banking industry is not competition but performance" (Federal Reserve Bank of Chicago, *Proceedings of a Conference on Bank Structure and Competition, 1968.* [Chicago, 1968], p. 122).

[22]"Competition and Efficiency in the Banking System—Empirical Research and its Policy Implications," *Journal of Political Economy*, LXXV (August, 1967, Pt. 2), p. 462. (Article is included in this text.)

ogy and in the demand for banking services.

The precise meanings to be attached to these criteria are elaborated in more detail in Greenbaum's article, but they accord rather closely with the intuitive meanings one would attribute to them.

Even such a simple listing of criteria as this constitutes a major advance, inasmuch as such efforts are almost wholly lacking in earlier studies of banking structure. Why this should be true of the academic literature on the subject, as opposed to the pronouncements of public officials desirous of avoiding controversy, is somewhat puzzling. But it may simply reflect the currency of the view that, with so much to be learned about specific relationships between structure and performance, discussion of the optimal banking structure was a bit premature.[23] However justified such an attitude may have been in the not-too-distant past, there appears to be a growing feeling that the time has come for a consolidation of existing knowledge, a fitting together of the bits and pieces, so to speak. Insofar as this need is met by a summary of the literature, Professors Guttentag and Herman have provided us with what has to be the authoritative work, although there are signs that it is rapidly going out of date only two short years after its initial publication.[24] It

would appear, however, that something more is called for, namely an actual description of the "optimal banking structure," given some broadly acceptable judgments regarding the desired results of such a structure and existing knowledge, limited though it be, of the relationships between structure and performance. What is proposed here is simply to sketch the procedure that one might follow in carrying out such a mandate and to attempt to anticipate some of the results.

As has already been indicated, however, any further progress toward a description of the optimal banking structure requires that one specify what it is that one wishes to optimize. Professor Greenbaum has provided us with a set of plausible and, I think, broadly acceptable, arguments of a social welfare function. What is lacking is a meaningful way of combining them so that situations which involve giving up something in terms of one citerion in order to get more of another can be evaluated and ranked in terms of their desirability relative to other situations. This is necessitated by the fact, emphasized at length by Greenbaum himself, that the existence of economies of scale in banking means that all goals cannot be attained simultaneously; rather, there is a tradeoff among goals determined by the parameters of the production function and other behavioral relationships found in banking.

In principle, at least, one could reconcile the marginal criteria of allocative efficiency with economies of scale through the introduction of public-utility rate regulation into banking. This alternative is not considered here, partly out of an unreasoning faith in free enterprise, partly because I don't think experience with Regulation Q indicates that the banking agencies are qualified to administer such regulation. Thus, it is necessary to trans-

---

[23]This seems to be what Bernard Shull had in mind at the Conference last year, when he said, in response to a question regarding the criteria applied by the Federal Reserve in deciding bank merger cases: "There's relevant economic evidence, as everybody here knows, on the relationship between numbers of banks in market areas, concentration ratios, and bank performance. There's evidence on scale economies—whether or not a bank is of adequate size to perform efficiently. It's in this frame of reference that the research has been done in the last five or six years. Surely, there's no blueprint for an optimal banking structure at this point but on these lesser questions, we do have some answers." (Federal Reserve Bank of Chicago, *Proceedings, 1968*, p. 182).
[24]Jack M. Guttentag and Edward S. Her-

man, *Banking Structure and Performance*, Institute of Finance, Bulletin No. 41/43 New York: New York University, 1967.

late Greenbaum's criteria into a meaningful optimization rule.

A promising approach is that suggested by Oliver Williamson in a recent article in the *American Economic Review*.[25] In dealing with the same type of tradeoff under discussion here, Williamson suggested that the "net social benefit" of a merger be measured by its effect on the sum of total revenue and consumer's surplus less social cost. If this quantity is increased, the merger should be permitted; if not, it is a legitimate target for antitrust. There is much to be said for utilizing some variant of this approach in deriving the characteristics of an optimal banking structure. As it stands, however, Williamson's measure is potentially inconsistent with one of Greenbaum's criteria. To the extent that the reduction in numbers required for the realization of economies of scale increases producer's surplus at the expense of consumer's surplus, a policy aimed solely at the maximization of the measure suggested by Williamson would violate the third of Greenbaum's criteria of optimality, namely the "absence of exploitation." As Williamson points out, there would be major difficulties involved in any attempt to integrate a formal distributional criterion into the administration of the antitrust laws. Yet it is quite obvious that such considerations have motivated the banking agencies on many occasions. It would be both anomalous and politically out of the question to administer policies that have very profound distributional effects as if they had none.

OUTPUT MAXIMIZATION

An alternative policy goal that encompasses, to some degree, both efficiency and distributional criteria is the maximization of output. Deferring for the mo-

ment the question of which output, which arises immediately when one considers the multiproduct nature of commercial banking, it may be of interest to examine the relationship betwen the goal of output maximization and Greenbaum's four criteria. Efficiency is taken into account in both its technological and allocational aspects in the sense that the maximization of output is incompatible with either the extremely high costs of an atomistic banking structure or with the deliberate restriction of output and elevation of price that might follow from monopoly, except in those cases where the market is extremely small. The consumer is protected from exploitation in the sense that he is confronted by a price-locational convenience package which encourages him to purchase the largest output of banking services achievable short of direct rate regulation. The criterion of "allocative neutrality" is not sufficiently well-defined to permit an assessment of its compatibility with the goal of output maximization, although it is difficult to see why there should be any major conflict. Finally, the factors conducive to "maximum responsivity to market and technological change" constitute a *terra incognita* that must be largely ignored here. Suffice it to say that the available evidence from industries other than banking does not suggest that "responsivity" in Greenbaum's sense requires any greater concentration than seems to be called for by economies of scale.[26] The major advantages of the output maximization goal, aside from its tentative—and perhaps tenuous—relationship to Greenbaum's more basic criteria, are its intuitive attractiveness and simplicity. By collapsing several competing criteria into a single unambiguous measure, it permits the analysis to be cast in terms of a relatively straightforward maximization problem. On the other hand, it is not proposed as the best of all possible guides

---

[25]Oliver Williamson, "Economies as an Antitrust Defense: The Welfare Tradeoffs," *American Economic Review*, LVIII (March, 1968), pp 18-36.

[26]For a summary of the evidence, see R. E. Johnson, "Technical Progress," *Oxford Economic Papers*, XVIII (July, 1966), pp. 158-76.

to policy, but simply as a means of unifying the discussion.

CONSTRAINTS

In view of the fact that the solution to essentially all economic problems involves optimization subject to constraints, it is rather surprising that the extant literature on the optimal banking structure has not formulated the problem in these terms or sought to specify the objective function and constraints of the programming model that is implied. In the previous section we have discussed, essentially, the appropriate "objective" to be maximized. What remains is to specify the precise form and arguments of the objective function and the nature of the constraints. Finally, a very simple example will be used to illustrate the procedure.

Perhaps the most important constraint that must be taken into consideration in designing an optimal banking structure is that which has plagued students of industrial organization for years—the real or apparent conflict between technological efficiency and the requirement of a sufficient number of competing units to assure independence of action. To be sure, the problem is better described as the consequence of the dispersion of population over a very large area and, hence, the geographical segmentation of markets for banking services. If the market for all banking services were national, for example, there would be room for about 20 banks the size of the Bank of America. Although all of the conceptual, methodological, and data problems associated with the measurement of banking costs and their relationships to bank output have not been resolved to everyone's satisfaction, every study of which I am aware has reported the existence of some economies of scale, in most cases over the full range of bank sizes studied, and at least up to some optimal scale after which costs again begin to rise. This scale, more-

over, is quite large relative to the size of most local banking markets, however defined.

It should be emphasized, of course, that these results relate to economies of plant, rather than firm size, except where the two coincide. Most, though not all, studies have indicated that the attainment of scale through combining two or more geographically separated plants into one firm—i.e., by branching—largely offsets the pure scale effect. Given the spatial distribution of demand for banking services, which, except in the case of a few very large unit banks in large cities that specialize in wholesale banking, limits the size of the individual banking office, this might seem to suggest that something like the existing wide array of bank sizes was, after all, not too far from the optimum.

Unfortunately, it is precisely in the important problem area of the relative costs of branch and unit banking that extant studies are weakest. Most have adopted one of two doubtful means of handling the problem, either the arbitrary assumption of a simple dichotomy with unit banks in one category and all banks with two or more offices in another, or a slightly more detailed classification by number of branches. None has made what would seem to be crucial distinctions regarding the character of the branches— their size, the nature of their business, their distance from the head office, etc. —which one would expect to have an important influence on costs. These observations are not meant as criticisms; the data which would allow such factors to be taken into account have not been readily available.[27] But they do point up the shaky character of the evidence on

[27]The absence of data on branch size has been remedied in part by the Federal Reserve's development of Individual Bank and Office Data, collected bi-annually since 1966. The raw material for measuring the distance of branches from the head office has long been available in the form of the branch addresses listed in *Polk's Bank Directory* and Rand McNally's *International Bankers Directory*.

this important and controversial question.

Additional confusion has resulted from the interpretation usually given to data regarding the costs of branching. The studies by Alhadeff and Powers assume, either implicitly or explicitly, that the relevant comparison is between a unit bank and a branch bank of the same size.[28] Consequently, they draw the conclusion, perfectly valid within the bounds of their conceptual framework, that expansion of output by the establishment of additional plants, as opposed to the enlargement of the scale of a single plant, involves increased costs that offset any economies due to a pure scale effect. However, as Paul Horvitz and Stuart Greenbaum have pointed out, the more relevant comparison of costs is between those of a group of unit banks and those of a branch banking system composed of an equal number of offices of the same size and character.[29] It would seem to be a rather obvious proposition—and, indeed, George Hall stated it very clearly at this Conference two years ago, only to have its import lost in the subsequent discussion, which bordered on chaos—that a unit bank is not a satisfactory substitute for a branch bank of the same size. The provision of banking facilities at a number of locations is as much a dimension of banking service as is the rate paid on savings deposits or the speed with which loan applications are processed. If this were not so it might be wise, given the findings regarding technological economies of scale, to do as George Hall suggested and replace our inefficient banking system by a single gigantic unit bank located in the center of Kansas. The satisfaction of public demand for convenience means that banking facilities must be provided at numerous locations and the appropriate question is simply whether these should be unit banks or branches of a larger institution.[30]

Among many possible reasons for questioning the significance of the reported efficiency disadvantage of branch banks is the widespread belief that large branch banks tend to be more aggressive in marketing their services, and that their higher observed costs reflect major differences in the nature and variety of services offered. And, indeed, there is substantial evidence to support this belief. Studies have indicated that branch banks have higher loan-asset ratios and a higher proportion of consumer loans, charge lower interest rates on instalment and real estate loans, and pay higher interest rates on time and savings deposits than do unit banks of similar size and/or location.[31] They provide greater mobility of funds from "surplus" to "deficit" communities.[32] Moreover, they offer a broader variety of services and provide greater convenience, in that branching results in somewhat more numerous banking facilities in moderate- and large-sized nonmetropolitan areas.[33] To be sure, a 1964 study by Jessup and Weintraub suggests that size,

[28]See David A. Alhadeff, *Monopoly and Competition in Banking* (Berkeley: University of California Press, 1954), p. 83, and John Powers, "The Existence of Economies of Structure and of Economies of Scale in Commercial Banking," Staff Memorandum, Federal Reserve Bank of Chicago, January 1967, p. 33.

[29]See Stuart Greenbaum, "A Study of Bank Costs," *National Banking Review*, IV (June, 1967), 428-33, and Paul Horvitz, "Economies of Scale in Banking," in *Private Financial Institutions*, Commission on Money and Credit, Supporting Papers (Englewood Cliffs: Prentice-Hall, Inc., 1963), p. 37. In contrast to Greenbaum's finding of cost savings from integrating unit banks into a branch system, Horvitz reported that "four $15 million unit banks can be operated at lower cost than a $60 million branch bank."

[30]Some of the difficulties involved in measuring the economies or diseconomies of branching have been discussed by Guttentag and Herman (*Banking Structure and Performance*, pp. 193-96).

[31]Horvitz and Shull, "Impact of Branch Banking," p. 176.

[32]See Verle B. Johnston, "Comparative Performance of Unit and Branch Banks," Federal Reserve Bank of Chicago, *Proceedings of a Conference on Bank Structure and Competition, 1967* (Chicago, 1967), pp. 13–14.

[33]Horvitz and Shull, p. 147.

rather than type of organization, is the major factor determining the variety of products offered by a bank.[34] However, in all but the largest cities, large size can be attained only through branching.

Yet there remains the problem of reconciling these findings with respect to economies of scale and the advantages of branching, which point unmistakeably in the direction of a banking structure comprised of fewer and larger banking firms, with the widely shared desire to maintain an adequate number of independent alternatives in local banking markets. The most recent studies have, if anything, tended to confirm Franklin Edwards' pioneering but controversial finding of a small but statistically significant association between concentration in local banking markets and the level of interest rates charged by banks.[35] After Theodore Flechsig's study for the Board of Governors, which seemed to cast doubt on certain aspects of Edwards' methodology and essentially all of his results[36] and Almarin Phillips' study of one- and two-bank towns in Minnesota,[37] which failed to reveal any strong evidence of a relationship between structure and performance, a long and growing list of studies have appeared which seem to indicate, within the limitations of available data

and analysis, that there is indeed such a relationship. Among the more recent studies one may mention Almarin Phillips' study of the relationship between concentration and business loan rates in major metropolitan areas,[38] Richard Aspinwall's finding of a significant relationship between concentration in commercial banking and interest rates on conventional mortgages,[39] and Bell and Murphy's recent and highly sophisticated analysis of the relationship between concentration and service charges on regular checking accounts.[40] A recent study that failed to find any evidence of a relationship between structure and performance is Charles Taylor's study of competition and interest rates on loans in the Sixth Federal Reserve District.[41] Nevertheless, until the reported findings of a significant relationship between concentration and the prices of banking services can be shown to be incorrect, either through a demonstration of faulty methodology or inadequate data used by the investigators or through the presentation of a preponderance of new evidence to the contrary, it would appear that the presumption in favor of maintaining a banking structure conducive to competition cannot be dismissed lightly, even by those who place their entire emphasis on performance.

THE OPTIMIZATION PROBLEM

The situation faced by the policymaker concerned with achieving the optimal

---

[34]Robert Weintraub and Paul Jessup, *A Study of Selected Banking Services by Bank Size, Structure, and Location.* U. S. Cong., House, Committee on Banking and Currency, Committee Print, 88th Cong., 2nd Sess., 1964.

[35]"Concentration in Banking and Its Effects on Business Loan Rates," *Review of Economics and Statistics*, XLVI (August, 1964), pp. 294–300.

[36]Theodore G. Flechsig, *Banking Market Structure and Performance in Metropolitan Areas: A Statistical Study of Factors Affecting Rates on Bank Loans* (Washington: U. S. Board of Governors of the Federal Reserve System, 1965).

[37]Almarin Phillips, "Relations Between Market Structure and Performance for Small Banks in Minnesota Towns," (unpublished paper, April 1, 1963). Actually, the evidence presented in this paper appears to be more consistent with the viewpoint that there is such a relationship, but it has been widely interpreted as supporting the opposite conclusion.

[38]Almarin Phillips, "Evidence on Concentration in Banking Markets and Interest Rates," *Federal Reserve Bulletin*, LIII (June, 1967), pp. 916–26.

[39]Richard Aspinwall, "Market Structure and Commercial Bank Mortgage Rates," (unpublished paper, October, 1968).

[40]Frederick W. Bell and Neil B. Murphy, "Impact of Market Structure on the Price of A Commercial Banking Service," *Review of Economics and Statistics*, LI (May, 1969), pp. 210–13.

[41]Charles T. Taylor, "Average Interest Charges, the Loan Mix, and Measures of Competition: Sixth Federal Reserve District Experience," *Journal of Finance*, XXIII (December, 1968), pp. 793–804.

banking structure may be illustrated by a simple—perhaps simpleminded—example. Assume, to begin with, that only one local banking market is involved. There is only one banking product—say, consumer loans—and the total market demand for such loans, measured in physical terms, is given by the following function of price, r, and banking offices, M:

$$Q = g - hr + kM \qquad h, k > O \quad (1)$$

The inclusion of the number of banking offices in the demand function takes account of the importance of convenience to consumers of banking services and makes explicit the fact that some elements of banking structure themselves constitute part of the terms on which banking services are offered.

In this simple version of the problem, it is assumed that all banks in the market are of the same size measured in terms of output, q, and that branch banks are yet to be invented—i.e., there are only unit banks, and the number of banks, N, equals the number of offices, M.

The constant elasticity-type of cost function found by Benston and Bell and Murphy is simply approximated by a quadratic function of the following form:

$$C = bq - aq^2 \qquad b, a > O \quad (2)$$

Dividing through by q to obtain average cost, one gets

$$\frac{C}{q} = b - aq \quad (3)$$

On the assumption that pure competition or some close approximation to it prevailed, the rate of interest on consumer instalment loans would equal average cost, $\frac{C}{q}$, also expressed as an annual rate:

$$r = \frac{C}{q} = b - aq \quad (4)$$

Price is equated to average cost rather than marginal cost for the simple reason that the latter would mean sales at a loss, given a long-run average cost curve that slopes downward throughout the relevant range. In other words, it is assumed that each bank's long-run average cost curve is tangent to its sales curve, as in the familiar Chamberlinian tangency solution, but that neither is horizontal.

It is further assumed that, as the number of sellers grows smaller, tacit collusion develops which raises the rate charged on consumer loans above the average cost of producing them. With only one seller the excess over average cost will be

$$e = d - b + aQ \quad (5)$$

where d is the profit-maximizing price and b-aQ is the average cost of the monopolist producing for the whole market. As additional banks enter the market, tacit collusion is made more difficult, and the excess over average cost declines according to, say, the following law:

$$r - \frac{C}{q} = \frac{e}{N} \quad (6)$$

where N is the number of banks. Clearly, as N tends to infinity, the deviation of price from average cost approaches zero.

But this does not mean that the interest rate charged declines monotonically as additional banks enter the market. Under the above assumptions, total market output, Q, is shared equally among the N banks. This means that the size of each bank, q, varies inversely with the number of banks in the market:

$$q = \frac{Q}{N} \quad (7)$$

Given the shape of the cost function, average cost varies directly with N.

Putting all of these relationships together, one finds that the rate on consumer loans is equal to the average cost of production plus a monopoly revenue that declines with the number of banks:

$$r = b - aq + \frac{e}{N} \quad (8)$$

Substituting for q, one obtains r as a function of Q and N:

$$r = b - a\left(\frac{Q}{N}\right) + \frac{e}{N} \quad (9)$$

Upon substitution into the demand equation one obtains the following expression:

$$Q = g - h \left(b - a \frac{Q}{N} \right) + \frac{he}{N} + kN \tag{10}$$

After solving for Q, this becomes

$$Q = (N - ha)^{-1} [(g - hb)N + kN^2 - he] \tag{11}$$

Differentiating with respect to N gives:

$$\frac{dQ}{dN} = (N - ha)^{-2} \{[(g - hb) + 2kN)](N - ha) - [(g - hb)N + kN^2 - he]\} \tag{12}$$

or

$$\frac{dQ}{dN} = (N - ha)^{-1} \{kN^2 - 2khaN + h[e - a(g - hb)]\} \tag{13}$$

Upon setting the derivative equal to zero, one gets the quadratic equation

$$kN^2 - 2khaN + h[e - a(g - hb)] = 0 \tag{14}$$

The roots are easily found by application of the quadratic formula to be

$$N = + ha \pm \sqrt{h^2a^2 - \frac{h}{k}[(e - a(g - hb)]} \tag{15}$$

Thus, given the optimization criterion applied here, one can obtain a solution for N in terms of the structural parameters.

It may be of some value to describe the implicit assumptions contained in the model, some of which accord very well with the real world and some of which would have to be removed before it could be applied to the analysis of an actual banking situation. As a means of reconciling equilibrium in the market with a downward sloping average cost curve, spatial product differentiation is assumed. Rather than being an abstraction from reality, this is a very important characteristic of banking markets. Other as-

sumptions are less readily justified. For example, the assumptions that all banks are of the same size, have the same long-run cost curve, and supply a single product that is completely homogeneous from the cost side and nearly so from the demand side correspond to Chamberlin's symmetry assumptions and the assumptions of elementary orthodox price theory, respectively, and were adopted solely for the sake of simplicity. Implicit in the above is the further assumption that banks are free to change their locations within the market, so that they are able to retain equal shares of the market when entry occurs, while charging the same rate as all other banks.

The specification of a reciprocal form of the relationship between numbers and independence of pricing, on the other hand, has rarely been used and even then with indifferent results. Most of the studies that have related prices to the number of banks in the market have employed either a linear or logarithmic form. Both George Kaufman[42] and Richard Aspinwall[43] have reported somewhat improved results using a logarithmic form. Aspinwall, the only one I know to have used a reciprocal relationship, reported results inferior to those obtained by using either a linear or logarithmic form of the structural variable. Nevertheless, there are some strong theoretical reasons for using the reciprocal, or some negative power of the number of banks, in such an equation. In the first place, the deviation from the "competitive" price would be expected to approach zero as the number of banks increases. Secondly, the effect of a given absolute change in the number of banks would be expected to be greater when numbers are smaller than when there is already a large number of banks in the

---

[42]Bank Market Structure and Performance: The Evidence from Iowa," The Southern Economic Journal, XXXII (April, 1966), pp. 438–39.

[43]"Market Structure and Commercial Bank Mortage Rates," (unpublished paper, October 8, 1968, pp. 12–13).

market, a property of the logarithmic and reciprocal forms, but not of the linear one.

The assumption that branching is impossible is, rather obviously, the least defensible in an analysis of what would be optimal banking structure. Accordingly, it should be the first to be dropped as the analysis becomes progressively more complicated.

Clearly, this primitive illustration of the general nature of the optimization problem faced by those in search of the optimal banking structure is not to be taken seriously in its present form. Nevertheless, it does suggest certain considerations that do not often receive explicit attention. As it stands, for example, it suggests that the best way of reconciling the existence of economies of scale with the desirability of having a number of competing banks in the market is by requiring that no bank operate more than one office in the local market. For example, the optimal banking structure for Chicago might include one branch of the Bank of America, one branch of Chase Manhattan, etc. Indeed, there would be much merit in such a system, in that banks could grow to essentially any size, but would have little hope of monopolizing any major banking market through a preemptive branching policy.

However, certain considerations omitted from the model weigh against such a proposal. For one thing, there is a certain convenience that attaches to the possibility of doing business with the same bank at a number of locations within the same area, which would seem to indicate that banks be permitted at least a few branches in the same market. The weight that should be attached to such convenience, as against the added competition that a larger number of individual banks would offer, requires another value judgment. In this case, guidance could be obtained by a study aimed at determining how many customers of branch banks in fact use more than one branch and the importance they attach

to the maintenance of such an option.

Another rather obvious, but largely uninvestigated, problem concerns the additional costs that might be incurred if branch banks were forced to look to markets hundreds of miles away to expand their branching systems. Some years ago Paul Horvitz observed that branch banks in New England tended to restrict the area within which they established branches, but was unable to determine whether this reflected a lack of aggressiveness on the part of the banks or the negative attitude of the regulatory authorities.[44] It may have resulted from the higher marketing costs or difficulties of supervision that accompany branching over a broad area. At least, this is suggested by the tendency of even nonregulated businesses—e.g., supermarket chains—to specialize to some extent on a regional basis. In any case, the question opens the door to additional research.

Expansion of the optimization model to take into account these and other considerations is possible in principle and should be feasible in practice as well, given the capacities of the modern computer. However, the complexities mount exponentially as additional aspects of reality are introduced. The most that is likely to be realized for some time are certain insights that would remain unexamined until brought to the attention of the investigator by the attempt to state the optimization problem explicitly.

One problem that should not be allowed to pass without an attempt to come to grips with it is that of specifying what is to be maximized when there are a number of banking services to be considered rather than one. At this point it becomes perfectly clear that the Benston-Bell and Murphy measures of output in physical terms, which have such desirable properties so long as one is concerned only

---

[44]Paul M. Horvitz, *Concentration and Competition in New England Banking*, Research Report No. 2 (Boston: Federal Reserve Bank of Boston, 1958), p. 24.

with measuring the costs of individual bank functions, are wholly inadequate to the task. If physical measures of output are to be used at all, they must be given value weights, as both Stuart Greenbaum and John Powers have argued in connection with their studies of banking costs.[45] On the other hand, I find quite convincing Donald Hester's criticism of gross operating revenue or Greenbaum's estimated yield-weighted average of earning assets as measures of banking output.[46] By omitting imputations for certain services rendered and received by banks for which no explicit charge is made, they understate both output and expenses. Moreover, there is no assurance that the value weights used by either Greenbaum or Powers accurately measure the social value of output. Both are subject to distortion through the differential effects of market power in the markets for different banking services, Greenbaum's in the sense that his weights are the "average" yields in monopolistic and competitive markets and Powers' in the sense that he

explicitly specifies that the effects on price of monopolistic output restriction should be counted as enhancing the "level of service provided by banks."[47]

It has occurred to me that the way out of this box is to measure the outputs of individual bank functions in terms of the physical units provided by functional cost data and then to combine these into a measure of overall banking output by weighting them by the average costs that would obtain if the banks producing them were of optimal scale, as determined by the various criteria under consideration in this paper.

In the sense that they reflect the social costs of production these are the valuations that a perfectly competitive market would place on the various outputs of a bank. Whether such a wedding of the two approaches to measuring output is really feasible or not, it warrants some experimentation. One thing is quite certain: until we can make explicit just what it is that we would like to see optimized, talk of the optimal banking structure is as idle as discussion of the "good life"; and like the latter, it lies outside the competence of the economics profession.

[45]Greenbaum, "A Study of Bank Costs," pp. 415–21; and Powers, pp. 6–21.

[46]Donald D. Hester, "Comment," *Journal of Political Economy* LXXV (August, 1967, Pt. 2), pp. 479–81.

[47]Powers, p. 21.

2. Exogenous Forces in the Development of Our Banking System*

George W. Mitchell†

The U.S. banking system has been changed significantly in the past 25 years by a number of important exogenous factors—such as the growth of non bank competitors, as well as indirectly by changes in the U.S. nonfinancial economy. On the other hand, George Mitchell does not see the banking industry itself as innovative in the past.

For the future, Dr. Mitchell sees banks receiving new impact from technological change, such as electronic data processing and from changing money use. He anticipates that the effects of these developments may be to make banks innovators for the first time, through creation of new methods of obtaining loanable funds and through introduction of new lending techniques and instruments.

Some firms and industries have created a product or service, built up public awareness and acceptance for it, and, using generative, adaptive, and innovative forces from within, have established a role and importance for their own enterprise. The result is a *de novo* industrial-commercial business or complex.

Banking is not such an enterprise or industry. It has had a pattern of traditional services, an imposed molecular structure, and a pedestrian operating technology, none of which it could call its own. It has not innovated its service products nor shown much adaptive ingenuity in their promotion. Its favorite image has been a passive conformity to the mores of its better customers. Its competitive aggressiveness has been schizophrenic, with large sectors of the industry advocating or supporting publicly administered price ceilings for time deposits, public prohibitions against the absorption of exchange, and a variety of regulatory devices or postures that by sanction or promise dilute competitive ingenuity.

In some measure this unflattering characterization of banking simply reflects the extraordinary economic vicissitudes experienced by banking institutions in the 1930s and in World War II and its aftermath. The Great Depression conditioned bank managements and bank regulators for a long time to a deadening apprehension of future commitments and a dedication to liquidity. World War II inflation and vigorous growth in demand deposits produced banking euphoria by flooding the system with loanable resources and restricting the use of these resources to the alternatives of a wartime economy. Even in the postwar years, the major challenge of banking management still revolved around managing a portfolio of government securities. These features of the early postwar banking system are evident from the balance sheets of the time.

As late as the end of 1947, 73 percent of commercial banking's deposit resources was in the form of demand deposits—65 percent being deposits of individuals, partnerships, and corporations and 8 per-

---

*From *Law and Contemporary Problems*, Winter 1967. Copyright Duke University, 1967. Reprinted by permission of the author and publisher.

†Member, Board of Governors of the Federal Reserve System.

cent deposits of the federal government, states, and municipal subdivisions. In the $130 billion aggregate of deposits, time and savings accounts amounted to only $35 billion, and passbook savings accounted for over 90 percent of that figure. In those days the banking system was getting its resources almost effortlessly.

Portfolio and loan totals of the time also reveal the lack of aggressiveness in bank managements. Treasury securities made up 60 percent of the total of loans and investments, and tax exempts and other securities added another 8 percent. Total loans amounted to only $38 billion out of the $114 billion of loans and investments. And commercial and industrial loans were nearly 50 percent of the loan total.

1. SOME EXTERNAL INFLUENCES

The banking system has been changing significantly since those early postwar years, but most of the forces making for change have been exogenous; change has been induced by the performance and innovation of nonbank competitors, by the penetration of consumer credit markets by vendors, by the proliferation of financing alternatives for borrowers—both as to instruments and institutions—and indirectly by changes in the U.S. nonfinancial economy and the goals that have been set for it.

Recently, and for the future, two developments have been having important and potentially revolutionary effects on banking. One of these—electronic data processing—is purely technological, while the other—a change in money use—is institutional as well as technological. The effects of both of these developments will be transmitted mainly by altering the manner in which banks obtain resources to loan or invest. The changes being wrought will test the innovative and adaptive powers of the banking system to an extent not yet fully recognized.

A. Money Use

The change in money use is an evolving trend toward more rapid turnover and a corresponding retardation of growth in demand deposits. Between 1949 and 1955, turnover outside of New York City rose about half as rapidly as the Gross National Product, but in the period 1955-1966 it rose at approximately the same rate. Turnover in New York City, which is at very much higher levels, rose in step with GNP in the earlier period and at double the rate of GNP increase in the second period. In line with these turnover trends, demand deposits grew one-half as rapidly as GNP in the earlier period and only one-third as rapidly from 1955 through 1966. These postwar trends in demand deposits and turnover are important for banking because over 80 percent of the nation's money is in the form of demand deposits, and demand deposits make up about 50 percent of the deposit resources of U.S. commercial banks. As this source of funds continues to decline in relative importance, banks will suffer a corresponding decline in investable resources unless they adopt policies to expand time deposits or borrowing or can reverse the trend toward economization of demand deposits by attaching to them useful secondary characteristics that they do not now have.

B. Automation

The advent of automation in banking and check transactions is now apparent to everyone. Nearly 90 percent of the checks being written today are sorted and accounted for electronically. The Federal Reserve System has announced that after September 1, 1967, it will not accept checks or drafts for regular processing unless they are machinable, that is, unless they can be handled by high-speed electronic equipment. Utilizing proven technology, we are moving rapidly toward an entirely different system of money settlement which will make federal funds transfers available for all nonlocal transactions of any significant size.

As these and related developments appear on the horizon, a good many bankers and students of banking are trying to evaluate the impact of electronics and automation on the services and structure of banking. For example, will the economies and convenience of electronic accounting for money settlement be confined to large banks? When tied into bank customers' payroll, billing, and receivables bookkeeping and analysis, will the service package be of such size and dimension that banking will take on a major new function, that of the community's accounts keeper? If banks decide thus to make their institutions local binary factories, will they find such operations so profitable and expansible that their first concern will be that of a bookkeeping service bureau and that banking will become their secondary concern? And does this powerful new service potential offer a route for escaping regulatory confinement on corporate growth? Even now, account-keeping packages are becoming an important feature of the services provided by some banks, and the practice is spreading as rapidly as the needed electronic hardware and software become available.

What are the implications of automation for smaller banks? It seems possible that, with recourse to service bureaus, cooperatives, or correspondent facilities, they will not necessarily be seriously handicapped in competing with institutions that operate on a scale which permits on-premises electronic equipment and processing. There are some psychological, or perhaps fancied, advantages to keeping banking operations "under one roof"—one corporate roof, that is. Control of quality, performance, and confidentiality are often mentioned. These arguments, however, seem a bit artificial, for all sorts of eco-

nomic services are already being contracted by business to outside experts with an actual gain in quality and performance. A loss in confidentiality appears chimerical too—after all, the computer offers a numbered account to everyone, and while all of the attributes of a Swiss-type numbered account are not legally available, electronic bookkeeping is a large step toward anonymity from what we now have.

Regardless of the size of bank, automation is bringing retail banking—the servicing of medium- and small-sized accounts and loans—into a more profitable focus. In the future, dependence on large personal, government, or corporate customers may very well lessen, and, as it does so, bank assets and liability structures will shift to accommodate a new mix of customers made possible by computer facilities which can profitably process the financial needs and transactions of heretofore marginally-sized bank customers.

II. INTERMEDIATION—THE ROAD TO GROWTH

A. Nature and Significance

In the broadest sense, modern commercial banking can be described as an industry which gathers up financial resources from the whole community of money owners: businesses, households, and governments, and relends them to an equally broad spectrum of private and public users. Over the years the business of acting as a go-between, or intermediary, for owners and users of money and credit has been built up as a personal or institutional relationship. It has not depended on sophisticated products or processes or on complex machinery.

Attracting demand deposits has been a matter of providing a variety of banking services at convenient locations and, for some customers, the assurance of access to bank credit. Attracting time deposits, the other major source of lending capacity, has involved providing much the same convenience facilities and a somewhat more limited range of services, but these deposits are primarily obtained by the payment of competitive interest rates. The advantages that banks, as well as other intermediaries, offer a large number of investors is a combination of yield, liquidity, and convenience which market instruments, their major competitors, seldom can match. Indeed, several kinds of depository-type financial institutions—commercial banks, savings and loan associations, mutual savings banks, and credit unions—have become extraordinarily facile at the technique of intermediation, the art of borrowing short and lending long.

Though it looks like alchemy and depends to a degree on financial intuition for its profitable use, the transformation of funds serving real liquidity needs for depositors into long-term loan commitments for borrowers is not only practicable but is also a sound operation. Both experience and statistical analysis show that exposure to the liquidity demands of small and medium-sized depositors is, under most circumstances, modest in proportion and predictable in timing and, therefore, manageable. The stability of these pools of funds in the aggregate is dependable, though to a lesser degree than the stability of demand deposits at commercial banks; commercial banking learned long ago that ordinarily money claims (withdrawals) against demand deposits simply roll around the community from one account to another and that if a bank could attract a balanced panel of depositors from various economic and geographic sectors in its service area it could count on surprising stability in the aggregate of its demand deposits.

As the U.S. financial economy grew in stability and strength after the banking reforms of the 1930s, experience with somewhat less liquid claims—time deposits and share accounts—encouraged intermediaries to work greater and greater transformations of liquidity promises and attractive yields into long-term loans against

which they extended commitments. Without a doubt this process has made saving easier and more profitable, and it has accommodated the interest and convenience of much broader groups of savers and investors. It has had an equally beneficent effect of users of loan funds, who have had the benefit of a more competitive environment and in many cases access to credit resources not heretofore available. Increasingly, intermediation became the best of all possible worlds for everyone—the intermediary, the saver, and the borrower.

B. Recent Changes in Banking's "Raw Materials"

The growing significance of intermediation to the commercial banking system is revealed in Table 1, which compares capital accounts and liabilities (excluding interbank) of all insured commercial banks as of the end of 1956 and 1966. In 1956, demand deposits comprised 66.2 percent of the total compared to 45.4 percent at the end of 1966. Time and savings deposits comprised only 24.5 percent of the 1956 total, but had grown to 41.6 percent by the close of 1966. Most of the growth in the time and savings category occurred in time deposits of individuals, partnerships, and corporations ("IPC").

The extent to which the sources of banking's "raw materials"—deposits, borrowings, and capital—are changing is undoubtedly significant for future developments. Projecting historical trends by reference to existing deposit and debt instruments, however, will not take into account the financial innovations on which banks may become increasingly dependent.

For example, the Federal Reserve System conducted a survey of the ownership of time and savings deposits held by Federal Reserve member banks in June 1957, and again in May 1966. The survey was repeated on January 31 of this year. These data are shown in Table 2 and show the structural changes within the IPC time and savings category. In the 1957 survey

TABLE 1
Capital Accounts and Liabilities (Not Including Interbank)
of All Insured Commercial Banks in the United States
(dollars in millions)

	December 1956		December 1966	
Capital Accounts	$ 16,301	7.6%	$ 31,609	8.2%
Borrowings				
Federal funds			2,824	0.7
Other liabilities for borrowed money	74	0.0	1,893	0.5
Total	74	0.0	4,717	1.2
Demand Deposits				
Mutual savings banks and savings & loan			3,075	0.8
Other IPC	111,048	52.0	141,620	36.9
U. S. Government	14,339	6.7	4,975	1.3
States and political subdivisions	10,449	4.9	14,951	3.9
Foreign	1,794	0.8	2,653	0.7
Certified & officers checks	3,785	1.8	6,956	1.8
Total	141,415	66.2	174,230	45.4
Time and Savings Deposits				
Savings deposits	48,193	22.6	89,706	23.3
IPC time deposits			49,986	13.0
States and political subdivisions	2,384	1.1	13,414	3.5
Foreign	1,254	0.7	4,470	1.2
Special accounts	235	0.1	2,226	0.6
Total	52,066	24.5	159,802	41.6
Acceptances outstanding	755	0.4	2,233	0.6
Other liabilities	2,813	1.3	11,412	3.0
Total of Capital Accounts and Liabilities	213,424	100.0	384,003	100.0

Source: *Federal Reserve Call Reports.*

there were four categories of time accounts tabulated: the largest—regular savings accounts—was 87 percent of the total. In the 1967 survey nine categories were tabulated, and, while regular savings accounts was still the largest category, it had shrunk to 60 percent of the total.

Accelerated growth in time deposits began early in 1957 as a result of increases in deposit rates announced by banks late in 1956. These were in response to an upward revision in the maximum limits on rates which banks were permitted, by government regulation, to pay on such deposits, effective January 1957. By June of that year, total time and savings deposits of Federal Reserve member banks had increased to $44.7 billion from the $41.2 billion in June 1956. (Demand deposits had increased only $0.4 billion dur-

ing the same year.) Of the $44.7 billion total time and savings deposits in June 1957, only $1.9 billion, or 4.4 percent, were in certificates of deposit, and most of these ($1.3 billion) were held in country banks. Certificates of deposit had traditionally been used by country banks in the Midwest, and were more important in Federal Reserve districts such as St. Louis and Minneapolis than in the banking centers of New York and Chicago. There is no breakdown of these certificates according to denomination, but it is safe to assume that almost all of these C/Ds were under $100,000, and were for all practical purposes nonnegotiable. The remaining $0.6 billion held by the reserve city banks were divided as to type (the survey at that time gave no exact breakdown), and it can be seen that the large negotiable

TABLE 2
Types of Time and Savings Deposits of Individuals, Partnerships, and Corporations
Held by Member Banks on June 6, 1957, May 11, 1966, and January 31, 1967
(dollars in millions)

	June 6, 1957*		May 11, 1966†		Jan. 31, 1967†	
Saving Deposits	$35,737	87.4%	$ 72,871	65.7%	$ 70,701	60.5%
Consumer-type Time Deposits (less than $100,000)						
Savings bonds			856	0.8	1,409	1.2
Nonnegotiable C/Ds			12,363	11.1	17,435	14.9
Negotiable C/Ds			3,197	2.9	4,381	3.7
Open account time deposits			1,244	1.1	1,856	1.6
Total			17,660	15.9	25,081	21.4
Business-type Time Deposits ($100,000 or more)						
Negotiable C/Ds			13,815	12.4	13,018	11.1
Nonnegotiable C/Ds			1,968	1.8	2,814	2.4
Open account time deposits			975	0.9	1,826	1.6
Total			16,758	15.1	17,658	15.1
Total C/Ds	1,961	4.8				
Total open time deposits	2,254	5.5				
Christmas saving & other special accounts	931	2.3	3,655	3.3	3,450	
Total	40,883	100.0	110,944	100.0	116,890	2.9

*44 *Federal Reserve Bulletin* 424 (1958).
†53 *Federal Reserve Bulletin* 518 (1967).

C/D had not yet made an important appearance as a money market instrument.

Table 2 also shows that by May 11, 1966, nonnegotiable C/Ds of under $100,000 had grown to over $12 billion. These are in the category that are regarded as "consumer-type" time deposits. The "business-type" time deposits ($100,000 or more and negotiable) had grown to over $13 billion. The importance of this instrument is underestimated in the table because only the IPC component is shown. An additional $5 billion of such instruments is held by state governments, foreign holders, and others. The table shows that consumer-type C/Ds have continued to increase to an important extent since May 1966.

Throughout the postwar period, banking's role as a supplier of funds to the economy has grown steadily, as Table 3 discloses. In the first five postwar years

banks supplied less than 20 percent of total funds raised; but by 1962-1965 the share had risen to about 35 percent. Most of this gain was paralleled by a decline in the proportion of funds raised through the sale of market securities directly to the nonfinancial public, but the market share of nonbank financial intermediaries also declined somewhat from a peak of about 50 percent reached in the years 1952-1956. Market shares for the year 1966 were temporarily distorted by monetary restraint which impaired the capacity of both bank and nonbank intermediaries to attract funds in competition with security markets.

C. Intermediation in International Financial Markets

In recent years U.S. commercial banks have extended their intermediation to international financial markets, again pri-

TABLE 3
Share of Funds Supplied
(in percent)

	Commercial Banks	Nonbank Financial Institutions	Nonfinancial Public
1947-51	18.9	41.8	26.7
1952-56	23.1	49.8	20.4
1957-61	24.7	47.6	16.5
1962-65	35.1	42.8	10.6

Note: The components do not add up to 100 percent because the government and foreign sectors are not included.

marily because of exogenous factors. First, the evolution of the U.S. dollar as a vehicle currency in international transactions and as a reserve asset enhanced the importance of New York as an international financial center and led to the development of the so-called "Eurodollar" market in Europe. A recent estimate by the Bank for International Settlements puts the volume of this market at about $13 billion.

Second, the formation of the European Economic Community, with its greatly expanded market and its vigorous rate of economic growth, provided incentives for U.S. business to expand this area, and for U.S. banks to increase their activity in order to meet these new requirements of their regular customers. But U.S. banks have been expanding elsewhere also.

One way of measuring the increasing importance of the international money market as a source of funds to banks is to look at the rates of growth in their short-term liabilities to foreigners. In the five years between the end of 1957 and the end of 1962, short-term liabilities to foreign banks (including foreign branches of U.S. banks) and other foreigners expanded at an annual average rate of about $450 million. Between 1962 and the end of 1966, the average annual increment was about $1.4 billion, even without counting negotiable certificates of deposit. While we do not have separate figures for them, we assume that negotiable C/Ds held by

foreigners also increased significantly in the latter period.

In part, this growth in banks' short-term liabilities to foreigners is the counterpart of increasing bank claims on foreigners, which went up by an average of about $1.2 billion a year in the period 1960-1963 and by a record $2.5 billion in 1964 following the imposition of the interest equalization tax on foreign security issues. It was this last development, by the way, which did much to lead to the extension of the interest equalization tax to long-term bank loans and the announcement of the voluntary foreign credit restraint program in February 1965. But to a great extent the increase in deposit liabilities reflects the ability of American banks to tap this source of funds.

Operations of foreign branches of U.S. banks have been very prominent in acquiring these funds. The number of these branches has increased from 117 at the end of 1955 to 244 at the end of 1966; during the same period total assets of the branches have increased by over six times —from $2 billion to $12.4 billion. A large part of this increase has been in the dollar, or "international," business of the branches as distinguished from transactions in other currencies, their "domestic" business.

A dramatic example of the ability of the branches to acquire funds occurred during the scramble for liquidity in the latter part of 1966. During this period the branches passed on to their head offices for use in the U.S. market about $2.5 billion in funds acquired from foreign holders of dollar balances, including other foreign banks. It is quite clear that from now on the international market will have to be regarded as an important source of funds which American banks may tap when they find it attractive.

III. BANKING STRUCTURE: DO COMPETITIVE RESTRAINTS IMPEDE BANK RESPONSE TO MARKET OPPORTUNITIES?

A. Constraints of Regulation

The structure of banking in the United States is generally thought to reflect in a rather large way the constraints of state laws with respect to banking operations. These restrictions impair the freedom of banks to move from their original location, to branch, to merge, or to exploit opportunities outside of their immediate demand deposit service areas. The presumption of statutory containment, however, is often carried too far. It fails to hold up as a complete explanation for the banking system's slowness to develop and respond to market opportunities.

Banks are multiproduct or multiservice firms, and there are many markets in which they are able to participate without significant statutory constrictions. A good example is in their asset acquisitions, where they can compete freely on a nationwide basis with the other banks, other financial institutions, nonfinancial businesses, and individuals for Government securities, corporate securities, state and local securities, mortgages and consumer paper (to some degree), and for business loans of the larger and more important corporations. In these markets, Pacific Coast banks compete with New York, Boston, Chicago, Philadelphia, or Dallas institutions. The ability of banks to make loans and investments and, to a lesser degree, to attract deposits from far beyond their home office locations has

served to relax significantly the performance constraints of state laws restricting bank location. But despite the fact that banking in the United States as a whole has been able to respond reasonably well to many needs of our over-all economic system and to business practices and consumer habits, there is no gainsaying that in some economic and geographic sectors the efficiency and services of banking have been circumscribed by regulatory policies and the confinement of state laws and conforming federal practices.

B. Structural Constraints

1. DESCRIBING BANKING STRUCTURE. The term "banking structure" is used frequently and easily without specification as to its precise meaning, but generally the reference is to number, size, and location of banks. Thus, there were, at the end of 1966, 13,770 commercial banks operating out of 30,000 offices with $330 billion in deposits (excluding deposits of other commercial banks). On the average, there was an office for every 6,700 persons, but in actual fact a large number of the 30,000 offices were in relatively small communities, and in these locations they ordinarily served populations of less than 1,500. In the nation, outside of metropolitan areas, there were 7,600 one-office towns, and nearly all of these were the sole office of an independent bank. There were 1,600 communities with two offices and 900 with three or more. All of the other banking offices were in metropolitan areas.

While such demographic data are useful in understanding the functioning of our banking system, the concept of "banking structure" should be expanded to consider the degree and nature of a bank's participation in various asset or deposit markets. Banks of similar size and location do not *necessarily* evidence similar operating opportunities—but the structure of their assets and liabilities ordinarily reveals the determining influence of various environmental conditions.

Moreover, when we refer to a bank in the United States it may be to an institution with a few million dollars of deposits oriented to the needs and outlook of sparsely populated farming areas, or it may be a multioffice and multibillion dollar institution serving the population of an entire metropolitan area or state, and experiencing rapid economic growth.

The large banks are growth- as well as profit-minded. They cultivate customers on a nationwide, if not a worldwide, scale, even though their local base of operations may be eroded by confining legislation and economic stagnation. On the other hand, the small community banks are locally oriented and resigned to accepting the community's economic growth and development as a limiting factor in their growth goal.

The problem of characterizing banking structure by size, location, and concentration involves criteria for size and a method of determining significant market areas. Bank size can be defined, for example, in terms of total resources, or total deposits, or demand deposits, or demand deposits of individuals, partnerships, and corporations, or demand deposits IPC under $100,000, or demand deposits IPC under $25,000 or $10,000. These are alternative measures; some are better than others, given a particular purpose. Total deposits is probably the best measure of size despite its shortcomings as an indication of local activity—a shortcoming that arises from the fact that it includes both local and nonlocal deposits, for, as is well known, many banks have deposits from firms and individuals far removed from their home office, sometimes as far removed as a distant state or nation.

For a measure of size in a local market, helpful proxies are available in the number of demand deposit accounts or the amount of demand deposits in accounts with balances of less than $100,000 or even $25,000. The logic of the proxies using size-of-account data is that, while there is no sure way of knowing how many deposit accounts over $100,000 are nonlocal, it is fairly sure that many of them are of this character. And as to the accounts under $25,000, we can be quite sure that most of these deposits are of a strictly local character—owned by local individuals, businesses, or corporations. This fact makes the size group of under $25,000 a reasonable proxy for bank participation in the local deposit and credit markets.

2. MEASURING BANKING CONCENTRATION. A major source of interest in banking structure arises from its impact on banking competition. The geographical areas that encompass important banking markets may be local, regional, or national. The local markets are usually a metropolitan area, a city, a county or town, or even a neighborhood. The regional markets can be approximated by regarding a state or group of states as a significant area. The advantage of regarding a state as a market area is that more pertinent economic and demographic data are available for states. Moreover, aggregate state data can be viewed as an average structure, reflecting both the over-all economic environment of the state and the statutory freedom or constraint imposed by the state's banking laws.

For any given geographical area and size criterion, there are data and a technique for summarizing structural characteristics. From periodic (approximately quarterly) call reports for all insured banks in the United States, a uniform balance sheet and supplemental exhibits detail a variety of assets and liability items by bank. These data can be tabulated for any classification or array of banks by any asset or liability category on the call.

For example, using the entire United

States as the geographical area and total deposits as a measure of size, we derive the following table on banking concentration (as of December 1965):

$$\text{The largest} \begin{Bmatrix} .1\% \\ 1\ \% \\ 5\ \% \\ 15\ \% \end{Bmatrix} \text{of the banks,} \begin{Bmatrix} 13 \\ 131 \\ 659 \\ 1,969 \end{Bmatrix}$$

$$\text{in number, have} \begin{Bmatrix} 25\% \\ 53\% \\ 71\% \\ 82\% \end{Bmatrix} \text{of total deposits.}$$

Looking at the other end of the spectrum:

$$\text{The smallest} \begin{Bmatrix} 25\% \\ 50\% \\ 75\% \\ 85\% \end{Bmatrix} \text{of the banks,} \begin{Bmatrix} 3,283 \\ 6,585 \\ 9,847 \\ 11,160 \end{Bmatrix}$$

$$\text{in number, have} \begin{Bmatrix} 1.6\% \\ 5.1\% \\ 12.2\% \\ 17.5\% \end{Bmatrix} \text{of total deposits.}$$

These concentration characteristics for the nation are also rather surprisingly typical for a large number of individual states with a variety of banking structures. For example, states where as much as 50 percent of the deposits are held in 1 percent of the banks are as diversified in banking structure as California (statewide branching), Georgia (limited branching and holding company), Illinois (unit only), Minnesota (unit and holding company), and New York (limited branching and holding company). In these states and in several other groups of states, dissimilar banking laws have led to some obvious differences in structure, but the concentration figures are very much alike. On the other hand, there are instances, particularly in the South and Southeast, where branching restrictions, or their absence, seem to have had a marked effect on concentration. The Carolinas and Virginia, for example, show the effects on concentration of branching freedom, just as Arkansas, Mississippi, and West Virginia show the results of branching restraints.

Without doubt, the variegation in state banking structures is greater because of the differences in regulatory constraints, but state-to-state differences in economic environment are often an overriding factor tending to accentuate or moderate those constraints. And the response of bankers themselves to the combination of the economic and regulatory environment is still another significant factor affecting the banking structures actually existing.

CONCLUSION

Whatever phase of commercial banking one examines, the imprints of environment, precedent, and authority are evident. In the beginning "bankers' money" —demand deposits or notes—was an adaptation of the "sovereign's money"—coin and currency—with the identical problem of confidence and a similar opportunity for gain. In our time, the development of new lending techniques and instruments, the introduction of credit to new users and uses, and the competitive tapping of loanable resources are, by and large, innovations taken over by the banking system after experimental and developmental costs have been charged off by someone else. Banking has not done badly, profitwise, in its imitative, cautious role, but it may not—up to now—aspire to the reputation of a growth industry. However, the impact of automation and changing money use on banking is potentially capable of transforming the industry into an innovator for the first time in its existence.

3. Competition and Efficiency in the Banking System—Empirical Research and Its Policy Implications*

Stuart I. Greenbaum

This article is noteworthy for two reasons. First, it concisely summarizes all the important preceding studies on banking structure. Second, it provides an introductory definition of the "socially optimal" banking structure. Regarding the second reason, the article is often cited as the seminal work around which subsequent studies have evolved. This is brought out in the preceding article by Mote wherein particular significance is attributed to Greenbaum's efforts.

This paper focuses on the results and implications of recent cost studies in banking. Additional materials are discussed with a view toward placing the cost analyses in perspective. The following section provides a definition of a "socially optimal" banking structure in order to indicate the possible importance of returns to scale in banking. Succeeding sections consider the cost studies individually and provide an interpretation of their findings.

THE OPTIMAL BANKING STRUCTURE

"Governmental supervision of banks and restrictions on their operations long predate any comparable supervision of

other financial institutions, have always been more far-reaching and continue to be so today" (Friedman, 1960, p. 66). The present-day justification for public regulation of commercial banking appears to be twofold.[1] On the one hand, the banking industry serves as a conduit through which stabilization policy is transmitted to the economy at large. Regulation allegedly promotes stabilization and assures the continued usefulness of the banking system as a conduit. The second justification pertains to the "industrial organization" of banking. Regulation seeks to promote an ordering of the banking system that will foster allocative, distributive, and technological ends sought by the community. The ends relate to economic agents outside com-

[1]The term "regulation" encompasses all manner of governmental direct intervention in the prerogatives of commercial banks, including control of entry, merger, and branching; portfolio regulation—asset, liability, capital account structuring; regulation of interest rates on time and demand deposits; and usury laws. Unlike reserve requirements, open-market operations by the Federal Reserve System need not be viewed as a form of direct intervention. Operation of the discount window occupies a middle ground. To the extent that the System merely posts an interest rate at which it stands ready to lend to qualified borrowers, there is no interference with the operation of banks. However, the practice of "wrist-slapping" can be viewed as a form of portfolio control.

mercial banking as well as to the industry itself. Underlying the second rationale for bank regulation is the vaguely defined aim of promoting a socially optimal banking structure.[2] Congressional interpretation is suggested by the criteria for evaluating merger and holding-company applications set forth in the Bank Holding Company Act of 1965 and the Bank Merger Act of 1960. The criteria are neatly classed under three headings: "needs and convenience factors," "banking factors," and "competitive factors," but their ambiguity is amply demonstrated by the interpretive difficulties encountered by the bank regulatory agencies.

At the risk of plunging into controversy, I should like to offer an interpretation of "socially optimal banking structure" that may find acceptance among those interested in the problem. Setting aside considerations deriving from monetary policy, the socially optimal banking structure should be defined in terms of at least four desiderata.[3] First (not necessarily in order of importance), the optimal banking structure would be characterized by maximum productive efficiency. The social cost of producing banking services with an optimal structure would be equal to or less than the social cost of producing the same services with any other implementable banking structure.[4] Second, the optimal banking structure would be characterized by allocative neutrality, which means that the over-all allocation of resources in the

economy would not be appreciably influenced by any peculiarity of the banking structure.[5] The third desideratum can be considered a derivative of allocative neutrality. It would preclude exploitation of both consumers of banking services and sellers of banking inputs. Thus, banks could not behave like monopolists or monopsonists.[6] Finally, the optimal banking structure would be characterized by maximum responsivity to technological and demand-oriented changes. This criterion focuses on the time required by the banking system to adopt new technology and to adjust its operations to shifts in the composition and magnitude of the public's demand for financial services.[7]

The relationship between banking structure and responsivity to change has received scant attention, and yet it may ramify in numerous important ways. For example, slow responsivity in banking may explain the postwar proliferation and growth of special-purpose financial institutions, such as credit unions, per-

---

[2]The structure of banking relates to aspects of the ownership, organization, and control of the banking industry. Structure may be described by the number and size distribution of banks, the number of bank offices, the extent of holding-company and chain banking, as well as other properties. For example, if correspondent banking results in control of some smaller banks by city correspondents, this will be relevant to structure.

[3]It may be impossible to satisfy all four desiderata simultaneously, in which case the possibility of trade-offs arises. The question of social rates of substitution among desiderata will not be discussed in this paper.

[4]This means the industry is operating somewhere on its product transformation curve.

[5]In the presence of economies of scale, permitting concentration will increase efficiency, thereby affecting resource allocation. Thus, the norm would not be the resource allocation obtained under perfect competition. Allocative neutrality, as used here, is reciprocally analogous to the concept of excess burden, used in the literature on taxation (see Musgrave, 1959, esp. pp. 140–54). A more ambitious definition of allocative neutrality might require the banking structure to foster a resource allocation identical to that obtained if all markets in the economy were perfectly competitive. But, this is obviously a will-o'-the-wisp. It would require the implementation by the banking system of a most peculiar set of compensatory discriminating practices to correct for aberrations from competitive norms in other sectors of the economy.

[6]Allocative neutrality may be expressed as precluding monopolistic and monopsonistic behavior. The point in treating separately the exploitation desideratum is that it focuses on distributive as well as allocative problems.

[7]Maximum responsivity should be thought of as a first approximation to optimal responsivity, which, in fact, may be submaximal. This qualification was suggested by Richard Sutch. The responsivity criterion suggests the inclusion of inventive capacity among the desiderata. It is excluded here because intuitively it seems less compelling than the other criteria mentioned.

sonal-loan companies, and savings and loan associations. Any social advantages accruing from this recent growth must be weighed against the disadvantage of having a financial-services industry that is more vulnerable to cyclical phenomena.[8]

The question of proliferation has another, more complicated aspect. It has been argued that the postwar growth of the savings and loan industry may be partly attributable to the erstwhile indifference of commercial banks to both the mortgage market and the time depositor (see R. Robertson, 1962). During the fifties, commercial banks were offering time-deposit rates that were considerably below both the Regulation Q ceilings and the rates offered by savings and loan associations.[9] In addition, mortgages represented a small—as compared with today—component of commercial-bank asset portfolios.[10]

Having permitted the savings and loan industry to develop and demonstrate the profitability of this type of intermediation, commercial banks began to compete in earnest. Time-deposit rates were adjusted upward toward those offered by savings and loan associations. When the Regulation Q ceilings became an impediment, they were raised. At the same time, mortgage holdings of commercial banks grew faster than earning assets. In this competition, commercial banks enjoy the considerable advantage of being a general-purpose financial institution. The importance of consumer convenience suggests that when rate differentials between savings and loan shares and commercial-bank time deposits are narrowed, funds will be shifted to commercial banks.[11] In turn, this may imply the dissolution and bankruptcy of savings and loan associations and a general withering of the industry (see Fand, 1965, pp. 55–63, and J. Robertson, 1966). The social cost of such adjustments may not be staggering —their dimensions are unknown—but the adjustments probably could be obviated by more expeditious adaptation of operations by commercial banks.[12]

The line of influence running from regulation and structure to rates of innovation can be reversed. Technology may be an independent influence on structure. Automation of the payments system may affect banking structure by altering the production function, increasing the importance of economies of scale. Regulation could still frustrate the process of consolidation that might naturally follow, but the cost of doing so would become greater, and perhaps more obvious.

Automation of the payments system also may undermine the viability of thousands of smaller banks by reducing the importance of banking-facility proximity.[13] When banks followed a "live

[8]The vulnerability derives from externally imposed limitations on portfolio diversification. There may be additional cost disadvantages from the provision of financial services through specialized institutions.

[9]*The Savings and Loan Fact Book* (1965) indicates that average rates paid on savings and loan shares exceeded those on commercial-bank time deposits in each year from 1947–64. From 1947–53 the rate spread increased from 1.4 percent to 1.7 percent, and the average spread was 1.5 percent. From 1953–64 the rate spread declined, almost monotonically, from 1.7 percent to 0.83 percent, and the average spread was 1.19 percent.

[10]Real estate loans secured by residential properties at insured commercial banks have increased from $7 billion in 1948 to $30 billion in 1965. These loans rose from 6.7 percent of total earning assets to 10.5 percent (*Assets, Liabilities, and Capital Accounts, Commercial and Mutual Savings Banks*, 1948–65).

[11]The relevant cross-elasticities are unknown, but casual observation suggests they are not trivial. Also see Christ (1963, pp. 201–18).

[12]Capital that is specific to the savings and loan industry is probably not very great, and personnel can probably be retrained to work in commercial banks at little cost. However, the precipitous failure of large numbers of financial institutions has potentially deleterious effects on the community, with ramifications that are difficult to predict.

[13]Frequent trips to a banking office will be unnecessary when funds are transferred from employer to employee without a check, when credit cards become universally acceptable, and when most small loans are made through prearranged overdraft facilities.

and let live" policy toward the savings and loan industry, it was argued that they were valuable commercial-bank customers. Changed conditions and recalculations of profit opportunities have altered the attitude of commercial bankers on this point. The solicitousness of larger commercial banks toward their smaller counterparts is analogous to the earlier tolerant attitude of commercial banks toward the savings and loan industry. I have argued elsewhere that correspondent banking is a critical element in the viability of a sizable proportion of smaller banks (see Federal Reserve Bank of Kansas City, 1965a and b). The new payments technology may cause a re-evaluation of the benign attitude of large banks toward small banks. The likelihood of this occurring will be enhanced as the importance of physical proximity of banking facilities is diminished.

The structure of banking may also have implications for rates of innovation outside of the financial-service industries. Risk pooling suggests that a banking industry composed of large firms can hold greater amounts of high-risk earning assets than one made up of small firms with equal total risk to the industry. However, differences in attitudes toward assuming risk among banks of different size may nullify or magnify the possible effect of risk pooling. Furthermore, the community's attitude toward the assumption of risk by banks—the social risk aversion regarding bank portfolios—complicates discussion of the relationship between banking structure and rates of innovation outside banking.

The four optimal-banking-structure desiderata—maximum productive efficiency, allocative neutrality, absence of consumer and factor exploitation, and maximum responsivity to market and technological change—represent nothing more than a value judgment.[14] With some notable ex-

ceptions, these desiderata are approximated by fostering competition, and this is what many economists counsel.[15] It is not certain, however, that a socially optimal banking structure can be achieved by promoting competition. Indefinitely falling long-run average costs would rule out competition as a means of promoting the optimal banking structure defined here.[16] Indeed, the presence of U-shaped average cost curves is not sufficient to assure the success of a procompetitive policy. Cost curves could be U-shaped with the optimal-size firm being so large that competition would be ruled out in all but the largest market areas.[17] Cost studies should aid in determining whether the optimal banking structure can be approximated by promoting competition. Such studies should also provide esti-

---

[14]Many have argued the virtues of a decentralized—essentially unit—banking system in terms that suggest this might be an end in itself. However, except for possible political considerations, these arguments may be more accurately interpreted as supporting decentralized banking as a means toward achieving the ends mentioned above.

Some might wish to add depositor protection against bank failures to the desiderata mentioned. This criterion was omitted because the instrumentality for depositor protection is extant and its structure need not be altered with future changes in banking structure. If the minimization of insurance cost is made a desideratum, the topic cannot be disposed of so quickly. The insurance fee structure of the Federal Deposit Insurance Corporation has implications for banking structure which are discussed by Donald Jacobs (1964) and Sam Peltzman (1965).

[15]George W. Mitchell (1965, p. 236) has argued that "an economic and political case for a procompetitive policy in banking, like the case against sin, is an easy one to make." The precise meaning of a procompetitive policy is not entirely clear, especially with regard to mergers and acquisitions. In general, however, such a policy might be aimed at maintaining a large number of independent banks in all markets.

[16]The absence of externalities is another necessary condition for the success of a procompetitive policy. For a discussion of the relationship between competition and responsivity see Schumpeter (1947, esp. chaps. v–vii).

[17]The problem of defining bank markets has plagued much of the recent research on banking structure. Most of the concepts employed are expedients that few find entirely satisfactory. For one approach to the problem see David A. Alhadeff (1954, esp. chaps. ii–iv).

mates of the social costs—at least some of them—of pursuing a procompetitive policy in the presence of economies of scale.[18]

The ensuing discussion considers the contribution of recent bank-cost studies toward resolving the competition-efficiency dilemma. Findings of significant scale economies will suggest the need for alternatives to a procompetitive policy. In their absence, a procompetitive policy may be reasonably consistent with the ends sought, and the arguments of those who counsel less regulation and more scope for competition would be strengthened. On the other hand, findings of scale economies will not necessarily constitute an argument in support of the current regulatory framework. They would merely indicate that the promotion of competition cannot result in an approximation of the optimal banking structure.

RETURNS TO SCALE IN COMMERCIAL BANKING

The following discussion will focus on the cost studies of David A. Alhadeff

---

[18]Insured-commercial-bank data for 1964 indicate that a 10 percent reduction in operating expense would amount to over $1 billion per year. A 10 percent reduction in operating expense minus interest cost of deposits would amount to almost $700 million annually. According to my study (Greenbaum, 1964), the optimal-size bank in the Kansas City Federal Reserve District has average costs of better than 30 percent lower than those for all banks in the area. In the Richmond District, the optimal-size bank has average costs of more than 20 percent lower than those for all banks in the area. I also attempted to evaluate the savings, if any, attendant to the conversion of large numbers of small unit banks into branch systems, assuming the output of each plant (branch) fixed. A subsample of Richmond District branch banks suggested that average costs fall approximately 12 percent when firm size is expanded from the smallest ($3 million in assets) to the largest ($580 million in assets) observed while holding the average size of branches constant. These estimates do not include the savings from simpler regulatory procedures made possible by increased concentration. In recent years, the combined operating expenses of the Federal Reserve System, the Federal Deposit Insurance Corp., and the Comp-

(1954), Irving Schweiger and John S. McGee (1961), Lyle E. Gramley (1962), Paul M. Horvitz (1963, pp. 1–54), Stuart I. Greenbaum (1964), and George J. Benston (1965a and b). These studies are rich in detail and subtleties reflecting the complexities involved in analyzing bank costs. This brief survey cannot do complete justice to the authors. The following will sketch the approach employed in each study, the data used, and the findings obtained. The significance and position of each study within the collection of works will be indicated, but a detailed criticism of each study will not be attempted.

Recent bank-cost studies attempt to infer returns to scale from estimated long-run cost-function parameters.[19] Although common threads are found running through these studies—resulting largely from common data-availability problems—they are strikingly diverse in terms of model specification. Yet, with one exception (see Gramley, 1962) all are aimed at shedding light on public-policy questions. All of these studies employ concepts of private, as opposed to social, costs, and possible divergences have not been carefully considered. For example, the relationship between bank size or concentration and the cost of public regulation has been ignored, as has the fact that bank reserves are a scarce resource to the banking system but practically a free good to the community.[20]

Alhadeff's *Monopoly and Competition*

---

troller of the Currency's office have been at a rate of approximately $225 million per year. Combined expenses of the fifty state bank regulatory agencies are not readily available.

[19]Since returns to scale are essentially a property of the production function, the exclusive reliance on cost analysis is notable. This point will be considered later (see Greenbaum, 1966).

[20]Bank reserves are practically free to the community since they can be augmented at negligible production cost. In another sense, however, bank reserves are not a free good. If the goal of full

(*Footnote continued on next page*)

in Banking (1954) was seminal. However, the empirical aspects of his analysis are vulnerable to criticism.[21] Based on operating-ratio data for 1938–50 published by the Federal Reserve Bank of San Francisco, Alhadeff found that: "If unit costs for different size banks were plotted on a scatter diagram with unit costs on the ordinate, and size of bank (or level of output) on the abscissa, a curve drawn by least squares would decline fairly sharply in the early ranges [up to perhaps $5 million in total deposits], remain fairly constant over a wide intermediate range [up to $50 million or more in total deposits], and then decline again in the range of the largest banks [over $275 million in total deposits]" (Alhadeff, 1954, p. 83). The results show little difference between the costs of the largest unit banks and branch banks. Alhadeff believes this finding casts doubt on the alleged cost advantages of branch banking (1954, p. 106).[22]

Using tabular inspection, Alhadeff related operating expenses to a host of variables, the most important of which was total earning assets—loans plus investments. The signal importance of the earning-assets variable derives from Alhadeff's identification of it as his measure of bank output.[23] In fact, however, Alhadeff relates the ratio of operating expenses to earning assets to still another variable—total deposits—in order to derive his cost curves.

The problem of output definition pervades the literature and, therefore, justifies special consideration. If the ultimate findings of bank-cost studies are to have cogency, the measures of output employed must be related to community well-being. (The same point was made in a broader context by Kuznets, 1953, pp. 192–215). Output measures that cannot be interpreted in terms of the socially relevant services produced by commercial banks should be considered suspect.

The use of earning assets to measure output, as suggested by Alhadeff, implies that lending is the primary productive activity of commercial banks. This view finds support in the fact that in recent years approximately 90 percent of the banking system's current earnings were directly attributable to lending activity.[24] However, the use of earning assets as an output measure also implies that all forms of bank credit are perfect substi-

---

employment and stable prices dictates a unique level of bank reserves at each point in time—assume fiscal policy is fixed in the short run—then deviations from this level incur social costs in the form of unemployment or rising price levels.

[21]Alhadeff's originality is indisputable, and it should be remembered that present judgments are made with the benefit of twelve years' and five subsequent major studies' worth of hindsight. Benston (1965b, p. 543), in commenting on Alhadeff's study, as well as those of Schweiger and McGee (1961), Gramley (1962), and Horvitz (1963), asserts that: "Given the limited data they had available, they generally did all that could be done."

[22]This finding is based on comparisons of branch and unit banks of the same deposit size but different numbers of offices. Implicit in such comparisons is the assumption that the community is indifferent to changes in the number of banking facilities. The comparisons are not relevant for evaluating consolidations of unit banks into branch systems. Indeed, it is difficult to establish their relevance for any of the policy questions relating to banking structure.

[23]Alhadeff was keenly aware of many of the problems involved in defining and measuring bank output.

[24]The prohibition of interest payment on demand deposits reduces interest expense and noninterest earnings, leading to an overstatement of the relative importance of interest earnings. I estimated what current non-interest income of banks would be in the absence of the prohibition of interest payment on demand deposits by employing national bank data for 1927 and 1932. Assuming that the ratio of the interest rate on demand deposits to that on time deposits would now approximate the ratios prevailing in 1927 and 1932, interest on demand deposits at all insured commercial banks would have been between $1.25 billion and $1.96 billion in 1964. These amounts may be thought of as lower-limit estimates of the addition to current noninterest—or service charge—income that would result from explicit charges for all services provided at all insured commercial banks. Thus, explicit charges for clearing and other services might increase

tutes to the community, that is, a $100 consumer loan is the same as a $100 business loan, which is the same as a $100 interbank loan. The earning-assets measure may be thought of as a price-weighted index in which all the weights are of equal value. Observed differences in interest rates on various types of bank credit argue against the use of this type of output measure (see Greenbaum, 1964, and Hester and Zoellner, 1966).

Because earning assets is a balance-sheet variable—as are deposits and total assets—still other doubts are raised regarding its use as a measure of bank output. Although the use of stock variables to represent flow concepts is not uncommon,[25] when flow measures are readily available the reasons for substituting stocks should be explicit and reasonably compelling. Such arguments have not been made. In their absence, income-statement variables, such as current operating earnings, would appear to be preferable.[26]

Emphasis on the selection of an appropriate output measure has been questioned by those who have argued that earning assets, deposits, total assets, and current operating earnings are so highly correlated that the issue is more apparent than real. This contention is demonstrably false. In regressing current operating expense on the various suggested measures of output, I obtained adjusted coefficients of determination ranging from 0.015 to 0.701. Moreover, the estimated total cost equations were linear, quad-

ratic, or cubic depending on the measure used (Greenbaum, 1964, p. 247).

Horvitz (1963) employs essentially the same methods and model used by Alhadeff. However, he uses Federal Deposit Insurance Corporation data on all insured banks for the period 1940–60 and data provided by the Federal Reserve System on all member banks for 1959. Not surprisingly, Horvitz' findings are similar, in many respects, to those of Alhadeff. "Over most of the range of bank size the decline in costs is very small and only in the largest size class was the decline substantial. This result bears out the description of costs . . . in Alhadeff's work. . . . The important point . . . is that once a bank reaches the relatively small size of $5 million of deposits, additional size does not result in reduced cost to any great extent until the bank reaches the giant size of over $500 million. This indicates that a small bank can compete on even terms with very large banks" (Horvitz, 1963, p. 37). With reference to branch banking, Horvitz maintains that:

For any given size and time deposit ratio, the branch bank expenses were greater (with only one exception) than the unit bank costs. What is important is not only the fact that branch bank costs were higher but also the considerable spread between branch and unit bank costs. This spread was generally greater than the spread between banks of different sizes. This means, surprisingly enough, that four $15 million unit banks can be operated at lower cost than a $60 million branch bank. In fact, even the smallest size category of unit banks had lower costs, on average, than the largest size branch banks (except for banks with less than 25 percent time deposits). The differences here are small but they indicate that extension of branch banking need not mean the demise of the small unit bank [1963, p. 37].[27]

---

non-interest income from the current (1964) 12.7 percent of current operating revenue to somewhere between 19 and 23 percent. (*Annual Report of the Comptroller of the Currency, 1928,* 1929; *Annual Report of the Comptroller of the Currency, 1933,* 1934; *Annual Report of the Federal Deposit Insurance Corporation, 1964,* 1965.)

[25]Production-function studies often use capital-stock and labor-force measures to represent corresponding flow concepts.

[26]Alhadeff does not consider the possibility of using current operating earnings as an output measure.

---

[27]Horvitz' conclusion regarding the costs of four $15 million unit banks, vis-à-vis a $60 million branch bank, does not appear to be convincingly substantiated by the data he presents.

The Horvitz study is perhaps best viewed as an attempt to check Alhadeff's findings with data of broader geographic and temporal coverage. Consequently, it suffers similar shortcomings. The most striking among these are the inability to develop relevant comparisons between branch and unit banking and the questionable compromises in handling the problem of bank output.

The Schweiger-McGee (1961) study, "Chicago Banking," differs from those of Alhadeff and Horvitz because it uses regression analysis and, perhaps more important, because it employs a different cost-equation specification. The dependent variable in the Schweiger-McGee cost equation is the ratio of current operating expense to total assets, and the primary independent variable—the output measure—is total deposits. The regression equations are calculated using transformed data—which may cause serious estimating problems—for all member banks for the year 1959.[28] In addition, costs of member banks in the Chicago Federal Reserve District for 1959 are analyzed using tabular inspection. The authors summarize their findings as follows: "Banks of less than $50 million in deposits can realize marked cost savings by growing. Cost savings from larger size are very sharply reduced for banks larger than $50 million in deposits. Branch banks tend to have higher costs and lower net current earnings on capital than unit banks of the same size. But branch banks are of larger average size. As a consequence, a greater proliferation of banking offices can be achieved more cheaply, and with higher net current earnings by branch banks than by many

very small unit banks" (Schweiger and McGee, 1961, p. 215).[29]

In *A Study of Scale Economies in Banking*, Gramley (1962) went one step beyond Schweiger and McGee. It will be remembered that Alhadeff and Horvitz drew their inferences directly from tabular data while Schweiger and McGee employed regression analysis in conjunction with transformed deposit data. Gramley applied regression analysis to data from individual-bank earning and condition reports, perhaps the richest source of banking information. The data are a sample—approximately stratified randomly—of 270 Kansas City District member banks, and each observation was an average of annual data for the years 1956–59. The banks in the sample were virtually all unit banks. Gramley also differed from his predecessors in his specification of the cost equation. The ratio of current operating expense to total assets served as the primary independent variable.

Gramley is one of the few who displays serious concern about the output problem. He states that the primary argument of his cost function—total assets—is not to be interpreted as a measure of, or proxy for, bank output. Gramley's inability to handle the output problem to his own satisfaction led him to circumscribe carefully the interpretation of his findings. He states that "the study . . . does not seek to determine whether, from the standpoint of achieving maximum social efficiency, the banking system should be composed of small or large units" (Gramley, 1962, p. 4).

Gramley indicates that the cost-asset ratio is best expressed as a negative linear function of the logarithm of assets. Thus, average costs decline sharply with size increases among small banks, but the cost curve flattens out as banks become

[28]Instead of introducing deposits directly as an independent variable, Schweiger and McGee define nine deposit classes—under $2 million, $2-$5 million, . . . , over $500 million—and assign each class a number—from 1 through 9—in ascending order. Each bank is then assigned a number according to which deposit class it falls into, and the assigned numbers are introduced in lieu of deposits.

[29]The conclusion regarding the relative advantage of branch banking does not appear to be substantiated by the data presented.

larger. A subsequent acceleration in the decline of costs among larger banks is not observed, but the largest banks in Gramley's sample are considerably smaller than those in Horvitz' sample.

Although my study of bank costs was under way before the publication of Gramley's work, it can be viewed as an attempt to fill a gap in his study. To quote Gramley:

The Nation's economic welfare depends very much on how efficiently resources are employed in the banking industry as a whole as well as in other lines of activity. That is why many studies of scale economies are directed specifically toward the social concept of efficiency in resource allocation.

But to attempt an evaluation of scale economies in banking from so broad a perspective would entail a much more extensive investigation than is undertaken in the present study. The question of what constitutes "output" of banks, and how the various dimensions of output should be given weights representing social valuations, is quite profound; an attempt to answer it would involve an excursion into areas of economic theory and theories of social welfare [1962, p. 3].

These are the questions that define the focus of my study. Dissatisfaction with the measures of output used in earlier studies prompted the development of a new alternative designed to impart greater public-policy relevance to the findings of bank-cost studies. The new measure initially divides output into two components: lending and all other. Lending output was defined as the gross yield-weighted sum of the diverse earning assets in each bank's portfolio. Yield weights were obtained by experimenting with least-squares regression equations of the following general form:

$$\frac{Y_i}{A_i} = b_0 + \sum_{j=1}^{n} b_j \frac{Z_{ij}}{A_i} + \sum_{j=n+1}^{m} b_j X_{ij} + u_i,$$

where Y_i is the ith bank's gross operating income directly attributable to lending; A_i is total assets of the ith bank; Z_{ij} is the ith bank's holding of the jth type of earning asset; X_{ij} are variables designed to isolate systematic interfirm price variation attributable to imperfect output markets; $b_0, b_1, \ldots, b_m$ are calculated net regression coefficients; and u_i is a stochastic term. Experimentation indicated that sixteen classifications of earning assets provided ample disaggregation and satisfactorily homogeneous earning-asset groupings.

Output of the ith bank was defined as:

$$Q_i = \sum_{j=1}^{16} b_j Z_{ij} + W_i, [30]$$

where W_i is a measure of non-lending output—defined as the ith bank's current operating revenue minus Y_i. The less elegant treatment of non-lending output was the result of difficulties in finding quantity measures for non-lending services, but, in aggregate, less than 10 percent of current operating revenue was directly attributable to these sources. The chief merits of this output measure include its explicit recognition of: (1) the multiproduct nature of commercial bank output, (2) interbank price differences resulting from imperfect markets, and (3) production as a flow process. The principal shortcoming of the Q_i output measure is its failure to treat transaction size as a product characteristic. It is prima facie implausible to assume community indifference to variations in average transaction size of bank services: a $10,000 loan is not a perfect substitute for twenty loans of $500.[31] If average

---

[30]Contrary to expectation, an intercept significantly greater than zero was obtained in the estimating equation. Consequently, a second output measure, Q_i^*, was defined to include the intercept, which turns out to be the coefficient of the assets deflator. The cost curves obtained using the two output measures were sufficiently similar to render the intercept problem inconsequential.

[31]Persistent and significant interest-rate differences on loans of different size, but similar in all other characteristics, support this argument, provided such interest-rate differences are not totally explainable in terms of differential bargaining power of large and small borrowers.

transaction size is positively related to bank size, ignoring average transaction size will probably result in overstating economies of scale.

The basic data were obtained from 1961 earning and condition reports for 745 individual member banks in the Kansas City Federal Reserve District and 413 member banks in the Richmond Federal Reserve District. The Kansas City District is almost entirely a unit-banking area, whereas the Richmond District has a substantial number of branch systems. Regressing current operating expense on the output measure indicated U-shaped average cost curves in the Kansas City District, with optimal-size banks of approximately $300 million in deposits. In studying the Richmond subsample of branch banks, evidence of independent plant and firm effects on cost was found. Not only are there savings attendant to increases in plant size, but, in addition, cost reductions accompany increases in firm size when output per plant is held constant. This suggests that grouping independent unit banks into branch systems results in savings even if the output of each element in the system is unchanged.

Benston's study (1965a and b) has a number of attributes that set it apart from earlier works. Perhaps most interesting is the eschewal of a single-valued measure of output; "each bank was divided into six separate units—'producing' demand deposits, time deposits, mortgage loans, instalment loans, business loans, or securities" (Benston, 1965b, p. 509). Each type of output is measured in terms of numbers of loan or deposit accounts with the average dollar volume of transactions included among the arguments of the cost functions. Therefore, Benston avoids one of the major shortcomings of my formulation. However, Benston's approach has a number of questionable aspects.

Consider that elements from both sides of the bank's balance sheet—deposits and earning assets—are treated as types of output. From the viewpoint of the individual bank, deposits reflect borrowing while earning assets reflect lending. Banks pay others to hold deposits, not the reverse. In effect, deposits reflect the bank's purchase of the services of money. They may be thought of as a substitute for capital to the individual bank. These considerations suggest that deposits are more usefully thought of as a factor input to the bank.

The rejection of a unidimensional or single-valued index of output also introduces difficulties. If an over-all assessment of returns to scale is desired, some combinatorial scheme must be introduced. The stage of the analysis at which the output mapping should take place is open to question, but Benston presents disparate and unreconciled findings. Without additional bases for interpreting the findings, generalized interfirm comparisons are impossible, and the analysis stands incomplete.

Benston's data are generated by the *Functional Cost Analyses* published annually by the Federal Reserve Bank of Boston. Taken from questionnaires submitted by eighty to eight-three banks, the data apply to operations in 1959, 1960, and 1961. The surveyed banks range in asset size from $3.4 million to $55.0 million. It should be noted that Benston's results depend upon the individual banker's allocation of his expenses —according to prearranged guidelines— to the various output categories.[32]

Benston finds that although "there are economies of scale of direct cost with respect to the number of deposit accounts or loans, these are not great: efficiency of operations is not largely a function of bank size" (1965b, p. 541).[33]

---

[32]Benston recognizes the limitations inherent in the size range of his observations, but doubts whether the expense allocations represent a serious problem. The latter judgment may be open to question.

[33]One can accept the Benston analysis and yet question his judgment that economies of scale "are not great." His estimated elasticities

He also concludes that "branch banking does entail additional costs that are not offset by economies of scale" (Benston, 1965a, p. 330). The author expresses some doubts regarding this finding owing to the nature of his sample.[34]

INTERPRETATION

If the recent bank-cost studies are judged on the basis of whether they have supplied the reliable information necessary for evaluating regulatory policy, they have failed. But this is a harsh standard, especially since the first of these studies was published but twelve years ago. The gradual improvement among these studies and the nature of the shortcomings in the most recent works suggest that continued effort can yield handsome dividends in terms of the sought-after information.[35] The increasing attention devoted

to conceptual problems is especially noteworthy. This is evidenced in the later studies by advances in defining bank output and more relevant comparisons between branch and unit banking. Improvements in the techniques of bank-cost analysis are esspecially significant in light of the imminence of automated payments, which will inevitably alter the underlying production function. Only the scope of this change remains in doubt, and those who have studied the question argue that automation of payments will have a profound impact (see Greenberger, 1965, and Mitchell, 1966). Therefore, current findings relating to economies of scale are likely to be obsolete in the near future. The transitory quality of such findings is in contrast to the probable transferability of advances in the techniques of cost analysis. The practical irreversibility of banking-structure policy changes and the imminence and estimated impact of automated payments might well counsel against policy changes based on convincing case-study findings, even if they were available.

The recent works also suggest the types of data, not now readily available, that may be required for the execution of more definitive work. The most obvious need is for transactions data. *Functional Cost Analyses* generate these data, but only for limited numbers and types of banks. Data applicable to branch operations are virtually ignored by the regulatory agencies, but may be crucial in evaluating alternative banking systems. Analogous data in a unit-banking milieu are those applying to correspondent bank relations. These too are sparse. There are reasons for believing that efficiently functioning correspondent banking facilities could serve as an effective substitute for branch banking in the presence of economies of scale (see Federal Reserve Bank of Kansas City, 1965a and b).

---

of direct expenses with respect to the number of accounts or loans range from 0.736 to 0.968 on the six categories of output he examines. At one extreme a 100 percent increase in "output" results in a 74 percent increase in cost, while at the other, direct expenses rise 97 percent. Each 1 percent reduction in current operating expenses for all banks implies a saving of approximately $110 million annually. Moreover, the one finding of U-shaped average cost curves (Greenbaum, 1964) indicated that the optimal bank size is approximately twelve times the present average bank size in the nation.

[34]Benston (1965a) defines the effects of mergers as the difference between the cost saving associated with expanding output while holding the number of branches fixed and the cost of expanding the number of branches while holding output fixed. Both components of this measure focus on the consequences of varying the size of branches, but this is only one aspect of the effect of mergers on costs. Remaining is the question of what happens to costs when the number of branches is expanded with the average size—output—of branches remaining unchanged. Mergers may influence costs by altering the size of banks—a firm effect—while leaving the size of plants unchanged. The firm effect will be of primary importance where bank mergers result in the conversion of banks to branches. Benston, however, recognizes only the plant effect in his analysis.

[35]Milton Friedman (1955, pp. 230–38) has argued, on quite fundamental grounds, that statistical cost analyses based on accounting data cannot yield the sought-after information. Partially convincing counterarguments are presented by Johnston (1960, pp. 186–94).

Recent bank-cost studies also indicate that much remains to be done. Students of bank costs still employ the assumption that private-cost concepts have social relevance. Study of the relationship between private and social costs may lead to new cost-function specifications and to more emphasis on the production function approach to the study of scale economies in banking (see Morrison and Selden, 1965, Appendixes B and C, and Greenbaum, 1966).

The explanation for exclusive reliance on cost functions is not entirely clear, but inattention to the production approach has undoubtedly retarded progress. Recognition of the relationship between cost and production analysis and parallel development of the two probably would have resulted in more attention to the vexatious conceptual problems. The use of deposits as an output measure might have been ruled out. Consideration of the problem of defining inputs also might have resulted in more attention to defining relevant measures of costs. Exclusive focus on the cost-function approach to analyzing scale economies has resulted in fundamental issues being ignored and obscured. Perhaps this is pardonable in light of some of the interesting results that have been obtained, but if the findings of such studies are to be compelling, more attention will have to be directed to framing relevant concepts of cost, inputs, and output and probably to the use of production analysis as a complement to cost analysis.[36]

I have emphasized that firm findings regarding economies of scale are not at hand. However, study of the literature cannot fail to convey some impressions on this question. My review of this literature has led me to the view that small banks—say $10 million or less in deposits—are probably grossly inefficient.[37] It seems likely that significant economies of scale prevail beyond the $10 million deposit size, but they are probably of a smaller order of magnitude. The conditions under which banks of more than $300 million in deposits operate are much more difficult to judge. The studies done have run the gamut, observing rising costs (Greenbaum, 1964), falling costs (Alhadeff, 1954, and Horvitz, 1963), and essentially constant costs (Gramley, 1962). Thus, the optimal bank size is unknown.

The inefficiency of smaller banks may be attributable to their inability to spread overhead costs, limitations to specialization among employees, high transactions costs of moving funds in small amounts, loan risk interdependencies, and limitations on risk pooling. Some of these problems can be overcome by correspondent banking facilities, but the impression is that they are not overcome. This suggests that correspondent facilities leave much to be desired.[38]

The aforementioned impressions regarding scale economies pertain to the real resources used in producing bank output through firms of various size with

---

[36]Under certain circumstances the production-function analysis of returns to scale will possess greater generality than a comparable cost-function analysis. Some production functions yield different returns to scale depending upon the prevailing factor prices. Since the cost-function analysis proceeds on the basis of a given set of factor prices, its returns to scale findings will be more limited than those of the production function, which can allow for various results without reference to a specific set of factor prices.

[37]As of the year end 1965, 72.8 percent of all (13,818) commercial banks had deposits of less than $10 million, and 89.6 percent had deposits of less than $25 million. Banks with less than $10 million in deposits had 11.8 percent of total deposits, and those with less than $25 million in deposits had 22.5 percent of total deposits (*Annual Report of the Federal Deposit Insurance Corporation, 1965*, 1966).

[38]"Frictions within the correspondent system evidently impede the free flow of funds to and from the smaller unit banks" (Guttentag and Herman, 1967, p. 27). The current trend toward operating correspondent facilities on a fee basis may improve matters, since one problem appears to be lack of information on the cost and availability of services. The elimination of the prohibition of interest payment on interbank demand balances would be one means to encourage the use of explicit charges for correspondent services.

equal numbers of offices. The sparse evidence on the effects of consolidating unit banks into branch systems suggests that important savings result, even if the output of the consolidated banks does not exceed the output of the components. As might be expected, the savings from such consolidations are not so great as those obtained when numerous unit banks are consolidated into one larger unit bank, but they are still far from negligible. Consolidations of the former type may exploit the advantages of economizing managerial talents, risk pooling, and greater mobility of funds, even if some advantages of lower overhead are unavailable.

In the absence of regulation of entry, merger, and branching, and further assuming no improvement in correspondent banking facilities, small banks probably would be eliminated gradually and replaced with branches of larger institutions.[39] The extent of consolidation that would occur is uncertain, but international comparisons suggest that the industry might ultimately be composed of fewer than one hundred firms, perhaps fewer than fifty (see Sayers, 1962).[40] Such a consolidation might result in real savings on the order of $1 billion per year.[41] The distribution of such savings among factor services in banking, consumers of bank services, and the community at large would remain to be resolved. In any case, the $1 billion per year may be viewed as the cost of the present regulatory framework and should be weighed against the advantages inherent to present policies.

The question of the non-cost advantages of a decentralized banking system of the type extant, vis-à-vis one of the type visualized above, opens a Pandora's box that I cannot hope to explore thoroughly in this paper.[42] However, the alleged allocative and exploitative advantages of decentralized or unit banking do not appear to be supported. Indeed, the weight of evidence appears to favor more concentration in banking on these grounds (see Edwards, 1964; Horvitz and Shull, 1964; New York State Banking Department, 1964; Shull and Horvitz, 1964; Edwards, 1965; and Kaufman, 1966).[43] Although research on the efficiency, allocative, and exploitative issues in banking structure has not been entirely convincing, and research on the responsivity issue is practically nonexistent, the burden of proof appears to lie with those who favor a decentralized type of banking system.

REFERENCES

Alhadeff, David A. *Monopoly and Competition in Banking.* Berkeley: Univ. of Calif. Press, 1954.

---

[39]One effect of such consolidations might be the erection of natural barriers to entry which would replace the current regulatory barriers.

[40]Assets data for all insured commercial banks, December 31, 1964, indicate that an optimum-size firm of $300 million in assets would imply an industry of 1,150 firms. In a one hundred-firm industry, average asset size would be $3.5 billion (*Annual Report of the Federal Deposit Insurance Corporation, 1964, 1965*).

[14]See n. 18.

---

[42]Although the responsivity question has received little attention, research on the allocative and exploitative issues has been voluminous. The extent of research is suggested by the length (200 pages) of Guttentag and Herman's (1967) survey of selected publications on banking structure. For additional survey and bibliographical material see Robert Holland, Tynan Smith, George Hall, and Wm. Paul Smith (1964) and Tynan Smith (1966). Also see *Studies in Banking Competition and the Banking Structure: Articles Reprinted from the National Banking Review* (1966). A non-cost advantage of centralization that has received little attention relates to monetary-policy formulation and implementation. A more centralized banking system probably would result in more consistent—spatially and temporally—responses to monetary-policy actions. This would enhance the neutrality of policy and, therefore, would be desirable on equity grounds. Centralization might also simplify prediction of reactions to policy (see Federal Reserve Bank of Kansas City, 1963).

[43]Franklin Edwards' (1964) findings have been seriously challenged by Theodore Flechsig (1965). George Kaufman's (1966) findings are also ambiguous in that they rest on the assumption that all banks in his sample have essentially identical loan portfolios.

————. "A Reconsideration of Restrictions on Bank Entry," *Q.J.E.*, LXXVI (May, 1962), 246–63.

Annual Report of the Comptroller of the Currency, 1928. Washington: U.S. Government Printing Office, 1929.

Annual Report of the Comptroller of the Currency, 1933. Washington: U.S. Government Printing Office, 1934.

Annual Report of the Federal Deposit Insurance Corporation, 1963. Washington: Federal Deposit Insurance Corp., 1964.

Annual Report of the Federal Deposit Insurance Corporation, 1964. Washington: Federal Deposit Insurance Corp., 1965.

Annual Report of the Federal Deposit Insurance Corporation, 1965. Washington: Federal Deposit Insurance Corp., 1966.

Assets, Liabilities, and Capital Accounts, Commercial and Mutual Savings Banks, Nos. 29–74. Washington: Federal Deposit Insurance Corp., 1948–65.

Benston, George J. "Branch Banking and Economies of Scale," *J. Finance*, XX (May, 1965), 312–32. (*a*)

————. "Economies of Scale and Marginal Costs in Banking Operations," *Nat. Banking Rev.*, II (June, 1965), 507–49. (*b*)

Christ, Carl F. "Interest Rates and 'Portfolio Selection' among Liquid Assets in the U.S.," in Christ, Carl F., *et al. Measurement in Economics: Studies in Mathematical Economics and Econometrics in Memory of Yehuda Grunfeld*. Stanford, Calif.: Stanford Univ. Press, 1963, pp. 20–118.

Edwards, Franklin R. "Concentration in Banking and Its Effect on Business Loan Rates," *Rev. Econ. and Statis.*, XLVI (August, 1964), 294–300.

————. "The Banking Competition Controversy," *Nat Banking Rev.*, III (September, 1965), 1–34.

Fand, David I. "Financial Regulation and the Allocative Efficiency of Our Capital Markets," *Nat. Banking Rev.*, III (September, 1965), 55–63.

Federal Reserve Bank of Kansas City. "Banking Structure and Reactions to Monetary Stringency or Ease," *Monthly Rev.* (March–April, 1963), pp. 9–15.

————. "Correspondent Banking," *ibid.* (March–April, 1965), pp. 9–16. (*a*)

————. "More on Correspondent Banking," *ibid.* (July–August, 1965), pp. 14–23. (*b*)

Flechsig, Theodore G. *Banking Market Structure and Performance in Metropolitan Areas: A Statistical Study of Factors Affecting Rates on Bank Loans*. Washington: Board of Governors of the Federal Reserve System, 1965.

Friedman, Milton. Comment on "Survey of the Empirical Evidence on Economies of Scale," *Business Concentration and Price Policy*. New York: National Bureau of Economic Research, 1955.

————. *A Program for Monetary Stability*. New York: Fordham Univ. Press, 1960.

Golembe, Carter. "The Deposit Insurance Legislation of 1933: An Examination of Its Antecedents and Its Purposes," *Polit. Sci. Q.*, LXXV (June, 1960), 181–200.

Gramley, Lyle E. *A Study of Scale Economies in Banking*. Kansas City: Federal Reserve Bank of Kansas City, 1962.

Greenbaum, Stuart I. "Banking Structure and Costs: A Statistical Study of the Cost-Output Relationship in Commercial Banking." Ph.D. dissertation, Johns Hopkins Univ., 1964.

————. "Costs and Production in Commercial Banking," *Monthly Rev.* (Federal Reserve Bank of Kansas City) (March–April, 1966).

Greenberger, Martin. "Decline and Fall of the Check," *Bankers Magazine*, CXLVIII (Summer, 1965), 84–89.

Guttentag, Jack M., and Herman, Edward S. "Banking Structure and Performance," *Bulletin* (New York Univ., Graduate School of Bus. Admin., Inst. of Finance), Nos. 41–43 (February, 1967).

Hansen, Alvin H. "Bankers and Subsidies," *Rev. Econ. and Statis.*, XL (February, 1958), 50–51.

Henderson, James M., and Quandt, Richard E. *Microeconomic Theory: A Mathematical Approach*. New York: McGraw-Hill Book Co., 1958.

Hester, Donald D., and Zoellner, John F. "The Relation Between Bank Portfolios and Earnings: An Econometric Analysis," *Rev. Econ. and Statis.*, XLVIII (November, 1966), 372–86.

Holland, Robert; Smith, Tynan; Hall, George; and Smith, Wm. Paul. "Research into Banking Structure and Competition," *Federal Reserve Bull.*, L (November, 1964), 1383–99.

Horvitz, Paul M. "Economies of Scale in Banking," in Commission on Money and Credit. *Private Financial Institutions.* Englewood Cliffs, N.J.: Prentice-Hall, Inc., 1963, pp. 1–54.

Horvitz, Paul M., and Shull, Bernard. "The Impact of Branch Banking on Banking Performance," *Nat. Banking Rev.* II (December, 1964), 143–88.

Jacobs, Donald. "The Framework of Commercial Bank Regulation: An Appraisal," *Nat. Banking Rev.,* I (March, 1964), 343–57.

Johnston, J. *Statistical Cost Analysis.* New York: McGraw-Hill Book Co., 1960.

Kaufman, George G. "Bank Market Structure and Performance: The Evidence from Iowa," *Southern Econ J.,* XXXII (April, 1960), 429–39.

Kuznets, Simon. "National Income and Economic Welfare," *Economic Change: Selected Essays in Business Cycles, National Income, and Economic Growth.* New York: W. W. Norton & Co., 1953, pp. 192–215.

Mitchell, George W. "Mergers among Commercial Banks," in Almarin Phillips (ed.). *Perspectives in Antitrust Policy.* Princeton, N.J.: Princeton Univ. Press, 1965, pp. 225–43.

————. "Effects of Automation on the Structure and Functioning of Banking," *A.E.R.,* LVI (May, 1966), 159–66.

Morrison, George R., and Selden, Richard T. *Time Deposit Growth and the Employment of Bank Funds.* Chicago: Association of Reserve Bankers, 1965.

Motter, David C. "Bank Formation and the Public Interest," *Nat. Banking Rev.* II (March, 1965), 299–350.

Musgrave, Richard A. *The Theory of Public Finance: A Study in Public Economy.* New York: McGraw-Hill Book Co., 1959.

New York State Banking Department. *Branch Banking, Bank Mergers and the Public Interest.* New York: N.Y. State Banking Dept., 1964.

Peltzman, Sam. "Determinants of Bank Entry." Ph.D. dissertation, Univ. of Chicago, 1964.

————. "Bank Entry Regulation: Its Impact and Purpose," *Nat. Banking Rev.,* III (December, 1965), 163–77.

Phillips, Almarin. "Competition, Confusion, and Commercial Banking," *J. Finance,* XLX (March, 1964), 32–45.

Robertson, James L. "An Alternative to Fossilization." Remarks at the Diamond Jubilee Anniversary Convention of the Ill. Bankers Association, Peoria, Ill., May 17, 1966.

Robertson, Ross M. "Memorandum on the Growth of Financial Intermediaries." Unpublished study paper, Commission on Money and Credit, New York, 1962.

Samuelson, Paul A. "The Effect of Interest Rate Increases on the Banking System," *A.E.R.,* XXXV (March, 1945), 16–27.

The Savings and Loan Fact Book. Chicago: U.S. Savings & Loan League, 1965.

Sayers, R. S. (ed.). *Banking in Western Europe.* London: Oxford Univ. Press, 1962.

Schweiger, Irving, and McGee, John S. "Chicago Banking," *J. Bus.,* XXXIV (July, 1961), 203–366.

Shull, Bernard, and Horvitz, Paul M. "Branch Banking and the Structure of Competition," *Nat Banking Rev.,* I (March, 1964), 301–41.

Schumpeter, Joseph A. *Capitalism, Socialism, and Democracy,* 2d ed. New York: Harper & Bros., 1947.

Smith, Tynan. "Research on Banking Structure and Performance," *Federal Reserve Bull.,* LII (April, 1966), 488–98.

Smith, Wm. Paul. "Measures of Banking Structure and Competition," *Federal Reserve Bull.,* LI (September, 1965), 1212–22.

Studies in Banking Competition and the Banking Structure: Articles Reprinted from the National Banking Review. Washington: Administrator of National Banks. U.S. Treasury, 1966.

4. One-Bank Holding Companies: A Banker's View[*]

John R. Bunting, Jr.

One-bank holding companies (congenerics), this article argues, answer a pressing need and make available enormous opportunities for certain banks. The author focuses on important issues, as seen by the practitioner, and presents some commonly overlooked points which modify the claims that unfair competition, excessive monopoly power, and institutional convulsions will result from the one-bank holding company movement. This article and the next provide, respectively, a comprehensive view of the advantages and disadvantages of the financial congeneric.

The one-bank holding company movement is one of banking's few authentic revolutions. Usually change comes in a slow, evolutionary manner to commercial banks, which *Business Week* once called the "Stepin Fetchits" of the business world. One-bank holding companies, however, burst on the scene with dramatic suddenness. Virtually unheard of 18 months ago, this new form of organization now accounts for more than $100 billion in deposits—about one-third of the national total.

At the roots of this revolution are the desire of progressive, modern banks for freedom from outmoded and oppressive regulations governing their conduct, and the general inflation psychology that leads all financial institutions to want a "piece of the action."

The implications of the movement are

tremendous. The Federal Reserve System's William McChesney Martin, Jr. has said, "The whole capitalistic system in the United States could be profoundly affected by the use of one bank holding companies."

As I see it, these companies offer the best way now available for banks to adapt to the fast-changing needs of their customers and thus better serve the nation in the coming decade.

SEEDS OF REVOLT

Like most revolutions, this one has been in the making for quite some time. It was brought about by basic changes in the economy which began a number of years ago. Not only have banks come under increasing *pressure* to find new ways to increase their earnings, but the more enterprising banks also have been attracted to major new *opportunities* for improved profits.

Growing Pressures

The early 1960's offer a good vantage point from which to observe the changes just mentioned. Demand deposits had entered a period of moderate growth while savings had begun to expand rapidly. In 1961 the Federal Reserve raised the interest ceilings on time deposits and encouraged the development of negotiable certificates of deposit. So armed, commercial banks began to compete more aggressively for loanable funds.

[*]From *Harvard Business Review*, May/June, 1969. Copyright 1969 by the President and Fellows of Harvard College; all rights reserved. Reprinted by permission of the publisher.

They were eminently successful. Time deposits at Federal Reserve member banks swelled from $54 billion in 1960 to $155 billion in 1968. But this achievement was a costly one, for it sharply increased the proportion of deposits on which banks had to pay interest. A study of 25 major banks across the country made by the brokerage firm of M. A. Schapiro & Co., Inc. revealed that interest costs in 1967 were more than five times greater than in 1960.[1] Because of rising interest payments alone, the average break-even point of the banks in the survey tripled in less than eight years.

Banks also found other sources of funds in the 1960-1968 period—all of them expensive. The rapidly developing Federal Funds and Euro-dollar markets provided large amounts of money but at high rates. Even demand deposits on which interest could not be paid grew more costly. Competition for them became keener, and banks were forced to increase advertising expenses and to offer more free services as a lure to depositors.

As a result of rising costs, many banks found themselves in a difficult position. They had a lot of new money, which had to earn more because it cost more, but traditional lending and investing opportunities would not yield significantly greater returns. Usury laws, all sorts of restrictions on the character of bank assets, and the growth of competing sources of credit such as commercial paper and consumer finance companies placed effective limits on bank earning power.

The effects of this squeeze show up when we carefully examine bank earnings. At first glance we see that the dollar volume has increased substantially; the Schapiro study shows that operating earnings have grown by about 50 percent since 1960. But look again. When earnings are related to payout on stock or the volume of earning assets, their appearance becomes much more disappointing. The Schapiro report shows that:

1. The percentage of payout on common stock has been virtually constant since 1960.
2. Pretax profits per $1,000 of loans and investments have declined by $7.20, from $24.20 to $17.

Accelerating inflation, like rising costs, forces banks to seek higher earnings. Inflation hurts creditors because it makes the dollars they receive in repayment worth less than those they lent in the first place. Interest is supposed to make up for declines in the value of money out on loan, but with prices now rising 5 percent a year, rates would have to be much higher than they are even now to provide adequate compensation. Such a level of rates would severely disrupt the entire economy and, I am sure, will not be permitted by the monetary authorities.

In short, banks find themselves in need of new and more profitable ways to employ the high-cost money they have been obtaining in the past few years. This is not just "cloud nine" talk, for the extensive computer facilities that most large banks now possess give them the technological *ability* to diversify what they do and where they do it. But this isn't all the story.

Exciting Opportunities

All the while that pressures on banks have been growing, so also have new opportunities to increase profitability in new ways. The growing diversity of the U.S. economy, trends in technological development, the quickening pace of economic change—these and other developments have combined to "explode" the possibilities of business growth and expansion. Many of the new fields which have been opening up are of particular interest to entrepreneurial bank executives. Not only are these executives likely to be well

---

[1] M. A. Schapiro & Co., *Bank Stock Quarterly*, September 1968, p. 2.

trained in the kinds of financial analysis and management called for by the new enterprises, but they can perhaps sense the profit potentials better than most men can.

To be more specific, consider how radically the needs and desires of bank customers have changed during the past decade or two. It is true that because of their increased ability to finance themselves internally and because of the growth of alternative credit sources, business organizations have become less dependent on banking's old-time mainstay, the short-term commercial loan. Because company treasurers have sharpened their pencils and put idle cash quickly to work, demand deposit balances are kept to a bare minimum. However, this does not mean that business customers have reduced their over-all requirements for financial services. Far from it. Customers have simply developed different, more varied needs:

1. As corporations have grown—many of them now operating regionally, nationally, or internationally—they have come to require new varieties of financial service: automatic payment plans, mortgage services, equipment leasing, factoring, plant location advice, acquisition and merger services, credit information, foreign trade promotion and financing, property management, and a long list of others.
2. As for smaller businesses, they have special new needs for data processing and accounting services; and frequently they require credit under terms far different from those established by banking tradition.
3. Increasingly affluent consumers also seek a far wider range of financial services: credit cards, trust accounts, mutual funds, insurance, mortgage placement, small loans, travel services, revolving credit, and so on. With consumers today, convenience is a key item; they prefer all their financial ser-

vices to be available at one spot, just as they find more and more of the other things they buy grouped together in department stores and shopping centers. Already some insurance companies and mutual funds are trying to team up to provide more centralized services.

All these trends have indeed produced a revolution in the environment—and at first blush it would appear to be a congenial revolution for banks. Strong pressures to expand and diversify services, customers with a desire for such expansion and diversity, opportunities which progressive banks are especially well suited to seize—it all sounds like an ideal match. But it has not come off. Why?

'Banker, Stay Home'

The trouble is that banks in this country are hemmed in by all sorts of laws and regulations. Bank operations are subject to restrictions placed by the U.S. Congress, all the state legislatures, at least four federal agencies, and 50 state banking departments. I shall return to the subject of regulations later; suffice it to say here that banks, until recently at least, could not find adequate legal means to accomplish the expansion which seemed such a good idea for all concerned.

To make matters worse, when some government regulation is relaxed a bit and banks are permitted to operate beyond traditional fences, established interests usually feel threatened and initiate long, costly court fights to keep banking where they think it belongs—doing only the things that it always has done. To cite a few examples:

1. The Federal Reserve ruling which permits banks to set up loan production offices anywhere in the United States is now under legal attack in several states.
2. The right of national banks to perform computer services for customers is being challenged in court.

3. The right of national banks to underwrite revenue bonds, which were granted by the Comptroller of the Currency several years ago, has been denied by a federal court in the District of Columbia.

ENTER THE NEW ORGANIZATION

I don't know who first thought of the one-bank holding company as a solution to bankers' frustrations, but he deserves to have his statue placed alongside those of the other great emancipators of history. In 1956 a law was passed which prohibited holding companies involving two or more banks from owning nonbanking businesses. Organizations that included only one bank were specifically exempted. This exception recognized the fact that many organizations—such as R. H. Macy & Co., the Goodyear Tire & Rubber Company, Hershey Foods, the United Mine Workers, and even the trustees of Dartmouth College—long had owned banks which almost invariably were small and relatively insignificant.

In 1967 this exception in the 1956 law was remembered and used to turn a big bank into a holding company, which then was free to acquire and operate other financial firms. Thus a way was found to achieve the expanded spectrum of services and increased earning potential that banks so badly needed but theretofore had found so hard to get.

How It Works

A bank wishing to convert itself into a holding company usually creates a corporation which establishes a subsidiary, "phantom" bank existing only on paper. The original bank then is merged into the phantom, and the original bank's stockholders exchange their stock for shares in the corporation. In other words, the stockholders wind up owning the corporation, which at this point holds the bank as its only asset.

The bank continues to operate as before, subject to the same rules and regulations. As for the new corporation, since it is not itself a bank, it can operate with the same freedom enjoyed by any other business corporation in its state.

Theoretically, the new corporation could enter any legitimate business it desired—manufacturing, automobile dealerships, or what have you—either by acquiring existing companies or by starting new ones. Nevertheless, all banks which have formed one-bank holding companies or announced plans to do so have strongly emphasized their intentions to confine themselves to financial activities. Examples of ventures that may interest the company's management are mortgage service companies, factors, consumer finance and small loan companies, equipment financing operations, data processing facilities, and insurance.

Significant Advances

Why is the one-bank holding company the solution that entrepreneurial bankers have been looking for? It offers these specific advantages and opportunities:

DIVERSIFICATION WITHOUT DISPUTE. Through its subsidiaries, the one-bank holding company can offer the kind of one-stop financial service that modern businesses and consumers desire. Not being a bank, the holding company need not worry about the hobbles placed on banks by the regulatory authorities and by the lawsuits of fearful competitors seeking to keep banks out of their backyards. It can create financial subsidiaries—an equipment leasing firm, say, or a data-processing service—and locate them near the bank.

OPERATIONS ANYWHERE. Some of the most liberal states permit banks to merge or establish branches anyplace within their borders. However, other states restrict branching to certain groups of counties, and some states prohibit it entirely. I must admit I cannot understand why bank operations should be confined to tight little boxes when few if any other industries are so restricted. The rule makes no sense today.

Fortunately, one-bank holding companies play by the rules that apply to everybody else and thus are able to operate wherever they can find a demand for their nonbanking financial services. A bank in, let us say, Detroit would have to keep its branches located in the area prescribed by Michigan law, but other financial subsidiaries of the holding company could be located in other parts of the state or in other states.

This mobility will be a tonic to competition. It should be beneficial to all banks except inefficient, high-cost institutions which have survived only because their little fiefdoms were protected by law.

ATTRACTING THE RIGHT PEOPLE. In spite of recent improvements, the banking industry still has a stodgy image. The standard explanation is: "We deal with other people's money, so we have to be conservative." Personally, I think there is a big difference between "can't do" conservatism and "can do" carefulness. At any rate, the fact is that the stodgy image has hurt banks in the ever keener competition for bright young executive talent.

It used to be that the top executives of a bank had to have worked themselves up through various departments and learned all the details about making loans. Now, as Walter B. Wriston, president of The First National City Bank of New York, puts it, "There is a need for a different kind of bank management . . . good administrators who don't necessarily read the fine print . . . people who deal in broad concepts."[2] Such people are too much in demand everywhere to be enticed by a narrowly confined bank.

In my opinion, one-bank holding companies will create a new exciting image for banking and help it to attract dynamic talented executives. The new form of or-

ganization also offers tangible advantages to employees. The various firms in the holding company family will be able to hire experts in specialized fields at going rates. Moreover, opportunities for advancement and participation in policy formation should be greater in a number of semiautonomous companies than in a single large bank without a corporate family.

Further, one-bank holding companies permit more flexibility in stock option plans, which have become almost standard incentives for executives in many other industries.

LEVERAGE ON PROFITS. Banking laws and regulations place numerous special restrictions on the issuance of debt securities. Holding companies, however, have greater latitude in borrowing money. They can make greater use of debt issues to acquire subsidiary companies. Such leverage potentially increases the return on the equity of the holding company stockholders.

What is more, additional profits will enable management to plow back more money to the various firms under the holding company umbrella. I can think of many ways extra funds would enable a bank to improve its services to customers and community. Augmented research is one possibility. While U.S. manufacturers spend billions of dollars each year on research to discover new products and improve old ones, very few banks (or other financial institutions) conduct formal research programs to develop and test new and better services.

Also, increased profits should enable a bank to participate more fully in the solutions of today's critical urban problems. Although, as my bank has discovered, a program of loans to black businessmen does not necessarily lose money, risks and administrative costs are high. Having greater profits to work with, the bank member of a holding company should be able to invest more in efforts to encourage capitalism in the ghettos and to hire and

---

[2]"Why Citibank Is More Than a Bank," *Business Week*, November 16, 1968, p. 80.

train "hard core" unemployed workers from ghetto areas.

KNOWING WHAT THINGS COST. The management of a one-bank holding company can break the operations controlled into distinct units. It also might be able to spin off certain departments of the bank itself, such as data processing or travel, and operate them much like separate companies. On the other hand, some service functions, such as investment analysis, research, and printing, could be consolidated to serve the entire family of companies. In so doing, management can gain better cost information about an operation—and control it better—than if it were merged with other activities. By virtue of its size and freedom of operation, the management of a holding company can go further in this respect than can the management of an independent bank. (I do not deny, of course, that many banks could do a great deal more to separate operations for purposes of cost and control.)

In addition, more knowledge about costs could make it easier to switch more services performed for correspondent banks to a fee basis. While I have no personal grudge against the time-honored system of compensating balances, I think its imprecision can be unfair to both parties involved. A more equitable method might be to charge fees that cover the cost of the work done, as is now the practice with demand deposit accounting.

PRESERVING THE DUAL BANKING SYSTEM. The one-bank holding company device enables the management of state member banks to do all the things national banks, with their more liberal regulations, can do and then some. I do not mean to rule out the possibility that The First Pennsylvania Bank and others will switch to a national charter some day, but the chance to become a one-bank holding company should keep many state member banks in the fold. So many important banks already have switched to national charters that a few more conversions

might weaken the state sector enough to cause a fundamental change in the character of U.S. banking, i.e., a change from the philosophy that both state and federally regulated banks should exist in ample numbers in order to distribute regulatory authority.

Now, I do not feel that there is anything sacred about the dual banking system, but it does have its desirable aspects. The possibility of switching between national and state charters provides a kind of safety valve for banks should regulations in one or the other category become unusually harsh and restrictive. The presence of a choice is healthy, I believe, because it helps keep the regulatory agencies on their toes by providing a type of competition between them. The option to form a one-bank holding company will help to keep the choice a real one, not a theoretical one.

QUESTIONS AND CONCERNS

While one-bank holding companies present great opportunities and advantages to bank managements—and also to the public, as Paul S. Nadler points out in the next article—the revolution with its speed and drama has caused considerable concern, some of it justified and some the result of unrealistic "hang-ups." I shall comment on several of the most important fears and criticisms of the movement.

Unfair Competition?

The commercial banking system has the ability to create demand deposits within limits set by the Federal Reserve Board. A bank's access to money in its cheapest form worries nonbank lenders in particular, for they must pay going rates for their funds. They are afraid that firms in a one-bank holding company, possessing direct access to bank credit based on demand deposits, will be able to underprice their services and force competitors not so affiliated out of business.

I agree that one-bank holding companies will increase competition in many financial fields, and I heartily approve. After all, it has been national policy for more than half a century to encourage competitive conditions in most sectors of the economy. No doubt some of the most inefficient producers *will* fail because of the rise of one-bank holding companies. But the weeding out of weak sisters and the gradual increase in the size of productive units are long-standing trends which have been in large measure responsible for the nation's present standard of affluence.

Yet to say that one-bank holding companies will be *unfair* competitors is just not being realistic. Consider these points:

1. Direct access to bank credit is hardly a special advantage anymore because, as earlier pointed out, "free" demand deposits have declined sharply in relation to interest-bearing time deposits.
2. The loans that banks make to affiliates are strictly controlled by federal law. No bank may lend more than 10 percent of its capital and surplus to any one affiliate, or more than 20 percent to all affiliates combined. I think it likely that holding company banks will bend over backward to avoid even a hint of conflict of interest, and that, in practice, they will restrict loans to affiliates even more severely. For the same reason, these banks will make every effort not to discriminate against unaffiliated nonbank institutions whether or not they compete against members of the holding company. For many years banks have done business with dealers and finance companies which compete with their own installment loan department.

As a matter of fact, it is probable that many one-bank holding companies themselves will face what might be termed unfair competition when they attempt to acquire affiliates and find they have to bid against nonbank conglomerates.

The hard-nosed empire builders of the conglomerates have a lot more experience in corporate wooing than do banks. They also have an important dollars-and-cents advantage. The stock of many conglomerates sells at a higher price in relation to book value and earnings than does bank stock; since the latter will dominate a holding company's own price-earnings and price-book value ratios, at least until other subsidiaries are going concerns, the holding company stock also will sell at a lower ratio than that of many conglomerates. This means that conglomerates can offer a package of stock for an acquisition with far less dilution of existing stockholder equity than a one-bank holding company would incur with a package of similar market value.

Lack of sufficient management talent is another factor that should limit the growth and competitiveness of one-bank holding companies. In the beginning, at least, most acquisitions are expected to be going organizations that can run themselves, but the holding company still must provide overall direction and policy. This need, plus the extra burden of managing the holding company itself, will require a considerable amount of executive time and talent.

Much of the talent must come from the bank's existing management—but I know of very few banks that have an overabundance of qualified people. Even though it should be easier to attract executives from outside the company because of the excitement and opportunities generated by the new organization form, one-bank holding companies are starting with such important managerial shortages that they will generally have to expand slowly, I prophesy, for quite some time to come.

Indeed, the one-bank holding company concept is not for all banks—not even for all major banks. It should not be adopted unless adequate financial and managerial resources are available. It is a complex, expensive operation that easily could fail to justify its cost. Nor is it a surefire way to change a bank's image or increase the price of its stock. I view the one-bank holding company as an organizational device with considerable potential; but I hasten to warn that it is *how the device is used, not the device itself,* that determines ultimate results. Accordingly, I urge any bank thinking about becoming a one-bank holding company to give the matter the most serious and careful consideration before it plunges ahead.

Too Much Monopoly Power?

Many people are fearful that the new movement will lead to the creation of massive concentrations of economic power. Part of their concern must be due to the unusual speed with which one-bank holding companies have spread and to the size and importance of the banks involved. In a year and a half, 34 of the 100 largest U.S. banks, including 9 of the top 12, have either adopted the new form of organization or have announced their intention to do so.

At the roots of the concern that one-bank holding companies will become too big and powerful must be the widespread distrust of monopolies and of something vaguely thought of as "Wall Street," which dates back to the latter part of the nineteenth century. Many people, including members of Congress, still retain the aversion to concentration of financial power that William Jennings Bryan and the Populists incited almost 75 years ago. In reality, though, I cannot see how any one-bank holding company could achieve enough economic power to be socially harmful. The natural forces of competition will work to prevent it. I refer to outside competition from other strong and well-established financial institutions, and most certainly also to head-to-head competition between one-bank holding companies themselves. For this reason one might well argue that the greater the number of one-bank holding companies formed, the better.

The Supreme Court of the United States has taken a position on what constitutes concentration of financial power. In the 1963 Philadelphia National case it ruled that commercial banking comprises a market totally distinct from other financial services such as mortgage servicing, consumer finance, and savings banking. We can infer from this that, in the view of the Court, the combination of banking and financial services in a holding company does not produce a concentration that is inimical to the public interest.

The 1930's All Over Again?

Some members of the regulatory agencies fear that the present wave of one-bank holding companies ultimately will lead to a convulsion in the banking system similar to the one that occurred in the early 1930's, when almost 10,000 banks failed in a four-year period. Governor J. L. Robertson of the Federal Reserve Board said recently, "A decade marked by great permissiveness, the 1920's, brought almost unrestrained expansion followed by collapse and a depression that caused untold suffering." Now, he added, referring to one-bank holding companies, "we appear to be drifting toward a repetition of serious errors that the banking industry fell into in the 1920's."[3]

Not all federal regulators share this opinion. Comptroller of the Currency William B. Camp gave tacit approval to the one-bank holding company trend when he stated, "A revitalized banking industry, released from long-standing fetishes, has enormously expanded the range and depth of its financial services to the public."[4]

It should be remembered that the economy in general and banking in particular have changed a great deal since the 1930's. While I don't defend banking's dismal

---

[3]Address at the Convention of the American Bankers Association, September 30, 1968, Chicago, Illinois.
[4]Ibid.

record in the Depression, it is only fair to say that the collapse of the banking system was brought about as much by the breakdown of the entire economy and misguided monetary and fiscal policies as by anything else. Today our economy has been strengthened in so many ways that anything like the disaster of the 1930's seems out of the question. Moreover, banking itself has become infinitely stronger in the past 35 years. Amortized loans, deposit insurance, better audit and examination procedures, modern management techniques—one could fill a page with the changes that have buttressed our industry. It is significant that bank suspensions have averaged fewer than five a year since 1960.

In short, it is an entirely new ball game today. Yet banking is still weighed down by restrictions and regulatory philosophies that were conceived to deal with the conditions that existed in the 1930's. The old suspicion that bankers cannot quite be trusted to conduct their affairs with honor and integrity still remains in certain quarters of Washington.

I sometimes get the impression that we are thought of as second-class citizens who will blunder or scheme our way into all sorts of trouble if we are not watched closely. There seems to be a sort of double standard: one-bank holding companies are automatically suspect because they are created by bankers, while conglomerates (at least, those made up from related industries) put together by "wheeling and dealing" businessmen are less cause for concern. This double standard persists in spite of the fact that the bank in a one-bank holding company remains subject to all the same regulations imposed on any other bank of the same class.

May not the one-bank holding company actually make banking *safer*? If this method of expansion and diversification were not available or were severely restricted, many banks might soon be compelled to seek higher earnings by reaching into riskier loans and into investment situations. A similar reach got a great number of banks in trouble during the depression.

A CHANCE TO PERFORM

At the time this is written the status of legislation involving one-bank holding companies is very much in doubt. The House Banking Committee is conducting extensive hearings into all facets of the situation, and several bills have been introduced. There is no point in speculating here about what legislation, if any, will result or what features might be included.

I can only say that I feel banking deserves a chance to show what it can do with one-bank holding companies before crippling legislation is passed to guard against what might *conceivably* happen but is not a realistic possibility. I firmly believe that one-bank holding companies represent the best way now available for certain banks to deal with their cost/earnings problem and meet the dramatically changing needs of their customers in the coming decade. When an opportunity is so important to banks, why not let them test it?

5. One-Bank Holding Companies: The Public Interest*

Paul S. Nadler

It is acknowledged that the one-bank holding company "will help make commercial banks more effective competitors in the market place—better able to provide lowest cost service of quality." On the other hand, it is pointed out that some restrictions on inter-affiliate and parent company dealings involving the bank are necessary. This article complements the previous one by presenting the important regulatory issues from the public's standpoint.

The fact that in little more than a year bank-sponsored one-bank holding companies have expanded from virtual non-existence to encompassment of nearly one fourth of all U.S. banking assets makes it obvious that this structural form offers many advantages to the commercial bank. But from the viewpoint of the general public, the benefits from this stampede to form financial congenerics are by no means so clear-cut.

Undoubtedly there will be real benefits to the public from the trend. Prime among these are the new services that innovative banks should be offering and the development of a more intensely competitive financial environment.

But there are also potential drawbacks of significance. These include the fear that the congeneric structure may lead to riskier bank lending policies and that operation of one-bank holding companies

*From *Harvard Business Review*, May/June, 1969. Copyright 1969 by the President and Fellows of Harvard College; all rights reserved. Reprinted by permission of the publisher.

may result in violations of anti-trust law.

Subsidiary issues also arise, such as whether the trend toward formation of congenerics will alter drastically the competitive balance among banks and change the structure of banking in the nation.

But the key question is: Are banks special institutions whose money-creating power, legal protection from excessive competition, and tremendous financial strength require that they be more limited than other corporations in ability to diversify and buy nonbanking companies?

This is the question that must be answered in determining whether the congeneric trend is in the public interest. It is also the reason why so many proposals for legislative and regulatory control of one-bank holding companies are being considered as this article is written.

ANCILLARY QUESTIONS

Before taking up the critical issue of diversification, it is useful to discuss the implications of other aspects of this development for the public and users of bank services.

Profit Centers & Pricing

The financial congeneric can use the differentiated functions of its various subsidiaries to separate its accounting operations and ascertain where profits originate. The banking industry only recently has been gaining some thorough understanding of its costs—since the advent of third-generation computers—and the ability to break operations down into profit centers should help in this task.

This is of little concern to the public, except that it promotes financial soundness. Banks that have poor cost accounting procedures sometimes "give away" services below cost, then, to ensure profitability, they find it necessary to offset the deficiency by overcharging elsewhere or skimping on service.

Connected with this differentiation is more clear-cut pricing of bank services. At present, in many cases a bank will offer a new service only to find that the customer expects it to be paid for out of balances he has on deposit.

Under the operation of a congeneric, however, many of the new services that banks are providing these days will be offered by nonbank subsidiaries. So, management assistance, data processing services, and other functions must be paid for strictly through fees to subsidiaries, rather than compensated with balances.

To the borrowing public, this is to a degree beneficial, although on the surface it may appear not to be. For bank pricing has frequently been inequitable—with the sharp corporate treasurer gaining far more service from his bank than is justified by his company's balances maintained and fees paid. Bank compensation and profitability thus have depended rather too much on the less aggressive treasurer and individual who leaves balances above those needed to back the services provided.

While the corporate treasurer who has been getting more bank service than he paid for may consider better accountability an unfavorable trend, the treasurer who desires to compensate his bank fairly but not lavishly can determine more accurately what a fair fee for services rendered is. In other words, segregating of accountability of functions through the congeneric can be beneficial to the customer, as it is to the bank struggling to isolate each of the complex costs involved in its operation.

Capital Flexibility

One of the major benefits the commercial banking business is likely to gain from the trend toward financial congenerics is greater capital flexibility. The congeneric can utilize debt to a greater degree in capital structure than a bank alone can.

Use of debt capital in a bank is just as valuable as such leverage is to any nonbank corporation. If a bank raises equity capital, it must share ownership, control, and future profits with the new stockholders. But if new capital is borrowed through the sale of subordinated capital debentures or use of other debt forms, the bank can leverage the difference between the cost of money—currently 3 percent to 4 percent after taxes—and its return on capital—generally around 10 percent or more after taxes.

But banks are required to maintain a certain capitalization, as a protection of the depositors' funds, and the regulatory authorities can instruct a bank to raise more capital if they feel it is undercapitalized. And often they stipulate that this must be equity capital. These requirements limit a bank's ability to leverage and often force dilution of its equity position.

While the bank cannot borrow for capital purposes, the parent holding company can borrow as much money as lenders will grant, through the capital markets, term loans from unrelated banks, and other sources.

The parent company can then turn around and use the borrowed funds to buy the common stock of the subsidiary bank—a procedure that provides the bank with the required equity capital, while still gaining for the holding company and its shareholders the increased leverage that borrowed money provides.

The one-bank holding company is also

in a better position to improve leverage, if it happens to be overcapitalized, than the bank is. A bank can do little to eliminate excess equity capital and improve leverage unless or until deposits grow or a merger can be arranged with a bank in need of more capital. For regulatory supervisors do not allow a bank to reduce its capitalization by paying out capital or surplus in higher dividends; and even when undivided profits are large and dividends can be increased out of this pool of funds, many stockholders do not want a higher payout, as it increases their income tax liabilities.

Under the congeneric structure, however, the bank with excess capital can pay higher dividends to the holding company, and the parent company in turn can make use of this money for other ventures of other subsidiaries instead of paying out dividends to stockholders.

The Public Can Gain: What is the public interest here? It would appear that the public has little to lose from the greater leverage and possibly something to gain. The public would not be hurt when banks use debt to cushion depositors' funds instead of relying exclusively on equity capital.

To the depositor it makes little difference whether the funds that cushion his deposit are in equity or debt form, as long as the capital is subordinated to deposits. Far more important to him is whether enough capital is available to absorb losses out of capital, leaving deposits unscathed.

And even though debt capital must eventually be repaid, the repayment provisions are far from onerous. If a bank's percentage of capital to deposits is 8 percent, the maximum amount of debt capital as a percentage of deposits will be about 2 percent. If the term of this debt is 20 years, the cash drain of debt repayment equals one-tenth of 1 percent of deposits per year! Most banks experience greater cash drains in meeting a single routine withdrawal by a corporate customer during the course of a normal business day.

So, as long as the lenders who provide the debt capital do not fear for the safety of their funds, it is hard to see how the bank, its depositors, or anyone else can be harmed when a bank uses debt as part of its capital structure.

When the subsidiary bank of a financial congeneric raises equity capital by selling shares to its parent, the bank and its depositors do not face even the extremely slight repayment problem that debt capital usage involves. Whether the parent itself is as secure if it uses leverage to provide the subsidiary bank with capital is a slightly more complicated question.

One can assume that the congeneric's creditors will not allow the company to overborrow, so there will be no doubt of its ability to repay its debts. Even in the rare event that the holding company does overborrow and eventually goes bankrupt, the subsidiary bank is legally unaffected; its equity is now owned by a receiver instead of by the holding company.

There is, however, the question of whether the public would lose confidence in a bank whose parent company has experienced financial difficulty. If this happened, the bank might suffer serious deposit drains, however strong it otherwise remained. This is the only possible occurrence detrimental to sound banking and the public interest in the greater capital flexibility the congeneric offers.

Otherwise, the proper use of leverage can help create more profitable and viable banks, even when regulatory authorities, in their belief that debt capital is not as safe as equity, are overcautious in their capitalization requirements for the subsidiary bank.

DIVERSIFICATION QUESTION

The areas of possible public concern, then, appear limited to the questions of functional and geographical diversification. The fear is that diversification will bring:

1. Less sound banking operations.
2. Concentration of economic power.
3. Alteration of the present competitive balance in banking structure.

Each of these is worth examination and will be discussed in turn in the sections that follow.

Risk to Bank Soundness

Opponents of the development of congenerics express concern that a holding company's affiliate bank might make loans to and investments in its nonbank operations which are so unsound that they threaten the stability of the subsidiary bank and thus jeopardize the safety of depositors' funds.

For example, the bank might make a loan to an associated subsidiary that it would refuse because of excessive risk were there not the close relationship. And while most banks follow the temptation to act slowly in calling a loan that appears to be turning sour, the temptation would be much greater if the borrower were a subsidiary of the same company. In other words, does prudent lending get diluted when the bank and the borrower are related?

There are safeguards to prevent this. The Federal Reserve Act states that no loan or extension of credit may be made by a national bank or a member of the Federal Reserve System to any affiliate of the same holding company unless that loan is secured from 100 percent to 120 percent, depending on the type of security. Moreover, there are strict limitations on the amount that any Federal Reserve System member may invest in the stock of an affiliate of its own holding company.

Those supporting the view that no additional risk to the subsidiary bank is inherent in diversification through the congeneric form also point out:

1. The bank which becomes a part of a financial congeneric in no way insulates itself from the full weight of bank regulation as it has developed over the last 150 years.
2. The one-bank holding company may well serve as a better vehicle than the traditionally organized bank if activities involving increased risk are being considered. For if the bank were to engage in these activities, it alone would suffer any loss; while if the congeneric engages in these activities, institutions separate from the bank itself would bear any loss.

Proponents of congenerics also point out that, under the Financial Institutions Supervisory Act of 1966, the federal bank regulatory agencies have substantial powers to issue cease-and-desist orders for any unsafe or unsound practices of a subsidiary bank. As a report prepared for the Association of Corporate Owners of One Bank puts it:

"The language appears to be more than sufficient to permit a Federal banking agency to assert jurisdiction and to take proper action in a case in which it believes the solvency or the liquidity of the bank is likely to be threatened."[1]

This may well be true. But the question remains as to how much regulatory agencies can do beyond examining the operations of the nonbank subsidiaries of the one-bank holding company, since the cease-and-desist order would apply to the bank only.

The loan collateralization requirements and limits on bank loans to affiliates of 10 percent of its capital to one affiliate and 20 percent to all of them may lessen the possibility of bank failure or difficulty in the event a nonbank affiliate experienced financial trouble.

Even so, a nonbank affiliate's trouble is bound to reflect on the bank and raise

---

[1]Carter H. Golembe Associates, Inc., *The Nature and Control of One Bank Holding Companies* (New York, 1968).

doubts as to its solvency. Since bank deposits become extremely volatile when fear of financial stress is bruited about, a subsidiary bank would have difficulty continuing unscathed in such a situation.

This is one risk to bank operation in the establishment of the financial congeneric that appears unresolved at present. There may be no solution short of either government regulation of the nonbank affiliates or at least acceptance of cease-and-desist orders that can be applied to those affiliates as well as to the subsidiary bank operation.

Concentration of Power

Judging by the ruling of the U.S. Supreme Court in the Girard Trust-Philadelphia National Bank case of 1963,[2] it appears that financial congenerics have no antitrust problems to worry about. The court ruled in that case that banking is a "unique line of commerce," and each commercial bank competes only with other commercial banks.

This decision, unrealistic as many observers consider it to be, should give banking a free hand to enter related financial areas without fearing antitrust action. If commercial banking is "unique" and noncompetitive with other financial institutions, then the public interest should not be hurt by bank diversification either directly or through the financial congeneric route.

Despite the legal freedom, there is a real reason to worry about the potential power to restrain trade that a financial congeneric can wield. For while the volume of loans that the bank of a one-bank holding company can make to the nonbank affiliates is strictly limited by law, and collateralization requirements are severe, there is nothing to prevent the bank from lending funds to the other subsidiaries on very favorable terms.

[2]*United States* v. *Philadelphia National Bank* et al, 374 U.S. 321 (1963).

By offering credit to the nonbank subsidiaries at below market interest rates or by merely providing funds at times when money is extremely tight, the bank could help an affiliate obtain a larger share of its market.

Similarly, a congeneric that owns both a bank and, say, a factoring or finance company could establish a policy that those who want bank credit must also use its finance company for part of their credit needs.

The holding company may also be able to obtain much more capital through the open market and other sources than could an independent finance company, mortgage company, or other operation, because of the greater strength and stature of a corporation owning a bank. The congeneric can then use this capital to make its finance or mortgage subsidiaries dominant in their markets in the same way that a well-financed supermarket chain can become dominant over small retail food outlets.

Does a commercial bank's ability to create deposits, its role as the repository of the public's funds, and its protected position—because of the availability of federal deposit insurance and regulatory restraints on entry into the marketplace of new banks and branches—give banking a special role in the economy that requires extra restraint on diversification?

This is the key question, even among bankers. They proclaim that banks should be allowed free rein to establish or buy companies in other financial fields (and a few bankers say that banks should be allowed entry into nonfinancial fields as well). Yet when other companies seek to acquire control of commercial banks as part of their diversification, many bankers object to this intrusion into their domain and plead that banking is a special field with a public trust that merits protection from the vagaries of normal financial operations.

Certainly there is something special

about banking. Thus few believe that a bank should be allowed to buy a savings and loan company in its own market or that a major bank should be allowed to affiliate with a large industrial company—because of the anticompetitive potential that would result.

The commercial banks are charged with the principal handling of the payments function in the nation, and they have the responsibility of being sole guardians of our checking account deposits. So there is potential restraint of trade inherent in allowing banks to combine with a host of other enterprises, even with the available restrictions on bank loans to other subsidiaries of the same parent company.

Awareness of this potential restraint of trade is undoubtedly a major reason why many of the 200 company-owned one-bank holding companies—the companies that happened to own one bank before the bank-initiated financial congenerics began to be formed—have generally taken a hands-off attitude toward their banks. They make sure that the bank and its affiliates have no mutual dealings that might be construed even tangentially as collusion to restrain trade. (This caution, in fact, has been a drawback to effective operation of holding companies owning single banks).

The desire to maintain a hands-off approach has been reinforced by the fear that if the bank worked too closely with any nonbank affiliate, other companies in the industry of that affiliate would look elsewhere for banking services.

But while the banks and their owners have fairly effectively regulated themselves to prevent antitrust violations in their unregulated holding company operations, is this enough protection of the public interest? True, the antitrust laws apply to bank relationships with nonbank subsidiaries of the same corporation, so the Justice Department could halt any blatant abuses. But the potential is great for minor abuses of privilege in lending that may go undetected.

With the present trend toward diversification by banks and purchase of banks by nonbank corporations, more specific guidelines on the credit relationship between banks and other affiliates of the same company are in order for the protection of the public interest.

The commercial banks' unique role in our economy, their huge resources, and their need for safety have given them special protection from free market competition. In return, the public must have absolute assurance that bank lending will take place solely with the goal of gaining the best combination of profitability, risklessness, and liquidity.

Once other goals affect the lending decision, the banker is assuming a responsibility to determine the allocation of funds in the economy that violates the trust of his privileged, protected position.

Competitive Changes

The trend toward heavier competition, through geographical expansion and diversification and otherwise, is a very favorable aspect of the new banking picture.

Commercial banks are limited in geographical scope because of restricted entry into the industry and strict limits on branching or its complete prohibition in three fifths of the states. But the financial congeneric, of course, can establish plants, branches, and offices of its nonbank operations with the same freedom with which any other business can expand its geographical scope.

Since the congeneric will not establish such operations except where it thinks a market for them exists, obviously the geographical expansion of the nonbank operations provides needed new services to the public or intensifies competition in providing those services. Both developments serve the public interest in a free market economy.

Even though commercial banking always has been considered to be a special industry deserving of protection, as I have noted, there is a real question whether our geographical limitations on bank operations are too severe.

The restraints that prevent branching altogether, or that protect a bank from having to face any competition in the locality where it has its home office, have caused us to become a nation with a great many banks.

But the fact of a large number of banks by itself does not mean competition. Rather, it often means that local banking monopolies flourish, little affected by competition. Since the convenience of bank location is usually the most important determinant of where the public banks—despite the frequent availability of lower cost credit, higher rates on savings, and broader services only a few miles away—the customer will still generally patronize the bank nearest his residence or place of work.

The financial congeneric may play a significant role in altering our banking structure drastically as time passes.

It is obvious that only banks with large resources of cash and especially talent can undertake diversification, either by function or geographically. This undoubtedly means that the congeneric trend will encompass far more larger institutions than smaller banks.

Already some less aggressive small institutions are beginning to face stiffer competition in traditional bank operations. Despite the geographical protection that independent banks frequently enjoy in their communities, larger institutions are now chipping away at their deposit structures by offering the public —besides lower cost banking and a greater variety of services—credit cards, bank-by-mail service, in-plant banking, and other means of making convenience of bank location less compelling.

The movement toward greater geographical competition should be intensified as time goes on and as techniques for payment through the telephone and other electronic devices are perfected.

Smaller banks are experiencing other troubles that are forcing them into a losing battle with their larger competitors. These include:

1. Inability to satisfy customers' full credit needs.
2. Higher relative costs of operation, when the larger institutions are benefiting from computerized data processing.
3. Difficulty in hiring and retraining high-quality personnel.
4. Problems in raising capital.

The Federal Reserve Board has recognized such a trend. In establishing, under its Regulation Q, rate ceilings on the interest a bank may pay on savings and time deposits, it has kept ceilings rather low relative to marketplace interest rate levels. This was done to protect institutions that cannot afford to pay higher savings rates from suffering severe outflows of savings to higher paying institutions—an eventuality that would compound their weakness.

The erosion of banks' protected markets, however, may be too far along for even the Federal Reserve Board's efforts to halt. And not all its members favor attempts to insulate banks from competition. One of them, George W. Mitchell, recently stated:

"I opt for less regulation and more competition because I think it abundantly clear that banks cannot, given present-day conditions and technology, be insulated from nonregulated nonbank competition; they face a lot of it. They cannot even be effectively insulated from regulated nonbank competition.

"If regulators cannot protect banks from competitive inroads on their markets through chartering policies that deny new entry in 'overbanked' areas, they should relax constraints on banking's competitive efforts if they expect this industry to attract capital and management talent."[3]

One result of this turmoil may be that the financial congeneric will serve as a catalyst for a change in the banking structure from almost 14,000 banks—most of them extremely small—to a structure of many fewer institutions which are multifaceted financial services, competing widely on a basis of rate and service, rather than strictly commercial banks.

The development of the congeneric, with its great need for capital and talent—as well as its potential for greater service and profitability—makes the emergence of larger, more competitive banking organizations even more necessary than it was before.

CONCLUSION

For the bank, the one-bank holding company trend has great advantages, which are discussed elsewhere. As for the public, the trend will help make commercial banks more effective competitors in the marketplace—better able to provide lowest cost service of quality.

But the purchase or establishment by banks of nonbank operations and purchase of banks by nonbank corporations also have drawbacks from the public viewpoint.

To be sure, when the vitality of banks that have entered new fields or territories makes competitors more alert to the public need and convenience, it is beneficial. Similarly, if a nonbank company takes over an unenergetic bank and makes this institution more attuned to the needs of its market, this also is advantageous to the public. And, naturally, when the bank diversifies by offering services not available before, it is beneficial.

[3]"Bank Competition in the '70's," *Banking*, January 1969, p. 25.

Thus the congeneric trend can help improve operating efficiency in many of the fields which banks are entering, while the geographical expansion of congeneric operations and the entrance of nonbank corporations into banking have made banking itself more aggressive in some areas of the nation.

But there are dangers to the public interest:

1. The subsidiary bank might be damaged and subjected to loss of public confidence because of the excesses of an affiliate or of the parent company.
2. There is potential for excessive concentration and restraint of trade when a bank, with its privileged position, strength, and resources joins in an organization with nonbank companies which can improve their market power through the availability of lenient bank credit.
3. Banking might become too closely allied with nonfinancial functions and develop great financial-industrial combines with excessive political as well as economic power.

To prevent any of these eventualities, some restrictions should be imposed. The bank operations of financial congenerics and conglomerates should be limited to financial services—however inexact the definition of a financial service is. (For example, can a bank own a company that builds bank buildings?)

There should be closer supervision of acquisitions by banks and stiffer limits on purchase of banks by nonbank companies, to lessen the potential for injury of a bank and its depositors by actions of nonbank affiliates. Closer scrutiny of the operations of these affiliates is necessary; regulators have too little control of them to prevent abuses.

But whenever restraints are placed on one-bank holding companies, the impact of the "congeneric era" on banking and the public will be positive. For the competitive atmosphere and the push toward innovation and expanded services are sure to survive.

Freedom from any regulatory restraint on congeneric operations will soon become a thing of the past, judging from the pending legislation. The banking system and the economy should be left with more flexible legislation which maintains the traditional U.S. separation of banking from commerce, while at the same time providing a better mix than before of efficient, competitive commercial banking and sensible public policy.

Chapter II
INTERNATIONAL FINANCE

6. International Operations of U.S. Banks: Growth and Public Policy Implications*

Franklin R. Dahl†

Banking structure in the United States has undergone considerable change over the last decade. Banks in this country have likewise been at the forefront of significant developments in the international sphere. This article provides an in-depth look at these developments. It examines the evolution of U.S. banking activities in international markets and the institutional framework within which these activities are carried on.

Change and innovation dominate the contemporary banking scene both in this country and abroad. In the United States,

---

*From a symposium, *Banking—Part II: Developments in Banking,* appearing in *Law and Contemporary Problems* (Vol. 32, No. 1, Winter 1967), published by the Duke University School of Law, Durham, North Carolina, Copyright, 1967, by Duke University. Reprinted by permission of the publisher and the author.

†Assistant Director, Division of Examinations, Board of Governors of the Federal Reserve System.

The views expressed herein are those of the author and do not necessarily represent those of the Board of Governors.

considerable attention has been directed to a number of changes in banking that have already occurred, are taking place, or are in prospect as they affect the structure of financial institutions, the functioning of markets for money and credit, and the ways in which financial transactions are effected. Automation, credit cards, the checkless society, the role of banks as financial intermediaries—these are but a few of the current topics of study, discussion, and debate. Abroad, too, though perhaps to a less marked degree, the face and character of banking are undergoing changes of similar far-reaching significance.

One of the major areas of change in American banking in the past decade has been international operations. This rather short period has seen an unusually rapid expansion of the international activities of American banks and the extension of a growing number of domestic banking institutions into international banking and financial operations.

In contrast to the rather passive character of these operations in the early 1950s, major American banking institutions are today operating large networks of branches encircling the globe. Affiliations have been established with banking and financial institutions on every continent. Foreign loans and credits at banks in this country have undergone a nearly six-fold expansion. This lending now encompasses a full range of borrowers—foreign banks, governments, subsidiaries of U.S. corporations, and others; and, in addition to traditional financing of this country's foreign trade, credits are extended to provide working capital, to finance large-scale capital projects, and for a variety of other purposes in countries ranging from Australia to Zambia. Major American banks, together with their foreign branches and affiliates, are important intermediaries for the channeling of funds among international financial centers in quick response to changes in interest rates and in demand and supply relationships for money. Funds obtained in foreign financial markets have been used to support bank lending and investment activities in the United States, and, for a few banks, one quarter or more of their earnings are attributable to their international operations.

The expanded international operations of American banks have introduced or accelerated change in foreign banking markets and in foreign banking practices. In a number of foreign countries greater competition for deposits among banks, improved personal service to bank customers, the use of credit cards, and better accounting practices on the part of bank borrowers are traceable to the entry and subsequent activities of American banks. In turn, some of the experience acquired in overseas operations has been applied in domestic operations. For example, some major banks are currently advertising and promoting systems of personal loans which are adaptations of the personal overdraft systems used in many foreign countries.

I. GROWTH OF INTERNATIONAL BANKING AND INTERNATIONAL FINANCIAL OPERATIONS

A. History

American banks are not newcomers to the field of foreign banking and financing. Early efforts by American banks to widen their foreign financing activities and to develop a foreign banking organization date back beyond the turn of the century. Prior to 1914, however, these activities remained incipient, and banking organization for this purpose was embryonic. London was the dominant financial center, and the financing of U.S. foreign trade continued to remain largely in the hands of London banks.

Early development of the foreign activities of American banks was hampered by the lack of powers of national banks to accept drafts or to establish foreign branches. This deficiency was rectified only with the passage in 1913 of the Federal Reserve Act, which included provisions granting these powers to national banks.[1] Two other pieces of legislation contributed materially to the powers of commercial banks to conduct their foreign business. The first passed in 1916, amended section 25 of the Federal Reserve Act[2] and permitted national banks to invest in state-chartered corporations engaged in international or foreign banking and operating under an agreement with the Federal Reserve Board delineating their activities—so-called "agreement corporations." The second, which added section 25(a) to the Federal Reserve Act, was passed in 1919 and has come to be known as the

[1]Federal Reserve Act § 13, ch. 6, § 13, 38 Stat. 263 (1913), *as amended,* 12 U.S.C. § 372 (1964); Federal Reserve Act § 25, ch. 6, § 25, 38 Stat. 273 (1913), *as amended,* 12 U.S.C. § § 601–04a (1964, Supp. II, 1965–66).

[2]39 Stat. 755 (1916), *as amended,* 12 U.S.C. § § 601–03 (1964, Supp. II, 1965–66). See generally text at note 18 *infra.*

Edge Act.[3] This act provided for federally chartered corporations—so-called "Edge corporations"—to be organized for the purpose of engaging in international or foreign banking and financial activities.

These wider powers facilitated the upsurge in foreign banking activity by U.S. banks that took place in the aftermath of the First World War. The abnormal amount of foreign banking activity associated with postwar reconstruction credits tapered off in the early 1920s, however, and through the remainder of that decade and through the 1930s the pattern and extent of the international activities of American banks paralleled movements in world trade. A substantial contraction in the volume of these activities and in banking organization abroad occurred in the 1930s, and banks' foreign business was further constricted by the dislocations of the Second World War. At the end of 1945, the number of foreign offices operated by U.S. banks and their subsidiaries had shrunk to seventy-eight, less than half as many as a quarter of a century earlier.

In the decade following the war, substantial recovery occurred in the volume of foreign lending, and there was some renewed growth in the number of banking offices maintained abroad by American banks. In this period, too, the groundwork was laid for much of the subsequent expansion in these operations. Nevertheless, as a broad generalization, it is fair to characterize the international operations of American banks up to the mid-1950s as essentially passive, comprising mainly a service operation related to the financing of U.S. foreign trade.[4]

In the period of little more than a decade since that time, the volume and scope of these operations have been many times enlarged. Moreover, in a number of

banks the international banking department has attained a position of major importance in the over-all business and workings of the bank. An indication of this growth in international operations is provided by the following comparisons. At the end of 1966, dollar loans and acceptance credits to foreigners of banks in the United States totaled $9.6 billion, as compared with about $1¾ billion at the end of 1955.[5] Over the same period, the number of foreign branches of U.S. banks and banking corporations increased from 115 to 248 and foreign branch assets from $2 billion to $12 billion. Parallel growth occurred in Edge and agreement corporations over this eleven-year span: at the end of 1955 there were only seven such corporations in operation; by the end of 1966 the number of such corporations had increased to forty-five, owned by thirty-three banks and bank holding companies.

B. Reasons for Growth

No single or simple explanation can be offered for the remarkable transformation of U.S. banks into large-scale, sophisticated international lenders and major participants in global financial transactions. Clearly, the present volume and character of these activities are the product of many and complex forces. Among the more fundamental or underlying ones that may be cited are the emergence of the United States in the postwar period as the principal economic and financial power in the world economy; the growth and, by historical standards, the fundamental health of the world economy since about 1950; the progressive dismantling of restrictions on international trade and capital move-

---

[3]41 Stat. 378 (1919), *as amended,* 12 U.S.C. § § 611–31 (1964). See generally text at note 19 *infra.*

[4]See generally Tamagna & Willis, *United States Banking Organization Abroad,* 42 Fed. Reserve Bull. 1284 (1956), for an account of the

international activities of U.S. banks in the first half of this century.

[5]These figures relate to all banks in the United States reporting claims on foreigners to the U.S. Treasury and include branches and subsidiaries of foreign banks in the United States. Unfortunately, these data are not available for U.S. banks alone.

ments; the needs of the American economy for additional resources from abroad; and the demands of U.S. consumers with rising incomes and widening tastes for an increasing variety of goods and services. These elements have all helped to create an environment conducive to the exploitation of opportunities for trade, investment, and lending on an international scale.

More direct impetus to the development of the international business of U.S. banks has been provided by the upsurge of direct investment abroad by U.S. corporations since the early 1950s. Corporations embarking on or enlarging their international ventures naturally turned to their banks for financial assistance and for information and advice on the multifaceted problems encountered in international operations. As the business of more and more U.S. corporations became globally oriented and with the emergence of the multinational corporation, it became increasingly imperative for major banks to establish an international banking organization and to acquire the competence and experience needed to provide banking services on a world-wide scale. As the movement of U.S. corporations abroad gained momentum, interior banks were initially at a disadvantage compared to those banks, particularly New York City banks, with an existing fund of experience in conducting foreign business. Corporations unable to obtain a full range of international banking services from their local bank consequently turned to banks in New York City. Faced with a potential drain of corporate business and corporate deposits, a number of interior banks had quickly to establish themselves in the international field. The widening circle of banks engaged seriously in international banking is a clear reflection of these competitive forces at work.

Two accommodating factors may also be mentioned among the forces underlying the development of international banking in U.S. banks. First of all, the techno-logical advances in transportation and communication have greatly eased the tasks of banks in maintaining continuous and informed surveillance of foreign markets and of their overseas operations. Foreign markets and foreign customers, no matter how distant, are now easily accessible to direct contact by bank lending and supervisory officers. The second accommodating element was the easy monetary conditions that prevailed in the United States in the period 1960-65. Without that monetary environment, the speed and timing of the expansion of international business in U.S. banks would clearly have been quite different.

C. International Operations in Structural Perspective

Up to this point emphasis has been placed on the growth and altered position of international operations in American banks. In the ensuing paragraphs, too, attention will be directed to the changed and changing nature of these operations. Yet it is important to keep in mind that, despite the growth of recent years, these operations still form a very small portion of the over-all business of U.S. banks. Moreover, participation in this development has been confined to a small number of banks. For example, foreign credits account for less than 5 percent of the loan portfolios of all banks in the United States, and the number of banks significantly involved in international lending is about fifty at the most.

The confinement of this business to a relatively small number of banks is a reflection of the fact that, by its very nature, international banking is a province of the very largest banks. The provision of full-scale international banking services requires sizable organization and resources, and a substantial amount of international business is needed to support the provision of those services. Not surprisingly, therefore, the fifty banks actively engaged in international banking are, with few exceptions, among the fifty largest banks in the United States.

The concentration of international banking among U.S. banks is in fact greater than just suggested. The three largest banks in the United States alone account for more than one-third of total bank-reported claims on foreigners, and twenty banks account for nearly 85 percent of these claims. However, these banks are all major money market banks, are among the most aggressively growth-minded, and in general rank high among the innovators in the commercial banking industry. For some of these banks, foreign credits run as high as 25 percent of their loan portfolios.[6] The commitment of these banks to international banking, taken together with the leading, if not dominant, role of these banks in the banking system, clearly enlarges the importance of international operations in the U.S. banking system beyond that indicated by crude aggregative comparisons.

II. A PROFILE OF INTERNATIONAL OPERATIONS OF U.S. BANKS TODAY

A. Organizational Mechanisms for Carrying on International Banking

Traditionally, the foreign business of banks has been carried on from offices in this country using the facilities of correspondent banks in foreign countries. However, the larger banks have found it imperative to have some form of direct representation abroad and some means of direct participation in foreign banking and financial markets if they are to become and to remain fully able to meet the global banking needs of their customers. This need has led to the construction of elaborate and extensive overseas or-

ganizations to supplement and to some extent to supplant correspondent bank relations. Besides representative offices, these overseas organizations consist (with considerable variation from bank to bank) of foreign branches, foreign subsidiaries, and substantial affiliations with existing foreign banks and other financial institutions. A contemporary account of the international activities of American banks must therefore include the foreign lending and other international activities done at head offices in this country, the operations of foreign branches, and their relations with foreign subsidiaries and affiliates. In this account, the last named will be discussed in connection with the operation and uses of Edge and agreement corporations which until recently were the sole vehicle for the holding of ownership interests in foreign institutions.

1. HEAD OFFICE ACTIVITIES. The international banking departments of the major banks carry on a wide range of banking, administrative, and service functions. Their banking activities usually encompass all of the credit and deposit transactions of foreigners plus the international business of the bank's domestic customer. These include the usual range of banking services in connection with foreign trade transactions—letters of credit, acceptance financing, collections, remittances, etc., and foreign exchange. In addition, the credit function includes general purpose loans and advances to foreigners. In conducting this business, the department operates almost as a "bank within a bank" with a net creditor or net debtor position vis-à-vis the rest of the field.[7] In most cases, these departments directly conduct the bulk of the bank's interna-

---

[6]The figures and comparisons used in this paragraph relate solely to loans and other claims booked at offices in this country; for those banks with extensive branch systems abroad, the proportion of foreign credits to total loans would be higher.

[7]This element enters in an undefinable way into the complex equation by which a bank's resources are allocated among alternative uses. Those departments with an excess of international deposits over international credits apparently find it somewhat easier to obtain senior management approval for the extension of additional credits than do those in the reverse position.

tional banking business. For banks with extensive overseas organizations, however, the locus of their international banking activities has been shifting to their offices abroad; and in these banks, a principal task of the department is to supervise and coordinate the credit and other activities of foreign branches and subsidiaries. A major service function of the department is to provide information, advice, and other assistance to international customers, particularly on the financial aspects of conducting business in foreign countries and over international frontiers. Most of the large banks maintain a small but growing corps of experienced officers for the express purpose of assisting with such corporate problems.

In a subsequent section, the international lending done at banks in this country is described in more detail to illustrate the changing nature of U.S. banks' international business.

2. FOREIGN BRANCHES. In conducting their international banking business abroad, direct branches are the organizational form generally preferred by U.S. banks. In terms of size of operations, branches are far more important than subsidiaries or affiliated banks; moreover, the over-all activity of branches runs a fairly close second to the international operations of head offices. The advantage of the branch form of overseas operation is that the branch is legally an integral part of the parent bank with the full resources and organization behind it; in many countries, this provides stature to a branch that would not exist in the case of subsidiaries or affiliated banks. Administra-

tively, too, the branch can be and is operated as part of the parent bank. The principal disadvantage for foreign branches is that a branch usually starts *de novo* in a foreign market with the concomitant problems of a foreign bank attempting to build up a local deposit base. For a number of banks, this disadvantage has proven an insurmountable obstacle.

Because of the need for large resources and a large organization to support branch activity overseas, only twelve banks had established direct foreign branches by the end of 1966. Extensive overseas branches are operated by only three banks: First National City Bank, Chase Manhattan Bank, and Bank of America. The other banks have branches in only a few foreign countries, and a number of them maintain branches solely in London. The geographic distribution of foreign branches by number and relative size at the end of 1966 are shown in Table 1.

The three large branch networks operate on a world-wide basis. This global orientation gives them a distinction not found in other overseas banking organizations. For example, the British overseas banks, while operating a far larger number of branches in many cases, generally confine their activities to one or two geographic areas, none directly operates on a world-wide basis. A global network enables a bank to meet the banking needs of large multinational companies by acting as lenders and depositories in a wide number of foreign locations and as advisers on the broad range of complex and often unfamiliar financial problems encountered by corporations with far-flung

TABLE 1
Foreign Branches of U.S. Banks, December 31, 1966

	Latin America	England	Other Europe	Japan	Other Foreign	U.S. Overseas Territories	Total
Number of branches ...	102	21	27	12	53	29	244
Branch assets ($ millions).	1,052	6,411	2,056	1,239	840	787	12,385

operations. Moreover, for the corporate treasurer of a multinational company, they afford a means of dealing with one bank in a number of markets and also a channel for almost instantaneous transfers of funds among the companies in his international operation. The First National City Bank has developed the most extensive network of foreign branches consisting at the end of 1966 of 124 branches located in forty countries. The Chase Manhattan Bank operated forty-two foreign branches, and Bank of America had forty-four branches located overseas at the end of 1966.

Located in such a large number of diverse countries, the range and nature of branch activities within the three large branch networks show a large degree of variation. Some branches are located in highly developed and sophisticated loan and money markets, and in these markets the branches do a bank-to-bank business as a full market participant. In some other markets, the branches do a retail banking business in full competition with the local banking institutions. In still others, and especially among some of the newer nations, the local banking market is relatively underdeveloped, and the range and scope of branch activities is necessarily limited. These branches have also to operate within highly diverse legal systems, banking and exchange control regulations, and customary systems of banking practice and operation.

The principal locus of foreign branch activity is London. Twelve U.S. banks have established branches, and about half of all foreign branch assets are centered there. Attracting U.S. banks has been the continued status of London as a major world financial center, a status considerably enhanced by the emergence in the mid-1950s of the Euro-dollar market centered in London.

American banks in London are major participants in the Euro-dollar market and have been prime contributors to its development. The bulk of their activity, in fact, is confined to that market inasmuch as only limited business in sterling is available and sterling lending in recent years has been curbed by the Bank of England. As active participants in the market for dollars as it has developed in London, American banks offer and take dollars in the interbank market and obtain dollar funds from the market for corporate clients. The three banks with world-wide networks of branches are able to garner funds throughout their branch systems and funnel them in and out of London in response to needs and availabilities in widespread money centers. Deposits placed with these branches are not subject to any interest rate limitations such as apply to deposits at offices in the United States, a fact which together with the names of the banks has attracted large deposits from corporations abroad. Participation in this market, however, involves a highly sophisticated money and foreign exchange operation inasmuch as the basis for operations consists of potentially volatile "bought" deposits and lending operations can involve complex swap operations in and out of all the major foreign currencies.

Growth in activity at London branches surged in 1965 and 1966 as a result of the rechanneling of international financing to London and to the Euro-dollar market in the wake of the institution of the voluntary foreign credit restraint program in the United States and the imposition of the interest equalization tax on term loans by U. S. banks. Borrowers in foreign developed countries turned to the Euro-dollar market to obtain funds, and U.S. banks close to or above their foreign credit ceilings sold off parts of their foreign loan portfolios to their London and other foreign branches. Total assets of London branches more than doubled in this period from $2.7 billion to $6.4 billlon, and alone accounted for two-thirds of the asset growth of all foreign branches of U.S. banks.

Access to the London market through a branch proved especially advantageous to U.S. banks in the summer of 1966 as monetary conditions in the United States tightened progressively. Those U.S. banks faced with substantial run-offs of certificates of deposit in this period as well as heavy domestic loan demand were able to obtain resources by borrowing in the Euro-dollar market through their London branch.[8] This was an expensive way to obtain additional funds as rates in the Euro-dollar market rose to 7 percent for ninety-day funds (one and a half points higher than permissible rates on C/Ds), but with the degree of pressure on the banks, the availability of funds was of far greater importance than their cost. In the latter half of 1966, head office liabilities to foreign branches (and mainly to those in London) rose by over 2 billion. Banks without direct access to the Euro-dollar market through a London branch were somewhat disadvantaged, being forced to rely on the federal funds market or to borrow from the Federal Reserve discount window to maintain their reserve positions. Largely because of this experience, recent months have seen further interest by some banks previously without foreign branches to seek to establish a branch in London.

Of the many other diverse types of banking conducted by foreign branches of U.S. banks, one of particular interest is the business of branches in centers such as Nassau, Beirut, Geneva, Hong Kong, and, to some extent, Panama. These centers have in common rigid banking secrecy, a favorable tax climate, reasonable political stability, and all the virtual absence of exchange controls. In consequence of the resulting advantages to corporations and investors, they became financial centers in their own right, serving as gathering points for liquid wealth and other funds seeking tax or political haven or as way stations in the international movement of corporate cash balances. The U.S. branches attract a sizable portion of the funds entering these centers by reason of their association with the largest names in U.S. banking. The branches are able through the world-wide connections of their parent institutions to channel these funds into appropriate investment outlets.

3. "EDGE" AND "AGREEMENT" CORPORATIONS, INCLUDING FOREIGN AFFILIATES. The third major institutional framework through which U.S. banks conduct their international operations consists of subsidiary corporations, the so-called "Edge" and "agreement" corporations. The activities, focus, and the size and number of these corporations, like other aspects of banks' international activities, have undergone considerable change since the mid-1950s. At the end of 1955 there were three Edge corporations and four agreement corporations in existence. Eleven years later, the aggregate number of these corporations had grown to forty-five, owned by thirty-three banks.

As these corporations have developed in size and number in the last decade, three distinct functions have appeared. First, for the non-New York banks, the Edge corporation has offered a permissible corporate vehicle for the establishment of a New York office. Second, all banks have employed these corporations as holding companies through which to acquire and hold their interests in foreign subsidiary or affiliated banks and in other foreign financial institutions. Finally, the ability of these corporations to acquire and hold shares has enabled American banks in their foreign operations to extend some equity as well as loan financing.

---

[8]Deposits at foreign branches are not subject to reserve requirements, nor are the rates paid for such deposits subject to the interest rate limitations applied to deposits at offices in the United States. Also, liabilities of head offices to their own foreign branches (i.e., borrowings) are not considered as deposits at head offices and hence are not subject to reserve requirements or to interest rate ceilings.

Establishing a New York Office by Non-New York Banks. In the mid-1950s there were only two Edge or agreement corporations located in New York and owned by non-New York banks: Bank of America, New York, established in 1949, and First of Boston International Corporation (now known as Bank of Boston International). Because of New York's dominant position as this country's center of international trade and finance, a substantial portion of the financing of import and export transactions flows through New York City; the international customer also wants to be able to make and receive payments in New York City. The interior or West Coast bank can, of course, use the services of its New York correspondent bank in the negotiation of foreign drafts, collections, and in making and receiving foreign payments. However, in doing so, the bank's identity with the foreign financing is mitigated, if not lost, and the risk is run, under present competitive conditions in American banking, that all of the foreign business of that customer, and possibly the domestic business as well, may be lost to the New York bankers. Where a substantial amount of foreign business is involved, then, as Edge corporation offers the interior bank a means of conducting part of its foreign business in New York.

Bank of America's experience with its New York Edge subsidiary, in particular, has proven the precursor to the entry into the New York market of a number of other non-New York banks. The incentive for interior and West Coast banks to establish such a New York subsidiary has grown as their own foreign business has grown and as competition among banks in general has become more acute. At the end of 1966, there were nine Edge corporations operating in New York, which were in effect arms of the international banking departments of banks in Boston, Minneapolis, Pittsburgh, Chicago, Los Angeles, and San Francisco. These New York subsidiaries carry on full-scale international banking services. However, they are limited by law and regulation to the conduct of only such business as is related to international transactions.

Affiliations with Foreign Banks and Other Financial Institutions. The ability of Edge and agreement corporations to hold stock in other companies has been used by U.S. banks for the most part to acquire subsidiary banks and ownership interests in other financial institutions abroad. Affiliations with foreign commercial banks are motivated primarily by a desire to obtain a degree of direct representation in a foreign market or markets.[9] The nature of these affiliations naturally varies with the over-all market strategy of the bank as tempered by the exigencies of foreign market conditions. By and large, existing affiliations are of three types. First is the wholly-owned subsidiary, either established by the U.S. bank or resulting from the purchase of an existing bank. Banks strongly oriented toward overseas expansion through branches have preferred such subsidiaries in markets were legal impediments precluded the establishment of direct branches. In these cases, the subsidiaries are pure substitutes for branches and are for the most part operated as if they were branches. Examples of this type of affiliation are the First National City Bank (South Africa) Ltd. and The Mercantile Bank of Canada, another First National City Bank subsidiary.

A second broad type of affiliation is the controlled subsidiary with a substantial minority interest held by local shareholders. These affiliations are also close substitutes for the bank's own branches, but in these cases either local law or policy or opportunities for acquiring a larger participation in a going local institution

---

[9] See generally Pringle, *Why American Banks Go Overseas,* 116 The Banker 770 (1966), for an illustrative list of these affiliations with foreign banks.

have prevented the establishment of direct branches or the acquisition of a wholly-owned subsidiary. Sometimes, too, the presence of substantial local ownership interests assists in maintaining the indigenous character of the foreign bank, an attribute that can be advantageous in those countries with a strong nationalistic bias. The integration of such controlled but not wholly-owned subsidiaries into the international operations of the U.S. bank can pose difficulties. At times, for example, consideration of the interests of minority stockholders acts as a constraint on the operation of the foreign bank on American bank lines. In any case, it takes time to instill American standards of efficiency and American operating practices into a foreign affiliate.

A third type of affiliation is the minority interest with the ownership interest ranging from about 10 to 40 percent. These affiliations may be characterized as a cementing of correspondent relations or as the establishment of a closer working relationship. This type of affiliation has been used primarily by those banks without a pronounced strategy for overseas branches or without sufficient resources to man and support branches abroad. For some, the minority affiliation has been employed as a means of gaining entry in geographic areas where they would not, for reasons of policy, be prepared to establish branches in any event. While some earlier affiliations of this type involved the acquisition of less than a 10 percent interest in the foreign bank, recent acquisitions have all been in excess of 10 percent, and banks have shown a preference for an even larger interest. Banks have discovered through experience that a greater than 10 percent interest in the foreign bank is required if the U.S. bank is to have a significant say in the management and policy of the foreign institution and if its own needs are to be properly cared for.

Aside from affiliations with foreign commercial banks to provide direct banking facilities abroad, banks have acquired through their Edge or agreement corporations numerous equity interests in a wide range of other financial institutions. At the end of 1966, affiliations ranging from wholly-owned subsidiaries to purely nominal shareholdings in such institutions numbered upwards of 150 and included interests in government-sponsored development banks, private investment banks, finance companies, factoring operations, and equipment leasing firms.

In less developed countries, a number of token investments have been made in government-sponsored development banks such as the Industrial Credit and Investment Corporation of India, the Pakistan Industrial Credit and Investment Corporation, and the Nigerian Industrial Development Bank. These investments serve to associate the investing U.S. bank with the long-term development of these countries and to cement their relationships with those governments. Other and more important interests in less developed countries are in private investment companies providing loan and venture capital to private industrial and commercial firms and in sales finance companies providing credit to finance business receivables and consumer credit extensions. In some countries, these institutions have offered specialized financing facilities not otherwise available. For the U.S. banks these investments provide, in addition to monetary returns, collateral benefits in the form of business contacts, improved knowledge of local economic and financial conditions, and an added means of providing financial services in various markets to their international customers.

In Europe and other advanced countries, these affiliations have been fewer in number, but interest in these types of affiliations has been marked recently. The emergence of the Euro-bond market, the growth of "offshore" financing by U.S. corporations, and the improvements and adaptations in European capital markets generally, have prompted several recent investments by U.S. banks, in conjunction with other European banks, in new financial institutions intended to provide medium- and longer-term financing of enterprises. An example of this type of venture is Ameribas, jointly owned by Bank of America and the Banque de Paris et des Pays-bas, which has already floated a major bond issue in Europe to finance its operations.

Equity Financing of Foreign Enterprises. The third principle use of Edge corporations has been to provide equity financing in conjunction with the international lending operations of the banks. At one time, a number of banks believed that this would be a relatively important function of their Edge corporations, believing or anticipating that U.S. corporations establishing subsidiaries overseas would seek equity participations by their U.S. bankers. These expectations have failed to materialize as U.S. corporations have preferred to establish either wholly-owned subsidiaries abroad or joint ventures with local interests. Hence, acquisitions of shares by Edge corporations in nonfinancial business have amounted to less than 5 percent of their stock investments. Usually these stock acquisitions have resulted from participations in loan-equity financing projects of the International Finance Corporation or from exercise of stock rights obtained to improve the terms of loans.

Edge and agreement corporations have, on the whole, proved flexible devices by which U.S. banks seeking to develop their international banking businesses could augment their facilities and expand their organizations in a variety of ways. The New York office is almost indispensable to the internationally oriented bank located in other sections of the country. Equally indispensable are the affiliations with foreign banks and other financial institutions, for these add to the overseas banking organization needed if the American bank is to be able adequately and imaginatively to meet the banking and financial needs of globally-minded customers.

B. A Profile of International Lending

Lending is the dynamic sector of a bank's business, and this is equally true in the international business of banks. It is this sector that has seen the most profound changes as U.S. banks have developed their international activities. Earlier, an indication was provided of the credit operations at branches located abroad. In this section, attention is directed to the international lending done at banks in this country. A profile of that lending is provided together with some indication of the changes that ocurred in recent years.[10]

At the end of 1966, dollar credits reported by banks in the United States totaled $9.6 billion. An indication of the composition of these credits is given in Table 2. Several points of interest emerge from an examination of this table. First of all, it reveals the dominant position of Japan, which alone accounts for nearly one-fourth of all foreign credits of banks in the United States. The phenomenal growth in these credits (a twenty-fold expansion in eleven years) paralleled an equally extraordinary growth of Japan's economy and its foreign trade. These Japanese borrowings have played a catalytic role in the development of the interna-

---

[10]A major distinction between the international lending done at banks in this country and that at branches and affiliates overseas is that the overwhelming bulk of the credits extended from the U.S. are denominated in dollars. For example, dollar credits to foreigners reported by banks in the United States totaled $9.6 billion at the end of 1966, but claims payable in foreign currencies totaled only about $400 million. Of this amount, more than half represented deposits with foreigners—that is, principally working balances with foreign correspondent banks. At foreign branches and affiliates, foreign currency lending predominates (with important exceptions such as London).

TABLE 2
Bank Credit to Foreigners, December 31, 1966
(in millions of U.S. dollars)

	Europe	Latin America	Japan	Other Asia	All Other Countries	Total
Short-term:						
Loans						
Banks and official institutions ..	352	726	562	295	16	1,996
Other	248	395	14	69	216	1,140
Acceptances	304	637	1,392	129	78	2,540
Long-term:						
Loans*	1,186	1,220	304	391	818	3,919
Total	2,090	3,176	2,272	884	1,173	9,595

*Long-term loans are all loans with an original maturity of more than one year.
Source: U.S. TREASURY DEPARTMENT, TREASURY BULLETIN, Feb. 1967.
Data related to loans and acceptance credits denominated in U.S. dollars.

tional business of U.S. banks. In order to meet their international credit needs, Japanese bankers sought to establish credit lines not only with banks in New York but with major banks throughout the country as well. For many banks making their initial excursions into international lending, the acknowledged credit standing of the Japanese banks and their strong demands for credit offered a prime outlet for their lendable funds. The initial expansion of the international activities of a number of banks can in a sense be said to have been underwritten by Japan.

A second point of interest in the Japanese credits is that they are acceptance credits for the most part. As such, these credits are (directly or indirectly) associated with the financing of foreign trade. However, the larger portion of these credits is not for the financing of U.S.-Japanese trade but for the financing of movements of goods outside the United States. It is this financing of so-called third-country trade that is particularly indicative of the changed role of U.S. banks in the financing of international transactions. Illustrative of this point is the fact that in 1955 acceptances outstanding to finance movements of goods between foreign countries accounted for one-sixth of total acceptances; eleven years later, they accounted

for 44 percent of the total. Use of the acceptance instrument by Japanese borrowers as a means of obtaining credit in the United States also contributed importantly to the revival of the market for bankers' acceptances in this country, thereby adding to the facilities of New York as an international financial center.

Another feature of this portfolio is the high proportion of term loans it contains. At the end of 1966, over 40 percent of total outstanding bank credits to foreigners were loans with original maturities of more than one year. In some banks, the proportion was considerably higher. U.S. banks making international loans are the same large banks that are heavily engaged in term lending domestically. These banks have sought to adapt the techniques of term lending learned and developed domestically to the financing requirements of international borrowers. Aggregate figures, such as those presented in Table 2, do not show the degree of success attained by the banks in this type of lending, even when those data are viewed over time. For the proportion of term loans in the total foreign loan portfolio has not changed significantly over the past decade. The change has occurred in the composition and characteristics of the term lending undertaken.

In earlier years, longer-term foreign loans by U.S. banks were extended for the most part to foreign governments and official institutions. Longer-term credit to less developed and nonindustrial countries continues to be mainly to official bodies, usually in connection with large-scale development projects. Part of these credits have taken the form of participations in the shorter maturities of loans extended by the World Bank, the International Finance Corporation, and other international financial institutions. On the other hand, by the early 1960s the banks began to extend term loans to commercial and industrial borrowers in developed and financially stable countries abroad. Prime foreign corporations in countries, especially in Europe, with inadequate local facilities for longer-term financing or without access to foreign securities markets, sought and were able to obtain medium-term financing from U.S. banks for plant expansion, working capital, or refinancing of short-term debt. The high proportion of term loans in credits shown in Table 2 for Europe and All Other Countries (which category includes Canada, Australia, and South Africa) is an indication of this development. To take a more specific example, major Italian corporations borrowed heavily in 1963 and 1964 when the Italian economy went through a balance-of-payments crisis, a period of severe monetary restraint, and an industrial recession; these credits assisted importantly in the needed strengthening of the financial structures of these corporations, then heavily indebted at short-term to Italian banks, to meet the altered economic circumstances of the time; a side benefit of these credits, of course, was that they also served to shore up Italy's external reserve position. Other major uses of term loans have been to finance additions to the shipping fleets of Scandinavian and other shipping companies, and to finance purchases of commer-

cial jet aircraft in the United States by foreign airlines, in both developed and underdeveloped countries.

The attraction of these loans to the banks extending them and to the foreign corporate borrower is that they provide a flexible means of medium-term financing (from two to eight years, though clustering more in the three- to five-year range) with terms and conditions tailored to specific financing needs and in the context of a corporation's over-all financial program. The provisions for regular amortization payments over the life of the loan also adds to the liquidity of the bank's loan portfolio.

Following the upsurge in this type of lending, however, the interest equalization tax[11] was applied early in 1965 to bank loans to developed countries with original maturities of more than one year and for purposes other than financing U.S. exports. Imposition of this tax, which effectively raised the interest rate on such loans by 1 percent per annum, was part of the Government's program to improve the balance of payments position by restricting the growth of bank lending abroad. Another part of that program, the voluntary foreign credit restraint effort, has applied to all bank lending to foreigners. Following the introduction of those measures, new term loans to developed countries effectively ceased, and as regularly scheduled repayments have been received the outstanding term loans have fallen. Whether this type of general corporate lending would be resumed on a significant scale if existing restraints were relaxed or removed is not certain, for, in the interim, important changes have taken place in European capital and credit markets, including the establishment of new banks and financial institutions by U.S. and European banks which could provide a

---

[11]Interest Equalization Tax Extension Act of 1965, 79 Stat. 954, INT. REV. CODE 1954, § § 4911–20.

good deal of medium-term financing facilities hitherto lacking.[12]

The composition of this portfolio is also a reflection of the special considerations and risks encountered in international lending. For in addition to the strength and nature of foreign credit demands, the size, geographic distribution, borrower characteristics, and maturity of credits in this portfolio represent a collective judgment by the lending banks as to the political and financial stability of foreign countries. An appraisal of the so-called country risk inherent in any foreign credit is the major distinction between domestic and international lending. Besides assessing the credit-worthiness of the individual borrower, the bank has to exercise a judgment on political, economic, and social conditions in the country of the borrower as they are likely to affect foreign exchange availabilities at the time of repayment of the loan. The possibilities of exchange rate changes, foreign exchange controls, political upheaval, and the like are myriad in the large number of heterogeneous countries in which banks are lending.

Assessing the credit risk of a borrower located far from the head office is alone no easy task; in attempting to do so, the bank encounters widely varying standards of business conduct, differing financial practices, the absence of meaningful financial statements, and other imperfect credit information. The balancing of all these considerations is a delicate and subtle task requiring wide-range knowledge, experienced judgment, and often just a keen instinct. In this task, banks avail themselves of information gathered through foreign branches, affiliated foreign institutions, foreign correspondent

banks, and frequent visits to foreign banking markets and foreign customers by lending officers.

Technological developments in communications and especially in transportation have clearly eased the job of supervising and developing international banking business in the past decade as American banks have gone through the learning process of becoming informed and knowledgeable international lenders. Still, the best information and expertise do not fully protect the bank against the risks faced in this lending. Other means employed are diversification of portfolio among countries, discrimination as to borrowers, variation in maturities, and the extensive use of guarantees from third parties—foreign banks, foreign governments, and U.S. corporations in the case of loans to their subsidiaries. In areas of political and financial instability—for example in many Latin American countries – U.S. banks have limited short-term credits to foreign trade financing and longer-term lending is largely confined to foreign governments and official institutions; lending to other borrowers is usually contingent on appropriate guarantees from banks and foreign governments.

CONCLUSION

The present size and significance of international operations in many banks are less surprising when viewed in retrospect and in full appreciation of the strength and nature of the forces underlying their growth. What is far less certain is whether these activities have attained their full maturity in the context of the over-all development of American commercial banking. That the future will bring further growth and development of the banks' international operations cannot be questioned, for those forces and elements underpinning the thrust of American banks into international banking in the past decade are still present

---

[12]See generally Rothschild & Leach, *Recent Developments in the International Capital Market*, 117 THE BANKER 297 (1967), for the view that those facilities are no longer dependent on the existence of U.S. Government restrictions on foreign borrowing in the United States.

and for the most part, still strong. It is rather the extent and rapidity of future growth and the shape of these activities in the years to come that are matters of conjecture.

Three factors are likely to slow the future growth of international operations of commercial banks. First, virtually all the largest banks in the United States are now committed to provide full-scale international banking services in this country and in varying degrees abroad as well. Possibilities of a new wave of banks entering significantly into this field are consequently limited. Second, increasing difficulty is being encountered in establishing and developing overseas banking organizations. The number of foreign markets not already penetrated by American banks is now relatively small, and nationalistic and other foreign restrictions are hindering new entrants into these markets. Third, efforts of the U.S. government to improve this country's international payments position are for the foreseeable future likely to result in conditions less conducive to

the expansion of international operations than conditions in the early 1960s.

Another uncertainty for the future is how well the U.S. banks have learned the international lending business. The few significant loan or other losses sustained in the last decade of expansion would seem to indicate a sucessful learning process. However, this period has been one of exceptional growth in the world economy and one of few major financial crises. The test of successful banking and bankers and of the quality of credits they have extended comes when less favorable conditions prevail. U.S. banks have yet to meet that test in their international operations.

As the international operations of U.S. banks continue to evolve, the monetary and banking authorities are faced with the task of resolving some of the issues explored in this paper. More generally, they are faced with the challenge of appraising the changing nature of those activities and of attempting to discern their changing implications for public policy.

7. The Euro-dollar Market: Its Nature and Impact[*]

Jane Sneddon Little

Euro-dollars have been called both a bless-ing and a burden—a blessing in the sense that they comprise an additional source of funds and help to integrate national financial mar-kets; a burden because they can complicate a particular country's monetary policy. This ar-ticle provides a definitive description of the origin and operation of the Euro-dollar market. It also analyzes the relation of this market to balance of payment problems as well as its possible influence on monetary policy in the United States and other countries.

During recent periods of tight money, the Euro-dollar market has become the focus of a great deal of excited attention. Almost daily the financial press discusses the latest figures on Euro-dollar borrow-ings made by U. S. banks and reports at length the opinions of bankers and gov-ernment officials on these developments. Frequently, these comments are contra-dictory, for some observers see the Euro-dollar market as a source of funds which "cushion" the overly harsh impact of tightening monetary policy in the short run but permit no long-term escape from its dictates. Other reporters, however, direly describe the market as a "bottom-less pit" of funds which allows the bank-ing community to weaken the effective-ness of Federal Reserve System decisions drastically. Much of this contradiction and confusion stems, of course, from the fact that the Euro-dollar market is still evolving and that its operations and im-pact on monetary policy here and abroad are only beginning to be understood. This article attempts to provide a synthesis of current thought on the origin of the Euro-dollar market and its modus operandi. It also offers some analysis of the mar-ket's impact on U. S. monetary devel-opments.

EURO-DOLLARS AND THEIR MARKET: A DESCRIPTION

According to a broad but generally acceptable definition, the term "Euro-dollar" refers to dollar balances depos-ited in banks outside the United States, including foreign branches of U. S. banks. The dollars may, of course, be owned by American residents or foreigners. Because the decision to make a Euro-dollar de-posit does not involve the physical re-moval of dollars from the United States, the assets which correspond with new Euro-dollar deposit liabilities generally take the form of claims on American banks.[1] The Euro-dollar market, in turn, is created by the banks, including foreign branches of American banks, which ac-cept and relend these deposits. These banks, referred to as Euro-banks, are lo-cated throughout Western Europe and Canada but are even found in such wide-spread places as Lebanon, Nassau and,

---

[*]From *New England Economic Review*, May/June, 1969. Reprinted by permission of the publisher, the Federal Reserve Bank of Boston.

[1]Thereafter, of course, the Euro-bank may choose to make a loan on the basis of its dollar claim in which case this first asset will be re-placed by a claim on the Euro-dollar borrower.

perhaps in the near future, Singapore. Because of the London bankers' traditional expertise in international finance, however, that city developed without question as the center of the market. Although many of these Euro-banks also make a market in other foreign currencies, no other Euro-currency has attained the importance of the Euro-dollar. As one of the largest markets for short-term funds in the world, the Euro-dollar market is particularly significant because of its high degree of freedom, flexibility and competition. Because of these characteristics and the widespread international demand for dollar assets, the market greatly facilitates the rapid transfer of capital to the areas where the shortages are most acute.

The Euro-dollar market is largely a wholesale market characterized by a high proportion of interbank activity. A typical Euro-dollar transaction involves a round amount ranging from $1 million to $5 million placed for a standard maturity running from call to one year, although maturities of up to 5 years can be negotiated. Since 1966, Euro-dollar CD's have also been available. Because these transactions usually involve prime customers, Euro-dollar interbank loans are made in a matter of minutes or hours with practically no questions asked—even on loans of over 6 months. The actual transfers are made by telephone or teletype with a letter of confirmation as the only customary documentation.

Limiting the amount loaned to any one customer or any one country is one of the few safeguards these Euro-banks like to maintain. As another safeguard, many Euro-banks prefer to act as intermediaries only, dealing primarily with banks and having little contact with commercial and industrial borrowers. They, thus, reduce their risk and yet perform a useful service by bringing together the major international banks with loanable funds but limited knowledge of local markets and the large number of smaller banks which lend dollar deposits.

Because so many Euro-dollar transactions are large scale and low risk, they are considered practically costless additions to normal banking and foreign exchange business requiring few additional facilities or personnel. For this reason, the banks which operate in this market are willing to work with much narrower margins between Euro-dollar deposit and loan rates than American banks—or European banks for that matter—would find acceptable for any sizable portion of their domestic loan business. Because the Euro-dollar market is a wholesale operation and thus not available to all depositors and borrowers, reducing margins on Euro-dollar business does not force the European banks to adopt the practice for domestic currency transactions.[2]

While these considerations explain the ability of the Euro-banks to adopt narrow margins, the necessity for their so doing results from the high level of competition in this largely unregulated international market. On the demand side too, the development of a large number of multinational corporations presents the Euro-banks with a group of very sophisticated borrowers with many alternative sources of funds.

Naturally, the actual margin between deposit and lending rate on a given loan depends on the risk involved. The margin for prime name banks, for instance, is $\frac{3}{32}$ percent to $\frac{1}{4}$ percent while that for prime industrial or commercial firms is about $\frac{1}{2}$ percent. From these levels, the margins rise as high a 2½ percent depending on the type of borrower, his country, etc.

THE ORIGIN OF THE MARKET

The world had never before seen anything quite like the Euro-dollar market

[2]Paul Einzig, however, foresees that the competition of the Euro-dollar market eventually will result in the development of wholesale domestic banking with reduced profit margins on loans to large prime borrowers (*The Euro-dollar System*, London, Macmillan & Co. Ltd., 1964).

when it first became recognizable in 1958. The Euro-dollar market produced, for the first time in history, a unique structure of international interest rates, distinctly different from any schedule of national rates. To be sure, Euro-dollar rates are affected by rate levels and movements in New York and elsewhere, but the Euro-dollar market owes its very existence to the differentials between national interest rates and their variations over time.

Not surprisingly, since there's very little that is entirely "new under the sun," some limited aspects of the Euro-dollar market have developed before. For example, a thriving business in sterling and dollar deposits grew up in Berlin and Vienna in the 1920's; however, these activities were not directly comparable to the Euro-dollar market. During the 1920's, for instance, the proceeds of foreign currency deposits were generally converted immediately into domestic currency resources. The subsequent relending of these foreign demand deposits, which is of major importance in the Euro-dollar market, is a new phenomenon.

Requirements for a Market in Foreign Currency Deposits

How and why then did this unique market develop? The major theoretical requirements for the creation of a banking system based on foreign currency deposits are: 1) the existence of interest rate differentials between national credit markets; 2) a sufficient degree of freedom from exchange controls to permit investors to take advantage of the rate differences; and 3) sufficient confidence in the vehicle currency to permit the potential for profit to outweigh the risk.[3] Although many observers have argued to the contrary, a U. S. balance of payments deficit is not among these theoretical requirements.[4] In theory a foreigner's decision to hold dollars for liquidity and transactions or investment purposes and his separate decision to place these dollars in a bank outside of the United States rather than in the New York market are not dependent upon a particular U. S. payments position.

In the context of post World War II history, however, the large and continuing U. S. deficits as well as the role of the dollar as a key currency were probably important prerequisites for the development of the market. They allowed for the development of a large pool of highly acceptable and interest elastic assets and a sufficient degree of international liquidity to permit the removal of exchange controls.

Evolution: 1945–1958

At the end of World War II, the United States held a large proportion of the world's monetary gold reserves; thus, as a matter of practicality, under the international payments system established in 1947, nations included foreign exchange (dollars and pounds sterling) among their official reserve assets. At the same time the United States was the only nation capable of producing or financing the vast resources required for reconstruction. Thus, policies designed to encourage the transfer of reserve assets, over and above the required real resources, resulted in large and almost continuous balance of payments deficits for the United States from 1950 on. Because, despite these deficits, the United States was the world's major exporter and possessed the world's strongest and only freely convertible currency (except for the Swiss franc), the

---

[3]A certain basic degree of confidence in the foreign currency used in such a banking system is undoubtedly a necessity—especially during its developmental stages; however, considerable fluctuations in this trust may occur without destroying the market since counteracting movements in the interest and forward exchange rates will tend to maintain the advantages inherent in the system.

[4]Carl H. Stem, "The Euro-dollar System: An Analysis of its Credit Function and Impact on the International Financial Position of the United States," unpublished Ph.D. thesis, Harvard University, 1968. This valuable analysis provided the framework for this and a later section on the volume of intermediated loans.

dollar became an internationally acceptable means of payment and the most functionally important official reserve asset. Under these circumstances, the U. S. deficits resulted in a growth of short-term liabilities to foreigners of about $8.5 billion between 1950 and 1958 in addition to a slowly rising outflow and redistribution of gold.

Because a large part of this deficit resulted from U. S. Government payments for military and aid purposes, many of the transferred dollars went directly to foreign official hands. Gradually official monetary institutions began to look for investment opportunities for at least a portion of the dollar balances which they were accumulating for balance of payments contingencies. At the same time much of the private sector still wanted the convertible dollar to finance international trade. During the 1950's most dollars which foreign officials and others chose to invest were channeled to private European borrowers through the New York money market banks. All through this period, however, indications of a growing European market for dollar deposits were beginning to appear. In the early 1950's, for instance, East European banks began to deposit their dollar balances with their correspondents in London and Paris rather than in the United States, undoubtedly fearing that the United States might block these balances during any crisis. It probably did not require too much ingenuity for the accepting banks to develop a loan business in these and other dollar deposits.

A major impetus to the expansion of Euro-dollar business, moreover, developed in 1957 when the British, after a series of balance of payments crises, curbed the use of sterling for the finance of non-sterling trade. With London a traditional center for trade finance, the British bankers decided that it was not important *how* trade was financed as long as it continued to be financed *through* London; thus, they substituted the dollar, already frequently used for trade finance, for the pound.

Until 1958, however, a major barrier to the full development of a Euro-dollar market, continued to persist—the entanglement of exchange controls. But by that year, the U. S. balance of payments deficits had contributed sufficient international liquidity to permit the major European countries to make their currencies freely convertible into the dollar. This return to freedom from exchange controls is perhaps the most important link between the U. S. payments deficits and the development of the Euro-dollar market.

Required Interest Rate Relationships

The demand for an internationally acceptable currency and other special postwar problems apparently explain the first appearance of the Euro-dollar market. However, with the return to financial freedom in 1958, the interest rate structures in the United States, Europe and the Euro-dollar market became relevant too and gave its growth momentum.

As mentioned above, without rate discrepancies between national credit systems, a market in foreign currency deposits can have little reason for being. While questions of confidence and convenience in working hours and communications etc. may sometimes override interest and forward rate differentials, generally unless rates on Euro-dollar deposits are higher than those available in the United States and rates on Euro-dollar loans are lower than those on domestic currency alternatives, foreigners will have little reason to hold or borrow Euro-dollar balances. If, for instance, it were cheaper (including the cost of covering the exchange risk) to borrow domestic currency for use in buying dollars on the foreign exchange market than to borrow Euro-dollars directly, few borrowers would choose the second alternative. In addition, Euro-banks must compete with the loan rates offered by financial institutions within the United States when U. S. banks are free and willing to make such an offer, or again little demand for their new facilities will develop. Thus, the competitive rates prevalent in the United States set the lower limits for Euro-dollar deposit rates but only the approximate upper limits for Euro-dollar loan rates.

In the case of deposits, where U. S. rates do form a fairly firm floor, the return on balances placed in the Euro-dollar market must variously compete, according to the status of the investor, with the current rates on official foreign deposits, which are exempt from Regulation Q, and with competitive money market rates like those on Treasury bills or, in the last few years, CD rates.

As for Euro-dollar loan rates, before the U. S. voluntary credit restraint program began in early 1965, the cost of U. S. loans to foreigners provided a partial ceiling. Because European banks do not engage in the American practice of requiring that a certain percentage of a loan be kept as a demand deposit with the lending bank, the "effective" prime rate in the United States is about 20 percent above its nominal level as far as European borrowers are concerned. These compensatory balances, thus, permitted the Euro-dollar loan rate to rise above the nominal U. S. prime rate. In addition, since very few foreigners who are considered prime names in Europe can obtain the same treatment in the United States, the ceiling on Euro-dollar loan rates could have been well above the U. S. prime rate for most borrowers. In fact, a sizable group of foreigners would find U. S. banks unwilling to make loans to them at any price. Thus, for these Euro-dollar borrowers the effective ceiling would have been the rates available on domestic currency loans. Since 1965, of course, given the U. S. voluntary credit restraint program, this last qualification applies to most foreigners, and

Euro-dollar loan rates are indeed free to rise as high as the cost of domestic currency.

Development: 1958 to Present

By 1958–1959, when the removal of exchange controls had set the stage for the rapid development of the Euro-dollar market, such rate discrepancies became of crucial importance for the first time. During this period Euro-dollar deposit rates at 3⅞ to 4 percent had risen well above 2½ percent maximum permitted on 90-180 day deposits by Regulation Q. In addition to disappointing yields, the U. S. market also did not offer sufficient flexibility to attract bankers' deposits since no interest at all could be earned on a deposit made for under 30 days. Moreover, while U. S. banks were charging the equivalent of 5¾ percent (including the compensatory balance), Euro-banks were offering dollar loans of similar risk etc. for 4½ to 5 percent. With boom conditions in Europe and rates on domestic currencies often set by cartel arrangements in addition, Euro-dollar loans were also usually cheaper[5] than available domestic currency loans. It is hardly surprising, thus, that the Euro-dollar market rapidly became very popular on both sides of the Atlantic.

Obviously, artificial barriers, such as Regulation Q and cartel agreements, have been of great importance to the development of the market. More recent restrictions, such as the Interest Equalization Tax and the voluntary balance of payments program, have also greatly stimulated the growth of the market since these measures forced Europeans who had borrowed directly from the United States to turn to the Euro-dollar market and required that a sizable group of U. S. foreign subsidiaries join them. During 1966 and again within the last few

---

[5]This rate includes the cost of covering the exchange risk incurred by switching the dollars to the desired currency.

months, tight money conditions in the United States have also provided a significant spur to the growth of the market.

THE SIZE OF THE MARKET

As of this year the size of the Euro-dollar market is estimated to be about $30 billion. Measured from 1960 when the market stood at about the $1 billion level, its compound annual rate of growth has been over 50 percent a year. Unfortunately any estimate about the size of the Euro-dollar market is very much an estimate because few satisfactory data sources are available. One problem, for instance, is that the nature of the Euro-dollar market with its large number of interbank deposits makes data reporting net Euro-dollar positions vis-à-vis various countries with no distinction between banks and nonbanks very likely to include double counting. However, the Bank of England, the Bank of Canada and the Bank for International Settlements have published data series since 1964 which, despite their incompatibilities, make some approximations possible.

THE EURO-BANKS' CUSTOMERS

Unfortunately, the available data do not permit a very precise discussion of the sources and the uses of Euro-dollars by type of customer or by function. Again, however, a few generalizations may be made.

Euro-dollar Depositors

When the Euro-dollar market first developed, central banks were probably the most important sources of funds. In fact, the late Oscar Altman of the I. M. F. estimated that as of 1962 over two-thirds of all Euro-dollars were owned by central banks and official agencies. By 1967, however, Mr. Altman was suggesting that only one-third of the Euro-dollar deposits were owned by these institutions.[6] The explanation for the decrease seems to be two-fold: first, foreign official dollar holdings have been increasing less than non-official dollar holdings; and second, after Regulation Q was amended in 1962 to exempt foreign official deposits from its ceilings, the Euro-dollar rates no longer looked so attractive in comparison. Nevertheless, central banks and official agencies still remain important Euro-dollar suppliers for domestic and international policy reasons. Many central banks take advantage of the Euro-dollar market, for instance, in their efforts either to expand or reduce domestic liquidity, as will be described in more detail below. In addition, European monetary authorities, including the B. I. S. and often in cooperation with the Federal Reserve System, may pour dollars into the market to maintain orderly conditions. During the fall of 1967, for example, the German, Swiss, Dutch and Belgian central banks and the B. I. S., drawing on swap lines with the United States, channeled $1.4 billion into the market to prevent Euro-dollar rates from flaring too high in response to the sterling crisis. Generally, international crises tend to lead to shortages within many parts of the Euro-dollar market as few investors want to *own* dollars but many speculators want to *borrow* them to buy the currencies which appear to be in the strongest position. Apparently this latter group chooses to borrow Euro-dollars rather than domestic currencies to avoid exchange controls and possibly reduce the cost of their gamble. Central banks, particularly those in the strong currency countries, must then intervene in the foreign exchange markets to buy the dollar and prevent their currencies from rising too far above par. Faced, thus, with a deluge of dollars from the private market and the consequent creation of domestic reserves, these central banks often try to reverse the flow by selling spot dollars to their com-

[6]Oscar L. Altman, "Euro-dollars," *Finance and Development,* IV (March 1967).

mercial banks in exchange for domestic currency and offering to repurchase the dollars in the future at particularly favorable rates. By reducing the forward discount on the dollar in these situations, the authorities raise the return which banks can earn on Euro-dollar investments. This benefit occurs because the return must be calculated by subtracting from the interest earned the loss incurred by selling the dollars forward at less than their spot value to cover the exchange risk. Frequently, however, such a policy merely produces a vicious circle with the same dollars returning promptly to the central banks as speculators go short in borrowed dollars by using them to buy another currency without bothering to cover the exchange risk.

Foreign commercial banks make up a second major group of depositors in the Euro-dollar market when they accept domestic currency liabilities and convert the corresponding excess reserves to dollar form. Like the central banks, they find the flexibility of the Euro-dollar market with its abundance of short-term investment opportunities and good yields very attractive. Particularly in countries like Germany, France and Italy where broad and varied money market facilities have been slow to develop, the commercial banks have welcomed the opportunity to diversify their investments and to adjust the ratio of the average maturity of their liabilities to the average maturity of their assets. If, for instance, they can lend Euro-dollars at call, having borrowed them for 90 days, they feel justified in employing a larger proportion of their other resources in a less liquid form. The Euro-dollar market provides them with additional opportunities for this kind of adjustment. Moreover, when banks face an atmosphere of high domestic liquidity and low interest rates, they often transfer their excess funds in dollar form to a nation in a more expansionary phase. The use of the dollar greatly facilitates this type of transfer since many lenders who are willing to accept a foreign liability in dollars would not be willing to accept a liability in pesos or yen.

Of course, nonbanks like insurance companies and large international businesses compose a third important group of suppliers. In addition to questions of safety and convenience, these depositors are undoubtedly influenced by rate incentives, for Euro-dollar returns are often higher than those available on domestic deposits of most of the world's major currencies, including, as has been stressed, dollar assets held in the United States. These firms may find it convenient and profitable, thus, to deposit even their working balances or the proceeds of Euro-bond issues floated in advance of need in the Euro-dollar market.

Until 1965 U. S. resident companies were depositing substantial quantities of dollars in Canada and Europe. In response to the voluntary balance of payments program, however, most of these funds were repatriated.[7] Now the substantial majority of Euro-dollars are dollars already owned by foreign residents (including the subsidiaries of American companies abroad) or are purchased by them for foreign currency.

Euro-dollar Borrowers

As for the borrowers of Euro-dollar funds, when the market first developed most Euro-dollar loans were made to borrowers who used them to finance international trade. Trade was considered to be the Euro-dollar's natural purpose and even countries like France, which have restricted the borrowing of Euro-dollars for domestic reasons, have usually not tried to discourage this use. At present a substantial amount (one-quarter in 1967 according to some authorities)[8] of world trade is still financed by Euro-dollars.

Since the market first developed, how-

---

[7] The funds placed in the market by the Delaware corporations represent an exception to this statement.

[8] Peter Oppenheimer, "Short-Term Capital Flows," *The Banker*, CXVII (August 1967).

ever, commercial banks have found many other investment opportunities for Euro-dollars. These investments may, of course, include loans in dollars or in some other currency bought with dollars. Currently a major outlet for these funds is the large volume of loans made to U. S. banks which borrow Euro-dollars to adjust their reserve positions. As this activity will be discussed in detail below, it seems sufficient here merely to indicate that these loans account for more than one-third of all final Euro-dollar investments. Canadian "street loans" provide another important example of loans to U. S. residents.

Loans to British local authorities are relatively important examples of borrowings made to finance domestic transactions where the dollar is not the national currency. Many Euro-banks located in Britain at times solicit Euro-dollar funds specifically for the purpose of converting them on a covered basis into pounds for local authority loans. Italian and Japanese banks are also prime illustrations of institutions which lend Euro-dollars for domestic purposes whenever borrowing dollars and converting to domestic currency on a covered basis becomes less costly than borrowing domestic funds directly. In Japan a substantial fraction of the large quantity of Euro-dollars that Japanese banks borrow abroad may be used for local financing.[9] Euro-dollar loans made for domestic purposes may merely reflect the determination of commercial banks to make loans in the face of restrictive monetary policy, although the central banks may, of course, take offsetting action. Such loans may also occur, however, with official acquiescence because the monetary authorities are more willing to permit an increase in the domestic money supply which is accompanied by an inflow of capital and official reserve assets than they would be without such advantageous offsets.[10] Still a third

explanation for this development may be that in countries where investors traditionally prefer highly liquid assets, the Euro-dollar market provides their industries with access to lower-cost intermediate-term funds than are available from the domestic banking system.

Finally, in contrast to their important role as suppliers of Euro-dollar funds, central banks—with the important exception of several Communist states and the Belgian Treasury—seldom borrow in the Euro-dollar market. The Belgian Treasury often turns to the Euro-dollar market because of the Belgian National Bank's firm ceiling on its advances to the government.

THE EURO-DOLLAR MARKET AND TOTAL DOLLAR CREDIT EXTENSION

One of the many controversial questions concerning the Euro-dollar system involves the impact of this new market on the total volume of intermediated dollar credit which can be extended worldwide. While some observers deplore the "limitless" chains of interbank loans and the precarious "pyramids" of dollar credit, others express doubt that any additional credit at all can be extended on the basis of Euro-dollar intermediation.

Interbank Loans

Because the term "multiple credit extension" applies only to credit available to final nonbank borrowers, the questions actually have no direct relevance to a large portion of Euro-dollar transactions —the use of dollars for redeposits with other Euro-banks. Since these deposits usually move very rapidly in response to small interest differentials, intermediation may give rise to a long chain of interbank loans on the basis of a given dollar deposit in a U. S. bank. The economic

[9]Einzig, op. cit.

[10]See Francesco Masera, "International Movements of Bank Funds and Monetary Policy in Italy," Banca Nazionale del Lavoro Quarterly Review, December 1966, for a description of the Italian policy between November 1962 and August 1963.

significance of this activity, however, is the rapid transmission of funds from the savers to the ultimate borrowers in whatever part of the world they may be. Although this interbank intermediation does tend to minimize excess reserves, it does not actually add to the means of payment available to the nonbank sector. The accompanying T-accounts demonstrate how a chain of interbank deposits can be consolidated to show clearly that the Euro-banking system as a whole still has just one liability, the deposit due to the original owner, and one asset, the loan made to the final borrower. The first set of accounts shows the bookkeeping effects of Individual A's decision to transfer his dollar balance from Bank B in New York to a new account with Bank C in Paris. With this decision a new Euro-dollar deposit is created. As these first accounts and the next two sets—which depict a series of interbank loans—demonstrate, Bank B keeps transferring its demand deposit liability from one new owner to another (in Paris, London and Tokyo), while each new bank owner substitutes an earning asset, a Euro-dollar deposit, for its demand deposit with Bank B. Finally, as the consolidated accounts show, when Bank E decides to make a nonbank loan to Individual F, the banking system has in effect lent Individual A's Euro-dollar deposit to Individual F in the form of a demand deposit with Bank B—without creating any net new assets or liabilities.

In theory, this chain of loans could go on indefinitely, instead of involving merely four banks. In fact, however, there are two basic limits to the process. In the first place, a variety of voluntary and official reserve requirements impose a limit. To the extent that reserves are voluntary, however, they may tend to be very low because the narrow margins would be wiped out by any sizable retention of reserves.

Perhaps more basically, the length of the chain will also be determined by the cost of intermediation. Naturally, each bank will want to make more by lending the dollars than it is paying to acquire them, and as the chain grows, and smaller, less well-known banks become involved, the required margin will tend to widen. Since the rate at which the ultimate nonbank borrower obtains the loan will include all these costs of intermediation, the limit will be reached when that rate approaches the cost to the nonbank borrower of obtaining funds in the United States (or domestically in his own currency).

Mechanics of Euro-dollar Credit Extension

On the other hand, when a Euro-bank eventually does make a loan to a nonbank borrower, dollar credit totaling a multiple of a given dollar balance held in the United States may be extended to final borrowers within the Euro-dollar system. However, the extent of this credit extension will be very limited. The process is, of course, in many ways similar to credit extension by nonbank financial intermediaries in the United States on the basis of excess cash balances held as demand deposits with commercial banks.[11] When, for instance, the owner of a dollar balance decides to deposit these dollars—or dollar claims on an American bank as

---

[11]In this regard, Euro-banks are much like S & L's in the United States, for like S & L's they hold their liquidity reserves as demand deposits with commercial banks. In addition, the assets they create, like S & L shares, generally do not add to the total means of payment available. According to Fred H. Klopstock (The Euro-dollar Market: Some Unresolved Issues, Princeton, N. J., Princeton University, March 1968), except in Switzerland and Canada where dollar demand accounts are not uncommon, most Euro-dollar investments are call and time deposits held for the sake of the return rather than for transactions purposes. A Euro-bank may thus act like a commercial bank when it authorizes its borrowers to make overdrafts or provides them with checking facilities; however, as long as its original deposit liability is not a demand deposit, the Euro-bank is merely passing along an already existing means of payment when it makes a loan on the basis of that deposit.

T-Accounts for a Chain of Interbank Loans*

STAGE I: CREATION OF THE EURO-DOLLAR DEPOSIT

Individual A

1. DD with Bank B	$100
2. {DD with Bank B	−$100
{E$D with Bank C	+$100

Bank B, New York

1. Cash	$100	DD due A	$100	1.
2.		DD due A	−$100	
		DD due C	+$100 }	2.

Bank C, Paris

| 2. DD with Bank B | +$100 | E$D due A | + $100 | 2. |

STAGE II: REDEPOSIT I

Bank C, Paris

1. DD with Bank B	$100	E$D due A	$100	
2. {DD with Bank B	−$100		−$100	
{E$D with Bank D	+$100		+$100	

Bank B, New York

1. Cash	$100	DD due Bank C	$100	1.
2.		DD due Bank C	−$100	
		DD due Bank D	+$100 }	2.

Bank D, London

| 2. DD with Bank B | +$100 | E$D due Bank C | + $100 | 2. |

STAGE III: REDEPOSIT II

Bank D, London

1. DD with Bank B	$100	E$D due A	+ $100	1.
2. {DD with Bank B	−$100			
{E$D with Bank E	+$100			

Bank B, New York

1. Cash	$100	DD due Bank D	$100	1.
2.		DD due Bank D	−$100	
		DD due Bank E	+$100 }	2.

Bank E, Tokyo

| 2. DD with Bank B | +$100 | E$D due Bank D | + $100 | 2. |

STAGE IV: EURO-DOLLAR LOAN TO FINAL BORROWER

Bank E, Tokyo

1. DD with Bank B	$100	E$D due Bank D	$100 1.
2. {DD with Bank B	-$100		
{E$L to F	+$100		

Bank B, New York

1. Cash	$100	DD due Bank E	$100 1.
		DD due Bank E	-$100 } 2.
		DD due F	+$100 } 2.

Japanese Importer F

2. DD with Bank B	+$100	E$L due Bank E	+$100 2.

CONSOLIDATED POSITIONS

Individual A

E$D with Bank C	$100

Bank B, New York

Cash	$100	DD due F	$100

Banks C, D, and E

Bank C	E$D with Bank D	$100	E$D due A	$100
Bank D	E$D with Bank E	$100	E$D due Bank C	$100
Bank E	E$L to F	$100	E$D due Bank D	$100

Japanese Importer F

DD with Bank B	$100	E$L due Bank E	$100

*The use of T-accounts to illustrate the process of interbank lending was suggested by a similar usage in Klaus Friedrich, op. cit.

T-Accounts for Euro-dollar Credit Extension*

(assuming a 10 percent reserve)

STAGE I

Individual A

1.	DD with N. Y. Bank	$100	
2.	{DD with N. Y. Bank	−$100	
	{E$D with E-bank 1	+$100	

Euro-bank 1

2.	DD with N. Y. Bank	+$100	E$D due A	+$100	2.
3.	E$L to B	+$ 90	DD due B	+$ 90	3.

New York Bank

1.	Cash	$100	DD due A	$100 } 1.
			{DD due A	−$100 } 2.
			{DD due E-bank 1	+$100 } 2.

Individual B

3.	DD with E-bank 1	+$ 90	E$L due E-bank 1	+$ 90	3.

STAGE II

Individual B

1.	DD with E-bank 1	$ 90	E$L due E-bank 1	$ 90	1.
1.	{DD with E-bank 1	−$ 90			
2.	{Goods bought from C	+$ 90			

Euro-bank 1

1.	{DD with N. Y. Bank	$100	E$D due A	$100 } 1.	
	{E$L to B	$ 90	DD due B	$ 90	
2.	DD with N. Y. Bank	−$ 90	DD due B	−$ 90 } 2.	

Individual C

1.	Goods	$ 90
2.	{Goods sold to B	−$ 90
	{DD with N. Y. Bank	+$ 90
3.	{DD with N. Y. Bank	−$ 90
	{E$D with E-bank 2	+$ 90

Euro-bank 2

3.	DD with N. Y. Bank	+$ 90	E$D due C	+$ 90	3.
4.	E$L to D	+$ 81	DD due D	+$ 81	4.

STAGE III

Individual D

1. DD with E-bank 2	$ 81	E$L due E-bank 2	$ 81 1.
2. { DD with E-bank 2	–$ 81		
{ Goods bought from E	+$ 81		

Euro-bank 2

1. DD with N. Y. Bank	$ 90	E$D due C	$ 90]	1.
{ E$L to D	$ 81	DD due D	$ 81]	
2. DD with N. Y. Bank	–$ 81	DD due D	–$ 81	2.

Individual E

1. Goods	$ 81
2. { Goods sold to D	–$ 81
{ DD with N. Y. Bank	+$ 81
{ DD with N. Y. Bank	–$ 81
3. { E$D with E-bank 3	+$ 81

Euro-bank 3

3. DD with N. Y. Bank	+$81	DD due E	+$81	3.
4. E$L to F	+$72.90	DD due F	+$72.90	4.

SUMMARY OF FINAL CONSOLIDATED POSITIONS

Individual A

E$D with E-bank 1	$100

New York Bank

Cash	$100	DD due Consolidated E-bank $100

Consolidated Borrower (Individuals B, D etc.)

Goods Purchased	$900	E$L due Consolidated E-bank	$900

Consolidated Euro-bank

DD with N. Y. Bank	$100	E$D due A	$100
E$L	$900	DD due Consolidated Seller	$900

Consolidated Seller (Individuals C, E etc.)

DD with Consolidated E-bank $900	

*The use of T-accounts to illustrate the process of Euro-dollar credit creation was suggested by a similar usage in Klaus Friedrich, *op. cit.*

they actually are—with a bank outside the United States, the bank can use these claims to make a loan to a nonbank borrower. If the borrower spends the dollars and the new owner again chooses to deposit the dollars with a Euro-bank, a new round of credit extension may occur—*ad infinitum*—unless reserve requirements are imposed. A second group of T-accounts illustrates this process when the reserve requirement is assumed to be (an overly high) 10 percent.

Whether or not reserve requirements on foreign currency deposits exist, and they sometimes do, banks tend voluntarily to hold larger reserves against nonbank deposits than they do against deposits made by other banks; thus, as in the United States, reserve requirements, legal or voluntary, do limit the amount of credit extension possible.

In contrast to the situation in the United States, where dollars tend to remain within the banking system, leakages out of the Euro-dollar system are fairly common. Although the dollar is almost universally acceptable for international payments, foreigners must usually convert dollars to domestic currencies to meet their general payments needs. For this reason, dollar balances lent by Euro-banks cannot be assumed to return automatically to the Euro-dollar system. The second round of Euro-dollar credit extension may never occur, thus, if the new owner does *not* choose to deposit his dollars with a Euro-bank. He may instead choose to invest them in the United States in which case they are permanently lost to the Euro-dollar system, or he may choose to sell them on the foreign exchange market or transfer them in payment to someone else. In the last two cases, the outcome is indeterminate since the new owners will again face the same four alternatives: 1) transferring them as a means of payment to someone who is not resident in the United States; 2) selling them on the foreign exchange market; 3) returning them to the United

States; or 4) depositing them in a Euro-bank. Because these choices can be made with each round of credit extension, the leakage of dollars out of the Euro-dollar system constitutes the most serious limit on the amount of dollar loans which can be made on the basis of a single injection

While the system does, then, permit a multiplication of dollar loans, it seems likely, according to Fred H. Klopstock's estimate, that only about 30 to 40 percent of the total number of Euro-dollar deposits could have been created in this way.[12] In other words, the transfer of $1 million to the Euro-dollar market from a U. S. bank might eventually result in approximately $1.5 to $1.9 million in Euro-dollar deposits. This estimate is a far cry from the "unlimited" expansion which has dismayed some observers.

Volume of Intermediated Loans

Now that the mechanics of credit extension within the Euro-dollar system have been illustrated, it may still be asked whether the Euro-dollar market enlarges the potential worldwide volume of dollar loans provided by financial institutions. Does the appearance of Euro-banks as a new group of intermediaries able to extend dollar loans imply that a *given quantity of dollar reserves* may result in a greater total of dollar credit than before?[13] The answer is not necessarily "yes" but depends upon the kinds of

---

[12]Klopstock, *The Euro-dollar Market: Some Unresolved Issues.*

[13]In fact, of course, the very process of intermediation implies that the amount of credit made available by original savers to final borrowers will be below the level it would have reached if this credit had been extended directly, say through the sale of equities. This reduction would occur because financial intermediaries always hold some fractional reserve against their liabilities. It seems very unlikely, however, that American or French investors would have been willing to make credit available to Japanese firms through the sale of equities to anywhere near the extent or at the same cost that they have in recent years with the help of financial intermediaries.

assets which the new Euro-dollar deposits replaced and the types and proportions of reserves held against these assets.

As Carl Stem frequently points out in his study, it may be assumed at one extreme that the total volume of Euro-dollar deposits at a given time largely reflects a demand for dollars which, in the absence of this new market, would have been satisfied by other forms of investments in the United States. Naturally, the existence of the Euro-dollar market may itself have increased the demand for dollars since Euro-dollars may have advantages that U. S. dollar assets do not. Under present balance of payments conditions, however, without the development of the Euro-dollar market, foreign monetary authorities would merely have acquired a larger proportion of the foreign-owned dollar assets than they hold at present.[14] Had the Euro-dollar market never developed, therefore, owners—although perhaps a different group of owners—of approximately $27 billion Euro-dollar deposits at the end of 1968 could be assumed instead to have held $27 billion in U. S. commercial bank demand or time deposits, in deposits with nonbank financial intermediaries, or in marketable securities such as Treasury bills.

Because, as should be reemphasized, Euro-dollar reserves take the form of demand deposits with U. S. commercial banks, Euro-dollar loans may be made as an addition to the credit provided by U. S. financial institutions. As the Euro-dollar market developed, therefore, and balances which were once due to individuals or foreign officials became due to foreign banks, the activities of U. S. commercial banks as a group were unaffected

—except as the transfers raised the proportion of demand deposits to other assets held in the United States.

Because Euro-dollar deposits generally answer an investments rather than a payments need it is actually quite likely that the assets they replaced were CD's or Treasury bills rather than demand deposits. To the extent that Euro-dollars replaced these investment-type assets, then, a more limited expansion of the potential volume of intermediated dollar loans would have occurred than if demand deposits had been transferred. In this case, the additional Euro-dollar credit made available by the growth of the market would have been partially offset by a reduction in credit extended by U. S. commercial banks or other financial institutions. If CD's were transferred, for instance, U. S. bank credit would have been curtailed because once dormant time deposits would have been replaced with active demand deposits due to foreign banks. The change would have increased required reserves from 6 to 17.5 percent. If, similarly, the Euro-dollars replaced investments in U. S. Government securities, a similar or even larger reduction in the total volume of dollar assets might have resulted. Because government securities—unlike deposits—must be passed on to other investors, the final outcome of the transfer would be the substitution of a demand deposit due to a foreign bank for a time deposit or asset with a nonbank financial institution. In the latter case reserves would rise from about 1 percent to 17.5 percent.[15]

On the other hand, another Euro-dollar activity which affects total dollar credit extension should also be considered. The Euro-dollar credit multiplier probably falls as low as somewhere between 1.5

---

[14]To the extent, however, that official monetary institutions might have preferred to exchange additional dollar balances for gold, these purchases would probably have led to a more restrictive monetary policy in the United States, thereby reducing the amount of dollar credit available on a global basis below the level possible under present circumstances.

[15]Because nonbank financial institutions hold their liquidity reserves (of about 5 percent) as demand deposits with commercial banks, less than 1 percent (.175 x .05) of a given asset held with a nonbank financial institution is withdrawn from circulation.

and 2.0, because of the sizable leakages of dollars from the system. One of the most important of these drains takes the form of borrowings by U. S. banks. As the press has made abundantly clear in recent months, foreign branches have been requested to hold as much as a third or more of their Euro-dollar assets in the United States partly because balances due to these branches released a portion of required reserves and, thus, expanded the potential for domestic credit extension. Because Euro-dollar balances borrowed by American banks are not considered deposits, they are not presently subject to reserve requirements; thus, each borrowing by an American bank reduces required reserves by 17.5 percent of the loan. Just recently, of course, the Federal Reserve Board has proposed a 10 percent marginal reserve requirement to be imposed on that portion of U. S. bank Euro-dollar borrowings which rises above the daily average of these liabilities in the 4 weeks ending May 28, 1969. Under present market conditions, the cost of carrying these new reserves may discourage U. S. banks from turning to the Euro-dollar market for additional funds. To the extent that U. S. banks choose to increase these Euro-dollar liabilities above the base level, however, each new borrowing would reduce required reserves by only 7.5 percent rather than 17.5 percent of the loan.[16]

Because the two considerations which might modify the effect of Euro-dollar credit extension generally do little more than cancel each other out, the conclusion remains that on a given dollar reserve base the Euro-dollar market permits a slightly larger volume of dollar credit to be extended worldwide than would have been possible without its development. The much-feared pyramiding effect appears to be quite minor indeed.

More importantly, however, the economically significant portion of this credit extension, the part resulting in additional means of payment, is even more limited. Only in the relatively few cases when Euro-banks extend credit on the basis of Euro-dollar demand deposits does this activity enlarge the means of payment available to investors and consumers. In the majority of transactions, Euro-banks are acting merely as nonbank financial intermediaries passing along the means of payment yielded to them by savers.[17]

It should also be pointed out that the credit extended by Euro-banks could generally have been made available to borrowers in some other way—at a price, and assuming a flexible reserve base. In the absence of the Euro-dollar market

---

[16]How then do all these offsets and counter-offsets balance out? To take a hypothetical, but plausible, example (except that it neglects the important possibility of cash drains), assume that $1 billion is transferred from a time deposit in the United States to the Euro-dollar market. While Euro-banks might make loans totaling $1.5 to $2.0 billion on the basis of that deposit, banks in the United States would find that their required reserves had risen by $115 million ($1 billion times the difference between the reserve on time deposits, or 6 percent, and the reserve on demand deposits, or 17.5 percent). As a consequence, they would have to contract their loans by about $650 million (1/.175 times $115 million). It is also likely, however, that the U. S. banks would choose to borrow an amount totaling

about one-third of the resulting new Euro-dollar assets, as they have on the average. If, therefore, they borrowed $500 to $700 million Euro-dollars from their branches, their reserves on that amount would be reduced from 17.5 percent to 0, and the commercial banks as a group would be able to make somewhere in the vicinity of $500 to $700 million in additional loans from the released reserves of $88 to $122 million. Of course, with the new Federal Reserve proposal for a marginal reserve requirement, if this borrowing raised U. S. bank liabilities to foreign branches above the base level, required reserves would be reduced by only $37.5 to $52.5 million and potential new loans would equal $215 to $300 million. Quite obviously then, the effects of the asset shift caused by transfer of the time deposit to the Euro-dollar market and of the release of reserves occasioned by the Euro-dollar borrowing generally do little more than cancel each other out. Even assuming the new reserve requirement, the ability of the Euro-banks to make additional loans seems likely to outweigh the probable net offsets.

[17]See footnote 11.

(and before the U. S. voluntary credit restraint program) borrowers needing dollar balances could turn to banks in the United States or could borrow other currencies and convert them on a covered basis to dollars. Thus, the most important aspect of Euro-dollar intermediation is that it makes a given amount of dollar, and frequently non-dollar, credit available at a lower cost than would otherwise be possible. As a consequence, the market encourages the use of the dollar as a vehicle currency.

EURO-DOLLARS AND BALANCE OF PAYMENTS PROBLEMS

Before discussing the Euro-dollar market's implications for monetary policy here and abroad, it seems best to consider first its influence on another variable which the monetary authorities must keep in mind in making their policy decisions. This variable is, of course, a nation's balance of payments.

The U. S. Position

Because we in the United States tend to be primarily concerned with the market's effect on our own balance of payments, this discussion will focus on the U. S. payments position; however, it may be well to remember that changes in our deficit or surplus may sometimes affect other nations' accounts in such a way as to cause a countervailing policy reaction.

Again to begin with theory, the Euro-dollar market may influence the U. S. payments position in four principal ways— two positive and two negative. The existence of the Euro-dollar market may: 1) entice U. S. residents to place additional capital abroad to obtain the higher interest rates that have generally prevailed there; 2) reduce foreign lending by U. S. banks because of Euro-bank competition; 3) reduce the quantity of dollar balances held in the United States required to satisfy the private demand for

dollars abroad and thus, *ceteris paribus*, increase foreign official dollar holdings; and 4) raise the private demand for dollar assets and thus, other things again remaining equal, reduce foreign official dollar balances. The first pair of countervailing influences may be relevant to either the liquidity or official settlements balance, while the second pair assumes importance only when the official settlements balance is considered.

Under the present credit restraint program, the U. S. payments position is being partially shielded from impact #1—increased foreign investment by U. S. non-banks—the most obviously negative influence which the Euro-dollar market exerts. Until 1965, as has already been mentioned, international corporations and other U. S. residents were making deposits in the Euro-dollar market on a significant scale. Thereafter the transfer of dollar balances by U. S. corporations from domestic to foreign banks was curbed by regulation and exhortation and contributed only moderately to the volume of Euro-dollars. During the second quarter of this year, however, exceptionally high Euro-dollar rates appear to have led to renewed outflows from the United States.

Similarly, impact #2, which falls on U. S. bank loans with a positive effect on the U. S. balance of payments, has also become less important during this period of tight money and restraint on foreign lending. Theoretically, however, since a capital outflow from the United States causes a negative entry on our payments accounts, to the extent that dollar loans from foreign banks including our foreign branches compete with and replace loans from U. S. banks, the result for the U. S. payments position is positive.

Once a dollar balance has reached the Euro-dollar market, its movements within the market do not alter the U. S. payments position as long as the U. S. liquidity balance is kept under consideration. According to this liquidity definition, the U. S. balance is measured by the change in U. S. reserve assets and liquid liabilities to foreigners, both official and private; thus, the following discussion will point out the change (or lack of it) in the volume of liquid liabilities to foreigners caused by Euro-dollar movements.

When a foreigner receives dollars in payment, for instance, for the export of a shipment of lace and deposits them as part of his working balance of dollars with his commercial bank in Paris, the bank acquires a liquid claim on a bank in the United States as the asset which matches its new deposit liability. Although the Paris bank may then start a long, international chain of interbank dollar deposits, the U. S. liquid liability to foreigners is not increased in any way. The United States remains liable only for the original dollar deposit, and not for some multiple thereof. Alternatively, the Paris bank, or any bank along the chain of interbank deposits, may make a dollar loan to a nonbank customer, thereby possibly beginning a round of credit extension. In this event the United States again remains liable only for the original dollar balance which was transferred to Paris on the books of the two banks involved. No change in the U. S. balance of payments takes place.

If a U. S. bank borrows Euro-dollars from a foreign bank (including, for balance of payments purposes, one of its own branches abroad), there is again no resulting change in the size of the U. S. deficit as measured by the liquidity balance. The borrowing bank will incur a liquid liability to a foreigner while in a counteracting transaction another U. S. bank will transfer its liability for the original dollar balance from a foreign bank to the borrowing U. S. bank. Similarly, any movement of Euro-dollars to the United States on a short-term basis, except the repatriation of a dollar balance owned by a U. S. resident, will leave the total of U. S. liquid liabilities to foreigners unchanged with the net effect being that a different U. S. resident may hold the liquid liability to a different foreigner. Altogether then, to state the matter very briefly, unless a U. S. resident creates a new Euro-dollar deposit or subsequently destroys one, no movement of Euro-dollar balances will have any effect whatsoever on the U. S. *liquidity balance*.

In the case of the U. S. *official settlements balance*, which is measured by a change in its reserve assets plus certain liquid and non-liquid liabilities to foreign *official* monetary institutions, however, Euro-dollar movements may indeed have an effect. It is when using this measure that the still operative, negative influences of impact #3 come into play. As Carl Stein emphasizes in his analysis, Euro-dollar deposits may substitute for dollars held directly in the United States. Because, as he also points out, only a portion of the Euro-banks' assets—the fractional reserves they hold against their Euro-dollar liabilities and the balances borrowed by U. S. banks—must be fully reflected in dollars held in the United States, the Euro-banks may find a large part of their dollar deposits excessive to their needs. The growth of the dollar market is likely, thus, either to increase the flow of superfluous dollars to official hands or to reduce the quantity of dollars which must be purchased from officials in order to fill a given gap between the private foreign demand and supply.

On the other hand, Euro-dollar interest rates, flexible Euro-dollar facilities, and the possibility for making dollar investments with local banks may all raise the demand for dollars above the level it would have reached in the absence of the market. Because the rapidly growing Euro-dollar market offers foreigners these many incentives for holding dollar balances, impact #4 may reduce the flow of dollars to official monetary institutions. This reduction would in turn lessen the U. S. deficit on the official settlements basis. In addition to these private reactions, to the extent that monetary institutions take advantage of the alternative of holding dollar reserves indirectly in the Euro-dollar market, rather than directly in U. S. Government securities, the U. S. balance of payments on the official settlements basis should show an improvement. According to the same logic, the existence of the Euro-dollar market also undoubtedly reduces the official institutions' purchases of gold. This result would serve to strengthen international confidence in our currency.

How then do these counteracting influences balance out? With impacts #1 and #2 largely inoperative, the effect of the Euro-dollar market on the U. S. liquidity deficit would appear to be fairly neutral at present. We are then left with the question of whether the substitution of Euro-dollars for dollar assets fully reflected in balances held privately in the United States is great enough to offset the effect of an increased demand for dollars. Clearly it is difficult to measure these impacts; however, a glance at the growth in official and private foreign holdings of dollar balances from 1945 to 1958 and from 1958 to 1968 seems suggestive. During the early period official dollar balances reported by U. S. banks grew at an average rate of 8.3 percent a year, while private dollar holdings increased just slightly faster, at an average rate of 9.2 percent. In the later period, however, once the Euro-dollar market had developed, the average rate of growth in official dollar balances dropped to 3.1 percent a year while the growth in private holdings jumped to 21.8 percent. While these figures are not conclusive, they would suggest that on balance the Euro-dollar market may have contributed to an improvement in the U. S. official settlements balance.

The View from Outside

While inflows into Euro-dollar investments instigated by foreigners may strengthen our official settlements balance, these inflows frequently represent outflows from investments in another currency, and as mentioned above, their effect on another country's balance of payments or reserve position will be damaging. Euro-dollar balance of payments effects may be another reason for remembering the cliché that "when the United States sneezes, the rest of the world catches a cold." An important example of potentially harmful effects, of course, would be the arbitrage movements which sometimes flow in to British local authority loans and sometimes flow out to dollar investments, thereby reducing official reserves. Another example is the loss of foreign official assets occasioned by increases in Euro-dollar borrowings by American banks.

"Real" Impact

Difficult as it may be to measure these surface-level accounting impacts, the Euro-dollar market's indirect effects on the U. S. payments position appear equally contradictory and even more difficult to judge. Because the long-term "real" repercussions are of greater economic importance than the accounting effects discussed, this question obviously deserves study. Within the scope of this article, however, it may be sufficient merely to suggest some of the most obvious possibilities. To the extent that the Euro-dollar market reduces future U. S. bank earnings, for instance, its impact will be negative. However, inasmuch as the existence of the Euro-dollar market presently permits U. S. banks and corporations to invest abroad despite the credit restraint program, it will tend to increase the inflow of their future profits from overseas. Perhaps more importantly, if the Euro-dollar market increases the availability of credit and the difficulty of imposing monetary restraint outside of the United States, the result would probably stimulate our exports. In addition as Euro-dollar borrowings used for conversion to domestic currency increase official reserve assets, the monetary authorities may pursue more expansionary policies than otherwise—again to U. S. advantage. On the other hand, because changes in U. S. monetary policy exert a powerful influence on Euro-dollar rates and flows, especially through U. S. bank branches abroad, adjustments to our balance of payments difficulties via equilibrating capital flows may have become even more unlikely than in the past. As explained below, the pull of U. S. monetary restraint may result in a multiple contraction of credit abroad in direct opposition to U. S.—and perhaps European —objectives. At present then, these contradictory examples merely suggest the importance of another set of questions not yet thoroughly understood—the implications of the Euro-dollar market for monetary policy here and abroad.

EURO-DOLLARS AND THEIR IMPLICATIONS FOR MONETARY POLICY

Under any system of fixed exchange rates, capital movements in response to interest rate differentials may reduce the effectiveness of monetary policies set by individual nations. Without much doubt, however, the Euro-dollar market facilitates these movements. Clearly, the very existence of a well-integrated market for widely acceptable vehicle-currency assets encourages these flows. Furthermore, the relative lack of regulation on Euro-dollar transactions permits capital movements which domestic currency controls would prevent. Thus, Euro-dollar flows tend to circumvent artificial restrictions, like exchange controls or cartel arrangements, and work to eliminate national interest rate differentials.

Monetary Policy Abroad

At times, as mentioned previously, the Euro-dollar market has actually facilitated officially induced short-term capital

flows which help to achieve certain policy goals. The German, Italian, Swiss and Dutch monetary authorities, for instance, have frequently used dollar swaps for reducing domestic liquidity. By providing their commercial banks with spot dollars in exchange for domestic currency and offering to buy the dollars forward at a higher price than the market rate, these central banks have increased the incentive for commercial banks to invest their cash reserves in the Euro-dollar market instead of in domestic currency loans. In the Italian case, where the central bank has the power to instruct the commercial banks to reduce their net liabilities to foreigners, Euro-dollar swaps and flows have been used as an effective tool for offsetting balance of payments surpluses and curbing domestic inflation.[18] Following the opposite policy goal, central banks have sometimes deposited dollars with their commercial banks without requiring domestic currency in exchange specifically in order to expand domestic liquidity. The Italian policy of 1961 is again a good example.[19] From time to time central banks have also encouraged their banks to borrow abroad to cover a payments deficit or to protect the level of official reserves.

Frequently, however, Euro-dollar movements are not at all welcome to the monetary authorities whose intentions they set awry. When, for instance, a government seeks to impose credit restraint, higher interest rates may attract Euro-dollar funds from abroad. Because in most nations no domestic reserves are required against foreign currency deposits, this inflow will in no way reduce the banking system's ability to extend credit in domestic currency. On the contrary, the nation's banks will then be able to make additional loans either in dollar form or,

---

[18]See Masera, *op. cit.*, for a description of the period from late 1963 to 1965.

[19]See Masera, *op. cit.*

by selling the dollars on the foreign exchange market, in domestic currency. To the extent that the central bank is required to absorb dollars on the foreign exchange market, these dollar sales will force an injection of new domestic currency reserves into the banking system, thereby permitting a burst of multiple credit extension. Of course, the monetary authorities can choose to offset this increase in the reserve base—but usually only at the expense of raising interest rates and drawing in additional funds from abroad.

In the opposite situation, when monetary authorities may wish to stimulate the economy, high interest rates in another part of the world may again thwart their efforts. At present, for instance, with the pull of monetary stringency in the giant U. S. economy, conversion of other currencies into dollars for placement in the Euro-dollar market is leading to a multiple contraction of credit abroad. Partly for this reason, a majority of the West European nations recently raised their discount rates—under audible protest. In addition, during the last few months France, Italy and Belgium have asked their banks to limit the flow of capital to the Euro-dollar market or to return some of the funds already placed there.

Of course, as suggested previously, capital flows in response to interest rate differentials could cause similar problems whether or not the Euro-dollar market existed. Because Euro-dollar flows tend to be exceptionally interest sensitive, however, they may aggravate these difficulties.

Implications for U. S. Monetary Policy

If Euro-dollar movements can play havoc with monetary policies abroad, are they equally troublesome to monetary authorities here in the United States? Certainly a great deal of recent discussion suggests that the massive Euro-dollar borrowings by U. S. banks may be thwarting the Federal Reserve's efforts to tighten monetary conditions.

Quite obviously the practice of borrowing Euro-dollars has grown as a recent response to tight money conditions. Before 1964 relatively few banks borrowed Euro-dollars from their overseas branches, and not until the summer of that year did total head office liabilities to their branches remain at a level of $1 billion or above. During the summer of 1966, however, with business loan demand intense, Federal Reserve pressure tightening and money market rates rising above the Regulation Q ceilings, banks found themselves priced out of the domestic financial market and experienced a serious loss of funds through CD runoffs. To cushion Federal Reserve pressure and live up to loan commitments, banks with foreign branches bid aggressively in the Euro-dollar market to get the funds which they could not obtain at home. Because balances acquired by their foreign branches are not subject to Regulation Q, and because the supply of Euro-dollars is very interest sensitive, the effort was apparently most successful. U. S. banks were able to raise their Euro-dollar takings by a starting $2.7 billion during 1966. When credit eased in late 1966 and early 1967, the use of branch balances fell rapidly. By the fall of 1967, however, liabilities to branches had risen above the amount outstanding at the height of the credit "crunch." This second surge took place in an atmosphere of relative ease and seemed to indicate that a group of American banks had realized the potential of the Euro-dollar market and come to see it as another normal source of funds when the price was right. During this most recent period of tight money, from December 1968 to the present, U. S. bank Euro-dollar liabilities have again leaped to unprecedented heights, jumping about 90 percent in the first half of this year. For the large New York City banks, the group which borrows Euro-dollars most actively, liabilities to foreign branches totaled over 200 percent of outstanding CD's at the beginning of June 1969.

REASONS FOR BORROWING EURO-DOLLARS. Why have U. S. banks rushed to borrow Euro-dollars in this fashion? What are the advantages to be gained from so doing? As already suggested, one of the great merits of the Euro-dollar market from the point of view of the American banks is that since balances acquired by their foreign branches are not subject to Regulation Q, they can gain access through their branches to a large quantity of funds that they cannot attract directly themselves. As another advantage, these borrowed funds are not presently subject to reserve requirements or FDIC fees. Of course, Euro-dollar liabilities are not unique in this respect, for banks have several alternative methods of acquiring funds which are not subject to reserve requirements. The Fed Funds market gives them access to such balances, for instance. Up to the present, however, Euro-dollar borrowings have provided another short-term advantage which Fed Funds frequently do not, although the Federal Reserve System has proposed a change in Regulation D to prevent this practice. When a foreign branch transfers its claims on dollar balances to its head office and thus instructs the U. S. bank currently holding the deposit to issue a cashier's check payable to that head office, the parent bank's "items in the process of collection and balances due from banks" increases. As a reasonable accounting procedure, banks are permitted to deduct these "items in the process of collection" from their gross demand deposits in computing their reserve requirements so that they are not held responsible for reserves on deposits before they have received the cash balances which are the offsets to their new liabilities. In the case of Euro-dollar borrowings in the process of collection, however, since balances due to foreign branches

are not subject to reserve requirements, the effect is to reduce required reserves.[20] By borrowing Euro-dollars for one day and rolling them over constantly, the American banks have transformed this loophole from an incidental to a considerable advantage. Because Fed Funds are usually transferred by wire the same day rather than by a check taking one or more days to clear, transactions in Fed Funds generally do not have a similar impact on "items in the process of collection" or required reserves.[21] Since the marginal reserve requirement proposal will leave a large volume of Euro-dollar borrowings free from reserves, a change in Regulation D will still be necessary if this loophole is to be closed.

PRIMARY IMPACTS ON BANK CREDIT AND THE MONEY SUPPLY. How, then, does the American banks' large-scale use of Euro-dollar balances in adjusting to tight money conditions affect the strength of Federal Reserve decisions? In marked contrast to the situation in other countries, Euro-dollar borrowings by U. S. banks do not increase the *total reserves* available

---

[20]In order to prevent this original advantage from being offset when the Euro-dollar borrowing is repaid, the parent must use a "bills payable" check in making the transfer. Outstanding bills payable checks, which can be used to repay bank borrowings, are not included in demand deposits subject to reserve requirements in contrast to cashiers' checks. (See Fred H. Klopstock, "Euro-dollars in the Liquidity and Reserve Management of United States Banks," Federal Reserve Bank of New York, *Monthly Review*, L (July 1968).

[21]An additional advantage occasioned by the delays in district check clearing practices has led to the use of overnight Euro-dollars to finance weekend reserve positions. While the borrowing bank receives Euro-dollars on Thursday and repays them on Friday according to bookkeeping entries, it does not receive the funds in the form of reserves with the Federal Reserve Bank until Friday after the check has passed through the Clearing House. And as the check written on Friday to repay the loan will not be cleared until Monday, the borrowing bank is actually left with the use of the funds over the entire weekend. Naturally, the loan rates reflect the practice, and the price of Thursday overnight Euro-dollars is very close to three times the Friday Federal Funds rate, the cost of alternative financing.

to the American banking system.[22] As the third set of T-accounts indicates, while Euro-dollar loans provide the individual borrowing bank with new cash reserves, this bank's gain reflects another U. S. bank's loss almost entirely. When a foreign branch requests that dollar deposits which it holds in the United States be transferred to its head office, the parent bank receives cash already held by other banks in the system. Only because total deposits are reduced in this process, thereby releasing required reserves, does the borrowing bank gain more than another bank loses.[23] Required reserves in the U. S. banking system are released when the Euro-dollar borrowing is made because the *deposit* due to the foreign branch, which must carry reserves, is extinguished and replaced by the parent bank's *liability* to the branch, which is reported among "other liabilities" and is not presently subject to reserve requirements.

In the context of tight money, these released reserves are undoubtedly used to make multiple new loans. Assuming, as a textbook example might, that 1) the liability due to the foreign branch replaces a demand deposit, 2) the cash drain is negligible, and 3) each new loan is returned to the banking system in demand deposit form, by the end of the multiple credit extension process, these new loans would total approximately as much as the original borrowing. However, the total is actually likely to be less than the original borrowing (the theoretical amount also shown in the T-accounts) because the cash drains are

---

[22]An exception to this statement occurs when the B.I.S. or other foreign central banks draw on their swap lines with the United States in order to channel funds to the market.

[23]Foreign branches of U. S. banks generally hold the dollar balances behind their Euro-dollar liabilities with their own head offices and then place these assets at the disposal of the parent banks from time to time; thus, the transfer of cash to the head office and a given Euro-dollar borrowing may not occur as immediately consecutive steps.

probably quite significant and the liability to the foreign branch may ultimately have replaced a time deposit. (See page 90.)

Euro-dollar borrowings, thus, are similar to other available adjustment techniques like purchases of Fed Funds or sales of security holdings. Potentially these borrowings permit the U. S. banking system to acquire a larger volume of earning assets on the basis of a given quantity of reserves. In addition, they may make it possible for banks to continue to accommodate important loan customers in the face of tightening credit conditions.

The published money supply is not likely to show an immediate increase as a result of Euro-dollar borrowings—despite the multiple extension of loans which they permit—for reasons to be discussed below. However, these borrowings may raise the balances used for purchasing goods and services within the United States—again by an amount approximately equal to the new loans created on the basis of the released reserves. Under the assumptions outlined in the theoretical example just above (including a negligible cash drain, and the transfer of assets to the Euro-dollar market from demand deposits only), a jump of $3 billion in liabilities to foreign branches during the first quarter of 1969 might represent the equivalent of close to a 1.6 percent increase in the money supply (as defined by demand deposits and currency less an estimate of the dollar balances held behind Euro-dollar deposits which are not borrowed by U. S. banks) from its level at the beginning of the year. Such an increase could have a sizable impact on real economic activity.

SECONDARY OFFSETS. On the other hand, it seems highly unlikely that any such sizable offsets to monetary restraint have actually occurred—whether bank credit or the money supply used to purchase U. S. goods and services is considered the target to watch. In the case

T-Accounts Showing the Release of Reserves Effected by Euro-dollar Borrowings
(assuming a 20 percent reserve requirement)

STAGE 1: CREATION OF EURO-DOLLAR DEPOSIT AND
SIMULTANEOUS CREDIT EXTENSION IN UNITED STATES

Bank 1 (Boston)

1. Cash	$100	DD due A	$100 1.
		DD due A	−$100 } 2.
		DD due Bank 2 Paris Br.	+$100 } 2.
3. Loan to B	+$ 80	DD due B	+$ 80 3.
4. Cash	−$ 80	DD due B	−$ 80 4.

Individual A

1. DD at Bank 1	$100
2. { DD at Bank 1	−$100
{ E$D at Bank 2 Paris Br.	+$100

Bank 2 (Paris Branch)

2. DD due fr. Bank 1	+$100	E$D due A	+$100 2.

American Banking System at End of Credit Extension Process

Cash res.	$100	DD due Bank 2 Paris Br.	$100
Loans	$400	DD due U. S. Depositors	$400

STAGE 2: EURO-DOLLAR BORROWING AND RELEASE OF RESERVES

Bank 2 (Paris Branch)

1. DD due fr. Bank 1	$100	E$D due A	$100 1.
DD due fr. Bank 1	-$100		
2. Bal. due fr. Bank 2 Hd. Off.	+$100		

Bank 1 (Boston)

1. {Cash res.	$ 20	1. DD due Bank 2 Paris Br.	$100 1.
{Loan	$ 80		
		2. DD due Bank 2 Paris Br.	-$100 } 2.
		DD due Bank 2 Hd. Off.	+$100 } 2.
3. {Loan	-$ 80	3. DD due Bank 2 Hd. Off.	-$100 3.
{Cash	+$ 80		
{Cash	-$100		

Bank 2 (Head Office, N.Y.)

2. DD due fr. Bank 1	+$100	2. Bal. due Bank 2 Paris Br.*	+$100 2.
3. {DD due fr. Bank 1	-$100	(*no res. requirement)	
{Cash (excess res.)	+$100		
4. Loan to C	+$100	4. DD due E	+$100 4.
5. Cash	-$100	5. DD due E	-$100 5.

American Banking System at End of Credit Extension Process

Cash	$100	Bal. due Bank 2 Paris Br.	$100
Loans	$500	DD due U. S. Depositors	$500

of bank credit, as suggested in the discussion of the Euro-dollar market's impact on credit extension; a growth in Euro-dollar deposits implies that investors are decreasing their holdings of other types of assets, frequently other dollar assets. Since these transfers may also have an effect on required reserves, etc., they should be taken into account in any consideration of net credit extension permitted by Euro-dollar movements.

With Euro-dollar deposits estimated to have grown by approximately $8 billion during 1968[24] while U. S. Euro-dollar takings rose about $2.7 billion, it seems likely that much of the increased demand expressed by U. S. banks has been met by new flows into the market rather than by sizable reductions in borrowings by other users. In the past, for instance during the 1966 period of credit restraint, the Euro-dollar supply has generally proved itself to be remarkably interest elastic. Since most U. S. resident corporations are restrained from making deposits in the Euro-dollar market, and private foreign nonbanks actually increased their assets in the United States last year, it appears that the most important source of the funds recently channeled into the Euro-dollar market has been the liquidation of private foreign currency assets. Ultimately, however, this liquidation must have occurred at the expense of foreign official balances, particularly—since a large part of these assets take this form—at the expense of holdings of U. S. Treasury bills. At times increased Euro-dollar borrowings may actually lead to sales of U. S. Government securities by foreign officials. During periods of increasing U. S. deficits, however, as in the first quarter of this year, a rise in the level of U. S. bank Euro-dollar borrowings may largely have been reflected in reduced foreign official purchases of U. S. Treasury bills.

Since such increased sales or reduced purchases of Treasury bills would tend to raise U. S. bill rates, these transfers would —other things being equal—also have induced a secondary CD runoff over and above the losses caused by restrictive monetary policy. Such a secondary runoff would partially, perhaps even largely, have offset the reserves released by Euro-dollar borrowings.[25]

Thus, reserve adjustments to restrictive monetary measures in the form of Euro-dollar borrowings merely produce market reactions very similar to those occasioned by other possible adjustment techniques, such as the sale of government securities by the banks themselves. In both cases, faced with a loss of time deposits, the adjusting banks acquire cash ultimately at the expense of a further loss of CD's.

It is possible, of course, that the Federal Reserve System may choose to stabilize interest rates over the short term; thus, in response to a rise in the bill rate caused by foreign official sales (or reduced purchases) of U. S. Government securities, it may feel compelled to buy bills, thereby providing additional reserves. Of course, producing fresh reserves in this way is not a unique attribute of Euro-dollar borrowings. Most other available adjustment techniques, such as the sale of securities by banks themselves, also drive up interest rates and could lead to similar offsets by the Federal Reserve System.

On the whole, then, it appears that Euro-dollar borrowings *in themselves* may have a rather insignificant impact on the imposition of credit restraint.

As for the implications of Euro-dollar borrowings for the U. S. money supply— a second possible target of monetary policy—the offsets outlined in connection

---

[24]Bank for International Settlements, *Thirty-Ninth Annual Report*, Basle, June 1969.

[25]While the potential increase in cash items in the process of collection may occasion an additional release of reserves not discussed here, this loophole appears likely to be eliminated in the near future.

with bank credit again come into play. When the Euro-dollar borrowing first occurs, the published money supply (demand deposits plus currency) is likely to fall since foreign branches tend to hold their dollar balances in the United States in demand deposit form until they are borrowed by their head offices and become "liabilities to foreign branches" which are not included in the published money supply figure. Until this point the published money supply overstated the "real" figure at least to the extent that Euro-dollar balances were not borrowed by U. S. residents or used to purchase exports from them. Thereafter, as the reserves released by the Euro-dollar borrowing are used to make new loans, both the published figure and the effective money supply (demand deposits plus currency used for investment and consumption purposes within the United States) are likely to rise toward the level the published data had indicated before the borrowing. However, as the rise in Euro-dollar rates causes investors to substitute Euro-dollar deposits for assets in foreign currencies and foreign officials sell (or reduce their purchases of) U. S. Treasury bills to supply dollars to the market, the ultimate effect in the United States is likely to be the substitution of a demand deposit due to a foreign branch for a CD.[26] Thus, the published money supply will spurt ahead while the real money supply used to engender U. S. economic activity will drop back toward its level before the borrowing occurred. However, the rise in required reserves brought about by the transfer of a CD to a demand deposit is likely to cause both the (somewhat overstated) published and effective money supplies to fall. At the end of this series of impact and offset, the published money supply is likely to be somewhat higher than it was before the U. S. bank Euro-dollar borrowing while the effective money supply is likely to be somewhat lower.

---

[26]To the extent that the Treasury bills are sold to investors who would otherwise have held assets with nonbank financial institutions, the published money supply would not rise since these institutions hold their liquidity reserves as demand deposits with banks. In this case, the net result of the transfers would be that a demand deposit due to a foreign bank would replace a demand deposit due to a nonbank financial institution. The institutions' reduced capacity to make loans would also have no effect on the real or published money supply.

8. The Euro-dollar Market: Some First Principles *

Milton Friedman

Professor Friedman posits that there is general confusion concerning the origin and growth of Euro-dollars. He states that "their major source is a bookkeeper's pen." The article explains this statement and applies the explanation to the question of the effect of Regulation Q and restrictive monetary policy on the demand for Euro-dollars by U.S. banks.

The Euro-dollar market is the latest example of the mystifying quality of money creation to even the most sophisticated bankers, let alone other businessmen. Recently, I heard a high official of an international financial organization discuss the Euro-dollar market before a collection of high-powered international bankers. He estimated that Euro-dollar deposits totaled some $30 billion. He was then asked: "What is the source of these deposits?" His answer was: partly, U.S. balance-of-payments deficits; partly, dollar reserves of non-U.S. central banks; partly, the proceeds from the sale of Euro-dollar bonds.

This answer is almost complete nonsense. Balance-of-payments deficits do provide foreigners with claims on U.S. dollars. But there is nothing to assure that such claims will be held in the form of Euro-dollars. In any event, U.S. deficits, world-wide, have totaled less than $9 billion for the past five years, on a liquidity basis. Dollar holdings of non-U.S. central banks have fallen during the period of

rapid rise in Euro-dollar deposits but by less than $5 billion. The dollars paid for Euro-bonds had themselves to come from somewhere and do not constitute an independent source. No matter how you try, you cannot get $30 billion from these sources. The answer given is precisely parallel to saying that the source of the $400 billion of deposits in U.S. banks (or for that matter the much larger total of all outstanding short-term claims) is the $60 billion of Federal Reserve credit outstanding.

The correct answer for both Euro-dollars and liabilities of U.S. banks is that their major source is a bookkeeper's pen.[1] The purpose of this article is to explain this statement. The purpose is purely expository. I shall restrict myself essentially to principle and shall not attempt either an empirical evaluation of the Euro-dollar market or a normative judgment of its desirability.

---

[1] The similarity between credit creation in the U.S. fractional reserve banking system and in the Euro-dollar market has of course often been noted. For example, see Fred H. Klopstock, "The Euro-Dollar Market, Some Unresolved Issues," *Essays in International Finance*, No. 65 (Princeton, March, 1968), p. 6. A recent excellent analysis is given in an article by Joseph G. Kvasnicka, "Euro-Dollars—an Important Source of Funds for American Banks," *Business Conditions*, Federal Reserve Bank of Chicago, June, 1969. A useful examination of the Euro-dollar market is Jane Sneddon Little, "The Euro-Dollar Market: Its Nature and Impact," *New England Economic Review*, Federal Reserve Bank of Boston, May/June, 1969. (The last article is included in this text.)

*From *Morgan Guaranty Survey,* October, 1969. Reprinted by permission of the publisher (Morgan Guaranty Trust Company) and the author.

Another striking example of the confusion about Euro-dollars is the discussion, in even the most sophisticated financial papers, of the use of the Euro-dollar market by U.S. commercial banks "to evade tight money," as it is generally phrased. U.S. banks, one reads in a leading financial paper, "have been willing to pay extremely high interest rates . . . to borrow back huge sums of U.S. dollars that have piled up abroad." The image conveyed is that of piles of dollar bills being bundled up and shipped across the ocean on planes and ships—the way New York literally did drain gold from Europe in the bad—or good—old days at times of financial panic. Yet, the more dollars U.S. banks "borrow back" the more Euro-dollar deposits go up! How come? The answer is that it is purely figurative language to speak of "piled up" dollars being "borrowed back." Again, the bookkeeper's pen is at work.

WHAT ARE EURO-DOLLARS?

Just what are Euro-dollars? They are deposit liabilities, denominated in dollars, of banks outside the United States. Engaged in Euro-dollar business, for example, are foreign commercial banks such as the Bank of London and South America, Ltd., merchant banks such as Morgan Grenfell and Co., Ltd., and many of the foreign branches of U.S. commercial banks. Funds placed with these institutions may be owned by anyone—U.S. or foreign residents or citizens, individuals or corporations or governments. Euro-dollars have two basic characteristics: first, they are short-term obligations to pay dollars; second, they are obligations of banking offices located outside the U.S. In principle, there is no hard and fast line between Euro-dollars and other dollar-denominated claims on non-U.S. institutions—just as there is none between claims in the U.S. that we call "money" and other short-term claims. The precise line

drawn in practice depends on the exact interpretation given to "short-term" and to "banks." Nothing essential in this article is affected by the precise point at which the line is drawn.

A homely parallel to Euro-dollars is to be found in the dollar deposit liabilities of bank offices located in the city of Chicago—which could similarly be called "Chicago dollars." Like Euro-dollars, "Chicago dollars" consist of obligations to pay dollars by a collection of banking offices located in a particular geographic area. Again, like Euro-dollars, they may be owned by anyone—residents or nonresidents of the geographic area in question.

The location of the banks is important primarily because it affects the regulations under which the banks operate and hence the way that they can do business. Those Chicago banks that are members of the Federal Reserve System must comply with the System's requirements about reserves, maximum interest rates payable on deposits, and so on; and in addition, of course, with the requirements of the Comptroller of the Currency if they are national banks, and of the Illinois State Banking Commission if they are state banks.

Euro-dollar banks are subject to the regulations of the relevant banking authorities in the country in which they operate. In practice, however, such banks have been subject neither to required reserves on Euro-dollar deposits nor to maximum ceilings on the rates of interest they are permitted to pay on such deposits.

REGULATION AND EURO-DOLLARS

The difference in regulation has played a key role in the development of the Euro-dollar market. No doubt there were minor precursors, but the initial substantial Euro-dollar deposits in the post-World War II period originated with the Russians, who wanted dollar balances but recalled that their dollar holdings in the U.S. had been impounded by the Alien Property Custodian in World War II. Hence they wanted dollar claims not subject to U.S. governmental control.

The most important regulation that has stimulated the development of the Euro-dollar market has been Regulation Q, under which the Federal Reserve has fixed maximum interest rates that member banks could pay on time deposits. Whenever these ceilings became effective, Euro-dollar deposits, paying a higher interest rate, became more attractive than U.S. deposits, and the Euro-dollar market expanded. U.S. banks then borrowed from the Euro-dollar market to replace the withdrawn time deposits.

A third major force has been the direct and indirect exchange controls imposed by the U.S. for "balance-of-payments" purposes—the interest-equalization tax, the "voluntary" controls on bank lending abroad and on foreign investment, and, finally, the compulsory controls instituted by President Johnson in January 1968. Without Regulation Q and the exchange controls—all of which, in my opinion, are both unnecessary and undesirable—the Euro-dollar market, though it might still have existed, would not have reached anything like its present dimensions.

FRACTIONAL RESERVES

Euro-dollar deposits like "Chicago deposits" are in principle obligations to pay literal dollars—i.e., currency (or coin), all of which consists, at present, of government-issued fiat (Federal Reserve notes, U.S. notes, a few other similar issues, and fractional coinage). In practice, even Chicago banks are called on to discharge only an insignificant part of their deposit obligations by paying out currency. Euro-dollar banks are called on to discharge a negligible part in this form. Deposit obligations are typically discharged by providing a credit or deposit at another bank

—as when you draw a check on your bank which the recipient "deposits" in his.

To meet their obligations to pay cash, banks keep a "reserve" of cash on hand. But, of course, since they are continuously receiving as well as paying cash and since in any interval they will be called on to redeem only a small fraction of their obligations in cash, they need on the average keep only a very small part of their assets in cash for this purpose. For Chicago banks, this cash serves also to meet legal reserve requirements. For Euro-dollar banks, the amount of literal cash they hold is negligible.

To meet their obligations to provide a credit at another bank, when a check or similar instrument is used, banks keep deposits at other banks. For Chicago banks, these deposits (which in addition to facilitating the transfer of funds between banks serve to meet legal reserve requirements) are held primarily at Federal Reserve banks. In addition, however, Chicago banks may also keep balances at correspondent banks in other cities.

Like cash, deposits at other banks need be only a small fraction of assets. Banks are continuously receiving funds from other banks, as well as transferring funds to them, so they need reserves only to provide for temporary discrepancies between payments and receipts or sudden unanticipated demands. For Chicago banks, such "prudential" reserves are clearly far smaller than the reserves that they are legally required to keep.

Euro-dollar banks are not subject to legal reserve requirements, but, like Chicago banks, they must keep a prudential reserve in order to be prepared to meet withdrawals of deposits when they are demanded or when they mature. An individual bank will regard as a prudential reserve readily realizable funds both in the Euro-dollar market itself (e.g., Euro-dollar call money) and in the U.S. But for the Euro-dollar system as a whole, Euro-dollar funds cancel, and the prudential reserves available to meet demands for U.S. dollars consist entirely of deposits at banks in New York or other cities in the U.S. and U.S. money market assets that can be liquidated promptly without loss.

The amount of prudential reserves that a Euro-dollar bank will wish to hold—like the amount that a Chicago bank will wish to hold—will depend on its particular mix of demand and time obligations. Time deposits generally require smaller reserves than demand deposits—and in some instances almost zero reserves if the bank can match closely the maturities of its dollar-denominated liabilities and its dollar-denominated loans and investments. Although a precise estimate is difficult to make because of the incompleteness and ambiguity of the available data, prudential reserves of Euro-dollar institutions are clearly a small fraction of total dollar-denominated obligations.

This point—that Euro-dollar institutions, like Chicago banks, are part of a fractional reserve banking system—is the key to understanding the Euro-dollar market. The failure to recognize it is the chief source of misunderstanding about the Euro-dollar market. Most journalistic discussions of the Euro-dollar market proceed as if a Euro-dollar bank held a dollar in the form of cash or of deposits at a U.S. bank corresponding to each dollar of deposit liability. That is the source of such images as "piling up," "borrowing back," "withdrawing," etc. But of course this is not the case. If it were, a Euro-dollar bank could hardly afford to pay 10 percent or more on its deposit liabilities.

A HYPOTHETICAL EXAMPLE

A Euro-dollar bank typically has total dollar assets roughly equal to its dollar liabilities.[2] But these assets are not in cur-

---

[2]Which is why it is not subject to any special foreign exchange risk simply by operating in the Euro-dollar market. The balance sheet of its

rency or bank deposits. In highly simplified form, the balance sheet of such a bank—or the part of the balance sheet corresponding to its Euro-dollar operations — must look something like that shown in the adjoining column (the numbers in this and later balance sheets are solely for illustrative purposes).

It is the earnings on the $9,500,000 of loans and investments that enable it to pay interest on the $10,000,000 of deposits.

Where did the $10,000,000 of deposits come from? One can say that $700,000 (cash assets minus due to other banks) came from "primary deposits," i.e., is the counterpart to a literal deposit of cash or transfer of funds from other banks.[3]

EURO-DOLLAR BANK H OF LONDON

ASSETS

Cash assets*	$ 1,000,000
Dollar-denominated loans	7,000,000
Dollar-denominated bonds	2,500,000
Total assets	$10,500,000

LIABILITIES

Deposits	$10,000,000
Due to other banks	300,000
Capital accounts	200,000
Total liabilities	$10,500,000

*Includes U.S. currency, deposits in N.Y. and other banks, and other assets immediately realizable in U.S. funds.

The other $9,300,000 is "created" by the magic of fractional reserve banking—this is the bookkeeper's pen at work.

Let us look at the process more closely. Suppose an Arab Sheik opens up a new deposit account in London at Bank H (H for hypothetical) by depositing a check for $1,000,000 drawn on the Sheik's de-

---

Euro-dollar operations balances in dollars; if it is, for example, a British bank, the balance sheet of its pound sterling operations balances in pounds. It is operating in two currencies but need not take a speculative position in either. Of course, it may take a speculative position, whether or not it operates in the Euro-dollar market.

[3]Note that even this is an overstatement, since most of the deposits at N.Y. banks are themselves ultimately "created" rather than "primary" deposits. These are primary deposits only vis-à-vis the Euro-dollar market separately.

mand deposit account at the head office of, say, Morgan Guaranty Trust Company. Let us suppose that Bank H also keeps its N.Y. account at Morgan Guaranty and also as demand deposits. At the first stage, this will add $1,000,000 to the deposit liabilities of Bank H, and the same amount to its assets in the form of deposits due from New York banks. At Morgan Guaranty, the transfer of deposits from the Sheik to Bank H will cause no change in total deposit liabilities.

But Bank H now has excess funds available to lend. It has been keeping cash assets equal to 10 percent of deposits—not because it was required to do so but because it deemed it prudent to do so. It now has cash equal to 18 percent (2/11) of deposits. Because of the $1,000,000 of new deposits from the Sheik, it will want to add, say $100,000 to its balance in New York. This leaves Bank H with $900,000 available to add to its loans and investments. Assume that it makes a loan of $900,000 to, say, UK Ltd., a British corporation engaged in trade with the U.S., giving corporation UK Ltd. a check on Morgan Guaranty. Bank H's balance sheet will now look as follows after the check has cleared:

ASSETS

Cash assets	$ 1,100,000
Dollar-denominated loans	7,900,000
Dollar-denominated bonds	2,500,000
Total assets	$11,500,000

LIABILITIES

Deposits	$11,000,000
Due to other banks	300,000
Capital accounts	200,000
Total liabilities	$11,500,000

We now must ask what UK Ltd. does with the $900,000 check. To cut short and simplify the process, let us assume that UK Ltd. incurred the loan because it had been repeatedly troubled by a shortage of funds in New York and wanted to maintain a higher average level of bank balances in New York. Further assume that it also keeps its account at Morgan Guar-

anty, so that it simply deposits the check in its demand deposit account.

This particular cycle is therefore terminated and we can examine its effect. First, the position of Morgan Guaranty is fundamentally unchanged: it had a deposit liability of $1,000,000 to the Sheik. It now has a deposit liability of $100,000 to Bank H and one of $900,000 to UK Ltd.

Second, the calculated money supply of the U.S. and the demand deposit component thereof are unchanged. That money supply excludes from "adjusted demand deposits" the deposits of U.S. commercial banks at other U.S. commercial banks but it includes deposits of both foreign banks and other foreigners. Therefore, the Sheik's deposit was included before. The deposits of Bank H and UK Ltd. are included now.

Third, the example was set up so that the money supply owned by residents of the U.S. is also unchanged. As a practical matter, the financial statistics gathered and published by the Federal Reserve do not contain sufficient data to permit calculation of the U.S.-owed money supply—a total which would exclude from the money supply as now calculated currency and deposits at U.S. banks owned by nonresidents and include dollar deposits at non-U.S. banks owned by residents. But the hypothetical transactions clearly leave this total unaffected.

Fourth, Euro-dollar deposits are $1,000,-000 higher.

However, fifth, the total world supply of dollars held by *nonbanks*—dollars in the U.S. plus dollars outside the U.S.—is $900,000 not $1,000,000 higher. The reason is that interbank deposits are now higher by $100,000, thanks to the additional deposits of Bank H at Morgan Guaranty. This amount of deposits was formerly an asset of a nonbank (the Arab Sheik); now it is an asset of Bank H. In this way, Bank H has created $900,000 of Euro-dollar deposits. The other $100,000 of Euro-dollar deposits has been transferred from the U.S. to the Euro-dollar area.

Sixth, the balance of payments of the U.S. is unaffected, whether calculated on a liquidity basis or on an official settlement basis. On a liquidity basis, the Arab Sheik's transfer is recorded as a reduction of $1,000,000 in short-term liquid claims on the U.S. but the increased deposits of Bank H and UK Ltd. at Morgan Guaranty are a precisely offsetting increase. On an official settlement basis, the series of transactions has not affected the dollar holdings of any central bank or official institution.[4]

---

[4]It is interesting to contrast these effects with those that would have occurred if we substitute a Chicago bank for Bank H of London, i.e., suppose that the Arab Sheik had transferred his funds to a Chicago bank, say, Continental Illinois, and Continental Illinois had made the loan to UK Ltd., which UK Ltd. again added to its balances at Morgan Guaranty. To simplify matters, assume that the reserve requirements for Continental Illinois and Morgan Guaranty are the same flat 10 percent that we assumed Bank H of London kept in the form of cash assets (because, let us say, all deposit changes consist of the appropriate mix of demand and time deposits).

First, the position of Morgan Guaranty is now fundamentally changed. Continental Illinois keeps its reserves as deposits at the Federal Reserve Bank of Chicago, not at Morgan Guaranty. Hence it will deposit its net claim of $100,000 on Morgan Guaranty at the Chicago Fed to meet the reserves required for the Sheik's deposit. This will result in a reduction of $100,000 in Morgan Guaranty's reserve balance at the New York Fed. Its deposits have gone down only $100,000 (thanks to the $900,000 deposit by UK Ltd.) so that if it had no excess reserves before it now has deficient reserves. This will set in train a multiple contraction of deposits at Morgan Guaranty and other banks which will end when the $1,000,000 gain in deposits by Continental Illinois is completely offset by a $1,000,000 decline in deposits at Morgan Guaranty and other banks.

Second, the calculated money supply of the U.S. and the demand deposit component thereof are still unchanged.

However, third, the money supply owned by the residents of the U.S. is reduced by the $900,000 increase in the deposits of UK Ltd.

Fourth, there is no change in Euro-dollar deposits.

Fifth, there is no change in the total world supply of dollars.

Sixth, the balance of payments of the U.S. is affected if it is calculated on a liquidity basis but

Clearly, there is no meaningful sense in which we can say that the $900,000 of created Euro-dollar deposits is derived from a U.S. balance-of-payments deficit, or from dollars held by central banks, or from the proceeds of Euro-dollar bond sales.

SOME COMPLICATIONS

Many complications of this example are possible. They will change the numbers but not in any way the essential principles. But it may help to consider one or two.

a) Suppose UK Ltd. used the dollar loan to purchase timber from Russia, and Russia wished to hold the proceeds as a dollar deposit at, say Bank R in London. Then, another round is started—precisely like the one that began when the Sheik transferred funds from Morgan Guaranty to Bank H. Bank R now has $900,000 extra deposit liabilities, matched by $900,000 extra deposits in New York. If it also follows the practice of maintaining cash assets equal to 10 percent of deposits, it can make a dollar loan of $810,000. If the recipient of the loan keeps it as a demand deposit at Morgan Guaranty, or transfers it to someone who does, the process comes to an end. The result is that total Euro-dollar deposits are up by $1,900,000. Of that total, $1,710,000 is held by nonbanks,

---

not if it is calculated on an official settlements basis. On a liquidity basis, the deficit would be increased by $900,000 because the loan by Continental Illinois to UK Ltd. would be recorded as a capital outflow but UK Ltd.'s deposit at Morgan Guaranty would be regarded as an increase in U.S. liquid liabilities to foreigners, which are treated as financing the deficit. This enlargement of the deficit on a liquidity basis is highly misleading. It suggests, of course, a worsening of the U.S. payments problem, whereas in fact all that is involved is a worsening of the statistics. The additional dollars that UK Ltd. has in its demand deposit account cannot meaningfully be regarded as a potential claim on U.S. reserve assets. UK Ltd. not only needs them for transactions purposes; it must regard them as tied or matched to its own dollar indebtedness. On a official settlements basis, the series of transactions does not affect the dollar holdings of any central bank or official institution.

with the other $190,000 being additional deposits of banks (the $100,000 extra of Bank H at Morgan Guaranty plus the $90,000 extra of Bank R at Morgan Guaranty).

If the recipient of the loan transfers it to someone who wants to hold it as a Euro-dollar deposit at a third bank, the process continues on its merry way. If, in the extreme, at every stage, the whole of the proceeds of the loan were to end up as Euro-dollar deposits, it is obvious that the total increase in Euro-dollar deposits would be: 1,000,000 + 900,000 + 810,000 + 729,000 + ... = 10,000,000. At the end of the process, Euro-dollar deposits would be $10,000,000 higher; deposits of Euro-dollar banks at N. Y. banks, $1,000,000 higher; and the total world supply of dollars held by nonbanks, $9,000,000 higher.

This example perhaps makes it clear why bankers in the Euro-dollar market keep insisting that they do not "create" dollars but only transfer them, and why they sincerely believe that all Euro-dollars come from the U.S. *To each banker separately in the chain described, his additional Euro-dollar deposit came in the form of a check on Morgan Guaranty Trust Company of New York!* How are the bankers to know that the $10,000,000 of checks on Morgan Guaranty all constitute repeated claims on the same initial $1,000,000 of deposits? Appearances are deceiving.

This example (involving successive loan extensions by a series of banks) brings out the difference between two concepts that have produced much confusion: Euro-dollar creation and the Euro-dollar multiplier. In both the simple example and the example involving successive loan extensions, the fraction of Euro-dollars outstanding that has been created is nine-tenths, or, put differently, 10 Euro-dollars exist for every U.S. dollar held as cash asset in New York by Euro-dollar banks. However, in the simple ex-

ample, the Euro-dollar multiplier (the ratio of the increase in Euro-dollar deposits to the initial "primary" deposit) is unity; in the second example, it is 10. That is, in the simple example, the total amount of Euro-dollars goes up by $1 for every $1 of U.S. deposits initially transferred to Euro-dollar banks; in the second example, it goes up by $10 for every $1 of U.S. deposits initially transferred. The difference is that in the simple example there is maximum "leakage" from the Euro-dollar system; in the second example, zero "leakage."

The distinction between Euro-dollar creation and the Euro-dollar multiplier makes it clear why there is a definite limit to the amount of Euro-dollars that can be created no matter how low are the prudential reserves that banks hold. For example, if Euro-dollar banks held zero prudential reserves — as it is sometimes claimed that they do against time deposits—100 percent of the outstanding deposits would be created deposits and the potential multiplier would be infinite. Yet the actual multiplier would be close to unity because only a small part of the funds acquired by borrowers from Euro-dollar banks would end up as additional time deposits in such banks.[5]

b) Suppose Bank H does not have sufficient demand for dollar loans to use profitably the whole $900,000 of excess dollar funds. Suppose, simultaneously, it is experiencing a heavy demand for sterling loans. It might go to the Bank of England and use the $900,000 to buy sterling. Bank of England deposits at Morgan Guaranty would now go up. But since the Bank of England typically holds its deposits at the New York Federal Reserve Bank, the funds would fairly quickly disappear from Morgan Guaranty's books and show up instead on the Fed's. This, in the first instance, would reduce the

[5]This is precisely comparable to the situation of savings and loan associations and mutual savings banks in the U.S.

reserves of Morgan Guaranty and thus threaten to produce much more extensive monetary effects than any of our other examples. However, the Bank of England typically holds most of its dollar reserves as Treasury bills or the equivalent, not as noninterest earning deposits at the Fed. It would therefore instruct the Fed to buy, say, bills for its account. This would restore the reserves to the banking system and, except for details, we would be back to where we were in the other examples.

THE KEY POINTS

Needless to say, this is far from a comprehensive survey of all the possible complications. But perhaps it suffices to show that the complications do not affect the fundamental points brought out by the simple example, namely:

1. Euro-dollars, like "Chicago dollars," are mostly the product of the bookkeeper's pen—that is, the result of fractional reserve banking.

2. The amount of Euro-dollars outstanding, like the amount of "Chicago dollars," depends on the desire of owners of wealth to hold the liabilities of the corresponding group of banks.

3. The ultimate increase in the amount of Euro-dollars from an initial transfer of deposits from other banks to Euro-dollar banks depends on:

a) The amount of their dollar assets Euro-dollar banks choose to hold in the form of cash assets in the U.S., and

b) The "leakages" from the system— i.e., the final disposition of the funds borrowed from Euro-dollar banks (or acquired by the sale of bonds or other investments to them). The larger the fraction of such funds held as Euro-dollar deposits, the larger the increase in Euro-dollars in total.

4. The existence of the Euro-dollar market increases the total amount of dollar balances available to be held by nonbanks throughout the world for any given amount of money (currency plus deposits at Federal Reserve Banks) created by the Federal Reserve System. It does so by permitting a greater pyramiding on this base by the use of deposits of U.S. banks as prudential reserves for Euro-dollar deposits.

5. The existence of the Euro-dollar market may also create a greater demand for dollars to be held by making dollar balances available in a more convenient form. The net effect of the Euro-dollar market on our balance-of-payments problem (as distinct from our statistical position) depends on whether demand is raised more or less than supply.

My own conjecture—which is based on much too little evidence for me to have much confidence in it—is that demand is raised less than supply and hence that the growth of the Euro-dollar market has on the whole made our balance-of-payments problem more difficult.

6. Whether my conjecture on this score is right or wrong, the Euro-dollar market has almost surely raised the world's nominal money supply (expressed in dollar equivalents) and has thus made the world price level (expressed in dollar equivalents) higher than it would otherwise be. Alternatively, if it is desired to define the money supply exclusive of Euro-dollar deposits, the same effect can be described in terms of a rise in the velocity of the world's money supply. However, this effect, while clear in direction, must be extremely small in magnitude.

USE OF EURO-DOLLARS BY U.S. BANKS

Let us now turn from this general question of the source of Euro-dollars to the special issue raised at the outset: the effect of Regulation Q and "tight money" on the use of the Euro-dollar market by U.S. banks.

To set the stage, let us suppose, in the framework of our simple example, that

Euro-dollar Bank H of London loans the $900,000 excess funds that it has as a result of the initial deposit by the Arab Sheik to the head office of Morgan Guaranty, i.e., gives Morgan Guaranty (New York) a check for $900,000 on itself in return for an I.O.U. from Morgan Guaranty. This kind of borrowing from foreign banks is one of the means by which American banks have blunted the impact of CD losses. The combined effect will be to leave total liabilities of Morgan Guaranty unchanged but to alter their composition: deposit liabilities are now down $900,000 (instead of the $1,000,-000 deposit liability it formerly had to the Sheik it now has a deposit liability of $100,000 to Bank H) and other liabilities ("funds borrowed from foreign banks") are up $900,000.

Until very recently, such a change in the form of a bank's liabilities—from deposits to borrowings—had an important effect on its reserve position. Specifically, it freed reserves. With $1,000,000 of demand deposit liabilities to the Arab Sheik, Morgan Guaranty was required to keep in cash or as deposits at the Federal Reserve Bank of New York $175,000 (or $60,000 if, as is more realistic, the Sheik kept his $1,000,000 in the form of a time deposit). With the shift of the funds to Bank H, however, and completion of the $90,000 loan by Bank H to Morgan Guaranty, Morgan Guaranty's reserve requirements at the Fed fell appreciably. Before the issuance of new regulations that became effective on September 4 of this year, Morgan Guaranty was not required to keep any reserve for the liability in the form of the I.O.U. Its only obligation was to keep $17,500 corresponding to the demand deposit of Bank H. The change in the form of its liabilities would therefore have reduced its reserve requirements by $157,500 (or by $42,500 for a time deposit) without any change in its total liabilities or its total assets, or in the composition of its assets; hence it would

have had this much more available to lend.

What the Fed did effective September 4 was to make borrowings subject to reserve requirements as well. Morgan Guaranty must now keep a reserve against the I.O.U., the exact percentage depending on the total amount of borrowings by Morgan Guaranty from foreign banks.[6] The new regulations make it impossible to generalize about reserve effects. A U.S. bank losing deposits to a Euro-bank and then recouping funds by giving its I.O.U. may or may not have additional amounts available to lend as a result of transactions of the kind described.

If Bank H made the loan to Chase instead of to Morgan Guaranty, the latter would lose reserves and Chase would gain them. To Chase, it would look as if it were getting additional funds from abroad, but to both together, the effect would be the same as before—the possible release of required reserves with no change in available reserves.

The bookkeeping character of these transactions, and how they can be stimulated, can perhaps be seen more clearly if we introduce an additional feature of the actual Euro-dollar market, which was not essential heretofore, namely, the role of overseas branches of U.S. banks. In addition, for realism, we shall express our example in terms of time deposits.

Let us start from scratch and consider the head office of Morgan Guaranty in New York and its London branch. Let us look at hypothetical initial balance sheets of both. We shall treat the London branch as if it had just started and had neither assets nor liabilities, and shall restrict the balance sheet for the head office to the part relevant to its CD operations. This set of circumstances gives us the following situation:

---

[6]The required reserve is 3 percent of such borrowings so long as they do not exceed 4 percent of total deposits subject to reserves. On borrowings in excess of that level the required reserve is 10 percent.

NEW YORK HEAD OFFICE

ASSETS

Deposits at F. R. Bank of NY . $	6,000,000
Other cash assets	4,000,000
Loans	76,000,000
Bonds	14,000,000
Total assets . . . . $	100,000,000

(Note: Required reserves, $6,000,000)

LIABILITIES

Time certificates of deposit . . $	100,000,000
Total liabilities . . . . $	100,000,000

LONDON OFFICE

ASSETS

$ 0

LIABILITIES

$ 0

Now suppose a foreign corporation (perhaps the Arab Sheik's oil company) which holds a long-term maturing CD of $10,000,000 at Morgan Guaranty refuses to renew it because the 6¼ percent interest it is receiving seems too low. Morgan Guaranty agrees that the return should be greater, but explains it is prohibited by law from paying more. It notes, however, that its London branch is not. Accordingly, the corporation acquires a time deposit at the London office for $10,000,000 "by depositing" the check for $10,000,000 on the New York office it receives in return for the maturing CD—or, more realistically, by transfers on the books in New York and London. Let us look at the balance sheets:

NEW YORK HEAD OFFICE

ASSETS

Deposits at F.R. Bank of NY . $	6,000,000
Other cash assets	4,000,000
Loans	76,000,000
Bonds	14,000,000
Total assets . . . . $	100,000,000

LIABILITIES

Time certificates of deposit . . $	90,000,000
Due to London branch	10,000,000
Total liabilities . . . . $	100,000,000

(Note: Required reserves, before issuance of new regulations, $5,400,000; since issuance of new regulations, between $5,400,000 and $6,400,000).

LONDON OFFICE

ASSETS

Due from N.Y. office . . . . $	10,000,000

LIABILITIES

Time certificates of deposit . . $	10,000,000

Clearly, if we consolidate the branch and the head office, the books are completely unchanged. Yet these bookkeeping transactions: (1) enabled Morgan Guaranty to pay a rate in London higher than 6¼ percent on some certificates of deposit; and (2) reduced its required reserves by $600,000 prior to the recent modification of Regulation M. The reduction in required reserves arose because until recently U.S. banks were not required to keep a reserve against liabilities to their foreign branches. With the amendment of Regulation M, any further reduction of reserves by this route has been eliminated since the Fed now requires a reserve of 10 percent on the amount due to branch offices in excess of the amount due on average during May.[7]

HYPOCRISY AND WINDOW DRESSING

This example has been expressed in terms of a *foreign* corporation because the story is a bit more complicated for a U.S. corporation, though the end result is the same. First, a U.S. corporation that transfers its funds from a certificate of deposit at a U.S. bank to a deposit at a bank abroad—whether a foreign bank or an overseas branch of a U.S. bank—is deemed by the Department of Commerce to have made a foreign investment. It may do so only if it is within its quota under the direct control over foreign investment with which we are still unfortunately saddled. Second, under pressure from the Fed, commercial banks will not facilitate direct transfers by U.S. corporations—indeed, many will not accept time deposits from U.S. corporations at their overseas branches, whether their own customers or not, unless the corporation can demonstrate that the deposit is being made for

---

[7]An amendment to Regulation M effective September 4 established a 10 percent reserve requirement on head office liabilities to overseas branches on that portion of such liabilities in excess of the average amount on the books in the four-week period ending May 28, 1969.

an "international" purpose. However, precisely the same results can be accomplished by a U.S. holder of a CD making a deposit in a foreign bank and the foreign bank in turn making a deposit in, or a loan to, the overseas branch of a U.S. bank. As always, this kind of moral suasion does not prevent profitable transactions. It simply produces hypocrisy and window dressing—in this case, by unnecessarily giving business to competitors of U.S. banks!

The final effect is precisely the same as in the simple example of the foreign corporation. That example shows, in highly simplified form, the main way U.S. banks have used the Euro-dollar market and explains why it is that the more they "borrow" or "bring back" from the Euro-dollar market, the higher Euro-dollar deposits mount. In our example, borrowing went up $10,000,000 and so did deposits.

From January 1, 1969 to July 31, 1969 CD deposit liabilities of U.S. banks went down $9.3 billion, and U.S. banks' indebtedness to their own overseas branches went up $8.6 billion. The closeness of these two numbers is not coincidental.

These bookkeeping operations have affected the statistics far more than the realities. The run-off in CD's in the U.S., and the accompanying decline in total commercial bank deposits (which the Fed uses as its "bank credit proxy") have been interpreted as signs of extreme monetary tightness. Money has been tight, but these figures greatly overstate the degree of tightness. The holders of CD's on U.S. banks who replaced them by Euro-dollar deposits did not have their liquidity squeezed. The banks that substituted "due to branches" for "due to depositors on time certificates of deposit" did not have their lending power reduced. The Fed's

insistence on keeping Regulation Q ceilings at levels below market rates has simply imposed enormous structural adjustments and shifts of funds on the commercial banking system for no social gain whatsoever.

CORRECTING A MISUNDERSTANDING

A column that appeared in a leading financial paper just prior to the Fed's revision of reserve requirements encapsules the widespread misunderstanding about the Euro-dollar market. The Euro-dollar market, the column noted, has:

". . . ballooned as U.S. banks have discovered that they can ease the squeeze placed on them by the Federal Reserve Board by borrowing back these foreign-deposited dollars that were pumped out largely through U.S. balance-of-payments deficits. Of this pool of $30 billion, U.S. banks as of last week had soaked up $13 billion . . .

"Thanks to this system, it takes only seconds to transmit money—and money troubles—between the U.S. and Europe . . . The Federal Reserve's pending proposal to make Euro-dollar borrowing more costly to U.S. banks might make their future demands a shade less voracious, but this doesn't reduce concern about whether there will be strains in repaying the massive amounts already borrowed."

Strains there may be, but they will reflect features of the Euro-dollar market other than those stressed by this newspaper comment. The use of the Euro-dollar market by commercial banks to offset the decline in CD's was primarily a bookkeeping operation. The reverse process—a rise in CD's and a matching decline in Euro-dollar borrowings—will also require little more than a bookkeeping operation.

Chapter III
INTERMEDIATION AND DISINTERMEDIATION

9. Changes in the Structure of Bank and Nonbank Competition in the United States[*]

Ernest Bloch

Over the last two decades, commercial banks and their principal competitors (savings and loan associations, mutual savings banks, and credit unions) have traded leadership positions in the quest for deposits: In the 1950's, nonbanks prevailed; in the 1960's, commercial banks. Ernest Bloch documents this change in competitive position. It is argued that nonbank supremacy in the earlier period was due in large part to the unwillingness of banks to compete. The working hypothesis is that "more aggressive competition by banks in the sixties necessarily reflected a revolutionary willingness to take the risk that higher and costlier time deposit rates would cut into the bank's own monopoly in providing demand deposits."

Introduction

From the end of World War II until the beginning of the decade of the sixties, nonbank financial institutions in the United States experienced a far greater growth rate than did commercial banks.

So rapid indeed was the growth of those industries generally referred to as non-banks—namely, savings and loan associations, credit unions and mutual savings banks—that the commercial banking industry in the United States seemed to be well on the way of losing its primary status among financial intermediaries. But with the advent of the 1960's the commercial banking industry in the United States began a competitive drive that raised its growth rate at home to such an extent that it came to be called a "banking revolution." And that same "revolution" was accompanied by a sharp rise in the competitiveness of U.S. banks in foreign countries as well. Indeed, the international expansion of U.S. bank financing, usually dated with the advent of sterling convertibility, may be better understood once the domestic background of competitive forces is exposed. The following study will attempt to explore this change in the competitive position of the U.S. banking industry.

[*]From *Banca Nazionale Del Lavoro Quarterly Review*, March, 1968. Reprinted by permission of the publisher.

Before the "banking revolution" began, however, academic discussion in the United States during the decade of the fifties was concerned about an apparent relationship between the slow growth of commercial banks and the revival of U.S. monetary policy in 1951, particularly as monetary policy tended to place occasional restraints on bank credit expansion. It was contended that the policy impact of restrictive open market operations (or other aspects of monetary policy) tended directly to impinge on the banking system, thereby thwarting its general capacity to expand. Aside from the inequity associated with this process, it was argued, this "discriminatory" impact of policy was on the way of becoming selfdefeating as the relative importance of the banking system within the financial sector was being reduced, in part as a result of these same policy constraints.[1]

By contrast, in the 1960's the growth rate of commercial banks sharply accelerated, while that of the nonbanks held rather stable. Most discussions of these changes attribute the banks' surge in competitive capacity to the more permissive administration of interest-rate ceilings on time deposits by the Federal Reserve System (called Regulation "Q"); the nonbanks' lesser ability to compete was associated typically with their relatively rigid rules of asset administration. This is part of the truth, but not nearly the whole truth. For increases in interest-rate ceilings will not, by themselves, induce a change in the competitive efficiency of banks. Witness, for example, the fact that original Regulation Q ceilings were set up in the 1930's, and were no bar to competition for time deposits in the early 1950's; the banks simply chose not to compete for time deposits.[2] Accordingly, this study will attempt to document the banks' *willingness* and *ability* to compete hard for time liabilities. For it is that change in attitude which is of greatest significance for the future of financial competition in the U.S. and worldwide.[3]

As a working assumption, the following accepts the Gurley-Shaw proposition buttressed by Tong Hun Lee,[4] that the liabilities of nonbanks (i.e., savings and loans, mutual savings banks, and credit unions) are reasonably close substitutes for some type of bank liabilities. The analysis will not be directly concerned with the money-near money substitution controversy, however. It will be argued, instead, that more aggressive competition by banks in the sixties necessarily reflected a revolutionary willingness to take the risk that higher and costlier time deposit rates would cut into the banks' own monopoly in providing demand deposits. The major theme of the paper will be that the banks' willingness to compete is directly quantifiable by reviewing their willingness to accept narrower profit margins. These narrower margins resulted from a faster rise in TD rates than in rates of return on bank credit; it was the banks' acceptance of the new set of cost/return functions that helped them to bid funds away from nonbanks. Finally, a rise in leveraging of capital accounts and faster asset growth by banks allowed them

---

[1]The theoretical approach that came to grips with these problems has been generally identified with the work of Professors John G. Gurley and Edward S. Shaw. For an exposition, see their *Money in a Theory of Finance*, The Brookings Institution, 1960.

[2]Indeed, a study published in 1959 argued that bank competition for time deposits would be of "doubtful benefit" in view of the high break-even yield required on assets financed with new time deposits. See WARREN L. SMITH, "Financial Intermediaries and Monetary Controls", *Quarterly Journal of Economics*, November 1959, pp. 533–53.

[3]That notion has also been proposed by M. A. Rozen. See his "Competition for Funds Between Commercial Banks and Savings Institutions" in Pontecorvo, Shay, and Hart. eds., *Issues in Banking and Monetary Analysis*, New York, 1967, pp. 60–72.

[4]"Substitutability of Non-Bank Intermediary Liabilities for Money: The Empirical Evidence", *Journal of Finance*, September 1966, pp. 441–457.

to maintain profit rates, while, under that same competitive pressure, nonbank profit rates receded.

1. BANK AND NONBANK PERFORMANCE

The results of the banks' changes in willingness to compete are shown by the growth rates of the relevant financial inputs (that is, claims, or deposits) as given in Table 1 (p.116). The sluggish growth rate of the banks through the fifties is clearly illustrated, and the concern expressed by Gurley-Shaw is supported by the actual decline in bank growth between the first half and second half of that decade. Contrasted with that performance, the nonbanks appeared to be going from strength to strength through the fifties, experiencing rates of increase about triple those of the banks for each of the periods shown through 1960 (compare column 3 and 7).

In the decade of the sixties, however, that entire pattern was changed. By aggressively doubling the growth rate of time deposits (TD) between the second half of the fifties and the sixties, the banks nearly tripled their total growth rate even though DD growth did not exceed the rate of rise of the early fifties.[5] And as a result of the competition for TD, the growth rate of savings and loan (S&L) liabilities in particular began to recede below the rates obtained in the fifties.

---

[5]The rapid growth of U.S. bank deposits at home was even exceeded by deposit growth abroad. Taking data for the United Kingdom alone, U.S. banks there experienced a truly phenomenal deposit growth rate of 40 percent *per year* (compound annual rate of change, year-ends 1959–1966). In the same period, foreign and Commonwealth banks grew at about a 15 percent rate per year, while the large London clearing banks expanded at less than 4 percent. Indeed, at the end of 1966, the deposits of the American banks made them the second-largest group of financial institutions in the U.K., ranking behind the London Clearing Banks, and well ahead of Accepting Houses, Scottish banks, foreign banks, etc.

By paying higher rates for time deposits on the financial input side, the banks could compete some household sector funds away from nonbanks, if monetary authorities permitted. But the banks went further. They became discriminating monopsonists in their purchase of financial inputs. By offering a variable menu of certificate-of-deposit maturity/rate combinations that could be finely tuned to changes in the money market, capital notes, etc., the banks attracted funds into TD from *non*household sectors of the economy that otherwise could have moved into near-money assets such as Treasury bills, or to other liabilities of the banking system, notably DD, or "money." The banks' willingness to *take* that last risk, of having to experience a switch from interest-free DD to "costlier" TD, is more interesting from the point of view of the "banking revolution" than the fact that the growth of DD did *not* suffer in the last period shown.

2. BANK AND NONBANK COMPETITION

The essential difference in the character of bank/nonbank competition between the fifties and the sixties was that in the latter period banks were willing to enter rate competition, as indicated. During most of the fifties, banks had used DD as their primary input to expand credit output; through 1957, for example, the volume of DD still was more than twice that of TD.[6] As interest rates generally rose in the fifties, however, so rose relative attractiveness to the public of interest-bearing deposits, or other forms of "near money" as opposed to DD (that is, money proper). Put differently, the public's demand for holding non-interest bearing

---

[6]To be sure, some credit expansion could also occur at the cost of reduced liquidity. But this factor, likewise, has been used by both industries, although it is limited by supervisory authorities. See discussion below of Federal Home Loan Bank Board policies in 1966.

TABLE 1
Annual Growth Rates of Depositary-Type Assets Held by Public, Selected, Periods, 1946-66
(compound annual rates of change, in percent)

Periods	Commercial Bank Deposits			Nonbank Deposit-type holdings				Total Deposit-type Holdings of Public
	Demand (Adj.)*	Time†	Total	Mutual Savings Banks	Savings & Loan Assoc.	Credit Unions	Total Nonbank	
	1	*2*	*3 (1 + 2)*	*4*	*5*	*6*	*7 (4 + 5 + 6)*	*8 (3 + 7)*
1946–50	2.2	1.9	2.2	4.4	13.3	15.8	7.7	3.3
1950–55	3.3	6.3	4.2	6.9	18.0	21.0	12.4	6.2
1955–60	0.9	8.0	3.3	5.2	14.1	15.8	10.6	5.6
1960–66	3.3	16.7	9.4	8.7	12.9	15.5	11.6	10.2

*Demand deposits at all commercial banks, other than those due to domestic commercial banks and the U.S. Government, less cash items in process of collection and Federal Reserve float, and foreign demand balances at Federal Reserve Banks.

†Time deposits at all commercial banks, other than those due to domestic commercial banks and the U.S. Government. Data are for December 31 call data where available.

Source: *Federal Reserve Bulletin*, Flow-of-Funds Accounts.

inputs of intermediaries as a share of its liquid assets declined, and as the public learned to make do with smaller transactions balances in relation to transactions volume (i.e., DD velocity rose) the rate of input flows to the *banks* increased less than to the nonbanks.[7]

Why did the banks necessarily have an advantage over nonbanks in interest-rate competition? For nonbanks and banks, the interest rates paid to depositors (or in the case of DD, compensating services) are themselves a function of the rates of return earned on assets, leaving an appropriate spread for profit and risk taking. Now assume a period of rising rates. In such a period a competitive advantage would tend to accrue to the intermediary with the greatest adaptability built into its asset portfolio. For the more responsive the asset structure is to rising rates, the greater the capacity to pay for inputs and growth. And the greater the competitive edge for inputs, the higher the rate of intermediation, or what we shall call the rate of throughput of funds for the successful competitor.

---

[7]This is just another way of putting the Gurley-Shaw phenomenon.

A. Markup and Throughput Concepts

Beyond the mere productivity change, or rate responsiveness of assets to changes in credit conditions, another factor that affects bank/nonbank ability to compete is the elasticity of compression of the spread between input rates and output rates.[8] This proposition was first put by Tobin,[9] and we will now proceed to illustrate this point. To do so we will consider a typical bank—called American Bank and Trust Company—from the point of view of competitive capacity. Figure 1 should look familiar to every student of econom-

---

[8]It may be noted here that we are not so much concerned with intra-industry competition (bank against bank) or economies of scale, which are measures of the efficiency with which a given firm in the industry may perform its function. Our purpose here is to analyze inter-industry competition. Although many studies of bank costs have been made recently, none has been made to give a comparison of costs of banks with costs of savings and loans to this writer's knowledge. Our working assumption will be, therefore, that the efficiency of individual institutions *within* each of the major financial industries is distributed in a roughly equal way.

[9]In "Commercial Banks as Creators of 'Money'", D. Carson, ed., *Banking and Monetary Studies*, R. D. Irwin, 1963, pp. 408–19.

FIGURE 1
The Theory of the Firm as a Bank

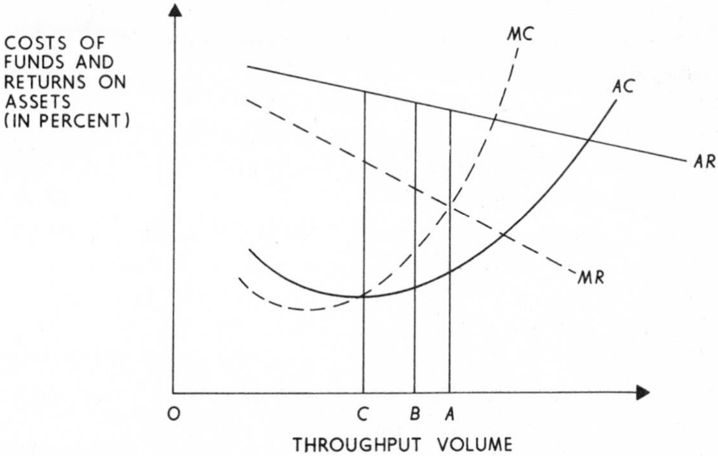

ics since it applies the theory of the firm to the monopolistic competition for funds.

Consider, first, American Bank and Trust's average revenue and marginal revenue functions. As department stores of finance, banks make many types of loans ranging from consumer credit through mortgage loans (both residential and corporate) to business loans of various types. As a result, the loan portfolio may be built up from various combinations of types of loans, each carrying a different rate of return. These rates of return have been arrayed in the figure in descending order (i.e., in declining interest costs to borrowers) to indicate the bank's conventionally sloped supply curve of credit (R). Accordingly, the bank can increase the supply of credit (or throughput) from any one point only as it is willing to accept a reduced rate of income. Within this declining credit supply (or AR) curve, the average bank typically will have a substantial share of its loan portfolio in short-term loans.[10] Thus, at

any one time, the average revenue from the bank's loan portfolio will reflect its ability to discriminate on rate as well as on nonrate terms, and on that account alone, the negative slope of the AR function is well established. (The lesser discrimination probably associated with the banks' investments portfolio—whose importance may be declining—should only slightly modify that slope). The MR function is derived from AR in the usual way.

On the other side of the ledger, the average cost (AC) function represents what it takes to acquire financial inputs from the public. And in order to attract the maximum volume, the AC curve (and the related MC curve) is shaped and sloped much like that of any other corporation. For the willingness to attract more inputs—either DD or TD—will involve a rise in costs. This cost increase may have considerable visibility, such as an advertised increase in interest rates paid for TD in the form of CD's. Likewise, a rise in costs may be associated with an increase in services provided, say, to business type holders of DD, such as payroll

[10]An important point occurs here with respect to monopolistic competition in finance that will occupy us further below. When it comes to the *maturity terms* on loans made, banks may be maturity-*makers* to a much greater extent than maturity-takers. On the other hand, since savings and loans are mortgage lenders almost exclusively, they tend to be maturity-

takers in the main. As we shall note in more detail, the greater rigidity implicit in the mortgage portfolio of an S & L (as opposed to more flexible maturity pattern of a bank) carries a true "lock-in effect" with respect to earnings.

bookkeeping, bill collecting, etc. The intent of both measures is the same: to expand the scale for the bank or, in other words, attract more inputs to raise its rate of throughput.

Now consider the typical firm that lurks between the covers of any economics text. It will be recalled that its optimum point of doing business—at maximum profits—should lie at the point of intersection of MC and MR. But for a bank the equilibrium point lies elsewhere.

As Tobin pointed out, the law that requires banks to hold "legal reserves" against their deposit liabilities in noninterest bearing form necessarily cuts into the productivity, or yield, of their aggregate asset structure. To the extent, then, that banks hold required reserves with the central bank, or vault cash in excess of transactions needs, some assets at the margin earn nothing. And as a result, the bank acting as a profit maximizer cannot push throughout to the point where MC = MR. But now assume that the monetary authorities reduce reserve requirements of the banking system. A number of reductions in reserve requirements were made in the period 1958-1962 when actual reserve percentages behind DD were lowered, and when vault cash was recognized as "reserves"; in 1962, required reserves behind TD were lowered as well, so that required reserves then stood at 16½–12 percent for DD and 4 percent for TD.[11] It is clear that such reductions in reserve requirements allow banks in effect to push throughput closer to the point where MC = MR because banks can then carry a greater proportion of earning assets.

That this is so can be seen from the following example. In 1957, the banking system held the equivalent of 13 percent of aggregate credit extended in the form of required reserve-type assets, contrasted to about 8 percent in 1966. This reduction in effective reserves required was not sole-

ly the product of official action, however. For banks were able to cut total reserves behind total deposits as they shifted the deposit mix away from DD and toward TD. To be sure, this switch involved the acquiescence of monetary authorities. Nevertheless this also required an important decision by the banks to compete by cutting unit profits as AC could be expected to rise, and AR to drop (i.e., higher rates were paid on TD while the rise in throughput implied reductions in MR). The result of both sets of decisions was that as effective required-reserve ratio fell, the bank moved closer to the MR = MC position.[12]

Going back to Figure 1, we can conceive of American Bank and Trust Company operating in the late fifties some distance to the left of the optimum profit position. Now the difference between AR and AC functions will give us the "markup" per dollar of throughput, and the maximum markup is clearly at point OC (when MC = AC). At that point, inputs could include relatively high DD volume, and a correspondingly high volume of required reserves, or non-earning assets. With relatively fewer *earning* assets, therefore, a higher markup may have been desired by the banks.

Recapitulating the foregoing, we note that to raise total profits from point OC banks will have to bid for higher-cost funds (a rise in AC), and the net increment of funds now available to bid for

----

[11]Required reserves behind some classes of TD were raised again in late 1966, however.

[12]In most of the discussion to follow, the concept of "profit" will not be, strictly speaking, what is the usual concept, namely, rate of return on equity. Since a crucial element of the following involves a comparison of bank experience to nonbank, and since nonbanks are primarily mutual-type firms (while banks are equity-type firms), a difficult problem of comparison arises. As a result, the spread between cost of time-money to banks and nonbanks, and rate of return on assets, which can be more clearly stated and compared, will be our primary proxy for the profit concept. However, we shall have some things to say about rate of return to bank equity as compared with a profit-proxy for nonbanks below.

new financial assets was bound to raise asset prices, resulting in a drop in AR. But because the banks operate in a throughput area in which MR exceeds MC they can, in effect, choose to increase competitive pressure, quite unlike nonbanks, for reasons that will become clearer below. Thus banks will operate somewhere between OC and OB, depending on what compromise they make between maximum *average markup* (move closer to OC) or total profit (move to OB). In any event, a shift from OC toward OB will be shown by the bank's acceptance of a lower markup to expand throughout and total profit. And the implied reduction in required reserves as DD/TD ratio declines will tend to make MR drop fast and make AR function more elastic as throughput expands. In the short run, then, the more competitive bank is willing to allow MC to rise and MR to decline as long as aggregate profits keep on rising. In a more dynamic sense, the more competitive bank would be accepting a lower markup to achieve faster growth while maintaining profits. This trade-off, during the 1960's, was made possible by a drop in the ratio of bank capital accounts to risk assets.[13] In sum, a rise in leverage allowed the banks to maintain earnings per share (see below) in spite of a narrowing of AR/AC markup.

To the extent, therefore, that higher-cost inputs and lower markups are brought into play, throughput in that longer-run sense should mean a faster/liability growth than in prior periods. A brief look back to Table 1 will suffice to show that bank liability growth rates in the 1960's were better than twice those achieved in prior comparable periods. What remains

to be shown is, first, empirical support to the proposition that bank AR-AC markups have narrowed and secondly, that this narrowing of markups was associated with improved performance on the asset side in competition with nonbanks.

B. High Markup vs. High Throughput: Toward an Empirical Verification

As a proxy for the typical bank's (i.e., American Bank and Trust's) average revenue function (AR) we shall use Federal Reserve member bank data shown in Table 2 indicating annual ratios of total operating revenue[14] to total assets. (The use of member bank data as a proxy for the industry, as well as for the "average" bank, is appropriate since total member bank assets have tended to be about four-fifths of total commercial bank assets in the United States.) We can call the ratio of operating revenue/total assets "AR" because it obviously represents the average earnings on the *stock* of outstanding assets for any year. More important, from our point of view, that rate also reflects the average of all of the rates produced by a given year's throughput or assets of the industry. For banks to a significant extent are *maturity*-makers as well as rate makers since their loan portfolios, say, may contain variable proportions of short-term business loans, term loans, mortgage loans, etc., as their preferences may dictate. Moreover, even though bank loan maturities have tended to lengthen, on balance, they still hold a large proportion of assets at short term. As a result banks can make the *level* of their AR for any year respond fairly quickly to changes in interest rates and other market forces. Accordingly, in the 1952–1966 period, in which interest rates were generally on the rise, banks were able to raise their AR levels. Nevertheless, banks were subject to the dis-

---

[13]For all member banks, the ratio of total capital accounts to total assets less cash and government securities moved in the narrow range of 14.2 percent – 14.9 percent in the period 1956–1961. From a level of 14.5 percent in 1961, however, that ratio fell continuously to reach 11.4 percent in 1966, a decline of more than 20 percent. For New York City banks, the comparable decline came to better than 26 percent.

[14]As shown in the footnote of Table 2 below, there was a slight change in data coverage that, however, does not significantly affect our results.

cipline of the market on the *output* side, for in periods of slow credit demand, the year-to-year rise in AR slowed down; indeed, in one recession year (1961) the general upward shift in the AR function was slightly reversed, albeit only temporarily.

The banks' average interest *costs* (AC) likewise underwent year-by-year increases (see column 2, Table 2).[15] The empirical

TABLE 2
Analysis of Member Bank
Revenue, Cost, and "Markup" Data 1952–1966
(in percent)

Year	Ratio of		
	Total Operating Revenue* to Total Assets	Interest Paid on TD/TD	"Gross Markup"
	1	2	3 (1–2)
1952	2.71	1.13	1.58
1953	2.93	1.23	1.70
1954	2.96	1.30	1.66
1955	3.13	1.36	1.77
1956	3.47	1.58	1.89
1957	3.75	2.08	1.67
1958	3.76	2.20	1.56
1959	4.07	2.36	1.71
1960	4.37	2.61	1.76
1961	4.28	2.73	1.55
1962	4.38	3.23	1.15
1963	4.44	3.34	1.10
1964	4.56	3.47	1.09
1965	4.62	3.73	0.89
1966	4.97	4.11	0.86

*For period 1952–56 ratio was total earnings/total assets; change in series probably is insignificant since for period of available overlap (1957–61) difference in ratios was 1–2 basis points for most years.
Source: *Federal Reserve Bulletin*, "Income Ratios by class of Bank", May 1967, pp. 867 ff, and earlier articles in that series.

proxy used for average costs (AC) is the ratio of interest paid on time deposits (TD) to total TD outstanding, or what might be called the "direct" cost of TD.

---

[15]These upward movements took place, particularly in the 1960's, under a more permissive regulation of interest-rate ceilings (Regulation Q of Federal Reserve Board). The first change in Regulation Q since 1936 was made in 1957; in the 1960's upward revisions came in 1962, 1963, 1964 and 1965.

By not including other banking costs, we are assuming that the manufacturing and overhead costs attributed to TD and/or to DD (demand deposits), as well as for savings accounts at savings and loans and other nonbanks, are roughly comparable. Further, these direct TD costs are quite directly related to the banks' decision to compete; the nonbanks' capacity to meet that competition will be highlighted in this manner. In any case, more precise attempts to specify production costs in bank and nonbank industries would necessarily require a heavy dose of judgment, for banks in particular and nonbanks to a lesser extent, are multi-product firms whose production outlays cover a wide variety of *assets* as well as the liability costs.[16] Finally, we are mainly concerned with the period of the "banking revolution" of the sixties, when competitive bidding for TD made them grow in importance to first equal, and then overshadow DD in magnitude. A comparison of direct TD costs thus appears appropriate.

Now to the proof of the pudding, namely, that the banks' markup between AR and AC was held rather high during the relatively slow throughput years of the 1950's, but that it was reduced in the 1960's as the banks opted for more volume and larger *aggregate* profits, albeit at the cost of cutting their unit profits (or markup). Consider the data in column 3 of Table 2 called "gross markup." In the 9 years 1952–60, we find but two in which markup was below 1.66 percentage points,

---

[16]For a useful summary of the problems of costing bank services see STUART I. GREENBAUM, "Costs and Production in Commercial Banking", *Monthly Review*, Federal Reserve Bank of Kansas City, March–April, 1966, pp. 11–20. For a treatment of some technical aspects of that problem see J. P. FURNISS and P. S. NADLER, "Should Banks Reprice Corporate Services", *Harvard Business Review*, May–June 1966, pp. 95–105, and H. C. CARR, "Pricing of Correspondent Banking Services", *Bankers Magazine*, Summer 1967, and J. M. GUTTENTAG and E. S. HERMAN, *Banking Structure and Performance*, Bulletin, N.Y.U. Institute of Finance, 1967, esp. Chapter 4 and appendixes.

while markup during the period averaged 1.70 percentage points. Following 1960, however, when the banks began aggressively to compete for TD with deposit-type nonbanks in order to raise throughput volume, their markup dropped sharply indeed: in 1962–64, markup fell to a 1.10–1.15 percent range, and in 1955–66 to less than 90 basis points. In those last two years, in sum, the markup as defined had dropped to half its 1960 level!

From these data we may readily conclude that the average bank has, in fact, shifted the throughput rate in the 1960's much closer to the optimum profit position than it ever had been before. In other words, our American Bank and Trust Company, shown in Figure 1, moved much nearer to the point where MR = MC, and in the process it had become a much tougher competitor for other banks—who were compelled to follow suit—as well as for the nonbanks.[17]

3. HOW DID THE COMPETITION COME OUT?

In the preceding section we explored the extent to which the bidding for deposits, and particularly for interest-bearing deposits escalated as between the banks and the nonbanks. By concentrating our attention on the changes in markup that the banks were willing to accept we, in effect, examined the bank pricing decisions for inputs and outputs. The time has now come to examine the effects of these changes on bank vs. nonbank competition as measured by the rate of throughput. Or, in other words, we will now assess how "badly" the banks fared during the "high markup" days of the fifties contrasted to how well the nonbanks did then;

we will then bring the story up to date by analyzing how these institutions are doing today.

In Table 3 we attempt to get the broadest possible perspective on the banking industry's throughput volume by using the Federal Reserve's flow-of-funds data to relate: (a) intermediary *inputs* to (b) the use made of *outputs* by ultimate borrowers, namely, the *nonfinancial* sectors. In the process of attributing input/output shares to banks and to nonbanks we will be able as well to assess (c) the extent to which these two competing groups of institutions have been able to raise their "sales" of liabilities to the public in order to provide for the credit needs of the nonfinancial area of the economy as a whole.

To take the last point first, consider our analysis of the banks' and nonbanks' total throughput shown in column 7 of the table. In the period 1952–60, we note a rather variable pattern in annual share of credit supplied to nonfinancial sectors that is attributable to deposit expansion of deposit-type intermediaries. This type of intermediary throughput ranged between the lowest shown, of 18 percent in 1959, and highs of 59 and 52 percent, respectively, in 1954 and 1958. A quick glance at column 6 indicates that nonbank throughput during that period was rather stable, and that it was the extreme variations of commercial bank-type intermediation to which the wide variability of deposit-type institutions (shown in column 7) can be attributed. Indeed, during the two peak years of total throughput of 1954 and 1958, bank credit (column 3) constituted 32 and 31 percent, whereas in all other years prior to 1961 it only reached about ⅔ of that figure at best, and was frequently below that. And as columns (1) and (2) indicated, TD were just as unstable as DD. Taking the entire 1952–60 period together, the volume of financing of "real" sectors attributable to intermediary throughput averaged 39 percent per

---

[17]Other aspects of the attempts to raise throughput and *aggregate profits* (rather than high markups), albeit at a price, involved, among other techniques, the sale of capital notes, premium bids for Federal funds, as well as repatriation of Eurodollar balances, particularly in 1966. For further discussion see E. BLOCH, *Eurodollars: An Emerging International Money Market*, N.Y.U. Institute of Finance, 1966.

TABLE 3
Relation of Increases in Intermediary Liabilities
to Net Funds Raised by Nonfinancial Sectors, 1952–66
(in percent)

	Commercial Banks			Nonbanks			Banks and Nonbanks
	DD	TD	Total	S & L	MSB	Total°	
Years	1	2	3 (1 + 2)	4	5	6 (4 + 5)	7 (3 + 6)
1952	9	9	19	9	5	16	35
1953	3	12	15	13	6	20	35
1954	17	15	32	18	8	27	59
1955	9	3	12	13	5	19	31
1956	5	7	13	17	6	25	38
1957	4	17	21	15	5	21	42
1958	12	19	31	14	5	21	52
1959	†	2	2	12	2	16	18
1960	−1	16	15	21	4	27	42
1961	11	20	31	18	4	24	55
1962	3	26	29	17	5	23	52
1963	5	23	28	18	5	25	53
1964	6	22	28	16	6	24	52
1965	9	28	36	12	5	18	54
1966	†	19	20	5	4	10	29

°Includes credit unions, which averaged between 1–2 per cent per year.
†Less than 1 per cent.
Source: *Federal Reserve*, Flow of Funds Accounts.

year, with the nonbanks contributing more than half that figure, or about 21 percent, and leaving but 18 percent to the banks.

In the 1961-66 period, on the other hand, just about everything in the pattern was reversed. To begin with column 7 again, we now find rather extraordinary stability in total throughput rate, and at the much higher rate through 1965 of 52 to 55 percent. Further, this general pattern of stability is now more characteristic of bank throughput than of nonbank. Moreover, bank throughput now contributes the lion's share (averaging 29 percent out of a total of 50 percent) rather than nonbank; and finally the banks' expanded role in financing throughout is shown to be almost exclusively a function of sharply rising TD.

To be sure, during the year of "credit crunch" in 1966, banks and nonbanks both had to restrict throughput. But as the data in the last line clearly suggest, a tight monetary policy that initially placed increasingly great pressure on the banks, paradoxically affected the throughput of the nonbanks far more than that of the banks! Nonbank throughput, at 10 percent, fell to the lowest level for the entire period, whereas that of the banks shrank only to a level that in any year prior to 1961 would have been counted a good year. In sum, the improved competitiveness of the banks enabled them to hang on to a respectacle share of the 1966 market shrunk by very tight monetary policy, even though the impact of that restrictive policy hit them first.

The explanation for the banks' improved ability to compete in the 1960's as well as in 1966, when money got very tight, has been attributed above to the ability to expand TD. Earlier on, we noted that the banks were willing to do this by buying more TD inputs at "prices," or rates, that were rising faster than revenues because they were willing to undergo a shrinkage in unit margins to raise total profits. Table 4 indicates how rates paid by banks on TD approached rates paid

TABLE 4

Comparison of Savings Rates Paid by Savings
and Loan Associations and Commercial Banks, 1950–66
(in percent)

Years	S & L's Percent	Commercial Banks Percent	Spread Percent
	1	2	3 (1–2)
1950	2.5	0.9	1.6
1951	2.6	1.1	1.5
1952	2.7	1.1	1.6
1953	2.8	1.1	1.7
1954	2.9	1.3	1.6
1955	2.9	1.4	1.5
1956	3.0	1.6	1.4
1957	3.3	2.1	1.2
1958	3.4	2.2	1.2
1959	3.5	2.4	1.2
1960	3.9	2.6	1.3
1961	3.9	2.8	1.1
1962	4.1	3.1	0.9
1963	4.2	3.3	0.8
1964	4.2	3.5	0.7
1965	4.2	3.7	0.5
1966 e	4.4	4.1	0.3

e: Partly estimated.
Source: *Savings and Loan Fact Book*, 1966, p. 17.

by S&L's ever more closely (see columns 1 and 2). Column 3 of the table, called "spread," reflects the competitive stimulus of the banks, and the response of the nonbanks, particularly as the banks began to raise rates in 1957 following a change in ceiling rates of TD.

Taking the competition in chronological order, the 1950-1956 period shows S&L rates drifting up slightly from 2.5 to 3.0 percent, while deposit rates of other nonbanks such as, e.g., Mutual Savings Banks followed suit.[18] In that period of "com-

[18]Owing to wide interregional differences in interest rates, the country-wide averages used here can claim to be no more representative than any average. That there are wide differences by region on rates paid on even such homogeneous items as short-term business loans of $10,000 to $99,999 can be seen from the Federal Reserve's revised loan series (see May 1967 *Federal Reserve Bulletin*, p. 725); such loans carried a rate of 6.32 percent in the Southeast, while on the West Coast the rate was 6.90 percent. The range is even wider for mortgages, for at the end of 1965, conventional mortgage rates on new homes ranged from a low of 5.24 percent in Boston to

petitive quiet," 1950–1956, the nonbank-bank deposit spread held fairly steady in the neighborhood of 150 basis points. The table also indicates that banks *could* have competed more aggressively under the Reg. Q ceiling of the early and mid 1950's, but they *chose* not to do so. Following the Regulation Q change effective in 1957, banks began more aggressive bidding since the spread fell to 1.2 basis points as bank rates rose faster than nonbank. And when the banks' rate ceilings again were raised successively in 1962, 63, 64 and 1965, the competition for funds began in earnest. Spreads sharply narrowed as a result, to reach the ½ percentage point in 1965 and a low of .3 percentage point in 1966. In sum, Table 4 indicates three competitive phases in bidding for TD by the banks against the nonbanks: the quiet period of high spreads (1½ percentage points) prior to 1956; the acceleration in TD rate advances 1957-61, and finally the period of active competition as an aspect of the banking revolution of the 1960's. And the rapidly improving *rates* paid on TD help to explain the rapid growth of TD as inputs to feed the accelerating throughput of banks shown earlier in Table 3.

The question now arises, why did the S&L's not retaliate by raising *their* liability rates—as rates rose on assets—so as to maintain their competitive spread over banks at, say, 80 points or better? That spread, through 1963 at least, had allowed them to provide between 18 and 20 percent of net funds raised by nonfinancial sectors (Table 3). The answer is simple: in the mid-sixties the character of, and returns earned on, their assets did not

a high of 6.10 percent in Houston. The range on rates paid on savings balances by associations in 1965 was similarly wide, with a low of 4.03 percent paid in the Indianapolis Home Loan Bank District, and a high of 4.72 percent in San Francisco District. At our level of abstraction, however, comparisons of country-wide averages are appropriate for institutions with country-wide coverage, such as banks and S & L's.

TABLE 5
Comparison of Rates Earned on New Convention Mortgages,
Savings Rates Paid to Public, and "Savings Spread"
(in percent)

Year-end	Rates on new conventional mortgages*	Five-Year Moving Average†	S & L Savings Rates	"Savings Spread"
	1	2	3	4 (2–3)
1961	5.97		3.9	
1962	5.93		4.1	
1963	5.81		4.2	
1964	5.80		4.2	
1965	5.83	5.87	4.2	1.7
1966	6.40	5.95	4.4e	1.6

e: Partly estimated.
*FHA series for full period available. Mortgage rate for 1961 year-end is that for January 1962, the earliest date available.
†Average for 5 years placed in *fifth* year.
Source: *Federal Reserve Bulletin.*

allow them to push up income rates—that is, their AR function could not rise as fast as that of banks. Recall that S&L's and MSB's, and other nonbanks as well, have a heavy stake in such long-term assets as residential mortgages; moreover, there is no ready secondary market for "turning over" a large portfolio of mortgages.[19]

To be sure, most residential mortgages are refinanced prior to maturity, thereby permitting some upward rate (and nonrate) adjustments on a share of this portfolio, and some 15–20 percent of the nation's housing stock has tended to turn over in the average postwar year. Given even the upper range of that rate of turnover, institutions specializing in mortgages could expect that about 1/5 of the AR of existing portfolio (which includes amortization of all mortgages) would be adjusted to reflect a rise in rates. Higher rates would, of course, also be placed on mortgages financing *new* construction. As a result, it might be supposed that better returns on refinanced and new mortgages would substantially raise the ability of nonbank mortgage lenders (especially

[19]By contrast, the municipal, U.S. Government, and corporate securities carried by banks in their investment portfolios all enjoy relatively liquid secondary markets.

S&L's) to compete for financial inputs. But the ability to compete for inputs is a function of *average* revenue of mortgage portfolio, and some 4/5 of that revenue is fixed at earlier rate levels. In view of the fact that rates in the early 1960's were lower than in the mid 1960's, the upward adjustment of aggregate earnings on a mortgage portfolio is quite sluggish because the weight of the lower rates on mortgages made as long ago as 5 years and earlier pulled down the earning power of the portfolio.

The sluggishness of upward adjustment of average revenue (AR) can be illustrated by the data in Table 5. Here we show rates placed on new *conventional* mortgages (column 1) for each of the years for which such data have become available. And we can see that while these rates fluctuated by fairly small amounts in the period 1961-65, they really jumped in 1966, rising to 6.40 percent. But now consider the 5-year moving average (column 2) computed to indicate a rough proxy for AR of a mortgage portfolio. For the exercise it was assumed that 20 percent of such a portfolio consisted of 1966 mortgages although this tends to overstate the improvement in AR owing to the sharp cut in 1966 S&L and mortgage throughput indicated in Table 3. Nevertheless, the

AR of portfolio in the exercise is improved by less than 10 basis points, a rate that is consistent with data derived by U.S. Savings and Loan League (see below).

In effect, an aggressive campaign by S&L's to attract more savings capital in a period of rising rates would require a quick upward adjustment in rates paid on *inputs* (AC). Yet, as noted, the average revenue (AR) of a mortgage portfolio moves upward but sluggishly even if, in any one year, mortgage rates do zoom. Inevitably, then, the maintenance of a given throughput rate of financing on the capital markets would require the S&L's to sharply cut the difference between stable AR and rising AC. In other words, markups would have to decline, for only a willingness or an ability to cut markups would allow S&L's to meet rate competition for inputs.[20] To meet bank competition on more or less even terms, S&L markups probably should have contracted by as much as did bank markups, which, as noted, were halved between 1960 and 1966.

Were S&L's able to shave markups? Consider the fact that in 1965, when S&L's already experienced some difficulty in attracting and holding on to savings capital, their "savings spread" (as computed in column 4 of Table 5) was 1.7 percentage points. Using slightly different data that go back to the 1950's (provided by U.S. Savings and Loan League) we find that comparable savings spreads fell but little, from about 1.8 percent in the 1950's to about 1.6 percent in 1966. In 1966, indeed, savings and loans generally raised savings rates, but the Federal Home Loan Bank Board restrained rate increases as the "savings spread" was squeezed below the level that the Board deemed to be appropriate. An important factor in that decision was the decline in portfolio quality

experienced by member associations. To begin with, in early 1966, the annual rate of nonfarm real estate foreclosures rose to about 5 per 1,000 mortgaged structures, a rate about twice that of 1960, and a record for the postwar period. Worse yet, the first line of defenses of portfolio quality as a whole, namely, the growth of total reserves, fell very sharply in 1966.[21]

In point of fact, the basic constraint on competitive capacity of S&L's is the slow turnover of mortgage assets that, in periods of rapidly rising interest rates, necessarily places a ceiling on aggregate earnings, and by extension, on the capacity to hold, much less attract, new rate-sensitive savings capital. In addition, each of the recent periods of monetary tightening (e.g., 1959 and 1966) were accompanied by much faster increases in short-term rates than in long-term—that is to say, yield curves tended to flatten as they rose, thereby helping holders of short-dated assets, such as banks. It should be recalled, further, that during a good part of the mid-1960's Federal debt management policy, called "operation twist," was intended to press down on longer-term rates while shoring up short-term rates. As a result, a structural income problem was building up for nonbank holders of long-term assets, namely, a lower rate of AR for some time in the future. This set of problems can be illustrated by the much sharper reduction of S&L profit rates in 1966 than the decline in bank profits; for, while bank profits fell a bit between

---

[20]It should be emphasized that owing to a variety of technical reasons, this exercise is meant to be rather illustrative more than anything else. For example, it omits nonrate mortgage income, such as initial fees, etc., as well as offsetting higher *costs* of servicing a mortgage portfolio.

[21]The capital accounts of financial institutions represent, for the supervisory authorities, the first line of defense against declines in asset values. From the point of view of the FHLBB, the sum of reserves and retained earnings—or net worth—is the proxy for capital accounts of largely mutual member association. In the period 1950-1962, the net worth of associations grew, on average, by about 14 percent per year. From that point on, however, annual increments to net worth fell, to reach a low of less than 7 percent in 1966. In view of the rising 1966 foreclosure rate, the FHLBB apparently decided that a year of slowly rising reserve cushion was not the time to permit a further rise in AC, particularly in the face of very sluggish rise in AR.

TABLE 6
Share of Funds Supplied Directly to Credit Markets by Selected Groups, Annually, 1956-66
(in percent)

Years	Private Domestic Nonfinancial	Commercial Banks	Nonbanks*	Total	Memo Item: Market Rates on 90-day Treasury Bills†
	1	2	3	4 (1 + 2 + 3)	5
1956 16		17	57	90	2.62
1957 25		16	52	93	3.23
1958 8		37	45	90	1.78
1959 38		8	39	85	3.37
1960 1		24	62	87	2.87
1961 5		35	48	88	2.36
1962 8		34	45	87	2.77
1963 9		34	48	91	3.16
1964 13		32	43	88	3.54
1965 12		40	37	89	3.95
1966 30		26	30	86	4.85

*Savings and loans, mutal savings banks, and credit unions.
†Annual averages.
Source: *Federal Reserve Bulletin,* Flow-of-Funds Accounts; and tables on Money Market Rates.

1960 and 1966, the decline experienced by S&L's, particularly after 1962, was greater and much more abrupt.[22]

Perhaps the most direct way of looking at this new effect of monetary policy (which is the reverse of that worried

[22]The differential effect on banks and S & L's of financial policies, regulations, and other factors in the 1960's can be illustrated by a comparison of profit rates of the two groups. For member bank profits we use net income as a ratio to average bank capital accounts; for a "profit proxy" for the largely mutual S & L's we use the annual rise in reserves and retained profits to average net worth during the year. The results are, in percent:

Year	Profit proxy, S & L's	Bank net income Capital accounts
1960 .... 12.6		10.1
1961 .... 13.6		9.6
1962 .... 13.3		8.9
1963 .... 10.0		9.0
1964 .... 9.1		8.8
1965 .... 10.9		8.7
1966 .... 6.0		8.6

Source: *Federal Reserve Bulletin,* May 1967, p. 716, and Federal Home Loan Bank Board, *Annual Report* 1966, Washington, 1967, Appendix Table 13.

about by Gurley-Shaw) is to consider the extent to which the rising interest rates of the tight-money period of 1966 have influenced the through-put rate of the entire intermediation process. For if, as indicated by Gurley-Shaw, both bank and nonbank intermediation creates new credit, a monetary policy designed to restrain a rise in total credit must needs reduce the rate of intermediation. In an operational sense, there should be a decline in the dollar volume of funds supplied to credit markets by intermediaries (or throughput) and this decline might well be associated with a rise in direct investment by nonfinancial public—or in disintermediation. And we should find out whose throughput was most affected.

The development of substantial *disintermediation* in 1966 is clearly illustrated by Flow of Funds data presented in Table 6. In column 1, we show that transactors such as households and business,[23] which provide most inputs of intermediaries, di-

[23]In the Flow-of-Funds accounts, and Table 6, these units are called "private domestic nonfinancial."

rectly contributed in 1966 nearly one-third of the funds used by credit markets, contrasted to a share averaging about one-tenth in the preceding five years. It may be noted that in prior periods of relatively tight money (1957 and 1959) disintermediation also was relatively high. Now how were potential "depositors" induced to do their own investing? Column (5) of the table gives the answer in the form of sharply rising yields on Treasury bills. In the years 1957, 1959, and 1966, these bill rates (and other comparable yields) not only rose very rapidly, by between ⅜ to 1½ percentage points over the prior year, but in each case their rates approached or exceeded rates available on time deposits or on the country-wide average for S&L shares (compare with Table 4).

If a tightening monetary policy does produce disintermediation, which intermediaries lose out, and by how much? Columns (2) and (3) of the table readily indicate how little the nonbanks were affected in the late fifties (in contrast to a drop to 8 percent by the banks in 1959), whereas in the sixties the banks show up much better, and the nonbanks comparatively less well. Put slightly differently, a rise in open-market rates associated with greater restrictiveness of monetary authorities places a premium on capacity to meet the competition of these (higher) open-market rates. In the short run, financial intermediaries can raise rates on their liabilities and compete by accepting a (unit) profit squeeze. Such a squeeze becomes acceptable if upward adjustments can be made soon on rates carried by a significant proportion of assets. The shorter-term structure of bank assets allows the banks to do this far more readily than nonbanks, as noted. And further, as noted, the banks' longer-run decision to buy faster throughput, or growth, with the acceptance of lower unit markups improved their competitive position. By contrast, the nonbanks were locked into long-

term assets (which have virtually no secondary market) and as the quality of their portfolios declined, supervisors were loath to allow the nonbanks aggressively to compete for funds that might have led to further deterioration in portfolio quality. For all of these reasons, the throughput rate of banks held up much better than that of nonbanks in 1966.

An overview of our analysis can be based on the approach presented in Figure 1 by using cost-return and throughput data together, as we have in Figure 2.[24] The comparisons made refer to throughput performance derived from Flow-of-Funds accounts in Table 3 for two representative years, 1957 and 1966, and for both banks and nonbanks.[25] Taking the throughput performance of the *banks* first, Table 3 indicated virtually the same throughput rate for both years, at 21 and 20 percent, respectively. It should be noted, however, that the 1966 data refer to a dollar total of $71 billion, or more than twice the dollar volume of $33 billion in 1957. Interestingly enough, the throughput rate of the *nonbanks* in 1957 also was at 21 percent rate.[26] But in 1966, the nonbank rate of throughput was cut by more than half, to 10 percent. A quick glance at the x-axes of Figure 2 shows that in 1966 tight money was tougher to live with for nonbanks than for banks.

This is only part of the story, however. For the banks held on to their throughput share only at a price: a halving of their average markup (compare y-axes of Figure 2). Whereas in 1957 bank AR ex-

[24]The truncated bits of AR and AC curves in the Figure are provided for illustrative purposes only.

[25]The year 1957 was chosen because it was the first year during which a postwar Regulation Q *change* became effective. As a result, the banks had begun to compete for funds even in the period prior to the banking revolution of the 1960's. And for this reason banking throughput had already shifted to the right of minimum AC (see Figure 1), and no longer reflects a maximum cost/return spread.

[26]That 21 percent share also represents the throughput *average* for nonbanks in the period 1952-60.

FIGURE 2
Comparisons of Markup and Throughput Rates for Banks and Nonbanks, 1957 and 1966
(in percent)

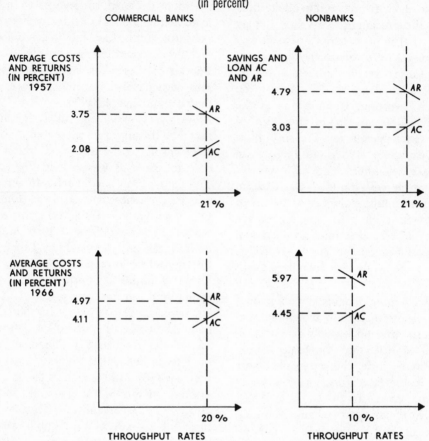

Note: Throughput volume, in dollars, was: $33 billion in 1957 and $71 billion in 1966.
Sources: Table 2, 3, 4.

ceeded AC by about 1.7 percentage points, that markup had fallen to .9 percent in 1966. On the other hand, the markup of the nonbanks fell by no more than 20 basis points from 1.76 percent (1957) to 1.55 percent (1966). Finally, because the reduction in bank markups has come to a greater extent from higher rates paid by banks on *input* rates, which roughly doubled between 1957 and 1966, it is understandable that the banks could better hang on to their share of inflows of funds, thereby maintaining capital market throughput. In the short run, higher rates could be paid by banks because their greater asset flexibility had a shorter

built-in time lag between raised costs and raised revenues. Even in the longer view, the banks were willing to accept lower markups for some time because, with faster growth, and by accepting a decline in capital/risk asset ratios, they were able to maintain earning rates.[27] But whatever their immediate reason, the acceptance by banks of lower markups in 1966 helped them to maintain throughput, thereby be-

[27]This process has raised some questions about "bank soundness" among bank supervisors. See speech by W. F. TREIBER, "Some Current Banking and Economic Problems", Federal Reserve Bank of New York, *Monthly Review,* Sept. 1967, p. 170.

ing hurt less by policy-induced disintermediation than the nonbanks were.

4. CONCLUSIONS

The foregoing has tested the extent to which banks have a unique means of expanding what has been called throughput in this study because they operate to the left of the MC = MR position. It was argued that the extent to which the banks succeeded in expanding throughput by reducing unit profits, the "banking revolution" was only partly attributable to the more permissive administration of Reg. Q. The point that this study has attempted to make is that the sufficient condition behind the banking revolution was the *willingness* of the banks to bid for higher-price funds. This willingness did *not* exist through most of the fifties as the early data on operating revenue/TD spreads clearly indicated (Table 2). The shift in management decision to aggressively seek out TD was illustrated by the halving of AR/AC spreads in the sixties. As a result of that decision, the outstandings of TD are now some 20 percent greater than DD. On another level of analysis, the narrowing of cost/return spreads has moved banks closer to the theoretical profit optimum (as suggested by Tobin). And the inability of S&L's to compete for inputs was related to their inability to cut their cost/return spreads, which was associated, in turn, with the long-term nature of their asset structure.

Looked at from the point of view of the S&L's, their less flexible asset structure and the absence of a large-scale secondary market for mortgages made it difficult to adjust to the increasing and cumulative pressures of governmental financial policies and bank competition. Thus, in retrospect, the extent to which "operation twist" was a success in the early sixties implied that sometime later S&L's would experience a lower rate of AR than would otherwise have occurred. When this was followed by a restrictive monetary policy associated with rising rates and a flattening yield curve, the competitive position of S&L's worsened further. In the words of the Federal Reserve's *Annual Report*, the ". . . impact of tighter credit conditions (fell) heavily on nonbank institutions and therefore on the mortgage markets . . ."[28] and in July 1966 the Board voted to provide for "emergency credit facilities . . . through Federal Reserve Banks . . . to nonmember depositary-type institutions, including mutual savings banks and savings and loan associations."[29] Following the banking revolution, public policy concern has turned from the fate of the banks (Gurley-Shaw) to that of nonbanks—a turn of 180 degrees. For the competitive position of banks at home—as well as abroad—has probably changed for good.

---

[28]*Fifty-Third Annual Report*, Board of Governors of the Federal Reserve System, 1966, Washington, 1967, p. 28.

[29]*Ibid.*, pp. 29–30, p. 91.

10. A Historical Analysis of the Credit Crunch of 1966 *

Albert E. Burger

The "credit crunch" of 1966 was a unique and, in a sense, invaluable experience. Its examination shows how an apparently robust economy can be quickly weakened and brought to the brink of recession. It is a lesson in contrasts, both as to the offsetting actions of monetary authorities and financial intermediaries to affect the supply and demand for loanable funds, and to the value of monetary policy versus fiscal policy in economic stabilization. Though past history, "the 1966 experience has exercised an important influence on monetary policy decisions made since that time and on the procedures for raising funds used by the commercial banks." The article provides an in-depth analysis of the circumstances and actions surrounding this episode.

In early 1966 the U.S. economy was entering the sixth year of continuous economic expansion. The unemployment rate was at 4 percent, a level believed almost unattainable two or three years earlier, capacity utilization was close to 90 percent, and firms were faced with an exceptionally large backlog of orders. The economy had not only reached a state of full employment, but there was every indication that the "boom" would continue. To many, it appeared that the "New Economics" had finally removed the danger of recession or economic slowdown.

The year 1966 was not, however, to be remembered as a year of smooth economic expansion. The real sector of the

*From *Review*, September, 1969. Reprinted by permission of the publisher, the Federal Reserve Bank of St. Louis.

economy, operating at the full-employment level of real output, was forced to attempt to adjust the mix and amount of real output to meet the increased demands of both the private and government sectors. The two main topics in discussion of economic stabilization policy in 1966 were as follows: (1) the sharply rising level of Government spending for the Vietnam war, and (2) the emergence of inflation. At the start of 1966, firms operating at near capacity with record levels of backlogs of orders, when making plans for future capital expenditures, expected rising aggregate demand, a rising price level, and a "tighter labor market" with rising wage demands. These types of expectations are all precursors to a boom in capital spending.

As corporations and the government sector bid aggressively for funds, financial intermediaries and the securities markets were placed under increasing demand pressure. The aggregate demand for real output, and the ability of various sectors of the economy to acquire funds to make their desired command over real output effective, was such that, at existing prices, the demand for real output exceeded the productive capacity of the economy.

Reflecting demand pressures on the productive capacity of the economy, prices rose rapidly. Over the first nine months of 1966, the consumer price index rose at a 3.7 percent annual rate, and the wholesale price index rose at a 3.5 percent rate, compared to rises of 1.7

percent for consumer prices and 2.0 percent for wholesale prices in 1965, and compared to an average annual rate of increase of 1.2 percent for consumer prices and essentially no change for wholesale prices during the 1960–64 period.

In the summer of 1966 a policy of monetary restraint led to conditions popularly called the "Credit Crunch of 1966." The most publicized features of this period were (1) the development in August of an alleged near liquidity crisis in the bond markets and (2) a record decrease in savings inflows into nonbank financial intermediaries and the resulting reduced rate of residential construction. This article focuses on the first of these developments. The role of monetary policy and its impact on the commercial banks and the financial markets is discussed and analyzed.

The 1966 experience has exercised an important influence on monetary policy decisions made since that time and on the procedures for raising funds used by the commercial banks. The possibility of causing another "Credit Crunch," with all of its feared ramifications on the financial markets and the savings and loan and housing industries, acted as an important constraint on a decision to move toward a tighter monetary policy in the last half of 1967. These same fears, combined with overly optimistic expectations on the potency of the fiscal actions taken in mid-1968, constrained monetary policy decision-makers again in 1968 and 1969.

In 1966, for the first time, commercial banks experienced a period when the Federal Reserve actively used Regulation Q ceiling rates on time deposits as a means to restrict the banks' ability to extend credit. Since that time commercial banks have actively sought new methods, such as Eurodollar borrowings, to obviate the constraint of Q ceilings.

This article is divided into four major sections. The first section discusses conditions in the credit markets in the first eight months of 1966; the second section discusses and analyzes both the intent and impact of Federal Reserve policy during this period; the third section discusses the actions and reactions of the commercial banks during the first eight months of 1966; and then the last section presents a summary of developments in the remainder of 1966.

DEVELOPMENTS IN THE MONEY AND CAPITAL MARKETS: FIRST EIGHT MONTHS OF 1966

The greatest source of pressure in the financial markets coming directly from the Federal Government sector originated in the sale of securities by Federal agencies, not in direct debt financing. The amount sold by Federal agencies was three times as great as the $1.6 billion raised in the first eight months of 1965. In the months of May and June, at the same time that the financial markets encountered heavy demand pressures from corporations to meet their accelerated tax payments, Federal agencies raised $1.7 billion in new cash, about a billion dollars more than in the same two months of 1965. Such security sales were entered as reductions in expenditures in the Federal budget, and thus acted to reduce the reported spending totals and the cash deficit.

In August, the month of the so-called Credit Crunch in the financial markets, corporations and Federal Government agencies placed especially heavy demands for credit. Typically, a lull occurs in new issue activity in the securities markets in August. However, in August 1966 the government and private sectors of the economy raised an estimated $3.7 billion in new cash, a large increase from the $2.4 billion borrowed in August 1965. As shown in Table 1, estimated gross proceeds from new securities offered for cash by the U.S. Government and by state and local governments remained at about the same level as in August 1965. However, compared to the same period of 1965, corporations and Federal agen-

TABLE 1

Estimated Gross Proceeds from
New Securities Offered for Cash
in the United States
(millions of dollars)

	August 1965	August 1966	Percent Increase
All Offerings	2,354	3,676	56.2
U.S. Government ..	371	386	4.0
State and Local Governments ...	718	764	6.4
Corporations	930	1,712	84.1
Federal Agencies ..	239	799	234.3

Source: Securities and Exchange Commission, Statistical Bulletin.

cies issued a much larger volume of new securities. In August, the estimated new cash raised in the securities markets by corporations and Federal agencies was more than twice as great as in August 1965.

Rising Interest Rates

Reflecting primarily the heavy demand for credit in the first eight months of 1966, market interest rates rose to new peaks for the post World War II period. The weekly average of yields on Aaa-rated corporate bonds rose 64 basis points by the end of August. As shown by Table 2, yields on long-term Government bonds and state and local securities, and yields on short- and intermediate-term securities, also rose markedly over the first eight months of 1966.

The increased demand for credit by the business sector led to a sharp rise in interest rates on business loans. Commercial bank rates on short-term business loans, as reported in a survey of banks in 19 large cities, rose from an average of about 5 percent in the first three quarters of 1965 to an average of 5.82 percent in June of 1966 and then rose to 6.30 in September of that year. Market rates on four- to six-month commercial paper, which averaged 4.35 percent over the first three quarters of 1965, rose sharply to 5.51 percent in June 1966, and then increased to 5.85 percent in August 1966.

High Interest Rates Did Not Curb Corporate Expenditures

Once corporations had begun large capital spending programs, they were unwilling to allow rising market rates of interest to bring these programs to a sharp halt. Although by past comparisons interest rates rose to very high levels, many corporations found that even at higher rates of interest the rate of return they could earn on borrowed funds exceeded the cost of borrowing. *Fortune Magazine* (June 15, 1967), in its review of operations of the 500 largest non-financial corporations in the United States, found that in 1966 the median industry return on invested capital was 12.7 percent, up from 11.8 percent in 1965. Almost all industry groups in the *Fortune*

TABLE 2

Weekly Averages of Annual Yields on Selected Securities, 1966

	Early Jan.	Peak in Month		
		June	July	August
Corporate Aaa bonds	4.73%	5.07%	5.22%	5.37%
Long-Term Governments	4.44	4.63	4.78	4.87
State and Local Governments	3.40	3.60	3.77	3.94
3–5 Year Governments	4.92	5.02	5.25	5.79
3–Month Treasury Bills	4.50	4.59	4.89	5.06
4–6 Month Prime Commercial Paper ..	4.75	5.51	5.63	5.85

Source: Federal Reserve *Bulletin*, March 1967.

FIGURE 1
Bank Credit and Money Stock in Billions of Dollars
(monthly averages of daily figures
seasonally adjusted)

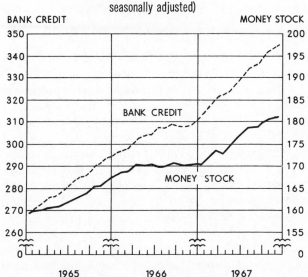

Sources: Board of Governors of the Federal Reserve
System and Federal Reserve Bank of St. Louis.

study showed an increase in their return on invested capital.

The main concern of corporations seemed to be more with the availability of funds than with the cost of these funds. Prime rate customers placed large orders for cash with the commercial banking system. As Jerome Behland, Treasurer of Owens-Illinois, Inc., remarked in an interview with *Business Week* in late August:

Our general corporate attitude is that you can't stop a $500 million program just because the cost of borrowing goes up. That's part of the cost of the program, and if it is one that is going to produce a more profitable operations for the corporation, then it must proceed.[1]

INTENT AND IMPACT OF FEDERAL RESERVE POLICY: FIRST EIGHT MONTHS OF 1966

In this section we first examine the intent of monetary policy in 1966, and

[1]*Business Week*, August 27, 1966, p. 23.

then discuss movements in money and bank credit, two commonly used indicators of the impact of monetary policy on the real sector of the economy. An analytical framework is presented which permits one to determine the impact Federal Reserve policy actions have on money and bank credit, and to analyze the causes of observed movements in money and bank credit.

Movements of Two Monetary Aggregates

Two widely used indicators of the effect of monetary policy on the real sector are (1) money, defined as currency plus demand deposits held by the non-banking public, and (2) bank credit, defined as the loans and investments of commercial banks.

MONEY STOCK. During the last four months of 1965 and through the first four months of 1966 the money stock expanded at a rapid rate. Over the last four months of 1965 the money stock increased by $3.6 billion, or at an annual rate of 6.8 percent. During the first four months of 1966 the money stock continued to increase markedly, rising at an annual rate of 6.4 percent. One of the most noticeable features of this rise was that it was a fairly steady month-by-month increase. After April, the money stock showed almost no noticeable change. Through January of 1967 it remained at approximately the level reached in April of 1966.

BANK CREDIT. Credit extended by commercial banks increased steadily at a rapid rate from early 1965 through June of 1966. Over the last four months of 1965, bank credit expanded at an annual rate of 10.4 percent. Bank credit continued to rise at a rapid rate over the first four months of 1966, rising at an 8 percent annual rate. Whereas the growth of the money stock stopped in April 1966, the stock of bank credit continued to grow at an 8 percent annual rate through July. The growth of bank credit throughout the whole period January 1965 to July 1966 was manifested in a very sharp increase in bank loans.

The growth of bank credit came to a temporary halt in August during the so-called Credit Crunch. By components, this halt reflected a deceleration of the rate of increase in bank loans and a decrease of $0.6 billion in banks' holdings of securities. In September bank credit increased sharply, but following September the growth of bank credit moderated noticeably until near the end of the year.

The Impact of Policy Actions on Money and Bank Credit

The three major policy instruments under the direct control of the monetary authorities are as follows: (1) the discount rate; (2) reserve requirements on member bank deposits; and (3) changes in the Federal Reserve's holdings of Government securities. In addition, a regulatory power of the Federal Reserve, Regulation Q ceilings on interest rates offered by commercial banks on time deposits,

has been used at times since mid-1966 as if it were also a policy instrument.

The Federal Reserve, by its policy actions alone, does not determine the equilibrium level of market interest rates. Likewise its policy actions are not the only factors which enter into the determination of the equilibrium stocks of money and bank credit. The amount of money and bank credit supplied to the economy also depends upon behavioral actions of the commercial banks and the public. To understand how the Federal Reserve, with its policy instruments, can control the money supply and bank credit processes, and to analyze and predict the effects of policy actions on these aggregates, one must use a framework which incorporates the behavioral responses of the commercial banks and the public.

THE ANALYTICAL FRAMEWORK. The Brunner-Meltzer Nonlinear Money Supply Hypothesis is such a framework.[2] Money (M), defined as demand deposits and currency held by the nonbanking public, and bank credit (BC) are defined therein as:

$$M = m \, B^a$$
$$BC = a \, B^a$$

where B^a is the adjusted monetary source base, and m and a are multipliers. In this article the monetary source base is adjusted by removing member bank borrowings, and is defined as shown in Table 3.[3]

The adjusted monetary source base (B^a) is an asset supplied to the private

---

[2]For a complete discussion of the Brunner-Meltzer hypothesis, see Albert Burger, *An Analysis and Development of the Brunner-Meltzer Nonlinear Money Supply Hypothesis*, Working Paper No. 7, available from Federal Reserve Bank of St. Louis.

[3]In alternative formulations of this multiplier-base framework, member bank borrowing may be included as a component of the base and the base adjusted for reserve requirement changes. For a more complete discussion of the sources and use of the monetary base, see Leonall C. Andersen and Jerry L. Jordan, "The Monetary Base: Explanation and Analytical Use," this *Review*, August 1968, available as Reprint No. 31.

TABLE 3
Adjusted Monetary Source Base (B^a), April 1966
(not seasonally adjusted)

	(Millions of Dollars)
Federal Reserve holdings of U.S. Government securities	$40,758*
Float	1,934
Gold Stock	13,632
Treasury currency outstanding	5,768
Less:	
Treasury cash holdings	941
Treasury deposits at Federal Reserve banks	311
Foreign deposits at Federal Reserve banks	148
Other (net)	903
Equals adjusted monetary source base	59,789
Federal Reserve holdings of Government securities as per cent of B^a	68%

*Includes $129 million of acceptances not shown separately.

sectors of the economy by the monetary authorities. The users of the monetary source base by the banks and the public are member bank deposits at the Federal Reserve banks, banks' holdings of vault cash, and currency held by the nonbank public. The source base is considered an important quantity because:

1. The magnitude of B^a, given the portfolio decisions of the banks and the public, determines the size of the stocks of money and bank credit;
2. Empirical evidence shows that changes in the amount of base money supplied to the public and banks have been, on average, the major cause of changes in the stocks of money and bank credit; and
3. From the sources side, the amount of base money supplied is under the complete control of the Federal Reserve.[4]

The monetary base and the multipliers jointly determine the supply of money and bank credit. Given the stock of base money, the value of the money multiplier (m) determines the outstanding money stock. Likewise, the value of the bank credit multiplier (a) determines the amount of bank credit that will be supported by a given stock of base money. For example, if the value of m is 2.5, then each dollar of base money supports $2.50 of currency and demand deposits held by the public. Given a one dollar change in the stock of base money, and assuming the change in base money does not alter the equilibrium value of m, the result will be a change of $2.50 in the stock of money held by the public.

The numerical values of the money and bank credit multipliers are determined by:

1. Policy actions of the Federal Reserve System. The policy parameters that enter into the determination of the values of the multipliers are: (a) legal reserve requirements on member bank demand and time deposits; (b) the discount rate and administration of the

[4]This does not mean that the Federal Reserve determines Treasury cash policy or that the Federal Reserve determines the surplus or deficit in the balance of payments. It means that, through open market operations, the Federal Reserve can offset any movements in Treasury cash policy and inflows or outflows of gold. Also, this does not mean the Federal Reserve will

choose to offset changes in either of these factors affecting the supply of base money. However, by open market purchase and sale of government securities the Federal Reserve has the power, if it wishes to exercise that power, to determine the magnitude of base money supplied to the economy.

discount window; and (c) Regulation Q interest rate ceilings.

2. Portfolio decisions by the public. Among these decisions are: (a) the decision of the public as to its desired allocation of bank deposits between demand and time deposits; (b) the decision of the public as to its desired allocation of money balances between bank money and currency, and (c) the public's desired allocation of bank deposits between member and non-member banks.

3. Portfolio decisions by the banks. For example, (a) the banks' desired holdings of excess reserves relative to deposit liabilities, and (b) the amount of member bank borrowing from the Federal Reserve given the discount rate.

4. Treasury policy as to holding of deposits at the commercial banks versus at the Federal Reserve.

Exact forms of the multipliers are given in footnote 5 below.

In this multiplier-base framework, Federal Reserve policy actions have two major effects. First, through its open market operations the Federal Reserve can determine the amount of base money. Secondly,

by changing the other policy parameters under its control the Federal Reserve can influence the amount of money or bank credit a given stock of base money will support.

THE IMPACT OF OPEN MARKET OPERATIONS. Federal Reserve holdings of Government securities is the component of the adjusted monetary source base that is under the direct, day-to-day control of the Federal Reserve System. The Federal Reserve does not dictate the administration of the Treasury General Fund. Gold movements reflect principally past movements in the balance of payments, and nonseasonal changes in the level of float reflect mainly such things as weather conditions and transportation disruptions.

To measure the impact of Federal Reserve open market operations on the monetary aggregates, it is not sufficient simply to discuss changes in the System's holdings of Government securities, as shown in Table 4.[6] To the extent that the System's open market operations only offset other factors, such as gold flows, float, and Treasury actions, and no change occurs in the amount of base money, no net expansionary or contractionary effect is transmitted to the monetary aggregates and bank credit.[7]

For example, in June 1966 Federal Reserve holdings of Government securities rose by $543 million, but adjusted mone-

---

[5]The money multiplier in its explicit form is:

$$m = \frac{1 + k}{(r-b)(1+t+d)+k}$$

The total bank credit multiplier in explicit form is:

$$a = \frac{(1+t+d)[1+n-(r-b)]}{(r-b)(1+t+d)+k}$$

where:

$$k = \frac{\text{currency held by the public}}{\text{demand deposits held by the public}}$$

$$t = \frac{\text{time deposits}}{\text{demand deposits held by the public}}$$

$$b = \frac{\text{member bank borrowing}}{\text{total bank deposits}}$$

$$r = \frac{\text{total bank reserves}}{\text{total bank deposits}}$$

$$d = \frac{\text{Treasury deposits at commercial banks}}{\text{demand deposits of the public}}$$

$$n = \frac{\text{capital accounts}}{\text{total bank deposits}}$$

The k, t, b, r, and n ratios reflect behavioral responses of the banks and the public to (1) economic factors; and (2) the policy parameters, legal reserve requirement ratios, discount rate, and Regulation Q, which are determined by the Federal Reserve System. The d-ratio reflects mainly actions by the Treasury.

[6]See "An Explanation of Federal Reserve Actions (1933–68)" by Michael Keran and Christopher Babb, this *Review*, July 1969.

[7]To the extent that open market operations affect market interest rates, and these open-market-induced changes in interest rates affect the multiplier, then open market operations affect the monetary aggregates.

TABLE 4
Monthly Changes in the Adjusted Monetary
Source Base and Federal Reserve
Holdings of Government Securities*
(millions of dollars)

	Adjusted Monetary Source Base	Federal Reserve Holdings of Government Securities
1965		
January	− 20	−442
February	260	368
March	190	263
April	210	322
May	200	474
June	210	729
July	270	409
August	250	69
September ..	160	−210
October	510	493
November ..	260	527
December ...	540	757
1966		
January	100	−259
February	250	9
March	80	−237
April	480	231
May	220	500
June	50	543
July	600	549
August	60	59
September ..	430	455
October	140	102
November ..	210	510
December ...	380	413

*Not seasonally adjusted

tary base increased by only $50 million. Although on balance the System made quite large purchases, expansion of the adjusted source base was only slightly greater than the normal seasonal increase. Hence the *net* expansionary influence of open market operations in June was quite small.

In contrast, in July 1966 the Federal Reserve purchased the same amount of Government securities as in June. However, the increase in the source base in July was 12 times as great as the increase in June. Looking at the $600 million increase in the source base in July, we would assert that the System's open market operations had a very expansionary *net* effect on the monetary aggregates.

ANALYSIS OF MOVEMENTS IN MONEY. A complete analysis of the movements observed in the money supply and bank credit involves not only the analysis of movements in the base, but also changes in money and bank credit resulting from changes in the multipliers.

To analyze the behavior of money and bank credit, we divide the change in each one of these aggregates into two major components: the percentage change resulting from the change in base money, and the percentage change due to the change in the multiplier.[8]

Looking at Table 5 we see that the expansion of M over the last part of 1965

[8]To partition the effects on money and bank credit of changes in the base and changes in the multpiliers, the following expressions were used:

$$\frac{M_t - M_{t-1}}{M_{t-1}} \cdot 100 =$$

$$\frac{m_{t-1}(B^a_t - B^a_{t-1})}{M_{t-1}} \cdot 100$$

$$+ \frac{B^a_{t-1}(m_t - m_{t-1})}{M_{t-1}}) \cdot 100$$

$$+ \frac{(B^a_t - B^a_{t-1})(m_t - m_{t-1})}{M_{t-1}} \cdot 100$$

For example, the percentage change in money in February,

$$(\frac{M_t - M_{t-1}}{M_{t-1}}) \cdot 100$$

is found by letting

M_{t-1} = money stock in January
B^a_{t-1} = adjusted monetary source base in January
M_t = money stock in February
B^a_t = adjusted monetary source base in February

$$\frac{m_{t-1}(B^a_t - B^a_{t-1})}{M_{t-1}} \cdot 100$$

= the percentage change in money in period t resulting from the change in B^a in period t assuming no change in the multiplier.

$$\frac{B^a_{t-1}(m_t - m_{t-1})}{M_{t-1}} \cdot 100$$

= the percentage change in money in period t resulting from the change in the multiplier in period t assuming no change in B^a.

TABLE 5

Major Components of Monthly Percentage Changes in Money*

	Change in Money (M)	Change in Money Resulting From Change in:	
		Monetary Base (B^a)	Multiplier (m)
1965			
January	.19%	−.04%	.22%
February	.25	.46	−.21
March	.12	.34	−.21
April	.31	.37	−.06
May	.12	.35	−.23
June	.50	.37	.13
July	.43	.47	−.04
August	.49	.43	.06
September	.49	.28	.21
October	.73	.88	−.15
November	.30	.44	−.14
December	.66	.92	−.25
1966			
January	.66	.17	.49
February	.42	.42	−0−
March	.35	.13	.22
April	.65	.80	−.15
May	−0−	.37	−.36
June	.12	.08	.04
July	−.35	.99	−1.33
August	.06	.10	−.04
September	.29	.70	−.41
October	−.17	.23	−.40
November	−0−	.34	−.34
December	.12	.61	−.49

*Columns two and three may not add exactly to column one because of the cross product term.

was wholly a base phenomenon. The multiplier acting alone *decreased* the stock of M in the last three months of 1965. However, an expansionary open market policy resulting in an increase in the stock of base money more than off-set the multiplier, and the money stock showed a marked increase.

During the first quarter of 1966 the effect of open market operations was much less expansionary. The base increased at only a 3 percent annual rate, much reduced from the 7 percent rate over the last half of 1965. Consequently, the impulse transmitted to money and bank credit by open market actions was considerably reduced.

In the first four months of 1966, the money stock continued to increase. How-

ever, in the first three months of this period the increase in M was largely a multiplier phenomenon. Although the stock of base money was increasing at a slower rate, it supported a larger stock of publicly held money balances than previously, due to the rise in the multiplier. Almost one-half of the percentage change in M was accounted for by an increase in the multiplier. The major cause of this increase was a reduction in the desired reserve ratio. As the banks adjusted to the large increase in base money occurring in the last half of 1965, and in response to the higher yields on business loans, banks reduced their desired reserve-to-deposit ratio, and this was reflected in a rise in the stock of bank money. April shows a sharp percentage increase in M, but this is entirely explained by a very large increase in the supply of base money. After April the rapid expansion of the money stock came to an abrupt halt.[9]

During the first three months of 1966 the banks and the public apparently were still reacting to the rapid increase in base money that occurred in the last part of 1965. As the increased stock of base money was absorbed into the asset portfolios of the banks and the public, the growth rate of M slowed. By April the increase in the money multiplier had stopped.

ANALYSIS OF MOVEMENTS IN BANK CREDIT. Referring to Table 5, we see that the increase in bank credit over the last part of 1965 was also primarily attributable to the growth of the monetary base. During the first quarter of 1966 the growth rate of base money slowed, but bank credit continued to expand at a rapid rate. As was the case with M, the increase in bank credit during the first three months of 1966 was not solely a base-dominated phenomenon. The rise in the bank credit multiplier (a) accounted for almost half of the increase in bank credit.

In contrast to the money multiplier, the bank credit multiplier continued to increase after March, contributing significantly to the percentage increase in bank credit from March through June. In the May through June period the percentage increase in bank credit was dominated by the increase in the bank credit multiplier.

The increase in (a) over the first part of 1966, and its continued increase after the money multiplier stopped rising, can be largely explained by the success of commercial banks in acquiring time deposits, which raised the t-ratio. The t-ratio (the ratio of time deposits to demand deposits of the public) is of crucial importance when analyzing the movements of monetary aggregates and bank credit. It is important because, other factors constant, changes in the t-ratio are accompanied by changes in opposite directions of money and bank credit. An increase in the t-ratio lowers the value of the multiplier associated with the money stock and raises the value of the multiplier associated with bank credit. In other words, a decision by the public to hold a larger portion of their bank deposits in the form of time deposits increases the amount of bank credit a given stock of base money can support and decreases the size of the money stock a given amount of base money can support.

Over the last three months of 1965 the t-ratio average 1.1184, compared to an average of 1.0396 over the first three months of 1965. In the first three months of 1966, the t-ratio continued to increase, rising to an average of 1.1264. The t-ratio then rose very sharply over the next three months, reaching an average of 1.1508 over this period.

Given that the Board of Governors raised Q ceiling rates in December, and given the increasing profitability of business loans for banks, the longer lag in adjustment of bank credit is not surprising. As long as banks could acquire funds via time deposits, and as long as the marginal cost of these funds remained less than the marginal revenue from business loans, banks could be expected to continue to bid aggressively for time deposits.

Over the four months from April through July, the banks were using what

---

[9]The marked percentage change in money (−1.33 percent) resulting from the multiplier acting alone in July reflected changes in several components: a sharp rise in the ratio of time to demand deposits (t); an increase in the reserve ratio (r) resulting from the July increase in reserve requirements on time deposits; a marked increase in the currency ratio (k); and a rise in the ratio of Government deposits to demand deposits of the public (d). The percentage changes in the multiplier from June to July resulting from the change in each of these components are as follows:

t .... −.411   k .... −.504
r .... −.376   d .... −.234

TABLE 6

Major Components of Monthly
Percentage Changes in Bank Credit

| | Change in Bank Credit | Change in Bank Credit Resulting From Change in: | |
		Monetary Base (Bᵃ)	Multiplier (ᵃ)
1965			
January	.67%	−.04%	.71%
February	.86	.46	.39
March	.92	.34	.58
April	.99	.37	.61
May	.43	.35	.08
June	.46	.37	.10
July	.61	.47	.13
August	.78	.43	.34
September	.56	.28	.28
October	1.29	.88	.41
November	.55	.44	.11
December	.89	.92	−.03
1966			
January	.51	.17	.34
February	.61	.42	.19
March	.34	.13	.20
April	1.11	.80	.30
May	.63	.37	.23
June	.36	.08	.27
July	.99	.99	−0−
August	−.13	.10	−.23
September	.55	.70	−.15
October	−.32	.23	−.55
November	−0−	.34	−.34
December	.55	.61	−.07

might be called "the financial slack in the economy" to expand their flow of credit to the business sector. This was accomplished primarily through time deposits.[10] By raising their rates on time deposits, banks induced the public to markedly increase its desired ratio of time-to-demand deposits (t-ratio). The purchase of banks' debt obligations (time deposits) by the public with bank money "freed" reserves from required reserves and permitted banks to expand their flow of credit to business. A crude calculation of the effect of the increasing t-ratio on the supply of bank credit indicates that

$3 to $4 billion of the $9.3 billion increase in bank credit from March through July was due to the increase in the time deposits relative to demand deposits.[11]

The bank credit multiplier remained constant in July, and the large increase in bank credit reflected solely the very large increase in base money resulting from the Federal Reserve's open market actions. Although the t-ratio rose sharply in July, by itself increasing the bank credit multiplier, this was offset primarily by a marked rise in the reserve ratio.

[10]To an extent this was also accomplished by banks reducing their ratio of excess reserves to deposits and liquidating Government securities (see the following section).

[11]This estimate is made by recalculating the total bank credit multiplier for July, substituting the t-ratio value for March. This new value for the multiplier is then multiplied by Bᵃ for July and the new value for bank credit is compared to the actual value for bank credit.

The rise in the reserve ratio reflected the increase in reserve requirements on time deposits which went into effect in the last part of July. By raising reserve requirements, the Federal Reserve reduced the amount of bank credit a given stock of base money would support. However, at the same time, the Federal Reserve, through open market purchases, permitted the stock of base money to rise by $600 million, thus offsetting the contractionary effect on bank credit of the higher reserve requirements.

In August we observed a marked reversal of the impact of open market operations on the monetary aggregates. The system purchased net only $60 million of securities compared to $550 million in July. Most importantly, this reversal in open market actions resulted in virtually no change in the stock of base money in August. Therefore, open market policy became much more restrictive in August than it had been over the previous four months.

ACTIONS AND REACTIONS BY COMMERCIAL BANKS: FIRST EIGHT MONTHS OF 1966

This section first presents a historical development of the banks' portfolios as they existed in early 1966. Next, portfolio adjustments by the banks in the months leading up to the Credit Crunch are discussed. The impact of Regulation Q on the banks and consequently on the money supply and bank credit processes is discussed. Finally a discussion of the banks' portfolio reactions in August, the month of the Crunch, is presented.

A Historical Development of the Banks' Portfolio Positions in 1966

To understand the development of the Credit Crunch in August 1966, it is useful to review briefly the historical development of two closely related phenomena. The first of these is the increased use by commercial banks of negotiable time certificates of deposit as a means of acquiring deposits. The second is the growth of state and local government obligations (municipals) as a component of the commercial banks' asset portfolios.

NEGOTIABLE CD's. Until the late Fifties commercial banks did not bid actively for time deposits. In the early Sixties large commercial banks, faced with rising loan-deposit ratios and the possible loss of deposits of business firms to other higher-yielding market assets, began actively to seek deposits by issuing large CD's. This action by the banks marked a significant change in banking practice. The banks began to compete for funds in the most interest-rate-sensitive sector of the money market. CD's were in competition with such interest-rate-sensitive assets as Treasury bills and commercial paper. Also, the attitude developed among some banks that CD's could be used as an avenue to borrow funds whenever attractive investment opportunities appeared.

From 1960 through mid-1966 large commercial banks increasingly relied on CD's, especially large denomination negotiable CD's, as a means of attracting deposits. Time deposits, acquired by issuance of large denomination CD's, accounted for 40 percent of the increase in time and savings accounts at weekly reporting member banks from 1961 to the end of 1965. Total outstanding CD's in denominations of $100,000 or more at member banks rose from $2.9 billion on December 30, 1961 to $17.7 billion on May 18, 1966, and the number of member banks issuing large CD's rose from 232 to 632.[12]

As commercial banks sought to issue an increased volume of CD's in an environment of generally rising market interest rates, the cost to the banks of acquiring these funds rose. After remaining at

---

[12]Parker B. Willis, *The Secondary Market for Negotiable Certificates of Deposit*, Board of Governors of the Federal Reserve System, 1967.

around 2.5 percent through the middle of 1963, the new issue rate on CD's rose steadily, reaching an average of 4.07 percent in the last quarter of 1964 and then increased to an average of 4.58 percent in the fourth quarter of 1965. After the increase in Regulation Q ceilings in December 1965, yields offered by banks rose sharply, reaching the Regulation Q ceiling of 5½ percent in the third quarter of 1966.

The rising cost of acquiring deposits by bidding in competition with other short-term money market instruments meant that the banks had to begin to acquire assets with yields high enough to cover this increased cost. Over the 1961 through mid-1965 period the rate on bank short-term business loans remained very stable at around 5 percent. The prime rate, which represents a minimum rate on somewhat longer-term business loans, was set at 4.5 percent by commercial banks in August 1960 and remained at this level until December 6, 1965. Given supply and demand conditions for bank credit by the business sector until mid-1965, commercial banks were unable to employ funds acquired from CD's at higher yields in short-term loans to business.

BANKS' MUNICIPAL PORTFOLIOS EXPAND. Commercial banks, looking for higher yielding assets in the Sixties, increased sharply their acquisition of tax-exempt municipal securities. Prior to the Sixties commercial banks had not held a large portion of newly issued municipals. In 1960 commercial banks had about 7½ cents of every deposit dollar invested in municipals. By mid-1965 banks' municipal portfolios accounted for almost 12 cents of every deposit dollar. From 1961 through mid-1965 commercial banks put 23 cents of each new deposit dollar into municipal securities, an amount large enough to purchase over 50 percent of the net volume of municipals issued annually.[13]

The average maturity of municipals held by commercial banks lengthened noticeably from 1961 through 1965. For all national banks in 1965, 51.5 percent of their total portfolio of municipals had a maturity of 5 years or longer; and 25.5 percent of their portfolio of municipals was over 10 years to maturity. For large commercial banks the figures were even higher, at 54.7 percent and 33 percent, respectively.[14]

As we shall see later in this section, the increased reliance by commercial banks on the interest-sensitive certificate of deposit as a means of attracting funds, together with the increased portion of commercial bank portfolios in long-term municipal securities, had important implications for the developments occurring in the money and capital markets in August 1966.

Bank Portfolio Adjustments in 1966

HIGHER-YIELDING BUSINESS LOANS INCREASE. During the first eight months of 1966 the commercial banking system faced heavy borrowing demands from the business sector. Over this period the rates on bank business loans rose sharply. The interest rate charged by large commercial banks on short-term business loans rose from 5.27 percent to 6.30 percent. The prime rate—the interest rate at which commercial banks extend business loans to their highest-grade business customers —was raised by the banks in December 1965 from 4½ percent to 5 percent. This was the first increase in the prime rate since August 1960. During the first eight months of 1966 the prime rate was raised three more times: on March 10 to 5½ percent; on June 29 to 5¾ percent; and on August 16 to 6 percent—at that time the highest prime rate in over 30 years.

Even with sharply rising interest rates, the demand for bank credit by the business sector remained strong. Commercial

[13]Jack C. Rothwell, "The Move to Municipals." *Business Review*, Federal Reserve Bank of Philadelphia, September 1966, p. 3.

[14]Rothwell, p. 7.

FIGURE 2
Commercial Bank Rates on Short-Term Business Loans

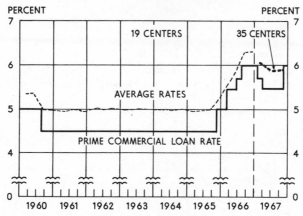

Note: Average rates on short-term business loans plotted in two segments to emphasize the increase in sample size to 35 financial centers in February 1967 (see Federal Reserve Bulletin, May 1967, page 721–27).

banks rapidly expanded their business loans as yields on these loans rose. Over the first seven months of 1966 commercial and industrial loans by large commercial banks increased $6.3 billion, or by 12 percent.

LOWER-YIELDING ASSETS DECLINE. To take advantage of the rising yields on business loans, commercial banks restructured their asset portfolios. During the first half of 1966, banks switched from lower-yielding securities to higher-yielding business loans. As can be seen from Table 7, this resulted in a sharp reduction in banks' holdings of Government securities, primarily Treasury bills. From the end of December 1965 through June 1966 commercial banks reduced their

holdings of Government securities by $6 billion.

This restructuring of the banks' asset portfolios reduced their liquidity. Government securities as a percent of banks' deposit liabilities decreased noticeably and steadily from early 1965 through the first seven months of 1966. This trend prevailed not only for the so-called money market banks, but for all banks. Also, over the period 1965 through July of 1966, banks reduced their ratio of excess reserves to deposit liabilities. This ratio was on average about 20 percent less in the period January through July of 1966 than in 1964.

CD'S AS A SOURCE OF FUNDS. Large commercial banks, which specialized in

TABLE 7
Selected Assets—All Insured Banks
(millions of dollars)

	December 31, 1965	June 30, 1966	Annual Rates of Change
Commercial and			
Industrial Loans	70,887	76,725	17.1
Total U.S. Government			
Securities	59,120	53,111	−19.3
(Bills and Certificates)	(13,134)	(9,174)	(−51.2)
Municipals	38,419	40,368	10.4

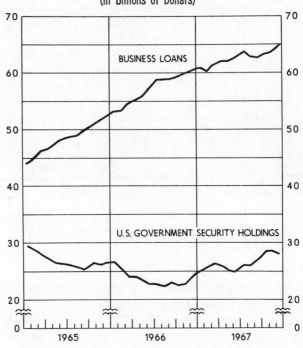

FIGURE 3
Selected Asset Items Large Commercial Banks
(in Billions of Dollars)

Monthly averages of Wednesday figures. Data for first half of
1965 are partially estimated.
Sources: Board of Governors of the Federal Reserve System and
Federal Reserve Bank of St. Louis.

business loans, relied heavily on the issuance of certificates of deposit as a source of funds in the first seven months of 1966. Individual commercial banks competed aggressively for funds by raising the rates paid on certificates of deposit to the Regulation Q maximum of 5½ percent. From the first week in January to the end of June 1966 large commercial banks increased their large denomination CD's outstanding by $2 billion.

Large commercial banks, restricted under Regulation Q to a maximum rate of 4 percent on passbook savings, began in early 1966 to compete aggressively for household savings by issuing small denomination non-negotiable certificates of deposit. By issuing these small denomination CD's, banks were able to compete directly with assets offered savers by other financial institutions.[15] In a survey of member banks covering the period December 1965 to May 1966, the Federal Reserve found that commercial banks with total deposits of $500 million and over increased their consumer-type time deposits by $3 billion.[16] As the spread between interest rates paid on passbook savings and non-negotiable CD's widened, the increase in consumer-type CD's was partially offset by a decline of $1.8 bil-

---

[15]Some large commercial banks began issuing consumer-type CD's in the form of 5-year discount bonds. Some of these CD's could be purchased in $25 multiples at prices below $20 and could be cashed-in 90 days after purchase, on any 90-day anniversary thereafter, or between 90-day periods with written notice.

[16]"Changes in Time and Savings Deposits: December 1965–May 1966," *Federal Reserve Bulletin*, August 1966.

FIGURE 4
Security Yields

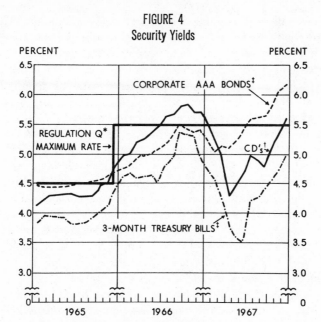

*Rate on deposits in amounts of $100,000 or more maturing in
90–179 days.
†Secondary market yields on negotiable certificates of deposits;
averages of weekly rates during the month.
‡Monthly averages of daily figures.
Sources: Board of Governors of the Federal Reserve System and
Solomon Brothers and Hutzler.

lion in passbook-type savings deposits at these banks.[17]

All of these factors operated to reduce the liquidity of the banks. The banks were not passively accommodating the demand for credit, but were responding in a manner that economic theory would predict of any profit-maximizing economic unit. As the rate of return on business loans rose relative to the rate of return on other assets, banks restructured their asset portfolios to contain more of the higher-yielding business loans.

THE EFFECTS OF REGULATION Q. Commercial banks are free to raise the yield they offer on CD's only up to ceiling

rates set by the Federal Reserve System with Regulation Q. In contrast, yields on competitive assets such as Treasury bills and commercial paper are not restricted by any artificial ceiling rate, but are determined by free market forces of supply and demand. Therefore, when short-term market interest rates rise above the Regulation Q ceiling rates on time deposits, commercial banks find their ability to attract and hold such deposits determined not by their willingness to pay the market price for funds in a free market, but dependent upon the willingness of the Federal Reserve Board to raise the Regulation Q ceiling rates.

In three previous periods in the Sixties, July 1963, November 1964, and December 1965, when the secondary market interest rate on outstanding certificates of deposit issued by commercial banks moved above the Regulation Q limit on newly issued CD's, the Federal Reserve System raised the Regulation Q ceiling.

---

[17]Large commercial banks appear to have taken the lead in competing for consumer-type deposits. In May 1966, of the member banks surveyed, 61 percent of the banks with deposits of $100 million or over were paying above 4.50 percent on consumer-type time deposits, while only 14 percent of the banks with deposits below $100 million were paying above 4.50 percent.

This policy action allowed commercial banks, by offering yields on time deposits competitive with other available market assets, to compete effectively with other borrowers.

However, when the market rate on outstanding CD's moved above the Regulation Q ceiling in the summer of 1966, the Federal Reserve System refused to raise Regulation Q ceilings. One factor influencing this decision was the pressure from the House Banking and Currency Committee to restrain commercial banks' competition with savings and loans and mutual savings banks for savings. In July 1966, in order to further restrict commercial banks in their attempt to attract consumer time deposits, the Federal Reserve lowered the maximum interest rate payable on multiple maturity time deposits from 5½ to 5 percent on 90-day or more multiple maturities and from 5½ to 4 percent on multiple maturities of less than 90 days.

In the first week of July, the secondary market rate on outstanding negotiable CD's rose above the maximum rate of 5½ percent on new issues. After early July, with CD's selling at a discount in the market, large commercial banks found it increasingly difficult to attract and hold these funds. New York banks were able to increase their outstanding CD's by only $46 million in July.

With the market yield on CD's rising above the ceiling rate on new issue CD's, and the Board of Governors refusing to raise Regulation Q ceilings and increasing reserve requirements on certain classes of time deposits, banks now realized they could no longer rely on time deposits to acquire funds to expand their flow of credit to the business sector. Further, the banks now expected a reversal of the flow of time deposits.

In August over $3.7 billion of outstanding negotiable certificates of deposit matured at large commercial banks, and $6.7 billion in negotiable CD's were scheduled to mature in the September–October period. By middle and late August there were expectations of a large loan demand converging on the commercial banking system just as the expected heavy runoff of certificates of deposit occurred. Large offerings of Treasury tax-anticipation bills were expected in late August, and the expected sale of Federal National Mortgage Association participation certificates and other Federal agency financings were slated to add to an already heavy schedule of new corporate and municipal offerings. There were growing fears in the capital and money markets that the major suppliers of funds would be unwilling to continue to supply funds at currently existing interest rates.

Hopes for a tax increase to halt inflationary pressures had faded in August. The feeling spread in the financial markets that the Federal Government did not or would not recognize the pressures its operations were placing on these markets. The conviction spread that the major burden of economic restraint would fall on monetary policy.[18]

Banks' Reactions in August

Banks had never before experienced a large outflow of time deposits. The expectations of a runoff of CD's and the uncertainty about the magnitude of the outflow and its effects on their operations led individual banks to desire to increase their liquidity, by acquiring a larger portion of the existing stock of reserves to meet the expected increase in required reserves as time deposits decreased and demand deposits increased. To continue to expand business loans while simultaneously building up their reserves, the in-

---

[18]On August 25, 1966, the Wall Street Journal reported that J. Dewey Daane, a member of the Board of Governors, had stated that if monetary policy was going to have to carry all the burden of fighting inflation, a further rise in interest rates was inevitable. He asserted that he believed such further increases in interest rates were coming.

dividual banks attempted to restructure their portfolios.

Over a period of time, if an individual bank wants to increase the liquidity of its portfolio, the three main ways it may accomplish this are:

1. Member banks may attempt to borrow from the Federal Reserve banks via the discount window;
2. Commercial banks may borrow short-term funds in the Federal funds market; or
3. A commercial bank may sell part of its investment assets and/or reduce its volume of loans.

Methods (1) and (2) are essentially short-term in nature. They are designed to permit commercial banks time to restructure their portfolios via method (3).

MEMBER BANK BORROWING. Federal funds and borrowings at Federal Reserve banks, to a large extent, may be viewed by individual member banks as alternative sources of short-term funds. The amount of member bank borrowing at the Federal Reserve discount window rose steadily from an average of $402 million in January to $722 million in May 1966. In June the rate on Federal funds passed 5 percent; in July most trading was at rates above 5.25 percent; and in August the rate moved above 5.5 percent wtih some trading occurring at the 6 percent level. However, after May, despite the sharply rising rates on Federal funds, and despite increasing demands by the banks for short-term funds (to permit them to adjust their portfolios to take advantage of the rising yields on business loans), member banks did not noticeably increase their borrowings at the Federal Reserve banks.

The question then arises why, in the summer of 1966, with the spread between the 4.5 percent discount rate and the market rate on Federal funds widening, there was no marked increase in the amount of member bank borrowings at the Federal Reserve banks.

This question can be answered largely by taking into consideration the Federal Reserve system's policy of discouraging continuous borrowing by any one member bank at the discount window, which tends to become progressively more restrictive as the aggregate level of member bank borrowing rises and remains at a higher level for an extended period. Although the Federal Reserve banks did not explicitly refuse credit to any member banks in 1966, there are strong indications that, as the level of member bank borrowing approached the $750–800 million range, rather than raising the cost of such borrowing to ration potential borrowers out of the market, the result of some Federal Reserve banks' tighter administration of the discount window was, in effect, to "close the window" to further increases in the level of member bank borrowing.[19]

Beginning in about June, the Federal Reserve banks may have used tighter administration of the discount window to force member banks to reduce their borrowings, or member banks may have felt that the Reserve banks would show great reluctance to extend additional accommodation. Also, some member banks may have decided to husband their "goodwill" at the discount window to meet expected future emergency cash demands.

BANKS LIQUIDATE MUNICIPALS. Since the banks had reduced their holdings of Government securities to near a minimum level, and believing that access to the discount window was limited, the banks in August attempted to adjust their reserve positions to increase their cash holdings by selling municipal securities. To do so, they had to induce other economic units to restructure their asset portfolios.

In the terminology of the financial com-

---

[19]Borrowing at the Federal Reserve Banks is a privilege which may be extended by a Reserve Bank to member banks in its district. It is not a right of member banks to demand accommodation. To a significant degree, each district Reserve Bank sets its own policies on lending to member banks.

munity, the market for municipal bonds could be described as much "thinner" than the market for Government securities. Within the bond markets a small number of specialists in the buying and replacement of securities, called dealers, perform an important function. These dealers broaden and add depth to the bond market by standing ready to buy and sell debt obligations of the Federal government, state and local governments, and corporations, and facilitate shifting these assets to other individuals or institutions. Hence, their operations tend to increase the liquidity of these assets. Dealers rely heavily on borrowed funds to finance their positions (holdings) in these securities; they are heavily dependent on commercial banks for their financing requirements, especially their residual financing.

Dealers are especially sensitive to changes in monetary conditions because of the special characteristics of their business. During periods when interest rates are falling, dealers are able to anticipate that if they buy securities, they can distribute these securities at a higher price as interest rates fall. Inspired by the profit motive, dealers actively add to their holdings and increase their participation in the securities market when rates are falling.

In periods of rising interest rates, dealers may find that they are unable to distribute their security holdings at prices above what they paid. Also, they find that the cost of borrowing funds to carry their positions rises. When dealers expect market interest rates to rise, they attempt to reduce their positions and engage less actively or withdraw from participation in the securities market. For those dealers who remain in the market, the residual financing function of the commercial banks becomes extremely important.

Commercial bank loans to dealers are viewed by the individual banks as a source of liquidity. Such loans are callable at the discretion of the lending bank.

Also, for the banks the cost of reducing dealer loans is less than reduced lending to business customers. During the summer of 1966 as the yields on business loans increased, commercial banks, especially New York banks, sharply increased their lending rate to dealers. The lending rate of New York banks to dealers in Government securities rose from a range of 5¼ to 5¾ percent for renewals and new loans in the first week of June to ranges of 6 to 6½ percent at the end of July. The lending rate to dealers then rose to 6⅜ to 6⅝ percent in mid-August.

Dealers responded to the sharply rising level of credit market interest rates and the increased cost of borrowing funds to carry their positions by (1) reducing their borrowing from banks, and (2) sharply reducing their participation in the bond market. From a high of $4.5 billion on July 6, loans by large banks to dealers and brokers for purchasing or carrying securities fell to $3.8 billion by the first of August, then fell by an additional $0.4 billion during the next three weeks. Dealers' positions in Government securities decreased from an average daily level of $3.6 billion over the first eight months of 1965 to an average daily position of $2.1 billion over the first eight months of 1966. In the July to August period of 1966, dealers' holdings of Governments was only half as large as in the same period of 1965. Dealers also attempted to shorten the maturity of their holdings. Government securities due within one year as a percent of total dealer positions in Goverments rose to 92.7 percent in the July–August period of 1966, compared to 82.5 percent in the same period of 1965.

After the middle of August, with banks attempting to reduce their holdings of municipal securities, with other principal purchasers of municipals themselves faced with large expected cash demands, and with dealers in the securities attempting to reduce their own positions, price quotations for those securities became almost nominal. Only a few dealers were willing to buy municipal bonds in the secondary market. Commercial banks found they could shift their holdings of municipals to other economic units only at sharply lower prices. Thus, banks found they could buy the liquidity they desired only at a rapidly rising cost.

BUSINESS LOANS.   Commercial banks maintained a high level of business loans in the early summer of 1966. After totalling $56.4 billion at the start of June, business loans by large commercial banks rose $2.3 billion by the first week of July.

Over the last part of July and in early August, credit market interest rates rose sharply, reinforcing the expectations by banks of significant run-offs in time deposits. There was no reduction in the business sector's demand for credit. Expecting high interest rates in the future and worried about the future "availability of credit," corporations, relative to past periods, placed record demands for credit. The banks reacted to the continued demand for business loans, the impact of Regulation Q, and the tighter monetary policy by attempting to reduce their holdings of municipals. A classic liquidity crisis in the municipal bond market resulted.

Compared to July no large increase in base money occurred in August. The drastic reversal of the impact of open market operations on the growth of base money and the full impact of higher reserve requirements on time deposits had a decided contractionary effect on the bank credit process. The statements of Federal Reserve officials indicated to the banks that the intent of policy was to maintain monetary restraint.

With all other avenues of adjustment exhausted, the banks reduced their lending to the business sector. Between the reporting dates of August 3 and August 17, large commercial banks reduced their business loans by $65 million. In the last half of August, banks decreased their flow of credit to the business sector at a much more rapid pace. In this period

large commercial banks' holdings of business loans fell by $668 million. As the commercial banks reduced their lending to the business sector, cries from the business sector, not only about the cost of funds but the actual availability of funds, were added to the cries of disorder and fears of a possible panic emanating from the financial markets.

SUMMARY AND CONCLUSIONS

The impact of Federal Reserve actions, through open market operations and reserve requirement policy became much more restrictive in July through August 1966, the period of the so-called "Credit Crunch." These actions took place within an economic environment much different from recent prior periods. This article has discussed and analyzed the effect of this changed economic environment on the money supply and bank credit processes. It was pointed out that in 1966, relative to previous periods in the current expansion:

1. The credit markets were faced with exceptionally large credit demands from the business sector and the Federal agencies;
2. The business sector increased its use of commercial banks as a major source of credit;
3. To take advantage of the profitable opportunities offered by rising rates on business loans, banks reduced their liquidity positions by decreasing their holdings of Government securities and excess reserves; and
4. For the first time, commercial banks faced a situation where Regulation Q ceiling rates severely restricted their ability to bid for time deposits.

Money and bank credit during early 1966 continued to expand at the very rapid rates prevailing in the last half of 1965. This expansion reflected increases in their respective multipliers which more than offset a reduction in the rate at which the monetary base was supplied by the Federal Reserve. After April, money remained about unchanged to the end of the year, as a result of a decrease in the money multiplier, which more than offset a resumption in April of growth in the monetary base at its late 1965 rate. Bank credit, however, expanded through July at an 8 percent rate, then slowed markedly to late 1966.

The Federal Reserve should not have been surprised that money and bank credit continued to expand through the first quarter of 1966, even though there was a desire to exert a restraining influence on total demand. The rapid expansion of base money in the last half of 1965, and the sharply rising yields on business loans reflecting strong demands by the business sector for bank credit, caused money and bank credit to rise rapidly in early 1966. An increase in the stock of base money must be absorbed into the asset portfolios of the banks and the public, and such an adjustment is not an instantaneous process. In early 1966, as this adjustment process proceeded (reflected in a rise in the money and bank credit multipliers), market interest rates and prices increased, and the stocks of money and bank credit expanded .

In the first seven months of 1966 the individual commercial banks behaved in a manner that economic theory would predict for any rationally behaving profit-maximizing economic unit. As the yields on business loans increased, the banks used every avenue available to expand their holdings of these high-yielding assets. With the opportunity cost of liquid assets rising, banks responded by reducing their holdings of lower yielding liquid assets—Government securities, excess reserves, and dealer loans.

The continued increase in bank credit after the money stock ceased to expand can be largely explained by the success of banks in acquiring time deposits. An increase in the ratio of time deposits to demand deposits increases the bank credit

multiplier but decreases the money multiplier. With rising yields available on business loans, banks bid aggressively for time deposit funds to meet business demands for credit. Operating on past experience, banks did not expect that the Federal Reserve would permit Regulation Q ceiling rates to prevent them from bidding competitively for time deposits.

In July policy actions by the Federal Reserve began to exercise a much more restrictive effect on the commercial banks. The refusal of the Federal Reserve to raise Q ceilings as credit market interest rates rose restricted the ability of banks to compete for time deposits. In late July the increase in reserve requirements on time deposits exercised a further restrictive effect on the bank credit process. The Federal Reserve, by its open market actions, offset most of the contractionary effect of these two policy actions. In July the stock of base money rose by $600 million.

Given the large increase in base money in July, the Federal Reserve should also not have been surprised at the large rise in bank credit in that month. Rather, given the upward trend in the bank credit multiplier over the previous months, the central bank should have been warned by the fact that the increase in bank credit was not much greater and by the fact that the money stock showed no change.

In August the marked reversal of the impact of open market operations on the growth of base money added a further restraining influence. The banks were forced to make a portfolio adjustment. This portfolio adjustment took the form of an attempt by banks to reduce their holdings of municipals. The result of this attempted portfolio adjustment was manifested in the credit crunch in August.

In a period of time in which the commercial banks are forced by monetary policy to restructure their asset portfolios, one would expect there to be "above average pressure" in the financial markets. That banks are forced to reduce their rate of production of bank money and reduce the credit they extend to the rest of the economy are the key elements of a tighter or more restrictive monetary policy. This is a necessary preliminary to the desired policy goals of reduced aggregate demand and hence a reduced rate of increase of prices.

In 1966 the intent of monetary policy was to slow the growth rate of aggregate demand and hence reduce the inflationary pressures building up in the U.S. economy. This goal was achieved in the first part of 1967, as increases in aggregate demand and prices slowed very markedly. This beneficial result was preceded by a severe but short-lived liquidity crisis in the money and capital markets in August 1966.

A historical analysis of the 1966 period suggests that by following a less drastic contractionary policy in August (permitting less of a decline in the stock of base money), and by following a more contractionary policy with respect to the growth rate of base money over the remaining months of 1966, the Federal Reserve could have achieved the desirable ultimate results of policy mentioned above. Also, more gradually restrictive policies would quite likely have prevented the severe wrenching of the money and capital markets that occurred in August. Such a policy, of course, would not have removed the necessity for banks to make adjustments in their portfolios. It would have permitted this adjustment to be spread over a longer period of time, thereby reducing the threat of near-panic selling, and allowing a smoother adjustment to a policy of monetary restraint.

SECTION TWO
New Directions in Asset, Liability, and Capital Management

Chapter IV
BACKGROUND

11. Theories of Cyclical Liquidity Management of Commercial Banks*

G. Walter Woodworth

The liquidity problem of financial institutions in general and commercial banks in particular is unique. Few if any industrial groups have as high a proportion of short-term liabilities; and only commercial banks have checking accounts or deposits which must be paid on demand. The providing of liquidity with minimum sacrifice in profitability has traditionally been viewed the basic task of "asset" management. In the 1960's however, emphasis shifted to "liability" management—that is, the providing of liquidity through equity sources or bank borrowing in short-term and long-term markets. This article analyzes the evolution and development of liquidity management theory and application in commercial banking from colonial days to the present.

Prior to the second World War, commercial banks often maintained excessive positions of cyclical liquidity. Since that time, however, the opposite error has been more common. Many commercial banks,

*From *National Banking Review*, June, 1967. Reprinted by permission of the publisher, Office of the Comptroller of the Currency.

finding themselves with large excess reserves during recessions, have reached for more current income by purchasing too many intermediate- and long-term bonds and too few liquidity (secondary) reserve assets. The penalty was paid during the last phase of all four succeeding cyclical-expansion periods when, in order to meet customer loan demands, investments were sold at substantial capital losses. These losses greatly exceeded the additional income from the longer-term as compared with shorter-term issues; consequently, net profits actually declined in most boom years even though net current earnings (before adjustments for capital gains and losses) recorded substantial increases.

It is the purpose of this paper to trace and analyze the various cyclical liquidity theories. Four different theories can be identified: (1) the commercial loan theory; (2) the shiftability theory; (3) the anticipated income theory; and (4) the liabilities management theory.

I. THE COMMERCIAL LOAN THEORY

The commercial loan theory had its origins in England during the 18th century,[1] and it prevailed in the United States until after the first World War. In fact, its philosophy permeated both the National Bank Act of 1864, as amended, and the Federal Reserve Act of 1913. In 1923, the Federal Reserve Board expounded a variant of this theory, called a "system of productive credit,"[2] which was widely accepted throughout the 1930's.

According to the commercial loan theory, earning assets of banks should consist principally of short-term, self-liquidating loans to business firms for working capital purposes; that is, loans to finance the movement of goods through the successive stages of production, transportation, storage, distribution, and into consumption. Loans for long-term purposes —to finance plant, equipment, permanent working capital, real estate, consumer durables, and speculation—were not regarded as appropriate for commercial banks. The logical basis for the doctrine was that bank deposits are demand or near-demand liabilities, and should therefore be committed to obligations that are self-liquidating within a short period in the normal course of business operations.

II. THE SHIFTABILITY THEORY

Soon after establishment of the Federal Reserve System, some economists challenged the traditional commercial loan theory. They called attention to the wide divergence of actual commercial bank assets from those that qualified as automatically self-liquidating in a short period of time. In 1917, B. M. Anderson analyzed bank assets and concluded, "that the great

bulk of banking credit in the United States, even of commercial banks, is not commercial credit. . . . Most of it, . . . represents advances to the permanent financing of corporate industry."[3] In another bank asset study in 1918, H. G. Moulton found that: "The statistics of all commercial banks show that something like 50 percent of all *loans* is devoted to investment uses; and that in the neighborhood of two-thirds of all the credit extended by commercial banks goes for fixed rather than working capital."[4]

The shiftability theory of bank liquidity, which Moulton originated, may be summarized as follows:

1. The greater part of business loans of banks supports permanent working capital and fixed capital needs. Such loans are not usually paid at maturity but are renewed to accommodate the customer. Only seasonal-type loans are paid at maturity, and the cash flow from them is not steady nor dependable, particularly in cyclical financial crises. ". . . the commercial paper of a bank's own customers is among the least reliable of all bank assets as a means of replenishing depleted reserves."[5]

2. Other loans of banks—largely secured by bonds, stocks, equipment, and real estate—represent principally fixed-capital financing, and do not provide an automatic cash inflow from maturities. However, loans secured by marketable stocks and bonds "are more reliable as a secondary reserve than commercial paper loans to customers."[6]

3. Recognizing the lack of liquidity of loans, banks in practice have long safeguarded their liquidity by other methods, principally by holding secondary reserves in the forms of open-market commercial

---

[1]See Adam Smith, *An Inquiry into the Nature and Causes of the Wealth of Nations*, Everyman's Library Edition, I, pp. 269, 272.

[2]See Federal Reserve Board, *Tenth Annual Report*, 1923, pp. 33–34.

[3]B. M. Anderson, Jr., *The Value of Money*, 1926 Ed., New York: The Macmillian Co., 1926, pp. 511–512.

[4]H. G. Moulton, "Commercial Banking and Capital Formation," *The Journal of Political Economy*, July 1918, p. 729.

[5]*Ibid.*, p. 709.

[6]*Ibid.*, p. 713.

paper and marketable notes and bonds which could be sold to replenish depleted reserves. ". . . the way to attain the minimum in the matter of reserves is not by relying on maturities but by maintaining a considerable quantity of assets that can be shifted to other banks before maturity as necessity may require. *Liquidity is tantamount to shiftability.*"[7]

4. "Among the most shiftable, and hence among the most liquid, of assets are bonds and stocks, both as direct investments and as collateral. The development of the corporate form of enterprise has largely undermined the theory of commercial banking as elaborated to fit the conditions of early nineteenth-century England. The share and bond as claims to fixed capital have a ready transferability; indeed the active securities that are listed on the exchanges have in normal times an almost instantaneous convertibility into cash. The result is that securities are from the standpoint of any individual bank incomparably more liquid in ordinary times than commercial paper of customers—assuming that no special machinery, such as reserve banks, has been developed to permit the same shifting of commercial paper."[8]

The shiftability theory gained an increasing number of adherents with the passage of time, but a traditional theory, even though outmoded, dies slowly and vestiges of the old commercial loan theory persisted through the 1930s.

III. THE ANTICIPATED INCOME THEORY

A new theory of commercial bank liquidity, designated "the anticipated income theory," was developed in 1949 by Herbert V. Prochnow. It grew out of a comprehensive study of bank term loans in which he found that:

"In every instance, regardless of the nature and character of the borrower's business, the banker planned liquidation of the term loan from the anticipated earnings of the borrower. . . . It (liquidation) is not by the sale of assets of the borrower as in the commercial credit or traditional theory of liquidity, nor by shifting the term loan to some other lender as in the shiftability theory of liquidity, but by the anticipated income of the borrower."[9]

Although Prochnow's study was primarily concerned with term loans, he noted that the anticipated income theory applied also to consumer loans.[10] He also recognized that: "In the event of widespread and large withdrawals in the entire banking system, ultimate liquidity is to be found in the central bank or Federal Reserve System."[11]

The early 1930's marked a new era in the terms of bank loan contracts, with highly significant consequences for the liquidity of bank loan portfolios. Loan officers began systematically to adapt loan repayment schedules to the anticipated income or cash receipts of the borrower. Under the new loan contracts with systematic repayment schedules, a continuous cash inflow could be expected from all types of amortized loans. In a growing economy, banks tend to experience cash outflows from their lending operations— from long-term growth in normal years, and from cyclical loan expansion in prosperous years. But in periods of cyclical decline, loan repayments may exceed the amount of new loans with a resultant net cash inflow. Within limits, loan officers can control the net cash flow by policies with respect to (1) granting new loans, and (2) collection of outstanding loans. However, the net cash inflow under the anticipated income theory is not available to meet an increase in total loans during expansion periods, but only in economic contractions to meet possible shifts of de-

---

[7]*Ibid.*, p. 723; italics supplied.
[8]*Ibid.*, p. 730.

[9]Herbert V. Prochnow, *Term Loans and Theories of Bank Liquidity*, New York: Prentice-Hall, Inc., 1949, pp. 401–402.
[10]*Ibid.*, p. 408.
[11]*Ibid.*, p. 411.

posits to other banks and withdrawals of currency.

It remains to mention that the anticipated income theory can be used to explain a degree of liquidity for the entire commercial banking system which is not implied in either the commercial loan theory or the shiftability theory. Since liquidity in this theory is expressly derived from the flow of income, total loans (and total deposits) may be reduced by savings from borrowers' incomes. This does not in itself increase total cash reserves of banks, but it releases required and working reserves needed to support deposits. In contrast, the commercial loan theory contemplates repayment of loans by the sale of the goods, rather than from income, and it implies the shifting of a repaid loan to another bank and another borrower. The shiftability theory also usually implies the sale of securities or the shifting of loans to other banks, perhaps including the Reserve banks, so that no reduction in total bank credit takes place. However, the exception should be noted that if the banks sell securities to individuals, business corporations, and other nonbank interests, a reduction of total bank loans and investments (and therefore of deposits) takes place. In this event, required reserves are released and the entire banking system becomes more liquid.

IV. THE LIABILITIES MANAGEMENT THEORY

During the 1960's, a new theory of cyclical bank liquidity emerged, which may be labelled the "liabilities management theory." According to this new doctrine, it is unnecessary to observe traditional standards in regard to self-liquidating loans and liquidity reserves, since reserve money can be borrowed or "bought" in the money market whenever a bank experiences a reserve deficiency. There are seven possible sources from which the individual bank may acquire reserves by the creation of additional liabilities: (1) acquisition of demand deposits; (2) issuance of time certifiicates of deposit; (3) purchase (borrowing) of Federal funds; (4) borrowing at the Federal Reserve; (5) issuance of short-term notes; (6) raising capital funds from the sale of capital notes, preferred stock, or common stock, or from retained earnings; and (7) the Eurodollar market.

A. Demand Deposits

The acquisition of demand deposits as a means of meeting cyclical liquidity needs might have been feasible before 1933, when banks were free to pay whatever rates they wished in bidding for such deposits. But the Banking Act of 1933 prohibited these interest payments. Moreover, there has been a definite tendency for total demand deposits to decline during the last half of cyclical expansion periods, largely in response to the tight rein of Federal Reserve policy. Banks must draw these deposits competitively from a smaller total reservoir by aggressive promotion and effective enforcement of balance requirements. Management cannot count on opening this valve whenever cyclical funds are needed.

B. Time Certificates of Deposit

The predominant liability source of reserve money for the individual bank since the early 1960's has been the issuance of time certificates of deposit, mainly in negotiable form. The negotiable certificate market was launched in early 1961 by the large money-market banks of New York City, mainly as a means of attracting deposits of large corporations. Prior to this time, New York City banks paid no interest on corporate time deposits as a matter of policy. But during the first quarter of 1961, they began to offer negotiable certificates with original maturities ranging between 90 days and one year at rates competitive with Treasury bills, commercial paper, bankers' acceptances, Federal agency securities, and other money market instruments. At the same time, the large bond dealers began to develop a secondary market in CD's which materially enhanced their liquidity features. Growth in the amount of CD's was meteoric, rising steadily from zero in early 1961 to $18.6 billion in August 1966—$7.4 billion in New York City and $11.2 billion in other cities.[12] With some time lag, the practice spread—first to the large banks outside New York, and later to intermediate-size banks throughout the country, although certificates of the latter were not ordinarily negotiable and did not reach the secondary market. A better idea of overall growth is conveyed by the fact that "other time deposits of individuals and businesses" (largely certificates) of all member banks increased from $7.1 billion in April 1961 to nearly $28.7 billion at the end of 1965.[13] Thus, a vigorous new segment of the money market, second only to short-term Treasury securities, grew to maturity in an incredibly short time.

The relative ease with which the large city banks could buy reserve money by the issuance of CD's masked some of the limitations of this source under tight credit conditions. Such conditions almost invariably develop sometime during the last stage of cyclical expansion, and in the current expansion they began to appear in the last half of 1965. Demands for bank credit continued their upsurge, and on the supply side of the Federal Reserve tightened the credit reins another notch. Net free reserves of member banks,[14] which had shown a substantial surplus since the last quarter of 1960, moved to a deficit position in the first quarter of

1965 and averaged about $150 million during the remainder of the year. Further restraint was applied in 1966, and by July net borrowed reserves exceeded $400 million. Meanwhile in December 1965, the Federal Reserve discount rate was raised from 4 to 4½ percent. In this setting, open-market rates moved up sharply. The 3-month Treasury bill rate rose from 3.99 percent in August 1965 to 5.66 percent in September 1966, and the 4- to 6-month prime commercial paper rate increased in the same period from 4.58 percent to 6.26 percent.[15] In order to compete for money, the leading banks were forced to make corresponding increases in the rates offered on CD's—from 4.50 percent in August 1965 to 5.50 percent by midyear 1966 on certificates of 30 days and more.

This situation points up a major limitation on CD's as a dependable source of reserve money during boom conditions, namely, Federal Reserve control of maximum rates payable. If the structure of rates on competing money market instruments—principally Treasury bills, Federal agency securities, commercial paper, and repurchase agreements for Federal funds —rises above the ceilings on CD's set by the Federal Reserve, the banks can no longer sell them. And if this situation should persist, the amount of outstanding CD's would shrink as maturities occur. Since maturities of outstandings range from one day to one year or a little more, the drain on reserves of the individual bank would begin immediately and would continue until all interest-sensitive CD's were liquidated.

Another limitation of CD's as a dependable source of reserves is the fact that the Federal Reserve authorities are almost certain to implement a monetary policy of restraint, thereby changing adversely the whole environment of the money market with respect to availability of reserves. In contrast with conditions of

---

[12]*Federal Reserve Bulletin,* September 1966, p. 1369.

[13]Board of Governors of the Federal Reserve System, *Summary Reports of Assets and Liabilities of Member Banks,* April 12, 1961, p. 3; December 31, 1965, p. 3.

[14]Excess legal reserves less borrowing at Federal Reserve banks.

[15]Rates adjusted to comparable basis—actual yield on 360-day year.

business recession when the Federal Reserve is typically on the side of the banks in providing abundant reserves at low rates, it shifts to the opposing side sometime during the last stage of cyclical expansion. Witness 1952–1953, 1956–1957, 1959, and 1966—all periods of rising net borrowed reserves, and of sharply increasing money rates. In large part, these conditions were created, or at least validated, by Federal Reserve policies and actions—whether by sales of U.S. securities, by raising legal reserve requirements, by rationing advances and increasing the discount rate, or by some combination of these methods. Although this limiting factor affects all means of replenishing reserves, it applies uniquely to CD's because of Regulation Q. In contrast, a bank can always sell short-term U.S. securities to repair its reserve position; and if they are sold to non-commercial-bank investors, deposits decline correspondingly in the banking system and total required reserves are reduced.

In addition to the issuance of negotiable CD's to large corporations, a significant new development took place at the retail level in non-negotiable CD's and other time deposits, beginning in December 1965. On December 6, 1965, the Federal Reserve Board raised the maximum rates payable on time deposits with maturities of 30 days and over from 4½ to 5½ percent. This opened a new door through which commercial banks could compete for savings. Previously this door had been nearly closed by the rate ceilings, which were below rates paid by savings and loan associations and mutual savings banks, and below yields obtainable on open-market securities.

C. Federal Funds

The third source from which the individual bank may acquire reserve money by the creation of additional liabilities is the purchase (borrowing) of Federal funds. This is the market in which banks with deficient legal reserves borrow from other banks having excess reserves. Lenders and borrowers are brought together by two or three broker-dealers in New York City who receive reports by wire from banks all over the country in regard to bids and offers of funds, and by a few large money-market banks that act in part as dealers and in part as brokers and clearing centers of information. There are two principal methods of dealing in this market: (1) straight one-day loans; and (2) repurchase agreements. The great bulk of Federal funds is loaned on a one-day, unsecured basis, although a significant part is secured by U.S. securities. Banks also utilize repurchase agreements under which the borrowing bank actually sells U.S. securities under contract to buy them back in one or more days at a predetermined rate and price. Rates are very sensitive in response to changing currents of supply and demand. They are closely related competitively to other rates in the money market, and particularly to those on Treasury bills. Also, in ordinary times the Federal Reserve discount rate marks the upper limit of their fluctuations, since banks seldom choose to pay more when they can borrow at the discount rate. But in periods of strong loan demand and tight money, the Federal funds rate may rise well above the discount rate. This situation, which existed during the last half of 1965 and the first three quarters of 1966, developed from a combination of credit rationing by the Reserve banks, a relatively low discount rate, and exceptionally inviting loan and investment opportunities.

A more specific idea of the market's background is conveyed by the fact that in September 1966, total member bank legal reserves were $23,239 million while required reserves were $22,847 million, so that excess reserves were $392 million. The greater part of the excess reserves—$291 million—was held by the smaller country banks, with only $101 million in the large reserve-city banks, including New York City and Chicago.[16] It should be noted that the average size of excess reserves in the banking system materially understates the availability of Federal funds. This is true since the reserve position of each individual bank varies widely from day-to-day and within each day during the reserve computation periods—one week in reserve-city banks and two weeks in country banks. The lightning-like turnover of available Federal funds is indicated by the fact that combined purchases and sales of 46 major reserve-city banks during the first four weeks of September 1966 amounted to $19.7 billion—an annual rate of $1,022 billion.[17] More relevant to the present purpose, average borrowings of Federal funds by weekly-reporting large banks during September 1966 amounted to $5.8 billion—over two-fifths of their total legal reserve balances.[18]

The limitations of the Federal funds market as a dependable source of cyclical reserve money for the individual bank are similar in some respects to those of CD's, but there are also significant points of difference. A summary of the similarities will suffice. The first is that the banks must compete actively among themselves for existing reserve money when it is scarce during the last phases of business expansions. This may lead to a very high cost of funds, as illustrated between August and November 1966 when Federal funds typically traded at 6 percent while the Federal Reserve discount rate was 4½ percent. The other similar limitation is the fact that a bank must face the high probability of a restrictive Federal Reserve policy in boom periods whether it expects to acquire reserves through CD's or Federal funds. This magnifies the degree of reserve scarcity.

There are three significant differences between Federal funds and CD's as dependable cyclical sources of reserve money. First, the Federal fund rate is not subject to Federal Reserve regulation, nor is such regulation likely. On this count, Federal funds have a distinct advantage over CD's, which are subject to maximum rates under Regulation Q. However, the price may be too high to contemplate in practice when other alternatives to provide liquidity are considered, and under extreme conditions of restraint this source may nearly dry up at any price.

Second, there is no legal reserve requirement against the borrowing of Federal funds, whereas a reserve requirement of between 3 and 10 percent applies to time deposits. This difference has both a positive and negative aspect. On the positive side, the net cost of borrowing Federal funds is somewhat lower than the net cost of CD's when market rates are the same. But, on the other hand, there is no release of required legal reserves in the banking system when borrowings of Federal funds are increased.

Last, Federal funds are bought and sold by banks on a very short-term basis —predominantly for one day only, and seldom for more than one week, while original issues of CD's are for considerably longer periods. Most of them have maturities in the range of 3 to 12 months, although a significant part has maturities after one year and beyond two years.[19] The exceedingly short-term nature of Federal funds borrowing makes this source inconvenient and undependable for cyclical purposes.

D. Borrowing at Federal Reserve Banks

The fourth source of reserves by creation of liabilities is borrowing from the Federal Reserve. In fact, the founders of the Federal Reserve System visualized the

[16]*Federal Reserve Bulletin*, October 1966, p. 1468; preliminary figures.

[17]*Ibid.*, p. 1470.

[18]*Ibid.*, pp. 1486–1489.

[19]*Federal Reserve Bulletin*, April 1963, p. 465.

discount window as the principal pipeline through which high-powered reserve money would be released and withdrawn from commercial banks. The use of the term, "high-powered," calls attention to the profound difference between this source and those just discussed—CD's and Federal funds. When a member bank borrows from a Reserve bank it adds, other things being equal, to total bank reserves. This multiple expansion feature does not apply to either CD's or Federal funds, since these markets deal only with existing bank reserves and do not in themselves bring forth newly-created reserves. However, both markets do have a multiple-expansion effect insofar as they bring about a more complete utilization of existing legal reserves—that is, insofar as dealings through them reduce the amount of "excess legal reserves" in the banking system, or activate shifts of demand deposits to time deposits. This effect is a significant one during boom conditions when bank reserves become relatively scarce and money rates rise sharply. For example, excess reserves exceeded $700 million during the recession of 1960–1961, but as the economy recovered and interest rates rose they gradually declined, and during the first half of 1966 they were in the vicinity of $350 million.[20]

In practice, member bank borrowing at the Reserve banks predominantly takes the form of a renewable promissory note for 15 days or less secured by U.S. securities. Seldom utilized are other possible forms of borrowing, namely: (1) discounting of eligible customer notes with remaining maturities not in excess of 90 days;[21] and (2) a promissory note with a maximum maturity of four months and secured by any satisfactory bank assets. However, in the latter case a penalty of ½ percent above the regular Federal Reserve discount rate applies.

Regardless of the method of borrowing, the Reserve banks observe certain guiding principles in the administration of discounts and advances. Federal Reserve credit is generally granted as a privilege rather than a right to meet day-to-day and seasonal liquidity needs of member banks. Under ordinary conditions, dependence on borrowing for longer-term purposes, including cyclical loan expansion, is not regarded as appropriate. Also, advances are not to be used in support of speculative activities in securities, commodities, or real estate. Only in unusual situations arising from national or local difficulties can a member bank count on borrowing continuously for longer periods.[22] In practice, a Reserve bank seldom refuses the first application for an advance to meet a purpose in line with the foregoing principles, but a large member bank which has borrowed continuously for three or four reserve-computation periods is likely to be called on the carpet.

E. Short-Term Notes

A fifth source from which the individual bank may acquire reserve money by the creation of additional liabilities is the issuance of unsubordinated, short-term, promissory notes. This new member of the money-market family was launched by the First National Bank of Boston in September 1964. The unsecured notes were offered in negotiable form with maturities to suit corporate and other large short-term investors. Shortly afterward, First Boston Corporation announced that it would make a market in the notes. Other large banks and security dealers followed suit, and with the blessing of the Comptroller of the Currency and the Federal Reserve Board the new market seemed to be off to a promising start.

There were significant advantages of

---

[20]*Federal Reserve Bulletin*, July 1966, p. 988.
[21]Nine months in the case of agricultural paper.

[22]Board of Governors of the Federal Reserve System, *Regulation A*, 1955 Revision, Foreword-General Principles.

such notes over CD's. Since they were not classified as deposits they were not subject to maximum-rate regulation (Regulation Q). For this reason, a bank could regard them as a more dependable reserve source because there was no obstacle in bidding up rates to attract or to retain funds. This constituted a special advantage for banks outside the circle of leading money-market banks. The smaller institutions had to offer somewhat higher rates on CD's to compete, and whenever market rates approached the rate ceiling they tended to lose CD's to leading banks. Another advantage of the notes was that they were officially classified as borrowed funds and not as deposits. Consequently, they were not subject to either legal reserve requirements or to deposit-insurance assessments. This represented an annual cost saving at the time of about 0.2 percent.

The only apparent disadvantages of the notes were certain legal restrictions on borrowing. A national bank was prohibited from borrowing in excess of capital stock and 50 percent of surplus, and state-chartered banks were also restricted in this regard. In addition, the banking law of New York was interpreted to bar the issuance of such notes, whether negotiable or non-negotiable. Without a legal change, this would of course seriously limit growth of the market, since the great money-market banks in New York City were excluded. In August 1965, partial relief came to New York banks when the State Banking Department ruled that *non-negotiable* short-term notes, issued for specific periods in units of $1 million or more, were permissible. With this assurance, several large New York banks sold significant amounts of non-negotiable short-term notes to corporations and others.[23] However, the prohibition of negotiable notes in New York remained a major obstacle to development of an

active secondary market, and to the potential growth of the new market. Pending a permissive change in the New York banking law, it seemed improbable that a major national market could be established in view of the predominance of New York City as a financial center.

Even if the New York banking law should be amended to permit issuance of negotiable notes, their future growth is called to question by restrictive measures taken in June 1966 by the Federal Reserve Board. Effective September 1, 1966, short-term promissory notes of banks became subject to the regulations governing reserve requirements and payment of interest on deposits. The Board's purpose was, "to prevent future use of these instruments as a means of circumventing statutory and regulatory requirements applicable to bank deposits."[24] This action erased the advantages of such notes over CD's, except perhaps for use in individual situations. Moreover, in view of the limits on bank borrowings, the legal barrier to negotiable notes in New York, and the great head-start of the CD market, it now appears unlikely that a comparable new market in notes will develop.

Now that short-term promissory notes of banks have become subject to legal reserve requirements, the analysis of their effects on the money market becomes identical with that pertaining to CD's. That is, the individual bank may acquire liquidity through their issuance only by drawing existing reserves and deposits from *other* banks. The only difference is that the process involves a shift in the banking system from demand deposits or time deposits to note liabilities; whereas in the case of issuance of CD's there is a shift only from demand deposits to time deposits. In both cases, there is a reduction in the amount of required legal reserves when the shift is from demand deposits to a liability against which a materially lower percentage reserve re-

---

[23]*The Wall Street Journal*, September 3, 1965, p. 8.

[24]*Federal Reserve Bulletin*, July 1966, p. 979.

quirement applies. The general conclusion is also the same as that with respect to CD's; Short-term notes are not a dependable source, except to a limited extent, to meet the liquidity needs of the individual bank during the last phase of cyclical periods of expansion.

F. Capital Funds

The sixth source from which the individual bank may acquire reserve money by the creation of liabilities is by raising capital funds in any one of several forms —sale of common stock, preferred stock, or capital notes, and retention of earnings. While these forms differ in character, the effect of their increase on the asset-liquidity position of the individual bank and the banking system is the same. When Bank A, having a legal reserve deficiency of $10 million, increases its capital funds by this amount, say by sale of common stock, its cash reserve is increased and so is its common stock account. Assuming that the stock is paid for by checks on other banks, total demand deposits of the banking system are immediately reduced by $10 million. At the same time, required legal reserves are reduced by $1.5 million when the reserve requirement is 15 percent. Given time, the released reserves provide the basis for loan and investment expansion (and therefore deposit expansion) of $10 million, so that the demand deposits initially extinguished may be recreated. Thus, the end result, assuming net free reserves of zero at the outset and full utilization of the released reserves, is no change in total demand deposits, an increase of $10 million in total capital accounts, and an equal increase in total loans and investments. It should also be noted that these transactions have made no change in total legal reserves of the banking system. Hence, the cash reserves that Bank A gained were drawn away from other banks which, collectively, are assumed to have excess reserves of $10

million—just enough to provide for Bank A's reserve deficiency. Thus, as a generalization, deposits are the immediate source of additional capital funds in the banking system, and an increase of capital funds of the individual bank causes a redistribution of existing cash reserves rather than an increase in total reserves.

Table 1 shows the changes in capital accounts of all member banks between 1961 and 1965. Over half the total increase of $6.3 billion came from retained earnings. Much dependence on this source does not seem practicable, since in periods of increased earnings stockholders expect higher rather than lower dividends. Issuance of preferred stock may also be dismissed in view of its insignificance in the banking field, and because of the depressed level of preferred stock prices during periods of high interest rates.

The sale of common stock likewise has a very small potential for this purpose. Bank stock prices are likely to be depressed by the high interest rates associated with boom conditions. For example, the index of bank stock prices reached a peak in the third quarter of 1964 and had declined one-fourth by June 1966, while Standard and Poor's index of industrial stock prices rose 8 percent during the same period.[25] In addition, banks are often reluctant to issue more common stock because of dilution of per-share equity, and because of control considerations.

One possibility for use of common stock in this connection would be issuance at an earlier stage of the business-expansion cycle when the price is favorable, as in 1964. Proceeds could be held in short-term U.S. securities and other liquidity reserves which then offer attractive yields. But the practicability of such a program is open to serious question. Success would depend on a higher degree of accuracy in business forecasting than past experience demon-

[25]M. A. Schapiro & Co., Inc., *Bank Stock Quarterly*, June 1966, p. 5.

TABLE 1

Capital Accounts of All Member Banks, 1961 and 1965

(in millions of dollars)

	December 30, 1961	December 31, 1965	Increase	Percentage Distribution
Common stock*	5,512	7,002	1,489	23.7
Capital notes & debentures	16	1,553	1,537	24.4
Preferred stock	7	32	25	0.4
Surplus and other capital accounts ..	13,102	16,341	3,238	51.4
Total	18,683	24,926	6,288	100.0

*An unknown part of the increase in common stock took place as a result of stock dividends which capitalize surplus or undivided profits. Hence, the table over-states to that extent the raising of new capital funds in this manner, and under-states retained earnings as a source of new funds. Any discrepancies in totals are the result of rounding.

Source: Board of Governors of the Federal Reserve System, Summary Report, December 30, 1961, p. 3; December 31, 1965, p. 3.

TABLE 2

Capital Accounts of Reserve City Member Banks, 1963 and 1965*

(in millions of dollars)

	December 20, 1963	December 31, 1965	Increase	Percentage Distribution
Common stock	3,640.2	4,237.8	597.6	23.2
Capital notes & debentures ...	78.4	1,294.5	1,216.2	47.2
Surplus and other capital accounts	8,959.1	9,721.4	762.3	29.6
Total capital accounts	12,677.7	15,253.7	2,576.1	100.0

*Includes New York City and Chicago member banks. Any discrepancies in totals are the result of rounding.

Source: Board of Governors of the Federal Reserve System, Summary Report, December 20, 1963, p. 3; December 31, 1965, p. 3.

strates, and also on timely action in accordance with the forecast. Although bank officers may wish to sell common stock as part of an over-all liquidity program, the uncertainties and limitations commit it to a minor role.

Capital notes have become a major source of capital funds since December 1962, when the Comptroller of the Currency approved their issuance if they were subordinated to deposits. As shown by Table 2, between 1963 and 1965, they represented 47 percent of the increase in total capital funds and over three-fourths of total capital raised in the investment market by reserve-city banks.[26] In New

[26]Allowing for the fact that an appreciable part of the increase in capital stock occurred by transfer from surplus and undivided profits.

York City, the proportion of the increase in total capital funds represented by capital notes was appreciably higher during the same period—58 percent. Thus, it is evident that the banks eagerly grasped the opportunity to acquire liquid funds by this method during this phase of business expansion. It afforded the advantage of tax-free capital at a relatively low interest cost when customer loan demands were strong.

G. The Eurodollar Market

In an immediate accounting sense, borrowing in the Eurodollar market by a U.S. bank does not represent a net addition to the reserves of the banking system. This follows from that fact that Euro-dollars have demand deposit counterparts on the books of U.S. banks.[27] A change in ownership of a Eurodollar time deposit from one foreign owner to another brings about a corresponding shift of U.S. demand deposits, usually from one bank to another.

But, more basically, it is possible that borrowing in the Eurodollar market by U.S. banks may lead to an improvement of the reserve position of the domestic monetary and banking system. This would take place (1) if the Federal Reserve banks purchase foreign moneys by expanding their credit, such as in recent swap arrangements with foreign central banks; (2) if Federal Reserve credit is extended domestically in any manner; (3) if the Treasury borrows foreign moneys from the International Monetary Fund; and (4) if the Treasury or the private sector of the economy borrows more heavily abroad. Thus, it may be that increased borrowing by U.S. banks in the Eurodollar market will generate a train of circumstances leading to an increase in the total reserves of the banking system, and to an increase in the size of the Eurodollar market.

H. Summary and Conclusion

The potentialities of liabilities management as a source from which the individual bank may meet liquidity needs during the last phase of periods of cyclical expansion may be summarized as follows:

1. All sources with the exception of Federal Reserve borrowing have in common the fact that, assuming a fixed stock of legal reserves, the individual bank can acquire reserves only at the expense of other banks in the system.[28]

2. However, an individual bank may utilize any one of these sources as a means of capturing a larger share of total existing reserves.

3. The tight credit policy typically adopted by the Federal Reserve authorities during boom conditions strictly limits the availability of reserves, and may bring about an absolute reduction in total reserves. Therefore, the bank that needs more reserves at such a time is confronted with a highly-competitive situation in which other banks are also seeking more reserves.

4. The acquisition of demand deposits cannot be counted on as a source of cyclical liquidity because banks are prevented by law from paying interest on such deposits.

5. CD's and other time deposits are not dependable sources, except for short-term liquidity needs (including seasonal), to meet requirements in the first half (or even three-fourths) of a cyclical expansion period. The unique reason for this is the probability of maximum-rate regulation by the Federal Reserve Board.

6. The exceedingly short-term character of Federal funds, and their scarcity during boom conditions, largely restrict their employment to day-to-day, week-to-week, and seasonal adjustments of a bank's liquidity position.

7. Borrowing at the Federal Reserve has traditionally been reserved by law and policy for short-term and emergency purposes.

8. Rate regulation largely eliminates the sale of short-term notes as a dependable source of cyclical liquidity.

9. Common stock or capital notes may represent a source of cyclical liquidity if they are sold before the last phase of a cyclical expansion. The markets for both bank stock and capital notes are usually depressed during boom conditions by the sharp rise of interest rates. In view of the general reluctance of banks to sell additional common stock, the issuance of capital notes has a materially larger potential for this purpose.

10. The Eurodollar market merits a

---

[27]In some cases, the Eurodollar counterpart is a loan payable to foreign banks by U.S. banks.

[28]This generalization is subject to the qualification that issuance of CD's involves a shift from demand to time deposits and therefore releases required legal reserves.

limited place in the cyclical liquidity program of a large money-market bank.

If the management of bank liabilities can make only a limited contribution to cyclical liquidity, by what methods can a bank provide for this essential need? Briefly, the answer lies in the management of asset liquidity. This may involve

some loss of current income during the greater part of a cyclical expansion, but it is likely to avoid a far greater capital loss during the last phase of expansion. The essence of asset-liquidity management is to equate the probable earlier loss of income with the subsequent probable loss, taxes considered.

12. Commercial Banks as Multiple-Product Price-Discriminating Firms[*]

Bernard Shull[†]

Even in a banking system commonly described as atomistic in structure, most banks operate in a local or regional market best described as oligopolistic. Bernard Shull offers a hypothesis and a rationale in the following article for commonly pursued asset management policies. The basic argument presented here is that banks sell a homogeneous product insofar as costs are concerned, but because they are able to classify customers effectively, they can exploit various credit sub-markets individually, as if the product sold in each sub-market were different. Hence, profit-maximizing behavior should lead to an asset allocation such that marginal profitability in each sub-market is equated.

There is currently a widespread desire to preserve and encourage competition among commercial banks. One major dif-

ficulty in attaining these objectives is a lack of systematic knowledge on the process and results of rivalry and non-rivalry among banks. It is hardly possible to judge what sort of market structure and performance constitutes "workable" or "effective" competition when the process of competition in banking is still so shallowly explored.

In the following pages it will be argued that there is a model of the firm, not yet utilized, that seems particularly appropriate for analyzing the process of competition in banking. This is the multiple-product, price-discriminating model developed by Eli Clemens.[1] The theory

[*]From Deane Carson (ed.), *Banking and Monetary Studies* (Homewood, Illinois: Richard D. Irwin, Inc., 1963), pp. 351–68. Reprinted by permission of the publisher.

[†]I would like to acknowledge the helpful comments of Professors Eli W. Clemens and Lester V. Chandler, and those of former colleagues in the Federal Reserve System, including Clay J. Anderson, Bong Suh Lee, Robert Lindsay, Paul S. Anderson, and J. C. Rothwell. These highly constructive critics, of course, are in no way responsible for any errors that may remain.

[1]Eli W. Clemens, "Price Discrimination and the Multiple-Product Firm," *The Review of Economic Studies*, Vol. XIX (1950–51), pp. 1–11. Reprinted with alterations in Heflebower and Stocking, *Readings in Industrial Organization and Public Policy* (Homewood, Ill.: Richard D. Irwin, Inc., 1958), pp. 262–76. Clemens views the firm as a combination of Joan Robinson's price-discriminating monopolist and Edward Chamberlin's product-differentiating monopolistic competitor. He attempts to unite the insights of both Robinson's and Chamberlin's views into a more realistic picture of the modern firm. See John Robinson, *The Economics of Imperfect* (Footnote continued on next page)

seems to offer reasonable explanations of certain kinds of banking behavior and may provide insights into the causes and effects of bank mergers. It leads to additional conclusions on how effective competition in banking should and should not be measured.

As will be indicated below, much of the behavior explained by the theory can be explained in other, more customary, terms. But this fact, in and of itself, does not vitiate the model. It and the customary explanations are more complements than substitutes. The model's own value lies in the purpose it serves.

THE COMPETITIVE PROCESS IN BANKING

The theoretical exploration of the competitive process in banking has generally proceeded by borrowing models developed for industry in general and applying them to banking. In 1938 Lester Chandler wrote: "In their analyses of the markets in which the prices of bank credit and of banking services in the United States are determined, most students have utilized the assumptions of pure competition. . . . In the following pages it will be shown . . . that it is the theory of monopolistic competition, rather than the theory of pure competition, that is the more useful. . . ."[2] Chandler went on to demonstrate structure characteristics of banking markets and conduct characteristics of banks that are inconsistent with the assumptions and predictions of pure competition. He noted that both the theories of monopolistic competition and oligopoly are helpful in explaining behavior and performance in banking markets.[3]

Subsequent writers have also taken the position that banks generally operate under conditions of imperfect competition. David Alhadeff, pointing to Chandler's lead, stated, "The groundwork there established can be elaborated profitably to focus more sharply on those features of banking market structures which are relevant in considerations of policy alternatives."[4] Alhadeff provided an extensive description of the imperfect market structure and performance of banking, especially in small towns. Hodgman has explored the oligopolistic implications of the prime rate and compensating balance conventions in business loan markets.[5] More recently, Bachman and Sametz have emphatically stated that "The economist's concept of pure and perfect competition . . . does not provide a usable standard to determine the efficacy of competition in banking."[6]

Thus, it seems generally agreed that the "banking industry" is not appropriately represented by the model of pure competition. Most writers seem willing to cite characteristics that suggest some banking markets are monopolistic, others oligopolistic, and still others monopolistically competitive. But aside from such references, there has been little analysis of the way the imperfectly competitive banking industry, as a whole, actually operates.

The difficulty of implementing public policies without an appropriate theory was demonstrated recently in the suit brought by the Justice Department to prevent the proposed merger of the Phila-

Competition (New York: St. Martin's Press, Inc., 1950), pp. 179–208, and Edward Chamberlin, *The Theory of Monopolistic Competition* (Cambridge, Mass.: Harvard University Press, 1948), pp. 56 ff.

[2]Lester V. Chandler, "Monopolistic Elements in Commercial Banking," *Journal of Political Economy*, Vol. XLVI, No. 1 (February, 1938), p. 1.

[3]*Ibid.*, pp. 17–21. Some of Chandler's analysis, especially in regard to the fluctuation of rates in

different credit markets, anticipates the analysis developed below with the help of the multiple-product, price-discriminating model.

[4]David A. Alhadeff, *Monopoly and Competition in Banking* (Berkeley and Los Angeles: University of California Press, 1954), p. 20.

[5]Donald R. Hodgman, "The Deposit Relationship of Commercial Bank Investment Behavior," *The Review of Economics and Statistics*, August, 1961, pp. 257–68.

[6]Jules Bachman and Arnold W. Sametz, "Workable Competition in Banking," *The Bulletin of the C. J. Devine Institute of Finance*, 1962, p. 9.

delphia National Bank and Girard Trust Corn Exchange.[7] The Justice Department contended that commercial banking—including individual credit and deposit markets—should be looked at separately to gauge the effects of the proposed merger.[8] The judge, however, stated, ". . . it is not the intention of this court to subdivide a commercial bank into certain selected services and functions. . . . It is the conglomeration of all the various services and functions that sets the commercial bank off from other financial institutions. Each item is an integral part of the whole, almost every one of which is dependent upon and would not exist but for the other."[9]

This approach permitted Judge Clary to designate commercial banking as "a separate and distinct line of commerce within the meaning of the statute."[10] He then reached a conclusion as to the probable effect of the proposed merger on the commercial banking line of commerce as a whole.

The conclusion, whatever its legal basis, cannot but seem somewhat arbitrary since it is not supported by any detailed analysis of how the individual services and functions of commercial banking *depend* upon one another and *integrate* into the whole. Until a more realistic picture can be drawn, there is bound to be extreme controversy over the effect of mergers on banking competition and on the workability of competition in banking generally.

The theory of multiple-product production and price discrimination seems to

summarize the strategic characteristics of banking, and relates the structures of the markets in which banks operate to the objectives of the bank's management. It holds some promise of extending our understanding of the process of competition among banks.

THE THEORY

In his article on price discrimination and multiple production, Clemens sees the firm as producing and selling a number of distinct products to "separable" groups of customers with different elasticities of demand. He equates multiple-product production with price discrimination and illustrates each product and each separated group of customers by means of individual demand curves. Each "market," composed of one product sold to one distinct group of customers, has its own demand curve. At the same time, the firm sells a homogeneous product with respect to costs—the firm does not sell products, but its capacity to produce.

The firm diversifies into new product lines, discriminates among customers, generally invading new markets over a period of time—going from the most profitable to the least profitable market. Strong and weak markets are exploited at different profit margins. The limiting or marginal market would be highly elastic—the one in which marginal cost just about equaled demand price. Prices, of course, would vary from market to market. The assumptions are basically as follows:

1. The resources within the firm are mobile, and the firm can produce a wide variety of products. The case of joint costs and fixed product proportions is excluded.

2. Units of output, without distinction as to product, have equal direct costs under standard conditions. This means that the output, as far as its effects on short-run costs go, is assumed homogeneous. Marginal costs are thought to rise gradually through normal ranges

---

[7]*U.S.* v. *The Philadelphia National Bank and Girard Trust Corn Exchange,* 201 F. Supp. 348 (1962).

[8]*Ibid.,* p. 361. The defendants took essentially the same position, but did not include commercial banking in its entirety as a line of commerce and emphasized the importance of substitute products.

[9]*Ibid.,* p. 363.

[10]*Ibid.;* the Supreme Court, which reversed the District Court decision, also accepted commercial banking as the relevant "line of commerce." *U.S.* v. *The Philadelphia National Bank, et al.,* 374 U.S. 321 (1963).

of output and then move steeply beyond some given level of ouput.
3. Demand curves, resulting from the different products and customers with different elasticities, are not related.
4. Equilibrium will result when profit is maximized. Profits will be maximized when two conditions are met:
   a) *Market diversification requirement:* When there are no more accessible markets where demand price exceeds marginal cost.
   b) *Marginal requirement:* When marginal cost in the least profitable market equals marginal revenue in this market, and marginal revenue in all markets are equal.

The operation of this model can best be understood with the help of a diagram developed by Clemens. (See Figure 1.) The diagram shows a series of five markets represented by demand curves (D_1 to D_5) and associated marginal revenue curves (MR_1 to MR_5). The markets are aligned from left to right in order of

profitability and, as Clemens assumed, in order of their chronological entry. Each market has its own zero output axis.

We can view the firm as entering the most profitable markets first and, finding itself with excess capacity, expanding into other markets of less profitability rather than lowering its price in the old market. This diversification continues until there are no more accessible markets in which the price customers are willing to pay exceeds the marginal cost. Production is carried to a point established by the equation of marginal cost (MC) and marginal revenue in the marginal market (D_5). Marginal revenue is then made equal in all other markets by adjusting output and prices. The equal-marginal-revenue line (EMR) traces this equality and establishes the market prices (P_1 to P_5) and outputs (O_1 to O_5).

Several *conclusions* can be drawn from this analysis.

1. Marginal cost will at least roughly equal demand price in the marginal mar-

FIGURE 1

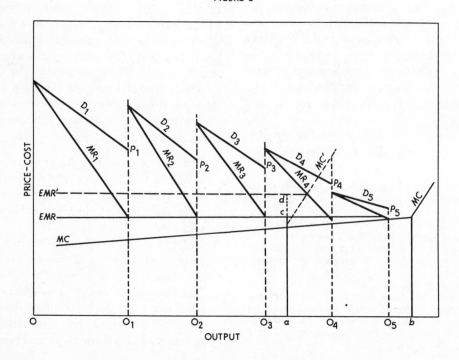

ket. There will, in other words, be production which is just barely profitable.

2. As a firm moves to less profitable markets, prices will rise somewhat and production will be somewhat restricted in the more profitable markets. This follows from the profit-maximizing rule that marginal revenue should be equal in all markets and that marginal cost is gently rising. As Clemens puts it, "The extension of production to the point where marginal cost is equal to demand, increases total output but encourages the restriction of output in individual markets."[11]

3. The marginal or limiting market would be one in which the elasticity of demand is greatest; it could be infinite. Thus, the firm can be viewed as possessing different degrees of market power in different markets.

4. The more prices that can be established—the more markets that can be separated—the greater the profits. It is in the firm's interest to break up the demand curve into as many markets as possible and break up each market into as many submarkets as possible. Through the techniques of "quantity discounts" and other terms on which purchases are made, such segmentation becomes possible. In the limiting case, the monopolist obtains the demand price for each unit of output. Consumer surplus is entirely eliminated. This analysis, Clemens notes, is applicable to a custom order firm that sets prices on a negotiated basis.[12]

5. Since most, if not all, firms are seen as trying to maximize profits in this way, and this process may be carried on by large numbers of competitors, no more than normal profits may be earned. "Normal profits . . . are obtained only insofar as average revenues . . . are equal to average costs."[13] An average revenue curve is derived from the prices in each market.

There is a striking resemblance between the kind of firm Clemens pictures and the commercial bank. Banks are multiple-product firms, producing many kinds of credit; in recent years, they have expanded into many new markets. Banks do make distinct separations among classes of customers for pricing purposes.[14]

Theoretical Assumptions and Observed Behavior

The basic assumptions underlying Clemens' model seem fairly appropriate in banking.

1. A bank's resources are highly mobile. The principal resource is its reserves —generalized purchasing power. Banks can readily change their product mix.

2. The output of banks, for purposes of analysis, can be considered homogeneous with respect to costs. The assumption is that excess capacity at any level and in any given amount (including excess labor, machines, and reserves) can be directed into any kind of credit without significantly different increases in cost. It is recognized that different kinds of credit actually do involve different direct costs. Nevertheless, at this stage of the analysis, these differences may not be too important. We may base this assumption on the view that "deposits" or "money"

---

[11]Eli W. Clemens, "Price Discrimination and the Multiple-Product Firm," *Readings in Industrial Organization and Policy, op. cit.,* p. 270.

[12]*Ibid.,* p. 274. This analysis is derived from A. C. Pigou's treatment in *Economics of Welfare* of perfect or first degree price discrimination.

[13]*Ibid.,* p. 273.

[14]It is possible to look at banks as multiple-product price discriminating firms in deposit markets as well as in credit markets. Banks engage in product differentiation in these markets, as has been clearly indicated most recently by the development of negotiable time certificates of deposit. The price banks pay for different kinds of deposits are highly regulated, but there is still a "free range" within which different prices need not and do not reflect different costs. In this paper there will be no systematic attempt to incorporate discrimination and differentiation in deposit markets with the analysis in asset markets. This position is taken on the belief that knowledge may be advanced by concentrating on structure and behavior in asset markets, and that the conclusions reached reflect tendencies that exist independently of structure and behavior in deposit markets.

are the principal and strategic variable input in banking, and that credit of all types is homogeneous with respect to the cost of money.[15]

3. Demand curves in some banking markets are probably related. For example, the demand for credit by consumers

---

[15]It is recognized that different types of money have different costs. Money in the form of demand deposits, time deposits, and capital funds involve different cost elements and do not under normal circumstances cost the same. In the argument above, short-run cost curves are assumed to reflect an aggregate cost of money schedule experienced by the bank as it expands its output of credit. The shape of the schedule, as well as its level, would reflect the composition of the "money" the bank has obtained. To pursue the analysis under fairly simplified conditions, it will be assumed the composition of the money input is constant.

In the functional cost analysis of commercial banks developed by the Federal Reserve Bank of Boston, it is assumed that the total cost of money—demand, time, and capital funds—can be allocated in a proportional fashion to the several types of earning assets the bank has purchased in order to determine the net return on each type of asset. The implication is that the several kinds of assets ("products") are homogeneous with respect to the cost of money. For a given dollar increase in either, say, instalment loans or business loans, is in effect assumed to involve the same dollar amount of funds coming from a common "pool of funds." This amount would cost the same no matter what credit use was made of it.

Analysis of the functional cost data suggests that differences in the cost of money is extremely important in explaining differences in earnings among banks. It was found that the allocation of funds among different kinds of earning assets was relatively unimportant in explaining earning differences. See "Looking Behind Bank Earnings," *Business Review*, Federal Reserve Bank of Boston, December, 1961. This finding tends to confirm the appropriateness of the decision to ignore differences in the unique costs associated with different kinds of output at this stage in the analysis and to concentrate on the cost of money.

In Clemens' article, which deals with industrial firms, the assumption of homogeneous output is based on data developed from time and motion studies, and a definition of "units of output" as "blocks of output" produced under "standard conditions." See Clemens, *op. cit.*, p. 265. For an explanation of "direct costs under standard conditions" or "standard costs," see C. C. Balderston, V. S. Karabasz, R. P. Brecht, and R. J. Riddle, *Management of an Enterprise* (New York: Prentice-Hall, Inc., 1949), pp. 352 ff.

and by finance companies could well show a substantial amount of interdependence. But it will be assumed that demand interdependence is not the general case in banking and that, in the short run at least, there is no more "relatedness" than for the kinds of industrial firms Clemens had in mind.

4. There is no way of telling, at this stage of our knowledge, how profit motivated bankers really are, or the extent to which marginal analysis is applicable. We will simply have to assume that many important banks do try to maximize profits and see how far this assumption gets us.

The behavioral characteristics that the model posits also seem appropriate to banking.

1. Banks do produce in marginal markets—markets that appear only marginally profitable. At times, investment in some types of government securities appears to represent such markets. Banks seem to produce up to the capacity dictated by their reserve positions and up to a point where marginal costs just about equal demand price. We would expect different profit margins in different banking markets.

2. Banks do seem to diversify into new markets rather than lower prices in old markets. For example, business loan rates have, at times, appeared very sticky, while bank reserve positions have increased and credit has expanded for new types of loans and investments.

3. Banks do apparently discriminate in price in the economic sense of the term. Since the pricing process involves private negotiation and extensive revelation of all pertinent facts by the potential borrower, this should be expected. Chandler has observed:

The wide differentials in the elasticities of different customers' demands for loans at an individual bank render rate discrimination profitable; . . . even at the same bank, different customers pay widely different rates. . . . Many of these differences cannot be explained by the differences in risks, maturities and expenses to the loans; they must be ascribed rather to the differences in the alternative available to customers.[16]

Alhadeff has stated that the market for business loans "is divided into submarkets corresponding to the different mobility of different groups of business borrowers."[17] In effect he is saying that discrimination is both possible and profitable.[18]

4. Bank profits, overall, do not seem excessive. Bogan has argued that they are deficient.[19] Bachman and Sametz also maintain that they are quite low.[20] But the level of profits is not crucial to the theory itself. The theory is consistent with normal as well as excessive profits.

Interpretation of Recent Performance

In terms of the key assumptions and observation of general behavior and performance, the theory of multiple-product production and price discrimination seems applicable to banking. With the aid of the model, some recent banking behavior and performance will now be analyzed.

REACTIONS TO MONETARY POLICY. For purposes of this analysis, one direct and simplified central bank effect will be considered. Changes in monetary policy toward ease or tightness will be viewed as changing the point at which marginal costs begin rising steeply—expanding or contracting the output capacity of individual commercial banks. When monetary policy eases, the point of steeply rising marginal costs will move to the right along the output axis of Figure 1. When monetary policy tightens, we will assume that the reverse happens—the bend in the marginal cost curve will shift to the left along the output axis.[21]

Central bank policy will also affect the level of marginal costs. When monetary policy tightens, banks may find that at least a portion of their marginal cost schedule rising due to increased costs of borrowed funds, and possibly due to more intense competition from other financial institutions for deposits. When monetary policy eases, the reverse may be true. As an effect on countercyclical policy, however, we will consider this second effect a subsidiary one. When the monetary authority sets a maximum on time deposit interest rates, the effect on the level of the marginal cost curve is, on the other hand, primary. This will be discussed below.[22]

When the full capacity point shifts to the right, during a period of transition from tightness to ease, banks will increase the amount and proportion of their resources devoted to marginal markets, e.g., short-term government securities. The line of equal—marginal—revenue (the horizontal EMR lines on the diagram) should fall and, as a result, output should rise and prices should fall in other markets.

As can be seen on Figure 1, the expansion in capacity involved in the movement from MC' to MC is measured by the distance ab, which induces a smaller change in the line of equal marginal revenue, measured by the distance cd.

[16]Chandler, op. cit., pp. 5-6.

[17]David A. Alhadeff, "Bank Mergers:: Completion versus Banking Factors," Southern Economic Journal, January, 1963, p. 218.

[18]However, a recent study has failed to confirm the hypothesis that banks discriminate between large and small borrowers. See Albert M. Levenson, "Interest Rate and Cost Differentials in Bank Lending to Small and Large Business," The Review of Economics and Statistics, May, 1962, pp. 190-97. The author admits, however, that his conclusions ". . . are very tentative."

[19]Jules I. Bogan, The Adequacy of Bank Earnings, A Banking Research Study by the Graduate School of Business Administration, New York University.

[20]Bachman and Sametz, op. cit., p. 43.

[21]The central bank does not typically decrease the absolute level of bank capacity. The shift to the left assumes that over time the demand curves in all markets are shifting to the right as the result of economic growth.

[22]A third effect would be on the market demand and supply curves in some markets in which banks deal. In pursuing any particular policy through open-market operations, the Federal Reserve will have some impact on the level and shape of the curves in government security markets.

During a period of transition from ease to tightness, the point of full capacity shifts to the left. The amount and proportion of resources that banks devote to marginal markets would decline. In other markets, rates would tend to rise and outputs tend to fall.

The relative extent of price and output changes in the several credit markets would mainly depend on the structures of these markets. In a marginal market submerged by a restriction in capacity, the output reductions by individual banks would be relatively large, and the aggregate reduction for all banks would be relatively large. We would expect market rates of interest to rise steeply. In a period of ease, when the expansion of capacity permits the marginal market to emerge again as, at least, marginally profitable, we would expect the large aggregate increase in output to produce a sharply falling interest rate. In more profitable markets, small aggregate reductions in credit during periods of tightness and small aggregate increases during periods of ease would tend to produce relatively stable rates.[23]

The kinds of behavior sketched above, based on the theory of multiple-product production and price discrimination, seem to conform fairly well to actual experience.

Banks have sold government securities when monetary policy has tightened. In the expansion of 1955–57, to take an extreme example, commercial bank hold-

ings fell to very low levels. Interest rates during the period climbed rapidly.

On the other hand, when monetary policy has eased during recessions, banks have quickly accumulated government securities and interest rates have plunged at times to below 1 percent.

The fluctuations in the structure of interest rates have been apparent throughout the postwar years, and widely noted. This relationship between market structure and interest rate structure has been recognized before. In 1938 Chandler observed:

. . . monopoly affect(s) the structure of interest rates in the United States. . . . The conditions under which interest rates on short-term, open market loans are determined conform much more nearly to the requirements of pure competition than do those under which rates on bank loans to customers are determined. . . . Open market rates vary widely with credit conditions. . . . But interest rates on bank loans to customers without ready access to the open market or to distant banks show no such variation. . . . Open market rates could not rise so high in boom periods if bankers did not deem it wise to limit their lending in the open market "to take care of their customers" in order to retain "good-will." And open market rates could not fall so low in periods of credit ease if banks engaged freely in price competition for customers' loans in their respective cities instead of maintaining interest rates on customers' loans at the same level and "dumping" credit in the open market, where each bank tends to neglect its effects on rates.[24]

CHANGE IN REGULATION Q. In January, 1962, the Board of Governors of the Federal Reserve System raised the maximum interest rates payable by member banks on savings and time deposits. On money deposited for a year or more, the maximum rate was raised from 3 percent to 4 percent. For money deposited for shorter periods of time, maximums were similarly raised. Many banks subsequently

---

[23]It should be noted that in the case of the individual bank, the relative price fluctuation would seem to be just the opposite. A change in the *EMR* line induced by a change in capacity might appear to result in relatively small price changes in the weaker markets and larger price changes in the more profitable markets. But this observation, depending on the differing elasticities of demand confronting the individual bank, is misleading. The individual and aggregate output changes are large in the weak markets and small in the strong markets; it is these market supply changes that determine the actual changes in the structure of prices (interest rates) that result when the marginal cost curve is altered.

[24]Chandler, *op. cit.*, pp. 18–19.

raised the rates they actually paid depositors.[25]

The increase in rates on time deposits seems to be closely associated with a readjustment of bank portfolios. During 1962, weekly reporting member banks expanded their holdings of mortgages by over $2 billion; they expanded their holdings of corporate and municipal securities by over $3.5 billion. At the same time, these banks reduced their holdings of short-term government securities by $1.7 billion, and their holdings of other federal government securities by over $700 million. Many bankers have explained this switch in preference toward higher earning assets as an attempt to increase gross revenues in the face of rising money costs.[26]

This explanation of bank response to rising rates on time deposits raises an intriguing question. If municipals and mortgages were more profitable than other securities after the increase in interest rates, they must also have been more profitable before the increase. It could be argued that bankers are not profit maximizers but aim at some target profit amount or return. It could further be argued that when costs increased and their targets became doubtful under current policies, they relaxed somewhat their preferences for safety and liquidity.

A supplementary explanation, based on the view of banks developed in this paper, might proceed as follows: the increased cost of money raised the level of the marginal cost curve. This increase tended to submerge all or part of a marginal market—short-term government securities. It also tended to raise prices and reduce

outputs in other markets in which banks were producing credit. Since the point at which marginal costs begin increasing rapidly did not shift as the result of interest rate increases, banks were initially confronted with the possibility of excess capacity. They could not allocate this capacity to existing markets and increase profits unless marginal revenue exceeded marginal cost. This motivated a search for new markets in which marginal revenue did exceed marginal cost—some markets within the areas of municipal and mortgage securities.

This analysis can be carefully followed with the aid of Figure 2.

The original situation is shown in 2(a). When the cost of money increases, the marginal cost curve shifts from MC to MC', as is shown in 2(b). The marginal market is submerged by this upward shift, and a new marginal market is established by the equation of marginal cost and revenue at a higher level and the establishment of price P_4'. Prices in all other markets also rise, and outputs in these markets decrease. The increase in excess capacity is the distance $O_5' - O_4'$. This is composed of the decrease in output in what was formerly the marginal market plus the decreases in outputs in all other markets.

More profitable markets existed prior to the rise in interest cost and had not been exploited. To this extent, bankers did not maximize profits prior to the change. But it may still be true that given the set of markets in which banks operated, bankers did maximize profits prior to change. The analysis suggests, in other words, that bankers are profit maximizers in markets in which they produce, but also conservative in invading and exploiting new markets. Strong motivation, stemming from the threat of excess capacity, was required to spur bankers into new markets.

LOAN-ASSET RATIOS. In a recent study of "Chicago Banking" by Schweiger and

[25]"Supplement to Regulation Q," *Federal Reserve Bulletin*, December, 1961, p. 1404. See also Caroline H. Cagle, "Interest Rates on Time Deposits, Mid-January 1962," *Federal Reserve Bulletin*, February, 1962, p. 147.

[26]J. C. Rothwell, "The Long and the Short of It: Bankers Are Reaching out for Longer-term Securities," *Business Review*, Federal Reserve Bank of Philadelphia, April, 1962, p. 11.

FIGURE 2

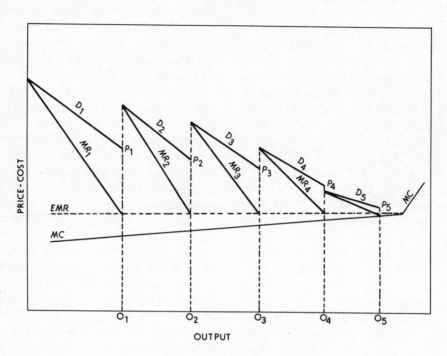

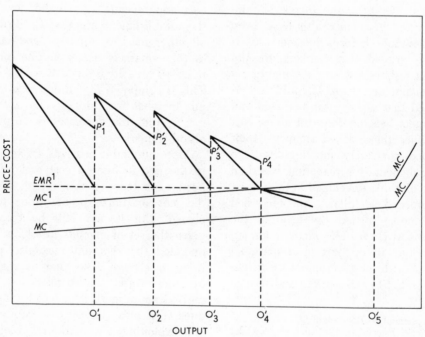

McGee, it was found that branch banks tend to lend a larger proportion of assets than unit banks of comparable size in areas of comparable lending opportunities; and that the difference is largely concentrated in loans of special importance to the local community.[27] In a critical review, Jacobs and Lerner have argued that such differences are relatively unimportant and imply no weakness in unit banking. They state: "Various loan-to-asset ratios do not indicate imperfections in the market."[28]

It is true that differences in loan-to-asset ratios need not reflect market imperfections. There are a number of possible explanations for this finding, involving the relative "aggressiveness" and efficiency of branch banks. Schweiger and McGee, themselves, have explored some of the possibilities.

Nevertheless, "various loan-to-asset ratios" might also be explained, at least in part, by the hypothesis that banks are more isolated from competition in local loan markets in unit bank communities than in branch bank communities. In the simplest of terms, we may consider a bank, investing its funds in local loans and government securities, similar to a producer selling in a monopolistic market domestically and a competitive market abroad. For profit maximization, the output in each market must be such that marginal revenues in each market are equal. The lower the elasticity of demand in the domestic market, the smaller would be the domestic output, and the lower the ratio of domestic output to total output.[29] It follows that for two comparable firms, the comparative ratios of domestic output to total output would depend on the comparative elasticities of demand in the domestic market.

Given two banks, the same in all respects with the exception that the first faced less elastic demands in local loan markets, we would expect the first to have a lower ratio of local loans to total earning assets. The excess resources would find their way into more competitive markets in which marginal revenue exceeded marginal costs. In banking, the funds might be invested in short-term government securities, where the demand curve facing the bank is close to, if not actually, infinitely elastic.

MEASURING COMPETITION AND BANK MERGERS. In a recent monograph on competition in banking, Bachman and Sametz have argued that banking is workably competitive.[30] They have pointed out that banks do not perform like traditional monopolists. Banks do not restrict total credit nor do they earn excessive profits. They also argue that banks do not restrict credit in loan markets to earn greater profits.

Restrictions on total output are imposed on banks in the aggregate by the monetary controls of the Federal Reserve System. Individual banks may well limit their loan portfolio, by adhering to a given loan/deposit ratio. But this is done in the interests of liquidity *not* profitability and would promptly be modified if deposits rose or required reserves were lowered. To restrict output of loans affects profits adversely. Thus, even if banks had the uninhibited power to restrict output (loans), it would not be to their advantage to do so.[31]

From the discussion above, it seems clear that neither the absence of total credit restriction or excessive profits can serve to indicate the existence of effective competition.[32] It also seems clear that credit restriction in particular markets is a profit-maximizing type of behavior. The

---

[27]See "Chicago Banking," *Journal of Business,* July, 1961, pp. 15–38.

[28]D. P. Jacobs and E. M. Lerner, "A Critical Review," *Journal of Business,* October, 1962, pp. 414–15.

[29]Joan Robinson, *op. cit.,* pp. 184–85.

[30]Bachman and Sametz, *op. cit.,* p. 43.

[31]*Ibid.,* pp. 42–43.

[32]For a further discussion of bank profits as an indicator of competition, see this writer's "Competition in Banking: A New Old Problem," *Business Review,* Federal Reserve Bank of Philadelphia, January, 1963, p. 18.

logic of profit maximization by a multiple-product, price-discriminating firm would lead one to look at credit restriction and profit margins in individual markets, and the extent and duration of price discrimination among different groups of customers purchasing the same product.

In merger cases, where the degree of actual and potential competition is an important consideration, the extent of competition in particular product-customer markets should be studied. But the theory suggests that the effect of the merger may involve more than simply a change in the number of competitors in particular markets.

Many mergers can be looked at as attempts to establish banks in new markets. The new market may be composed of a new group of customers set off by their geographic location or financial needs or both.

A merger between a city bank and a suburban bank may be motivated primarily by the city bank's desire to gain a foothold in an area of expanding income and population. A merger between one city bank and another may be motivated primarily by the bank's desire to grant larger loans to larger customers. In both cases, a desire to increase the bank's capacity to extend credit as well as the demand factors alone would be intertwining motivations.

The inducement of increasing returns to scale may be very important. But the demand-inducement to merger should not be ignored. The theory suggests that the new market which the banks wish to enter by merging need not be more profitable than the old market; it need only be marginally profitable. The total advantage of a merger that establishes a bank in a new market will include the addition to profit earned by devoting resources to its new market and squeezing its older and more profitable markets. This advantage is quite aside from any reduction in the elasticity of demand in the old markets resulting from a decrease in

the number of alternative sources of credit available to customers.[33]

THEORY AND PUBLIC POLICY

The theory that has been developed is based on assumptions and behavioral observations that are consistent with commercial banking. It offers a reasonable explanation in a unified manner of a number of kinds of banking performance, some of which are puzzling, others which can be explained in an *ad hoc* manner. There seems to be a presumption, then, that the model does accurately portray an important facet of commercial banking and can be useful in understanding and predicting future developments.

The presumption is, of course, not conclusive. It can be argued that the behavior of banks noted above can be explained on other grounds. The diversification of banks into many different product lines has traditionally been understood as reflecting a need for asset diversification to minimize risk (required in part by banking regulations) and a need for liquidity to meet the potential demands of depositors. The separation of customers into classes for purposes of charging different rates has typically been thought of as reflecting different degrees of customer "credit-worthiness."

The need to diversify to minimize risks, legal restrictions which require diversification, and liquidity needs help explain why banks produce in marginal markets. Differences in credit-worthiness of customers also help expain why banks charge different rates for the same type of loan. The movement of banks into marginal markets when monetary policy eases has been explained as an attempt to restore liquidity lost in the previous expansion. The movement out of governments when monetary policy tightens has been under-

---

[33]See Judge Clary's reference to Warren Smith's testimony in *U.S. v. The Philadelphia National Bank and Girard Trust Corn Exchange Bank,* 201 F. Supp. 348, 367–68.

stood as an attempt to increase profits and a failure of the "lock-in" effect; bankers are presumably willing to forego the added liquidity they so recently restored during the period of recession when profit opportunities improve and customer demand picks up.

These kinds of behavior are nevertheless believed to proceed against a background of shifting demand curves in the various markets and a willingness on the part of bankers to shift reserves into the most profitable markets. Clemens' model really says no more than this. It points out, however, that the most profitable product mix is one in which diversification and discrimination proceed to the fullest extent possible.

The behavior of banks may be determined by a number of causes. The behavior discussed above may be understood in both customary terms and on the basis of Clemens' model. The explanations are not really conflicting, but complementary.

The chief problem in developing public policies to preserve competition in banking may be to separate the competitive or enterprise behavior from the behavior resulting from regulation and tradition. Both profit maximization and traditional banking practices require diversification of portfolios, provision for adequate liquidity, and different prices to different customers. However, to the extent bankers diversify and discriminate to increase short-run profits, certain policy conclusions seem appropriate.

1. The absence of total credit restriction and excessive profits are not necessarily reflections of the absence of monopoly power in banking either at the individual bank level or in the banking industry. Conventional performance tests of this sort do not tell us whether banks are workably competitive.

2. The effects of the exercise of monopoly power by a bank might be revealed in the extent and duration of price discrimination among customers purchasing the same product, though the problems of measuring this are undoubtedly difficult. Monopoly power may also be revealed in the way the bank directs its resources. A bank with considerable market power in specific markets could restrict loans and raise rates in these markets; it would divert some of its capacity to marginal markets.

3. Mergers can be looked at as attempts to establish banks in a new market. The new market need not be more profitable than the old markets; it need only be marginally profitable. The total advantage of a merger involves not only increased profit in the new market, but a more profitable use of resources in the old markets as well. The advantage goes beyond any reduction in the number of competitors.

4. A bank may earn no more than normal profits and still injure competition among the customers through discrimination and/or injure some portion of its market—perhaps the local community—through its portfolio management. In such a situation, interference with the bank's policies, by increasing the number of competitors in the market, for example, may seriously affect the stability of the bank, while the absence of interference may seriously affect the prosperity of its customers. As in so many cases, a careful balancing of the alternatives must be made.

Chapter V
ASSET MANAGEMENT

13. Deposits, Reserves and Bank Earnings[*]

Harry L. Johnson

It may be said that a bank's earnings are indirectly a function of its reserves. This article examines the relationship between bank earnings and the loss of reserves through the clearing house. It is hypothesized that the smaller the loss of reserves the greater the individual bank's capacity to purchase earning assets. If this is true, it is reasoned, banks in branch banking states will possess relatively greater lending power and earning potential than banks in unit banking states.

Attempts in English-speaking countries to explain the operations of commercial banks began with their inception in the second half of the 17th century. Some explanations reveal an understanding that the lending operations of commercial banks increase the quantity of the circulating medium and that this contribution is a function of the reserves which are to be held against deposit liabilities. A fractional reserve system permits a bank and/or the banking system to contribute a multiple of available reserves. For example, if reserves requirements are 20 percent of deposits liabilities, the system may create five dollars of bank credit for each additional dollar received in reserves.[1]

There will be no attempt here to delineate the commercial banking process; rather, the objective is to explore the implications which it has for commercial bank earnings. Earnings derived primarily from the assets structure of commercial banks is properly viewed as a function of the amount of credit which banks have extended. That is, as banks purchase earning assets (extend credit), earnings rise. If the amount of credit which banks extend is determined by available reserves, it follows that earnings are indirectly a function of reserves.

In other terms, earnings for the banking system are determined by the quantity of

---

[*]From Bankers Magazine, Spring, 1968. Reprinted by permission of the publisher, Warren, Gorham & Lamont, Inc.

[1]A thorough treatment of the relation between commercial bank reserves and credit expansion may be found in Clifton H. Kreps, Jr., and Olin S. Pugh: Money, Banking and Monetary Policy, second edition, The Ronald Press, New York, pages 174–190.

reserves and the percentage of surplus reserves devoted to the purchase of earning assets. For the individual bank, earnings are also affected by the loss of reserves through the clearing house.[2] The clearing house drain directly affects the ability of the individual bank to purchase earning assets. The smaller the loss of reserves through the clearing house (the larger the proportion of intra-shifted deposit debits to total debits-to-deposits), the greater the ability of the individual bank to purchase earning assets. The significance of clearing house drains to bank earnings is pointed up by a recent work of Professor Chester Phillips which develops the thesis that a bank's lending power is inversely related to the clearing house drain.[3]

To assess the significance of this hypothesis to the commercial banking industry it is necessary to observe the relationship between bank debits, loan-to-deposit ratios, and earnings on loan portfolios for banks located in states that have unit, limited branching, and statewide branch banking. This statistical analysis is based upon the assumption that as a bank increases in size relative to its market, the proportion of intra-shifted deposit debits to total deposit debits also increases. Banks located in states permitting branching (especially on a statewide basis) will tend to experience a higher proportion of intrashifted deposits than banks located in unit banking states. As a result, banks where branching is allowed will have a greater lending ability and earning potential.

For each of the three types of the banking structure indicated (branch, limited branch, and unit banks),[4] the following data were observed for the period from 1955 to 1964: total debits-to-demand deposits, (excluding United States government and inter-bank deposits); the ratio of loans and discounts to demand deposits; and interest income derived from loans and discounts. These data reflect the deposit-turnover ratios which in turn describe the reserve position, lending ability, and earning power of banks. As implied above, banks experiencing a high proportion of intra-shifted deposits to total deposits (low deposit turnover) will be able to maintain a higher ratio of loans to total deposits and as a result will have a higher return of its loans and discounts.

CREDIT EXPANSION AND EARNINGS

The amount of earning assets which the banking system will acquire is a function of the ratio of reserves to the amount of reserves available for credit expansion. That is, the asset structure of the commercial banking industry is determined by the amount of total reserves less legal reserve requirement, the working reserve necessary to satisfy the day-to-day cash demands of customers, and the mixture of demands (time and demand).

---

[2]The reserve position of an individual bank consists of three categories of reserves—legal reserves, working reserves, and surplus reserves. For a discussion of the interdependence of these three divisions of reserves and earnings see Edward S. Shaw: *Money, Income, and Monetary Policy*, Richard D. Irwin, Chicago, 1950, pages 122–229.

[3]For a more complete illustration of this position see Chester A. Phillips: "Intra-Shifted Deposits: Their Nature and Significance," *Iowa Business Digest*, August, 1965, Volume 36, Number 8, pp. 3–10.

[4]The states included in the study are: branch-banking states—Connecticut, Delaware, North Carolina, the District of Columbia, California, and Nevada; limited-branch-banking states— Alabama, New York, New Jersey, Indiana, Georgia, and Michigan; and unit-banking states —Montana, New Hampshire, Texas, Colorado, West Virginia, and Florida. The sample was chosen on a qualitative rather than a random basis because it permits diversification on the basis of geographic location, financial environment, population, nature of the business community, etc. The data used were gathered from three sources: (1) Debits to demand deposits were assembled from Bank Debits and Deposit Turnover published by the Federal Reserve System; (2) loan turnover figures were abstracted from the semi-annual reports of the Federal Deposit Insurance Corporation and (3) data for income from loans and discounts was taken from the annual reports of the F.D.I.C.

This relationship is best illustrated with a numerical example. For this purpose, let us consider the case of a commercial banking system that has $100 million in total reserves, legal reserve requirements are 20 percent demand deposits, and ten percent for time deposits, the ratio of time deposits to demand deposits is one to one, and working reserves are 10 percent. The potential credit expansion of the system, therefore, is approximately $525 million.

However, the amount of the potential credit expansion is not realized because individual banks are reluctant to devote all their excess reserves to the purchase earning assets. In other words, the amount of excess reserves devoted to credit expansion tends to be less than the amount of reserves available for expansion. The differential consists of reserves devoted to holding for check clearing purposes and unexpected contingencies.

In a one-bank system, the clearing house drain would equal zero. The cash demands of customers would be the only avenue through which reserves were drained from the bank. As the number of banks in a system increases, the loss of reserves through the clearing house becomes a reality for individual banks; in a banking system composed of several banks, any one bank will experience a loss of reserves through the clearing house. The greater the number of banks, the greater the probability that reserves from any one bank will be drained through the clearing house—and the smaller the proportion of reserves devoted to the purchase of earning assets.

The structure of banking in the United States suggests that banks in unit banking states should experience a higher loss of reserves through the clearing house than banks in limited branching states or banks in states which permit statewide branching. In other terms, total debits-to-deposits in unit banking states should contain a smaller percentage of intra-shifted de-posits, than similar debits in limited branching states and states permitting statewide branching, respectively. If intra-shifted deposits are correlated to bank earnings, it follows that banks in unit-banking states will experience a lower ratio of earnings to debits-to-deposits than banks in branch-banking states.

Evidence Available

Data providing an insight into the relationship of debits-to-deposits to bank earnings and loan turnover for branch, limited branch, and unit banking systems are presented in Table 1. These data reveal that banks operating under a branch-banking system experienced the highest average annual increase in debits-to-deposits and the lowest average annual increase in loan turnover. In contrast are the earnings of banks in unit-banking systems—these banks had the highest average annual increase in income from loans and discounts.

The relationship between loan turnover and debits-to-demand deposits is further exemplified by a simple regression analysis. This analysis shows that banks in unit-banking systems experienced a loan turnover ratio of approximately .533 for every billion dollar of debits-to-demand deposits, while banks in limited-branching systems and statewide branch-banking systems witnessed a similar ratio of .218 and .097, respectively. In other terms, for each billion dollar increase in check clearings, banks in unit systems experienced a 53 percent turnover in loans, while banks in statewide branching systems and limited branching systems experienced a turnover of loans of 10 and 22 percent, respectively. A regression of income from loan portfolio to debits-to-deposits shows that banks located in unit-bank states experienced an increase in earnings of approximately $1.05 per $100 increase in debits-to-demand deposits. Banks in limited branching and statewide branching states

TABLE 1
Annual Percentage Increase in Debits-to-Deposits, Loan Turnover and
Earnings on Loan Portfolio 1955–64

	Average Yearly Increase		
	Debits to Demand Deposit Accounts	Loan Turnover	Income from Loans and Discounts
Branch States:			
Connecticut	8.399	8.336	11.321
Delaware	16.204	5.203	7.849
North Carolina	8.278	5.288	11.624
District of Columbia	9.987	6.643	11.703
California	9.273	5.731	13.201
Nevada	10.313	6.523	16.107
Limited Branching States:			
Alabama	7.431	6.329	11.458
New York	9.424	7.293	11.449
New Jersey	7.317	6.195	11.331
Indiana	6.235	6.812	10.854
Georgia	8.145	4.671	11.100
Michigan	6.355	8.180	11.457
Unit States:			
Montana	4.479	8.469	11.713
New Hampshire	5.759	6.962	12.008
Texas	6.851	5.951	11.376
Colorado	8.293	7.528	12.542
West Virginia	3.898	4.962	8.970
Florida	8.877	6.612	15.230
Categories of States:			
All Branch States	10.409	6.287	11.967
All Limited Branching States	7.484	6.580	11.275
All Unit States	6.359	6.747	11.973

experienced an increase of approximately .44¢ and .52¢, respectively, per $100 increase in debits-to-demand deposits.

Results of this statistical analysis suggest that banks operating in branching systems tend to lose a smaller portion of reserves through check clearing and as a result they are able to support a higher loan-to-deposit ratio than banks in unit systems. The observed behavior of bank earnings, however, does not coincide with the prediction that a low clearing house drain is highly correlated to income earned from the lending activities of commercial banks. Unit bank systems experienced the highest level of earning even though their loan portfolio was characterized by the highest turnover.

VALIDITY OF THE IMPLICATIONS

The findings described only indirectly suggest that the pattern of intra-shifted deposits are consistent with predictions. The smaller turnover of loans experienced by banks located in statewide branching systems infer a greater retention of lending ability. This conclusion is reiterated by the relatively high average loan-to-deposits ratio experienced by banks in branch-banking states (Table 2). In other terms, the loan coefficient of banks in states permitting branch banking is greater than in unit bank states. An excursion into the history of commercial bank loan activity appears to provide an explanation of the

TABLE 2
Loan to Deposit Ratios for Selected States, 1955-64

States	Years									
	1964	1963	1962	1961	1960	1959	1958	1957	1956	1955
Statewide Branch Banking:										
Connecticut	.73	.71	.68	.65	.63	.60	.55	.53	.50	.46
Delaware	.54	.59	.54	.52	.49	.49	.45	.45	.46	.44
N. Carolina	.58	.58	.55	,52	.50	.49	.44	.45	.43	.42
Dist. of Col.	.57	.55	.54	.50	.50	.49	.45	.46	.45	.42
California	.64	.63	.59	.55	.58	.57	.51	.53	.53	.48
Nevada	.63	.60	.57	.53	.57	.50	.43	.45	.45	.42
Limited Branch Banking:										
Alabama	.51	.51	.48	.48	.46	.45	.41	.41	.39	.38
New York	.70	.70	.66	.62	.63	.65	.58	.60	.59	.55
New Jersey	.61	.60	.55	.53	.53	.50	.46	.47	.45	.43
Indiana	.50	.50	.47	.44	.45	.43	.38	.39	.36	.34
Georgia	.58	.57	.55	.51	.52	.51	.46	.46	.47	.46
Michigan	.55	.53	.50	.49	.49	.48	.43	.43	.41	.37
Unit Branch Banking:										
Montana	.54	.52	.49	.44	.46	.44	.39	.38	.38	.38
New Hampshire ..	.78	.77	.72	.69	.67	.64	.61	.60	.58	.54
Texas	.54	.53	.50	.47	.46	.45	.43	.43	.41	.42
Colorado	.60	.58	.56	.51	.52	.52	.46	.44	.43	.42
W. Virginia	.48	.48	.46	.43	.44	.41	.38	.38	.37	.36
Florida	.48	.47	.44	.40	.41	.42	.38	.37	.37	.34

difference between the predicted and observed relationships between debit-to-deposits, loan turnover, and earnings from loan portfolios.

To accomplish the dual objective of high profit and liquidity, banks have traditionally pursued a conservative policy of credit extension. The history of banking is characterized by a tendency to purchase only those assets that are self liquidating.[5] Inter and intra-industry competition, shifts in the type of credit demanded, and changes in the overall banking structure have altered this concept of banking. Today commercial bank lending activity is properly described by the shiftability doctrine or the doctrine of anticipated income. The quality of the assets acquired by commercial banks is viewed as a function of their ability to be converted into cash in secondary security markets and/or the ability of borrowers to meet the obligations of the debt from present and future income.[6]

The history of banks, however, suggests that, when possible, bankers tend to practice a policy of credit extension which emphasizes safety (liquidity) rather than earnings. Ideally, the commercial banker desires an asset structure of highly liquid short-term debt securities – e.g., U.S. Treasury bills, short-term loans to businesses, and similar items. Competition from other lenders, the necessity of pro-

[5]A thorough treatment of the conventional theories of banking is found in Lloyd W. Mints, *A History of Banking Theory,* University of Chicago Press, Chicago, 1945.

[6]The new approach of bank liquidity–doctrine of anticipated income, has grown out of the extension of term loans to consumers and businesses. See Herbert V. Prochnow, "Bank Liquidity and the New Doctrine of Anticipated Income," *The Journal of Finance,* Vol. IV, No. 4, December 1949, pp. 298–312; and Paul S. Nadler, "Changing Concepts of Liquidity," *Savings and Loan News,* May 1967, pp. 22–27.

tecting their sources of money, and the desire for earnings, however, compels him to hold a portion of his assets in less liquid, more risky forms (consumer loans, real estate loans, etc.). It appears that the asset structure of a commercial bank tends to be directly related to the degree of competition prevailing in the market in which it operates.

Example of a Dilemma

To illustrate this position, let us delineate the bankers' problem of choosing between earnings and liquidity with a hypothetical example of a bank having assets of $100 million. The banker is confronted with the choice of holding assets in liquid or non-liquid form or a combination of liquid and non-liquid assets. Acting rationally, he will choose neither of the extremes but will hold a mixture of liquid and earning assets. The ratio of liquid assets to earning assets is a function of the bankers' willingness to substitute earnings for loss of liquidity and vice versa. For instance, the banker may feel that 20 percent of total assets (excluding legal reserves) should be held in the form of vault cash, deposits in other banks (primarily correspondent banks), and highly liquid securities such as Treasury bills and Federal funds. Remaining assets will be in the form of U.S. Government bonds, state and local government bonds, corporate bonds, and loans and discounts.

In his choice of earning assets, the banker is confronted with an array of securities and credit instruments that have varying degrees of liquidity and earnings. Possessing a natural bias for the more liquid assets, the banker will tend to sacrifice earnings for safety of principal. There will be a tendency to discriminate in favor of the highly low earning assets. The ability of the banker to discriminate is a function of his bank's market power and the supply of earning assets available for purchase. Institutions located in one-bank towns will tend to enjoy a strong

market position (a localized monopoly). As a result, they discriminate in favor of the higher quality earning assets; that is, their asset mixture will favor high quality, short-term, low-yielding assets.

An examination of the asset structure of banks located in unit banking states and banks located in one-bank towns, reveals a higher proportion of earning assets in the form of U.S. Government, state and local bonds, and in commercial loans, than is the case for banks in states permitting branching and banks located in cities and towns with two or more banks.[7]

One-Bank Town Banks

To illustrate this behavior, a review of the activities of a commercial bank operating in a one-bank town with no close competitors or substitutes for its services may be helpful. Since the bank is faced with many demands for credit, it will tend to select the best quality from each sector of the market. For example, in the selection of earning assets, the bank will choose, first, to satisfy the credit demands of business firms with unquestioned credit ratings. With no competitors it, within limits, possesses the power to fix the price for each type of service (credit). The nature of the bank's liabilities and its power to fix the price for each service offered permits the banks in a one-bank town to build an asset structure which optimizes liquidity and profits. This is accomplished through an asset structure favoring highly liquid government securities, federal funds, and so forth. The loan portfolio of such a bank will be composed of prime personal and commercial loans with collateral and terms favorable to the bank. That is, the loans will be self-liquidating, of short maturity, and offering high yields.

A comparison of banks operating under

---

[7]See Call Reports, *Assets, Liabilities, and Capital Accounts Commercial and Mutual Savings Banks*, Federal Deposit Insurance Corporation, Washington, D. C.

these conditions with banks operating in states permitting branches (especially statewide branching), suggests a high loan turnover and higher earnings from loans for unit-system banks. On a comparative basis, the balance sheets of banks in states permitting branching will contain:

1. A larger loan to deposit ratio;
2. Lower earnings on the loan portfolio;
3. A smaller turnover of loans; and
4. A smaller holding of highly liquid assets.

In summary, our studies indicate that banks in unit banking states experience the highest average annual rate of earnings from loans and the highest loan turnover. Instead of contradicting the thesis

that banks in states permitting branching will experience the highest ratio of intra debits-to-deposits to total debits-to-deposits and as a result possess greater lending and earning power, these findings suggest that the behavior of banks in unit banking states results from monopolistic powers. The results of this study suggest that banks in branching states—especially statewide systems, experience a smaller loss of reserves through the clearing house, hold a larger proportion of earning assets in loans, and earn less per unit of output.

These findings are not surprising since they tend to agree with other studies on the economies of scale in commercial banking.

14. Commercial Bank Tax Swaps[*]
Federal Reserve Bank of Boston[†]

As the 1970's began, interest rates on many securities were or had recently been at their highest levels in over a century. This article examines the controversial hypothesis that in times of rising interest rates, commercial-bank loan expansion is held below what it would otherwise be by an unreasoned or "predilected" reluctance to realize losses on marketable securities. Underlying this hypothesis is the principle that selling securities below their book values impairs reported bank capital and the opinion that it is unwise for a bank to allow its reported capital to be impaired. The study's findings are seen to have significant tax reform implications.

[*]From *New England Business Review*, March, 1968. Reprinted by permission of the publisher, the Federal Reserve Bank of Boston.

[†]This article is based on a technical supplement, "Is There a Predilected Lock-In Effect?" by Professor Edward J. Kane of Boston College. Copies of the supplement are available on request from this Bank's Research Department.

Tax swaps are security trades that commercial banks (as well as other financial institutions) can undertake to reduce their Federal tax liabilities. These transactions are profitable mainly because the law provides different treatment for net capital gains than it does for net capital losses. Capital gains are realized when banks sell securities at higher-than-purchase prices, while capital losses are taken when banks sell securities below cost. Net capital gains (on securities held for 6 months or longer) are taxed at 25 percent. Net capital losses are deductible from ordinary income which for large banks is taxed at a 48 percent rate. By swapping their security holdings so that book values rise and fall with the interest rate cycle, knowledgable commercial bankers can reduce taxes substantially and increase after-tax profits over a period of years.

To determine the extent to which commercial banks engage in tax trading, a detailed statistical analysis was made of the 1966 capital gains and losses on securities at 47 large commercial banks located in 27 states throughout the country. This study was limited to large banks—those with more than $200 million of total deposits because banks of this size have a strong incentive to engage in tax swaps. On the other hand, small banks have little incentive for engaging in these operations since the first $25,000 of bank income is taxed at a 22 percent rate. The year 1966 was especially interesting because security prices fell dramatically and book losses were particularly severe. Two major highlights of the analysis were:

1. The Nation's very largest banks—those with over $1 billion in deposits—generally exploited opportunities for tax swapping much more energetically than banks with deposits ranging from $200 to $999 million. Apparently, a very large securities portfolio is required to generate sufficient tax savings to cover the cost of implementing a policy of aggressive tax trading.
2. The stronger a bank's net worth and operating income positions, the more willing it was to realize capital losses. Banks with less favorable financial ratios were found to take less advantage of the tax-trading laws. This finding provides some support for the notion of a "lock-in effort," which is part of a popular postwar economic theory that attempted to explain how monetary policy could curtail economic activity without causing dramatic rises in long-term interest rates. According to this theory, bankers are unwilling to provide funds for loans by selling securities at losses for fear they would reflect unfavorably on management competence. This study shows that in 1966 at least the reluctance of bank management to take losses was related to the strength of the bank's capital position.

THE TWO WAY OPTION

The tax advantages arising from the different treatment for capital gains and losses are subject to two legal restrictions. First, it is not possible in any one year to write security losses off against ordinary income and simultaneously to apply the lower rate to capital gains. All capital losses must be subtracted from all capital gains to obtain the *net* amount of gains or losses for a given year. Thus, to take full advantage of opportunities for tax saving, a bank must plan in advance to concentrate its losses and gains in separate years. If gains are taken in a "loss year" or losses in a "gain year," tax advantages are wasted. Second, tax write-offs are not allowed for the sale and repurchase of "substantially identical" securities within a 30-day period. On the other hand, if a bank sells a large volume of securities when bond prices are depressed and then waits 30 days before buying back the same securities, bond prices may rebound in the interim. In this situation, the banks would be paying a higher price for securities and their potential capital gains would be reduced. To avoid this possibility, banks usually do not wait 30 days but immediately acquire securities of a type allowable as "different" by the Internal Revenue Service. Although bankers feel that the IRS has been generous in its allowances, management of a portfolio for maximum tax benefits still involves technical problems. These together with the treacherous planning problems of insuring that gains and losses occur in different years require the attention of senior management, adding considerably to bank cost.

Despite the complexities involved, there is a strong case for using swaps to realize losses roughly as they accrue. For example, suppose that bond prices decline one year, but in the next successive year they recover fully. Imagine a bank whose net operating income in each year is $225,000 and whose book losses on securities in the first year amount to $100,000. If the bank does no tax swapping at all, it will pay Federal taxes amounting to:

22 percent of the first $25,000 ..	$ 5,500
48 percent of $200,000	$ 96,000
Total	$101,500

If the bank realized all its book losses in the first year, however, its taxable income would be $125,000, and its taxes $53,500.

Then if it realized $100,000 in gains during the second year, its tax for that year would be $101,500 on its regular income of $225,000 + $25,000 in capital gains for a total of $126,500. Thus, the gross tax saving over the 2 years consists of $23,000 in tax liabilities forgiven completely. [(2 × $101,500) − ($53,500 + $126,500).]

This, of course, represents "gross" profit only. To calculate the net profit, information is needed on how much it costs the bank to execute the swaps and to plan the portfolio correctly.

THE COST OF PLANNING TAX SWAPS

While everyone knows that interest rates rise and fall with economic activity, predicting the precise path of bond prices is a difficult task. Moreover, to maximize tax savings, the timing of gains and losses is of paramount importance. The portfolio must be maneuvered so that virtually no gains are taken in a loss year and no losses in a gain year.

Maturing bonds are a particular problem. If purchased below par value, they will provide an unavoidable gain in the year when they mature. If purchased above par, their maturity will mean a loss. If plans are made to hold securities until maturity, there are substantial risks that gains at maturity will be achieved in a loss year, and vice versa. Decisions may

even include questions of whether to bypass profitable opportunities because raising additional funds by securities sales would waste the tax advantage. In short, necessary planning to take maximum advantage of the two-way tax option is far from costless. An efficient, highly specialized and well-trained staff is a basic requirement and the portfolios of many banks are too small to justify this cost.

Data from the 47 sample banks studied suggest that the most aggressive tax trading takes place at the very largest commercial banks, those with deposits in excess of $1 billion. At the beginning of 1966, the 21 sample banks in this size class, had unrealized losses averaging less than .2 of 1 percent of the par value of their U. S. Government Securities portfolio. In contrast, the 26 sample banks with deposits between $200 and $999 million had unrealized losses averaging over .6 of 1 percent. This shows that during 1965 the largest banks were able to realize a greater share of available losses. During 1966, the largest banks were able to generate total losses equal to 2.5 percent of their U. S. Government portfolios while the smaller banks averaged only about 1 percent. As these comparisons show, the largest banks were far more aggressive than the smaller banks in taking tax losses.

RESTRAINTS ON LOSS-TAKING

Bankers generally wish to maintain a fairly steady growth in their published figures for earnings and capital. Selling securities at prices below their book values may prevent them from achieving this goal if security losses are large and if, as a result, net income falls below the level of the previous year. If a bank attempts to maximize profits over a period of years by taking security losses for tax swap purposes, it runs the risk of appearing less sound in relation to its competitors in the current year. Thus, some banks limit their volume of swaps in a loss year in order to avoid revealing declines in earnings or capital ratios.

Larger banks are often more concerned about preserving the appearance of their financial statements than small banks. Large banks have a greater proportion of depositors whose deposits exceed the $15,000 F.D.I.C. insurance limit. These depositors may become concerned about the uninsured portion of their deposits, if there is any question about the bank's financial position. Moreover, large banks have large corporate customers whose need for credit may strain the banks' legal limit on maximum loans to one borrower. If a bank lets its capital account decline —or even fail to keep pace with customer and deposit growth—it runs the risk of having to deny a critical loan request that could otherwise have been filled completely. Thus, on two counts a decline in bank earnings or capital ratios increases the likelihood of unfavorable shifts in large depositor accounts.

Statistical tests based on data from the sample study of 47 banks show that in 1966 capital accounts were an important restraining factor in the securities sales of commercial banks. Numerous statistical tests were used in an attempt to explain variations in net losses on securities sales at individual banks by differences in net-worth positions, expected future interest rates, maturity preferences, deposit size and other portfolio characteristics, and operating-earning levels. In every case the tests showed that other things being equal, the stronger the net-worth position of a bank, the larger were its net losses in 1966.

IMPACT ON LENDING

The study did not uncover any direct evidence of what impact the reluctance to take security losses had on banks' lending policies. It must be recognized that although the desire to maintain net worth may restrain a bank from selling securities, loan expansion is not necessarily limited.

Most banks are willing to take *some* capital losses. Also maturing securities may generate loanable funds. Finally banks can raise funds by other means, particularly through sale of certificates of deposit.

Even though alternative sources of funds might have been available for most banks, the observed reluctance to realize capital losses in 1966 probably did exert a constraining influence on the lending behavior of at least a few of the Nation's larger banks.

POLICY IMPLICATIONS

Do tax swaps tend to obstruct policy in periods of monetary restraint? In theory at least, they enable banks to make tax savings by selling securities at a loss and encourage them to acquire loanable funds during such periods. Such action would weaken the effectiveness of restraint policies. Yet, the study has shown that in addition to tax savings, banks also considered their net-worth and earnings positions before selling securities. Thus, even though tax swaps may not be a major obstacle to policies of monetary restraint, such policies would function more effectively if tax swaps were not allowed.

Other issues that arise from studies of tax swaps concern tax policy. Does this provision in the tax law benefit the economy as much as it costs? Certainly it does provide some benefits. Among them are the following:

1. In financial crises when bond prices fall sharply, the provision for writing off capital losses against ordinary income softens the impact on banks of bond-liquidation losses (especially through loss-carryback and carry-forward provisions). Thus banks are enabled to maintain and rebuild their net-worth positions.

2. The cushioning of the impact of financial crises gives banks more operating confidence in general. As a result, they are probably encouraged to take somewhat riskier loan and investment positions than they would otherwise.

3. It helps bank earnings.

These benefits are not achieved without costs, however. First, Federal tax revenues are lost—which is why commercial banks engage in security swaps. Second, while swaps help bank earnings, this study shows that the largest banks benefit much more than smaller banks. Third, with simpler tax provisions, resources now devoted to security swaps could be employed in more productive pursuits.

One proposal for tax reform would eliminate low tax rates on security capital gains for financial institutions. This would simplify portfolio management and reduce inequities between large and small banks. Capital gains would be handled as ordinary income and taxed at the same rate. In essence, security portfolios of banks would be treated as stock-in-trade, and any gains and losses would be handled in the same way as inventory gains and losses of manufacturing and trade establishments. This would encourage banks to take losses roughly as they occur but to defer taking gains as long as possible.

This reform would maintain the full offset for security losses to protect financial institutions in the event of crises. Since such a tax system would simplify portfolio management, it would improve the competitive position of small banks in relation to large ones. At the same time, tax revenues would be increased at the expense of banks' net income.

Commercial banks, however, already pay higher taxes on retained earnings than such competing financial institutions as mutual savings banks and savings and loan associations. If the capital gains provision were eliminated, some readjustment would be needed to prevent deterioration in the competitive position of commercial banks. This could be accomplished by adjusting the treatment of tax-exempt transfers to loan-loss reserves at different types of financial institutions. At the present time the permissible level of reserves (as a percentage of loans) is much lower for commercial banks than it is for most of their competitors.

15. Investment Strategy of Pooled Funds*

Frank L. Voorheis

Pension funds, because of their size, have material impact in the security markets. Trust departments of commercial banks administer a large portion of private pension fund assets. A common procedure is to "pool" or lump together several funds (personal trusts) to gain investment advantages typically available to larger trusts only. This article describes and evaluates the investment management and performance of such pooled funds.

An estimated 36 million of the more than 70 million civilian workers now employed in the United States are covered by retirement programs other than social security. The growth of assets of these private employee benefit plans over the past three decades has been nothing short

*"Investment Strategy of Pooled Funds," Frank L. Voorheis, MSU Business Topics, Spring,

1969. Reprinted by permission of the publisher (the Bureau of Business and Economic Research, Division of Research, Graduate School of Business Administration, Michigan State University).

of spectacular. With reserves of less than $3 billion in 1940, assets of private pension funds, which include reserves of insured and non-insured plans, currently total more than $100 billion. This figure according to government estimates should exceed $225 billion by 1980.

Non-insured plans, which are usually funded through a trustee, have been the principal method utilized by employers for managing assets of private retirement programs. Comprising less than 54 percent of total reserves in 1950, non-insured plans now account for about 70 percent of private pension fund assets. Reserves of non-insured plans have increased from $6.5 billion in 1950 to $58.1 billion in 1965, and to $75.8 billion as of June 30, 1968.[1] A major portion of the assets of non-insured plans is administered by trust departments of commercial banks.

It is not surprising that the retirement programs of a few hundred giant corporations account for a very large percentage of total reserves of all private non-insured pension plans. Partly because smaller firms often experience higher operating costs, lower and more uncertain earnings, and greater enterprise mortality, they have lagged behind their larger rivals in adopting deferred compensation plans.[2] In recent years, however, the reserves of employee benefit plans of smaller companies have also risen quite dramatically as these employers have included defined retirement benefits as part of the wage package.

Since required contributions by small companies to an employee benefit plan

may be rather insignificant in amount, in some cases less than $1,000 annually, an adequate degree of diversification, liquidity, and operating efficiency in the investment process is not usually possible unless some type of pooling arrangement is employed. The purpose of this article is to discuss the nature and use of pooled funds as an investment medium for small-to-medium-sized employee benefit plans, to describe recent changes in the investment strategy adhered to in managing these funds, and to present performance records of several banks administering equity portfolios on a pooling basis.

The concept of pooling several personal trusts, each of which is too small to individually attain various investment advantages usually available only to larger trusts, is a well-established banking principle. Prior to 1955, however, the pooling concept could be employed only for managing assets of personal trusts, not for investing reserves of employee benefit plans. Reserves of private retirement plans could be invested only in accordance with Section 10 of Regulation F as promulgated by the Board of Governors of the Federal Reserve System. On June 13, 1955, Regulation F was amended to permit collective investment of reserves of retirement programs provided that each participating trust was exempt from federal income taxes. Further legislation was enacted on September 28, 1962, which expanded trust powers of national banks and transferred authority over these trust powers from the Board of Governors of the Federal Reserve System to the Comptroller of the Currency, where it now rests.[3]

HOW POOLED FUNDS OPERATE

Most collective investment arrangements are based upon either the balanced fund concept or the multi-fund concept.

[1] Sources: President's Committee on Corporate Pension Funds and Other Retirement and Welfare Programs, *Public Policy and Private Pension Programs—A Report to the President on Private Employee Retirement Plans* (Washington, D. C.: U. S. Government Printing Office, January, 1965), and *Statistical Bulletin,* Securities and Exchange Commission, August, 1967 and 1968.

[2] U. S. Congress, Senate, Subcommittee on Employment and Retirement Incomes of the Special Committee on Aging, *Hearing, Extending Private Pension Coverage,* Statement of Merton C. Bernstein, 89th Congress, 1st Session, 1965, Part 1, p. 18.

[3] "Years of Reform, A Prelude to Progress," 101st Annual Report, Comptroller of the Currency, U. S. Treasury (Washington, D. C.: U. S. Government Printing Office, 1963), p. 13.

Under a balanced fund approach, the reserves of participating trusts are collectively invested in a fund comprised of both debt and equity securities, the proportion of each being dependent upon the general investment requirements of the participating trusts. If the employees of most participating trusts, for example, are several years away from retirement, a relatively larger portion of the combined assets, perhaps as much as 75 percent, will be invested in equities since combating inflation would be an important investment objective.

Because of the greater degree of flexibility which can be attained by participating trusts, most banks now administer pooled funds on a multi-fund basis. In the late fifties and early sixties, this approach was often referred to as either a dual fund plan or a two fund plan. An equity fund was invested in common stocks and in securities convertible into common stocks while a fixed income fund was usually limited to bonds, preferred stocks, and other securities providing a fixed return. In recent years, several banks have added additional specialized funds to their collective investment programs to better enable participating trusts to tailor investment selections to income requirements. Most banks now offer a fixed income mortgage and real estate fund, the assets of which are invested in various types of mortgages and other real estate interests. Rather than offering a single common stock fund, many banks have split their equity portfolios into two divisions. Common stocks with only average growth potential make up one division, while the other is reserved for equities with greater growth potential, and thus with lower current dividend yields. Also, some eastern banks distinguish between pooled funds for pension plans and pooled funds for profit sharing plans, partly because the desired degree of liquidity under each plan may be different. The allocation of a participating trust's reserves among these various specialized funds is based upon several factors such as the number of employees covered by the plan, the average age of the employees, the presence of other employee benefit plans, and whether benefits are tied to a cost of living index.

The operation of a pooled fund is quite similar to that of a mutual fund. Like a mutual fund, a pooled fund offers new shares (or units as they are frequently called) for sale, and stands ready to redeem existing shares or units for cash at the request of a participating trust. While mutual funds usually determine their net asset value per share at least daily and sometimes more frequently, pooled funds generally limit valuations to the last day of each month. For smaller banks, valuations may be as infrequent as once each quarter. Deposits to or withdrawals from a pooled fund may be made only on the valuation dates. A unit is valued by summing the current market prices for all the fund's securities and assets, subtracting any liabilities of the fund (generally limited to audit fees and bank service charges), and dividing the remaining amount by the number of units outstanding. Any income received by a pooled fund in the form of interest and dividends is usually reinvested in additional securities rather than distributed to participating trusts. Therefore, reinvested income is reflected in the calculated unit values. For those banks which do not adhere to the policy of continuous reinvestment of current income, distribution of such income to unit holders is made on the valuation dates. If the cash is not needed by the participating trusts, additional units in the fund are purchased.

While banks generally levy no charge for managing a collective investment fund, a fee is imposed for administering the assets of each trust participating in a pooled fund. The fee is usually determined either quarterly or semi-annually and is expressed as a percentage of the market value of the assets of the participating trust. A typical fee schedule for a bank in the Midwest administering pooled funds for pension and profit sharing plans is as follows: 0.5 percent on the first $100,000 of trust assets, 0.25 to 0.33 percent of the next $900,000, 0.125 percent on the next $4 million, 0.067 percent on the next $20 million, and 0.05 percent on any excess over $25 million. The minimum fee is $250. In contrast, the average mutual fund deducts between 0.5 and 0.75 of 1 percent of net asset value from investment income to cover operating expenses. Mutual funds which are sold through stockbrokers and other seller organizations also levy a loading charge on the buyer which averages 7.5 to 8.5 percent of the selling price. There are of course, no selling charges for a bank-administered pooled fund. However, banks do charge a fee for providing participating trusts with various clerical services, which may include maintaining participants' records under profit sharing plans and preparing and mailing checks to benefit recipients.

GROWTH OF POOLED FUNDS

According to annual surveys conducted from 1960 through 1965 by *Trusts and Estates,* the number of banks administering pooled funds for employee benefit plans increased from 64 to 122 over the five-year period. Growth in terms of assets controlled by pooled funds was even more dramatic. Amounting to less than $440 million in 1960, the book value of pooled fund assets climbed to nearly $2.5 billion by 1965, a relative increase of over 400 percent. During this same five-year period, total reserves of all private pension and profit sharing plans increased from $52 billion to about $85 billion, a percentage increase well under that for pooled funds.

Data concerning the size and growth of pooled funds for the last few years are almost nonexistent. An estimate of the current amount of reserves in pooled funds can be obtained, however, by observing the historical relationship between pooled fund assets and total pension and profit sharing reserves in years for which data are available. Assets of pooled funds as a percentage of total private retirement assets increased from 1.15 percent in 1960 to 3.1 percent in 1964. If this trend has continued in recent years, assets of pooled funds should now account for over 6 percent of the estimated $103 billion of private pension and profit sharing reserves, or at least $6 billion.

INVESTMENT MANAGEMENT

Portfolio managers of pension funds, and particularly managers of pooled funds for employee benefit plans, probably have a greater degree of operating flexibility than any other investment administrator, including individual investors and institutions.[4] Since pension and profit sharing funds are usually approved for tax exemption by the Internal Revenue Service, income and capital gains earned on investments are tax free. Thus, tax effects need not be considered by the administrator when liquidating overpriced issues or acquiring high yielding securities. Also, in view of dramatic asset growth rates experienced in recent years by most employee retirement funds, and the expectation for continued high rates of growth over at least the next decade, there is little need for liquidity in most pension and profit sharing trusts. With new deposits greatly exceeding cash withdrawals, an extremely large proportion of a retirement program's reserves can be placed in long-term, high yielding securities. Moreover, large inflows of new money enable investment managers of pension trusts to restructure portfolios solely

---

[4]Jerome B. Cohen and Edward D. Zinbarg, *Investment Analysis and Portfolio Management* (Homewood, Illinois: Richard D. Irwin, 1967), p. 719.

through the purchasing of new issues, rather than through a combination of buying and selling which may result in depressing prices of securities sold in relatively thin markets. Although large cash inflows during periods of declining stock prices may dampen investment performance, in the longer run the advantage of abundant cash flows probably more than offsets the concomitant disadvantages. Finally, portfolio managers of pooled funds are afforded an additional degree of operating flexibility because participating trusts are not of sufficient size to influence either the selection of investments for the pooled fund or the timing of security purchases and sales. This may not be the case if a retirement trust is administered exclusively for a giant employer.

Several changes in the investment strategy followed in managing pension and profit sharing funds have taken place in recent years. Since there is little need for either current income or stability of principal in trusts of most employee benefit plans, increasing amounts of reserves are being allocated to equities. Common stocks now comprise about 55 percent of total assets of private pension plans, up from 47 percent in 1962.[5] The giant $6 billion AT&T fund at year-end 1967 had nearly 24 percent of its assets in common stocks, up markedly from 13 percent in 1964 and 9.9 percent in 1962.[6] Greater emphasis is being placed on the selection of growth stocks rather than income stocks. This increased emphasis is reflected in the growing number of special situation and growth stock pooled funds now available to participating trusts. Bank trustees are no longer content to follow a simple buy and hold policy, which was so widely adopted in the 1950s and early 1960s. Rather, fund managers are becoming more performance oriented, adopting

when possible the strategy of switching out of overpriced issues and into undervalued situations. The degree of diversification in bank-administered funds is being reduced as investments are concentrated among fewer issues. One of the largest banks in the Midwest, for example, has cut the number of issues in its pooled equity fund from 122 to 63 in the last five years. Some banks are no longer allocating the fixed income portion of a trust to fixed interest-bearing bonds.[7] Instead, funds once destined for bonds are being shifted to investment quality bank and utility stocks as well as to convertible bonds and preferred stocks. By switching to investment quality stocks, bank trustees feel investment returns will improve since the fund will be more heavily hedged against inflation. These more aggressive managerial tactics of bank trustees are being reflected in higher portfolio turnover rates. While portfolio turnover rates of less than 7 percent were commonplace as recently as three to five years ago, bank-administered pension funds may now experience turnover rates as high as 15 to 20 percent.

INVESTMENT PERFORMANCE

By adopting these more aggressive and imaginative portfolio management tactics, bank trustees hope to achieve higher returns on invested reserves, and thereby either raise employee benefits or reduce employer costs. An improvement of 1 percent in investment returns over a sustained period of time can increase benefits to employees by as much as 25 percent or decrease costs to employers by as much as 20 percent.[8] While bonds, preferred stocks, and other fixed income securities typically provide a major portion of a retirement fund's current income, overall

---

[5]*The Wall Street Journal,* February 7, 1968, p. 27.

[6]*The Wall Street Journal,* October 19, 1968, p. 31.

[7]*The New York Times,* June 5, 1968, p. 62.

[8]Paul L. Howell, "Common Stocks and Pension Fund Investing", *Harvard Business Review* (November, December, 1958), p. 93.

investment performance, which includes capital appreciation as well as dividend income, is largely dependent upon the performance of equity issues. Therefore, an examination of the performance records compiled by bank trustees administering pooled equity funds for employee benefit plans should provide valuable insight as to the level of investment returns banks are achieving when managing the assets of pension and profit sharing trusts.

Some indication of the level of investment performance being achieved by commercial banks administering a pooled equity fund as part of a collective investment trust for employee plans is provided by the performance records of four Michigan banks. The annual rates of return achieved by the four banks from date of fund inception through 1967 are shown in Table 1. These annual performance figures include all realized and unrealized appreciation or depreciation as well as the receipt of any current dividend income. The data reveal that, while the annual investment returns achieved by the four banks tend to move in the same general direction from year to year, the amount of the change among the funds varies greatly.

Table 2 presents annual rates of return that would be earned on a fund that was invested exclusively in the stocks com-

TABLE 2
Annual Rates of Return*
on Popular Market Averages
December 31, 1961—December 31, 1967
(percentages)

Year Ended Dec. 31	Dow-Jones Industrial Average	Standard and Poor's 425 Industrial Stock Index	Standard and Poor's Common Stock Index
1961 ..	22.8	27.0	27.1
1962 ..	(7.7)	(10.1)	(8.9)
1963 ..	20.8	24.1	22.9
1964 ..	19.0	16.6	16.5
1965 ..	14.4	13.2	12.4
1966 ..	(16.6)	(10.5)	(9.6)
1967 ..	19.3	27.2	23.3

*Adjusted for cash dividends.

prising one of the popular market averages. Since the investment of reserves of an employee benefit plan in the stocks included in one of the market averages (which would result, in effect, in an unmanaged investment portfolio) is an investment strategy available to administrators of most pooled equity funds, the use of such averages as performance benchmarks by trusts participating in a collective investment fund is quite appropriate. A comparison of Tables 1 and 2 reveals that the participating banks have usually not outperformed the popular market averages.

Table 3 presents rate-of-return data in a form more useful for evaluating longer-term investment performance of bank trustees. The data show the average annual compound rates of return earned through 1967 on the deposit of one dollar at the end of a selected year. For example, a deposit of one dollar in the pooled equity fund of Bank B earned 10.1 percent on an average annual compound basis over the seven-year period Dec. 31, 1960 through Dec. 31, 1967. Similar to the results shown in Table 1, the data in Table 3 reveal a considerable degree of dispersion among the cumulative returns of the four banks.

TABLE 1
Annual Rates of Return*
of Selected Pooled Equity Funds
December 31, 1961—December 31, 1967
(percentages)

Year Ended Dec. 31	Bank A	B	C	D
1961	—	22.6	21.7	—
1962	(8.9)	(9.6)	(9.4)	—
1963	17.1	18.1	16.9	15.3
1964	15.3	14.9	12.2	12.8
1965	10.2	16.3	(5.4)	8.9
1966	(11.1)	(6.5)	(12.3)	(10.8)
1967	24.7	20.0	21.1	16.8

*Adjusted for any cash dividends not reinvested.

TABLE 3
Annual Compound Rates of Return*
of Selected Pooled Equity Funds
for Selected Periods
(percentages)

Year Ended	Bank			
	A	B	C	D
1960–1967	–	10.1	5.5	–
1961–1967	7.2	8.1	3.0	–
1962–1967	10.8	12.1	5.7	8.1
1963–1967	9.2	10.7	3.0	6.3
1964–1967	7.3	9.3	.2	4.3
1965–1967	5.9	5.9	3.0	2.0
1966–1967	24.7	20.0	21.1	16.8

*Adjusted for any cash dividends not reinvested.

TABLE 4
Annual Compound Rates of Return*
on Popular Market Averages
for Selected Periods

Year Ended		Standard and Poor's	
	Dow-Jones Industrial Average	425 Industrial Stock Index	Composite Common Stock Index
1960–1967	9.2	11.4	11.0
1961–1967	7.1	9.0	8.5
1962–1967	10.3	13.3	12.4
1963–1967	7.9	10.7	9.9
1964–1967	4.4	8.8	7.8
1965–1967	(.2)	6.7	5.6
1966–1967	19.3	27.2	23.3

*Adjusted for cash dividends.

Table 4 shows the cumulative performance records of the three market averages being used as comparative yardsticks. A comparison of the data in Tables 3 and 4 indicates that the four institutions have usually failed to achieve cumulative returns in excess of those shown for the popular market averages. An investment in any one of the three market averages prior to 1965, for example, would have provided a greater average annual compound rate of return through 1967 than an investment of an equal amount in the pooled equity funds of either Bank C or Bank D. While the funds of Banks A and B have consistently outperformed the Dow-Jones industrial average on a cumulative basis, neither of these funds achieved returns exceeding those of either the Standard and Poor's 425 industrial stock index or the 500 composite stock index in a majority of the years studied.

Additional data concerning the performance of pooled equity funds have been provided by a recent study covering 43 of an approximate 49 funds in operation continuously over the five-year period 1960 through 1964.[9] A distribution of the

[9]Frank L. Voorheis, *Pooled Equity Funds for Employee Benefit Plans* (East Lansing: Bureau of Business and Economic Research, Graduate School of Business Administration, Michigan State University, 1967).

average annual compound rates of return achieved over the five-year period by the administering banks is shown in Table 5. The data reveal a considerable degree of dispersion among the cumulative returns realized. Compound appreciation varied from less than 4 percent to nearly 14 percent over the five-year period. The median return for the sample as a whole was 10 percent.

Table 6 compares the performance of the 43 funds with that of the popular market averages. The data reveal that a majority of the funds performed better than the Standard and Poor's composite com-

TABLE 5
Distribution of 43 Pooled Equity
Funds by Average Annual
Compound Rates of Return*
December 31, 1959—December 31, 1964

Average Annual Compound Rates of Return (percentages)	Number of Funds
Less than 5	1
5 and less than 7	3
7 and less than 9	10
9 and less than 11	16
11 and less than 13	12
13 and over	1
	43

*Adjusted for any cash dividends not reinvested.

mon stock index and the Dow-Jones industrial average in both 1960 and 1961. Between 1962 and 1964, most funds failed to match either of the indexes. Over the entire five-year period, 30 funds outperformed the Dow-Jones industrial average, while only 15 funds achieved an average annual compound rate of return superior to that of the Standard and Poor's composite common stock index. In general, these findings are similar to those shown above for the four Michigan banks.

TABLE 6
Performance of 43 Pooled Equity
Funds Compared With
Popular Market Averages*
December 31, 1959—December 31, 1964

	Number Outperforming	
Year Ended Dec. 31	Dow-Jones Industrial Average	Standard and Poor's Composite Common Stock index
1960	33	42
1961	25	34
1962	12	5
1963	5	8
1964	10	5
Five-year period 1960–64	15	30

*Adjusted for cash dividends.

CONCLUSIONS

Increasing from less than $440 million of reserves in 1960 to an approximate $6 billion today, bank-administered pooled funds for employee benefit plans have grown to become a popular investment medium for assets of small-to-intermediate-sized pension and profit sharing trusts. Accompanying this growth of pooled fund assets have been several discernible changes by managing institutions in investment strategy. Larger percentage allocations to equity issues, declining levels of investment diversification, replacement of bonds and preferred stocks in fixed

income funds with investment quality income stocks, and higher portfolio turnover rates are changes indicative of adherence to a more aggressive and imaginative investment philosophy by bank trustees.

While the performance data presented above on pooled equity funds probably do not fully reflect these recent changes in investment strategy, they do reveal that investment returns achieved varied greatly among administering banks, and that these returns were generally less than those shown for the popular market averages. Two comments regarding these findings are in order. First, given the large degree of dispersion in returns earned by the respective banks, it is evident that the selection of a bank trustee can have as much influence on investment performance (and hence on employee benefits or employer costs) as the selection of the investments themselves. Therefore, before the reserves of a retirement program are committed to a particular bank trustee for portfolio administration, the performance records of several banks offering investment management services ought to be thoroughly analyzed, using perhaps some of the techniques employed by a security analyst. Second, although the performance records of many of the banks examined are rather poor when compared to those of the popular market averages, it cannot necessarily be argued that a random investment strategy would have provided participating trusts with more favorable investment results. Investment returns are believed to be directly correlated with risk. Thus, if sponsors of employee benefit plans have a high aversion to risk, they may be quite content with below average returns together with a lower variability of return, for example, less than average risk. Whether the below average returns achieved by the banks were actually accompanied by lower degrees of variability is a question which cannot be adequately answered with the information made available.

16. Portfolio Strategies for Bank Holding Companies[*]

Paul F. Jessup

The portfolio policies of bank holding companies have been mainly concerned with acquisition of stock of subsidiary banks. Little attention has been given to the selling side. This posture, it is argued, has contributed to a burdensome regulatory structure. This article examines the recent growth of bank holding companies and suggests various portfolio strategies aimed at increasing both investment flexibility and profits.

Bank holding companies should focus more on portfolio management. Such a policy, which implies relatively reduced emphasis on directing and monitoring the operations of subsidiary banks, should benefit both shareholders of bank holding companies and the public.

At the present time, portfolios of bank holding companies consist principally of shares of subsidiary banks. At times a portfolio is increased by acquiring additional shares of affiliated banks and by acquiring shares in new affiliates. Rarely, however, are shares sold. The behavioral pattern is that of an investor who gradually adds to his holdings—but seldom reassesses them in order to sell those with the least potential.

Dynamic portfolio management involves constant reappraisal of current holdings in order to relate their probable performances to that of alternative investment opportunities. This approach, which is not new to bankers concerned about performance of trust accounts, emphasizes continual evaluations of risk-return relationships. When an alternative investment is judged preferable to a current holding, the new asset should be purchased and the less-promising asset sold. A similar emphasis on dynamic portfolio managemnt should be applicable to bank holding companies.

BANK HOLDING COMPANIES AS OPERATING SYSTEMS

By the early 1900's, there were chain systems of banks, whereby individuals or groups controlled more than one bank. Gradually, control of multiple banks was achieved through the corporate form—the bank holding company. With its indefinite charter, limited liability, and potentially greater depth of management and capital resources, the corporate form has become the preferred vehicle for owning multiple banks.

In states with laws prohibiting or limiting branch systems, holding companies were frequently organized by bankers as a method of approximating proscribed branch systems.[1] Not only might holding companies achieve some economies of scale, flexibility, and benefits of diversification; but they were seen as potential

[*]From Bankers Magazine, Spring, 1969. Reprinted by permission of the publisher, Warren, Gorham & Lamont, Inc.

[1]The motives summarized in this paragraph are presented and further developed by Gerald C. Fischer in Bank Holding Companies (New York: Columbia University Press, 1961), pp. 18–32.

branch systems should state legislation later permit branching or more extensive branching. In addition, holding companies might control banks in several states, while branch systems, with minor exceptions, were limited to one state or subdivision. Some holding company systems were developed to reduce the possibility of regional banking structures becoming dominated by holding companies based in other states; while others were to protect correspondent relationships from preemption by rival banks. Common to these motives for developing holding companies is a view of them as operating systems—to protect or extend established patterns of bank management.

After a period of rapid expansion during the late 1920's, growth of bank holding companies slowed during the 1930's. Confronted by years of crisis in the nation's financial structure, officials of bank holding companies had to focus on the survival of affiliated banks, reinforcing the traditional concern about operating characteristics of each bank in a system. A related feature of the national banking crisis was the Banking Act of 1933, the first Federal law providing for regulation of bank holding companies.[2] However, its provisions were believed to be inadequate by the Federal Reserve System, which advocated broader jurisdiction over bank holding companies.[3] Depressed economic conditions and regulatory uncertainties thus restrained the expansion of holding company systems during the 1930's and 1940's. In the early 1950's, until the Bank Holding Company Act of 1956 became law, holding companies accelerated their acquisition of banks before the probable advent of restrictions through new federal legislation.[4]

The Bank Holding Company Act of 1956

The principal objectives of the Bank Holding Company Act of 1956 were to control the expansion of bank holding companies and to require that they divest themselves of nonbank affiliates.[5] Under the Act, as amended, a company that directly or indirectly controls 25 percent or more of the stock of two or more banks, or that controls the election of a majority of directors or two or more banks, is a bank holding company.[6] It is required to register with the Board of Governors of the Federal Reserve System, and many of its activities are regulated by the Board.

The Act further specifies that a registered bank holding company: (1) must obtain prior approval of the Board before acquiring more than 5 percent of the voting stock of any bank; (2) may not control the voting stock of companies that engage in any business other than banking, managing banks, or furnishing services to subsidiary banks; and (3) may not acquire any control over an additional bank located outside the state in which the holding company has its principal office or conducts its principal business, unless the laws of the state in which the bank is located specifically authorize such action. (States retain authority to regulate bank holding companies and banks within their borders.) The Act, as amended and as interpreted by the Board of Governors, is the principal regulatory framework within which bank holding companies must function.

RECENT EXPANSION OF BANK HOLDING COMPANIES

After passage of the Bank Holding Company Act, aggregate expansion of

[2]"Group Banking in the United States," *Federal Reserve Bulletin* (Vol. 24, No. 2), February 1938, pp. 92–101, especially p. 97.

[3]*Thirtieth Annual Report of the Board of Governors of the Federal Reserve System*, 1943, pp. 34–37.

[4]Fischer, pp. 39–42.

[5]*Federal Reserve Bulletin* (Vol. 42, No. 5), May 1956, pp. 444–453, especially p. 444.

[6]The principal provisions of the amended Act outlined in this paragraph are largely quoted from Robert J. Lawrence, *The Performance of Bank Holding Companies*, Board of Governors of the Federal Reserve System, June 1967, pp. 1, 3.

TABLE 1

Changes in the Role of Registered Bank Holding Companies
in the American Banking System Since 1956

Item	Year-end Figures				
	1956	1960	1965	1966	1967
Number of holding companies°	49	42	48	58	65
Number of states†	35	31	32	35	35
Number of commercial banks in—					
Holding companies	433	426	468	561	603
United States	13,640	13,471	13,804	13,769	13,720
Percentage of commercal banks in holding companies	3.2	3.2	3.4	4.1	4.4
Percentage of commercial banking offices in holding companies	‡	6.2	6.7	7.8	8.6
Total deposits (billions of dollars) in—					
Holding companies	15	18	28	41	50
United States	198	230	332	353	396
Percentage of total deposits in holding companies	7.6	8.0	8.3	11.6	12.6

°Numbers are for separate bank groups. For example, on December 31, 1967, there were 74 registered companies; but they represented only 65 separate bank groups. Such differences arise because some groups are controlled by other registered holding companies.
†In 1966 and 1967 the District of Columbia is included.
‡Not available for 1956. At year-end 1957 the figure was 5.9.
Sources: Robert J. Lawrence, *The Performance of Bank Holding Companies* (Board of Governors of the Federal Reserve System, June 1967), Table 1, p. 2; and *Federal Reserve Bulletins.*

bank holding was minimal. During 1957–65 the number of holding companies decreased from 49 to 48, while the percentage of the nation's banks in holding company systems increased from 3.2 to 3.4 (Table 1). In the same time interval, holding company affiliates increased their percentage of the nation's bank deposits from 7.6 to 8.3. Apparently, officials of existing holding companies delayed possible acquisitions—and potential organizers deferred creation of new systems—until the Board of Governors' regulatory policy became more clearly defined. Another probable reason for delay was the need for clarification or amendment of state statutes affecting bank holding companies.

As indicated in Table 1, the relative role of bank holding companies has increased since 1965, whether measured by number of holding companies, percentage of banks controlled by holding companies, or percentage of bank deposits held by their affiliates. Two factors explain most of this change: (1) a 1966 amendment to the Bank Holding Company Act provided for inclusion of several systems that

had been exempt under the original Act; and (2) formation of new systems in such states as Florida, New York, Virginia, and Wisconsin. Creation of new systems has been largely due to revised state laws facilitating holding company expansion while continuing to circumscribe branching activities. Notably, all the new holding companies are *intrastate* systems; none has overcome the regulatory constraint on interstate expansion.

While formation of new intrastate holding companies has recently accelerated, some of the older companies have been constrained in their growth opportunities. They have grown, as measured by deposits, profits, and share prices; but these increases have been principally through internal growth of affiliated banks.

External Growth

External growth, through acquisitions and chartering of new banks, has been limited. During the years 1956–67, the ten largest bank holding companies applied to acquire 23 banks; and 16 of these applications were approved by the Board of Governors (Table 2).

TABLE 2

Regulatory Decisions on Applications by the Ten Largest Holding Companies to Acquire New Affiliates: 1956–67*

| | Application to Acquire | | |
Decision	Existing Bank	Proposed Bank	Total
Approval	16	7	23
Denial	7	4	11
Total	23	11	34

*These are the ten largest bank holding companies in continuous existence since passage of the Bank Holding Company Act of 1956.
Sources: Jules Backman, *The Bank Holding Company Act* (*The Bulletin of the C. J. Devine Institute of Finance*, April–June 1963), Appendix, pp. 48–52; and *Federal Reserve Bulletins*.

The same holding companies applied for permission to establish 11 new banks, and 7 of these applications were approved. The preceding figures undoubtedly understate the impact of regulatory policy. Other acquisitions or charters were probably desired but never formally requested because management assigned a low probability to obtaining regulatory approval. In ruling on holding company applications to acquire existing banks or establish new banks, the Board of Governors often has given principal weight to the probable effects of such acquisitions on competition in the relevant banking markets.[7]

Another procedure by which bank holding companies can try to grow externally is to have their affiliates acquire banks through direct mergers. This process, which is most feasible in states permitting the acquired bank to be retained as a branch, is regulated by federal supervisory agencies. As does the Bank Holding Company Act, the Bank Merger Act of 1960 (as amended) provides that the regulatory agencies evaluate the probable impact of a proposed merger on competition in the relevant banking market.[8] During the years 1956–67, bank affiliates of seven of the 10 largest holding companies acquired approximately 44 banks through merger processes; and two of the 10 holding companies accounted for 70 percent of these indirect acquisitions.[9]

Affiliates of the older bank holding companies have been generally unable to increase their percentage of state deposits from 1956–67, and in some cases their market share has declined (Table 3). Recognizing limitations to this measure, it does tend to confirm the inability of holding company systems to expand more rapidly than their aggregate state competition. (Furthermore, aggregate deposit figures for the systems may reflect aggressive use of negotiable certificates of deposit by the metropolitan banks rather than diversified expansion by each affiliate.) In view of present operating strategies within the regulatory environment, it is difficult (based on market share) for a bank holding company's portfolio of banks to outperform the state averages. If the portfolio is "inefficient," it is likely to perform more poorly than the averages.

Limited in their opportunities to grow by adding new banks to their systems, older bank holding companies have emphasized the internal growth of affiliated banks; and they have expanded in such areas as foreign branches, Edge Act corporations, and data-processing centers. Such areas of expansion accord with tra-

---

[7]Jules Backman, "The Bank Holding Company Act," *The Bulletin of the C. J. Devine Institute of Finance* (No. 24–25), New York University, April–June 1963, pp. 45–47. Also, George R. Hall, "Bank Holding Company Regulation," *The Southern Economic Journal* (Vol. XXXI, No. 4), April 1965, pp. 346–353.

[8]*Federal Reserve Bulletin*, March 1966, pp. 337–339. Also see *Studies in Banking Competition and the Banking Structure*, The Administrator of National Banks, United States Treasury, January 1966, especially pp. 3–96.
[9]This tabulation has been prepared from various editions of *Moody's Bank and Finance Manual* and *Polk's Bank Directory*. All mergers by holding company affiliates (particularly the smaller banks) may not have been reported in these sources, in which case the tabulation understates the extent of this merger process.

TABLE 3
Total Deposits in Affiliate Banks of Ten Registered Bank Holding Companies as a Percentage of Total Commercial Bank Deposits: by State°

Holding Company and State	December 31, 1956	December 30, 1967
BancOhio Corporation		
Ohio	6	6
Baystate Corporation		
Massachusetts	9	10
Citizens & Southern National Bank		
Georgia	22	20
First Bank System, Inc.		
Minnesota	30	30
Montana	31	29
North Dakota	18	18
South Dakota	8	11
Wisconsin	†	†
First Security Corporation		
Idaho	34	31
Utah	29	31
Wyoming	1	1
First Wisconsin Bankshares Corporation		
Wisconsin	21	17
Marine Midland Banks, Inc.		
New York	5	6
Northwest Bancorporation		
Iowa	6	6
Minnesota	27	24
Montana	13	15
Nebraska	10	10
North Dakota	18	17
South Dakota	24	23
Wisconsin	†	†
Shawmut Association, Inc.		
Massachusetts	12‡	11
Western Bancorporation		
Arizona	35	34
California	4	8
Colorado	4	5
Idaho	7	11
Montana	6	5
Nevada	76	59
New Mexico	14	14
Oregon	45	43
Utah	19	17
Washington	6	7
Wyoming	17	15

°These are the ten largest holding company systems in existence during the time interval, 1956–67.

To illustrate the derivation of these percentages, at year-end 1956 the affiliate banks of BancOhio Corporation had $599 million in deposits, while total deposits in all of Ohio's commercial banks was $10,158 million.

†Less than one percent.

‡This figure includes the deposits of National Shawmut Bank with those of its affiliate banks.

Sources: Tabulations based on figures reported in *Moody's Bank & Finance Manual*, 1957, 1958; *Polk's Bank Directory*, March 1957; *Annual Report of the Federal Deposit Insurance Corporation for the Year Ended December 31, 1956*, Table 103, pp. 100–101; *Bank Operating Statistics: 1967*, Federal Deposit Insurance Corporation; and "Subsidiary Banks of Bank Holding Companies: December 31, 1967," (mimeo) Board of Governors of Federal Reserve System.

ditional views of holding companies as bank operating systems.

A DYNAMIC APPROACH TO PORTFOLIO MANAGEMENT

A bank holding company can be viewed as a portfolio of shares of banks and related enterprises. With this view, strategies can then be analyzed that should contribute to maximizing the value of this set of assets. Dynamic portfolio management involves a continuous reappraisal of risk-return relationships of the shares in the existing portfolio and also of alternative opportunities. Where an alternative investment is judged to provide a greater return for an acceptable level of risk, then a less-promising asset should be sold and the proceeds invested in the more-promising asset. Through time, such a decision process will result in improved performance of the total portfolio.

Because of regulatory constraints, bank holding companies have been limited in their opportunities to buy shares of: banks outside their home state, nonbank-related enterprises, and even banks within their home state. Such restraints on entering new geographic and product markets limit the opportunities of registered bank holding companies to structure broadly diversified portfolios.

Paradoxically, the tightness of these constraints may be because bank holding companies have not been flexible portfolio managers. Since passage of the Bank Holding Company Act in 1956, only one of the ten major bank holding companies has sold or spun off any of its banks. That one was exceptional in that Firstamerica Corporation (now Western Bancorporation) sold the shares of a newly-created bank in order to avoid possible antitrust litigation.[10] Because bank holding companies have only added to their portfolios, legislation and regulatory decisions apparently have been seen as nec-

essary to restrain the accretion process. If acquisition of a bank by a holding company were not such an irrevocable addition to its system, regulatory decisions could be more flexible.

A portfolio of bank shares created before 1956 is unlikely to be an efficient portfolio in states experiencing major shifts in population patterns, industry location, and other economic variables. Among the collection of banks in such a portfolio, some must have relatively limited profit potential. By continuing to hold such assets, the potential rate of return on the total portfolio is reduced; and the opportunity to acquire potentially more profitable banks is limited.

By being willing to sell or spin off some of its assets, a holding company should be better able to acquire shares of other banks. In some cases these new assets may be banks requiring revitalization, whereby the holding company can use its resources of personnel, experienced operating systems, and capital to convert a formerly-inefficient bank to a high-profitable asset. The holding company's pool of resources also can be effectively used to develop new banks in areas of above-average potential. Whether it is revitalizing a formerly inefficient bank or developing a new bank in a growing area, a holding company's operating resources should result in a profitable bank that is an effective competitor, responsive to the public's banking needs.[11]

In some instances, bank holding companies have not been permitted to acquire banks in expanding metropolitan areas. Yet these companies were permitted to acquire some other banks, an apparent reason being that there were no other

---

[10]*Federal Reserve Bulletin* (Vol. 47, No. 2), February 1961, pp. 157–159. Also, *Moody's Bank and Finance Manual*, April 1968, p. 560.

[11]These statements imply that the market for shares of smaller banks is at times imperfect, such that a current price does not always precisely discount future earnings potential. The extent of such market imperfection is suggested in "The Market for Bank Stock," Subcommittee on Domestic Finance, Committee on Banking and Currency, U.S. House of Representatives, December 22, 1964.

TABLE 4

Portfolio Management: Northwest Bancorporation, 1944–48*

| Item | Total Deposits (Millions of dollars) | | Total Percentage Change |
	Year-end Preceding Sale (or Purchase) of Bank	Dec. 30, 1967	
Banks Sold†			
Minnesota:			
Northwestern State Bank, Appleton	1.4	3.0	
Peoples State Bank, Warren	2.0	4.3	
Scanlan-Habberstad Bank & Trust Co.,			
Lanesboro	1.8	3.3	
State Bank of Lake Park	1.3	3.1	
Montana:			
Bank of Sheridan	0.6	2.2	
The Continental National Bank, Harlowton ...	2.6	4.8	
First State Bank, Malta	5.7	10.5	
Miners and Merchants Bank, Roundup	3.4	6.0	
North Dakota:			
Farmers State Bank, Maddock	2.4	4.7	
Stock Growers Bank, Napoleon	2.0	3.6	
Wisconsin:			
The First National Bank, New Richmond	2.1	6.2	
Total	25.3	51.7	(+104)
Banks Bought†			
Minnesota:			
Northwestern Bank and Trust Co., St. Cloud ..	3.2	14.2	
Northwestern National Bank, Rochester	6.1	37.8	
Total	9.3	52.0	(+459)

*Five banks are omitted because they were subsequently merged or voluntarily liquidated.

†Bank names are those at time of transaction, except for the two purchased banks which are identified by their current names.

Sources: *Annual Reports*, Northwest Bancorporation, and *Polk's World Bank Directory*, March 1968.

potential buyers willing to meet the proposed selling terms.[12] The irony of this pattern is that holding companies have been excluded from potential growth situations and still have been willing to purchase possibly less-desirable assets. Such a process of acting as *buyer of the last resort* suggests that some acquisitions provide marginal benefits to a holding company's portfolio. In fact, some acquisitions may reduce the average rate of return on the portfolio.

While bank holding companies, with the one exception, have sold or spun off no banks since 1956, there have been historical episodes of holding companies

selling some banks. The reasons for such sales may have been diverse, but the outcomes of such actions provide important confirmation of the merits of a dynamic portfolio strategy. During 1944–48, Northwest Bancorporation sold 15 banks in four states (Table 4). These banks were predominantly small rural institutions. Eleven of these banks have continued through 1967 without mergers or voluntary liquidations. The deposit growth of the 11 banks from time of sale until December 1967 was 104 percent. Also during the period 1944–48, Northwest Bancorporation bought two banks, which subsequently had deposit growth of 344 percent and 520 percent. During the same basic time interval, the

[12]See, for example, *Federal Reserve Bulletin*, February 1968, p. 225.

total deposits of the holding company system increased 141 percent.[13]

Thus, measured in terms of deposit growth, disposal of the less-promising banks and purchase of more-promising banks contributed to improved performance of the system. A preferable measure would be the subsequent profitability of the sold and acquired banks in order to analyze their marginal impact on the total profitability of the holding company. However, the profit figures are not matters of public record. Also, if the sale and purchase prices were available, one could analyze how much of the relative performance of the banks had been discounted in the prices. Recognizing limitations of the comparisons, the relative deposit growth of the banks purchased and sold does provide preliminary evidence of the value of a dynamic portfolio strategy.

A Set of Portfolio Strategies

Although more appropriate for older bank holding companies—the portfolios of which were largely constructed before 1956—the following strategies should provide insights for new holding companies as they develop their networks of banks:

1. As previously outlined, the portfolio should be continually reviewed, and *less-promising assets should be sold*. By reinvesting in more-promising assets, performance of the total portfolio will improve through time. A further reason is that by occasionally selling banks, holding companies are more likely to be permitted to acquire assets with greater potential. Organizers of holding companies should not acquire banks with modest prospects if such acquisitions are likely to contribute to subsequent regulatory disapproval of more-promising acquisitions.

2. The regulatory agencies and courts often focus on "share of market" in their decisions about proposed acquisitions by bank holding companies.[14] This measure, which entails problems of defining the relevant product and geographical market, at times has been used to restrain the external growth of some bank holding companies. Therefore, a portfolio strategy would be to *spin off certain banks* so that the holding company's "share of market" will be reduced. In this way, a holding company often can demonstrate a reduced share of a local, metropolitan, or state market. The shareholders own the same banks; and the holding company, by reducing its "market share," may be able to acquire promising banks that might otherwise have been precluded from its ownership.

3. In addition to selling or spinning off banks, market valuation of a holding company's assets may be increased by *partial sale or distribution of shares in the portfolio*. Minority ownership of some of the affiliate banks may result in increased market valuation. Also a bank holding company should analyze the possible benefits of creating a market for minority shares in such affiliates as computer leasing companies and data processing centers. Such semi-autonomous firms may command a higher market valuation.

4. Under laws as of this writing, a company that controls only one bank is not required to register as a bank holding company; it is not subject to the provisions of the Bank Holding Company Act. The Board of Governors of the Federal Reserve System has advocated legislation to eliminate this one-bank exemption, and some legislation has already been introduced.[15] If the exemption is judged likely to persist, another portfolio strategy is for a registered bank holding

---

[13]*Annual Reports*, Northwest Bancorporation, 1943, 1947, 1967. Using year-end 1943 as the base, the increase was 242 percent.

[14]*Federal Reserve Bulletin*, February 1968, pp. 222–225.

[15]*Fifty-Second Annual Report of the Board of Governors of the Federal Reserve System*, 1965, pp. 236–237.

company to analyze the possible benefits of restructuring in order to *become a one-bank holding company*. By selling or distributing shares of some banks and possibly consolidating other units into a branch system, it could control one bank and acquire nonbank-related affiliates, a process closed to it under the Bank Holding Company Act. Such a strategy seems particularly relevant for some of the existing interstate systems that have banks in states permitting branching. Such banks could be spun off to become nuclei of one-bank holding companies. The profit potential of these one-bank holding companies may be sufficiently greater to result in increased market valuation of the shares.[16]

The preceding strategies, which follow directly from viewing a bank holding company as a set of assets amenable to portfolio management, are neither all-inclusive nor definitive. Features of the tax structure and analysis of the possible benefits of integrated operating systems may reduce the attractiveness of some of the proposed strategies.

Many nonbanking firms can grow externally by acquiring companies in the same industry or in unrelated industries. Some proponents of planned external growth claim there are benefits to synergism—the sum may be valued more highly than the component parts. Bank holding companies, however, are limited in their opportunities to acquire: additional banks in the same state, banks in other states,

and nonbank enterprises. Because of such constraints, it is probable that for bank holding companies, valuation of component assets may be greater than the valuation of the present holding company.[17]

Managers of bank holding companies must assess the probability of changes in the regulatory environment. If state branching laws were liberalized, the one-bank exemption removed, or regulatory decisions less concerned about "share of market," the value of some of the proposed strategies would be reduced.

Without working directly for change in regulations, bank holding companies may stimulate changes by adopting imaginative strategies. If holding companies begin restructuring themselves by selling and spinning off assets and forming one-bank holding companies, the regulatory agencies will have to reconsider the legislative framework and the administrative

---

[16]To provide a suggestive example, on July 1, 1958, to meet the requirements of the Bank Holding Company Act, Transamerica Corporation spun off its banking affiliates in the form of a new bank holding company. From 1958 through 1967, the per-share price of the registered bank holding company (Western Bancorporation) has increased about 67 percent while that of the parent, less constrained in its investment opportunities, has increased about 96 percent. (Percentage changes are based on mean price of yearly trading ranges and adjusted for stock dividends.) Might not one-bank holding companies, less restricted in their investment opportunities, similarly have greater potential for their shareholders?

---

[17]This hypothesis may be conceptualized as follows:

P_c = Market valuation of the registered bank holding company operating under a set of regulatory constraints.

P_j = Market valuation of each element of $j = 1, n$ the portfolio when some of the elements are unconstrained.

It is probable that $\sum\limits_{j=1}^{n} P_j > P_c$.

To consider one example:

P_1 = Valuation of the original holding company seeking to achieve greater profits by selling less-promising assets and buying banks with greater potential for revitalization and growth. (This assumes an imperfect market for banks—see footnote 11.)

P_2 = Valuation of the minority shares of a data processing affiliate that have been spun off to the holding company's stockholders.

P_3 = Valuation of a large bank spun off to become the nucleus of a one-bank holding company, which as a less-constrained entity should be able to achieve greater profit growth.

In this example it is probable that

$$\sum\limits_{j=1}^{3} P_j > P_c.$$

processes within the framework. As regulatory constraints are reappraised and probaby changed, bank holding companies may have greater flexibility to restructure their portfolios. Such a dynamic process should result in more efficient systems, in contrast to systems that have accrued through time—perhaps more because of chance historical opportunities than a carefully-formulated and continually-reviewed strategy of expansion.

BREAKING WITH TRADITION

Management of bank holding companies should focus more on objectives and techniques of dynamic portfolio management. This would represent a major shift in emphasis from the traditional view of bank holding companies as operating systems, a view apparently adopted because of certain historical objectives and experiences of bank holding companies. Ironically, by placing such emphasis on their operating characteristics, holding companies have contributed to a regulatory structure that has impeded their potential growth.

By adopting a portfolio approach, bank holding companies should be able to achieve increased values for their shareholders, without necessarily increasing risks. Bank holding companies should examine the net benefits of selling or spinning off shares of some affiliates. Not only is selling at appropriate times an attribute of dynamic portfolio management,

such a policy is particularly desirable in the present regulatory environment. By being willing to sell or spin off assets, holding companies should achieve more flexibility to buy assets with above-average potential.

Shifting attention to a portfolio approach need not detract from the operating aspects of bank holding companies. Characteristics such as management depth, operating experience, capital resources, and possible economies of scale, should continue to be analyzed. As outlined, however, possible operating advantages of bank holding companies may be better achieved by following a flexible portfolio strategy. By acquiring formerly-inefficient banks and banks in rapidly-growing areas, holding companies can effectively use their operating experience and skills. Not only will shareholders benefit, but the public should benefit from increased competition and from the fact that holding companies can, through time, directly influence the operating characteristics of a broader set of banks.

In developing a different—and potentially more productive—approach to management of bank holding companies, not all the conceptual and analytical problems have been resolved. Further attention must be directed to the myriad of possible regulatory, legal, and tax aspects of various strategies. However, by presenting a new approach to traditional procedures, the intention is to stimulate further reflection, discussion, and analysis.

17. Asset Management and Commercial Bank Portfolio Behavior: Theory and Practice[*]

Leonall C. Andersen and Albert E. Burger[†]

Two of the most important and perplexing questions in the entire area of bank management today are analyzed by Andersen and Burger in the following article. The first of these is whether banks actually seek to maximize profits, in the fashion prescribed by marginal theory, or whether they simply "accommodate" to loan demand, without regard to marginal profits, in adjusting the asset mix.

The second question is related to the first: However bank management has behaved in the past regarding asset allocation, have there been recent changes in the bank's loan demand function, i.e. an upward or downward shift in the demand function, or a change in the elasticity of demand for loans?

This paper reports the results of an investigation we have conducted regarding two aspects of commercial bank portfolio management. With regard to the first aspect, two alternative hypotheses regarding bank behavior are tested. These are the "accommodation principle" implied in the commercial loan theory of banking and the "profit maximization principle" implied in recent developments in bank portfolio theory and related research. The second aspect is an investigation into the proposition that there has been a significant change in bank portfolio behavior in recent years.

Knowledge of the first aspect of com-

[*]From *Journal of Finance*, May, 1969. Reprinted by permission of the publisher, The American Finance Assoc.

[†]Vice president and economist respectively, Federal Reserve Bank of St. Louis. The views expressed in this article are the views of the authors, they do not necessarily represent the views of either the Federal Reserve Bank of St. Louis or the Federal Reserve System.

mercial bank behavior is important for monetary management. The accommodation principle implies that the demand for bank loans determines bank portfolio behavior. On the other hand, the profit maximization principle implies that commercial bank responses to market forces determine their portfolio behavior. Expectations of bank response to actions of the Federal Reserve System differ according to which principle is accepted.

For example, under the accommodation principle, Federal Reserve open-market operations slowing growth in the reserve base could have little effect on growth in the volume of bank loans if the demand for such loans, at given interest rates, was expanding rapidly. Such would be the case if economic activity was expanding rapidly. Thus, loans could continue to rise at the previous rate or even to accelerate if demand should strengthen. Banks would tend to accommodate such demand by shifting out of investments. By comparison, in such circumstances of Federal Reserve restraint, profit maximization would induce banks to reduce the rate of growth of both loans and investments, at given interest rates, with loan growth continuing at its previous rate only if interest rates on loans rose relative to interest rates on investments.

Changes in bank portfolio behavior, the second aspect of this investigation, have important implications for monetary management. A change in commercial bank portfolio behavior may be reflected in a shift in a function, a change in the shape of the function, or both. For example, with regard to bank loans, a shift in the function explaining the desired level would be reflected in a change in its intercept. A change in its shape would be a change in the elasticity of the desired level of loans with regard to one or more of its arguments.

Monetary authorities, when attempting to forecast the asset behavior of banks in response to a given change in monetary policy, must take into consideration empirical evidence bearing on these questions. If the central bank attempts to forecast bank behavior based on a set of relations estimated from past observations of dependent variables such as borrowings, excess reserves, and loans and a set of independent variables, and if the conditions under which these estimated relations are proposed to represent bank asset behavior no longer hold, then the predictions of the response of commercial banks to monetary policy actions may be far from satisfactory. Furthermore, during different periods of time, banks may change their behavior, perhaps from accommodating business loan demand to responding more to market forces such as the relationship between short and long-term interest rates.

This report consists of four sections. First, recent literature and research into commercial bank asset behavior is surveyed with a view to delineating the accommodation and the profit maximization principles. Then, a model of bank asset behavior is constructed which provides the basis for testing these two principles. Next, the two rival hypotheses of bank asset behavior are tested. Last, evidence is presented bearing on the proposition that there has been a significant change in bank behavior in recent years.

I. REVIEW OF LITERATURE ON BANK ASSET BEHAVIOR

The study of commercial bank portfolio behavior is important for at least two major reasons:

1. Commercial bank portfolio behavior is an important explanatory factor for the magnitudes and changes in the magnitudes of the aggregate economic quantities (the money stock and bank credit).
2. At a less aggregate level, bank portfolio behavior is a key determinant of the cost and flow of credit to specific sectors of the economy.

For the purpose of discussion, monetary theory is defined as the set of theories concerned with the influence of the quantity of money in the economic system, and monetary policy as policy employing the central bank's control of the stock of money as an instrument for achieving the objectives of general economic policy. If one believes that changes in the magnitude of the money stock are an important explanatory variable for changes in real output, employment, and prices which are the goals of economic policy, then the study of factors determining the money stock becomes of crucial importance. Especially, if one is interested in monetary policy, knowledge about the linkage between operations that may be performed by the monetary authorities and changes in the magnitudes of economic quantities such as the money stock and bank credit becomes primary.

Recent research in the field of monetary theory has shown that, given the institutional structure in the United States, the magnitudes of the stocks of money and bank credit are determined jointly by the actions of the Federal Reserve, commercial banks, and the public.[1] The Federal Reserve, by its actions alone, does not determine the magnitude of the money stock. The immediate impact of a Federal Reserve operation, such as a purchase or sale of Government securities, may be to in-

[1]We might mention at this point that actions of the government sector, specifically actions by the Treasury in financing the debt, may enter as an explanatory variable in the actions of the monetary authorities. However, the actions of the monetary authorities determine the effect of a Treasury financing operation on the money stock.

crease or decrease the money stock. However, the equilibrium magnitude of the money stock is determined by the conjunction of the Federal Reserve action and the behavioral reactions of the commercial banks and the public to that action.

The behavioral responses of the banks and the public may be viewed as a portfolio adjustment process. The ability to predict the effect of a given action by the monetary authorities on the magnitudes of money and bank credit depends on being able to predict the behavioral responses of the banks and the public as they adjust their portfolios of financial and real assets.

In this section we present a summary review of some recent developments in the study of commercial bank portfolio behavior incorporating the profit maximization principle. This summary is followed by a brief analysis of the accommodation principle. Due to limitation of space and the nature of the content of the rest of our article, we concentrate primarily on bank portfolio behavior as it affects the holdings of excess reserves, borrowings from Reserve banks, and the volume of loans outstanding.

IA: Profit Maximizing Principle

At the micro-level, the individual commercial bank is viewed as an economic unit whose goal is to maximize profits. The commercial bank holds a portfolio of assets and, given the characteristics and distribution of its liabilities, the commercial bank attempts to structure its portfolio of assets in such a manner as to yield the greatest return subject to these constraints. The assets held by a bank may be divided into two broad classes, frequently called earning assets and non-earning assets. Earning assets are the two balance sheet items called loans and investments. Non-earning assets consist of the total reserves of the bank. Total reserves is then frequently partitioned into required reserves and excess reserves.

In most studies of bank portfolio behavior it is assumed that given such factors as the present and expected levels of market interest rates, loan demands and cash demands, the level of the discount rate, and actions by the Federal Reserve System, the individual commercial bank has a desired distribution of assets in its portfolio. If the existing distribution of assets held by the commercial bank is not the distribution desired, then the bank will attempt to adjust its portfolio of assets by increasing its holdings of some assets and decreasing its holdings of other assets.

Federal Reserve actions such as an open market purchase or sale of Government securities, a change in the legal reserve requirements on member bank demand and/or time deposits, or a change in the discount rate have their initial impacts in the commercial banking sector on total reserves. A purchase of Government securities by the Federal Reserve System leads to an increase in total reserves of the commercial banks. An increase in reserve requirements alters the composition of total reserves leading to an increase in required reserves and a decrease in the actual level of excess reserves. A change in the discount rate alters the cost for member banks of borrowing reserves from the Federal Reserve Banks.

Given that, before the action by the Federal Reserve System, commercial banks were holding their desired distribution of assets, these actions by the monetary authorities lead to a portfolio adjustment process on the part of the individual banks. For example, if an individual bank finds its total reserves increased as a result of the purchase of securities from the public by the Federal Reserve System, the bank will no longer be holding its desired distribution of assets. The proportion of non-earning assets to earning assets will be greater than the desired level. The bank will have an incentive to expand its earning assets by extending additional loans and/or purchasing securities.[2]

Assuming that the proportion of assets held in the form of required reserves is determined by the existing legal reserve requirements against commercial bank demand and time deposits, a commercial bank faces the decision of allocating its portfolio of assets between earning assets (loans and investments) and non-earning assets (excess reserves). Having chosen the desired distribution between earning and non-earning assets the commercial bank then decides what portion of its non-earning assets to hold in the form of free reserves (excess reserves less borrowings from Reserve banks). For member banks this involves a decision as to the level of borrowings from the Federal Reserve banks they desire to maintain.

Given the de jure and de facto status of the majority of their liabilities, and given that the individual bank cannot predict with certainty future deposit flows, loan demands, interest rates, and actions by the monetary authorities, commercial banks desire to have a portion of their portfolio of assets represent a stock of liquidity to act as a buffer against changes in these factors. One form in which commercial banks may hold this stock of liquidity is excess reserves. However, also available to banks are other assets, such as Treasury bills, which under most circumstances can be converted into cash with little loss of time or value, and unlike excess reserves yield an interest return to the bank. Also, member banks may borrow from Federal Reserve banks to meet reserve demands; and they also may acquire reserves in the Federal funds market.[3]

A considerable amount of research in the field of commercial bank portfolio behavior has been devoted to the question of what factors determine a bank's desired holdings of excess reserves. As recent research has highlighted, there are definite costs to the individual commercial bank in adjusting its portfolio of assets to meet changes in deposit flows, loan demand, and actions by the Federal Reserve System.

Although excess reserves yield no interest return as do other assets, they implicitly have a positive yield for the commercial banks. Excess reserves act as an immediate source of liquidity, and hence enable the individual bank to minimize the adjustment costs associated with restructuring its portfolio. Commercial banks desired holdings of excess reserves are postulated to depend on (1) the yield on Treasury bills which are the main alternative to holding excess reserves for liquidity purposes and hence represents the primary opportunity cost of excess reserves, and (2) the adjustment costs involved in restructuring the bank's portfolio. Such adjustment costs are the costs of alternative sources of funds to cover reserve demands. The primary alternative sources of short-term funds are borrowings from Federal Reserve banks and borrowings in the Federal funds market. Recent research by Peter Frost indicates that banks will permit their holdings of excess reserves to fluctuate within certain limits and adjust their holdings only when the return from doing so exceeds the potential cost of not making the adjustment.[4]

Sometimes the Federal Reserve discount rate is used as a proxy for the ad-

---

[2]Since interest rates are usually entered as an explanatory variable in bank demand functions for assets, the interest rate impact of the open market operation will also affect the adjustment process.

[3]The difference between these two sources of reserves is that by borrowing from the Federal

Reserve Banks total reserves of all commercial banks may be increased, while by borrowing in the Federal funds market reserves of the borrowing bank are increased and reserves of the lending bank are decreased with no change in total reserves of the system.

[4]Peter Frost, *Banks' Demand for Excess Reserves*, unpublished UCLA dissertation, 1966, University Microfilms: Ann Arbor, pp. XIV–XV, 279–287.

justment cost. However, as pointed out by several authors, the actual level of the discount rate may not fully represent the actual cost to a member bank of using this means to make adjustments in its portfolio.[5] Federal Reserve banks do not always set the discount rate and then allow member banks to determine the volume of the borrowings at that rate. They also "administer" the discount window and subject the use of borrowings of member banks to careful surveillance. This so-called "discipline of the discount window" has probably at times made the cost of borrowing from Reserve banks less attractive and hence raised the implicit return to commercial banks from holding excess reserves.[6]

Recent research by Stephen Goldfeld and Edward Kane has brought into question the assumption that all banks react in the same manner to changes in factors such as short-term market interest rates, the discount rate, availability of reserves and new loan demand. Goldfeld investigated commercial bank portfolio behavior using a stock adjustment model.[7] He fitted the structural model with quarterly, seasonally adjusted time series data from the third quarter of 1950 to the second quarter of 1962. Goldfeld concluded that for both country and city member banks the major determinants of excess reserve holdings appeared to be interest rate considerations (the differential between the bill rate and

the discount rate) and changes in the availability of reserves (as measured by a potential-deposit variable). However, the portfolio responses of the two classes of banks to changes in interest rates, deposit flows and new loan demand were markedly different. In the management of excess reserves the city bank sector was found to be more responsive to interest rate considerations than country banks. With respect to changes in borrowings to meet new loan demand, Goldfeld found that city banks increased their borrowings by $12 for each $100 of new loan demand while country banks borrowings rose only about $6 per $100.[8]

Kane and Goldfeld presented and estimated a model of member bank borrowing from Reserve Banks.[9] Banks were assumed to maximize utility which was postulated to be a function of the cost of acquiring reserves and borrowing. Utility declines as this cost of borrowing rises. Kane and Goldfeld suggest that, following an exogenous disturbance, banks may effect desired changes in their security portfolios through a series of partial adjustments. In the short-run a bank may prefer to borrow from the Federal Reserve rather than immediately liquidating its securities. Hence, banks may borrow more in the short-run than a static model would imply. They estimated the dynamic version of their model using weekly data on reserves and borrowings for four member bank categories from July, 1953 through December, 1965. The results using both seasonally adjusted and unadjusted data supported the importance of a distributed lag response. Also, they found that the speed of portfolio adjustment for country banks was slower than the speed of city bank portfolio adjustment.[10]

IB. Accommodation Principle

The accommodation principle of commercial bank behavior stems from an older

---

[5]See Stephen Goldfeld and Edward Kane, "Determinants of Member Bank Borrowing: An Econometric Study," *Journal of Finance,* September, 1966, pp. 499–514; and Murray E. Polakoff and William L. Silber, "Reluctance and Member-Bank Borrowing: Additional Evidence," *Journal of Finance,* March, 1967, pp. 88–92.

[6]The effect of Federal Reserve surveillance is extremely difficult to quantify. However, the existence of periods such as the middle of 1966, when the spread between the discount rate and the Federal funds rate rapidly widened while member bank borrowings did not increase, lends some credulence to the assertion of the existence of such an effect.

[7]Stephen Goldfeld, *Commercial Bank Behavior and Economic Activity: A Structural Study of Monetary Policy in the Postwar United States,* Amsterdam: New Holland Publishing Co., 1966.

[8]Goldfeld, pp. 149–152.
[9]Goldfeld and Kane, *op. cit.,* pp. 499–514.
[10]Kane and Goldfeld, p. 512.

concept of the proper role of banking in economic life. This older concept is known as the "commercial loan theory" or the "real bills doctrine" of commercial banking. According to this theory bank earning assets should be limited to short-term, self-liquidating loans related to the production and distribution of goods and services. Proper banking practice is to accommodate the "legitimate credit demands" of business, commerce, and agriculture.

This principle of banking is imbedded in the Federal Reserve Act.[11] Accordingly, the accommodation principle has been used as a basis for Federal Reserve supervision of banks, eligibility requirements for collateral for borrowing from Reserve banks, and Federal Reserve collateral for its issue of currency.

The accommodation principle has also played an important role in monetary management. The real bills debate over the proper types of securities for Federal Reserve open-market transactions points to the importance given this principle by monetary authorities. The Federal Reserve still views, to a considerable degree, its actions as accommodating loan demand.

The accommodation principle holds that commercial banks should primarily make business loans and agricultural production loans. The use of the term "accommodation" implies that the *demand* for such loans would mainly determine bank behavior regarding borrowing from Reserve banks, holdings of excess reserves, and the division of earning assets between loans and investments.[12] Thus, the response of demand for loans to such economic variables as interest rates and economic activity would also determine bank behavior regarding the above mentioned balance sheet accounts.

II. MODEL OF BANKING PORTFOLIO BEHAVIOR

Bank behavior regarding assets is viewed in this paper as a process of allocating a given amount of wealth (defined as total deposits) between non-earning assets (required and excess reserves) and earning assets (loans and investments). Once this allocation is determined, earning assets are allocated between loans and investments. We now proceed to set forth the factors influencing bank behavior with regard to this allocation process.

Since this study is concerned only with the behavior of member banks of the Federal Reserve System, the special considerations regarding the reserve requirements imposed on these banks will be applied. The following discussion is based on the assumption that banks are profit maximizers. Their behavior based on the accommodation principle will be presented later. Aggregate member bank behavior is used in the remainder of this article.

IIA. Bank Behavior Under the Profit Maximizing Principle

TOTAL DEPOSITS. Member bank total deposits (D) are constrained by their total reserves (deposits at Reserve banks and vault cash) and the average reserve requirement ratio. This relation may be expressed by the following identity:

$$D = \frac{1}{\bar{r}} R$$

In the above expression, R is member bank total reserves and $\bar{r}$ is the average

[11]See Clifton B. Luttrell, "Member Bank Borrowing: Its Origin and Function," *Quarterly Review of Economics and Business*, Bureau of Economic and Business Research, University of Illinois, Autumn, 1968, pp. 56–65.

[12]Some discussions of the Federal Reserve–M.I.T. Econometric Model seem to indicate that an accommodation hypothesis of bank lending behavior was assumed in constructing the model. For example, "Banks are assumed to accommodate short-run changes in loan demand by their business customers partly by changing their free reserve position." Frank de Leeuw and Edward Gramlich "The Federal Reserve–M.I.T. Econometric Model," *Federal Reserve Bulletin*, January, 1968, p. 14. Also see Robert Rasche and Harold Shapiro, "The F.R.B.–M.I.T. Econometric Model: Its Special Features," *American Economic Review*, May, 1968, p. 139, and footnote 19.

reserve requirement ratio. R consists of nonborrowed reserves (NB) and borrowings from Reserve banks (B). The term $\bar{r}$ is the average reserve requirement which takes into consideration the distribution of deposits between demand and time accounts and between reserve city and country banks.

The identity may be expanded to:

$$D = \frac{1}{\bar{r}} (NB + B)$$

With $\bar{r}$ constant, borrowing from Reserve banks or as a result of the Federal Reserve System increasing nonborrowed reserves, member banks as a group may expand their deposits, thereby allowing them to have more earning assets.

BORROWING. Member bank borrowing from Reserve banks, although relatively small compared with NB, is an important aspect of bank behavior. It is a liability item which allows banks some flexibility in their asset management within the constraint imposed by nonborrowed reserves.

The desired level of borrowings from Reserve banks (B*) is postulated as follows:

$$B^* = f_1 (i_s, i_d, i_F, C_b, D)$$

In this relationship, i_s is the short-term interest rate, i_d the Federal Reserve discount rate, i_F the federal funds rate, and C_b other costs of borrowing. B* is postulated to be positively related to i_s, i_F, and D and negatively related to i_d, and C_b.

EXCESS RESERVES. Holdings of excess reserves, other things constant, results in holdings of fewer earning assets; therefore banks hold excess reserves for returns other than earnings. Holdings of excess reserves constitute a buffer stock which allows banks to meet sudden withdrawals of deposits without requiring a reduction in earning assets. The desired level of excess reserves (ER*) is given by the following function:

$$ER^* = f_2 (i_s, i_d, i_L, C_{er}, D)$$

ER* is postulated to be negatively related to i_s and i_L and positively related to D, i_d, and C_{er} (costs of managing excess reserves).

LOANS. Earning assets in the form of bank loans consist mainly of loans to businesses, households, and financial institutions. The desired level of loans (L*) is given by the following relationship:

$$L^* = f_3 (i_s, i_d, i_L, C_1, D)$$

L* is postulated to be negatively related to i_L and i_d, and C_1 (transactions costs of lending) and positively related to i_s and D.

INVESTMENTS. Earning assets classified as investments consist mainly of holdings of government securities. The desired level (I*) is expressed as:

$$I^* = f_4 (i_s, i_d, i_L, C_i, D)$$

Investments are considered a residual item in this study; however, I* is postulated to be negatively related to i_s and i_d, and C_i (transaction costs of investments) and positively related to i_L and D.

IIB. Bank Behavior Under Accommodation Principle

Under the accommodation principle, bank behavior would mainly reflect the demand of customers for loans. For example, a rise in the demand for loans from banks (supply of this form of earning asset) would be met, subject to the deposit constraint, by reductions in investments and excess reserves and an increase in borrowings from Reserve banks. This implies that the factors influencing the demand for bank loans affect L*, I*, ER*, and B*.

The following equation is postulated as determining the supply of loans (viewed as earning assets of banks):

$$L^* = g (i_s, i_L, GNP, W)$$

L* is postulated to be negatively related to i_s and positively related to i_L, the level of economic activity (GNP), and to private nonbank wealth (W). These signs are the ones commonly developed on the basis of business maximization of profits and household maximization of satisfaction, subject to wealth and income constraints.

As stated above, the function g would be the relevant one for examining bank behavior under the accommodation principle. Incorporation of this principle into the functions for B*, ER*, L*, and I* in place of the profit maximization principle, introduces GNP and W into each function and reverses the signs for i_s in the B*, ER*, L* equations, and the sign for i_L in the L* equation.

IIC. Stock Adjustment Model

A stock adjustment framework is used as the basis of constructing the model of bank portfolio behavior. It is assumed that banks have a desired level of each of the balance sheet items under consideration (B*, ER*, L*, and I*) and that the stock of the item held is changed at a certain rate to close the gap between the actual and the desired level. This may be expressed as two equivalent equations:

$$X_t - X_{t-1} = \lambda(X_t - X_{t-1})$$
$$X_t = \lambda X_t + (1 - \lambda) X_{t-1}$$

In the above equations, X_t is the stock on hand at time (t); X^*_t is the desired stock, X_{t-1} is the stock in the previous period; and λ is a speed of adjustment coefficient. The desired stock depends on the economic factors spelled out in the preceding discussion. The speed of adjustment coefficient may range from zero to plus one. The closer it is to one, the faster the speed of adjustment.

III. Testing Two Rival Hypotheses

IIIA. Two Rival Hypotheses. Frequently, policymakers are confronted with conflicting policy advice. For example, one group of policy advisers starting from the assumption that banks passively accommodate business loan demand might predict one set of consequences for a policy action taken by the monetary authorities. Another group of advisers, assuming that banks behave as profit maximizers, might predict an alternative result for the same policy action. The policy results predicted by both policy advisers depend on whether initial assumptions about bank portfolio behavior do in fact represent the behavioral reactions of commercial banks.[13]

In this section we provide evidence on these two alternative assumptions about bank portfolio behavior. To compare the two hypotheses we first state each hypothesis so that it can be confronted with empirical evidence. Also, the two hypotheses must be stated in such a form that the available empirical evidence can discriminate between them. They must not, however, be formulated so that the empirical evidence is in good agreement with both. In section III-B the regression equations used in the formulation of the two hypotheses are presented. As we have formulated the two proposed explanations of commercial bank portfolio behavior, each of the two alternative hypotheses implies certain signs for the coefficients in the regression equations. These signs are presented in Exhibit 1 and discussed in Section III-C. The implied signs are used as the basis for testing the hypotheses.

IIIB. Estimation Procedures. Multiple regression analysis, using monthly observations for the period 1953–1967, is used to determine which of the two alternative explanations of commercial bank asset behavior, i.e., the profit-maximization or accommodation principle, is in better agreement with the empirical evidence. Lack of suitable data resulted in dropping the wealth variable and variables reflecting transactions and other non-interest costs. Also, the Federal funds rate was

---

[13]See Albert E. Burger and Leonall C. Andersen, "The Development of Explanatory Economic Hypotheses for Monetary Management," *Southern Journal of Business* (forthcoming).

EXHIBIT I

	i_s	i_L	GNP/D
Profit-Maximizing Hypothesis:			
B/D			
Expected sign	+	+,0	0
Sign of Regression Coefficient			
1953–1960	+	−	0
1961–1967	+	0	0
ER/D			
Expected sign	−	−	0
Sign of Regression Coefficient			
1953–1960	0	−	0
1961–1967	−	0	+
L/D			
Expected sign	+	−	0
Sign of Regression Coefficient			
1953–1960	+	−	0
1961–1967	+	−	0
Accommodation Hypothesis:			
B/D			
Expected sign	−	+,0	+
Sign of Regression Coefficient			
1953–1960	+	−	0
1961–1967	+	0	0
ER/D			
Expected sign	+	−	−
Sign of Regression Coefficient			
1953–1960	0	−	0
1961–1967	−	0	+
L/D			
Expected sign	−	+	+
Sign of Regression Coefficient			
1953–1960	+	−	0
1961–1967	+	−	0

omitted. Another variable, the ratio of country bank deposits (DCB) to total member bank deposits was introduced to take into consideration the possibility of differences in behavior between classes of member banks.

It was assumed that each function is homogenous with regard to deposits; hence, each variable measured in dollars was divided by D. The stock adjustment model thus becomes one involving the closing of a discrepancy between desired and actual ratios.

$$\frac{B}{D} = f_1 \left(i_s, i_d, i_L, \frac{GNP}{D}, \frac{DCB}{D}, \left[\frac{B}{D}\right]_{-1} \right)$$

$$\frac{ER}{D} = f_2 \left(i_s, i_d, i_L, \frac{GNP}{D}, \frac{DCB}{D}, \left[\frac{ER}{D}\right]_{-1} \right)$$

$$\frac{L}{D} = f_3 \left(i_s, i_d, i_L, \frac{GNP}{D}, \frac{DCB}{D}, \left[\frac{L}{D}\right]_{-1} \right)$$

In the above equations, all variables are

for the current period except the lagged ratios. All of the variables are seasonally adjusted monthly averages. Monthly data for GNP was developed by a straight line interpolation of quarterly GNP centered on the mid-month of each quarter. The 91-day Treasury bill rate was used as a proxy for the short-term interest rate, and the corporate Aaa bond rate was used for the long-term interest rate. Regressions were run using logarithms, thereby providing elasticity estimates. Two variables, i_s and i_L, were considered endogenous within a more complete model of bank behavior; hence, the two-stage least-squares estimation procedure was used.[14]

The regression results are reported in Table 1. The regression equations were run for the entire period 1953 through 1967. However, application of the Chow test indicated a significant structural change between the period 1953–1960 and 1961–1967. The F-value of the Chow test was 2.83 for B/D, 9.98 for ER/D, and 3.01 for L/D. All of these values are statistically significant at the 5 percent level. Therefore, the observation period 1953–1967 was split into two periods, 1953–1960 and 1961–1967. Only the results of the regressions for the separate periods are reported in Table I.

IIIC. EXPECTED SIGNS OF THE REGRESSION COEFFICIENTS. Following the above

[14]A complete model includes stock adjustment equations for demand deposits held by the public, currency in the hands of the public, and the public's holdings of time deposits. Also, there are balance sheet identities for demand deposits held by the public and bank total earning assets. In addition to the exogenous variables in the equations presented above, there are the lagged stocks of demand deposits, time deposits, and currency. Exogenous variables derived from the balance sheet identities include the factors affecting non-borrowed reserves and average reserve requirements for member banks. The balance sheet identity for private demand deposits is developed in Leonall C. Andersen's, "A Study of Factors Affecting the Money Stock: Phase One," *Staff Economic Studies*, Board of Governors of the Federal Reserve System, October 1965. The identity for earning assets is a slight alteration of the private demand deposit one.

discussions, Exhibit I presents the expected signs of the coefficients of the independent variables considered most relevant for the testing of the two hypotheses about commercial bank asset behavior. These variables are i_s, i_L, and GNP/D.

Exhibit I also presents the calculated signs of the regression coefficients. If the calculated t-value of a regression coefficient was not significant at the 5 percent level, a zero value for that coefficient is entered in this table.

An examination of Exhibit I reveals that the results of the regression analysis do not support the hypothesis that the factors influencing the demand for bank loans are the primary determinants of bank asset behavior. In neither period is it observed that bank behavior responds in the manner prescribed by the hypothesis that banks passively accommodate the demand for bank credit. However, the results tend to support the hypothesis that bank behavior responds to changes in i_s, i_L, and GNP/D in a manner that is consistent with the hypothesis that banks attempt to manage their asset portfolios in a way that is consistent with a profit maximizing explanation of commercial bank behavior.

In both periods, as the short-term interest rate rises, banks respond by increasing the ratio of loans to deposits. As the long-term interest rate rises, making investments more attractive relative to loans, banks restructure their asset portfolios by reducing the proportion of loans to investments in their portfolios. Lending behavior is not directly related to changes in GNP. These findings are consistent with the profit maximization hypothesis.

In both periods, as the opportunity cost of holding excess reserves increases (i.e., market interest rates rise), we find that banks respond by decreasing their holdings of excess reserves relative to deposits. This behavior is consistent with profit maximization. In the first period the long-term rate of interest is more important

TABLE I

Regression Results—Member Bank Behavior Borrowed Reserves, Excess Reserves, and Loans
(variables in natural logarithms)

	Intercept	i_s	i_L	i_d	GNP/D	DCB/D	Lagged Dependent Variable	Standard Error	R^2
B/D									
1953–1960									
	−.715	1.717* (.246)	−1.047* (.399)	−.709* (.235)	−3.434 (1.549)	−2.499 (3.958)	.517* (.069)	.197	.94
1961–1967									
	−14.660	1.557* (.632)	−1.978 (1.032)	.174 (.738)	1.879 (2.937)	−12.034 (6.260)	.622* (.122)	.268	.93
ER/D									
1953–1960									
	.131	−.103 (.063)	−.289* (.141)	.118 (.095)	−.271 (.849)	.956 (1.585)	.746* (.079)	.079	.89
1961–1967									
	−10.704	−1.246* (.223)	−.286 (.182)	.319 (.240)	5.258* (1.033)	−.505 (2.213)	.040 (.112)	.094	.93
L/D									
1953–1960									
	.702	.044* (.009)	−.041* (.015)	−.043* (.011)	−.169 (.136)	.479* (.176)	1.006* (.033)	.007	.99
1961–1967									
	−.038	.033* (.007)	−.019* (.007)	.015 (.013)	−.008 (.036)	.040 (.098)	.878* (.030)	.004	.99

Numbers in parentheses are standard errors of the regression coefficients.
*Statistically significant at 5 percent level.

than the short-term rate in determining the behavior of ER/D, in the more recent period the roles on the interest rates are reversed and the short-term rate becomes a more important factor in determining changes in ER/D. In the period 1953–1960 our regression results show that GNP/D does not enter as a significant influence on banks' excess reserves to deposit ratio. In the period 1961–1967, GNP/D appears as a significant influence on excess reserve behavior. The positive sign on the coefficient of GNP/D, indicating an increase in excess reserves given an increase in GNP, is clearly not in good agreement with the expected sign under the accom-

modation hypothesis. However, such a large positive influence on excess reserve behavior is also surprising given the expected sign of the coefficient under the profit-maximizing hypothesis of bank asset behavior.

With respect to borrowing behavior, we find that in both periods banks are sensitive to changes in interest rates in a manner consistent with the profit maximization hypothesis. A rise in short-term interest rates in both periods leads to a rise in borrowings by member banks from Reserve banks. Tentatively, these results indicate that banks may not be unaware of the profit opportunities inherent in a situation where the discount rate lags a rise in the short-term rate. In the period 1953–1960, as the discount rate rises, member banks reduce their ratio of borrowings to deposits. In the latter period, 1961–1967, our statistical tests indicate that the coefficient for i_d is not statistically different from zero. This may reflect the development of alternative sources of short-term funds in the more recent period. In neither period do we find that the independent variable GNP/D enters as a significant influence on commercial bank borrowing behavior.

IV. CHANGE IN BANK BEHAVIOR

Since about 1960, many new developments have occurred in the area of commercial banking. Observers of bank behavior since then have suggested that banks have become more aggressive competitors among themselves and in their relationships with other financial intermediaries. They appear to have become more profit oriented, i.e., basing to a greater extent than previously their decisions on assets acquired and liabilities offered on cost and yield considerations.

New liability forms have been developed such as marketable and consumer type CD's. This development suggests that banks have become more willing to compete for funds from many sources on the basis of rates paid. Asset adjustments, when required, appear to be made more on the basis of cost considerations. The development of the Federal funds market has created an important source of short-term funds for banks, and the proposition is frequently advanced that member banks now rely less on borrowing from Reserve bank for short-term adjustment purposes. Banks in their quest for profits have entered into new lending areas such as municipal bonds and mortgages. Recently, bank credits cards and a practice similar to over-draft checking have been started. Holdings of U.S. Government securities by banks have reached a low level.

The Federal Reserve System has also altered the economic environment of commercial banking. Open-market transactions since 1960 have been conducive to fairly long periods of quite uniform rates of expansion in bank credit and money. Furthermore, the period since 1960 has been characterized by a general economic expansion only interrupted by two mild plateaus, the first in 1962 and the second in the first half of 1967.

In response to these developments, economists have speculated about the impact of this new environment on commercial bank behavior regarding their holdings of excess reserves borrowing from Reserve banks, and acquisition of loans and investments. Such changes in bank behavior would involve shifts in functions and changes in the shapes of the functions.

TESTING FOR CHANGES IN BANK BEHAVIOR. Evidence presented in Table I is consistent with the view that a significant change in bank behavior has occurred. The Chow test, as mentioned previously, indicates that the set of parameters estimated for 1961–1967 are significantly different from those estimated for 1953–1960.

With regard to borrowing behavior, there was a downward shift in the function but no change in its shape. The intercept changed from −.715 to −14.660. Application of the test for differences in parameters of the independent variables indicates that there is no statistical significant difference for any of these parameters between the two periods. The downward shift in the borrowing function is consistent with the proposition that the development of the Federal funds market and the increased use of time deposits as sources of funds have led to a decreased preference for borrowing from Reserve banks as a source of funds.

The regression results for excess reserve behavior indicate both a downward shift in the function and a change in its shape. Its intercept changed from .131 to −10.704. There was a statistically significant change in the parameters for i_s, GNP/D, and the lagged ratio. The downward shift is consistent with a lower preference for excess reserves as a buffer stock as a result of the development of the newer sources of adjustment funds discussed under borrowing behavior. The elasticity of excess reserves to i_s increased from $-.103$ to -1.246; this is consistent with the proposition that banks have become more sensitive to the opportunity cost of holding excess reserves. The change in the coefficient for the lagged ratio indicates that in the latter period there was almost instantaneous adjustment to a discrepancy between desired and actual excess reserves, compared with a much longer adjustment period earlier. The coefficient for GNP/D also changed, but no explanation is offered here.

Bank lending behavior also underwent a marked change between the two periods. The intercept decreased from .702 to $-.038$. One explanation of this downward shift is the expansion of bank participation in the growing municipal bond market. The adjustment period decreased moderately, as indicated by the decrease in the coefficient for the lagged ratio. In the first period the coefficient for the discount rate is significant, but in the period 1961–1967 the coefficient for i_d is not statistically significant. The negative sign on the coefficient for i_d in the first period indicating a rise (fall) in L/D given a decline (increase) in i_d is consistent with a profit maximizing explanation of bank behavior. In the period 1961–1967, the absence of a significant effect of i_d on L/D may reflect, as discussed earlier, the institutional change reflected in the development of the Federal funds market.

REFERENCES

Leonall, C. Andersen. "A Study of Factors Affecting the Money Stock: Phase One," *Staff Economic Studies*, Washington, D.C.: Board of Governors of the Federal Reserve System, October, 1965.

Albert E. Burger and Leonall C. Andersen. "The Development of Explanatory Economic Hypotheses for Monetary Management," *Southern Journal of Business* (forthcoming).

Frank de Leeuw and Edward Gramlich. "The Federal Reserve–M.I.T. Econometric Model: Its Special Features," *American Economic Review*, May, 1968, pp. 123–149.

Peter Frost. *Bank's Demand for Excess Reserves*, unpublished dissertation – UCLA, 1966, University Microfilms: Ann Arbor, pp. XIV–XV, 279–287.

Stephen Goldfeld. *Commercial Bank Behavior and Economic Activity: A Structural Study of Monetary Policy in the Postwar United States*, Amsterdam: New Holland Publishing Company, 1966.

Stephen Goldfeld and Edward Kane. "Determinants of Member Bank Borrowing: An Econometric Study," *Journal of Finance*, September, 1966, pp. 499–514.

Clifton B. Luttrell. "Member Bank Borrowing: Its Origin and Function," *Quarterly Review of Economics and Business*, Bureau of Economic and Business Research, University of Illinois, Autumn, 1968, pp. 55–65.

Murray E. Polokoff and William E. Silber. "Reluctance and Member Bank Borrowing: Additional Evidence," *Journal of Finance*, March, 1967, pp. 88–92.

Robert Rasche and Harold Shapiro. "The Federal Reserve–M.I.T. Econometric Model: Its Special Features," *American Economic Review*, May, 1968, pp. 123–149.

18. The Commercial Paper Boom In Perspective*

Frederick M. Struble

A significant development in the latter part of the 1960's was the precipitous increase in commercial paper outstanding. This article reviews the trend and cyclical developments in this market. It also assesses the relevance of suggested explanations for the latest expansion: lack of internal sources of funds, high interest rates in capital markets, and the substitution of commercial paper indebtedness for commercial bank indebtedness. Regarding the last item, it is noted that "the commercial paper market already has cut substantially into the loan business of commercial banks with finance companies. The potential for similar inroads at nonfinancial corporations is clearly present."

Business indebtedness in the form of commercial paper—short-term, unsecured promissory notes issued by financial, commercial, and industrial firms—has more than doubled since 1965 and now totals more than $20 billion. Several explanations for this expansion have been advanced in recent discussions of this development. The sharp growth in total indebtedness at business concerns over this period, as internal sources of funds fell well short of requirements, has been mentioned frequently. The greater reliance placed on short-term sources of funds, because of the congestion and the high cost of borrowing in the long-term capital market, has also been mentioned. Finally, frequent reference has been made to the substitution of commercial paper

*From *Monthly Review*, November, 1968. Reprinted by permission of the publisher, the Federal Reserve Bank of Kansas City.

indebtedness for commercial bank indebtedness, a development primarily attributed to the rationing of loans by banks during the extremely tight credit situation of 1966 and to the subsequent reaction of their loan customers to this rationing process.

An assessment of the relative importance of each of these developments is presented in this article. Before considering this question, however, past trend and cyclical developments in this market are reviewed and compared with developments since 1965. The comparisons are made to provide a better basis for making this assessment and to provide insight into the question of whether it appears likely that this sharp rate of expansion can be maintained in the future.

TREND AND CYCLICAL DEVELOPMENTS IN THE VOLUME OF COMMERCIAL PAPER

The expansion in commercial paper which has occurred since 1965 extends a strong upward trend initially established after World War II. Commercial paper indebtedness increased at an exceptionally strong pace over the early years of this period, as the amount outstanding rose from a war-depressed low of slightly more than $100 million to nearly $1.75 billion by the end of 1952. Since then, growth in commercial paper indebtedness has continued to be impressive, as may be seen by examining Chart 1.

CHART 1
Commercial Paper Outstanding
(quarterly averages of monthly data, seasonally adjusted)

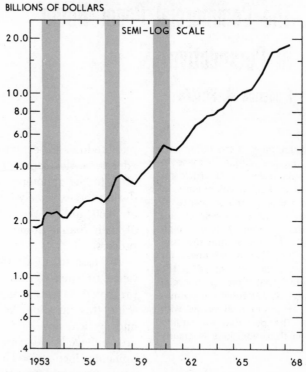

Shaded areas denote recessions as defined by National Bureau of Economic Research.
Source: Federal Reserve Bank of New York.

This secular growth in commercial paper was accompanied by considerable cyclical variation. During the 1950's the volume of commercial paper declined during the early stages of an upturn in business activity, increased during the remainder of the business expansion, and continued to increase on into the following period of recession in economic activity. A similar relationship between changes in the volume of commercial paper and the state of economic activity has prevailed during the 1960's. That is, the volume of commercial paper began to decline in the latter part of the 1960-61 recession, fell somewhat further during the early part of the current period of business expansion, and has increased since that time.

Focusing on the period since 1965, it is apparent that commercial paper indebtedness has been increasing at a sharper rate than earlier in the current expansion. The average quarterly rate of growth during the period was about 8 percent, compared with a rate of just more than 6 percent in the years 1961 to 1965. Relative to experience in the 1950's, the recent pace of increase is distinctly higher than that of the 1954-57 business expansion. On the other hand, it is just slighty less than the 8.7 percent average quarterly gain of the 1958-60 expansion.[1]

Thus, the recent advance in commer-

[1]The rates of growth for the periods prior to 1966 were measured from that date within the period of business expansion at which commercial paper reached its cyclical trough.

cial paper during a period of expanding business activity is generally consistent with its earlier cyclical behavior and the pace of the recent advance is not entirely without precedent. The composition of growth in commercial paper debt during the latest period has differed markedly, however, from what would have been expected on the basis of past trend and cyclical developments.

Expansion in dealer paper, that is, paper sold through commercial paper dealers, made a strong contribution to the recent advance in total commercial paper. Chart 2 shows that, during the 1950's, dealer paper rose sharply only during periods of business recession and, in contrast, declined steadily throughout most, if not all, of the periods of expansion in business activity. This relationship between changes in the volume

of dealer paper and economic activity was broken to some extent during the initial stages of the current period of expansion, as dealer-issued paper continued to grow. However, the volume outstanding stabilized by the end of 1962 and then tended to shade downward through 1965, so that in the period immediately preceding 1966, dealer paper showed definite signs of again conforming to its cyclical pattern of the 1950's. Thus, the strong growth in the volume of dealer-issued paper since 1965, occurring as it did well after the start of the current business expansion, quite clearly represents a sharp departure from its earlier cyclical pattern.

The recent growth in directly issued paper—notes sold directly to investors by borrowing firms—appears to be much more consistent with earlier trend and cyclical developments in this sector of

CHART 2
Commercial Paper Outstanding and Differential,
Bank Prime Rate and Prime Commercial Paper Rate
(1st Quarter 1953 to 2nd Quarter 1968)

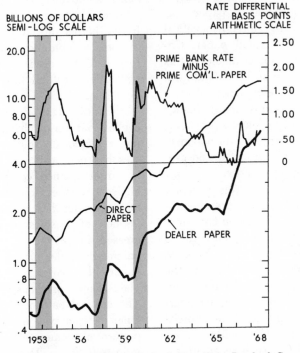

Source: Federal Reserve Bank of New York; Board of Governors, Federal Reserve System.

the market. The volume of directly issued paper declined during the early stages of the current business expansion period and has been increasing steadily since that time. As shown in Chart 2 these developments conform generally to the preceding strong uptrend and patterns of cyclical fluctuation in this sector of the market. However, as will be discussed later, the advance since 1965 has been generated by a different set of factors than those responsible for the growth in directly placed commercial paper in earlier periods of business expansion.

FIRMS ISSUING COMMERCIAL PAPER

Insight into the factors responsible for changes in the volume of commercial paper can be gained by viewing them within the context of corresponding changes in the level and structure of liabilities at firms issuing this paper. Ideally, the data reflecting liability positions at paper issuers should be classified according to the method used by firms in marketing their paper indebtedness, since dealer-issued paper has displayed a decidedly different cyclical pattern than directly issued paper. Unfortunately, data are not available in this form. However, flow of funds data reflecting liability developments at two major groups of business firms, finance companies and nonfinancial corporations, are available. Although they do not meet the ideal requirement, these data do provide a workable approximation.

About 30 percent of the firms presently issuing commercial paper are finance companies—firms which finance consumer instalment purchases, make cash loans to consumers, and provide funds to business for financing accounts receivable and the purchase of capital equipment on an instalment basis. The remaining commercial paper borrowers are nonfinancial corporations engaged in a wide variety of business activities, such as manufacturing, wholesale and retail trade, and

the operation of public utilities. Although finance companies constitute a comparatively small proportion of total commercial paper borrowers, they are extremely important in terms of the volume of total commercial paper debt. All directly placed paper is finance company paper. In addition, a considerable proportion of the paper placed through dealers is supplied by finance companies. Each of these generalizations apply for the entire period under consideration.

The number of finance firms placing their paper directly is but a small proportion of the total number of finance companies borrowing in the commercial paper market. However, these direct issuers are quite large relative to other finance companies and, as a result, their commercial paper indebtedness and their total indebtedness substantially exceeds that of all other finance companies. For example, at the end of 1967, directly placed finance company paper was equal to slightly more than 85 percent of total commercial paper indebtedness of all finance companies, just slightly below the ratio at the end of 1952. Direct issuers have a higher ratio of paper indebtedness to total indebtedness, however, so their total indebtedness is a somewhat smaller proportion of total finance company indebtedness.

In addition to differing in size, the cyclical pattern of changes in commercial paper issued by smaller finance companies has been different than the pattern at larger finance companies. The ratio of dealer finance company paper to total finance paper has generally declined in periods of business expansion and increased in periods of recession, as the volume of dealer placed finance company paper either varied inversely with directly placed paper or changed at a slower rate. The cyclical pattern of change in dealer finance paper was similar to the cyclical pattern of commercial paper issued by industrial firms. However, the ratio of dealer finance paper to total dealer paper generally declined during periods of recession and increased during periods of expansion, because the commercial paper indebtedness of nonfinancial corporations fluctuated more sharply over the cycle.

Since finance companies issuing their paper directly are relatively large, their liability positions generally dominate the data for all finance companies. Accordingly, the finance company data can be interpreted as providing a fairly good approximation of the changes in liability positions which coincided with fluctuations in directly issued paper. The relationship between dealer-issued paper and liability developments at nonfinancial corporations is quite obviously much less precise because a major proportion of this paper is issued by finance companies. Despite these problems, the association is close enough so that it is possible to gain a general impression of the relationship between fluctuations in dealer-issued commercial paper and associated developments in other liability accounts.

FACTORS AFFECTING THE VOLUME OF COMMERCIAL PAPER

Changes in the volume of commercial paper occur as issuing firms either alter their total indebtedness while holding the proportion of commercial paper unchanged or change the relative position of commercial paper in their liability structures. Fluctuations in the relative importance of commercial paper that are reflected in aggregate data also arise in part because of the entrance and exit of firms from the commercial paper market. Approximately 425 to 450 firms currently are borrowing in the commercial paper market, only slightly more than the 418 firms issuing paper in 1952. Thus, the long-run growth in the volume of total commercial paper outstanding has not been due in any significant way to this factor. However, some shifting has occurred in the composition of commercial paper borrowers and this did influence the growth of commercial paper debt at finance companies and nonfinancial corporations. More specifically, the number of finance companies issuing commercial paper increased from 95 to 130 over this period and those selling directly to investors increased from 4 to 20. In short, this shift in the composition of borrowing firms tended to stimulate growth in finance company paper and to restrain the growth in the volume of paper issued by nonfinancial corporations. Some alteration also occurred within the composition of nonfinancial corporations, as a number of earlier borrowers left the market and were replaced by new borrowers.

In general, the number of firms issuing commercial paper has increased during recessions and declined during business expansions. Changes in the number of nonfinancial corporations accounted for most of this cyclical fluctuation with one important exception. The total number of firms issuing commercial paper continued to rise during the early part of the current business expansion and then dropped off. By the end of 1965, the number of firms had fallen to 335. Since that time, many borrowers, most of them nonfinancial corporations, have returned to the market or have begun to issue commercial paper for the first time. Thus, the recent growth in commercial paper placed through dealers is attributable in part to an increase in the number of nonfinancial corporations issuing commercial paper.

The total indebtedness of finance companies increased from $7.6 billion in 1952 to $40.8 billion in 1967 as indicated in Table 1. If commercial paper had merely maintained the relative position it had in the liability structure of these firms in 1952, the volume of these notes would have risen to slightly more than twice the level outstanding in 1952. However, commercial paper increased at a stronger rate and the ratio of commercial paper to total liabilities rose substantially over

TABLE 1

Liability Positions of Financial Companies on Selected Dates

	Total Liabilities	Commercial Paper	Bank Loans	Ratio—Commercial Paper		
				To Total Liabilities	Plus Bank Loans To Total Liabilities	To Bank Loans
	(In billions of dollars)			(Percent)		
1952	7.6	1.4	3.6	18.4	65.8	38.9
1955	13.0	1.7	5.7	13.1	56.9	29.8
1965	36.2	8.3	11.6	22.9	55.0	71.6
1967	40.8	14.1	9.1	34.6	56.9	154.9

Source: Flow of Funds Accounts, 1945–67, Board of Governors of the Federal Reserve System, February 1968.

this period. Data for 1955 have been included in this table in order to show the temporary decline which occurred in the ratio of commercial paper to total liabilities between 1952 and 1955, and, more importantly, to emphasize the extent of the almost steady upward trend in this ratio since then. As can be seen, however, the advance in this ratio between the end of 1965 and the end of 1967 was much stronger than would have been expected on the basis of the trend established from the end of 1955 through 1965.

A general indication of the substitution process responsible for the increase in relative importance of commercial paper in the liability positions of finance companies is provided in the last two columns in Table 1. After declining sharply between 1952 and the end of 1955, the ratio of short-term liabilities to total liabilities declined slightly further during the following ten-year period, while the ratio of commercial paper to bank loans trended upward. The advance from 1955 to 1965 in the ratio of commercial paper to total liabilities then was due to the marked substitution of commercial paper indebtedness for commercial bank indebtedness.

The increase in the ratio of paper indebtedness to bank indebtedness which occurred between 1965 and 1967, an increase much stronger than would have been expected on the basis of the 1955–65 trend, stands out dramatically in this

table. Moreover, it should also be noted that the latest advance in this ratio was due not only to a comparatively sharp growth in total paper but also to an absolute decline in bank indebtedness. In contrast, during the preceding ten-year period, the change in the ratio was due to the relatively stronger expansion of commercial paper indebtedness.

Changes in level and structure of liabilities at nonfinancial corporations which occurred between 1952 and 1967 are presented in Table 2. It will be noticed that the ratio of commercial paper to total liabilities declined moderately between 1952 and 1955. This process of substitution was reversed after 1955, however, and commercial paper indebtedness increased at a somewhat faster rate than total indebtedness at these firms through the end of 1965. This growth in the volume of commercial paper indebtedness relative to total indebtedness between 1955 and 1965 was mainly due to a substitution of short-term indebtedness for long-term indebtedness, rather than the substitution of paper indebtedness for bank indebtedness. This contrasts with the substitution process observed at finance companies over this period.

Liability developments since 1965, on the other hand, have been similar to those recorded at finance companies. More specifically, commercial paper has increased in relative importance both as a source

TABLE 2

Liability Positions of Nonfinancial Corporations on Selected Dates
(dollars in billions)

| | | | | Percent Ratio Commercial Paper | | |
	Total Liabilities	Com- mercial Paper	Bank Loans	To Total Liabilities	Plus Bank Loans To Total Liabilities	To Bank Loans
1952	$113.2	$ .4	$19.5	.3	17.6	2.1
1955	135.7	.3	21.4	.2	16.0	1.4
1965	256.3	.8	48.4	.3	19.2	1.7
1967	310.6	3.0	59.1	1.0	20.0	5.1

Source: Flow of Funds Accounts 1945–67, Board of Governors of the Federal Reserve System, February 1968.

of total external finance and as a source of short-term funds vis-a-vis bank loans. However, in contrast to what occurred at finance companies, the rise in the ratio of commercial paper to bank loans did not reduce the relative importance of commercial bank loans in the total liability position of these firms. To the contrary, the ratio of commercial bank loans to total liabilities was at a record high for the 16-year period at the end of 1967 as a result of a strong expansion in these loans in 1965, 1966, and 1967.

The recent sharp increase in the ratio of commercial paper indebtedness to commercial bank indebtedness recorded at both groups of borrowers contrasts not only with past trends in this ratio but also with the fluctuation in these ratios during preceding periods of business expansion. This was particularly the case for nonfinancial corporations, as the ratio of commercial paper indebtedness to commercial bank indebtedness display a generally consistent pattern of decline during both the 1954–57 and 1958–60 periods of expansion in business activity. A drop in this ratio also was recorded from the beginning of the current business expansion to the end of 1965. These developments were due to a combination of a reduction in commercial paper indebtedness and an increase in commercial bank indebtedness.

Changes which occurred in this ratio at finance companies during the periods of business expansion of the 1950's were quite similar to those recorded at nonfinancial companies. This ratio declined during the 1954–57 period of expansion. During the 1958–60 period of expansion, the relative size of paper indebtedness and bank indebtedness remained unchanged, which must be interpreted as a cyclical decline if the upward trend in this ratio is considered. On the other hand, commercial paper indebtedness increased at a faster rate than bank indebtedness during the early years of the current expansion. The rate of advance in this ratio was much more modest than that recorded since 1965, however.

One factor which would ordinarily be expected to have a major influence on decisions to borrow in the commercial paper market as opposed to borrowing at banks is the relative cost of each form of indebtedness. A general indication of the relationship between the interest costs for each type of debt is provided by the top line in Chart 2, which shows changes which have occurred in the differential between the interest rate charged by banks on loans to their prime customers and the interest rate established in the dealer market on prime commercial paper notes with four to six months to maturity.

Two characteristics about the cost of commercial paper borrowing relative to bank borrowing stand out most dramatically in this chart. First, throughout most of the period since 1952, it was less expensive to borrow in the market than at commercial banks. Second, the relative cost of borrowing in the commercial paper market generally increased during periods of business expansion and declined during periods of business recession. These secular and cyclical relationships between borrowing costs provide a major explanation for the secular and cyclical changes in the ratio of commercial paper indebtedness to commercial bank indebtedness over the period through 1965.

Since fluctuations in this ratio will also be reflected by changes in the volume of commercial paper debt if other conditions remain the same, the influence of the relative cost of paper indebtedness on changes in the volume of commercial paper would also be expected to be quite strong. This relationship is quite apparent in regard to the volume of dealer-issued paper, the data for which has been replotted on Chart 2. A fairly close direct relationship through 1965 between the cyclical patterns of change in dealer-issued paper and the cyclical patterns of change in the size of this differential can be noted. However, the same close relationship between relative cost and changes in directly issued paper quite obviously did not exist. As previously indicated, this should not be interpreted as indicating any lack of cost sensitivity by borrowers issuing direct paper, for the behavior of the ratio of commercial paper indebtedness to bank indebtedness at finance companies generally declined during periods in which the cost of commercial paper borrowing was relatively high, at least until the current period of expansion. Instead, the growth in directly placed paper during periods of tight money and the decline in periods of easy money occurred despite the effects of the change in relative cost. It may also be

said that the variations in external financing requirements during these periods were so strong that they more than offset the influence of changes in relative cost on the volume of directly issued paper.

Although recognition of the influence of external financing needs reasonably explains why directly issued paper expanded sharply rather than declining in earlier periods in which the cost of commercial paper indebtedness was high relative to bank indebtedness, it clearly does not do so for the growth in both directly issued and dealer placed paper which has occurred since 1965. As previously indicated, the advances in the volume of paper indebtedness were attributable in part to growth in total liabilities, particularly at nonfinancial companies. A shift toward greater reliance on short-term sources of funds also played a part. However, the main source of growth was the sharp substitution of commercial paper debt for bank debt which occurred at both groups of borrowers, a development which contrasts sharply with what occurred during earlier periods in which similar cost conditions prevailed.

IMPLICATIONS FOR THE FUTURE

Because of the relatively high ratio of commercial paper indebtedness to bank indebtedness and to total indebtedness at finance companies, and because of the sharp increase in this ratio since 1965, there is some reason to believe that finance companies will not continue to substitute commercial paper for bank loans at a pace similar to that of the past two and a half years. Moreover, some shift from short-term indebtedness to long-term indebtedness may occur if the relative cost of long-term indebtedness declines. These observations taken together suggest that the rate of growth in directly issued paper in the next few years will be determined primarily by the rate of growth in total indebtedness at finance companies rather than by the substitution of commercial paper for other forms of indebtedness. As a result, it appears likely that the rate of growth of directly issued commercial paper will at best conform to past growth trends and may in fact expand at below this trend.

The outlook for growth in commercial paper sold through dealers, on the other hand, appears to be much more favorable. The ratio of commercial paper to total indebtedness at nonfinancial corporations remains quite low, even though it has increased since 1965. Thus, the possibility of substantial substitution of commercial paper for other forms of indebtedness appears quite strong, particularly in view of the strong growth which has occurred under what formerly would have been considered highly unfavorable conditions. The recent increase in the number of firms selling paper in this market, particularly the increase in the number of public utility firms, provides additional support for this judgment.

The implications of this latter projection are obvious. The commercial paper market already has cut substantially into the loan business of commercial banks with finance companies. The potential for similar inroads at nonfinancial corporations is clearly present.

19. Banks Move into High-Risk Commercial Financing*

Robert P. Shay and Carl C. Greer

Because of their various services, commercial banks are often called "Department Stores of Finance." Until recently however they had, for the most part, left high-risk commercial financing to the finance companies. This article examines bank activity in accounts receivable lending and the industry's entry into factoring. These developments are said to presage a more general invasion of the finance companies' historical domain.

In the period since World War II, commercial banks have become the major force in consumer financing. Sales finance companies once dominated auto-

*From *Harvard Business Review*, November/December, 1968 (copyright 1968 by the President and Fellows of Harvard College; all rights reserved). Reprinted by permission of the publisher.

mobile financing, but now the banks hold the majority of outstanding auto paper. In financing the purchase of other consumer durable goods, banks are second, mainly because of the financial subsidiaries of giant manufacturers and retailers. Finally, banks supply more personal loans to consumers than do either the consumer or sales finance companies.

And in their drive to meet all the financial needs or desires of their customers, the more aggressive big-city banks have branched into such fields as credit cards, mutual funds, and accounting and payroll services.

While many of the large banks have also become more opportunistic and imaginative in commercial financing, they have only moderately expanded higher-risk business, such as accounts receivable financing and loans secured by inventories or real property. This business represents the domain of the finance companies.

In the last few years, however, there have been signs that commercial banks may be ready to offer finance companies more competition in this area. Some of the leaders have ventured into factoring, mainly by acquisition. And more are making loans against accounts receivable, the other major form of short-term high-risk commercial financing in the United States.

The banks' move into factoring has given them a substantial, though minority, portion of this business. More important, it has brought men skilled in the acquisition, supervision, and collection of higher-risk commercial accounts into bank managerial ranks—men who have established that such accounts can be handled safely and profitably.

These men may well provide the know-how and impetus for a further extension of lending to customers who previously were able to obtain credit only from finance companies. If these bankers succeed in influencing their employers to solicit and accept higher-risk loans, competitive pressure will be exerted on other banks to follow their example.

In this article we shall examine the recent bank entries in factoring activities and the parallel development of "in-house" experience and expertise in dealing with more hazardous financing. We shall analyze the less altered situation with regard to accounts receivable loans, and search for clues to competitive trends in the banking and commercial finance industries.

STATE OF FACTORING

In factoring (which dates back to about 2000 B.C.), the lender underwrites the extension of credit by purchasing the accounts or notes receivable of his clients, typically without recourse to them for any credit losses. Consequently, the

factor must take responsibility for approving credits on sales made by manufacturers and merchants. The customers of these companies are notified that their accounts have been purchased and are payable to the factor on the due dates, usually within 60 days. The factor's compensation is a commission (usually 1 percent to 1½ percent) based on the face value of the purchased receivables, plus interest (usually 1½ percent to 2½ percent above the prime rate). The bulk of factoring activity is in textiles and allied fields, although other industries using factors include furniture, shoes, toys, lumber, and metal products.

Available figures on the current factoring volume are skimpy and imprecise. According to the National Commercial Finance Conference, in 1967 the volume of its member companies was $7.83 billion, compared with $2.7 billion in 1950. But its members do not include commercial banks or their subsidiaries. (This growth, incidentally, was substantially less than that of other forms of commercial financing done by its members, which increased from $2 billion to $18.25 billion in the same period.) According to the *Daily News Record*, in 1967 total volume was up to $8.99 billion.[1] This figure does include banks, but it also includes accounts receivable financing extended by factors, while excluding factors that do not have offices in New York City.

Most banks historically have been content to limit short-term commercial financing to high-grade borrowers under self-liquidating lines of credit. Companies qualified for such loans when their financial ratios and past earnings performance were satisfactory; but when the credit applicant was submarginal because of small size, no credit history, poor earnings performance, or weakening financial ratios, banks refused to extend credit. They were, however, willing to lend to

---

[1]February 5, 1968.

commercial finance companies, which seized the opportunity to develop factoring services for these risks and make loans against their accounts receivable.

Banks Move In

But, beginning with the darks days of the Great Depression, many banks began to search for new ways to bring in business. They attracted commercial customers, for example, with term loans. In the 1930's a few—notably, the Bank of America and the Trust Company of Georgia—even ventured into factoring. They were followed, in 1946, by the First National Bank of Boston and, in about 1960, by two others in Hawaii.

Most nationally chartered banks, however, showed little interest in factoring during and after World War II because federal law was interpreted as prohibiting such activity. To avoid this prohibition, the First National Bank of Boston designed its forms so that legally it was making advances against approved receivables, instead of purchasing them as factors do. The bank adopted all the other aspects of factoring agreements, including nonrecourse to the client for default on the receivables used to retire the advances.

In June 1963, James Saxon, then Comptroller of the Currency, issued a ruling that factoring was a legitimate bank activity. In this more permissive atmosphere, eight banks, including some of the largest and most energetic in the United States, have entered the field since 1965:

1. First National City Bank purchased Hubshman Factors.
2. Citizens and Southern National Bank of Georgia acquired Joel Hurt Factors, Inc.
3. United California Bank acquired Atlas Factors, Inc.
4. First Pennsylvania Banking & Trust Company started a factoring department.

5. Philadelphia National Bank purchased Congress Factors Corporation.
6. Chemical Bank New York Trust Company acquired L. F. Dommerich & Company, Inc.
7. Bankers Trust Company acquired Coleman & Company.
8. Chase Manhattan Bank agreed to acquire Shapiro Bros. Factor Corporation. (At this writing, the merger is awaiting the approval of the Comptroller of the Currency.)

It is important to note that, with one exception, these banks decided to buy going concerns rather than start in the factoring business from scratch. And even in the *de novo* exception, the First Pennsylvania's department was headed by former finance-company personnel. So all these financial institutions realized that it was essential to enter the business with persons knowledgeable and skilled in this specialty.

It is also worth noting that all these banks are located in areas with substantial textile or allied interests, where "old-line" factoring is an accepted practice. So it is not surprising that banks elsewhere have not followed their move. Evidently they are not willing to take a great leap into factoring when their corporate customers are not ready for it either.

With these recent entries into factoring, commercial banks have raised their share of the total business from a small one to a substantial one—38 percent by the end of 1967, by our reckoning from *Daily News Record* figures. Even so, only one bank, the First National Bank of Boston, ranked at that point among the top six companies in volume. It was third. (The others, not in order, were Meinhard—Commercial Corporation, James Talcott, Inc., William Iselin & Company, Inc., John P. Maguire & Company, Inc., and United Factors.)

Before we examine the commercial banks' entry into factoring more fully, let us take a look at the current state of

EXHIBIT 1
Banks Participating in Accounts Receivable Financing, 1940 and 1957
(number of banks in samples, 327 and 672, respectively)

| | Banks reporting participation on a: | | | |
| | "Regular" basis, 1940 | | "Relatively frequent" basis, 1957 | |
	Number	Percent	Number	Percent
All banks	89	27	342	51
By size of bank°				
Large	19	59	101	86
Medium	39	40	112	73
Small	30	15	129	32
By size of population center†				
Large	28	53	153	70
Medium	39	33	104	67
Small	22	14	85	29

°Size categories in millions:

	1940	1957
Large	Over $50	Over $100
Medium	$5 to $50	$20 to $100
Small	$5 or less	$20 or less

†Size categories: large, 500,000 and over; medium, 50,000 to 500,000; small, under 50,000.

Sources: Raymond J. Saulnier and Neil H. Jacoby, *Accounts Receivable Financing* (New York, National Bureau of Economic Research, 1943), Table C-1, p. 151; Board of Governors of the Federal Reserve System, *Financing Small Business* (Washington, D.C., 1958), Table 6, p. 405.

their activity in the accounts receivable business.

ACCOUNTS RECEIVABLE LENDING

Many more banks participate in accounts receivable financing than in factoring. How many more, and to what extent, is hard to tell; data on bank penetration into this market are even less complete and up to date than those on factoring. The most recent figures were issued in 1957. A comparison of a study made in that year with one done in 1940, shown in Exhibit 1, indicates that bank participation in this activity increased markedly during that period. As one might expect, the most active banks were the large ones in the larger population centers.

To get an inkling of the volume of bank participation, one has to turn back to 1955 for data. In October of that year, on request, member banks submitted to the Federal Reserve figures on their outstanding loans secured by the assignment of claims. The Federal Reserve later re-

ported the total to be some $2.81 billion.[2] But this figure lumped together loans secured by the assignment of contracts, and oil runs with accounts receivable. In a similar survey in 1945 accounts receivable loans represented 27 percent of the total,[3] suggesting that, if the same proportion existed in 1955, the value of accounts receivable loans in October 1955 was $759 million. If these loans turned over every 45 days, the implicit annual volume was about $6 billion in 1955. This admittedly very conjectural figure is significant when compared with the $4.9 billion volume of commercial financing (excluding factoring) in 1955 reported by members of the National Commercial Finance Conference. (Even so, the $759 million represented only 2.5 percent of all business loans held by member banks in October 1955.)

In 1967 we conducted interviews at

[2]*Federal Reserve Bulletin,* September 1959, Table 3, p. 1119.

[3]*Federal Reserve Bulletin,* June 1947, Table 1, p. 665.

nine leading commercial banks in Boston, New York, and Chicago, to assess their mood with respect to expanding accounts receivable financing and other related activities. Because any such moves would be directly competitive with commercial finance companies, we included four banks that were leading suppliers of loans to finance companies (none was in factoring), as well as five that were already active accounts receivable lenders (two were in factoring at the time, as well). These five banks (in New York and Boston) were generally classified as retail banks, while the other four (in Chicago and New York) similarly offered services to small depositors or borrowers, but concentrated on unsecured business loans to larger corporate customers.

In three of the five retail banks an innovative, expansionary spirit seemed to permeate accounts receivable lending. Two of these banks (First National of Boston and First National City of New York) were in factoring, and it appeared that they were more willing to accept higher risks when the two types of financing were handled in the same division or department. The third bank, though not engaged in factoring, had a strong finance-company orientation in its operating personnel and officers, which accounted for its aggressiveness. In one of the remaining two retail banks there was interest in moving into factoring among both its senior officers and its operating personnel, but it was evident that existing operations in accounts receivable lending were traditionally oriented away from any expansion into higher-risk business. The fifth bank in the group, the most conservative in its competition for accounts receivable borrowers, was not interested in factoring.

Since these banks were reputed to be the most active in accounts receivable lending in the New York and Boston areas, it did not appear likely that other large retail banks that had not entered factoring, or acquired finance-company personnel skilled in handling higher-risk financing, would be contemplating expansion of accounts receivable loans.

At the four wholesale banks there was an air of watchful waiting. They expected generally that commercial banks would become more competitive with finance companies in accounts receivable financing, but these bankers were not willing to take the lead. The banks saw a possibility in undertaking loan participations with a finance company, where the latter would service, supervise, and collect the loans while the bank would provide some portion of the funds supplied at a lower rate than that received by the finance company. In this way, finance-company accounts receivable financing could become more competitive with the lower rates charged by competitive retail banks, since a bank's participation would enable a borrower to obtain, on average, a somewhat lower rate. One of the four wholesale banks viewed participations as a means to acquire expertise so that its personnel could compete aggressively, independent of participations, in the future.

Slow-Growth Situation

Lest we give a wrong impression, we should stress that not many banks are aggressive in soliciting accounts receivable and other higher-risk loans. They do not advertise such services, and relatively few banks have set up separate departments to administer them. They confine themselves mainly to those borrowers who can be expected to "graduate" soon to unsecured loans or whose unsecured loans can be made safer by shifting them to a collateralized status. Big-city banks often participate in accounts receivable loans with their correspondents. And, as we mentioned, bankers are increasingly willing to participate in loans with finance companies, but even in this case they often retain the right to withdraw their participation on short notice. Using the most generous measures, loans secured by accounts receivable represent only a small fraction of total business loans among the large commercial banks we surveyed.

We checked our impressions from these interviews by sending questionnaires to nine large banks operating in the Midwestern and Southwestern United States. Only two of the seven banks that responded had separate departments for handling their accounts receivable loans, and in none did these loans account for more than 5 percent of total outstanding commercial loans.

None of the responding banks had shown an increase in the proportion of their loans secured by accounts receivable over the past few years, and only one expected an increase in the future. None participated in factoring because of assertedly insufficient return. Finally, all the responding banks engaged in participations with finance companies, and two of them felt that these would gain in significance in the future.

Obviously, judging from our interviews and questionnaires, banks contemplate only moderate growth in accounts receivable financing. When and if a rapid expansion occurs, it will be only when they are willing to accept risks that finance companies accept and charge comparable rates. It is axiomatic that rates must cover the greater costs of extending and policing higher-risk credits. The major source of loss in high-risk lending is fraud, and finance companies have developed successful procedures to minimize such losses. Banks must learn them.

One way to acquire the necessary expertise is to acquire a finance company, as some banks are doing. Another way is through participations with finance companies. This route is slower, and, if finance companies retain control of servicing and collection, banks personnel will learn little except what they can glean from the partner's auditing reports—however often bank auditors may accompany finance-company auditors when examinations are made.

It does not appear likely, either in our view or in the minds of the senior bank officials we interviewed, that employees now involved in accounts receivable financing in commercial banks are ready to adapt their present procedures to pursue high-risk borrowers.

THE BANKS IN FACTORING

Let us consider now why some commercial banks have turned to factoring and note the implications of their decision for the future expansion of higher-risk commercial financing. To obtain answers to this question, we supplemented our interviews on factoring and accounts receivable financing at the Frst National Bank of Boston and the First National City Bank of New York with interviews of officers at the four banks in New York and Philadelphia that entered factoring in 1967 and 1968.

Why They Did It

Those banks that entered factoring before the 1960's did so obviously because of their close contacts with customers in the textile industry. Those New York banks that entered factoring after the Saxon ruling, beginning with First National City Bank in 1965, had other reasons.

The move was a logical extension of the development of higher-risk lending which has occurred since the 1920's. First National City Bank, for instance, had first undertaken consumer installment lending in 1928, had moved with other banks into term loans and amortized mortgage loans in the 1930's, and had embarked on a still wider range of activities in the post-World War II period. In our interviews, all the bankers also cited the desire to become full-service institutions, catering to all of their customers' credit needs. And some mentioned more particular reasons:

1. Factoring is attractive because the business is relatively stable. The volume typically grows moderately from year to year. Factoring can be steadily profitable;

Hubshman Factors, for instance, made a profit every year from 1915 on, while it was an independent company. Customer turnover is low; clients tend to remain with their financing sources for eight or nine years. By way of contrast, in accounts receivable financing the average customer turnover is two to three years.

2. Consistent with the assumption of higher risk, the rates of return are higher than in most bank activities. While some old-line factoring companies are very profitable, commercial bankers argue that banks should be able to do better. They have a lower cost of obtaining funds because they do not depend solely on the money and capital markets, but can solicit deposits. While banks, too, are having to turn increasingly to these markets, they nevertheless believe they can keep a competitive advantage over their finance-company competition.

3. The ability of large-city banks to offer factoring services to their correspondent banks in other parts of the country is an important element. The city bank typically services the accounts for its correspondents, retaining the 1 percent to 1½ percent fee, and participates, if requested, in any advances of funds made to factoring clients. This adds to the city banks' factoring volume, which is an important element affecting costs and profitability of factoring operations. In the competition for correspondent balances, the advantage of being able to offer this additional service is also important.

4. The factored accounts receivable provide a source of future bank customers for either unsecured loans or deposits, since the evaluation of credit and the receipt of payments put the bank in contact with a large number of business firms.

Entry & Future Growth

The banks that have studied the possibility of establishing factoring departments in the past few years had many problems to consider in choosing between doing it *de novo* or acquiring an existing company. By that time, of course, the banks' managements had passed the point where they were worrying about whether they should risk tarnishing their image by accepting high-risk customers, or whether they should charge loan rates which the uninformed might regard as unconscionable.

De Novo Route. The time required to build volume, while absorbing start-up costs, and the recruitment of capable personnel are the principal problems in using this approach.

One banker experienced in finance-company factoring suggested to us that a volume of at least $100 million is needed to make money in this field. The close relation between a client and his factor makes it difficult for a competing institution to lure the client's business away. Bankers hope that the status of having one's receivables financed by a bank can draw business away from their finance-company competition. But more important is the client's confidence that the bank can provide the same degree of service, or better. Because of the necessity to build up volume quickly, the *de novo* bank department may have to undercut prevailing rates. But small rate differentials will not convince a satisfied factoring client that an untried bank can outperform his current factor easily. Moreover, a client does not want to make repeated announcements to his customers that he is changing factors.

Experienced persons capable of directing factoring operations soundly and profitably are scarce. The job requires a great deal of skill. For instance, a factor cannot set such restrictive credit standards that his clients' sales are affected in favor of his competitors. But the factor does not have recourse to his client if the account receivable is not paid. So liberality in approving credits must be balanced with a realistic appraisal of risk and intensive supervision and control of collections.

The First Pennsylvania Banking & Trust Company, as we have mentioned, is the only bank to have chosen the *de novo* department route in recent years. A substantial segment of the textile and apparel industry in Philadelphia has always been served by outside factors, so in the summer of 1967 First Pennsylvania decided to become the first local bank to enter the market. When the Philadelphia National Bank followed by acquiring Congress Factors in November of the same year, it, too, faced the problem of building volume in the Philadelphia area, since Congress was a New York-based company that was not a major force in the Philadelphia market.

These two banks will provide the first test of whether the acquisition of a going concern will prove to be a more effective method of market penetration than beginning from scratch. A question of greater importance is whether the two locally based banks can win clients away from "outside" competitors.

ACQUISITION ROUTE. The other way of entry into factoring poses different problems, particularly in availability of candidates.

Thus far, since the banks' acquisition interest has been mainly in the factoring part of high-risk commercial financing, they have made no acquisitions of large commercial finance companies with only a relatively small factoring volume—although some have been rumored in recent years. Those acquired have been factors whose assets were in the lower portion of the $25-million to $100-million size.

Banks are searching for consistently profitable companies with young but proven managerial talent. The search is intense because there is a shortage of independents. Of the 26 factors listed in the *Daily News Record* as having offices in New York City in 1967, six were bank-owned and six others were subsidiaries of manufacturers that factor their own accounts.[4] Of the 14 remaining companies, three were large (Meinhard-Com-

mercial, Talcott, and Heller), and only two showed factoring volume that was 95 percent to 100 percent of combined factoring and accounts receivable volume. Thus, if a bank's interest is limited to factoring, the number of potentially desirable companies to look at is small.

If a bank's interest also encompasses accounts receivable financing and related activities, the number of potential merger partners grows substantially. At the last check (June 1965), there were 40 companies in the $5-million to $25-million range of business receivables, and 18 companies in the $25-million to $100-million range.[5]

PROVISION OF FUNDS. The tight-money period of 1966 delayed the banks planning to enter the field. They were reluctant to allocate scarce funds for developing new activities at the expense of the demands of their usual business.

Once the banks had made the move into factoring, this question arose: How much money should be allocated to foster the new ventures' growth? It is apparent that First National City Bank allowed its Hubshman Division enough resources to grow rapidly throughout the tight-money experience of 1966. Hubshman's outstandings doubled during the first two years of Citibank's ownership, and its reported volume grew from $260 million in 1964 to $625 million in 1967.

The Philadelphia National Bank allows its subsidiary, Congress Factors, to go to the money market to raise its own funds, using its own commercial paper secured by a PNB letter of credit. The bank made these LCs available to its finance-company customers during 1966 for this purpose. PNB considers this technique as ensuring the availability of funds to its subsidiary during tight-money periods irrespective of Regulation Q, since commercial paper is not subject to the rate ceilings placed on certificates of deposit. This alternative is of course open only to those banks whose

---

[4]February 5, 1968.

[5]*Federal Reserve Bulletin*, April 1967, Supplementary Table 9, p. 550.

financing operations are carried on by subsidiaries, rather than departments or divisions.

COMPETITIVE EFFECTS

We believe that the movement of banks into factoring, as part of a general movement toward becoming full-service institutions, signals a general intensification of competition for higher-risk commercial customers. The move of many of the largest banks in the nation into factoring has brought persons skilled in handling these borrowers into commercial bank managements.

The earliest impact of these skills will be felt in the accounts receivable lending operations of New York City banks, which, we expect, will follow the example of First National City Bank and transfer these loans to their newly established factoring divisions. Then both accounts receivable loans and factoring services will be aggressively solicited, not only locally, but anywhere in the nation their correspondent banks are located.

It will take some time, however, for the competitive impact to be felt, because many of the banks that have just entered factoring did so primarily to be able to offer this new service, not to expand their accounts receivable loans. In some cases, the finance-company oriented bank officers will have to convince their managements that they should increase the proportion of business loans in higher-yielding accounts receivables financing as well as in factoring. And, once this point is won, these officers can press forward with more imaginative secured lending arrangements, such "package deals," where finance companies arrange a bundle of different types of collateral (i.e., inventory, accounts receivable, equipment, and real property) to secure a large loan, instead of using a single type of asset.

The senior officers we interviewed in the New York banks were philosophically ready to move in these directions; to them, the acquisition of factoring companies represented a first step. But they need the troops to carry out their plans. Absorbing the newly acquired units smoothly into the bank structure and harnessing the interests and objectives of previously separate management personnel cannot be done hastily. The second phase of expansion into higher-risk commercial financing will take time, even for those banks that have acquired factors.

The competitive effects of the steps already taken may hasten the action. Large banks that have not yet moved into factoring may try to catch up by buying out larger finance companies with well-developed commercial financing activities, including factoring.

Competitive responses from the finance industry could stimulate banks to expand indirectly into secured commercial lending via loan participations. The large wholesale banks and banks located outside the East Coast and West Coast factoring areas are prime customers for participations with finance companies, but the latter, until recently, have been reluctant to solicit their potential competitors. The outside threat from direct-lending retail banks may promote demand for participations from finance companies of all sizes.

Like accounts receivable lending on the part of banks, participations are now used only sporadically, to meet special needs. The finance companies' main motivation for seeking them is to lower the rate to the borrower. There are indications that rate competition will become more important when the large-city banks encourage their correspondents to promote factoring and accounts receivable financing services.

Finance Companies' Response

We expect that the commercial finance industry will be able to weather the initial impact of the banks' movement into factoring, as it has with accounts receivable financing. The invasion of the factoring field at present represents a transfer of companies, for the most part, from the label of "finance companies" to the label of "banks," by merger. The real test will come when the realignment has been completed and competition between the two stiffens.

Competition in factoring (and accounts receivable financing, if banks become more aggressive in this field) could at any rate have only a limited effect on the finance industry; it has already diversified so much that these two areas represent only a moderate part of their business. Factoring and accounts receivable financing accounted for only 5.6 percent and 10.8 percent, respectively, of gross outstanding receivables of these companies the last time they were reported to the Federal Reserve (as of June 30, 1965).[6] According to our calculations from figures in this *Federal Reserve Bulletin* article, commercial finance companies held only 60 percent of the accounts receivable financing and 53 percent of the factoring carried on by finance companies; sales and personal finance companies did the rest. There is no reason to believe that that situation has changed in the last few years. With the bulk of their receivables in business rather than consumer financing, commercial finance companies have substantial receivables in installment financing of business equipment, inventories, and leasing contracts.

The smaller commercial finance companies probably will continue to specialize in extending credit to higher-rate, higher-risk, smaller borrowers. The larger companies can be expected to retain an important share of the large-loan, lower-rate business because of their willingness to assume risk and their ability to devise new methods of making these loans. Entrepreneurship and innovation were the sources of the finance industry's initial growth, and it has depended on them for its survival.

---

[6]*Federal Reserve Bulletin*, April 1967, Supplementary Table 11, p. 553.

It is the medium-sized finance companies, the group most coveted by banks seeking expansion in factoring, that appear to be most vulnerable to bank competition. This group was recently squeezed for borrowed funds, especially in marketing subordinated debt issues, which provide the base for senior borrowings. The medium-sized companies cannot place their issues as readily as the larger ones because they often lack the depth in management skills that the larger companies possess. Nor are they small enough to permit lenders easily to appraise the effectiveness of their operations and ascertain the quality of their receivables. These companies are being acquired rapidly, not only by banks, but by other financial and nonfinancial corporations as well.

Acquisitions by corporations other than banks should strengthen the finance industry against commercial bank competition. Recently, many of the largest independent sales finance companies with considerable commercial finance receivables among their assets, have been merged into nonfinancial enterprises that see an opportunity to obtain greater leverage through owning financial subsidiaries. The resources of its new parent bolsters the finance company's borrowing power.

On the other hand, large finance companies have also acquired commercial banks to obtain a share of the deposit funds that permit banks to operate at relatively low cost; C.I.T. Financial Corporation's ownership of the National Bank of North America is an example. Both types of acquisitions can be expected to continue, as competition brings the functions of large banks and finance companies closer together.

CONCLUDING NOTE

The recent entry of several leading banks into factoring presages, we think, a more general movement of big-city commercial banks into higher-risk commercial financing. As banks develop more experience and managerial expertise, they should become more energetic in a related high-risk lending activity, accounts receivable financing. They may eventually take a more active role in package deals, in loans secured by inventories and real property, and other devices to supply working capital to borrowers who are unable to obtain funds through unsecured loans or who need larger amounts under revolving credit arrangements.

The recent bank movement into factoring has been almost entirely through merger. Until the banks can absorb their acquisitions completely and learn how to take advantage of their new skills and opportunities in higher-risk financing, competition between banks and independent commercial finance companies is not likely to be fierce. But in time it should develop, resulting in better service to high-risk borrowers from both the banking and the finance industries.

20. Consumer Credit in the Affluent Society[*]

David Caplovitz

The growth in use of credit by American households has been an outstanding feature of postwar financial markets and has left its imprint in many places. Professor Caplovitz reviews in the article which follows not only the facts regarding household use of credit, but, more importantly he also sets forth the implications which this radical change in the pattern of debt structure has for acquisition of consumer durable goods (and hence saving), the impact of credit on consumption patterns (especially among lower income groups), and the development of new merchandising and financial marketing practices.

A great deal has been written in the past decade or so about the affluence of American society, its increasingly high standard of living and the consumption-orientation of its citizens. One aspect of

the affluent society, however, that has gone largely unnoticed by sociologists is the extent to which it rests upon the institution of consumer credit. It can truly be said that the affluent society is also a *credit* society. The attitudes of Americans toward debt have undergone a remarkable change within the lifetimes of many of us. Whereas not too long ago, debt was viewed as the mark of the imprudent or poverty-stricken man, today it is part of the American way of life.

Consumer credit takes a number of different forms. By far the largest category, and the one we are most accustomed to, is mortgage debt. Outstanding mortgage debt has grown tremendously in the last few decades as government-backed low-interest loans have made it possible for vast numbers of families to realize their great ambition of home ownership. From 1950 to the second quarter of 1968, nonfarm mortgage debt grew from $45 billion to $243.4 billion.[1] Whereas 44 per-

[*]Reprinted with permission from a symposium, Consumer Credit Reform, appearing in *Law and Contemporary Problems* (Vol. 33, No. 4, Autumn 1968), published by Duke University Law School. Copyright 1968 by Duke University. An earlier version of this paper was presented at the Sixty-second Annual Meeting of the American Sociological Association, San Francisco, August 29, 1967.

[1]54 *Federal Reserve Bulletin,* No. 11, at A48 (1968).

cent of American homes were mortgaged in 1950, 57 percent were mortgaged in 1960, and the figure is undoubtedly much higher today.[2] In all accountings of consumer debt by economists and government, mortgage debt is sharply differentiated from other kinds, partly because it is long-term and partly because the purchase of a house is seen ≈ an investment rather than as purely consumption. The other kinds of consumer credit are referred to as personal debt or, somewhat confusingly, as consumer debt, the term now referring to debt other than mortgages. In this more narrow sense, consumer credit covers short-term noninstallment debt and somewhat longer-term installment debt. Noninstallment debt includes charge accounts, debts for professional services, and that new institution, the credit card.

Of particular significance has been the rapid development of installment credit, for which the consumer pays a fee for the privilege of paying the debt off over time. Installment credit far exceeds noninstallment credit in volume,[3] and the remainder of this paper will be concerned primarily with installment credit.

I. GROWTH OF THE CREDIT SOCIETY

Installment credit is by no means a new phenomenon. Expensive books, such a encyclopedias, were sold on the installment plan in the eighteenth century. The honor of inventing installment selling as we know it today belongs to the Singer Sewing Machine Company, which started selling its product in this fashion back in 1856.[4] For many years, installment credit

was viewed as somewhat disreputable and was engaged in more by the working classes than by the well-to-do. With the advent of the automobile, installment credit achieved legitimacy, but it did not fully come into its own until after the Second World War. In 1945, outstanding installment debt was a negligible $2.5 billion. A decade later it climbed to $29 billion, and today installment debt stands at over $80 billion. By now the great majority of American families have used installment credit.[5] A national survey conducted in January 1967 showed that 87 percent of American households had made installment purchases at one time or another; 75 percent had at some time obtained installment loans from banks or finance companies, and fully 93 percent had used either one or the other form of installment credit. Currently, more than 60 percent of America's families are making payments on installment debts.[6]

Much of what we knew about installment credit and what Americans think about it we owe to the research of George Katona and his associates at Michigan's Survey Research Center.[7] Katona's yearly surveys of consumer finances show that more and more Americans view installment buying favorably. In the early 1950s about half the population thought installment buying was a good idea; by the early 1960s this figure increased to 60 percent. Nor is installment buying indulged in only by those who cannot afford cash. One of Katona's surprising findings is that about a third of the installment buyers have sufficient savings to pay cash and yet choose to buy on credit anyway.[8]

The growth of consumer credit has been so rapid and so pervasive that we might well ask what have been the con-

---

[2]U.S. Bureau of the Census, Statistical Abstract of the United States 711 (1968).

[3]According to the Federal Reserve Board, installment credit outstanding in September 1968 came to $82.9 billion compared with $21.4 billion in noninstallment credit. 54 Federal Reserve Bulletin, No. 11, at A52-53 (1968).

[4]See Plummer, Installment Selling, in 8 Encyclopedia Society Science 74 (1932); see also H. Black, Buy Now and Pay Later 108–10 (1961).

[5]U.S. Bureau of the Census, supra note 2, at 461.

[6]These data come from a survey conducted by the National Opinion Research Center of the University of Chicago, on behalf of the author.

[7]See G. Katona. The Mass Consumption Society (1964) [hereinafter cited as Katona].

[8]Id. at 235.

ditions that have led to this transformation to a credit society? Of primary significance, of course, has been the growth of the economy in general, the rising income of the population, and the expansion of its consumer aspirations. As Katona has noted, America is the first society in history in which a majority of the population has discretionary income, that is, income beyond that needed for subsistence. But the growth of consumer credit is not merely a reflection of economic expansion, for installment credit has grown at a much faster pace than has either gross national product or disposable personal income. Thus between 1950 and 1964 installment credit grew at an annual rate of 10.5 percent, while GNP grew at a rate of 5.8 percent and personal income at a rate of 5.5 percent.[9]

The growth of consumer credit must also be understood in terms of the marked shifts in the occupational structure that have accompanied economic growth: the growth of the middle classes and more particularly the emergence of the new middle class of salaried employees and the decline of the old middle class of entrepreneurs. The status claims of the old entrepreneurial middle class rested upon the ownership of property. As entrepreneurs, its members operated in a world of risk, susceptible to the vicissitudes of the market place. Entrepreneurial success depended upon the judicious allocation of income to capital investment as well as to consumption. To the extent that its members acquired debts, it was for purposes of production rather than consumption. Only those who achieved considerable wealth could afford the luxury of conspicuous consumption.

In contrast, the new middle class, employed in large bureaucracies, has provided a ready market for consumer credit. This is for two reasons. First, the members

of this group, unable to rest their status claims on property, are under strong social pressures to acquire the consumer goods that symbolize the middle-class style of life, a pressure that is experienced even by those whose incomes are relatively low. Second, the new middle class is reasonably assured of job security and thus of a steady and even rising income. A steady income is essential to the development of a credit society, for buying on time means acquiring possessions with tomorrow's income. In the credit society, the traditional pattern of saving first and then spending is reversed; the purchase is made and then "saving" in the form of monthly payments occurs. For the credit transaction to take place, both the debtor and the creditor must be assured that the debtor's income is secure. Thus it may be hypothesized that the bureaucratization of the world of work is a structural prerequisite for the credit society. Unfortunately, there are not data relating occupation to credit usage, but Katona's annual surveys do show the connection between income and installment debt. Each year a majority of those in the middle income categories, especially those earning between $5,000 and $10,000, have installment debts. In contrast, only about a third of the very poor, those earning less than $3,000, and less than a third of the rich, those earning more than $15,000, have installment debts.[10] We might infer from the income data that installment credit does get its chief support from the middle classes and the higher-paid working classes.

Also relevant to an understanding of the growth of installment credit is the disjunction between the family life cycle and the income cycle of the salaried employee and, to a lesser extent, the wage-earner as well. To insure loyalty and commitment, large-scale organizations must provide not only job security but promotions and salary increases as well. Salaries tend to be low at the start, but improve

[9]See Shay, *Major Developments in the Market for Consumer Credit Since the End of World War II*, 21 J. Finance 369 (1966).

[10]Katona 232.

with time, reaching a peak when the employee is of middle age. But families are formed at a much earlier time, and consumer needs are particularly great when households are being established. Installment credit serves as a mechanism for bridging this gap. By mortgaging future income, the family is able to meet its current consumer wants. Thus installment credit is a device for leveling somewhat the income curve over the occupational career. This is particularly true of educational loans which allow the college student to pay for his education at a time when his income is substantially higher, but to some extent it is also true of loans that extend for only a year or two. The connection between the family life cycle and credit usage is shown by the findings of Katona's surveys. Young families, those with pre-school age children, are most likely to have installment debts. (Interestingly enough, Katona finds that older families use installment credit now more frequently than they used to, although still not as frequently as the younger families, a finding he interprets as due to the gradual dying off of those morally opposed to debt.[11])

The explosion in consumer credit is also intimately connected with the changing residency patterns of Americans, the development of suburbs, and the fantastic growth of home ownership reflected in the mortgage-debt data cited earlier. Between 1890 and 1940 the proportion of owner-occupied dwelling units remained fairly constant at around 46 percent. By 1950 this figure had shot up to 57 percent, and in 1960 it reached 62 percent.[12] The basic desire of American consumers to own a home has contributed to their readiness to accept other kinds of consumer debts. The home owner has, of course, substantial consumer needs. He must not only

fill his house with furniture and appliances, but, if he lives in the suburbs, he must have a car and the chances are his wife must have one as well.

Apart from the reasons why consumers may want installment credit, the growth of this institution also owes a great deal to the efforts of the business community to sell the idea of credit buying to the American public. When installment credit first came into being, it was a means for selling merchandise. But the business community has discovered that there is so much profit to be made in credit that now the relationship is reversed; merchandise has become a device for selling credit. It is increasingly difficult to buy things for cash in the face of the merchant's propaganda to buy on credit instead. The onslaught of installment credit has recently overtaken two of the more staid institutions of the business community—the large department store and that bastion of conservative financial policy, the bank. Department stores have invented revolving credit accounts which they hope will supplant the charge account. Banks have even more recently come up with the invention of check credit. Whereas banks once had a vested interest in training their customers to balance their accounts and never to overdraw them, they are now doing just the opposite; they are offering their customers credit plans that permit them to write checks for more money than they have on deposit, the overdrawn amount being treated as an installment loan. The banks have also invaded the credit card market with their highly dubious practice of mailing unsolicited credit cards. Bank credit cards, which require payment of interest, represent one of the fastest growing sectors of the credit industry today.

II. SOME IMPLICATIONS OF THE CREDIT SOCIETY

Having examined some of the reasons for the development of the credit society, I should now like to review some of its

---

[11]Id.
[12]B. Wattenberg & R. Scammon, This U.S.A.: An Unexpected Family Portrait of 194,067,296 Americans Drawn from the Census 241 (1965).

consequences. The system of mortgaging future income to satisfy today's wants functions relatively smoothly in a society of rising income. Anathema to the credit society are downward trends in the economy. If the cash society could ill afford the recessions of the business cycle, this is even more true of the credit society. The vast number of users of consumer credit might be viewed as a new interest group pressing for governmental control of the economy to insure that recessions will not occur. Political polls have traditionally shown that voters tend to be more sensitive to economic issues than to social issues or foreign policy, and one of the reasons for this might well be the debt burdens that they have assumed.

While on the macroscopic level the credit society requires an expanding economy, so on the microscopic level the individual user of installment credit is increasingly dependent upon job security. Katona has noted that the growth of the American family's contractual obligations has made it less tolerant of risk-taking and more committed to job security.[13] Just as the growth of bureaucracy has facilitated the development of consumer credit, so consumer credit would appear to help socialize individuals to bureaucratic employment. Whether installment credit is contributing to the demise of entrepreneurial spirit is a matter for empirical research. Such research might also investigate the connection, if any, between consumer credit and job mobility. Does consumer debt make workers less willing to change jobs as well as less willing to strike out on their own?

A. Installment Credit, Deferred Gratification, and the Family

One of the apparent victims of installment credit is that trait popularly assigned to the middle class known as deferred gratification. Social scientists have repeat-

edly pointed out that the middle classes, unlike the lower classes, are capable of deferring gratification. I suspect that in the credit society the distinction is no longer that sharp. With the availability of installment credit, there is less need to defer gratifications. Young couples need not delay marriage until they can afford to set up a household, nor are the young married confronted with the choice of either having children or acquiring material goods. Through installment credit they can have both. We are all familiar with the demographic data showing dramatic changes in family structure. For example, the age at which people get married has declined; the amount of time that elapses before the first child is born has declined (from 1.7 years a generation ago to 1.4 years today), and the elapsed time before the last child in the family appears has declined markedly. Today, childbearing ceases, on the average, only six years after marriage; and more and more married women, their childbearing completed, are entering the labor market.[14] The number of doubled-up households has declined markedly in the past generation. Thus in 1940, 6.8 percent of married couples were living in other people's households, presumably their parents'; by 1962 this figure had shrunk to 2.1 percent.[15] The greater independence of the younger generation, the more rapid separation of the generations, and the increasing fragmentation of the extended family suggested by these data may well be to some extent a consequence of consumer credit.

B. Installment Credit and Budgeting

Another function that has been attributed to installment credit is that it has reintroduced the idea of budgeting into family finances, or rather that it is a functional alternative to budgeting that permits the

---

[13]Katona 180–81.

[14]Wattenberg & Scammon, *supra* note 12, at 42.

[15]*Id.* at 37–39.

family to exercise more control over its income. Since the weekly or monthly paycheck is committed to a series of debt payments, the possibility of impulsive expenditures is supposedly reduced. Katona, in particular, is an advocate of this point of view, but it should be noted that others have attributed just the opposite outcome to credit. According to this second view, credit stimulates impulse buying and irrational expenditures by making it easier for families to make expensive purchases. The accusation of families living beyond their means is frequently heard in the credit society, and the suspicion is that such families are just as apt to be found in the middle class suburbs as in the ghetto. Obviously, research is needed on this point to find out the frequency of each outcome and the kinds of families that benefit from, or are hurt by, the ready availability of credit.

C. Installment Credit and the Poor

Until quite recently, it was rather fashionable for social scientists to point to the increasing homogeneity of American society, the blurring of class lines, as more and more people in all strata had access to the so-called standard consumer package of appliances and automobiles. The rediscovery of the poor and the war on poverty have served as a corrective to this picture of American society, reminding us that inequality is still very much with us. Nevertheless, it is still true that installment credit has provided the means by which even the poor can share some of the fruits of the affluent society, with the result that some symbols of status and class no longer serve as good indicators of social position.

This observation calls attention to the fact that the market for consumer credit is by no means limited to the new middle class. On the contrary, low-income persons, those near or even below the poverty line, also become consumers of such major durables as automobiles, television sets,

phonographs, and washing machines through the institution of installment credit. My own study of low-income families living in public housing in New York City showed that fully 95 percent owned a TV set,[16] and the comparable figure in a California study of even more impoverished families is 89 percent.[17]

Through the mass media, Americans in *all* walks of life are bombarded with messages to buy now and pay later. "Easy payments" and "no money down" are slogans luring even the poor into the market place, and in spite of the low credit status of the poor there are numerous merchants who are prepared to extend them credit. Nor is it very difficult to lure the poor into making costly purchases, for in some ways the ownership of goods takes on even more significance for low-income persons than for those in higher income brackets. Since the poor have little prospect of greatly improving their low social standing through occupational mobility, they are apt to turn to consumption as at least one sphere in which they can make some progress toward the American dream of success. If the upper strata observed by Veblen engaged in conspicuous consumption to demonstrate their social superiority, it might be said that today's poor are apt to engage in *compensatory* consumption. Appliances, automobiles, and the dream of a home of their own can become compensations for blocked social mobility.

In our low-income areas, a special kind of system of sales-and-credit has evolved to cater to the needs of the poor, one in which exploitation and fraud are more the norm than the exception. High-pressure tactics, "bait" ads and "switch sales," misrepresentation of price and quality,

[16]D. Caplovitz, *The Poor Pay More* 37 (paper ed. 1967).

[17]R. Stone & F. Schlamp, *Family Life Styles Below the Poverty Line* (Report to the California Social Welfare Board from the Institute for Social Science Research, San Francisco State College, 1966).

and the sale of used merchandise as new all flourish in the low-income market place. This deviant system rests in part upon the ignorance of low-income consumers and their vulnerability to fast-talking salesmen, but in large part it also rests upon the absence of meaningful alternatives to current practices. The poor, lacking the normal requirements of credit, cannot shop in the major department stores. Under present marketing arrangements in our society, unethical practices may be an inevitable consequence of serving the wants of the poorest risks. Society now virtually presents the very poor risks with twin options: of foregoing major purchases or of being exploited.

Quite apart from their greater exposure to fraudulent practices, the poor must pay more for their credit purchases. As a Federal Trade Commission study has recently shown, the mark-up of the low-income retailer is substantially higher than that of the general market retailer, in part because of his less efficient business practices.[18] To an unknown extent, these added mark-ups must be apportioned among various possible causes: the possibly greater risks and other costs of doing business in low-income areas, the weakness of competition where consumers are less informed and less mobile and where the more reputable retailers are less likely to operate, and the lower ethical standards prevailing in the community generally. Again the price of serving the poorest members of the society appear high, but amelioration of these costs seems possible through legal reforms, consumer education, and other efforts to bring the benefits of retailer competition to low-income areas.

The role of installment credit in the life of the poor has drawn public attention to two major issues. First, by making the poor into consumers, it has forced govern-

ment to include in its efforts to combat poverty ways of providing meaningful alternatives to the costly system of sales-and-credit. The discovery has gradually been made that improving the income of the poor is only one side of their economic plight. Equally important is the matter of how they spend what little income they have. If the poor must pay more for goods and services, the increments in their income may have little impact on their lives. Today the war on poverty includes numerous programs designed to cope with the consumer problems of the poor. Low-income credit unions have been set up in many areas, and food-buying clubs and other kinds of consumer cooperatives have been developed in ghetto communities.

Second, the access of the poor to installment credit has forced the legal profession to re-examine some traditional concepts. For example, the principle of freedom of contract has come into further question as it has become apparent that inequality in understanding and bargaining power can yield bargains that the courts cannot in good conscience enforce.[19] Even the venerable status of the so-called "holder in due course"—that is, one who takes a negotiable note innocently by endorsement and is freed of defenses that might be asserted against the payee —is also being threatened by the realization that unscrupulous merchants and co-operating finance companies are given an extraordinary legal advantage over the consumer.[20] Among other stimuli, the active efforts of dedicated lawyers in legal aid and OEO-sponsored neighborhood legal services programs have generated

---

[18]See FTC, *Economic Report on Installment Credit and Retail Sales Practices of District of Columbia Retailers* (1968).

[19]See note 23 *infra* on the gradual emergence of a principle of "unconscionability."

[20]See, e.g., Annotated Laws of Massachusetts ch. 255, § 12B (1968), *noted in* 75 *Harvard Law Review* 437 (1961). Uniform Consumer Credit Code § 2.403 would require consumer paper to be nonnegotiable, and § 2.404 provides alternative clauses specifying either that an assignee is subject to all defenses or the limited circumstances under which he would not be so subject.

new attention to the abuses possible in consumer credit arrangements, and the recent efforts at reform, which are the subject of this symposium, must be viewed as at least partially motivated by a new awareness of the credit problems of the poor. Whether the federal Consumer Credit Protection Act of 1968 and the newly promulgated Uniform Consumer Credit Code place too much reliance on disclosure as a means of promoting consumer self-help remains to be seen; the low-income consumer may still find himself victimized to an extent the society should continue to deplore. Perhaps consumer programs and cooperative efforts of the types noted above will be useful further remedies, but I suspect that, even more, we need stricter enforcement of the existing and proposed credit statutes. The enforcement machinery specified in the Uniform Consumer Credit Code holds out hope of more effective enforcement, but the dependence of the Code Administrator on legislative budgetary support reminds us that statutory power alone is not enough.[20a]

D. Credit Rating: A New Principle of Stratification

In the credit society, a new and increasingly important dimension of stratification has been introduced, one that is analytically independent of the older dimension of credit ranking. As our economy becomes more and more dependent upon credit, a man's credit rating becomes an increasingly important asset. A vast network of information exchange exists in the credit industry, and each city has a credit bureau in which information about consumers is assembled and collated. Automation has been introduced, and soon the credit rating system will be fully automated.

How one achieves or loses status in this ranking system is by no means obvious.

Considerable controversy is now going on in the credit industry as to whether a person's past performance with credit or whether some kind of index score based on the person's social status should be the basis for assigning rank in this system. Presumably, the person who has a known record of missing payments or defaulting on payments is assigned a low rank, but it is also true that the cash buyer, the person who prides himself on his solvency, is also denied a high rank. Many people who apply for credit for the first time are rudely jolted to discover that they cannot obtain as much credit as they would like even though they may have a high-paying, respectable job, for the simple reason that they have not yet demonstrated their reliability in credit transactions. This turns out to be yet another pressure forcing consumers into the credit economy. A number of the people interviewed in the Katona surveys explicitly stated that they bought on time in order to establish their credit rating.[21]

The pressure toward a probabilistic social index for determining credit ratings comes from the fact that such a procedure is easier to administer and fits more neatly into the computer age. Yet it also permits injustices, as errors inevitably occur—for example, when a persons neighborhood is used to assign him a high or low rank.

That a person's credit rating is not merely a reflection of his socioeconomic status is indicated by the fact that some relatively high-paying and respectable occupations are assigned low credit ratings by the credit industry. For example, musicians and entertainers have considerable difficulty getting credit because their income tends to be irregular and their jobs require them to move about a good deal. Conversely, not all unskilled workers are automatically assigned low ratings. Should the unskilled worker be employed in the public rather than the private sector, creditors will be more inclined to extend him

---

20aSee Curran, *Administration and Enforcement Under the Uniform Consumer Credit Code,* in this symposium, p. 737.

21Katona 235.

credit. Not only does such a person have more job security, but the public employer will more readily cooperate with the creditor on wage garnishments if they should prove necessary. It may be noted that although federal employees cannot be garnisheed, state and municipal employees ordinarily can be.

The notion of credit rating and the invisible industry of credit bureaus and information exchange systems soon to be fully automated pose a number of problems for the democratic society, problems that go beyond the issue of privacy that is now receiving much attention. As the system now operates, there is no institutionalized procedure whereby the consumer can find out his credit rating and check upon whatever derogatory information may appear in his credit folder. His dossier may contain erroneous or outdated information which severely damages his credit rating, and yet he does not have ready recourse for correcting the situation. The concept of due process does not exist in the credit rating system, although I suspect that, as the credit society becomes more fully institutionalized, something like it will have to develop.[22]

III. STRESSES AND STRAINS IN THE CREDIT SOCIETY

I should now like to turn to a consideration of some of the stresses and strains of the credit society. One undesirable consequence of the credit explosion has been a sharp rise in the amount of white-collar crime. Insofar as market transactions depended upon cash, sellers had less opportunity and incentive to employ deception and fraud. The consumer who could afford to pay cash for an automobile or expensive appliance was probably more deliberate and sophisticated in his shopping behavior, and there was no point in

trying to convince the person without cash to make an expensive purchase. All this changed with the advent of installment credit. Whether or not the consumer can afford the purchase is now a secondary consideration. Once the contract is signed, the seller has been able to count on the law to enforce his right to payment. Changes in contract law and the laws governing consumer credit have to this point lagged far behind the growth of our credit economy. The signed contract has for the most part continued to be treated as sacrosanct in courts of law, and the fraudulent techniques used to obtain the consumer's signature, so difficult to prove in court, have been largely ignored.[23] That the reform measures discussed in this symposium have been taken or are under consideration is to be noted with approval, although I am not now in a position to comment on the sufficiency of the legal steps themselves in meeting the problems I outline.

The recent report of the President's Crime Commission estimates that from $500 million to a billion dollars are lost annually to the victims of fraudulent home repair and improvement schemes.[24] Shady practices in the used-car field, in door-to-door selling of vacuum cleaners, deep freezers, and other expensive appliances,

---

[22]See Karst, " 'The Files': Legal Controls Over the Accuracy and Accessibility of Stored Personal Data," 31 Law and Contemp. Problems 342 (1966).

[23]This situation is slowly beginning to change. A few years back, a suit against a poor consumer in Washington, D.C., was dismissed on the grounds that the transaction stemmed from an "unconscionable contract." Williams v. Walker-Thomas Furniture Co., 350 F.2d 445 (D.C. Cir. 1965). The doctrine of the "unconscionable contract," which has been embodied in Uniform Commercial Code § 2–302, had never been applied to consumer credit until this case. See American Home Improvement, Inc. v. MacIver, 105 N.H. 435, 201 A.2d 886 (1964). Uniform Consumer Credit Code § 5–108 contains a derivative provision which would explicitly apply to consumer credit transactions. See Hogan, Integrating the UCCC and the UCC—Limitations on Creditors' Agreements and Practices, in this symposium, p. 686, 701, for a discussion of this section.

[24]President's Commission on Law Enforcement and Administration of Justice, Task Force Report: Crime and Its Impact—An Assessment 104 (1967).

and in the self-improvement field covering such things as dance courses and health courses, account for additional billions of annual losses to consumers. As I have already noted, the poor are particularly vulnerable to these exploitative schemes.[25]

Another strain in the credit society is that an increasingly large number of consumers find themselves unable to cope with the debt burdens they have assumed. According to Katona, this group is only a tiny fraction of the consuming public,[26] but I am not so sure. Certainly they are present in substantial numbers in the working and lower classes. Katona's own data show that in the early 1960s about 12 percent of all spending units had 20 percent or more of their income committed to installment payments.[27] Two firm indicators of the increasing frequency of debt problems are the rising number of wage garnishments and personal bankruptcies. There are no national statistics on garnishment, but in the cities where such records are kept, the pattern is clear. For example, in Chicago, wage garnishments increased from 59,000 in 1962 to 73,000 in 1966.[28] (I recently discovered that 10,000 persons employed by the City of New York had their wages garnisheed in 1966[29]—roughly one out of every thirty of the city's employees.) Personal bankruptcies in the country have risen at an alarming rate, from 16,000 in 1948 to approximately 191,000 in 1967.[30] A study now being conducted by The Brookings Institution shows that many of these bankruptcies resulted from efforts to garnishee wages.[31] Many workers who find that

their incomes will be reduced through garnishment have no alternative but to declare bankruptcy.

It should be noted that many employers will not put up with the nuisance of garnishment and do not hesitate to fire their employees who present them with this problem. There are no statistics on the number of workers who lose their jobs each year because of garnishments, although the Department of Labor recently estimated on a very impressionistic basis that this must happen to at least a hundred thousand workers a year. Moreover, once a worker is discharged because of a garnishment, he finds it very difficult to find new employment. Many employers will not hire persons with garnishment records. A recent study of the hard-core unemployed by the Department of Labor showed that some in this group were unemployable because of garnishment records. Thus installment credit is not only an important stimulus to economic growth and the means by which those in all strata can share in the country's affluence, it is also responsible for driving some people into the poverty class. Against this background, it is possible to note with approval those provisions of the federal Consumer Credit Protection Act of 1968 which limit the amount of wages subject to the garnishment remedy and the right of employers to fire employees on grounds of a single wage garnishment.[32]

The prevalence of fraud in the consumer credit field is a reminder that not all consumers who become trapped in debt and are driven into poverty are irresponsible credit users. Many of them have been victimized by firms that misrepresent price and quality; yet they, too, have suffered from the hardships that result from being hounded by bill collectors and the harsh but legally sanctioned collection procedures such as garnishment and the

---

[25]Caplovitz, *supra* note 16, at 12–31.

[26]Katona 242.

[27]*Id.* at 243.

[28]Personal communication to the author from the Chief Clerk of the Cook County, Illinois, Municipal Court.

[29]Personal communication to the author from the Director of the Garnishee Division of the Bureau of Administration, New York City.

[30]1967 Director of the Administrative Office of the United States Courts *Annual Report* 132, 136.

[31]D. Stanley *et al.*, Bankruptcy in the United States (forthcoming).

[32]§ § 303, 304, 82 Stat. 146. *See also Uniform Consumer Credit Code* § 5.106, which, where enacted, would prohibit *all* discharges because of wage garnishments.

attachment of real and personal property. The reform efforts discussion in this symposium attempt to strike new balances between creditors' rights and debtors' ability to resist payment of debts incurred in fraudulent transactions. Optimization of this balance will be difficult to achieve, but it is encouraging to see the pendulum swinging back.

Loss of job is not the only severe consequence of debt entanglement. Debt problems also turn out to be a factor in marital instability and illness as well. In the same national survey conducted in January 1967 that I referred to earlier, the respondents were asked if they knew anyone whose marriage had suffered or broken up because of debt problems. Some 23 percent answered in the affirmative. The respondents were also asked whether they knew anyone whose health had suffered because of a debt problem, and this time 21 percent answered "yes."[33] (Perhaps installment contracts should contain a warning that says, "Signing your name to this document may be hazardous to your health.")

Apart from the strains on those entangled in debt is the question of the strains consumer credit places on the economy itself. Economists agree that an excessively high debt-income ratio would lead to a recession since consumers would be forced to curtail their consumption to pay off old debts. But there is little agreement among economists as to where the danger point lies. In the early 1960s the debt-income ratio averaged about 14 percent;[34] some economists thought that this was too high,[35] and the ratio has presumably risen since then with no ill effects.

CONCLUSION: FROM THE CREDIT SOCIETY TO THE CHECKLESS SOCIETY

That economists cannot agree on the dangers of consumer debts is, I suspect, due to the fact that the credit society is still a new phenomenon. The strains that I have outlined might well be more symptomatic of the transitional period. As the credit society becomes more fully institutionalized and new structural arrangements emerge, these strains may disappear. There are already signs of this. For example, as this symposium details, government is beginning to take action to reduce the abuses associated with installment credit. The main thrust of the Consumer Credit Protective Act is to require full disclosure of credit costs so that consumers will be able to shop for credit. The federal act's curtailment of garnishments should go far to remove the hardships stemming from use of that remedy that I have mentioned, and the act provides legal machinery for a federal attack on that most merciless of predators, the loan shark, whose activities spawn terror and crime in the communities in which he operates. There is also increasing pressure to establish strong enforcement machinery that would curtail consumer fraud and other abuses.

The recently promulgated Uniform Consumer Credit Code promises a more far-reaching remedy for existing credit abuses to be enacted at the state level. Among the Code's desirable reforms are extensive finance charge disclosure requirements (largely paralleling those of the federal act); the setting of realistic and enforceable ceilings on the amount of finance charges in the place of exception-ridden usury laws; a new standard of "unconscionability" specifically applicable to consumer credit transactions; the curtailment of remedies available to lenders, particularly new restrictions on garnishments beyond those in the federal act; new remedies for debtors to invoke against creditors when credit is extended in violation of the Code; and the creation of an adequately financed enforcement agency to supervise compliance. While these are useful steps, my approval of the UCCC is at best qualified. For example,

---

[33]Survey, *supra* note 6.

[34]Katona 242.

[35]*See, e.g.,* J. K. Galbraith, *The Affluent Society,* 197–209 (1958).

I wish the Code had taken a less equivocal position on the holder-in-due-course doctrine by omitting the ninety-day notice option,[36] and I had hoped that it would abolish garnishment as some states have already done, even if this would mean an increase in the cost of credit. Most importantly, the Code's enforcement machinery leaves much to be desired. The Code makes no provision for class actions by consumers nor does it specify attorney fees for consumer plaintiffs. Without such incentives aggressive advocacy on behalf of consumers is not likely to occur.

Radical and significant changes will occur in the credit industry itself. Until recently, the structure of that industry has remained substantially the same in spite of the enormous growth of consumer credit.

Radical and significant changes will occur in the credit industry itself. Until recently, the structure of that industry has remained substantially the same in spite of the enormous growth of consumer credit. But it is now beginning to change, partly as a result of automation, but the pace of change would be dramatically increased by enactment of the Uniform Consumer Credit Code, which would eliminate most of the legal barriers that have prevented active competition among segments of the finance industry. With the elimination of the most restrictive licensing requirements and statutory provisions restricting particular types of lenders to particular types of business, competition for consumer credit business should produce more efficient operations, lower costs, and fewer abuses of the credit system. Given more alternatives and better disclosure to make alternatives meaningful, even low-income consumers should be able to obtain better service of their credit needs, and the consumer finance industry should assume a new shape.

Structural changes in the industry are likely to be produced by other forces as well. Because of automation, we shall eventually see what has been referred to as the "checkless society." This will be an elaborate, centralized system of transfer of payments in which both cash and checks become unnecessary. In this system, the bank or some comparable institution would serve as the intermediary between the consumer and his creditors. The system would require centralization of credit information. The bank would come to act as a financial adviser to the consumer since it would have the power to extend or withhold credit. Such a system would thus protect consumers from their own excesses, but it would also yield institutions of great size—needed for efficient operation—and power. Such a credit system is likely to require some added measure of governmental control to protect the public interest with respect to credit information and perhaps other matters as well.

A pervasive theme in the social analysis of our time focuses on the consequences of an historic shift from the problems of production to those of consumption, from those of scarcity to those of surplus, from those in which choices are constricted to those characterized by discretionary choices. In the emerging shape of the credit society we can discern not only new problematics but new solutions that will alter fundamental structures of modern society. It is superfluous to add that these problems and these solutions call for careful research and thought.

---

[36]For a more detailed critique of the UCCC, see N.Y. Consumers' Advisory Council, Dep't of Consumer Affairs, *Report on the Uniform Consumer Credit Code* (1969).

21. Credit and Credit Cards*

Robert Johnston

Bank credit cards and check-credit plans represent major forces in the movement toward a cash-less society. The first comprehensive survey of these forces was recently completed by the Federal Reserve System. This article summarizes that survey and enumerates current developments in this rapidly moving field.

Credit cards have become a regular fixture of the banking scene, especially in the West where credit-card plans are now available to consumers in every Twelfth District state. The total volume of activity is rapidly rising, and the character of plans is changing all the time. Credit-card operators are adding more banking services to the basic charge feature and are moving toward nation-wide coverage through interchange agreements. Moreover, the credit-card phenomenon goes hand in hand with the expansion of other kinds of revolving-credit plans of the check-credit or overdraft variety.

Credit-card and check-credit outstandings totaled $2,490 million nationally at the end of June 1969, roughly 64 percent above the year-ago figure and triple the level of early 1967. Of the two types of plans, credit cards are the more important and have also shown the higher rate of growth. Credit-card plans this June had $1,631 million outstanding, or 78 percent above the level of June 1968. In comparison, check-credit plan totals were

$859 million, 43 percent above the previous year.

The West continues to lead in credit-card plans, but the gap has narrowed as banks in other parts of the country have intensified their efforts in this field. A year ago, Twelfth District banks accounted for $434 million, or almost one-half of total credit-card outstandings. By this June they had built their outstandings to $574 million; however, this was just over one-third of the national total. This June also, Western banks had $191 million in check-credit outstandings, 22 percent of the total and slightly below their share of a year ago. Eastern banks now lead in this field, with New York District having the largest amount of check-credit outstanding.

The credit-card phenomenon is now a striking feature of the Western banking scene, no matter what yardstick is used. Credit-card outstandings account for 9 percent of instalment credit at District banks, as against 3 percent elsewhere. Moreover, such outstandings account for 25 percent of the sum of personal loans and non-auto consumer loans. Thus credit-card plans have become a major channel for short-term consumer lending in the West. Presumably the same end-result will occur elsewhere as these plans continue to proliferate.

All of this expansion has happened only in the last several years. Prior to 1966, bank credit-card plans were relatively unimportant except in California. Almost everywhere else, they were limited to local merchants and operated by small to medium-sized banks. But then came the breakthrough.

*Reprinted with the permission of the Federal Reserve Bank of San Francisco. This is an updated version of Robert Johnston, "Upsurge in Credit Cards," *Monthly Review* (F. R. Bank of San Francisco), September, 1968, pp. 177–85.

FIGURE 1

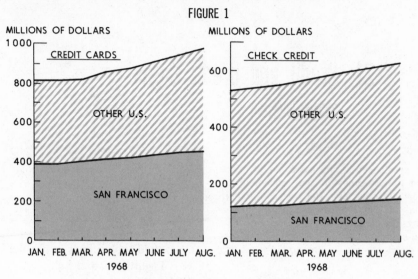

Western banks account for nearly one-half of bank credit cards
and one-fourth of check-credit activity

Several of the nation's largest banks, after a long period of hesitation, took the plunge in early 1966. At the same time, the largest operator in the field (Bank of America) announced the creation of the first nation-wide system through a national licensing scheme. And then the movement expanded even further, as still more banks decided to issue credit cards. By the end of 1966, new plans were either operating or in the planning stage in the Pacific Northwest, the Chicago area, and many areas of the East. By 1969, card plans were operating or planned in almost every part of the country.

Banks thus are relative newcomers to the field of "plastic credit," a field that was dominated for some time by the travel-and-entertainment (T&E) cards, such as American Express, Diners Club, and Carte Blanche, and the charge cards of department stores and oil companies. Despite their late start, banks are now deeply involved. They offer directly their own credit-card and check-credit plans, and to some extent they even help finance the T&E plans.

WHAT TYPE OF PLAN?

The charge privilege is the base on which the credit card rests. The bank credit-card customer can charge purchases at businesses signed to the bank plan and then be billed by the bank. The customer has a pre-arranged line of credit with the bank. He can pay in full within a specified grace period, usually 25 days, without paying service charges. He also has the option of repaying only part and putting the rest on a revolving basis, but in that case he pays interest charges on the unpaid balance.

It is this pre-arranged line of revolving credit that links credit cards and check-credit. But there is no equivalent in check-credit to the charge privilege of the credit card. In check-credit plans, tapping the line of credit immediately involves service charges. Beyond this common feature of a pre-arranged line of credit, the various bank plans diverge to present a wide range of features.

In credit-card plans, the line of credit

is activated by signing a sales draft at the store where the purchase is made. The bank in effect presents this sales draft for payment when it sends the customer his monthly bill. In check-credit plans, the customer makes his purchase by signing a check on his check-credit account, which the bank then covers by transferring funds to the account. The customer is then billed for the bank loan to his account.

In the original form of check credit, a special check-credit account is set up for these revolving-credit transactions, whether or not the customer already has a regular checking account. Thus borrowing is clearly separated from the customer's other banking transactions.

A more recent but now common variation, certainly the more common in this District, is the so-called overdraft plan. The name describes the plan. Whenever the customer overdraws his regular checking account, the bank automatically utilizes a pre-arranged line of credit to transfer funds to cover the check. The customer then has the option of repaying the bank on a revolving basis. This tie to the customer's regular checking account differentiates overdraft-type plans from standard check-credit plans.

The overdraft plan is particularly attractive. It does not require a separate account, as a standard check-credit plan does, and it protects the customer against the inconvenience of "bounced" checks. Moreover, many banks have begun to combine their overdraft plans with so-called check-guarantee cards,[1] to increase

further the attractiveness of their checking-account services.

With both types of check credit, the customer is usually able to tap his credit line directly for loans in cash. Charges on these plans show many variations, but the customer typically is charged interest on the average amount of funds borrowed. In addition, charges are frequently levied for each check used in standard check-credit plans, while the regular checking-account fee schedule applies to overdraft plans. But in either case, the check remains the instrument for making purchases, so that banks can adopt either variant with little effect on their existing banking procedures.

The familiar plastic card, not the check form, is the key instrument of the bank credit card. It serves a dual purpose: 1) identifying the customer to the merchant as someone eligible to charge purchases under the card plan, and 2) providing a convenient way of transferring information to the sales drafts used in the plan. (In principle, the card is not an inherent part of a bank-operated charge system, but until electronic transfer and identification devices come to be universally adopted, the card will be needed.) The merchant then presents the sales drafts recording the various charge purchases to his bank and immediately is reimbursed for the total less a percentage discount on the transactions.

The bank, not the merchant, provides the credit extended to the customers. It operates a central charge service for merchants, by maintaining the accounts of the individual cardholders and sending out monthly bills. As long as each merchant follows the terms of his agreement

---

[1] These check-guarantee cards are sometimes confused with credit cards since they are often made of plastic and have similar designs. Their function is to signify the bank's guarantee to honor checks presented using the card. The card will specify the terms of the guarantee, including the maximum amount covered. A guarantee card, unlike a regular credit card, does not permit the customer to make charge purchases and does not involve credit extension as long as the customer's checking account has sufficient funds to cover the check. Furthermore, guarantee cards are not characteristic only of overdraft plans. Some banks, as a courtesy to their better customers, issue them as a service independent of any revolving-credit plan. On the other hand, some credit cards can serve as check-guarantee cards. In this case, the credit-card design is printed on one side of the card and the check-cashing guarantee statement on the other.

with the bank, the bank is responsible for the collection of the credit and absorbs the loss. The merchant discount helps compensate the bank for its costs of operating the charge system.

Not all banks, by the way, operate a complete credit-card system. Many act in a limited way as agents of some principal bank which maintains a central accounting organization. Agent banks sign up merchants and accept their deposits of sales slips, but the principal bank actually issues the cards and carries all or the bulk of the resulting consumer credit. The principal bank is correspondingly responsible for credit-card losses. The agent-bank approach provides a way of obtaining geographic coverage and customer lists in unit-banking or limited branch-banking states.

For the customer, the bank credit card fits easily into habits already established by department-store and oil-company cards. In the public's mind, this is just another plastic credit card, but one acceptable at a number of different businesses. Moreover, there is no need to minimize the number of transactions in order to avoid service charges on checks, as would be the case with check-credit plans. There is also the further advantage of reducing the number of individual credit cards that have to be carried.

When the customer is billed by his bank, he has two options available to him: he may either repay the full balance within a grace period (typically 25 days) without any service charge, or he may repay on revolving credit with interest charged on the unpaid balance. There are no other charges for the credit card—the cards are issued free—nor is there any requirement to open an account with the bank. Thus, if a customer always pays within the grace period, the card is the equivalent of a charge account.

In practice, many customers choose the revolving-credit option, and their interest payments provide the bulk of bank's credit-card revenues. Merchant discounts, which were the major source of revenue

for the early credit-card plans, are now less important. Most Twelfth District banks, incidentally, now charge 3 percent or less for their merchant discounts.

Since the cardholder pays no membership fee and since the merchant pays only a modest discount, the interest from revolving credit must be the plan's main source of income. Thus, the bank's goal must be to stimulate the regular use of cards by a large number of people for a wide range of purchases. In other words, a high volume of card transactions is required to support the credit balances needed to produce sufficient interest income.

Credit-card managers also attempt to activate the largest number of accounts within the shortest amount of time when starting a new plan. Banks frequently resort to the mass issue of unsolicited cards, and willingly accept the higher risks entailed, since a high volume seems necessary as a means of recovering heavy start-up costs and attracting large numbers of participating merchants.* Check-credit managers, on the other hand, typically tend to limit their dealings to relatively small numbers of low-risk customers, each of whom has to apply for an account. The result normally is a lower-volume operation. The differences show up clearly in the Federal Reserve study, "Bank Credit-Cards and Check-Credit Plans."

As of September, 1967, credit-card plans covered 14.4 million accounts and $633 million outstandings, while check-credit plans covered 1.1 million accounts and $413 million in outstandings. Credit-card plans were offered directly by 197 banks and indirectly by about a thousand banks acting as agents, and these plans covered 371,000 participating merchants. Check-credit plans, on the other hand, were operated by 599 banks.

Not surprisingly, check-credit accounts

---

*Since publication of this article, unsolicited distribution of credit cards has been banned.

were more active than credit-card plans in the 1967 survey, 69 percent vs. 35 percent, respectively. Customers must apply individually for a check-credit account; there is no equivalent to mass mailing. Presumably someone who goes to the trouble of opening such an account is also more likely to use it.

The average line of credit was also higher for check credit, $1,100 compared to $350 for credit cards. Actual usage in 1967 was in proportion to the credit line: active check-credit accounts had an average balance of $610, and active credit-card accounts, $124. (The most recent figures for credit cards alone show average balances above $180.) Finally, the interest rate charged on outstanding balances was lower for check credit, commonly 1 percent per month compared to 1½ percent per month for credit cards, reflecting differences in risks and in operational costs for each type of plan.

Nonetheless, credit-card plans still dominate the field, in terms of both total number of accounts and total dollar volume. Besides, the lower rate of usage of credit cards may be due to nothing more than the relatively large number of new card plans. According to the 1967 survey, only 23 percent of the credit-card accounts started in the 1966-67 period were then active, as against a 61-percent rate of usage for plans started in 1958-59. Similarly, utilization of credit lines was much larger for the older plans. Thus, as the credit-card habit becomes established, we may well see a higher percentage of active accounts and larger average balances.

Of the 599 banks which operated check-credit plans at the time of the 1967 survey, 274 offered overdraft plans and 410 offered the standard type. (As figures indicate, many banks offered both types of plans.) Among the newer plans, the overdraft variant was the more popular choice—191 of the 312 new entrants nationally during the 1966-67 period were of the overdraft type—apparently because the overdraft type is both easier to institute and more appealing to customers than

the standard form of check credit. Overdrafts accounted for roughly three-fourths of all check-credit balances at Twelfth District banks on the survey date, and these banks have continued to emphasize overdraft plans ever since.

Some banks offer yet another alternative by affiliating with one of the major nonbank travel-and-entertainment credit-card plans, thereby combining elements of both credit-card and check-credit plans. under this type of arrangement, the bank does not set up a credit-card operation—this is done by the credit-card company—but instead it offers each customer an optional line of revolving credit in addition to the basic card privileges. The customer then can repay his T&E-card bills on revolving credit, rather than in full when billed. He can also borrow at the bank by drawing directly upon his line of credit.

With the bank credit card, the bank runs the entire operation, extending credit from the day a merchant deposits a sales draft to the time the cardholder pays his bills. With the T&E card, the bank becomes involved only if the cardholder, after signing the appropriate bank agreement, decides to let his bill go on a revolving credit basis or to use his card to borrow from the bank. Thus this option is not strictly a bank credit-card plan; from the bank's viewpoint it operates more like a check-credit plan.

The T&E card permits the bank to offer a credit-card service to its customers with a minimum of direct expense; the bank only has to set up an organization to administer revolving credit. But at the same time, the bank will not obtain as large a volume of operations from this plan as it would from its own plan. T&E cardholders generally have superior credit ratings and therefore are less likely to resort to revolving-credit to pay their bills; and when they do so, they tend to be in debt for only short periods of time.

Although a rather sizable number of banks offer this service, the total volume generated is not very large. In October, 1967, with 136 banks participating, credit extended through T&E-card plans amounted to only about 1 percent ($16 million) of total bank extensions of "plastic" credit. In fact, T&E balances held by consumers have shown no growth, having remained at $100 million between December 1967 and June 1969.

THE CUSTOMER'S ROLE

Do credit cards involve banks in heavy credit losses? The recent Federal Reserve study tried to answer this question by analyzing data on write-offs during the first half of 1967 and delinquencies as of September 1967.

The study revealed that credit cards involved heavier credit losses than check-credit plans, but it also showed that these losses were not excessive. In the period examined (first-half 1967), credit-card charge-offs amounted to 1.97 percent of outstandings, as against 0.23 percent for check credit. But the higher figure was partly due to the predominance of new plans among the credit-card plans studied. Charge-offs tend to fall quite sharply over time. Thus, the write-off ratio dropped to only 1.18 percent when the newest plans where excluded from the computations. The heavy losses involved in the new plans stemmed largely from fraud losses in new plans.

From the risk standpoint, credit-card lending perhaps should not even be compared with check-credit lending, which is a relatively low-risk enterprise. Instead, it would be more relevant to compare credit cards with that type of lending where there is a similar acceptance of higher credit risks and a similar emphasis on a mass market, that is, with other classes of consumer loans. Delinquencies as of September 1967 amounted to 0.97 percent of outstandings for check-credit and to 1.99 percent for credit cards, but on regular consumer installment loans, the rate was 1.4 percent, and on home-appliance loans (perhaps the closest category to credit-card plans), the rate was 2.19 percent.

Excessive losses thus are not an inherent feature of credit-card plans. Losses can be reduced to the levels acceptable in other types of consumer lending. The techniques of starting and operating a card plan are now better known than heretofore. Recent mass mailings avoided heavy fraud losses as banks learned from past experience. Although credit cards do involve risks to the banks involved, these are not extreme when compared with the risks encountered in other types of bank consumer lending.

Do credit cards encourage consumers to use their new-found credit excessively? According to the System study, this

FIGURE 2

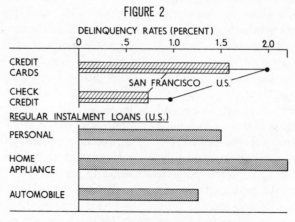

Credit-card delinquencies in line with those
on other consumer loans, as of September, 1967.

FIGURE 3

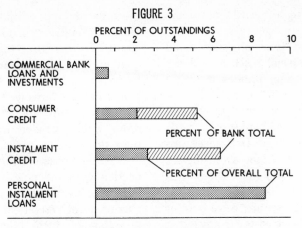

Credit cards plus check credit still represent
small share of total

danger has not yet materialized since credit-card outstandings now represent only a small proportion of total consumer credit and total bank loans. As of June 1969, credit cards and check credit together accounted for 2.1 percent of all consumer crdit, 5.2 percent of bank-held consumer credit, and only 0.6 percent of total bank loans and investments. Moreover, these two types of bank credit together accounted for only 8.7 percent of total personal loans. Finally, much of the increased bank credit is only replacing credit formerly granted by other lenders.

A similar answer applies to the charge that credit-card availability creates inflationary problems for the general economy. In view of their relatively small importance in the bank-lending scheme, credit cards could not exert, by themselves, a noticeable inflationary effect.

Sometimes, it is argued, merchants are forced to raise prices in order to cover the merchant discount on credit-card transactions, and therefore the growth of credit cards has inflationary implications. This argument rests on the assumption that the merchant discount can be considered in isolation. But this is not possible, for credit cards generate other changes.

First, some merchants who increase their sales volume substantially through credit-card plans find that their expanded volume tends to counteract any cost increases that may be associated with such a plan. Second, some merchants actually obtain a net reduction in costs if the bank plan is cheaper than their existing arrangement for financing accounts receivable. Third, the merchant discounts are usually small and are tending to become even smaller, having declined to 3 percent or below in many areas. Even if this were a et cost increase—which it does tend to be—it would be much less significant than other cost pressures on the economy, not to mention the excess demand forces which are basic to any inflationary situation.

There is also the argument that credit cards discriminate against cash customers by adding an additional ccst, the merchant discount, to other merchandising charges. In a sense, this same argument applies to any new service which does not benefit all customers equally. For example, to the extent a merchant provides free parking or free delivery, he can be said to discriminate against those customers who do not use these services. The merchant, when introducing a service, must decide whether it is more efficient to add the additional costs to general overhead or to attempt to recover only from those customers who actually use the service.

In the case of credit cards, as in the case of charge privileges generally, the usual choice is to treat any additional costs as part of the usual expenses of doing business. This decision implies it would not be worth the cost in terms of administrative expenses and lost sales to attempt to pass on the costs of bank credit cards to each charge customer. In a sense this is discrimination, yet as long as businesses offer a range of optional services, discrimination is always likely to be present. Again, however, there are questions of significance of the net costs (if any) that are involved at any particular store, and of the effect of such costs upon the store's pricing in a competitive market.

There is some substance to the charge that credit-card availability creates financial problems for certain individual borrowers, but this would be true of any broad-based consumer-credit plan. As a general issue, the response to this charge depends on how individual losses are weighed against the gains to other individuals of having such a plan available. The rapid spread of such plans indicates that large numbers of people do find credit cards to be convenient, and the relatively low loss record indicates that the bulk of bank customers do not have much difficulty in handling this type of credit. Furthermore, the banks in their own interest try to protect their customers from excessive borrowing. Bank plans have relatively low credit limits (averaging only about $350) and they often apply stricter lending standards than many other consumer lenders use.

A recent consumer survey made in connection with the new Truth in Lending law provides further evidence of the character of credit-card ownership. A sampling of 1,025 households indicates that, as of June 1969, approximately one-quarter of the survey group had a bank credit card. As would be expected, the percentage increased with income and education. For the group with post-graduate college education, 48 percent had a bank card, and for the group with incomes over $15,000, 44 percent held a bank card. At an income level between $8,000 and $10,000, the percentage holding a card was 29 percent, and at income levels below that, the percentage fell off to less than 20 percent. Over-all, the median income for cardholders was over $10,000. These figures not only confirm that bank credit cards are widely ac-

Ownership of Bank Credit Cards, June 1969

Selected Household Characteristics	Households in Subsample		Has Bank Credit Card	
	Number	Percent	Number	Percent
Total Responses*	1,025	100.0	258	25.2
Education Level:				
Grade school or less	177	100.0	29	16.4
Some high school	224	100.0	42	18.8
Graduated high school	312	100.0	81	26.0
Some college	142	100.0	43	30.3
Graduated college	104	100.0	33	31.7
Post-graduate college	60	100.0	29	48.3
Income Level:				
Less than $3,000	128	100.0	9	7.0
$3,000–4,999	122	100.0	22	18.0
$5,000–7,999	244	100.0	48	19.7
$8,000–9,999	170	100.0	50	29.4
$10,000–14,999	179	100.0	56	31.3
Over $15,000	124	100.0	55	44.4

*Note: Sum of the rows does not add to total row due to "no answers" to some of the specific questions.
Source: Board of Governors of the Federal Reserve System.

cepted by consumers, but also that they are largely in the hands of groups who can manage the amounts of credit usually extended by such plans.

Admittedly, some individuals are incapable of handling credit cards, and will get into trouble in spite of all reasonable safeguards. But on balance, it would appear that consumers do benefit from this new bank service.

IMPACT ON BANKS

One key to a successful credit-card program is effective control of credit. Banks must develop adequate controls over the distribution of cards (with their associated lines of credit). They must also develop adequate controls over their subsequent use to prevent excessive indebtedness and, most important, fraud. The task is generally greatest during the early years of card operation, but it then becomes more manageable as the bad cards are gradually eliminated. Credit supervision, although ultimately a technical problem, is by no means a minor one.

Another operating problem arises from the fact that credit card's initial impact is an increase in the amount of paper handled. While the credit card does tend to reduce the number of checks written, it also replaces former cash purchases so that banks end up by processing more pieces of paper. Ultimately, some have argued, the credit card is a step toward the "checkless society." This is true only in the sense that the system puts pressure on the banks to develop a technology capable of handling transactions more quickly and cheaply. The techniques which can process sales drafts can do the very same thing for checks. The credit card may ultimately have an indirect part in the development of a more sophisticated payments-transfer mechanism, but in the meantime it tends to increase each bank's paperwork burden. This fact is often forgotten.

This list of internal management diffi-culties should not obscure the important indirect advantages derived from an efficient credit-card operation. (This is in addition to the obvious benefits derived from revolving-credit revenues.) A credit-card plan, not being limited to depositors, allows a bank to make the equivalent of consumer loans to other banks' depositors. The requirement that merchants open an account for the deposit of their credit-card sales slips leads to new deposit business.

Moreover, the organization which processes retail sales slips can be readily adopted to handle other transactions. Most credit-card plans now allow card-holders to borrow amounts up to $500, depending on the bank. Not only does this privilege enhance the usefulness of the card but it allows the bank to process small loans more efficiently than it can through normal procedures. In fact, some banks funnel all their small loans through the credit-card organization by treating them as cash advances and setting up temporary accounts for non-cardholders. Similarly, overdraft plans for cardholders with checking accounts are often added and, as already noted, banks frequently use their credit card as a check-guarantee card.

Obviously, once a bank has borne the expense and solved the organizational problems of a full credit-card plan, it does derive significant competitive advantages. In particular, it can more easily match the check-guarantee and overdraft plans of competitors who cannot themselves reply fully without offering their own credit card.

How then can the small bank get a foothold in the credit-card field, in view of all the paperwork problems and (especially) the heavy start-up costs involved in credit-card operations? If credit-card plans should develop into the principal source of consumer credit, and if they should continue to require massive big-bank financial resources, the long-run competitive position of smaller banks presumably would be weakened. Fortunately,

FIGURE 4

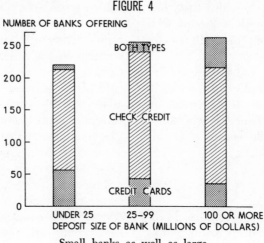

Small banks as well as large
operate credit-card programs

small banks which do not wish to operate independent plans have several alternatives open to them, including affiliation with a large credit-card organization or independent operation of a check-credit program.

In September 1967, roughly one-third of the banks with credit-card operations had deposits of less than $25 million, and another quarter had deposits of between $25 and $100 million. Many of these small banks have operated successful plans for years, even at times when larger banks were dropping out of the competition. Generally the small independents have not been forced to meet competing bank plans, and thus they have been able to maintain their schedule of merchant discounts at levels nearer 6 percent than the 3-percent competitive rate.

Although small banks may now find it increasingly difficult to start independent plans, this is not a major barrier. First of all the trend is away from independent plans, even for large banks, and towards joint plans. The development of large regional and statewide systems has made it easier for smaller banks to participate in these larger systems.

The most common form of participation is the agent-bank system. The agent bank does have only a limited role, but this limited participation has several advantages—minimization of costs, along with maintenance of long-standing relationships with local merchants.

Two other approaches permit smaller banks to join with large banks so as to offer a more-or-less complete credit-card program on equal standing with larger banks. Both of these approaches were developed by Twelfth District banks, the BankAmericard and Master Charge systems.

The BankAmericard franchise system licenses certain principal banks to issue BankAmericard in return for a fee. The licensee receives technical advice, including training of key personnel and development of computer programs, in order to operate its own BankAmericard system. In turn, the licensee offers so-called associate or sub-licensee status to other local banks, or alternatively, offers them agent status.

The associate signs up local merchants and issues cards bearing its own name to its own customers. It is responsible for the credit granted its cardholders and, in the eyes of its customers, it is offering its own credit card. The principal licensee provides its associate with a central computerized accounting system and other services, in return for fees based on the volume of business generated by each bank. The associate, in return for its fee payments, obtains a packaged credit-card plan and avoids the expenses of developing its own computer operation.

Master Charge is the product of the Western States Bankcard Association, a group of large and small banks originally organized at the initiative of four large California banks—Wells Fargo, Crocker-Citizens, United California Bank, and Bank of California. Their key contribution to this field was not the development of a common card name and design, though this was important, but rather the development of a unique type of credit-card organization.

The association, now composed of banks in California, Nevada, Utah, Washington, Oregon, Idaho, and Wyoming, operates the necessary central computer system for members who issue credit cards under the Master Charge name. The association administers the cardholder accounting, as well as the settlement of sales drafts between members, while the members sign up merchants and cardholders, carry cardholder credit, and absorb any resulting credit losses. The costs of the association's operations are borne by the members in proportion to their volume of credit-card transactions. Under this system, then, a small bank can issue credit cards on the same terms as a large bank. This form of organization thus has obvious advantages, such as pooling of expensive computer facilities and expansion of coverage through a common card plus interchange.

Several groups of banks in the East and South have adopted both the association form and, usually, the Master Charge name and card design. The Master Charge name and design can be used by single banks. On the other hand, this kind of association can be adopted without using the cards bearing the Master Charge name.

Elsewhere, less-centralized organiza-tions have been set up, as in the case of the Midwest Bank Card plan based in Chicago. Under these systems, the central organization arranges the interchange of sales slips, designs the basic credit card, and that is about all. The individual members themselves then have to operate the other elements of the credit-card organization. This type of system, sometimes described as a "compatible" system, thus is a half-way house between independent operation and membership in a credit-card association.

A small bank of course can become a licensee of a large-bank plan or strike out on its own, but these are the more costly alternatives. Less costly would be membership in a joint credit-card association. However, formation of such an association usually requires a nucleus of large banks to bear the initial organizing expenses. A small bank thus finds that its options are largely dependent upon the arrangements chosen by the dominant banks in its area. If the latter decide upon a Master Charge organization or on a sub-licensing arrangement with Bank-Americard, the barriers to entering the credit-card field are reduced for the smaller banks.

At the very least, a small bank in almost all cases has agent-bank status available to it. In fact, in many areas a small bank may become an agent of both Bank-Americard and Master Charge. The bank is then able to offer local merchants two credit-card services without having to have accounts at two banks. The larger banks are usually limited to their own plan, and to some extent the small bank thereby gains a competitive advantage.

INTERCHANGE

Just within the past three years, the bank credit-card industry has moved toward regional and national interchange and has shifted from the locally-oriented plans previously in vogue. In the past year, the decision of important single-bank and regional plans to join a national system has resulted in almost complete national coverage by these systems. At the same time, the trend is toward the development of only two nation-wide systems.

The first national system to be formed, BankAmericard, consists of BankAmericard licensees. The other, Interbank Card Association, is a nonprofit corporation made up of a number of banks operating their own plans. This system includes the Western States Bankcard Association and other regional associations (such as Midwest Bank Card) which has joined Interbank to get national interchange. Since May 1969, Interbank has taken over the licensing of the Master Charge name and card design. (While not all Interbank member banks and member associations issue Master Charge—many have kept their own designs for the present—use of the Master Charge format does entail membership in Interbank.) Some independent interchange systems and a declining number of independent one-bank plans still remain.

The object of interchange is to broaden the geographic coverage of a bank credit card and hence to increase its attractiveness to the cardholder. Banks agree to accept one another's cards on a reciprocal basis: that is, Bank A's merchants accept Bank B's cards, Bank A clears the sales slips to Bank B (the cardholder's bank), and Bank B then bills the cardholder in the usual fashion. The interchange agreement specifies how sales drafts will be cleared and how outstanding balances will be settled between banks.

In the West, the interchange concept reigns supreme. One or another of the two national systems has a member in every District state except Alaska, and in six states both are in operation. (One bank in Hawaii belongs to both systems.) There is also an independent interchange system operating in Utah and Idaho. Only two District banks, one each in California

and Alaska, remain with independent one-bank plans.

Each interchange system tries to insure that the cards of the various participating banks are readily identifiable and, hence, acceptable by merchants for charge purchases. BankAmericard, Master Charge, and the Midwest System have cards with a common design and some space for the individual bank's name. Interbank resolves the recognition problem by printing a common symbol, the letter "i" within a small circle, on cards whose general design otherwise can vary from bank to bank.

Within Interbank, there is a definite tendency for members to adopt the Master Charge design. The reason is that the Interbank symbol, the small letter "i", is simply too inconspicuous to insure ready acceptance of a card outside its own area. The adoption of Master Charge, the dominent design within Interbank, overcomes this shortcoming. Merchants tend to accept a Master Charge card without noticing whether the particular card was issued by a bank in New York or in California.

In the past year, long-established single-bank plans, such as those operated by First National City Bank of New York and Valley National Bank of Arizona, have replaced their present cards with Master Charge. Midwest Bankcard System, having now joined Interbank, is also considering dropping its present card design in favor of the Master Charge format. Most of the individual banks within the Midwest System have already shifted.

Although most credit-card transactions are still local in origin, the competitive pressures to offer a card with potential for wider use are quite strong. Most banks starting new plans within the past year have joined one or another of the interchange systems, as have many banks with older independent plans. Once one bank announces its intention to join an interchange plan, the other banks in the area typically make matching moves. The consequence is the cumulative growth of the interchange networks already described. The trend is thus pointing to membership in one of two national interchange systems—with a common card design within each system. There does not yet seem to be room for a third system.

Finally, both national interchange systems have gone international, establishing interchange privileges with foreign banks. Both have connections with Japanese and Mexican plans. Interbank has ties with some European card plans, and Bank-Americard interchanges with banks in Canada and Great Britain, as well as with banks on the Continent.

This international network should also grow.

Perhaps there are some areas where the plastic cards are still unknown, but this seems less and less likely as time goes on. Soon, it seems, the average bank customer will be able to utilize his credit card practically anywhere in the nation. Interchange systems must still improve their clearing processes and overcome their credit-control problems, but they have already created the general framework for a major new nationwide banking service. Despite the somewhat spectacular spread of interchange membership, it must be emphasized that this merely provides a framework on which the credit-card habit must be built. The rest of the country does not yet match the West in credit-card usage, and even in the West there remains room for growth.

Credit-card and check-credit plans will probably continue to expand because they perform a very useful banking service. But their overall importance must not be exaggerated. Despite the rapid growth in dollar outstandings, they still play a relatively minor role in the overall picture of bank lending and consumer credit, and will continue to do so for some time to come.

For small retailers, credit cards can improve their competitive position by opening to them charge services capable of matching those of the giant chains. For

U.S. Bank Credit-Card and Check-Credit Plans
(millions of dollars)

	Credit Cards			
	Volume extended		Outstanding (end month)	
1968:	12th District	Other	12th District	Other
January	72	75	387	428
February	59	61	390	427
March	61	64	395	427
April	74	84	411	448
May	69	83	417	461
June	71	84	434	480
July	79	93	446	499
August	81	95	462	521
September	77	96	477	547
October	81	113	480	586
November	71	114	484	627
December	117	201	532	733
1969:				
January	88	140	537	755
February	75	115	536	785
March	81	138	537	804
April	98	172	551	906
May	94	183	562	953
June	97	197	574	1032

	Check Credit			
	Volume extended		Outstanding (end month)	
1968:	12th District	Other	12th District	Other
January	32	53	128	403
February	29	49	131	412
March	29	47	130	419
April	37	58	137	433
May	37	60	139	447
June	35	58	143	457
July	37	66	147	475
August	36	67	150	494
September ...	35	68	153	512
October	39	71	157	530
November	35	64	159	635
December	47	87	170	569
1969:				
January	43	82	173	589
February	40	73	175	594
March	42	78	176	606
April	55	92	188	626
May	47	90	190	643
June	46	90	191	662

all retailers, credit cards can provide a means of shifting financing to banks, which are, after all, specialists in finance. For the general public, these plans can fulfill a need by providing a convenient source of revolving credit and, in the case of credit cards, a general purpose charge account. For the commercial banker, credit cards (and check credit, to a lesser extent) can pose complex management problems, but profitable opportunities, too, for the successful operator.

Chapter VI
LIABILITY MANAGEMENT

22. Corporate Treasurers and Their Depositories*

William F. Staats

Demand deposits of large firms are generally more profitable to banks than those of small firms. Because of this, commercial bankers aggressively compete for these funds. This article describes the nature of the market for corporate demand deposits and the factors that corporate treasurers of large firms consider in choosing a particular bank.

Commercial bankers trying to win demand deposits of large corporations have a difficult task. They face vigorous competition not only from other banks and institutions but also from financial markets. While banks aggressively vie for their business, treasurers of major corporations increasingly are turning away from banks. The volume of commercial paper is soaring as firms secure funds through that medium—depriving banks of the opportunity to grant credit directly

to corporations. And more sophisticated treasurers are keeping deposits at rock bottom by investing idle funds in commercial paper, Treasury bills, certificates of deposit and municipal debt.[1] So, banks are tending to miss out at both ends—they are losing lending opportunities as well as demand deposits to markets for other financial assets.

Nevertheless, corporate business still dominates the activities of many banks and corporate deposits still account for a huge chunk of total deposits, especially at bigger banks. Although the market for demand deposits of large corporations is just one of several in which banks compete, it deserves particularly close and continuous analysis by bankers who participate in it. Therefore, we have checked with treasurers of the nation's largest cor-

*From *Business Review*, March, 1969. Reprinted by permission of the publisher (The Federal Reserve Bank of Philadelphia) and the author.

[1]Just over 20 percent of the corporations in our survey owned municipal securities while nearly 30 percent held U.S. Government securities. Roughly 14 percent of the respondents invested in both federal and state and local debt.

porations to determine some of the characteristics and dimensions of this market.[2]

NATURE OF THE MARKET

The main struggle in the market for corporate demand deposits involves treasurers and bankers. Treasurers want to shrink their demand deposits to the bare minimum while each banker tries to expand deposits at his institution. Deposits are especially important to bankers because they are the main input for loans which are the principal earning assets of banks.

A banker may gain demand deposits by convincing a treasurer that his bank is a convenient place to keep temporarily idle funds. But this approach is proving less successful because treasurers are busy figuring out ways to minimize their idle funds. Rather than keeping funds in nonearning deposits, corporate officials are increasingly investing them in Treasury bills, tax-exempt municipal notes, and negotiable certificates of deposit. Each of these assets is highly liquid and each provides an explicit monetary return to the firm. So, bankers are finding that the pool of idle corporate balances is drying up—especially during periods of high interest rates.[3]

Bankers traditionally have required corporations to hold balances on deposit in exchange for other services provided by banks. Deposits, then, become a kind of medium of exchange with which firms purchase services. For example, at least part of the price of a bank loan is expressed in terms of deposit balances. Investment advice, payroll accounting, and numerous other services banks sell can or must be bought partly, if not entirely, with deposits. The barter system, long ago proven too cumbersome for efficient functioning of most markets, still hangs on in markets for bank services.

Despite the inefficiency of bartering, bankers cling to it for a couple of reasons. First, deposits are crucially important to a bank as a source of loanable funds, and the practice of requiring compensating balances helps maintain a bank's deposit base. Second, the practice also probably reflects a desire on the part of bankers to avoid explicit price competition in the market for deposits, thereby enabling them to compete on terms other than price. Of course, Regulation Q issued by the Board of Governors of the Federal Reserve System currently prohibits payment of interest on demand deposits and, consequently, provides a barrier to explicit price competition for such deposits. Prior to Regulation Q when banks did pay interest on demand deposits, they also required compensating balances for partial payment for other services.

NUMBER OF DEPOSITORIES

There is a lot of corporate business available for banks because most large corporations maintain deposits in a number of banks. Depositories fall into two categories—major ones where the bulk of the firm's working balance is kept and minor ones used primarily for payroll disbursements and lock-box receipts.[4] All respondents reported maintaining at least one major depository and four-fifths of them had one or more minor depositories.

---

[2]A questionnaire was sent to the treasurers of corporations included in *Fortune's* listing of the 500 largest firms. Responses to some or all of the questions were received from about 64 percent of the treasurers. Because only giant firms were included in the sample, information reported here may not apply to other corporations.

[3]Bankers are able to secure some corporate funds by selling certificates of deposit to the firms. Of course, banks must pay interest on these deposits. At times like the present, however, market rates on Treasury bills and other short-term investments may exceed the maximum rate permitted on C.D.'s.

[4]Many corporations use two types of major depositories. One type is called a concentration bank wherein receipts originally deposited in minor depositories are pooled. The other is a headquarters bank which provides a wide range of services to corporate customers.

	Ranked 1		Ranked 1 or 2		Ranked 1, 2 or 3	
	Number	Percent	Number	Percent	Number	Percent
Financial condition	120	38	173	28	217	24
Location	63	20	130	21	186	20
Size	43	14	113	18	185	20
Availability of adequate credit accommodation ..	56	18	132	21	187	20
Management contacts	23	7	59	9	108	12
Other	7	2	13	2	24	3

Well over half of the corporations had major depository relationships with 10 or more banks—and nearly 8 percent had over 50 major depositories.

Most corporations had more minor depositories than major ones. Over 70 percent of those firms having any minor depositories had 10 or more. About one-third had over 50, and over 5 percent kept deposits at more than 450 banks.

Not all banks holding a corporation's deposits get the opportunity to lend to the firm because corporations typically secure credit from fewer banks than they patronize with their deposits. Still, large firms tend to establish lines of credit at a number of banks. Nearly a third of the respondents reported borrowing or maintaining lines of credit at from 5 to 9 banks. Just under half of the firms had credit arrangements with 10 or more banks. And at the extreme, a few corporations borrowed or held lines of credit at more than 65 banks.

These data indicate that large firms spread their deposits about rather extensively and that their credit business is parceled out less widely. The large number of depositories stems principally from efforts of corporate treasurers to maximize available cash by streamlining systems for gathering and disbursing funds. Treasurers want to get their hands on customers' checks as quickly as possible. So, rather than waiting for the mail service to deliver a check from a customer in, say, Little Rock, to a headquarters bank in Philadelphia, a firm may direct the customer to remit to a depository bank in Memphis.

As soon as the money gets to the Memphis bank, the firm can speed the funds to a disbursing bank in some nearby state where the firm may have a plant or where suppliers may be located. The net result of such a system is efficient use of funds so that the minimum amount need be maintained. Lofty interest rates prevailing during the past few years have provided added incentive for corporations to use funds more efficiently.

WHAT TREASURERS LOOK FOR

Basically, corporate treasurers look at several factors—independently as well as collectively—in selecting a commercial bank. As shown in the table, there was not much agreement among respondents as to which of the factors was most important. However, when first, second, and third rankings for each factor were grouped together, four selection factors came out about the same (as shown in the far right column of the table).

FINANCIAL CONDITION. The financial condition of a bank is of first importance to more treasurers than is any other selection factor.[5] Much of the attention given to a bank's financial condition centered upon is capital position. More than nine out of ten treasurers expressed considerable concern over the adequacy of their depositories' capital and many treasurers

---

[5]This finding is consistent with that of a similar study made a dozen years ago. See George Hanc, "How Corporate Treasurers Select Their Depositories," *Banking*, (March, 1957).

have gone to great lengths to assess the adequacy of banks' capital.[6] But this concern over financial condition in general and capital adequacy in particular was prompted more by concern for the size of credit accommodation available than for safety of the corporation's deposits.

Financial officials at a number of major corporations believe that they need not worry about the safety of their deposits since the bulk of them is in the larger banks. Presumably, the view is that large banks cannot fail or, indeed, would not be allowed to fail by supervisory agencies charged with maintaining the viability of our banking system. Moreover, in the case of many major depositories, corporations frequently owe the banks more than the banks owe them. Consequently, as net borrowers, firms may feel they have little to lose should their banks become financially embarrassed.[7] In the case of minor depositories, the relatively small size of deposits at any of these banks may reduce the need for great concern over safety of these deposits.

Credit availability is tied to a bank's financial condition in several ways. For example, national banks as well as many state banks cannot lend to any one borrower an amount greater than 10 percent of their capital stock and surplus. So, the bigger a bank's capital, the more a corporate treasurer can probably borrow there.

Most treasurers also pay attention to other facets of a bank's financial condition

---

[6]See William F. Staats, "Corporate Treasurers View Bank Capital," *Banking* (June, 1966), for a discussion of some of the means and standards used by treasurers in appraising capital adequacy of banks.

[7]Perhaps these firms may be more exposed to loss than they think should the bank fail. The law usually does not provide the "right of offset." Consequently, a customer of a failed bank cannot deduct the amount of his deposit from the amount he owes. Receivers or trustees charged with wrapping up the bank's affairs can move to force payment of the loan balances.

—particularly the volume of loans already on its books. If a bank has loaned out about as much money as it may prudently lend, there may be little chance of the firm negotiating credit. This consideration probably has assumed greater importance in treasurers' eyes following the credit crunch of 1966 when firms were clamoring for more loans and larger lines of credit than banks could grant.

To keep tabs on banks' financial conditions, about 40 percent of the treasurers used ratio-analysis techniques. Favorite financial ratios were loans to deposits, capital to loans, loans to assets, and capital to total deposits.

LOCATION. For one-fifth of the respondents, the most important factor in choosing a depository was its location. Major depositories of the largest corporations usually are located near the firm's principal base of operations, in the nation's leading financial centers or, in the case of concentration depositories, in principal cities across the land. This means that banks outside of those places have to look primarily to locally based firms for corporate deposits.

Minor depositories used mainly for payroll accounts nearly always are located close to the facility which they serve. Lock-box depositories are selected mostly on a geographical basis in areas where corporate depositors have concentrations of customers. Because banks serving as minor depositories need not be particularly large, there are many banks competing in the sub-market. And the competition tends to be intense. There are indications, however, that once a bank has been selected as a minor depository, chances are good it will keep the account because large firms tend not to switch banks very much. Of course, they may add additional banks to their network of depositories but they rarely drop any.

SIZE. Fourteen percent of the treasurers said that size was the most important selection factor as far as they were concerned. Financial officials leaned toward larger banks in choosing depositories.

Larger banks, on balance, are able to offer a wider range of services required by treasurers. Specific services mentioned by respondents included investment advice, use of international facilities and contacts, and handling of pension funds. Moreover, treasurers reported that their depository relations with larger banks tend to insure availability of an adequate volume of credit.

Some financial officials of major corporations equate size with safety—the larger the bank, the less likely it will become insolvent. The reasoning apparently is that assets of huge banks are more widely diversified than those of smaller institutions. Also, some treasurers believe that the costs of failure of a giant bank is so great that supervisory agencies would not permit one to fail.

CREDIT ACCOMMODATIONS. Nearly a fifth of the respondents stated that availability of adequate credit accommodations was their principal criterion in selecting depositories for corporate funds.[8] The importance of bank credit to efficient operations of business firms is well understood and nobody understands it better than treasurers of giant corporations. Therefore, in choosing a depository, treasurers often reward those banks which promise and deliver credit when it's needed by the business.

Of course, most banks, both large and small, still follow the old custom of requiring borrowers to keep a deposit balance as partial compensation to the bank for granting a loan. This compensating balance, as it is called, usually equals 20

___

[8]The actual proportion of treasurers placing primary emphasis on availability of credit probably far exceeds the 20 percent figure. As indicated earlier, some of the concern over size and financial condition boiled down to concern over credit availability.

percent or so of the amount of the loan. Compensating balances increase the effective interest rate on loans because borrowers do not get to use all the money they borrow—yet they pay interest on the full amount. Just how much more costly compensating balances make a loan depends upon the average size of the borrower's usual working balance and the distribution of that balance among depositories. It is not surprising that many corporate officials who are able prefer to borrow in the commercial paper market, usually at lower interest costs. However, ability to raise funds in the commercial paper market partly depends on the firm's credit lines available at its bank. And banks granting lines of credit frequently impose compensating balance requirements.

MANAGEMENT CONTACTS. Only 7 percent of the treasurers said that personal contact between officials of the bank and the firm was the most important factor in selecting a depository. To some extent, of course, management contact is involved every time a depository is selected because bank management carries out the personal marketing effort. But only seven out of every hundred corporate treasurers believed management contacts were even more important than a bank's financial condition or its location. Some of these contacts may stem from interlocking directorates, mutual investments or just old friendships.

SUMMARY

Although sophisticated cash management techniques have reduced the total volume of temporarily idle funds for the typical giant corporation, at the same time they have increased the number of depositories the firm is likely to have. Because of the dearth of price competition in the market, the bulk of a firm's deposits goes to banks which are able to promote themselves on the basis of nonprice factors which the corporate treasurer looks at in selecting a depository. The most important of these factors were financial condition, location, size of bank (largely a proxy for variety of services available) and credit availability. Should federal regulations ever permit payment of explicit interest on demand deposits, bankers may have to abandon the barter system in which deposit balances are maintained in exchange for services performed by banks. A dollar price for each bank product would lead to more efficient markets for those products.

23. Businesses, Households, and Their Banks *

Robert D. Bowers

The preceding article (by Staats) dealt with large firms and their banks. This article analyzes the small firm sector. Further, it describes the nature of household banking markets. The studies which are examined show that demand for bank services by most households and small firms tends to be localized. Convenient location is found to be very important. The implications of these findings are significant —they suggest the tendency for banks to be viewed as homogeneous at the local level, and their pricing of services to be relatively unimportant to the local consumer.

Bankers are keenly interested in the preferences and behavior patterns of their customers. The wants of businessmen as well as of households and bankers' response to these wants determine the nature of banking markets. Two surveys undertaken by the staff of this Bank shed some light on the characteristics of banking markets in the central portion of Bucks County centered on Doylestown.[1]

BUSINESSES AND THEIR BANKS[2]

The business population of central Bucks County consisted mostly of small firms. Approximately 80 percent of the firms had 25 or fewer employees and about nine out of ten had a net worth under $75,000. Moreover, the omission from the sample of all branch firms with headquarters outside central Bucks County removed the influence of some larger firms from the survey results.[3]

MOST FIRMS BANKED LOCALLY. Busi-

---

*From Business Review, March, 1969. Reprinted by permission of the publisher (the Federal Reserve Bank of Philadelphia) and the author.

[1] The staffs of the Board of Governors of the Federal Reserve System and the Federal Reserve Bank of Philadelphia cooperated in the research

design of both surveys. A market research firm, Behavior Systems, Inc., of Philadelphia, was retained as a consultant in the business firm survey and to conduct the household survey.

[2] Information on the business-bank relationship was secured through personal interviews with firms in central Bucks County. The firms constituted a stratified random sample which was selected from a total business population of 687 firms, drawn from the Dun & Bradstreet listing of September 1, 1967. Of these, 179 were originally designated for sampling. Interviews were successfully completed in 147 cases. The interviewing was done in December, 1967 and January, 1968.

[3] This exclusion was based on the assumption that the home office, rather than the branch, normally makes decisions pertaining to selection and use of commercial banks and services.

FIGURE 1
Bucks County Pennsylvania

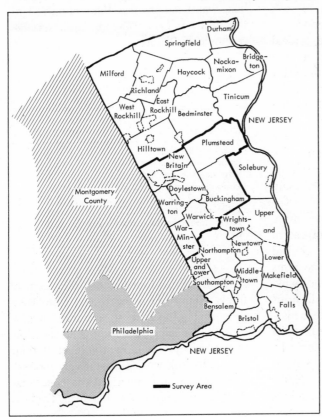

ABOUT THE AREA

The area covered by the two surveys is shown as the shaded portion on the map. Located within the Philadelphia Standard Metropolitan Area, Bucks County has undergone marked changes since 1950. Its industrial, commercial and residential expansion was accompanied by a more-than-doubling of its population during the 1950–60 decade. The most dramatic changes in its economic make-up took place in the lower portion of the county where the United States Steel Corporation built its integrated steel mill in Morrisville. In the 1960's, the expansion of economic activity carried into the county's central portion with the result that the area's pastoral and small-town setting began a transformation that most observers expect to continue to 1980 and beyond.

ness firms in central Bucks County had chosen as their primary banks those with an office, either the main office or a branch, nearby. Roughly two-thirds of the firms selected as their main bank one with its home office in Bucks County. Generally, the remainder used as primary banks ones having home offices outside the county, but with branch offices within the central Bucks County area.

For those firms with more than one banking connection, the same marked preference for local banks was in evidence. In fact, more than 60 percent of the firms in this group designated one or the other of the two Doylestown banks as their secondary bank.

While it is not known what factors motivated the firms in their initial selection of a primary bank, it appears that physical convenience was important. Approximately three-quarters of the businesses generally did their banking at an office that was within five miles and normally reached within 10 minutes. Only 10 percent of the businesses used a banking office that required 20 minutes or more travel time from the place of business.

MOST FIRMS USED ONE BANK. Approximately 70 percent of the business firms in central Bucks County used a single commercial bank for all of their banking needs. By contrast, 24 percent of the firms used two banks and 6 percent used three or more. Larger firms—those with an estimated net worth of $75,000 or more—showed, as expected, a higher incidence of multiple-bank usage than the smaller firms. Forty-two percent of these firms used two or more banks. Apparently, most of the area's business firms, being small, have not seen any reason to seek more than one banking connection.

In central Bucks County, the typical bank-business relationship is one of long standing. About three-fourths of the firms have dealt with the primary bank for at least five years, about one-half for ten years or more, and approximately a third for 20 years or more. Of course, since new firms would cause these results to be understated, the clear implication is that business firms change banks only infrequently.

Banks in recent years have placed more emphasis upon direct solicitation as a source of new business. In the central Bucks County area, one-third of the firms had been contacted by at least one bank. Given the large number of small firms in the area, it might be expected that marketing efforts of banks would have focused on the larger firms almost exclusively. But this was not the case. Only 41 percent of the larger firms (net worth of $75,000 or more) had been called upon by bankers seeking new customers. However, a few of these firms had been contacted, on several occasions, by three or more of the large Philadelphia banks.

Business firms in central Bucks County were generally well satisfied with the quantity and quality of services that they received from their banks. More than 88 percent of the firms rated the quality of their banks' services as being good or excellent. By contrast, less than 4 percent considered the service of their banks poor. Moreover, only 7 percent of the firms expressed a desire for additional banking services that were not being offered by the area's banks.

USE OF BANK SERVICES. Most of the firms in central Bucks County used two banking services: checking accounts and loans. Virtually all firms had one or more checking accounts with their primary bank, and about three-quarters had bor-

rowed from it. The next most frequently used banking service, the safe deposit box, was used by less than one-third of the business firms. Use of bank services is shown in Table 1.

TABLE 1
Services of Primary Bank Used

Service	Percent of Firms Using Service
Checking account	98.0
Bank credit (business loans)	78.1
Safe deposit box	31.1
Time deposits or C.D.'s	16.2
Business advice	13.6
Trust services	8.8
International banking services	2.0
Other	6.6

About three-fourths of the central Bucks County firms borrowed from their primary bank. Of these, roughly 70 percent had a loan outstanding at the time of the survey. For most, the level of their last borrowing was comparatively modest, reflecting in large measure the small size of the area's firms. As shown in Table 2, the last loan was under $5,000 for about 39 percent of the business firms. For 86 percent, it was under $25,000.

TABLE 2
Size of Last Loan at Primary Bank

Bank Size	Percent of Firms
Less than $5,000	38.5
$ 5,000 to $ 9,999	24.4
$ 10,000 to $ 24,999	22.7
$ 25,000 to $ 49,999	8.3
$ 50,000 to $ 99,999	2.6
$100,000 to $149,999	1.1
$150,000 to $249,999	0.9
$250,000 or more	1.4
	99.9*

*Because of rounding, percents do not add to 100.

A similar pattern existed for those firms dealing with more than one commercial bank. Of these, approximately four out of ten borrowed from their secondary bank and the majority had a loan outstanding at the time of the survey. Here, too, the general pattern of loan size was comparatively modest—about three-fourths of the firms indicated their last loan was under $25,000, with more than half under $5,000.

Most central Bucks County firms did not seek out alternative suppliers of bank credit—that is, they did not "shop" for loans. Nine out of ten of the borrowers had not discussed their credit needs with other banks. Of those who had borrowed from their secondary bank, the results were not substantially different. Of this group only 15 percent had discussed their credit needs with at least one other supplier. Failure to investigate alternative sources of credit may stem from the close, long-standing relationship between firms and their banks.

USE OF NONBANK FINANCIAL INSTITUTIONS. Roughly 16 percent of central Bucks County firms have had dealings with nonbank financial institutions. Firms named savings and loan associations, finance companies and insurance companies, in that order of frequency. Savings and loan associations and insurance companies were used most often for mortgages; finance companies generally were used to discount business loan paper.

HOUSEHOLDS AND THEIR BANKS[4]

BANKING SERVICES USED. On average, 19 out of every 20 households in central Bucks County used one or more commercial banking service. As expected, checking accounts were most widely used—88 percent of the households used one or more. This is substantially above the national average. The Survey Research Center at the University of Michigan estimates that 68 percent of the households in the United States had one or more checking accounts in 1967. One factor explaining the higher incidence of checking account usage in central Bucks County is that average family income is well above the national median.

Approximately 79 percent of the households had at least one savings or share account. One-third of them were with non-bank financial institutions, primarily savings and loan associations and mutual savings banks, and two-thirds were in the form of savings deposits with commercial banks.

Some of the 12 percent of the households which did not have checking accounts did use other services offered by banks. Nearly 8 percent of the area householders, while they had no checking account, had a savings account at a bank. The banking services used by the non-checking segment of the area's population are shown in Table 3.

Roughly half of the respondents indicated that they had not made use of services of financial institutions other than checking and savings deposits within the

[4]The household survey is based on completed telephone interviews with 1,452 householders drawn from central Bucks County. The population from which the sample was drawn consisted of all listed residential telephone numbers in the published telephone directory as of April, 1967, and those householders which had new or changed numbers between that time and December, 1967. In all, 3,759 telephone numbers were called. Of these, 13.8 percent were ineligible, 17.6 percent yielded a busy signal in three attempts, and 29.6 percent refused to be interviewed.

TABLE 3

Selected Banking Services Used by Central Bucks County Households that Did Not Have Checking Accounts

Service	Percentages Based on All Households in the Population
Savings account	7.6
Safe deposit box	2.3
Auto loan	2.0
Home mortgage	1.8
Personal loan	1.0
Savings certificates	.6
Home improvement loan	.2

past three years. About 25 percent of the households had received auto loans and mortgage loans during that period. Approximately three-fourth of those borrowing had obtained an auto loan from a bank, and the remaining one-fourth from finance companies and credit unions. By contrast, only 29 percent obtained mortgage funds from a commercial bank with the majority having borrowed from either savings and loan associations or mutual savings banks.

About one-third of the respondents indicated they had rented a safe deposit box. In nine out of ten cases, they got this service from a commercial bank.

FACTORS IN BANK SELECTION. Convenience to the home emerged as the single most important reason for selection of a particular bank as a depository for the main household checking account. Almost one-half of the respondents cited this reason, as shown in Table 4. By contrast, only about 10 percent of the households considered convenience to work as a deciding factor. The strength of the convenience-to-home motive is surprisingly strong inasmuch as there is substantial commuting to work in other parts of the Delaware Valley.

IMPLICATIONS OF THE FINDINGS

Because characteristics such as population, industrial mix, and personal incomes vary among geographical areas, information about banking markets in one area may not hold true for those in another region. But studies of markets in six areas have been completed and they do give rise to some general, if tentative, observations about the nature of banking markets.[5]

[5]George G. Kaufman, Customers View Bank Markets and Services: A Survey of Elkhart, Indiana (Chicago: Federal Reserve Bank of Chicago, 1967).

George G. Kaufman, Business Firms and Households View Commercial Banks: A Survey of Appleton, Wisconsin (Chicago: Federal Reserve Bank of Chicago, 1967).

TABLE 4
Reasons for Selecting Bank for the Main Household Checking Account

Reason	Percent[*]
Convenient to home	47
Convenient to work	11
Nice, friendly, like it	10
Family has always used it	6
Location was originally convenient, kept it after moving	4
Convenient to shopping	4
Recommended by friend, relative	4
Have mortgage, loan, etc., there	2
Only one there (at time), no choice	2
Other	19

[*]The sum exceeds 100 percent inasmuch as some respondents mentioned more than one reason.

LOCALIZED DEMAND FOR BANKING SERVICES. All of the studies confirm the prevailing belief that, for the majority of business and household customers, the demand for the services of commercial banks tends to be highly localized. Larger corporations usually take a broader regional or national view when considering banking connections, but evidence suggests this is not the case for smaller businesses and households. The small firm or family with primary banking connections beyond the local area stand as distinct exceptions.

High incidence of usage of local banks uncovered in the central Bucks County surveys has also been found elsewhere. In Appleton, Wisconsin, for example, more than 90 percent of the business firms used local banks while only 3 percent had

Lynn A. Stiles, Businesses View Banking Services: A Survey of Cedar Rapids, Iowa (Chicago: Federal Reserve Bank of Chicago, 1967).

Clifton R. Luttrell and William E. Pettigrew, "Banking Markets for Business Firms in the St. Louis Area," Federal Reserve Bank of St. Louis Review, Vol. 48, No. 9 (September, 1966), pp. 9–12.

Nathaniel Greenspun, "Measuring Customer Satisfaction with Bank Services," Bank Structure and Competition, A Summary of Discussion and Selected Papers Presented at a Conference at the Federal Reserve Bank of Chicago, March 16–17, 1967 (Chicago: Federal Reserve Bank of Chicago, 1967), pp. 19–20. This study covered the Racine, Wisconsin, area.

their primary banks in Chicago or Milwaukee. Virtually all business firms in Elkhart, Indiana, considered a local bank as their primary bank, while in only two out of 141 cases in Cedar Rapids, Iowa, was the principal bank located outside the area (Linn County, the Cedar Rapids SMSA). The same pattern of local bank usage by households emerged in each case that was studied. Even in the case of householders in Elkhart using bank-by-mail facilities, three-fifths used local banks and another one-fifth used nearby banks.

THE ROLE OF CONVENIENCE. The frequency with which householders in central Bucks County cited convenience in the selection of the primary bank has been noted. Perhaps surprisingly, the original bank choice of a large number of business firms is explained on the same grounds. Other surveys revealed similar, although not identical, findings. Convenience and personal preference were the reasons most often given by business firms in Cedar Rapids. In Appleton, convenience ranked second only to quality of services as a motive for the selection of a primary bank. The same general pattern emerged in Elkhart.

An implication of these findings is that for a large number of households, and a lesser but significant number of small business firms, banking output might initially be viewed as a "convenience good." Such a good, or in this instance, service, is one in which the buyer thinks it is not worth his time or trouble to investigate alternative sources of supply. If this is correct, it implies that some households and business firms approach the bank-selection decision with the belief that "banks are all alike" and the likely result is that customers chose the bank most conveniently located.

THE BANK-BUSINESS RELATIONSHIP. Finally, the empirical investigations of banking markets serve as factual reminders that, once established, the relationship of a business firm with its bank tends to be long-standing. The typical business firm does not take its banking connections lightly. Firms rarely shop for loans, attempting to play one bank against another in search of better price or terms. Bank switching is not common. For example, large firms in St. Louis, on average, had been customers of their primary banks for over a quarter of a century and 18 percent reported a relationship with their primary bank spanning more than 50 years.

The evidence further suggests that when a firm severs a banking connection, it is likely to be in response to what it considers to be a serious breach of a past relationship. Thus, a loan denial, curt or cavalier treatment by bank employees, or the like, rather than simply the firm's ability to obtain a "better deal" elsewhere are likely to lead to changes in banking connections.

In conclusion, these studies reflect patterns of bank usage in only six of the literally thousands of banking markets and submarkets in the nation. And, the studies of business firms tend to minimize the preferences of large corporate customers whose dealings with banks may be quite unlike those of the typical small firm. Thus, the reader is cautioned against making undue generalizations regarding all banking markets. Nonetheless, the analysis presented does serve to reveal some interesting common patterns of behavior in specific banking markets and suggests that such patterns may, in fact, exist in markets with the same general characteristics.

24. Deposit Turnover, Innovations, and Bank Profitability[*]

Kalman J. Cohen and Frederick S. Hammer[†]

The velocity or turnover of demand deposits has continually increased since the end of World War II. Among the primary forces responsible for this has been bank innovation. Many bankers, however, have had mixed reactions concerning the increased turnover and the innovative process behind it. They are unsure of the effects on profits. This article examines whether the greater velocity of money, induced by innovative services, has been of benefit to banking.

It is often said that problems are opportunities in disguise. If so, then opportunities permeate the entire fabric of the American banking community. In particular, banking is being confronted by a host of significant problems whose roots emanate from technical innovation. For the first time, the industry has found that it must come to grips with widespread technological change of breathtaking scope and intensity. Further, these developments, which in great measure focus around electronic computers and communications networks, seem to be progressing at an accelerating pace. As astute observers have commented, adaptations of traumatic magnitudes are being demanded of bankers weaned on conventional views concerning the proper functions of banks and traditional approaches to management problem solving.[1]

The continuing increase in the turnover of demand deposits during the post-war era furnishes one visible illustration of the changes taking place. Increased velocity has resulted, at least in part, from more intense competitive pressures in banking and heightened demands by customers for new and improved services. An oft-heard lament is that by responding to these demands and innovating certain new types of customer services, the so-called "progressive" banks are in fact undermining the basic health of the banking industry and are being shortsighted with respect to their own future position as well. As interest rates have risen and corporate treasurers have wielded sharper pencils, idle demand deposit balances have been pared. Consequently, bankers are finding it necessary to develop explicit methods of pricing their services. This has been found an arduous task both because of inexperience on the part of bankers in

[*]From *Bankers Magazine*, Spring, 1968. Reprinted by permission of the publisher, Warren, Gorham & Lamont, Inc.

[†]The authors wish to acknowledge the data gathering and computational assistance provided by Mr. Michael H. Kaericher (Ford Motor Company), Miss Margaret Kolouch (Federal Deposit Insurance Corporation), and Mr. Howard M. Schneider (Bankers Trust Company). In addition, Dr. Paul M. Horvitz, of the Federal Deposit Insurance Corporation, contributed several poignant suggestions after reading an earlier draft.

The opinions and conclusions presented in this paper are those of the authors and are not necessarily shared by either their colleagues or their institutions.

[1]See, e.g., "The Manager and the Moron," by Peter F. Drucker, and "Bank Management: The Unmet Challenge," by E. Everett Smith, *The McKinsey Quarterly*, Vol. III, No. 4 (Spring 1967).

this area and the general inadequacies of bank cost accounting systems.[2]

Conflicting views have been expressed concerning the net effect of bank innovations on the profitability of the banking system. Clearly, particular innovations will be initiated only in the expectation that they will lead to increased profits. Critics argue, however, that the innovative behavior by those banks introducing new services does not represent forward progress but, rather, a treadmill on which all banks are forced "to run harder just to stay even."

Bank innovations introduced in response to customers' demands have enhanced both the quality and quantity of banking services. Not only has the public benefited from these changes, the innovator banks have profited from their initiative. Thus, we find that Adam Smith's "invisible hand" works as well in modern banking as it does in the textbook: those banks most responsive to customer needs reap the harvest of increased profitability.[3]

REASONS FOR INCREASED VELOCITY

Since the end of World War II, there has been an almost continual increase in the velocity of money in the United States, stemming primarily from an increase in the turnover of demand deposits. In 1950, the average annual turnover rate of demand deposits in American banks was 22.6, while in 1967 it had reached 53.8, an increase of 138 percent.[4] This in-

crease in the velocity of money shows no signs of abating.

Some economists have indicated that the increase in the turnover of demand deposits stems at least in part from the attempts of corporate treasurers to adopt more efficient methods of cash management. This trend has been facilitated by the competitive activities of banks themselves. According to George Garvy:

Efforts to increase the efficiency of corporate working cash include projecting monthly, weekly, and even daily cash needs on the basis of cash budgets, centralizing the cash flows, speeding up the collection of remittances, reducing the amount of uncollected funds, and using more rapid means for the intracorporate transfer of funds. These efforts are stimulated by some large commercial banks, particularly by those in financial centers, some of which have special departments or officers working with corporate officials on the improvement of cash management. Efforts by commercial banks in financial centers to attract balances by assisting corporate treasurers in developing proper procedures for increasing the efficiency of cash management as well as higher interest rates have given a new stimulus to the trend toward economizing on balances in recent years.[5]

Paul S. Nadler has even more forcefully written that commercial banks have been responsible for the recent increase in the velocity of money. "But while a rise in monetary velocity hurts the banks as a whole, it is the new programs of the banks themselves that have made much of this rise possible. . . ."[6]

It might be well to consider some of the specific innovations in commercial bank services which have contributed to the increased turnover of demand deposits

---

[2]See James P. Furniss and Paul S. Nadler, "Should Banks Reprice Corporate Services?" *Harvard Business Review*, Vol. 44, No. 3, (May–June 1966).

[3]On the basis of economic theory, we would expect that the increased profits which stem from any particular innovation are of a short-run nature and will eventually be competed away. To the extent that a particular bank is successful in introducing a continuing stream of innovations, its profit performance will be relatively superior to its competitors.

[4]These average annual turnover rates apply to six leading centers, the only series which is more or less consistently defined over the 1950–1967 period.

[5]George Garvy, *Deposit Velocity and Its Significance*, Federal Reserve Bank of New York, November 1959, pp. 63–64.

[6]Paul S. Nadler, "Banks Speed Up Velocity of Money With Innovations, Hurt Themselves," *American Banker*, March 19, 1963.

either by creating new debits and/or lowering average balances.[7]

Innovations Affecting Business Checking Accounts

Banking innovations which have increased the velocity of business checking accounts include: the draft, the wire transfer, the lock box, drawing on uncollected funds, and less-strict compensating balance requirements.

Drafts allow corporations to reduce deposit balances in two ways: (1) funds need not be deposited until the drafts are presented for collection; (2) predetermined bank balances can be maintained since the firms are advised daily of the exact amount needed to cover the drafts presented that day. Thus, drafts enable corporations to release cash for investment, but they mean reduced demand deposit balances and increased turnover for the banks.

The *transfer of funds by wire,* although well-established, has only recently been promoted aggressively. This service reduces deposit balances both by decreasing float time and by providing certainty concerning the exact time when funds become available. In a similar manner, *lock-box plans* reduce float time and, hence, increase velocity.

As competition for corporate business has grown more keen, it has become increasingly common for banks to permit disbursements *against uncollected funds.* Similarly, banks on average have become less strict about *enforcing compensating balance requirements.* Such practices, by reducing demand deposit balances, lead to higher turnover rates.

Innovations Affecting Household Demand Deposits

Innovations which have increased the turnover rate of household demand de-

posits include: no minimum balance accounts, no-bounce accounts, bank credit cards, credit card plans and other new forms of consumer credit, the daily payment of interest on savings deposits, and the disbursement of funds through savings accounts.

In retail banking, the availability of *no-minimum-balance accounts* leads households to carry lower balances. Even more extreme is the *"no-bounce"* account under which a loan is created up to a predetermined amount to cover what otherwise would be an overdraft. Thus, this arrangement allows the customer to reduce his precautionary balance.

Bank credit cards, along with credit cards in general, increase deposit velocity by affecting deposit balances; non-bank credit cards also increase the volume of debits. Average demand deposits are decreased for two reasons: (1) by enabling consumers to predict with greater reliability the timing of future disbursements, transaction balances can be held to a minimum; (2) by providing a borrowing facility (in a manner similar to *check credit plans*), the credit card reduces the need for precautionary balances. Somewhat more subtle, perhaps, is the way in which non-bank credit cards increase the volume of debits. While non-bank credit cards may reduce the *number* of checking account transactions, they increase the *dollar volume* of these transactions.[8] It is the latter, of course, which constitutes the debit series used in computing deposit turnover.

The use of non-bank credit cards results in a doubling of the dollar volume of debits associated with the cardholders' purchases. With no credit card, a single check would be drawn by the cardholder to cover the purchase.[9] When a non-bank

---

[7]Garvy, *op. cit.,* ch. vii, presents a considerably more detailed discussion of some of the factors affecting deposit velocity.

[8]Increased deposit turnover stemming from this source may reduce, rather than increase, bank processing costs since it is accompanied by a smaller volume of checks to be processed.

[9]Note that whether this check is drawn to the vendor, or first to "cash" from which the vendor

credit card is used, however, not only does the cardholder draw a check (at a later date) to the credit card company, but in addition, this company must draw a check to the vendor. This "doubling of debits" does not prevail when a bank credit card is employed, since the crediting of the vendor's account by the bank is not reflected in the debits series. To the extent, of course, that bank credit cards reduce the dollar volume of purchases effected by non-bank credit cards, debits are thereby reduced.

By paying *daily interest on savings deposits,* banks motivate individuals to transfer temporarily idle funds from demand into savings accounts. More drastic in reducing average demand deposits is the practice of effecting *disbursements directly from savings accounts.* There are at least two forms that such plans take. Under the more usual system, funds are automatically transferred from savings to checking accounts whenever the checking account balance would otherwise fall below some predetermined minimum. A second, but less common, plan effects the disbursement through bank drafts rather than checks; whenever such a draft is presented to the bank for payment, a consumer loan (fully collateralized by the savings account), is automatically created.

IMPACT OF INCREASED VELOCITY

At first glance, it may appear that increases in monetary velocity have a negative impact on bank profitability. There are several "obvious" reasons for this. First, any increase in turnover of demand deposits not accompanied by increased efficiency leads to higher processing costs

for the banks. Second, the increasing velocity of money will, other things equal, cause the Federal Reserve System to reduce the growth rate of demand deposits. Lower deposit levels, or at any rate, smaller growth rates in deposits than would otherwise exist, reduce the levels of earning assets for banks, lowering their portfolio income.[10] Unless appropriate fee schedules are instituted which adequately compensate the banks for this reduction in portfolio income, gross revenues (i.e., portfolio income plus fees) will decrease. Because of both lower revenues and higher operating costs, the increase in the velocity of money which has resulted from the innovations of commercial banks may have been harmful for the banking system.

It is possible, however, that the Federal Reserve System may take offsetting actions which reduce the impact of slower demand deposit growth on the profitability of banks. While the Federal Reserve functions as the watchdog of the nation's money supply, it is also responsible, along with the other regulatory agencies, for maintaining a healthy and orderly banking system.

At least in the present political climate, it is not reasonable to suppose that the Fed would tolerate decreases in bank earnings sufficient to weaken very many banks. This may, in fact, account for the steady downtrend in reserve requirements during the postwar period. The recent support given by the Federal Reserve Board to proposed legislation which would establish graduated reserve requirements is the latest step in this direction. The Fed's support for this measure also indicates its concern for instituting appropriate measures designed to maintain the profitability of banks of varying

---

is paid, is immaterial in determining the dollar volume of debits. The differential effect of this "credit card-for-money" substitution is moot: while credit cards, for the reasons enunciated above, allow individuals to carry reduced demand deposit balances, these balances would necessarily be reduced if the individual were to carry a larger stock of cash.

[10]Nadler, *op. cit.,* concurs: ". . . this speed-up of deposit turnover is not only expensive, but is the main reason why checking account expansion has been so slow and why banks have had to rely far more on time and savings deposits for normal growth."

types as well as the overall banking system.

If the increased turnover of demand deposits were to result in an unhealthy profit picture for a significant number of commercial banks, another way in which the Fed can be expected to interpose itself is by injecting new reserves. During periods of monetary stringency, this type of action would not be required of the Fed. As can be easily verified, tight money periods (i.e., when interest rates are high) immediately precede the periods when commercial bank earnings are at their cyclical peaks. If bank earnings data were available on a quarterly basis, we would expect to see even closer connection between interest rates and earnings levels.[11]

Measuring Innovativeness

A statistical test of the effects of innovation of bank profitability can be conducted using a cross-section of large banks. A study conducted in early 1965 by the editors of *Fortune*[12] has provided a direct measure of the business community's opinions regarding the innovativeness of the nation's fifteen largest banks. One of the questions asked businessmen in this survey concerned the extent to which the nation's fifteen largest banks

---

[11]Bank profitability and interest rates (Regression Relations: 1950–66).

$$P_i = \begin{matrix} 7.28 + .55 \ T_{i-1} \\ (t = 3.5) \\ \text{adjusted } R^2 = .42 \end{matrix}$$

$$P_i - P_{i\,1} = \begin{matrix} -0.19 + 1.15 \ (T_{i-1} - T_{i-2}) \\ (t = 5.3) \\ \text{adjusted } R^2 = .64 \end{matrix}$$

Where

P_i = Net operating earnings as a percentage of Total capital accounts, all banks, year i

T_i = Treasury Bill rate, annual average, year i

Note that approximately two-thirds of the variability in bank earnings can be explained by simply referring to lagged values of annual averages on Treasury bill rates.

[12]*Fortune* Survey, "Business and Banking," Time, Inc., 1965.

". . . are known as innovators of commercial banking services." To avoid confounding the effects of general reputation and size with opinions concerning innovativeness, we have adjusted the businessmen's answers to this question by determining the percentage of respondents familiar with a bank who also regarded that bank as being innovative.

The resulting measure of innovativeness is presented in Table 1. The simple correlation between innovativeness and bank profitability provides weak evidence in the expected direction.[13] It is clear, of course, that the underlying relationship between innovativeness and profitability is masked because of the important impact on profitability exerted by other factors. In particular, one factor of overriding importance affecting a bank's expected profitability is the general risk structure of its balance sheet position. On average, those banks that incur greater risks expect to be more profitable. Thus, the effect of risks should, for statistical purposes, be held constant when trying to relate bank profitability and innovativeness.

One comprehensive measure of bank portfolio risk is provided by the capital adequacy tests defined by the examiners of the Federal Reserve Board of Governors.[14] Employing this measure, capital adequacy ratings for the nation's fifteen largest banks during 1964 are also displayed in Table 1. The table also presents data on the profitability of the fifteen largest banks, measured in terms of net operating earnings as a percent of total capital accounts.

---

[13]For 1964, the most recent year to which the innovativeness measure would be expected to apply, a simple linear regression of bank profitability as a function of innovativeness was run. The regression coefficient, although not highly significant, is positive. The simple correlation coefficient is .375.

[14]For an explanation of this risk measure, see Kalman J. Cohen and Frederick S. Hammer, "Linear Programming and Optimal Bank Asset Management Decisions," *"The Journal of Finance,* Volume 22, No. 2 (May, 1967), pp. 147–165.

TABLE 1

Fifteen Largest Banks, Base Data

Bank	1964 % Rating Innovative	Capital Adequacy Ratio	Net Operating Earnings as % Tot. Cap. Acct.
Bank of America	23.8	.57	9.7
Bankers Trust	5.2	1.00	7.9
Chase Manhattan Bank	17.7	.73	8.3
Chemical Bank-N.Y. Trust ..	4.5	.76	9.1
Continental Illinois	11.2	.86	7.7
Crocker-Citizens	3.7	.74	7.3
First National City Bank	23.3	.72	7.7
FNB of Chicago	5.9	1.06	7.1
Irving Trust	3.4	.61	7.9
Manufacturers Hanover	3.1	.96	7.4
Mellon National Bank	12.0	1.01	7.8
Morgan Guaranty Trust	11.5	.86	8.2
Security First	2.5	.65	8.9
United California	4.9	.62	6.8
Wells Fargo	2.7	.85	6.5

It is expected that, when risk is held constant, bank profitability is positively associated with innovativeness. Multiple regression analysis was used to test this hypothesis.[15] The results for 1964 are entirely consistent with the hypothesis. These conclusions, of course, must be regarded as suggestive rather than definitive. While the results are not strongly statistically significant, this is not surprising given the coarse nature of the data utilized. In addition, it should be remembered that this test is attempting to discriminate between relative degrees of innovativeness for a select group of banks which is undoubtedly on the extreme end of the innovativeness scale for American banks as a whole.

---

[15]Bank Profitability, risk, and innovativeness (Fifteen Largest Banks: 1964).

$$P_i = 8.924 - 0.0175\,K_i + .0405\,I_i$$
$$(t = 1.26) \quad (t = 1.36)$$

$$R^2 = .152$$

Where

P_i = Net operating earnings as a percentage of capital accounts, i^{th} bank

K_i = Rating on Federal Reserve Board of Governors Examiners' criterion as of 12/31/64, i^{th} bank

I_i = Adjusted rating of innovativeness in *Fortune* survey, "Business and Banking."

It has been argued that the innovations introduced by individual banks in response to customer demands for new and improved services have resulted in continued increases in monetary velocity. This in turn may well have led to higher processing costs and slower demand deposit growth. Nonetheless, on the basis of the rather limited evidence that one can muster, there is reason to believe that innovativeness and profitability are positively related in banking.

A LOOK INTO THE FUTURE

Is it reasonable to extrapolate past trends and project further increases of deposit turnover into the future? It is often argued that demand deposit balances have already been pared to their "hardcore" minimums. If true, the present volume of demand deposits is principally composed of working balances and excess, idle balances no longer exist. Implicit in this viewpoint is the conclusion that the past upward trend in monetary velocity will be slowed, if not arrested entirely.

This conclusion is difficult to accept. Essentially the same arguments have been advanced throughout the past decade. As recounted earlier, an ever-expanding array of new services is being introduced and diffused throughout American banking. These services provide bank customers with new methods and concepts for conserving deposit balances. The net impact of these innovations in banking services is to reduce the level of working balances needed to sustain a given volume of transactions.

Of all developments now visible on the horizon, perhaps the most dramatic in its potential impact on monetary velocity is the set of new customer services commonly labeled "the checkless society."[16] It is fairly easy to predict the probable reactions of bank customers to this innovation. First, there will be decreased time delays in transferring funds between accounts. Second, the costs involved in effecting these transfers will be greatly reduced. Finally, many of the uncertainties inherent in the flow of funds throughout the banking system will be resolved. All three of these factors point to a reduction in working balance requirements. Other things being equal, the effect of the "checkless society" will be to decrease the growth rate of total demand deposits in the banking system.[17]

In this environment, can it be argued that the prize of increased profitability will continue to be associated with innovative behavior? The answer to this question depends upon the extent to which the pioneering banks are successful in

adopting modes of behavior appropriate to the new situation. Asset management strategies must recognize that new sources of funds—other than demand deposits—should increasingly be relied upon.[18] Marketing perspectives must be adopted which incorporate realistic possibilities for substitutions and trade-offs between explicit fees and implicit payments through balances.[19] Central information files must be developed which portray a comprehensive picture of the interfaces between the bank and its customers.[20] Cost accounting systems must be implemented which properly measure the opportunity costs associated with providing various services to different classes of customers.[21] Managerial innovations such as these will be required if the profitability of banks is to be maintained in face of the continuing stream of innovative customer services.

All banks will not be equally successful in adapting to the changing environment. It is likely that smaller banks, lacking the necessary manpower and expertise, will find it difficult to maintain their relative position in a financial marketplace in which technological innovations are of growing importance. Knowledgeable observers have predicted that these changes may contribute to a decline in the role played by small institutions in providing

---

[16]A recent comprehensive discussion of the nature and implications of developments in this area may be found in Robert L. Kramer and W. Putnam Livingston, "Cashing in on the Checkless Society," Harvard Business Review, Vol. 45, No. 5 (Sept.-Oct. 1967), pp. 141-149. See also Martin Greenberger, "Decline and Fall of the Check," THE BANKERS MAGAZINE, Summer 1965, pp. 84-89; and Marvin C. Feinstein, "The Checkless Society," Bank Equipment News, April 1967, pp 14-18.

[17]For a corroborating viewpoint, see Paul S. Nadler, "Returning Canceled Checks Found Bothersome to Banks and Economy," American Banker, March 31, 1964, p. 4.

[18]See George R. Morrison and Richard T. Selden, Time Deposit Growth and the Employment of Bank Funds, Chicago, Illinois: Association of Reserve City Bankers, 1965; also G. Walter Woodworth, "Bank Liquidity Management: Theories and Techniques," THE BANKERS MAGAZINE, Vol. 150, No. 4 (Autumn, 1967) pp. 66-78. (A more detailed version of the Woodworth article is reprinted in this text.)

[19]See Nadler and Furniss "Should Banks Reprice Corporate Services?" op. cit.

[20]See Proceedings of Session A-2 of the 1967 National Automation Conference, American Bankers Association, New York, New York, May 7-10, 1967, and Donald R. Schnee and Walter E. Trabbold, Progress in Information Systems, Bank of Delaware, March 1967.

[21]See I. Miller and I. Plotkin, "Cost Structure of Banks," unpublished paper given at the Meeting of the Operations Research Society of America (June 1, 1967).

banking services to the American community.[22] If this is not to occur, it will be necessary for the bank regulatory agencies to revise their posture concerning the nature and extent of information and assistance which they will provide to the banking industry.

Some indications have already appeared that such revisions have already begun. For example, the Federal Reserve System has, for some years, been developing a method for functional cost analysis which it is providing to participating member banks.[23] In addition, the Federal Deposit Insurance Corporation has recently announced the initiation of efforts to establish a computer-based management information system for commercial banks.[24] Here again, flexibility and resourcefulness on the part of the regulatory agencies—which in many cases will require pervasive revisions in long-established modes of conduct—will be essential.

Many bankers will ignore the fundamental changes occurring about them and remain standing with both feet rooted firmly in tradition. Such bankers may eschew innovations in fear of possible adverse longer-run effects on bank profitability. Is this strategy viable?

Of course, there is no way in which an individual bank can prevent the adoption of any innovation simply by refusing to participate in it. If any one bank having both the technical and managerial abilities to introduce some innovation refuses to do so because it would rather not encourage its development, some more enter-

prising and more courageous bank will do so in its stead. Bank innovations which allow reductions in average demand deposit levels prove to be very attractive to bank customers. The remaining demand deposits tend to move toward those banks providing more vigorous and better services. For this reason, rewards await those innovative banks which are first in providing new customer services. Once a few banks have begun to introduce such innovations, it is clear that other banks must follow merely for defensive purposes, i.e., to retain their market shares.

The only effective ways in which an individual bank can block an innovation in new customer services is by colluding with other banks or by lobbying for prohibitive sanctions either through legislation or by appropriate actions from the various regulatory authorities. The long-term success of strategies involving collusion are virtually doomed to failure given the competitive character of the banking industry and the vigorous enforcement of anti-trust statutes. Attempts at instituting restrictive legislation are sometimes successful (witness the prohibition against paying interests on demand deposits). Legislative restrictions against specific innovations, however, are at best a short-run palliative since the more progressive banks will find alternative ways to offer equivalent services to their customers. Thus, the provision of so-called "free" services provides one example of ways in which progressive banks have found it possible to pay "interest" on customers' demand deposits.

Inherent in any attempt to predict the future is the possibility of incorporating grave error. In the absence of compelling evidence to the contrary, however, there is no reason to do other than extrapolate past trends. On the basis of the limited available evidence, and according to the dictates of economic theory, banks have profited from being innovative in providing improved customer services. The con-

---

[22]Refer to George W. Mitchell, "Effects of Automation on the Structure and Functioning of Banking," *American Economic Review*, May 1966, p. 159, and Paul S. Nadler, *Implications of the Automated Bank of the Future*, (New York University, New York; Graduate School of Business Administration, October 1966).

[23]See Federal Reserve Bank of Boston, *Functional Cost Analysis: The Workshop Bank and Trust Company, Yourtown, U.S.A.*, 1967.

[24]See Stanley Strachan, "FDIC To Award Pact For Major Research," *American Banker*, May 9, 1967, p. 1.

tinual demand for and acceptance of new services by banking customers demonstrates that service innovations do enhance the economic utility of the banking system to the overall community. Certainly, it seems that competition by enterprising banks for new business has resulted in benefits not only to bank customers, but also in increased profitability for the more innovative banks.

25. The Future of Demand Deposits at Big City Banks *

W. Giles Mellon

The preceding article (by Cohen and Hammer) discussed the large increase in deposit velocity over the postwar years together with relatively little change in volume of demand deposits. A continuation of these trends was also predicted. This article takes a contrary view. By examining the factors influencing long-term growth of the volume of demand deposits, it is reasoned that these deposits "may well expand during the 1970's above that of the late 1950's and early 1960's. In turn, the implications of this view, if it is correct, for bank management policies and earnings are extremely important."

A survey of the dozens of articles on commercial bank deposits written during the last few years would surely show that almost all have been concerned with the explosive growth of time money and the implications of this growth for bank portfolios and earnings.

In contrast, the few discussions of demand deposits have concentrated on the supposedly bleak outlook for long-term growth in this once preeminent source of bank funds.[1] These pessimistic projections

have been given added weight by a rash of recent statements suggesting that the eventual establishment of a "checkless society" will lead to a sharp reduction, if not virtual elimination, of demand balances. Particularly susceptible to such a development would be the larger commercial banks, whose business depositors would be in the forefront of the move toward sophisticated, computer-based methods for deposit management.[2]

This unfavorable appraisal of the future of demand deposits, however, seems significantly at odds with two sets of factors. The first is the strong recent showing of demand deposits at the nation's larger banks. The second, and far more important, is the result of a logical examination of the forces which will control the long-run growth of demand balances. As a consequence, it is possible to build a reasonably convincing case that demand deposits at the larger banks will not dwin-

---

for Demand Deposits?", *Business in Brief,* The Chase Manhattan Bank, Dec., 1967.

[2]Cf. The Remarks by Kalman J. Cohen and Frederick S. Hammer, "Deposit Turnover, Innovations, and Bank Profitability," THE BANKERS MAGAZINE, Spring, 1968, pp. 76–82. (Article is included in this text.)

---

*From *Bankers Magazine,* Autumn, 1968. Reprinted by permission of the publisher Warren, Gorham & Lamont, Inc.

[1]For an exception, see the author's "New Life

dle away to virtually nothing. In fact, they may well expand during the 1970's at a rate above that of the late 1950's and early 1960's. In turn, the implications of this view, if it is correct, for bank management policies and earnings are extremely important.

THE RECENT RECORD

During the late 1950's and the first part of the 1960's, net private demand deposits of the nation's larger banks, especially those of the very large banks headquartered in New York City, were virtually stagnant. Beginning in 1966, however, these deposits began to improve. During that year, net demand deposits of all weekly reporting banks averaged 2.9 percent above 1965, in 1967 the gain was 3.6 percent, and for the first half of 1968 the figures (adjusted for seasonality) showed a 3.2 percent gain over 1967. The equivalent figures for larger New York City banks were 2.8, 4.8 and 4.2 percent. All figures exclude U.S. Government deposits.

In absolute terms, these figures may seem unimpressive. But they are in sharp contrast to the virtual stagnation of demand deposits at such banks in previous years. The effects of this turn-around have already shown up in a dramatic fashion. A major part of the very sharp rise in earnings of the country's larger banks reported during the first half of 1968 reflects the fact that a significant portion of recent deposit growth—in contrast to previous years—has not consisted of expensive time money.

Of course, this period of improvement in demand deposit growth has been very short. Moreover, it is unquestionably true that much of the recent growth may have been heavily influenced by short-term, cyclical factors, such as the rebuilding of corporate liquidity, which took place in a period of slackening economic activity, and more recently perhaps by the sharp increase in stock market trading. Yet, this recent experience is impressive enough to suggest a closer examination of the question—to try to see if much of this recent improvement reflects underlying long-run forces which have already resulted in, and will continue to lead to, a significant growth in demand deposits.

THE "SUPPLY OF DEMAND DEPOSITS"

Like any other commodity, the future levels and "prices" of demand deposits will be determined by the joint interaction of supply and demand forces. Looking first at the supply side, this is determined, in turn, by the joint actions of the Federal Reserve and the banks themselves.

The Federal Reserve exercises an over-all control over the total of bank reserves and thus bank deposits through open market operations, reserve requirements, and administration of the discounting function. It also has a significant influence over the nationwide mix between demand and time deposits through its ability to vary the ceiling rates on time deposits under Regulation Q. It is, of course, extremely hazardous to make projections of future trends in the economy and in monetary policy. In addition, few academic or business observers are agreed on exactly what factors influence the Fed in the amount of reserves it will supply to the banking system under any given set of circumstances. Still, since monetary policy will exercise such an important influence on the future demand deposits, some assumptions about its future course must be introduced into our analysis.

Basically, it seems reasonable to work with the assumption that the gross national product of the American economy during the coming decade or so will grow at an annual rate of about six percent, and that a significant portion of this growth will reflect continued upward pressure on prices. At the same time, the experience with fiscal policy of the last two years suggests that monetary policy may have to play the major role in checking inflationary tendencies in the future. As a result, it seems plausible to project a future marked by a generally rapid expansion of bank reserves, but intermixed with periods of quite severe credit restraint.

A possible difficulty with this view of a rapid but widely variant growth in bank reserves is contained in the recent attempt by the Joint Economic Committee, under the leadership of Senator Proxmire, to influence the Federal Reserve to adopt a policy of a fairly steady growth in the money supply.[3] The implications of this development, which could be extremely critical to the industry, have received only limited discussion among bankers. For the purposes of this discussion, the assumption is adopted that the Fed will maintain its independence to vary bank reserves and deposits as it sees fit. It should be obvious, however, that any significant degree of control by Congress—for example, a restriction that the money supply, narrowly defined as currecy plus demand deposits adjusted, must grow at 4 to 6 percent a year—could materially alter the conclusions.

Some Expectations

With respect to the level of demand deposits which might be expected to result from our assumed provision of reserves to the banking system, several points can be raised:

First, there is the possibility that a somewhat larger proportion of the future growth in bank liabilities may reflect increased borrowings. This view is based on the recent Federal Reserve proposal to revise the discount mechanism.[4] While each dollar of borrowings can support several dollars of demand deposits, demand deposit growth still will be less under this system than it would if reserves were supplied via open market operations.

Second, there is the question of the administration of Regulation Q. Looking at recent experience, there can be little doubt that the Federal Reserve has used, and will probably continue to use, Regulation Q ceilings on time deposits to slow down the flow of such funds into the large money market banks, curtailing their extension of business credit during hyperboom periods. But, per se, such actions should have little direct effect on demand deposits of money market banks. Indirectly, though, if such banks cannot purchase time money to make loans, this will cut into compensating demand balances. A major direct effect would come, however, if the Fed allowed banks to pay for demand money. While such a move is not now probable, it is possible to build a plausible case that the larger banks may in coming years bring pressure to be allowed to pay something for certain types of demand balances. This, in turn, would obviously revise estimates of demand deposits upwards. On the other hand, if the banks should move to offer day-to-day time deposits to business, this might cut into existing demand balances.

Third, there is the issue raised by some authors[5] that, as improved methods of funds transfer come into existence, the velocity of circulation will rise. Thus the Fed will have to create less and less additional demand deposits to finance a given growth in GNP. There is considerable truth in this statement, properly qualified; as in the past, the money supply will probably continue to increase less rapidly in the long run than GNP.

---

[3]Joint Economic Committee, *Standards for Guiding Monetary Action,* Washington, July 2, 1968.

[4]Board of Governors of the Federal Reserve, *Reappraisal of the Federal Reserve Discount Mechanism,* Washington, July 19, 1968.

[5]For a most articulate expression of this view, see Paul S. Nadler, "Banks Speed Up Velocity of Money with Innovations, Hurt Themselves," *American Banker,* March 19, 1963.

Promoting Growth

Is there anything that the banking system—and especially the individual large commercial banks—can do to promote the continued growth of demand deposits?

Looking first at the question of the growth of bank liabilities as a whole, it is a mistake to believe, as many academicians and bankers do, that there is nothing bankers can do to influence the amount of reserves that the Fed will supply. On the contrary, the monetary authorities are, in the final analysis, interested in making sure that in the long run an adequate supply of credit is available to finance economic growth. Therefore, if the banking system aggressively tries to meet credit demands, it will usually be supplied the necessary reserves. If, on the other hand, banks relax and allow other institutions to supply the needed credit, the Federal Reserve will see no necessity to supply additional reserves to the banks.

There is also the question of what the individual large bank can do to try and make sure that as much as possible of its liability growth is in the form of demand deposits. The major factor here is the terms which the banks offer to holders of demand balances. If, for example, the banks provide services at competitive costs—services which involve the holding of demand balances—then such deposits will be held according to the demand for the services involved.

Despite sharp short-term swings, then, it would be expected that the monetary authorities will in the long run continue to supply bank reserves in substantial volume in coming years, although with some greater emphasis on member borrowing. Moreover, over the long run the Fed is not expected to try to significantly influence the division between time and demand deposits. Nor is it expected to directly curtail the inflow of demand deposits to larger banks. The commercial banks, for their part, are expected to continue vigorous efforts to meet the credit demands of the economy and to attract demand balances.

THE DEMAND SIDE

The other side of the coin is demand—the willingness of individuals, businesses, and non-bank financial institutions to hold a portion of their wealth in the form of demand balances. As already indicated, the Federal Reserve and the banking system obviously exercise a considerable control over the level of demand deposits. Still, barring only a policy whereby the Federal Reserve deliberately increased demand deposits by a fairly constant percent each year, growth in demand deposits will depend to a large degree on a growth in the willingness to hold funds in this form, certainly the public has the freedom to shift any increase in deposits from demand to time form. Even if the Federal Reserves did adopt a money supply target, the relative demands for demand deposits by various holders would still exercise a major influence over the distribution of such deposits among individual banks. These statements are especially true for any given group of banks, as opposed to the banking system as a whole. Thus, for the larger banks, demand deposits would not increase at all —despite an increase in the general money supply—if the depositors of this particular group of banks had no growth in their desires to hold this type of deposit. The possibility of this is shown by the stagnation of demand balances at such banks during the very easy money policies of the early 1960's.

MOTIVES OF INDIVIDUALS AND BUSINESS

To analyze this all-important willingness of depositors to hold demand deposits, we must look at the various motives for holding such deposits by the major classes of depositors.

For the large commercial bank, this group is by far the largest holder of demand deposits, with businesses much more important than individuals. Unfortunately, the Federal Reserve figures for reporting banks give only "gross" demand deposits by type of depositor—that is, including "float." But on this gross basis, growth in individual and business holdings accounted for the bulk of the recent increase in demand deposits, and, presumably, for the major part of the increase in net deposits as well.

What influences individuals and businesses to hold funds in demand form? Several sets of factors may be distinguished.

Transactional Needs

A significant amount of demand deposits are held for ordinary day-to-day transactions purposes. Looking for the moment at business balances only, these are governed by:

1. INTEREST RATES. The higher the short-term rates, the greater the incentive to economize on demand deposits.

2. THE LEVEL OF TRANSACTIONS. The higher the level of transactions, the higher —all other things equal—the level of demand deposits needed to handle them.[6]

3. TECHNIQUES OF DEPOSIT ECONOMIZATION. In recent years, corporate treasurers have developed considerable expertise in economizing on their holdings of demand deposits by various methods.[7] Since it is clear that short-term rates cannot possibly duplicate their rise of the last few years, the future of business transactional

balances will rest largely on the balance between two conflicting influences: Will businesses be able to continually devise and implement methods of economization to a sufficient degree to offset a steadily rising level of transactions?

Technology, to be sure, will take time to be developed and implemented. But assume for the moment that a nationwide system of instantaneous wire transfer of funds between commercial banks has been developed, and that every large corporation has a computer-based system which enables it to keep track of every dollar it has and to invest surplus funds in earning assets. What will be the logical effect of such a system on business demand balances?

For one thing, gross bank deposits would fall sharply, since bank "float"— cash items in the process of collection— would be virtually eliminated. This would affect total "footings," but, of course, it would mean no reduction in bank loanable funds.

For another, armed with such a system, we would expect the corporate treasurer to operate as follows: Demand deposits for transactions purposes would be kept at near zero. When a transaction was made and a check written, the system would automatically transfer the funds from some other source—say be selling treasury bills. Such "zero balance" systems already exist, and their number can be expected to grow as the level of technology increases.[8] Systems of this sort are expensive, but as firms grow either through expansion of sales or by merger, more and more will be able to afford the more elaborate cash control systems.

Are we to conclude from this that transactions balances of businesses at large banks are due to go to virtually zero in the near future? There are at least sev-

---

[6]Although, in general, it would not be expected that deposits would increase *proportionately* with transactions. Cf. Nevins D. Baxter, "Commercial Banks and the New Generation of Corporate Treasurers," THE BANKERS MAGAZINE, Winter, 1966, esp. p. 40.

[7]Cf. the discussion in Frederick Wright Searby, "Use Your Hidden Cash Resources," *Harvard Business Review*, March–April, 1968, pp. 71–80.

[8]Cf. the remarks made by John Leahy of American Machine and Foundry Company as reported by C. B. Axford, "Bank Corporate Ideas for Improving Cash Management," *Burroughs Clearing House*, May, 1968, pp. 31 ff.

eral reasons why this may not be the case:

1. Much of the economization of transactions balances which can take place under present systems of cash management and funds transfer may already have been effected. It is true that very sophisticated methods of cash control can probably cut these a good bit further, but the very large reductions could have been made —and probably have been made—by a clever corporate treasurer armed with paper and pencil.

2. While a nationwide funds transfer system will probably reduce transactions balances still further, it will be a number of years before such a system is in existence.

3. While even very small firms can be plugged into a nationwide funds transfer system, this does not mean that they can afford an elaborate system for investing excess funds. Below a certain size, such investments are currently impracticable— i.e., it could not pay to lend $10,000 in the dealer loan market. As a result, smaller firms will probably always hold some demand money for transactional purposes, even under the most elaborate of nationwide electronic cash transfer systems, unless some way of making day-to-day investments of relatively small sums of money can be devised.

4. There is ample evidence that as the corporate treasurers move toward cash economization, they also move toward a reduction of the number of banks in which they maintain deposits—toward a concentration of their remaining deposits in larger banks.

5. For some smaller businesses, an instantaneous funds transfer might actually increase the level of demand deposits held, since the drawer of the check could not count on his check not being deposited for several days. It is well known that numerous firms do, in fact, engage in such legal "kiting"—using mail and bank float to support current transactions.

6. As noted, there will probably be major pressure put on larger banks for sources of funds. If banks were in a position to pay a reasonable amount for such transactions balances, many businesses might find it more economical to take three percent from the banks, build up their bank relationships, and to dispense with an elaborate system to invest excess funds at five to six percent. And banks may find it better to push for such a system, rather than cut their own throats by offering competitive systems to businesses for investing excess demand balances in the money market.

In any case, however, some room for economization of demand balances by business must still remain. Latest Securities and Exchange figures, for example, show that corporate businesses decreased their holdings of net demand deposits by $1.7 billion during 1967. Thus, if the whole case for demand deposits rested on transactions balances of corporations, the best that could be expected would probably be a pattern of fairly steady decline, to a quite low level.[9] Fortunately, however, there are not only other holders, but also other reasons businesses want to or must hold demand balances.

Compensatory Balances

These come in two forms. The first are balances held against outstanding loans, lines, and commitments. Clearly, if we assume the next few years are ones of steadily increasing economic activity, business demands for credit will also increase. Commercial banks have to compete with other financial institutions and with the open market in supplying business credit, and this competition has intensified in the

---

[9]The above assumes, moreover, that the system for transferring funds remain in the hands of the banks. If, on the other hand, a "Giro" system, of the form which is apparently going into operation in Great Britain where the transactions balances and transfer mechanism are government held and operated, were adopted in this country, commercial bank demand balances would obviously be very adversely affected.

last two or three years. Still, given a growing economy, a reasonably liberal monetary policy, and a tendency on the part of larger banks to favor business customers, we can expect business loans to rise at a rate approximately equal to that of the economy as a whole. Moreover, in a period of generally strong credit demands, banks should be in a position to enforce compensating balance requirements.

The second type of compensatory balances are those held to repay the banks for services rendered. The trend in recent years has been for banks to shift somewhat toward a system of fees, while offering more and more services. As long as the banks remain competitive in offering services, therefore, some growth in balances to support these services may be assumed.

A significant amount of funds are already tied up in the form of compensating balances. For example, New York City banks had $23.1 billion of business loans plus another $1.5 billion of loans to financial corporations as of July 3rd of this year. At the same time, these banks held $21.1 billion of individual, partnership, and corporation deposits. At least 20 percent of this was float. Of the remaining $16.6 billion in "good" deposits, probably at least another 20 percent was individual money, leaving about $13.3 billion in corporate "good" funds. Assuming an enforced 20 percent compensating balance on outstanding loans to business, this would tie up some $4.9 billion directly, with a considerable extra amount tied up by balance requirements on lines and commitments, on which, unfortunately, there is little or no statistical information. Adding a reasonable allowance for compensating balances for services performed, and it would seem reasonable that at least one-half or more of all business deposits at New York banks are already tied up in compensating balances, then already a sizable amount is not subject to deposit economization techniques at all.

It is thus evident that a major part of the present and future of demand deposits depends on the continuation of the practice of requiring compensatory balances. While reduction of transactions balances could for a period of years outweigh rising compensatory balances, this process would eventually have to come to an end as transactions balances approached their minimum levels. At that point, the effects of compensatory balances would drive business demand deposits steadily upward.

As yet, there has been no concerted move away from the practice of requiring a balance against credits extended, although as we've seen, there has been something of a trend toward charging a fee for services rendered rather than requiring balances. It is indeed possible to make a theoretical case that the banks would be better off if they abandoned compensating balances altogether. Because of the existence of the 17 percent reserve requirement on demand deposits, it is possible for the bank to credit a customer with only 83 percent of his actual deposits since this is all that is actually available to the bank for loan and investment purposes. Actually, both sides might be better off profitwise if the bank charged a fee or interest rate which would allow the bank and its customers to split the return from investing the 17 percent of funds that would otherwise be wasted in non-earning reserve balances at the Federal Reserve. This, of course, would leave the banks short of loanable funds, but they presumably could purchase time money if there were profitable loan opportunities. There has been, however, no move yet toward this type of thinking on the part of the larger commercial banks.

Access-to-Credit Balances

A third type of demand balances are those held by businesses to promote a favorable long-term relationship with banks, mainly to help ensure favorable loan treatment during periods of tight money. Though this is hard to document, during the recent period of corporate liquidity building, there was considerable sentiment in the banking community that the reason business built up cash was to protect against a possible credit squeeze in 1968.

How important is such behavior likely to be in the future? The use of demand balances for this purpose is controlled by the costs of other means of guaranteeing access to bank credit: commitment fees, the rate on short-term investments, the demand for credit by business in relation to the supply of credit from non-bank sources. In the environment that we are projecting, however, this incentive to not cut demand deposits to the absolute minimum should continue to exist much of the time.

Liquidity-Emergency Balances

A final type of demand balances are those held in anticipation of emergencies, or in preparation for future investments. It would seem fair to assume, however, that the existence of such investments as negotiable C/D's plus reduced conservatism of corporate treasurers has already cut these balances to a minimum.

Individual Factors

Turning now to individuals, the future demand for demand balances will be determined by these factors:

TRANSACTIONS. Like businesses, individuals hold a significant amount of demand balances for ordinary transactions purposes, an amount which should increase, other things equal, as the volume of consumer spending rises. However, the introduction—again some years off—of a fully automated system of investment funds transfer for the individual could substantially offset the effects of rising transactions. It is possible to imagine a

system whereby all consumer transfer of funds is done automatically. The consumer purchases an item, inserts some sort of identification which the computer can verify, the computer checks his balance (and possibly his right to overdraw his account as granted by his bank), and then transfers the specified amount to the seller's account. Such a system would virtually eliminate "float" in individual accounts. More importantly, it would probably enable individuals to operate with a lower ratio of cash to expenses, especially if combined with a system in which demand funds above a certain level are automatically transferred to savings accounts or bank-run mutual funds.

In addition, the effect on consumer balances of several recent innovations in banking should be considered. The first of these is the widespread use of bank credit cards. It is unquestionably true that by carrying such a card a consumer can cut down on his use of coin and currency—and probably traveler's checks. It is an open question, however, if such cards cut into demand balances to the same degree. A second innovation is the granting of personal overdraft facilities, generally in connection with a credit card. The existence of such facilities does cut into the need to hold cash, although as soon as such facilities are utilized by checks drawn against them, demand deposits are created.[10]

An offsetting innovation, however, is the check guarantee card introduced by some large banks. Such cards increase the value of demand deposits, and should thus cause consumers to substitute deposits for other financial assets. On this count, they are clearly superior to credit cards, although on a profit and loss basis they may well be inferior.

A second offsetting innovation is also gaining ground. In a world where many people are making delayed payments via some credit card mechanism it is going

---

[10]Cf. Cohen and Hammer, *op. cit.*

to be eventually necessary to reward individuals who pay bills promptly. A widespread system of discount for cash would, in turn, increase the value of demand balances.

EMERGENCY-SPECULATIVE. A further portion of funds of individuals are held in demand form to cover emergencies or as funds accumulated to make purchases of physical items or securities at advantageous prices.

The existence of savings accounts and other short-term safe but liquid investments has unquestionably already cut sharply into this need to hold money balances for both emergency and unexpected investment. So long as they remain unused, overdraft facilities of the sort mentioned above clearly act as a substitute for actual cash reserves. However, if funds for such purposes have already been transferred to earning form, this may mainly adversely affect savings balances rather than demand accounts.

DEMOGRAPHIC FACTORS. In the next few years, family formation will be high, leading to a large growth in the number of individual accounts.

MINIMUM BALANCE REQUIREMENTS. For larger banks, regular checking accounts, rather than so-called "special" accounts, make up the great majority of individual deposits. Such accounts generally require a minimum balance of $200-$300 or more. The number of these accounts will increase as consumer income and population increase. Moreover, as banks provide more and more services, such balances will probably increase, unless a total fee system is adopted.

GROWING WEALTH. There is the effect of growing wealth on the part of consumers. It is true that really wealthy individuals tend to hold a much smaller proportion of their funds in demand and savings accounts and to invest in bonds and stocks. Still, as the great majority of Americans move into middle class income levels during the next two decades, we can expect that many individuals will acquire checking accounts who now do

not have them. This may be especially evident among disadvantaged minority groups in the cores of the larger cities. Also, as income rises, individuals can afford to be more careless about their cash management. After all, cash is in one sense an expensive luxury and one which gives a pleasant feeling of security.

Lumping these factors together, it would seem reasonable that the individual holdings on demand deposits in larger banks would contiue to grow steadily and more rapidly than business deposits. This has indeed been the case on a nationwide basis in recent years, as shown by the Federal Reserve's Flow-of-Funds figures. It was one reason why the large, money market banks, which concentrated on business accounts, were losing in relative share to smaller banks.

In the future, however, three factors can be expected to increase individual demand deposits at larger banks: (1) Such banks will exert still greater efforts to attract such balances by advertising and other means; (2) Greater liberalization of branching regulations should enable larger city banks to recapture individual depositors who have moved to suburban areas; and (3) Since larger banks will have an enormous advantage in offering future automated services to consumers because of economies of scale, such banks should gather a larger percentage of consumer demand balances than in the past.

COMMERCIAL BANKS

A second major holder of demand deposits at larger commercial banks are other banks. Deposits of mutual savings banks are relatively stable and insignificant, but commercial bank deposits account for a substantial proportion of demand deposits of larger banks.

The main reasons for the holding of correspondent balances are:

1. as compensation for services performed;
2. as liquidity reserves;

3. as required reserves for non-member banks;

4. as clearing balances.

Looking to the future, compulsory membership in the Federal Reserve would eliminate reason 3. but, while this has been widely proposed, it does not appear likely at this time. The future of 4. rests on what type of funds transfer system is eventually established, but there is no reason why the final system—at least with respect to the holding of the transfer balances—should not remain in the hands of commercial banks. The existence of an instantaneous clearing system, however, as in the case of individuals, will probably cut into the level of clearing balances.

Reason 1. depends on the future of the correspondent banking system in this country, which, in turn, depends on the structure of banking. Some increase in concentration can be expected. In general, though, one could expect that the correspondent system, and also the system of foreign agencies which is so important in New York City, will continue in much its present form for the foreseeable future. As the larger banks perform more and more services for correspondents, therefore, the level of compensating balances should continue to increase.

Finally, there is the question of interbank deposits for liquidity and similar purposes. Smaller banks have traditionally held fairly large amounts in correspondent balances over the amounts necessary for other purposes because of conservative management principles. As banks grow and management becomes more sophisticated, this practice should —and probably already has—become less and less prevalent.

GOVERNMENTS AND OTHERS

Government accounts come in two forms. The first are demand balances of the Federal Government, nearly all of which are so-called "Tax and Loan" accounts. Such accounts are outside the control of the banking system, although the individual bank can gain position by competing more efficiently for such balances.

Discounting these short-term swings and looking only at long-run trends, it seems improbable that these deposits will grow significantly or be reduced. With an assumed high level of borrowing rates, the Government will have a continuing incentive to keep demand balances as low as possible. Like other areas of the economy, eventual computer-based systems will eventually improve the efficiency of its cash management, but the volume of its transactions will continue to rise. It is possible, of course, that the whole tax and loan system will be altered. There have been, for example, sporadic attacks in Congress, generally led by Congressman Wright Patman, on the system, with demands that the banks pay interest on such deposits. An examination of the cost of services performed, however, suggests that Government balances are in no way excessively profitable for the banks, so such a development does not seem probable.

For larger banks, state and local deposits are much more important than Federal deposits. Many of these accounts do represent what are probably excessive holdings of cash. In an era of high interest rates, there will be continuing pressure on state and local officials to keep their funds invested. On the other hand, there has already been significant cutting by the larger and more sophisticated units of government which deal with larger banks, and the volume of state and local spending can be confidently expected to continue to grow in coming years, increasing transactional demands.

The other types of demand balances are:

CERTIFIED AND OFFICIAL CHECKS. This is a complex item, representing certified checks, officers checks, travelers checks, overdrafts, and other items, and one which is affected by the overseas operations of the larger banks. In gross terms, this item has grown rapidly in the recent period. While much of this growth is probably float, a moderate expansion in net deposits in this form is assumed.

FOREIGN BALANCES. These come in two forms: Demand deposits of foreign commercial banks and demand deposits of foreign governments, central banks and official institutions. The factors governing such deposits are too complex to handle in limited space, since they include such factors as confidence in the dollar, international interest rate differentials, and so on. In the absence of such analysis, a moderate growth in such deposits is projected.

PROJECTIONS

Given the complex pattern of uncertain and often opposing factors outlined, it is obvious that any observations about the future of demand deposits at the larger commercial banks must be highly tentative. Still, assuming that the economy grows as expected, that no drastic changes—such as the imposition of a fixed money supply target—occur in monetary policy, that automation proceeds at its recent rather slow pace, and that banks retain the practice of demanding compensatory balances, a growth rate over the next decade of approximately two to three percent per year at these banks seems reasonable. This reflects a projected growth rate of perhaps one to two percent in business demand

deposits—mainly the offsetting influence of compensating balances—a four to five percent growth in individual deposits, and something like three percent for inter-bank and other balances.

These are obviously guesses based on an attempt to quantify the various conflicting factors outlined above, but are thought to represent orders of magnitude fairly reasonably. To be sure, this is only about two-thirds the expansion rates of the last two years, and is probably a shade less than the expected rate of growth of the money supply nationally. As a result, larger banks will not be able to improve their share of the demand deposit market as they have in the recent period. Still, were these projections to hold, experience of these banks in the demand area would be far better than in the early 1960's.

As indicated earlier, the implications of such a trend for the profits of the nation's larger banks would be far-reaching. On an out-of-pocket basis, demand deposits are far less costly than buying an equivalent amount of time funds. Moreover, demand funds tend to be less variable than time, thus reducing the amount of funds which have to be tied up in lower yielding assets for liquidity purposes. All in all, the superiority of growing by demand deposit expansion is so manifest that the management of larger banks may be well advised to investigate in a careful manner the questions outlined somewhat superficially here. If such growth seems a reasonable potential, then steps should be taken to try to ensure that this potential is realized.

26. Negotiable Certificates of Deposit*

Federal Reserve Bank of Cleveland

Negotiable certificates of deposits were perhaps the most important innovation of commercial banks in the 1960's. Their introduction "reflected an attempt . . . to overcome the deterioration of their competitive position vis-a-vis nonbank financial institutions and the steady reduction in the proportion of total deposits accounted for by large banks." Today, CDs remain a significant money market instrument. This article documents the nature of this market and factors promoting its development.

A negotiable time certificate of deposit is a receipt issued by a bank in exchange for the deposit of funds. The bank agrees to pay the amount deposited, plus interest, to the bearer of the receipt on the date specified on the certificate. Because the certificate is negotiable, it could be traded in the secondary market before maturity.

The introduction of negotiable CDs reflected an attempt by some banks to overcome the deterioration of their competitive position *vis à vis* nonbank financial institutions and the steady reduction in the proportion of total deposits accounted for by large banks. This problem was especially acute for banks located in major metropolitan areas, such as New York City and Chicago. The volume of demand deposits at New York banks, for example, remained virtually unchanged during the 1950's. Throughout the post-World War II period, corporate treasurers adapted their cash management by placing increasing amounts of cash assets into

short-term, highly liquid investments. The slow but steady rise during the 1950's in short-term market rates of interest served as an incentive for corporate treasurers to keep demand deposits at a minimum and instead to invest temporary funds at higher rates of interest. Thus, the rise in short-term market rates contributed appreciably to the relative decline in corporate demand deposits held at "money market banks."

Nevertheless, these same money market banks were called upon to provide a larger share of total bank loans in the post-World War II period. This situation reflects, in part, the increased size of the loans required by large business firms that were growing internally, as well as through mergers. Because the maximum size of a loan that a bank may make to a single customer is limited by law and is determined by the size of the bank's capital and surplus account, many businesses in need of large loans can be accommodated only at larger banks.

In addition to the absence of a secondary market for CDs, the failure of banks to issue CDs on a large scale before 1960 also reflected the common belief that funds attracted to time deposits would, in effect, reduce demand deposits, and thereby increase bank costs (in the form of interest payments) without increasing total deposits. Nevertheless, larger banks, caught in the dilemma of increasing demands for credit and little prospect for increased deposits, chose to issue CDs in the hope that they would be able to retain some of the corporate funds that otherwise

*From *Economic Review*, July, 1969. Reprinted by permission of the publisher, the Federal Reserve Bank of Cleveland.

might have been invested in money market instruments, such as Treasury bills or commercial paper.

In retrospect, it appears that the bankers' fears about funds being drained away from demand deposits were largely unfounded. Time deposits at large Chicago and New York City banks increased nearly fivefold during 1961–1968; at the same time, demand deposits remained virtually unchanged in dollar volume during this period.

DEVELOPMENT OF THE SECONDARY MARKET

In February 1961, when a leading commercial bank in New York City announced it would issue negotiable CDs on a large scale, the dollar volume of outstanding CDs amounted to considerably less than $1 billion. Shortly after negotiable CDs began to be issued in substantial amounts, a U. S. Government securities dealer decided to trade in outstanding CDs. Thus, the secondary market for CDs was instituted. At yearend 1968, outstanding CDs with denominations of $100,000 and over amounted to nearly $23 billion. The growth in the dollar volume of CDs during the 1960s clearly demonstrates the success individual banks had in attracting funds to supplement bank reserves. Moreover, CDs emerged from a relatively insignificant position—in terms of volume—in the money market to a position second only to that of Treasury bills (of which $75 billion were outstanding at yearend 1968).

CERTIFICATES OF DEPOSIT AND BANK SIZE

Nearly two-thirds of the CDs outstanding at yearend 1968 were issued by banks with total deposits of $1 billion or more.[1]

In contrast, banks with total deposits of less than $200 million accounted for only 4.8 percent of the outstanding large CDs. As mentioned earlier, large banks have an advantage in selling large denomination CDs because these banks are located in leading financial centers and have on deposit working balances of many of the major corporations that buy large CDs. Nevertheless, banks with less than $1 billion in deposits have experienced a slight increase in their share of large CDs.

On the demand side, business corporations account for the bulk of CD purchases in the primary (or when-issued) market. Based on a Federal Reserve System survey, businesses were the original buyers of 69 percent of the large CDs outstanding at yearend 1962. A more recent survey revealed that this figure had increased to 80.1 percent as of January 31, 1967.[2] State and local governments, foreign governments and central banks, and individuals accounted for the remaining CD purchases at issue.

MATURITIES AND PRIMARY RATES

In the early 1960's, it was extremely difficult to issue CDs with maturities of less than six months because of the structure of Regulation Q ceilings. For example, until mid-1963, the maximum permissible rate for CDs with maturities of three to six months was 2.5 percent; until November 1964, the maximum rate payable for maturities of less than three months was only 1 percent. Beginning in 1962, however, rates on other three- to six-month money market instruments, such as Treasury bills and commercial paper, generally rose to above the 2.5 percent ceiling on new issues of CDs. Thus, CDs with original maturities of less than six months were relatively unattractive as a short-term investment, and banks were forced to issue most CDs with longer maturities. The permissible rates payable on such

---

[1] A special survey by the Federal Reserve System of 410 member banks found that at yearend 1961 nearly 50 percent of the negotiable CDs of all denominations had been issued by banks with deposits of over $1 billion. See *Federal Reserve Bulletin*, April 1963, p. 460.

[2] *Federal Reserve Bulletin*, April 1967, p. 519.

CHART 1
Distribution of Outstanding Negotiable Certificates of Deposit
(by Federal Reserve District)

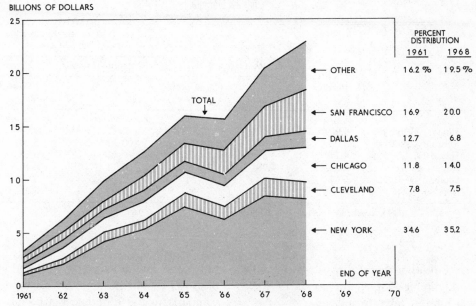

BILLIONS OF DOLLARS

	PERCENT DISTRIBUTION	
	1961	1968
← OTHER	16.2 %	19.5 %
← SAN FRANCISCO	16.9	20.0
← DALLAS	12.7	6.8
← CHICAGO	11.8	14.0
← CLEVELAND	7.8	7.5
← NEW YORK	34.6	35.2

TOTAL

END OF YEAR

NOTE: Data for 1963–1968 include outstanding certificates of deposit of $100,000 and over. Data for 1961 and 1962 include all denominations.
Last entry: 1968.
Sources of data: *Federal Reserve Bulletin* and Board of Governors of the Federal Reserve System.

---

issues were higher and more in line with yields on alternative money market instruments.*

In December 1965, Regulation Q ceilings were set at the same level (5.5 percent) for all maturities of CDs. The 5.5 percent ceiling remained in effect until April 1968 for CDs of $100,000 and over, regardless of maturity length. This ceiling enabled banks to issue shorter maturities of CDs during much of the December 1965–April 1968 period (except, of course, in the summer and fall of 1966, when most short-term market yields surpassed the 5.5 percent level). Following the 1965 changes in Regulation Q, the average maturity of outstanding CDs declined steadily in succeeding months, as more new issues were sold with maturities of three

months or less. At yearend 1968, the average maturity of outstanding CDs was about three months, compared with nearly four months in August 1964.[3]

Regulation Q, however, is not the only determinant of the average maturity of outstanding CDs. At times, banks attempt to lengthen or shorten the maturities of their CDs in accordance with their needs for funds and their evaluation of future interest rate trends. For example, if banks expect interest rates to fall in the near future, they will try to raise funds by issuing CDs with very short maturities—in the hope that they can renew the maturing issues at lower rates in the future.

---

*Editor's note: Reg. Q ceiling was eliminated in June 1970 with respect to Certificates of Deposit of $100,000 or more, maturing in 30–89 days.

[3]It has been estimated that the average maturity of large CDs outstanding before 1964 was much longer—more than 5 months in mid-1963 and 7.5 months in November 1962. See Parker B. Willis, *The Secondary Market for Negotiable Certificates of Deposit*, Board of Governors of the Federal Reserve System, 1967, p. 26.

TABLE 1

Primary Rates for Three-month Certificates of Deposit, Compared with Auction Discount Rates
for Three-month Treasury Bills, Selected Dates
(monthly average)

Month	3-month Certificates of Deposit	3-month Treasury Bills		Rate on Certificates of Deposit Less: 3-month Treasury Bill Rate	
		(Discount)	(Bond-yield equivalent)	(Discount)	(Bond-yield equivalent)
				(basis points)	(basis points)
January 1966	4.95%	4.60%	4.72%	0.35	0.23
February 1966	5.03	4.67	4.79	0.36	0.24
July 1967	4.77	4.31	4.42	0.46	0.35
August 1967	4.88	4.28	4.39	0.60	0.49
September 1968 ..	5.62	5.20	5.34	0.42	0.28
October 1968	5.83	5.33	5.48	0.50	0.35

Sources: *Weekly Bond Buyer* and *Federal Reserve Bulletin.*

On the other hand, investors in CDs would prefer long maturities if they expect interest rates to fall.

Detailed information for issuing rates on new CDs is not readily available. In general, primary CD rates are negotiated between the issuing bank and the buyer. Moreover, issuing rates may vary according to the size and reputation of the issuing bank and according to the denomination of the CD. Therefore, published rates in the primary market for CDs are usually described as approximations or guides to the actual rates. Nevertheless, the data in Table 1 confirm that when Regulation Q ceilings permit, CD rates on new issues are higher than rates on comparable issues of new Treasury bills. The actual difference or spread depends on the basis of the rates compared. As mentioned earlier, CDs are issued on a bond-yield equivalent basis, while Treasury bills are auctioned on a discount basis. Using this unlike comparison, issuing rates on three-month CDs averaged 35–60 basis points higher than rates on three-month Treasury bills during selected periods in recent years when Regulation Q did not act as a constraint on CD issuing rates. On the other hand, when Treasury

bill rates are adjusted to a bond-yield basis—as should be done for an unbiased comparison—the differences are considerably smaller, in a range of 23–49 basis points for the periods shown in Table 1.

THE SECONDARY MARKET

Although Regulation Q ceilings may, at times, eliminate certain CD maturities from the primary market, it is generally possible to obtain almost any maturity in the secondary market. As of 1968, virtually all the nonbank dealers and many of the bank dealers in U. S. Government securities bought and sold CDs and maintained inventory positions in these issues.

Trading volume, an important measure of activity in any market, is an indicator of the breadth of the CD market. During 1968, the volume of dealer transactions in CDs (purchases plus sales) averaged $59 million a day, compared with average dealer transactions of $1.9 billion a day in Treasury bills. The secondary market for CDs appears to be considerably thinner than the Treasury bill market, more so than would be indicated by the ratio of the outstanding volume of Treasury bills to that of CDs. One factor explaining

CHART 2
Dealer Activity in Negotiable Certificates of Deposit
(par value)

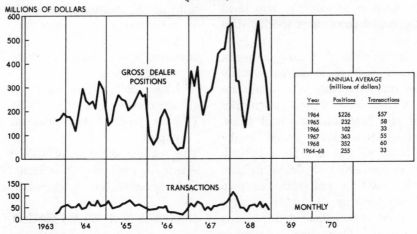

ANNUAL AVERAGE
(millions of dollars)

Year	Positions	Transactions
1964	$226	$57
1965	232	58
1966	102	33
1967	363	55
1968	352	60
1964–68	255	33

NOTE: Positions and transactions data are daily averages of monthly figures and are based on number of trading days.
Last entry: December 1968.
Source of data: Federal Reserve Bank of New York.

the thinner market might be the tendency of original corporate buyers to hold their CDs until maturity.[4]

As shown in Chart 2, dealer transactions and inventory positions in CDs varied widely in the 1963–1968 period,[5] but monthly fluctuations in the two series tended to be in the same direction. During the period under review, average daily transactions per year ranged from a low of $33 million in 1966 to a high of $60 million in 1968, while dealer positions on an average day varied from a low of $102 million in 1966 to a high of $363 million in 1967[6]

Dealers are reluctant to carry large CD inventories when interest rates are rising (prices are falling) because of the risk of capital losses on inventories that might have to be sold before maturity. Rising

interest rates explain in part the decline in both dealer positions and transactions in the summer and fall of 1966 and in the spring of 1968 (see Chart 2). The relative cost of carrying CD inventories, virtually all of which are financed through borrowed funds (short-term loans) rather than equity capital, also influences dealer positions and transactions. If the interest costs of financing inventory positions exceed the interest proceeds obtained from the inventory, dealers are likely to express their reluctance to acquire additional holdings by widening the difference between buying and selling prices; that is, by increasing the spread between bid and offered rates from the usual 4–5 basis points to 15 or more basis points.

Dealer financing to carry CD inventories can be obtained from several sources. Repurchase agreements are preferred, since ordinarily this method of financing involves the lowest costs. Most repurchase agreements are consummated with corporate investors, although insurance companies, state governments, and foreign banks also enter into such agree-

[4]See, for example, A. Gilbert Heebner, *Negotiable Certificates of Deposit: The Development of a Money Market Instrument* (New York: New York University, 1967), p. 39.

[5]Data for the period prior to 1963 are not available.

[6]In comparison, dealer positions in Treasury bills fluctuated around a daily average of $2.8 billion during 1968.

ments. The procedures are quite similar to repurchase agreements involving U. S. Government securities: dealers sell CDs, at the same time agreeing to buy them back at a stated price on a specific date in the future.

For any additional financing needs, dealers turn to bank loans that usually must be renewed daily.[7] In many instances, CDs held in dealers' inventories are used as collateral for the bank loans. As a rule, CDs originally issued by the lending bank are not used for collateral, because in the event of dealer default, the bank would be redeeming its own CDs before maturity. In addition, when a CD is used as collateral at the issuing bank, Regulation Q requires a 2-percent charge above the rate at which it was originally issued.

SECONDARY MARKET RATES

The fact that dealers stand ready to quote bid and offer rates for existing CDs suggests that there should be greater uniformity in interest rates in the secondary market than in the primary market. In the secondary market, the most common trading unit is $1 million, and dealers very rarely handle denominations of less than $500 thousand. Since most of the smaller denomination CDs are issued by smaller banks and have a greater range of interest rates, the absence of such denominations from the secondary market removes an important cause of rate variability.

The relative standing of CDs in the money market, insofar as interest returns are concerned, lies somewhere above Treasury bills and Federal Agency issues and slightly below finance company paper and bankers' acceptances. For example, a

comparison of rates (for three-month maturities on a bond-yield equivalent basis) for the 1966–1968 period reveals that CD rates in the secondary market averaged:
46 basis points above rates on Treasury bills,
26 basis points above rates on Federal Agency issues,
7 basis points below rates on bankers' acceptances, and
11 basis points below rates on finance paper.
The relative standing of CD rates was essentially the same before 1966, although yield differentials were somewhat smaller.[8]

CERTIFICATES OF DEPOSIT AND MONETARY POLICY

There is agreement that the rapid emergence of CDs and the development of the secondary market constitute highly significant innovations in commercial banking. The growth of CDs as a money market instrument has also had an important bearing on monetary policy, at times resulting in some controversy.

The role of Federal Reserve policy in the CD market stems largely from the authority of the Board of Governors to change (or not to change) the maximum interest rates payable on new issues under Regulation Q and the ability of the Federal Reserve System to influence other interest rates relative to the CD ceiling. The relationship between the Regulation Q ceiling and money market rates is very important. If the Regulation Q ceiling is below rates on other money market issues, banks may experience serious difficulties when offering new CDs or attempting to renew maturing CDs. That is, holders of maturing CDs may prefer to divert their funds into higher yielding money market instruments. In turn, when banks are faced with a loss of CD funds, they are apt to

---

[7]Nonbank dealers can often finance positions in Treasury bills and, to a lesser extent, bankers' acceptances through repurchase agreements with the Federal Reserve Open Market Account at the Federal Reserve Bank of New York. However, CDs have not been eligible for Federal Reserve repurchase agreements.

[8]For a more thorough discussion of rate spreads on money market instruments, see "Money Market Instruments: Characteristics and Interest Rate Patterns in the Current Economic Expansion," *Economic Review*, Federal Reserve Bank of Cleveland, February 1969.

restrict their lending and investing activity, or increase efforts to obtain funds from other sources.

The situation during the late summer of 1966 illustrates the effect on CD volume of Regulation Q ceilings that are out of line with rates prevailing on other money market instruments. As stated earlier and as Chart 3 shows, rates on three-month CDs in the secondary market and rates on three-month Treasury bills are closely associated. During the 1960–1968 period, the rate spread favored CDs. However, the spread between the Regulation Q ceiling and yields on other money market instruments, especially Treasury bills, is a more important indicator of the ability of banks to renew maturing CDs than is the secondary market rate. When the maximum rate on CDs of all maturities was raised to 5.5 percent on December 6, 1965, the Treasury bill rate was within 25 basis points of the Regulation Q ceiling (see Chart 3). The 1965 increase placed the ceiling rate substantially above other money market yields, thus enabling banks to compete more effectively for CD funds.

Between December 1965 and June 1966, however, money market yields advanced sharply. In the last week of June, three-month CD rates in the secondary market reached the Regulation Q ceiling and in early June exceeded that level. Thus, buyers of new CDs at ceiling rates could expect capital losses, because the price would move below par in the secondary market if the buyers sold before maturity. Banks experienced difficulties in renewing outstanding CDs, and the volume of outstandings began to decline in mid-August. At that time, the Regulation Q ceiling was about 30 basis points above the three-month bond-yield equivalent Treasury bill rate and about 15 basis points below the secondary market rate on three-month CDs. Between the week ended August 13 and the week ended December 10, the dollar volume of outstanding CDs dropped from $18.6 billion

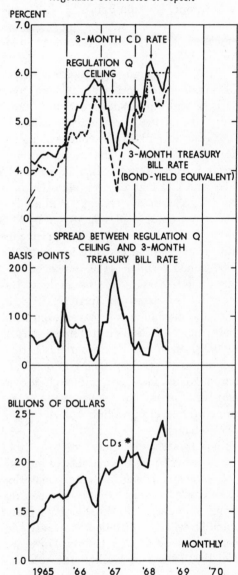

CHART 3
Interest Rate Relationships and Outstanding
Negotiable Certificates of Deposit

*Denominations of $100,000 and over.
Last entry: December 1968.
Sources of data: Salomon Brothers & Hutzler and Board of Governors of the Federal Reserve System.

to $15.4 billion. In several weeks during this period, the market rate on three-month bills exceeded the Regulation Q ceiling. Late in December 1966, the spread between the ceiling rate and the Treasury bill rate began to widen slowly, and by January, the spread was more than 50 basis points in favor of CDs. Banks then sold CDs in greater amounts; as a result, by mid-February 1967, the dollar volume of outstanding CDs approached the levels prevailing in mid-August 1966.

Banks were again faced with a loss of CD funds in the spring of 1968. In comparison with the 1966 experience, however, CD attrition was much smaller in 1968, due in part to the course of monetary policy. The decline in oustandings began in early March, when Treasury bill rates and CD market rates were close to the Regulation Q ceiling. Within five weeks, outstanding CDs decreased by $1.5 billion—a decline comparable in magnitude to that in the first five weeks of the 1966 runoff. Unlike 1966, however, the Board of Governors of the Federal Reserve System acted on April 19, 1968, to raise the maximum rate payable on most maturities of CDs with denominations of $100,000 and over. Following this action, CD drains stopped; in fact, CD outstandings actually increased, although it was mid-July before the dollar volume regained the level prevailing in early March ($21 billion).

SIGNIFICANCE OF CD LOSSES.   Other things being equal, the inability of individual commercial banks to renew maturing CDs weakens their ability to meet demands for new credit. Whether bank credit actually will be curtailed, however, depends on several other factors. For example, the decline in bank funds resulting from the CD drain can be offset by using other sources of funds (usually nondeposit sources). To the extent that banks are unsuccessful in tapping other sources, they have to sell assets or cut back lending.

For example, banks, at their own initiative, have attempted to offset CD losses by borrowing from the Eurodollar market through their overseas branches. This was, by far, the primary source used to balance CD losses in 1966 and 1968. As Table 2

TABLE 2

Liabilities of United States Banks to Their Foreign Branches and Outstanding Certificates of Deposit Selected Dates 1966 and 1968

1966	Borrowings from Foreign Branches (mil. of $)	Outstanding Certificates of Deposit (mil. of $)
July	$2,786	$18,294
August	3,134	18,194
September	3,472	16,996
October	3,671	15,738
November	3,786	15,498
Change for Period	+1,000	−2,752
1968		
February	$4,530	$21,094
March	4,930	20,196
April	5,020	19,708
May	5,888	19,543
June	6,241	19,538
Change for Period	+1,711	−1,556

NOTE: Data are as of the last Wednesday of the month.
Source: *Federal Reserve Bulletin.*

indicates, between the end of July and the end of November 1966, banks increased their liabilities to their foreign branches by $1.0 billion, thereby partially offsetting the decline of over $2.7 billion in CDs during the period. Over the period of four months from February through June 1968, the additions to United States banks' liabilities to their foreign branches amounted to more than the CD runoff for the period (see Table 2).

Bank borrowings from their foreign branches have been sporadic, increasing substantially during periods of CD attrition since 1965. Over the long run, however, banks have relied increasingly on all new sources of funds. Therefore, the increased use of Eurodollars in 1966 and 1968 should not be considered solely as a substitute for withdrawn CDs. In all likelihood, Eurodollar borrowings would have increased as part of the trend in recent years. However, in the absence of Eurodollar availability, the impact of CD drains in recent years on United States banks would probably have been more severe.

Between early December 1968 and June 1969, the outstanding volume of large CDs declined by about one-third, from $24.3 billion to about $15 billion. The implications of this recent decline for commercial banks, as well as for the financial markets, are beyond the scope of this article, because the decline has not ended. Thus, any evaluation of the effects of recent CD runoffs must be qualified. The current relationship between Regulation Q ceilings and interest rates on other money market instruments makes it extremely difficult for banks to renew maturing CDs and, needless to say, virtually impossible to attract new CDs at this writing. For example, the maximum rate now payable under Regulation Q on three-month CDs is 6 percent—a rate below that at which three-month Treasury bills were sold in most weekly auctions this year. Similarly, CD rates in the secondary market have generally been well above Regulation Q ceilings in most maturity categories (see Table 3). Thus, the price of a new CD generally falls below par immediately after issuance.

Predictably, commercial banks reacted to the recent CD drains by attempting to borrow from their foreign branches, as well as by tapping other sources of funds; for example, the sale of commercial paper

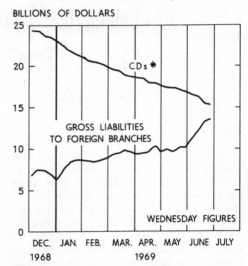

CHART 4

Outstanding Negotiable Certificates of Deposit and Eurodollar Borrowings

*Denominations of $100,000 and over.
Last entry: June 25.
Source of data: Board of Governors of the Federal Reserve System.

by bank affiliates and the sale of loan participation certificates; data on the extent of these transactions are not available. Thus far, however, Eurodollar borrowings have offset the bulk of the CD losses, as can be observed in Chart 4. Borrowings of United States banks from their foreign branches have increased by about $6 billion, from a total of $7 billion in early December to slightly more than $13 billion at the end of June.

The current CD attrition is much greater than that experienced in the summer and fall of 1966, when oustandings declined by about $2.7 billion. In evaluating the CD losses, it must be recognized that the two time periods involve several important differences associated with, among other things, the liquidity positions of corporations and banks, the Federal fiscal program, monetary policy, and relative levels of Eurodollar rates. Thus, the impact of a CD drain on credit markets is probably different today from what it was in 1966.

TABLE 3

Average Monthly "Bid" Rates* on Certificates of Deposit in the Secondary Market
January–June 1969

	Maturities			
	Three-month	Six-month	Nine-month	Twelve-month
January ..	6.65%	6.64%	6.72%	6.78%
February .	6.61	6.70	6.81	6.86
March ..	6.73	6.84	6.91	6.95
April	6.90	7.58	7.08	7.14
May	7.36	7.51	7.61	7.67
June	8.25	8.45	8.54	8.55

*Based on daily figures.
Source: Weekly Bond Buyer.

27. Commercial Bank Price Competition: The Case of "Free" Checking Accounts*

Steven J. Weiss†

Banks usually compete with one another on a non-price basis (e.g., convenient location, available services). The advent of "free" checking accounts is a notable exception to this. The following questions are examined in this study: "What sorts of banks first introduced 'free' checking? How did the phenomenon spread in space and time? Why have particular banks, or all banks in certain areas, resisted the trend? . . . What structural characteristics of retail banking markets appear to be most conducive to commercial bank price competition?"

An extraordinary new type of explicit *price competition* for a broad category of retail banking accounts has swept the New England states and many other parts of the country. Banks in many areas are actively promoting so-called "free" personal checking accounts that offer significant savings by eliminating service charges to individual checking account holders. This phenomenon, an unusual outbreak of genuine price competition, provides an excellent opportunity for an examination of competitive behavior in the retail sector of the commercial banking industry. It also offers a chance to investigate the extent to which banking market structure affects the performance of commercial banks.

Information for a detailed case study of "free" checking account competition was obtained through a complete survey of commercial banks in the six New England states, and an attempt has been made to put the regional experience into national perspective.[1] In order to illuminate certain aspects of competitive behavior, the most interesting questions posed in this study are the following: What sorts of banks first introduced "free" checking? How did the phenomenon spread in space and time? and Why have particular banks, or all banks in certain areas, resisted the trend? Underlying all these questions is a broader concern: What structural characteristics of retail banking markets appear to be most conducive to commercial bank price competition?

The first sections of this article describe the operations of "free" checking accounts in practice, the spread of "free" checking in the United States and New England in particular, and the most important factors affecting any bank's decision whether or not to adopt such a plan. Empirical data are then utilized to analyze banks' responses to price competition, in terms of their motivations and strategies in adopting (or not adopting) "free" checking ac-

*From *New England Economic Review,* September/October, 1969. Reprinted by permission of the publisher, the Federal Reserve Bank of Boston.

†Regional Economist, Research Department.

[1] A glimpse at the national picture was achieved by two informal methods, consisting of (1) examination of bank newspaper advertising in 57 cities (in 44 states and D.C.) and (2) telephone conversations with banking market specialists at other Federal Reserve Banks and other experts who generously contributed their time and valuable information.

count plans under various market conditions. The influence of general market structure characteristics is examined in a test involving the major metropolitan areas of New England. The principal results concerning the nature of retail banking markets and some still unan- swered questions about the implications of "free" checking account competition are reviewed in the concluding sections.

A brief review of the usual methods of commercial bank competition for the deposit and loan accounts of individuals reveals that the recent "free" checking account competition is indeed an extraordinary phenomenon in retail banking, where commercial banks generally compete vigorously, but not in terms of price. In this sector of the banking industry, a customer selects his bank largely on the basis of convenience. Many banks have found that they can draw a larger volume of customers by increasing the accessibility of their facilities, for example by establishing branch offices in convenient locations, by adding parking space or opening drive-in windows, or by extending banking hours. Advertising is also an important mode of competition. Through creative use of the media, some banks have achieved an attractive image, stressing their friendly or personal services, or their status as a small bank underdog—trying harder, of course.[2] Advertising campaigns are often combined with such gimmicks as baby photo contests, washing the windshields of customers' cars, or a wide variety of promotional giveaway offers to new customers, ranging from flatware to thermal blankets. Building attractive offices, adopting modern logos and offering "beautiful" checks are other items in the repertoire of appeals to retail customers.

The competitive devices described above share one important characteristic: they are all intended to attract customers by *non-price* means. Open price competition is rare in retail banking. In any given region, the prices in retail banking services (loan rates, checking account service charges, and other fees and charges) tend to settle at a "competitive" level that is relatively uniform among the banks in the area. There are exceptions, of course, but they are relatively minor in terms of total retail banking business.[3] Price competition on a wider scale is severely restrained by a plethora of state and Federal regulations designed to protect bank solvency, and also by customary industry practices[4] and a widespread distaste for "price-cutting" in banking. In this context, "free" checking plans, constituting price reduction in a significant segment of retail banking business, represent an important new competitive departure.

DESCRIPTION OF "FREE" CHECKING ACCOUNT PLANS: THE NITTY-GRITTY OF NSC

Most "free" checking accounts are not really free, for service charges are dropped entirely only if the account holder maintains a specified balance during the relevant statement period. Only in cases where the required minimum balance is *zero* are the checking accounts truly free. The general case is more appropriately described as a "No Service Charge-Minimum Balance" plan (NSC account). Bankers have contrived many variations within the general pattern of NSC account plans. The minimum balance re-

---

[2]An especially ingenious campaign to create a bank "personality" is described in an article by Frank J. Prial, "Friendly Little Bank Gives Cream Cheese with Deposit Slips," *Wall Street Journal*, June 26, 1968, p. 1.

[3]*E.g.*, Banks may offer some price advantage on certain kinds of accounts, for example by increasing effective rates on special types of savings accounts, offering bargain rates on certain types of loans, paying interest on club accounts, or cutting service charges slightly below prevailing levels.

[4]See Almarin Phillips, "Competition, Confusion and Commercial Banking," *Journal of Finance*, Vol. 19, (March 1964), pp. 32–45 for a lucid discussion of the restraints imposed by regulation and industry practices.

quired varies from the ultimate zero to $500 and higher. Some plans specify a required *average* balance rather than a minimum, and a few programs even provide an option, *i.e.* no service charges are imposed if a customer maintains a specified minimum balance *or* a given average balance during the statement period. Banks offering NSC accounts as a start-up promotional gimmick have sometimes required only a minimum *initial* deposit, after which there is no required balance level and the new customer may be guaranteed truly free checking "for life."

Variations of the basic NSC plan appear to be gaining in popularity, apparently inspired by the "total banking" concept of commercial bank marketing. For example, some banks are offering free checking accounts (with no minimum balance) to customers who maintain a $200 or $500 savings or time deposit. Other possibilities, which are not widespread at the present time, are to tie free checking plans to a combined total of the customer's demand and savings deposits or to set a minimum balance requirement in each category. A recent innovation by a leading Boston bank represents the latest step in the direction of "total banking" promotion via NSC accounts—the bank offers free checking to any individual who uses the bank's credit card to make purchases of at least $5 a month.

Banks ordinarily offer other types of checking accounts in addition to NSC plans. When NSC accounts are first introduced, existing customers may be offered an option to switch from regular or special checking accounts to NSC accounts. Other banks, usually new banks or banks that are first to introduce NSC plans in their area, automatically convert all eligible accounts (*i.e.* all accounts that satisfy the balance requirement) to the NSC plan.

If an NSC account does not satisfy the balance requirement in a given period, the customer is charged according to an ordinary service charge schedule, or a flat fee, or in some cases a combination of the two.[5] It is not unusual to find that charges for violation of the NSC balance requirement exceed the service charges that an individual would ordinarily incur under a regular or special checking account plan.

Some banks with NSC plans charge their customers for checks. The charge is usually quite low, however, approximating printer's costs of only about a penny apiece. An interesting result has appeared in Minneapolis, where most banks with NSC plans require a minimum balance of $90 and charge for checks; other banks offer plans with the minimum set at $100 but do not charge for checks.

Many banks offer free checking accounts to special categories of depositors. For example, churches, clergymen, and charitable groups have enjoyed free checking in many areas for quite some time. Similarly, many banks traditionally (and usually informally) waive service charges for personal checking customers who maintain fairly large and steady balances. The required balance in most instances of this type of long-standing free checking practice is ordinarily rather high, in most cases $1,000 or over, although several banks in Vermont and one in Rhode Island have offered NSC-type accounts with a $100 required balance for well over 10 years. It is not uncommon for small country banks to impose no service charges (or very minimal charges) on personal checking accounts; when this is true, it is often a matter of traditional practice at an institution that

---

[5]When a flat charge is imposed, it is typically in the range of $1 to $3. Under some plans the flat charge varies on a sliding scale depending on how far an account falls below the NSC minimum. Some banks impose a flat penalty charge *every time* an account's balance goes below the required level, but the usual practice is to impose only a single flat charge for each statement period when this occurs.

has never in its history adopted a "modern" schedule of service charges.[6] Another type of special case is more recent. Banks in many parts of the country are promoting NSC accounts for various classes of individual customers, e.g. retired or elderly citizens, students, servicemen, government employees, and even Girl Scouts. Such limited NSC plans, which are motivated by special factors in each case, must be distinguished from general NSC plans.

The most important features of "free" checking account plans discussed in this article are that they are new and that they are available to *all* individual demand depositors. These NSC plans offer a significant saving for cost-conscious individuals. They represent a real opportunity for aggressive banks that seize the initiative in their local areas; and they are a source of serious concern to many bankers who anticipate the spread of "free" checking in their own areas or resist the challenge of existing NSC competitors.

The attraction of NSC plans to individuals is quite clear. Consider, for example, a plan that requires a $200 minimum checking account balance. The relevant cost to the customer is the return he could obtain by investing $200 in a safe, liquid asset, which today would be about $10 annually. This represents the *maximum* opportunity cost to the customer, since he would maintain some positive balance through the year even without the attraction of an NSC account. Of course, the charges for violating balance

requirements give an incentive for maintaining a larger balance than would otherwise be the case, just as overdraft charges and complications in an ordinary checking account make it undesirable to keep too low a balance. When an NSC plan stipulates a minimum savings deposit and no minimum balance in demand deposits, the customer's maximum opportunity cost is even less. The "price" of checking accounts varies greatly from bank to bank, even within a single region.[7] Naturally, NSC plans are most attractive where the prevailing level of service charges is high. Most individual users of checking accounts can save from $10 to $40 annually by switching from ordinary accounts to NSC plans with low balance requirements.

"FREE" CHECKING: WHERE AND WHEN?[8]

"Free" checking accounts began to appear in an unlikely context: at roughly the same time many banks were *increasing* their service charges in response to rising costs and increasing awareness of the results of cost accounting studies indicating that many banks were not charging enough to cover the costs of personal checking accounts, even when earnings on deposit balances were taken into account.[9]

The first NSC plan known to the author that was clearly non-"traditional" and

---

[6]Service charge practices of many banks with *low* service charges resemble NSC plans in some respects, as the following examples illustrate: (1) monthly maintenance charge is dropped if average balance exceeds $100; (2) 10 free checks are allowed for every $100 in average balances; (3) maximum service charge per quarter is $1 if $100 balance is maintained. (4) one free check is allowed for every $10 in excess of $100 balance; (5) only service charge is a flat monthly fee scaled from 50¢ for accounts with balances over $300 or $2 for accounts with balances under $100.

[7]For a discussion of the various types of service charge arrangements and an examination of checking account costs to a "typical" customer, see Jared Hazleton, "Bank Service Charges in New England," *New England Business Review*, May 1968, pp. 2–7.

[8]This and all subsequent sections will contain no further discussion of limited free checking plans and "traditional" NSC-type practices.

[9]See, for example, the cost estimates contained in the article by Hazleton, *op. cit.* A study by F. W. Bell and N. B. Murphy concluded, however, that service charges (on regular checking accounts) of banks in the Federal Reserve System's functional cost program are closely, but inelastically, related to relevant costs, and when portfolio earnings are accounted for, the banks make a profit on regular checking operations ("Bank Service Charges and Costs," *National Banking Review*, Vol. 4, June 1967, pp. 449–457).

offered a low minimum balance ($100) was introduced by an aggressive "young" bank in suburban Boston in early 1964; in the fall of the same year, a new bank in Philadelphia introduced a similar plan that was "guaranteed for life."[10] Another "young" bank in suburban Boston introduced an NSC plan in 1963 but the minimum balance requirement was $300. Also, in early 1964, two new national banks in Fairfield County, Connecticut offered NSC plans, that initially required minimum balances of $300 and $400. Apparently predating this activity, large branch banks in California brought out NSC plans with $500 minimum balance requirements; other large branch banks in California have introduced similar programs with $300 minimums.

Two more banks in the Boston area offered $100 minimum NSC plans in 1965, and in the following year NSC accounts became available in most parts of Connecticut when the state's two largest banks introduced plans carrying $400 minimum balance requirements.

In Rhode Island and New Hampshire NSC plans with low minimum balance requirements appeared in 1967 and 1968, respectively, introduced in both cases by new banks.[11] By this time, NSC plans had appeared in many other parts of the United States, including North Carolina and the metropolitan areas of Milwaukee, Minneapolis, Chicago, St. Louis, Cleveland and Kansas City.

All of the NSC plans in effect by mid-

September 1969 in New England required a certain minimum demand deposit balance. At the same time, many variations of this basic NSC arrangement had cropped up in other parts of the country.[12] For example, plans tying free checking to savings account balances of $100 to $500 had been introduced by banks in Denver, Detroit, Cleveland, Washington, D. C. and suburban St. Louis.

There also appears to be some regional and sub-regional clustering of NSC plans by level of required balances. Table 1 illustrates this phenomenon for the New England states. The table shows that only in Connecticut does a substantial proportion of NSC banks require balances over $100. In Massachusetts, where only about one-tenth of the present NSC banks require minimum balances in excess of $100, all but one of the exceptions are located outside the Boston area. In the western states, higher minimum balances ($300 to $500) are more common, appearing for example in Utah, Idaho, Hawaii and California. Sliding scale charges for violation of the balance requirement, with a flat penalty fee varying according to how far an account falls below the NSC minimum, are common in these same areas. This sort of arrangement is almost nonexistent in New England where the NSC minimum is generally lower.

At the present time, over half the commercial banks in New England offer NSC personal checking account plans. NSC plans are most widespread in Massachusetts, where two-thirds of the banks now have NSC plans. Over half the banks in Connecticut offer NSC accounts; the corresponding proportions are approximately one-third in Vermont, Rhode Island, and New Hampshire, and one-fourth in Maine.

---

[10]The author is glad to report that both of these banks have prospered and grown rapidly in the intervening years. Another early entrant with low minimum balance was a new bank in the Virginia suburbs of Washington, D. C. This bank offered free checking with no balance requirements to customers opening an account with at least $300; the plan was limited, however, in that it was offered only during a period of opening celebration, and—apparently because the device proved successful—subsequently at several anniversary celebrations.

[11]Readers interested in details of the spread of NSC plans in New England can trace the geographic and temporal patterns by inspection of Maps 1 and 2 and Chart 1.

[12]Several variations have been introduced in New England since mid-September. A minor exception to the previous exclusive appearance of "basic" NSC plans in New England might be noted: one bank, apparently pursuing the "total banking" concept, requires a $100 minimum checking account balance *and* a $5 minimum savings account balance for free checking.

TABLE I
Distribution of Minimum Balance Requirements in New NSC Plans, by State
(New England)*

Minimum $ Balance	Connecticut	Maine	Massachusetts	Rhode Island	Vermont	New Hampshire	New England (Total)
0	1	1	1	0	1	0	4
50	0	0	2	0	0	2	3
75	0	0	5	0	0	0	5
99–100	7	6	86	5	11	21	137
200	6	2	9	0	0	0	17
300	5	0	1	0	1	0	7
400	12	0	0	0	0	0	12
Over 400	1	0	1	0	0	0	2
Total	32	9	105	5	13	23	187

*Includes only NSC banks with plans operational by mid-September 1969.
Source: Data from Federal Reserve Bank of Boston survey.

Chart I and the maps illustrate that the spread of NSC accounts in the region did not really begin to accelerate until late 1968 and early 1969.

THE BANKER'S-EYE VIEW OF FREE CHECKING

Bankers' attitudes toward "free" checking accounts are anything but uniform. Some banks have moved to NSC plans with great enthusiasm and considerable flourish. Others appear determined to resist the idea, preferring, in their view, to keep cool heads about it while all those around them are losing theirs. Regardless of his personal views, any banker would take certain factors into account when faced with the decision of whether or not to offer some type of NSC plan. Projected effects on income, costs, deposit growth, and other relevant variables will depend on particular characteristics of any given bank and the type of NSC plan it adopts as well as its strategy (timing and promotion) in introducing an NSC plan.

Loss of service charge income is an immediate and direct concern. This factor will obviously weigh most heavily on banks that derive a relatively high proportion of income from service charges, or banks that have a relatively high proportion of personal accounts (as opposed to commercial accounts) in total demand deposits. Many banks minimize service charge income loss by setting a high balance requirement, so that smaller accounts do not qualify for the NSC plan, or by maintaining other reasonably attractive checking account options and adopting procedures designed to discourage mas-

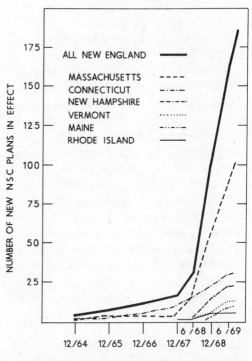

CHART I
Temporal Spread of New NSC Plans,
by State, New England*

*Most recent data are for 9/69.

MAP 1
Spread of "Free" Checking

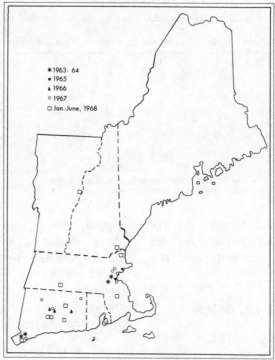

Each symbol denotes an NSC bank; time span denotes
period during which the bank adopted its NSC plan.

sive conversion of existing accounts to
an NSC basis.

Introduction of an NSC plan may entail added promotional costs or extra expenses for data processing systems or
software. However, if the bank already
has a successful advertising program and
commitments, the added costs of specific
promotion of NSC accounts may not be
very large. Similarly, a flexible computer
system already in operation should be
fairly easy to convert to handle NSC accounts. A more general concern is that
as customers become accustomed to free
checks they will write more checks than
usual, causing an attendant increase in
processing costs. One positive factor on
the cost side could partially offset these
possible negative effects, at least for NSC
plans that require a minimum checking
account balance. The minimum balance
provides a cushion against overdrafts,

which are not only irritating to customers
but also expensive for the bank to process.

Any expected loss of service charge income or increase in costs may be partly
or wholly offset by increased portfolio
earnings if a significant volume of new
deposits is drawn to the bank as a result
of an NSC attraction, or if a balance requirement induces an increase in the average level of personal checking account
balances.[13] Other positive offsets may be
realized since new customers can be expected to use the bank's facilities for
other, more profitable banking services.
Whether or not a significant increase in
new customers or deposit volume is

[13]However, a bank that as a matter of policy
informally gives free checking services to "good"
customers (*e.g.* those with balances of $1,000 or
more) may fear that such customers will draw
down their demand deposits if an NSC plan is
offered formally with a lower minimum balance
requirement.

achieved will depend largely on a bank's timing and promotional effort in bringing out an NSC plan.[14]

Other considerations may play an important role in decisions of specific banks. A bank that is heavily oriented toward wholesale banking functions may view promotion of NSC accounts as an entry wedge to help it get started in more diversified retail banking lines. If a bank does a large correspondent banking business, it may be reluctant to initiate NSC accounts for fear of antagonizing correspondents who might disapprove of such "price-cutting" competitive methods. Rival banks might attempt to win away some of its correspondent accounts by insinuating that a bank that would resort to such methods might not be an entirely suitable correspondent.

BANKS' RESPONSE TO FREE CHECKING: SOME DO, SOME DO NOT

Utilizing the survey results in combination with information from other sources, the market actions of individual banks can be viewed in the context of actual or anticipated NSC competition from direct and in some cases fairly distant competitors.[15] In terms of their actions and responses in the recent "free" checking competition, banks can be classified according to their timing of, motivation for and methods in introducing NSC accounts on the one hand, or their expressed intentions and revealed competitive positions in not doing so on the other.

1. *Early Entrants.* The New England survey revealed 55 banks that were clearly first in their service areas to offer or announce "free" checking plans. Of this number, roughly two-thirds (37) are either new banks or relatively small institutions, in either case banks on the competitive "fringe" of their respective market areas.

Promotion of NSC accounts has been a particularly popular device of new banks.[16] Thirty-two out of 38 new banks chartered in New England since 1964 have either accompanied their opening with mass advertising of NSC accounts or adopted such a program several years later. This pattern has been repeated in other parts of the country. New banks were first to offer NSC plans in the metropolitan areas of Washington, D. C., St. Louis, Philadelphia, Cleveland and Milwaukee. Brand new or relatively "young" banks comprise half of the group of New England banks that were first to offer "free" checking in their areas. Rapid deposit growth is a prime objective of these banks, and effective promotion of NSC accounts serves the dual purposes of drawing accounts of cost-conscious individuals and at the same time advertising the bank's existence. These banks clearly desire quick growth of deposits to achieve an efficient scale of operations and to build up their loan and investment portfolios. Foregoing personal service charge income is relatively minor consideration for them. Ten other banks in the group of 55 that initiated NSC plans in their respective areas are also relatively small "fringe" competitors. Deposit growth was specified as an important motivation by banks in this subgroup as well, and several respondents indicated that they initiated NSC plans in anticipation of the eventual spread of "free" checking into or near their service areas.

New and "young" banks are most likely, as a subgroup of NSC banks, to introduce NSC plans with procedures for automatic conversion of all eligible accounts. The

---

[14]A branch bank would appear to have some advantage over a unit bank in attaining a large volume response to a new NSC plan, unless the latter can draw bank-by-mail customers through advertising.

[15]The survey, covering every commercial bank in New England, made it possible to trace the spread of NSC plans in detail through the region. Banks that offer NSC accounts were asked to describe their plans and explain their reasons for introducing them. Banks that do not offer NSC accounts were asked to comment on whether they contemplate doing so.

[16]See "New Commercial Banks in Massachusetts," *New England Business Review,* September 1967, p. 5.

MAP 2
Spread of "Free" Checking

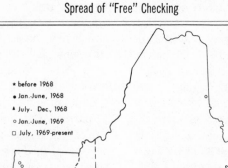

Each symbol denotes an NSC bank; time span denotes
period during which the bank adopted its NSC plan.

new and "young" bank subgroup comprises 42 percent of the 67 NSC banks
with automatic conversion provisions, as
against 26 percent of all NSC banks in
New England.

It is interesting to note that not all
banks adopted NSC plans or chose automatic conversion procedures entirely for
competitive reasons. Several banks responded that they switched all accounts
to an NSC basis in order to simplify their
checking account processing; one bank,
which is not yet on computers, noted
that its bookkeeping is now much easier.

Although only a handful of the banks
that led the way in introducing NSC
plans are large banks in absolute terms,
18 of the early entrants in New England
are large *relative* to their direct competitors, as distinct from the new banks
and "fringe" competitors discussed above.
About a third of these banks indicated

that they either sought to draw new accounts or to defend their prevailing positions against possible inroads by NSC
banks located outside their immediate
areas. Most of the other banks in this
group initiated NSC plans specifically because they wanted to be *first* in their areas
to do so and thus "get the jump on the
competition." For most of these banks,
therefore, adoption of NSC accounts was
a clearly offensive move (in general anticipation of competition), although several moved to NSC plans because they
knew that an NSC bank was about to
enter their area.

The New England survey revealed that
some of the larger early entrants got the
idea of NSC plans as a competitive device from holding company parents. Holding companies have not been especially
active in promoting NSC plans in New
England, but apparently they have done

so in Colorado, and possibly other states. A bank in New Hampshire, looking for a gimmick to attract deposits, adopted an NSC plan at the suggestion of a Boston director.

After the first round appearance of NSC accounts in a given area, the next step in NSC competition is reduction of balance requirements.[17] In Connecticut, and also apparently in California, where large branch banks led the way in many areas by introducing NSC plans with fairly high balance requirements, new or smaller banks competing with branch offices and larger banks in other cities have been able to enter the competition by undercutting prevailing balance requirements. This type of undercutting has been done primarily by new banks or by early entrants that reduced their balance requirements in order to retain their competitive advantage after other banks had followed their lead to NSC plans. Recently one of the first NSC banks in downtown Boston, which had started with a $100 minimum balance requirement in 1968, eliminated its balance requirement entirely, advertising that "Yes, Virginia, there really is a free checking account."

2. *Followers, "Quick" to "Laggard."* Two-thirds of the NSC banks in New England adopted "free" checking plans *defensively*, following the lead ("meeting the competition") of earlier entrants in their vicinity. At one extreme, some banks reacted almost immediately, responding to a competitor's NSC plan with one of their own. At the other extreme, the response of some banks lagged over a year or two. The principal factors determining a follower's reaction time are probably expectations regarding possible loss of accounts and the existence or absence of advance preparations for an NSC response. The following figures show the average and median sizes (in total deposits) of New England NSC banks classified as "quick followers" and "laggard followers" according to the speed of their response to an initial introduction of "free" checking in their areas:[18]

	Total Deposit Size (millions of dollars)		Number of Banks in Class
	Median	Average	
Quick Followers ..	14	39	52
Laggard Followers..	48	258	22

By either measure, it appears that smaller banks tended to respond more quickly to the challenge of NSC competition. Since smaller banks are largely dependent on retail accounts, they are more sensitive to any threatened loss of deposit balances.

The spread of "free" checking is impelled by several factors. Adoption of an NSC plan by a major bank in a given area appears almost certain to precipitate widespread and fairly rapid reactions. In situations where NSC plans are introduced first by small, "fringe" competitors, larger banks may be able to ignore the idea for a number of years without feeling much effect, but after a move to "free" checking by a major bank, resistance is likely to break down.[19] If a large branch bank or bank holding company adopts an NSC plan, the impact will be felt over a wide area, as the experiences of Connecticut, Vermont and Virginia demonstrate. Advertising by large banks can have quite far-ranging effects. For example, some bankers in northern New

[17]Preliminary rounds often include promotion of NSC plans for special classes of customers, as discussed above.

[18]By arbitrary definition, "quick" followers are generally those banks that responded by offering an NSC plan of their own within 3 months of an initial move by a competitor;"laggard" followers did not respond until over a year had passed. An intermediate class of followers, comprising 54 banks, has a median size of $16 mill. and an average size of $57 mill.

[19]This has been demonstrated rather dramatically in several cities of New England, notably Boston and Springfield, Mass. It will be interesting to see what happens in Chicago, where an NSC plan was recently introduced for the first time by a major bank.

England indicated that they felt the pressure of a large Boston bank's television and newspaper promotion of NSC accounts, and finally adopted a similar plan partly in response to inquiries by customers.

Quick followers are sometimes quite impressively quick. In some areas the response to an initial offering of NSC accounts has resembled a spontaneous reaction. For example, in Springfield, Mass., one of the four banks introduced "free" checking earlier this year; by the next month its three rivals were all offering competitive plans. This sort of rapid response has been quite common in New England.[20] After NSC accounts were first introduced on Cape Cod earlier this year, they swept the Cape from Buzzards Bay to Provincetown and seven out of nine commercial banks had operational NSC plans within 3 months. To paraphrase one banker's comment on a similar quick defensive reaction, "Bank A, believing that Bank B was about to introduce NSC checking, panicked and started a plan, so now we are all in it."

Banks that are less hasty to respond will typically study the local situation carefully before making a decision. Many believed (and some still hope) that NSC accounts represent only a passing phase in their areas. An early entrant will be closely watched for signs of success or failure with its NSC plan. Several banks refrained from offering NSC accounts until they noticed objective danger signs—a declining rate of new personal account openings or actual net loss of individual accounts.

Since following banks almost all introduced NSC accounts for defensive reasons—as one banker said, forced into it by "miserable competition"—it is not surprising that many did so very reluctantly.[21] Reluctant responses appear not to be

associated in any way with characteristics of the banks involved or with their reaction time. In fact, a few banks that *acted aggressively, e.g.*, were first in their area with NSC plans or undercut prevailing balance requirements, stated that they did so reluctantly; and other banks that were *"forced" into NSC competition* ultimately entered the fray with a positive approach and apparent enthusiasm. Banks in the latter category may follow a conscious mimimax strategy combining promotional efforts designed to attract new accounts with procedures intended to prevent too many existing customers from converting their accounts to the NSC plan. Under this type of strategy, the customer is presented with a choice; the virtues of alternative checking account plans are explained to him, and he must specifically authorize conversion of his account by signing a card at an office of the bank. A spokesman for a bank that adopted this sort of approach concluded that NSC checking, "if structured right, need not be the big giveaway that some tag it."

Banks that are forced into offering NSC accounts with extreme reluctance sometimes reveal their attitudes in the design of their plans and in the methods used to implement them. For example, some reluctant followers do not advertise NSC accounts at all. Their posture is purely defensive, intended only to prevent loss of existing accounts. Other banks will increase charges for ancillary services to NSC account customers. One respondent stated that by notifying potential NSC account holders that they would be charged extra for certified checks, stop orders, interim statements and other services, his bank had been able to "discourage quite a few." Another bank provided "horrible looking" signature cards specifically designed to discourage switching from ordinary checking to NSC checking.

3. *The Holders-Out.* Even though two-thirds of the NSC banks in New England adopted "free" checking more or less be-

---

[20]Particularly in 1969. It is possible to spot examples of this phenomenon on Map 2.

[21]A spokesman for one bank, a holding company subsidiary, stated that after the organization's lead bank decided to offer "free" checking his bank "had to go."

cause they were "forced" into it by competition, a good many other banks are still holding out. Many of the recent followers were obviously in the holding-out category half a year ago. The category of banks presently holding out against "free" checking includes those whose immediate service areas have not yet been touched by NSC plans, even though they may be right on the periphery. Many of these banks are constantly watching the spread of "free" checking, and many are prepared with "emergency plans" in case another bank in their area introduces NSC accounts.[22] In such a situation, where several banks in an area are prepared to act but unwilling to make the first move, a spontaneous reaction like the ones described above would appear quite likely some time in the future.

Spokesmen for many of the banks presently holding out voiced particular concern about prospective cost increases associated with a move to NSC accounts and expected seriously adverse effects on service charge income. A good number stated that their bank would hold out unless some specific competitor, Bank X, adopted an NSC plan, even though they already have experienced customers inquiring about NSC accounts. There is sometimes a tone of resignation in the statements from banks that are presently holding out against the trend. As one respondent remarked, "Banks often follow unprofitable programs simply for competitive reasons."

4. *The Resistance.* Some banks that are presently holding out against NSC accounts indicated by their responses to the survey a firm determination to resist the trend regardless of their competitors' future actions. Other banks may be classified as members of the resistance because of their refusal to move to "free" checking despite direct competition from NSC banks.

Several respondents offered specific reasons for resisting "free" checking. One bank, for example, conceded a loss of some customers to NSC competitors but claimed that it had achieved an offsetting gain in new accounts by competing in other ways, particularly by opening on Saturday mornings. Banks with low service charges sometimes argued that many of their customers would actually pay more for checking accounts under "free" checking plans that impose penalty charges for violations of balance requirements.[23] The most persistent theme in the statements of banks in this group is the familiar serious concern about the impact of any NSC plan on net income. For example, the following statement, from a bank that has directly confronted NSC competitors for several years, represents a view typical of the hard core resistance: "Banks shouldn't give away so much free service—our service charges are the highest in town."

It is not uncommon for banks that resist formal adoption of NSC plans to give unadvertised concessions, amounting to free checking, to longstanding customers who specifically request it or to customers who ordinarily maintain large balances and are considering leaving the bank because NSC accounts are unavailable. Branch banks will occasionally give unadvertised NSC accounts to customers at specific branches where they face open NSC competition.

Several respondents indicated candidly that banks in their immediate area had been in contact and decided to try to avoid introduction of any NSC plans. A spokesman for a bank in one of these areas gave expression to the apparent collective determination of the local banks to resist "free" checking. He said that although his bank was "besieged" by requests from customers, the bank had no plans to offer NSC accounts. A similar

---

[22]At least one holding company in the region has provided its affiliated banks with NSC checking "kits" in case the day of decision arrives suddenly.

[23]One respondent maintained that most NSC account promotion is "dishonest" insofar as the charges for violating balance requirements are not usually emphasized.

situation exists in one metropolitan area where a new bank has offered NSC accounts for over a year. The large banks in the city are standing pat, even referring customers who inquire about "free" checking accounts to the new bank.

5. *The Uninvolved.* Approximately 3 out of 10 banks in New England are essentially untouched by NSC competition at the present time. These are primarily banks in remote northern sections With only one or two exceptions, respondents from these banks were fully aware of NSC plans, and many expressed strong views on the subject. Their responses to the survey generally conveyed the impression that they enjoy being isolated from the "free" checking phenomenon.[24]

INFLUENCE OF MARKET STRUCTURE CHARACTERISTICS

The theory of industrial organization suggests that a firm's market behavior and performance are determined in part by the structure of the market in which it operates. A rough test of the hypothesized structure-performance nexus was carried out to see if any relationship is apparent in data obtained on the recent "free" checking account competition. The performance characteristic considered in the test is simply whether or not NSC accounts had been introduced by local banks in a given market by mid-1968. Market areas employed in the test are Standard Metropolitan Statistical Areas (SMSA's), areas which are generally accepted as reasonable approximations of retail banking markets. Three structural variables were derived for each market area—(1) the number of commercial banks with offices in the metropolitan area; and two standard measures of

market concentration, namely (2) the three-bank concentration ratio and (3) the Herfindahl Index.[25] The concentration measures were calculated using data by banking office on IPC Demand Deposits smaller than $10,000 in amount.[26] Data on these small demand accounts are especially useful for purposes of this test because they reflect the structure of retail banking markets better than any more aggregated deposit figures such as total deposits or total demand deposits.

Any simple measure of market structure is bound to be imperfect. In the present context, it should be noted especially that even perfect structural measures would fail to reflect particular behavioral relationships that are known to characterize some banking markets, such as the possibility of collusive action (tacit or explicit) suggested in some of the above examples of banks' resistance to NSC competition.

The SMSA statistics are presented in Table 2, where the SMSA's are grouped according to whether or not local banks had introduced NSC accounts by mid-1968. Any interpretation of the results of this classification must be impressionistic at best, due to the small sample size and the omission of other variables from explicit consideration.

On the basis of conventional theory, vigorous price competition by market participants should be positively related to the number of competitors and in-

---

[24]Some banks in New Hampshire will probably be able to remain uninvolved, shielded as they are from potential competition by that state's very restrictive branching law. Banks in isolated areas of the other New England states are not guaranteed such protection.

[25]The three-bank concentration ratio is merely the sum of market shares of the three banks in the market with the largest individual shares. The Herfindahl Index, by contrast, takes into account the market shares of all banks in the market, and to some extent reflects the total number of banks and the size-distribution of their market shares. For discussion, with particular attention to banking markets, and references, see Wm. Paul Smith, "Measures of Banking Structure and Competition," *Federal Reserve Bulletin*, Vol. 51, September 1965, pp. 1212-1222.

[26]The data are for June 1968. Source: Federal Deposit Insurance Corp., Summary of Deposits. IPC stands for "individuals, partnerships and corporations."

TABLE 2
Relation of Time of NSC Account Introduction and Market Structure

SMSA's Where Local CB's Introduced NSC Accounts before Mid-1968:	No. of Local CB's Offering NSC Acc'ts by Mid-1968	Total No. of CB's with Offices in the SMSA	Concentration Measures	
			3-Bank Concentration Rates	Herfindahl Index
Boston	13	72	33	62
Hartford	5	18	83	312
Springfield	3	15	76	242
Lawrence-Haverhill . .	1	8	88	304
Brockton	1	8	74	255
Norwalk	3	8	66	177
Stamford	1	7	81	269
Meriden	2	4	100°	369°
AVERAGE (excluding Boston)		9.7	81	275
MEDIAN (excluding Boston)		8	81	269
SMSA's Where Local CB's Had Not Introduced NSC Accounts by Mid-1968:				
Providence	†	17	76	234
New Haven	—	11	81	254
Worcester	—	7	89	299
Fall River	†	6	92	334
Bridgeport	—	6	88	311
Manchester	—	5	91	295
Pittsfield	—	5	86	261
New Britain	—	5	86	361
New Bedford	—	5	99	630
New London	†	5	94	418
Fitchburg-Leominster	—	5	94	330
Portland	—	4	94	330
Lowell	—	4	93	333
Waterbury	†	4	96	426
Lewiston-Auburn	—	4	93	333
AVERAGE		6.2	90	343
MEDIAN		5	93	330

Note: CB stands for commercial bank.
°These figures do not reflect a new bank that opened in April 1968.
†Branches of banks based outside these SMSA's introduced NSC accounts before mid-1968, but no local banks followed. In New London, the two largest banks in the state, which dominate the SMSA market, offered NSC plans; in the other three SMSA's NSC accounts were offered by outside banks with only one or two (in the case of Meriden) offices in outlying towns of the SMSA, representing extremely small market shares.
Source: Data from Federal Reserve Bank of Boston survey.

versely related to the level of market concentration. Where competitive behavior, conditioned according to the hypothesis by market structure, is relatively vigorous, market performance should be "better" (in terms of satisfying the consumer). This is the basis for expecting in the present application that "free" checking accounts are most likely to be offered in retail banking markets that are served by a relatively large number of banks and that are relatively unconcentrated.[27]

[27] A recent study concluded that the price of regular checking account services is positively and significantly related to concentration in metropolitan area banking markets. See F. W. Bell and N. B. Murphy, "The Impact of Market Structure on the Price of a Commercial Bank Service," *Review of Economics and Statistics*, Vol. LI, No. 2, May 1969, pp. 210–213.

The results of the test, reported in Table 2, support the hypothesized link between structure of the retail banking market and bank performance. Although of course there are some exceptional cases, the central tendencies are clear: in the group of metropolitan areas where NSC checking was introduced early, there is generally a larger number of commercial bank competitors and the retail banking markets are relatively less concentrated.[28] The Boston SMSA, which is clearly typical in that its number of banks is far greater and its retail banking concentration is far less than in other areas of New England, was excluded from the calculation of average and median figures for the first group in order not to distort the statistics for the more typical SMSA's in the group. The striking market structure characteristics of the Boston SMSA, where there is a great number of banks (including many new, small, "fringe" competitors), by themselves lend some support to the structure-performance hypothesis. It is in the Boston area that really intense and pervasive price competition in "free" checking accounts originated.

Reviewing the metropolitan areas where NSC accounts were introduced before mid-1968, it is significant to note that in every case except Hartford new or "young" banks were the first local institutions to offer NSC plans. In all of these areas, "free" checking has become more widespread in the past year and a half. By contrast, "free" checking has spread significantly in only 7 of the 15 metropolitan areas that make up the second group. In the other eight, NSC accounts are offered even now only by small competitors in the areas, branches of banks located outside the SMSA, or not at all.

REVIEW OF SOME EARLY RESULTS

At least one conclusion can be drawn quite clearly from the early experiences of New England banks with "free" checking accounts: a lot of individuals are definitely cost-conscious when it comes to checking accounts. Many new or small banks have achieved extremely rapid growth after leading the way and introducing the first NSC plans in their areas. In several cases, early entrants have drawn accounts from miles away, even from other parts of the country by promoting their NSC accounts and convenient bank-by-mail facilities. Some documented cases from New England and elsewhere illustrate that larger, established banks can also achieve significant deposit growth by moving quickly to lead, meet, or anticipate NSC competition in their areas.

Data from the New England survey confirm the reasonable expectation that new customer response to introduction of NSC checking is sensitive to the timing of a bank's move to adopt an NSC plan. The data are summarized in Table 3, which distinguishes banks that were first to offer NSC accounts in their areas, banks that were "quick" followers, and all other banks (i.e. intermediate and "laggard" followers). The success of banks in these three groups in drawing new customers by their NSC plans is rated from "very successful" down to "no significant volume of new accounts."[29] Table

---

[28]Statistical tests on the averages (sample means) for the two groups revealed that the differences are significantly different at around the 10 percent level of significance. (Differences between the concentration ratios and number of banks *almost* pass the test at significance levels of 2 percent and 5 percent, respectively.)

[29]The ratings are based on responses to the question "Do you think that [your NSC plan] has drawn new accounts to your bank?" The distinction between ratings of "very successful" and "moderately successful" was a matter of rather arbitrary interpretation in some cases. For example, if a bank gave an enthusiastic positive response or provided impressive statistics, new customer response was assumed to be "very successful." A simple "yes" answer, unsupported by statistics, was rated "moderately successful." The wary reader may prefer to regard a consolidated "successful" category.

TABLE 3

Effect of Timing on Customer Response to NSC Plans

Character of Response	Timing of NSC Plan Introduction by Number of Banks		
	First to Offer	Quick Followers	Other
Very Successful	26	13	8
(Many new accounts)			
Moderately Successful	16	14	17
Mediocre Response	3	10	18
No Significant Volume	5	15	24
Total Number of Usable Answers ...	50	52	67

Source: Data from Federal Reserve Bank of Boston survey.

3 shows fairly consistently that earlier entrants into the NSC competition in their areas generally have enjoyed a better response from new customers.[30] A few NSC banks noted that new customer response was less than they had hoped for; others noted that conversions to NSC plans by *existing* customers was considerably less than they feared—of course, customer response is sensitive to methods of introduction and promotion as well as timing. In cases where customer response was mediocre or insignificant, many bankers recognized that they had entered the competition too late to get any real advantage, and their adoption of an NSC plan had served primarily to prevent erosion of existing accounts.

In a limited number of cases, it was possible to make one- to four-year comparisons of demand deposit growth rates for early entrants in the NSC competition against growth rates of direct competitors that did not yet offer NSC plans. Almost without exception, the growth rates of early entrants were impressively higher during the period when an effective price differential existed in the local personal checking account market. Growth *rate* comparisons are not very meaningful in

all cases, however, because the early entrants were often new banks, but it is significant that the early entrants sometimes achieved greater *absolute growth* in demand deposits than even considerably larger banks in the same areas.

NSC banks have apparently found rather consistently that individuals with NSC accounts maintain higher average balances than special checking account customers. The survey results indicate that in roughly three-fourths of the NSC banks in New England the actual average NSC account balance is *at least* two and a half times the minimum required balance;[31] data obtained from 45 banks yield an (unweighted) average balance of $557 for NSC accounts with $100 minimum balance requirements.

What about loss of service charge income and increases in costs? The evidence so far is very incomplete, but several pieces are available. Regarding loss of income from service charges, many bankers expected a greater decline than actually took place. Growth of other types of checking accounts and low rates of conversion to NSC plans by existing personal checking account holders foiled gloomy projections in some cases; and

[30]Using a chi-square test on the classification scheme, the null hypothesis (that rows and columns are independent) is rejected at a level of significance of less than 0.1 percent.

[31]This result is based on responses from 56 NSC banks that provided specific data; 21 of these banks reported NSC balances averaging over five times the required minimum.

some banks (20 percent of the survey respondents)[32] increased ancillary checking account fees or service charges on other types of checking accounts. In any case over 6 out of 10 respondents reported that total service charge income had either *increased* since adoption of NSC checking or had declined somewhat, but not significantly. Not much can be said at this point concerning costs, except that "free" checking does appear to result in increased check volume, and therefore added processing costs. The picture on the cost side may not come into clear focus for some time. At least it is true that cost effects have not been immediately disastrous in New England. A sad tale (which many have become somewhat exaggerated in the telling) recounts the short history of a pioneer NSC bank in a western state. A new bank offered guaranteed lifetime free checking to anyone opening an account during its opening celebration; the quick response from a grateful public yielded 30,000 accounts —with an aggregate dollar volume of only about $1,000,000—and the bank shortly failed.

SUMMARY OBSERVATIONS ON THE NATURE OF RETAIL BANKING MARKETS

Retail banking markets are typically characterized by the existence of few sellers, a fairly high level of concentration, and often dominance by four or fewer relatively large banks. Retail banking products are generally homogeneous, notwithstanding banks' efforts to achieve differentiation through advertising. These structural characteristics closely fit the theoretical description of an oligopolistic market; furthermore, observed competitive behavior of banks in the retail banking market fits the mold of oligopolistic competition.

Since the payment of interest on de-

mand deposits is prohibited, competition for personal checking accounts has traditionally been restricted to non-price forms. With the exception of occasional undercutting of prevailing service charge rates, price policy has generally been "quiescent." The outbreak of "free" checking account competition, constituting effective and significant price-cutting, represents a sharp break from traditional practices resembling fairly effective price leadership.[33]

The results presented in Table 2 suggest a possible relationship between broad measures of market structure and the appearance of NSC competition. As the review earlier in this article of the characteristics and motivations of initial entrants in the recent NSC competition suggests, several specific structural features appear to be conducive to open price competition in retail banking markets.

Entry of new banks was crucial to the introduction of NSC plans in many areas and to their geographic spread. Many communities in New England and other parts of the country would not have a "free" checking account option today were it not for the chartering of new banks. Relatively small firms in any oligopolistic market are the ones most likely to start "price wars." Small banks on the "fringe" of many retail banking markets have been instrumental in the spread of NSC checking plans. Real price competition seems less likely to appear in markets where existing banks are roughly of similar size

---

[32]The number of respondents was 151, a subset of NSC banks excluding new banks.

[33]In New York City, for example, where NSC competition has not yet broken out, service charge schedules of the larger banks are apt to move together whenever a significant change is made. See William Zimmerman, "Rising Costs Cited as Chase, MHT Boost Special Checking Fees," *American Banker*, Vol. CXXXIV, (February 27, 1969), p. 2. Zimmerman cites the statements of an officer of one of the major banks that introduced a recent increase in personal checking account service charges, noting that "He said that if 'past history repeats itself,' there likely will be a general increase in these rates at the other banks, and that the bank does not anticipate losing many accounts from the hike" (p. 28).

or character. Where variety exists, differences in costs, sources of income, or management objectives arise, and such differences may furnish a sound basis for one competitor to perceive an opportunity for gain by resorting to price competition and introducing NSC accounts.

Banks that adopted NSC plans early discovered that significant numbers of personal checking account customers are quite cost-conscious, and other banks observed the effects of this indirectly as they lost existing or potential customers to NSC competitors. Without this price-elasticity—anticipated at first by early entrants and observed subsequently by other banks—in the demand for personal checking accounts, there would have been no incentive for any bank to cut prices.

A key determinant of market behavior in oligopoly is the "mutually recognized interdependence" on the part of major competitors in any given market. When this condition exists, a decision-maker in the market explicitly considers the reactions of his competitors to any market action he may take. A high and pervasive level of mutually recognized interdependence translates into a situation where market participants "play the game" to mutual advantage, and if this situation goes undisturbed, unilateral price reduction is not likely to occur. In many areas, where several banks were prepared to offer "free" checking for quite some time before the first move was made, no bank wanted to precipitate the price cut if its rivals were expected to follow quickly, resulting only in every bank's loss of service charge income, and so initial introduction of NSC accounts was stalemated. In some areas it still is, and in other areas larger banks are resisting initial moves to "free" checking by small rivals.

Changes in competitive behavior may influence market performance independently of structure, as occurred, for example, in one city when new management of a large, formerly conservative, bank decided to introduce "free" checking accounts as part of a program aimed at achieving a higher growth rate.[34]

The New England "free" checking account experience demonstrates that real price competition can break out even in highly concentrated retail banking markets. It is possible, as a perceptive banker suggested, that the nature of retail banking competition may be altered somewhat as a result of the "free" checking phenomenon. The appearance and promotion of NSC plans has perhaps awakened the ordinary bank customer's sensitivity to real differences among alternative banks, and he may not be so susceptible in the future to purely non-price attractions.[35]

PONDERING THE IMPONDERABLE

The available evidence leaves several important questions unanswered. Knowledge even of the "free" checking experience of banks to date is woefully incomplete since the returns are just beginning to come in. The future is no easier to predict than usual, so this discussion must enter the realm of conjecture.

Is FREE CHECKING HERE TO STAY? The current high money rates create a permissive condition for the introduction of NSC accounts since banks are able to obtain a handsome return on any new funds available for portfolio investment. It must be noted, however, that "free" checking began prior to current tight money conditions, and competitive pressures and reactions started early. If interest rates return to lower levels, NSC plans will clearly be less desirable for

---

[34]Restating some of the above points in behavioral terms, a new bank, a small "fringe" competitor, or a larger bank with some objective or characteristic that is not shared by its rivals, may introduce "free" checking because it recognizes a *unique advantage* inherent in *independent action.*

[35]Recently, the retail banking customer's price-awareness has also been stimulated by rising interest rates on savings instruments and alternative investments as well as publicity attending the introduction of regulations under "Truth-in-Lending."

many banks that now offer them. But would retreat from "free" checking be feasible? As long as one bank in an area remains willing to offer "free" checking, any other banks in the area would risk paying a high price (in loss of accounts) by retracting an established NSC plan.[36] If most banks find themselves in a serious earnings squeeze under "free" checking at some future date, pressures for collective action might be irresistible.

WHAT "FORCES" SOME LARGE BANKS TO ADOPT "FREE" CHECKING? Currently, regulatory and monetary policies have significantly limited banks' ability to raise loanable funds, and at the same time banks face great pressures of loan demand from customers whom they do not want to lose. Having limited recourse to other sources of funds, some large banks may be willing to pay a potentially high price for deposits by adopting NSC accounts, even though under more normal conditions they would not be sensitive to the loss of some personal checking accounts to NSC competitors. Additional deposits (or existing deposits retained) may carry such a premium when established customer relationships are at stake that some sacrifice of service charge income will be justified. While this sort of consideration is surely plausible, there is also solid evidence that direct competitive pressures have independently influenced decisions by large banks to offer NSC accounts.

IS "FREE" CHECKING A LOSING PROPOSITION? Before deciding to offer NSC accounts, a prudent bank will give careful consideration to the impact any given NSC plan will have on costs and income. Sophisticated techniques are available for

projecting these effects—with due allowance for expected changes in activity and other relevant factors—and arriving at a breakeven average balance for NSC accounts. This exercise can yield rather pessimistic results on the basis of full absorption functional costing. Under different assumptions or approaches, projected results look better. Accountants will argue with economists about the relevance of marginal costs in particular instances, or in *any* application to the banking industry. Bankers may attempt to estimate positive side-effects of "free" checking accounts in terms of contributing to their bank's total business—can they be justified as a loss leader? Meanwhile, if a bank is losing accounts to an aggressive competitor, (possibly a cost-unconscious competitor) the issue may be mooted as defense of the market share assumes paramount importance.

The next concern then becomes a search for new profit opportunities.

WHO WINS? Unless "free" checking induces a significant increase in individual demand deposits, which is unlikely, individual banks will gain deposits at the expense of others. The deposit gains to a given bank that initiates "free" checking may be only short run, or the promotion may have lasting positive effects. Cost and income prospects would appear unfavorable for NSC banks and, in the aggregate, the effects would imply a negative impact on net earnings. The only unambiguous winner is the consumer, the immediate beneficiary of price competition. One New England banker, conceding that he could be forced into "free" checking even though it "would be foolish," commented on all this as follows— "Competition is a terrible thing and a great one at the same time."

---

[36]A compromise move might be to raise balance requirements, but this would also be risky for the first bank or banks to do so.

Chapter VII
CAPITAL MANAGEMENT

28. Policies for Optimum Bank Capital: Summary[*]
Roland I. Robinson and Richard A. Pettway

All firms need a minimum amount of capital to begin operations and continue in business. This reading summarizes a detailed study of bank capital by the article's authors. Examined are: the question of capital adequacy, the role of bank capital, its measurement, and guidelines for individual banks in deriving optimum capital policies.

1. During the century and a half for which United States banking statistics are available, the capital of banks has grown less rapidly than their assets and liabilities. Thus, the relative amount of bank capital has persistently declined. The logical inference is simple: if capital were only barely adequate in the past, then either it is less than adequate in the present or the relative need for capital has declined. Since instability marred the history of banking in many earlier periods, it would have been hard to have argued that past

banking capital was excessive. Therefore, the only logical grounds on which present safety can be rationally assumed is that the relative need for banking capital has declined.

2. The question of capital adequacy has recently received renewed attention because commercial banks have become more aggressive, growth-minded institutions—and they have also become less liquid.

3. The function of bank capital is that of absorbing short and intermediate term losses resulting from events that managerial foresight cannot be reasonably expected to anticipate; a margin of safety that, preferably, would allow a bank to continue operations without loss of momentum and, at least, would buy time in which a bank could re-establish its operational momentum. If proper liquidity policies are pursued so that banks are not forced to liquidate good, but illiquid, assets under pressure and at unfavorable

*From *Policies for Optimum Bank Capital,* Association of Reserve City Bankers, February 1967. Reprinted by permission of the publisher.

times, then the risks to be covered are those which cannot be anticipated by actuarial or other probability methods. Some such risks can be covered by insurance; defalcation, for example. Many of the "losses" suffered by banks can be so anticipated—most loan losses and even those associated with short-term swings in business conditions. The type of losses for which capital protection is needed are those that cannot be anticipated: expropriation of foreign property, uninsurable disasters in the area in which a bank operates, and lapses of managerial judgment.

4. A bank needs capital to cover the hazards it faces as an individual bank; banks could not be expected to have enough capital to cover national hazards such as those that would be experienced in an attack upon the nation by nuclear weapons. Nor should banks be expected to have capital to cover gross errors in official judgment such as marked the banking difficulties of the Great Depression. Banks must be prepared for recessions, but it is not necessary that they compound this need by assuming that such recessions will be aggravated by uninformed public economic policy.

5. Since capital is needed to cover the hazards that cannot be anticipated, it follows that capital adequacy cannot be measured; it cannot be reduced to a formula; the only way in which it can be approximated is by the judgment of persons with mature financial experience. The honest label for this is "subjective" judgment.

6. The test of capital adequacy for a bank is not only the judgment of bankers themselves but also the judgment of their customers with money and credit availability at stake; also the judgment of bank supervisors as the agents for the general public interest.

7. Since direct measurement of bank capital adequacy is logically impossible, only indirect evidence can be marshalled.

Such evidence as could be assembled in this study, mainly the judgments of the second group mentioned above in (6), gave no hint of bank capital inadequacy. This essentially negative finding, however, does not prove adequacy. This evidence was mainly relevant to larger banks; the capital position of small banks was not tested.

8. Although direct evidence on the point could not be marshalled, the relative need for bank capital probably has declined. Fiscal and monetary policy are better equipped to deal with economic instability, and managerial methods of dealing with risk have been improved. However, new hazards may be encountered, even if they cannot be clearly discerned. World political instability could have drastic economic effects on the United States; technological revolution is not always beneficial to every segment of the economy.

9. Although no evidence of inadequacy was detected, the decline in relative bank capital protection is likely to continue unless some most unusual and unanticipated changes in conditions should occur. Even though indirect, testing should be continued; individual banks need to review their capital position regularly by application of such tests as are relevant. The public authorities probably will have to continue to take an interest in the problem, at least with respect to smaller banks.

10. Individual banks need a capital policy which, as a minimum, should embrace the following elements:

a) A bank should not only have enough capital to cover unanticipated losses but also enough more to keep on functioning without loss of institutional momentum.

b) Since profits are, and almost certainly will continue to be, the primary source of capital additions, a bank should aim to maximize the rate of return on its capital and not its size.

c) A bank should shape its financial

policies so as to minimize its cost of capital and cost of funds. An approximate test of minimization of funds cost is whether a bank is failing to secure deposits or paying a higher price for deposits than it would have to pay with more capital.

d) A bank should balance the profits in all special operations (trust departments, foreign operations, EDP services, even bank buildings themselves) against the cost of the added equity and debt capital required for such operations. This evaluation of capital expenditures parallels good practice in non-financial business.

e) The most important part of an individual bank's capital planning is its dividend policy. The evidence seems clear and unmistakable that bank share prices are influenced by dividend pay-out. If a bank retains earnings to increase its rate of capital growth, it increases its cost of external equity capital. Except for banks in areas of exceptionally fast growth, bank stocks have been considerably less than star price performers in post-war equity markets. It is not clear that different dividend policies would have improved the performance, but a general re-examination of dividend policy seems indicated. Rather than follow a median dividend policy, an individual bank may have to go to one or the other extremes: retain a larger part of earnings with consequent damage to its stock prices; or pay out rather generous dividends with the hope that such pay-outs will be more than returned in higher share prices when external equity financing is undertaken.

f) A bank should raise new capital externally only when it is possible to improve, or at least to maintain, the rate of return on existing equity capital. Another way of stating this rule is that a bank should raise equity capital only when it can be employed at a rate of return equal to or in excess of the cost of equity capital to that bank. The same rule should be applied to debt capital. During 1964 and 1965, when most capital notes and debentures were sold, they qualified under this rule. The sale of such obligations has since slackened, suggesting that this rule is already being followed by most banks.

11. The standards developed by the public authorities for screening or evaluation of bank capital adequacy cannot be said to have produced useful results. The public interest in banking safety would be discharged better if attention were focused on quality of bank management. As suggested above in (10a), rational bank managers would want at least as much as and possibly more capital than merely that required for public safety; they would want to be sure of more than barely covering losses; they would prefer to be able to keep operational momentum. The public interest requires no more capital than indicated by this standard. Negatively, it can be said that the public authorities should not press for added bank capital unless an adequate return can be earned on it. If an adequate return can be earned from added capital, then a bank itself would have reason to add capital from external sources voluntarily.

12. Earnings have priority as a banking problem over the capital problem. The social optimum is reached when the marginal returns to capital are equalized among all companies and industries. That point has not yet been reached by commercial banking as an industry, and the attainment of it should be a major objective, not only of individual banks, but of the industry as a whole.

29. Do Bank Capital Notes Merit Investment Stature?[*]

William H. Fichthorn

A major conclusion of past research has been that bank debentures were not particularly attractive investments because of low yield relative to risk and other features. This article questions that conclusion. It is contended that commercial banks have debt service ability which the traditional measures used in financial statement analysis do not reflect.

In the May–June 1966 issue of *Financial Analysts Journal,* an article questioned the relatively low level of yields on capital notes of commercial banks in view of the risks seemingly inherent in this type of security.[1] This article stated that yields on better-known bank capital notes should not command yields approaching those of Aa-rated corporate obligations. In support of this position, reference was made to the low level of the times interest earned characteristic of bank capital notes. This ratio—which is two times or less for most banks—has traditionally been regarded as an important indicator of debt service ability for nonfinancial business corporations.[2]

The purpose of this article is to examine those quantitative factors which determine the ability of a bank to service interest and principal on its capital notes. It is contended that the cost structure of commercial banks makes the times interest earned multiple of limited significance as a measure of safety for bank capital notes. Instead, the ratio of pre-tax operating profits to gross operating income constitutes a better measure of debt service ability out of bank income. Also, the *total* funds flow of commercial banks, which includes changes in assets and liabilities, shows that commercial banks have substantial debt service ability not reflected in either times interest earned multiples or profit margin calculations.

Much of the analysis in this article is based on data for all member banks so that conclusions will necessarily be general in character. The merits of the capital notes of a specific bank can be established only after analysis of that bank; its deposit structure, the economic characteristics of its service area, its competitive posture, management quality and depth and its past record and future prospects. Even so, this article suggests approaches for analysts to take in their evaluation of bank capital notes.

THE PROBLEM EXPLAINED

Debt servicing ability of corporations has traditionally focused on earnings coverage of *all* interest expense irrespective

[*]From *Financial Analysts Journal,* July/August, 1967. Reprinted by permission of the publisher, The Financial Analysts Federation.

[1]Eugene W. Lambert, Jr., "Bank Debt Securities: The Investor's Viewpoint," *Financial Analysts Journal,* May–June 1966, pp. 93–99.

[2]The terms "times interest earned multiple" and "overall coverage multiple" refer to the ratio of income available for interest expense on *both* time deposits and capital notes. Service of principal and interest on bank capital notes is subordinated to the obligation of the bank to its depositors.

of particular lien or other protective provisions.[3] Complications arise in applying this measure to bank capital notes because interest expense on time deposits is a high proportion of total bank expenses and has priority over interest expense on capital notes. Measured by the times interest earned multiple, commercial banks would seem to demonstrate limited debt servicing ability. In the period 1956–1963, all member banks of the Federal Reserve System showed an average times interest earned multiple of 2.9 times.[4] This level is substantially below the minimum standards proposed by Graham, Dodd and Cottle for corporate debt obligations generally.[5] These coverage standards are as follows:

Type	7–to–10 Year Average	Poorest Year in Period
Industrial	7×	5×
Railroad	5×	4×
Public Utility	4×	3×

Cates has refuted the charge of low coverage multiples by pointing out that there are functional differences between interest cost of deposits and interest cost of long term obligations.[6] In his opinion, interest on deposits is a variable cost depending on the general level of interest rates and, giving allowance to "stickiness" of rates on time deposits other than certificates of deposit, asset yields and deposit

interest expense will rise and fall together. Secondly, he states that deposit interest expense is only part of total deposit cost, probably the most flexible part. Other expenses, such as branch and teller expense, cost of services offered, and a share of general overhead would logically be included along with interest expense on time deposits in arriving at coverage multiples for bank capital notes. If this is done, he concludes, the times interest earned multiple becomes meaningless.

There are reasons not previously considered for taking exception to the conclusion that bank capital notes lack investment status. Attention will now be directed to the usefulness of the pre-tax profit and total funds flow of commercial banks as a basis for appraising capacity of banks to service capital notes.

LOW COVERAGE MULTIPLES AND HIGH PROFIT MARGINS

Interest expense of commercial banks is, and always has been, a high proportion of gross operating income. But this expense has been more than offset by the relatively low proportion of other operating expenses to gross operating income.[7] The following example shows how a commercial bank typically has a higher pre-tax profit margin than a manufacturing company even though its times interest earned multiple is decidedly inferior.

The substantially greater proportion of interest expense is responsible for the 1.8 times interest earned multiple of commercial banks as contrasted to the 7.5 × multiple of the manufacturing company. But the reader will note that the hypothetical commercial bank shows a pre-tax profit: operating income ratio of 25 percent,

[3]The reasons underlying this approach are stated in Graham, Dodd and Cottle, *Security Analysis*, 4th ed., (New York: McGraw-Hill Book Company, Inc., 1962), pp. 310–315. The fallacy of the "prior deductions coverage" method is discussed in Badger, Torgerson and Guthmann, *Investment Principles and Practices*, 5th ed. (Englewood Cliffs: Prentice-Hall, Inc., 1961), pp. 199–200.

[4]At December 31, 1965, total member bank resources were 82 percent of total resources of all commercial banks. *Federal Reserve Bulletin*, June 1966, p. 1000.

[5]Graham, Dodd and Cottle, *op. cit.*, p. 348.

[6]David C. Cates, "Bank Analysis for Bond Buyers," *Bankers Monthly*, September 15, 1964, pp. 19–23.

[7]The term "gross operating income" as applied to commercial banks refers to total income received from interest earnings on loans and securities and other income such as service charges on checking accounts, trust department services, etc. It does not include gains or losses on sales of securities.

TABLE 1
Selected Measures of Earnings Protection of Interest Expense

	Percent of Pre-Tax Profits			All Member Banks	
Period	All Member Banks, Gross Operating Income°	Manufacturing Companies Sales	Electric Utilities† Operating Revenue	× Interest Earned	% All Other Oper. Exp.: Gross Oper. Income‡
1956–58 Avg.	37.1%	12.8%	26.8%	3.8×	49.1%
1959–61 Avg.	35.5	11.2	26.4	3.1	47.7
1962–65 Avg.	28.3	11.8	26.0	2.0	44.5
1965	26.0	12.4	25.0	1.8	43.6

°Before deduction of bad debt losses, security gains or losses, or provision therefore.
†Investor owned.
‡Excludes interest expense.
Source of Data: Federal Reserve Bulletin, January 1962, p. 73, and June 1966, p. 869. The data in the 1962 issue are for 180 corporations and in the 1966 issue the data are for 177 corporations. Federal Reserve Bulletin, June 1966, pp. 785–789 and pp. 892–900.

MANUFACTURING COMPANY

Sales	$100
Cost of Sales and Operating Expenses[8]	85
Profits Before Interest and Taxes	$ 15
Interest Expense, Total	2
Profits Before Income Taxes	$ 13
Times Interest Earned	7.5×
Pre-Tax Profit: Sales	13%

COMMERCIAL BANK

Operating Income	$100
Operating Expenses, excluding Interest Expense	45
Profits Before Interest and Income Tax	55
Interest Expense, Total	30
Profits Before Income Tax	$ 25
Times Interest Earned	1.8×
Pre-Tax Profit: Operating Income	25%

twice as much as the pre-tax profits: operating income ratio of 13 percent for the manufacturing company.

---

[8]The figure of 85 percent used in this example compares with the ratio of total operating expenses to sales for selected post-World War II periods of 86.7 percent to 88.5 percent compiled by Stanford Research Institute. See Sidney Cottle, "Corporate Earnings: A Record of Contrast and Change," *Financial Analysts Journal,* May–June 1966, p. 79. Note that Cottle's figures *includes* interest expense while the 85 percent in the illustration *excludes* interest expense.

Commercial banks have enjoyed very satisfactory pre-tax profit: operating income ratios relative to pre-tax profits: sales ratios of other industries in the period 1956–1965. Table 1 shows that pre-tax profit: operating income ratios of all member banks have consistently been higher than similar ratios of manufacturing companies and electric utility companies in the past ten years. This is true even though the times interest earned ratio has never been as high as four times and was only 1.8× in 1965. Table 1 also shows the ratio of expenses other than interest expense to total operating income of all member banks in the 1956–1965 pe-expenses of commercial banks are perti-riod. Two points about the other operating nent here. First, such expenses constitute a low percent of bank operating income. Second, this ratio has experienced steady improvement in the past ten years. This undoubtedly reflects improved efficiency of bank operations due to such factors as adoption of electronic data processing, better systems and methods, better cost control, and adoption of new and profitable services. Reasons for the decline in the bank figures for times interest earned and for pre-tax profit margin in the selected periods shown in Table 1 will be discussed below.

The high proportion of interest expense

to gross operating income of commercial banks is further highlighted by comparing this ratio with the interest expense ratio of electric utilities in the past few years. This comparison is shown in Table 2.

TABLE 2
Interest Expense as Per Cent of
Gross Operating Income (Revenue).
Commercial Banks Compared to
Electric Utility Companies
1956–1965

Period	Banks	Utilities
1956–58 .... 13.8%		5.5%
1959–61 .... 16.8		6.1
1962–65 .... 26.0		6.1°

°1962–64 for electric utilities.
Source: Banks—see Table 1; Electric Utilities—Federal Power Commission, "Statistics of Electric Utilities in the United States, 1964, Privately Owned," (Washington: Government Printing Office, 1966), p. xxvii.

In contrast to the 5.5–6 percent interest expense ratio for electric utilities, the commercial banks experienced an interest expense ratio which rose from 13.8 percent in 1956–58 to 26 percent in 1962–65. Since the pre-tax profit margins of both banks and utilities were approximately the same in 1965, the substantially higher interest expense ratio of commercial banks necessarily causes a lower times interest earned multiple for commercial banks.

In substance, the figures for overall times interest earned on subordinated debentures substantially understate the margins of safety for coverage of total bank

interest expense. This arises because of the unusually high proportion of interest expense to gross operating income typical of commercial bank operations. But pre-tax margins of commercial banks as a whole compare favorably with those of the electric utility industry, which has had high investment standing for many years.

FIXED EXPENSES AND MEASURES OF DEBT SERVICE ABILITY

The high proportion of fixed operating expenses, other than interest expense, provides further support for the use of the pre-tax profit margin as the more appropriate measure of debt service ability of commercial banks. Generally speaking, the variability of operating expenses relative to changes in sales volume is important in deciding whether the pre-tax profit margin or the times interest earned multiple is the more suitable measure. This point is brought out by the following example which assumes a sales decline of 20 percent.

Company A, whose operating expenses are 100 percent variable, covers its interest expense eight times after a 20 percent sales decline. Company B, however, has no earnings to cover interest expense because its operating expenses are 100 percent fixed. Thus, the relevance of the times interest earned figure depends importantly on the variability of costs for given changes in sales; the greater the proportion of operating expenses which are fixed

		Operating Expenses		
	Company A 100% Variable		Company B 100% Fixed	
	Beginning	20% Decrease	Beginning	20% Decrease
Sales	100	80	100	80
Operating Expenses	80	64	80	80
Available for Interest ...	20	16	20	0
Interest Expense	2	2	2	2
Pre-Tax Profits	18	14	18	−2
Times Interest Earned .	10X	8X	10X	
Pre-Tax Profit Margin ..	18%	17.5%	18%	−2.5%

the less relevant is the times interest earned multiple as a measure of debt service ability.

Operating expenses other than interest expense of commercial banks are not likely to decline in proportion to declines in net operating income.[9] Thus, the pre-tax profit margin and the likely stability of gross operating income becomes the crucial determinants of the ability of commercial banks to service debt out of income. Table 1 shows that this margin for all member banks was 26 percent in 1965. This implies that bank operating income could decline 26 percent with out *any* decline in any operating expenses and all such expenses, including interest expense, could have been covered. In the light of the consistent upward trend in gross operating income of all member banks since World War II, the possibility of a 26 percent decline in gross operating income for banks in general is remote.[10]

TAX-EXEMPT SECURITIES AND PRE-TAX PROFIT MARGINS

The shift in commercial bank investment portfolios from taxable to tax-exempt obligations (obligations of state and local governments and subdivisions) in recent years and the increase in interest expense applicable to time deposits has lowered observed pre-tax profit margins and times interest earned multiples of commercial banks. To the extent that these observed declines have been caused by portfolio shift, the impression is misleading.

Since 1961 banks have increased the proportion of tax-exempt obligations in

their investment portfolios from 24.5 percent at December 31, 1961 to 40.5 percent at December 31, 1965.[11] This increased reliance on state and local government obligations, occurred in response to the increase in the interest rate ceiling on time deposits beginning in that year, has reduced pre-tax profit margins in the years 1962–1965 below levels of preceding years.

The shift to state and local government obligations was favorable for after-tax income of commercial banks because after-tax yields on these obligations were approximately 80 percent of pre-tax yields on U. S. government obligations of comparable maturity. But substitution of tax-exempt obligations for an equal amount of governments automatically *reduces* reported gross operating income of a bank since lower after-tax interest income is substituted for higher after-tax interest income.

These developments are summarized in Table 1 preceding and Table 3 following. Table 1 shows that the times interest earned multiple and pre-tax profit margin of all member banks declined throughout the 10-year period 1956–65. This decline was not due to poorer control of operating expenses other than interest expense; on the contrary, the ratio of these expenses to reported gross operating income decreased. Instead, Table 3 shows that the increase in the percentage of time deposits and the increase in interest rate paid on time deposits was accompanied by a corresponding increase in the percentage which state and local government obligations bore to total resources of all member banks. These developments put downward pressure on pre-tax profit margin.

For each of 43 commercial banks having capital notes outstanding throughout 1965, two sets of pre-tax profit margins were computed for that year. The first set was computed using reported figures for

---

[9]Roland I. Robinson, *The Management of Bank Funds*, 2nd ed. (New York: McGraw-Hill Book Company, Inc., 1962), p. 422. See also Howard D. Crosse, *Management Policies for Commercial Banks*, (Englewood Cliffs: Prentice-Hall, Inc., 1962), p. 71.

[10]Graham, Dodd and Cottle use the pre-tax profit margin as a quantitative measure of protection for interest expense on railroad obligations. Their suggested minimum average is 12 percent. Graham, Dodd and Cottle, *op. cit.*, p. 365.

[11]*Federal Reserve Bulletin*, June 1966, p. 850 and p. 892.

TABLE 3
Selected Data on Time Deposits
and State and Local Government Obligations
(all member banks, 1961–1965)

Date	Time Deposits: Total Deposits	Interest Expense: Time Deposits	State & Local Govt. Oblig.: Total Resources
12/31/61 .... 33.2		2.73	7.8
12/31/65 ..... 42.8		3.73	10.9

Source: Federal Reserve Bulletin, July 1962, p. 858
and June 1966, p. 850 and 897.

both gross operating income and net operating income before taxes. The second set was computed by adding an estimate of the tax savings due to the bank's investment in tax-exempt obligations to the reported figures of each bank for gross and pre-tax net operating income. The method of computing the estimated tax saving is described in Appendix A and the resulting margin computations for each bank is shown in Table 6 accompanying Appendix A. Summary statistics of this study are shown in Table 4.

Adjusting the gross operating income of each bank to reflect estimated income tax savings on tax-exempt obligations raises the median profit margin of the

TABLE 4
Pre-tax Operating Profit Margins
43 Commercial Banks Having Capital
Notes Outstanding Throughout 1965*

	Based on Reported Income	Based on Adjusted Income
Median	18.3	24.3
Q_1 (First Quartile)	15.5	20.0
Q_3 (Third Quartile)	25.3	29.1
$Q_3 - Q_1$ (Range of middle 50%)	9.8	9.1
X (Arithmetic mean)	20.6	25.0
O_x (Standard Deviation)	7.0	7.3

Based on reported gross operating income and on gross operating income adjusted for tax savings on tax-exempt securities.
*Source: Appendix A and Table 6.

43 banks from 18.3 percent to 24.3 percent, and the arithmetic average from 20.6 percent to 25.0 percent. The measure of dispersion—the range of the middle 50 percent of the items $(Q_3 - Q_1)$ and the standard deviation (O_x)—is similar for both unadjusted and adjusted profit margins. Perhaps of even greater significance is that three-fourths of the banks in the sample had adjusted pre-tax profit margins of 20 percent or better.

The adjusted pre-tax profit margins are approximations since the adjustment procedure made arbitrary assumptions regarding the mix of U. S. government and tax-exempt obligations in the portfolio of each bank and the average return thereon. Even so, it is clear that shifting from governments to municipal obligations in recent years has contributed to the decline in reported pre-tax profit margins of commercial banks.

FUNDS FLOW AND DEBT REPAYMENT ABILITY

Analysis of the debt repayment ability of commercial banks should also consider asset structure and funds flows characteristics. Funds flow characteristics are brought out by Table 5 which shows the funds flows of all member banks in the 1962–65 period. This period has been selected because it is current and it is a period of increasing pressure on bank liquidity.[12]

Table 5 shows that commercial banks acquired most of their funds in this period from deposit increases and that they were allocated largely to loans and to "other investments." Specifically, deposit increase represented 79.3 percent and internal funds generation from operations represented only 10.3 percent of funds sources. Of funds acquired, 11.6 percent were allocated to Cash Items, 18.3 percent to Other

[12]Robinson, op. cit., p. 118 points out: "The new character of business cycle developments may mean that there is more strain on banking liquidity at the top of booms than at the bottom of depressions, as was true in earlier periods."

TABLE 5
Funds Flow Analysis
Member Banks of the Federal Reserve System
Years 1962–65
(billions of dollars)

SOURCES OF FUNDS:

Internal Fund Generation
Operating Profits	$ 9.4		
Gains, Losses and Chargeoffs on Securities Transactions	.02	9.6	10.3%

External Sources
Increases in Deposits
Time Deposits	$49.9		
Demand and Other Deposits	23.8	73.7	79.3
Increases in Other Liabilities		4.6	5.0
Other Increases in Capital Accounts		0.3	0.3
Decrease in U. S. Govt. Obligations		4.7	5.1
Total Sources		$92.9	100.0%

USES OF FUNDS:

Increases in Assets
Cash Items	$10.8	11.6
Securities, other than U.S. govt. oblig. ..	17.0	18.3
Loans and Discounts	58.4	63.0
Other Assets, Including Fixed Assets	3.0	3.2
Cash Dividends°	3.7	3.9
Total Uses	$92.9	100.0%

°Includes interest on capital notes and debentures.
Source: Federal Reserve Bulletin, June 1966, p. 892.

Securities, and 63.0 percent to Loans. Only 3.9 percent of total funds raised were allocated to cash dividends. Despite increasing loan demands on banks during this period, banks did allocate 18.3 percent of total funds to the "other securities" category; this consisted mostly of investments in state and local government obligations.

This pattern of funds sources and uses in a period of liquidity pressure provides perspective on the ability of commercial banks to repay bank capital notes out of total funds flows. Let us assume that at December 31, 1961 member banks had outstanding capital notes equal to 50 percent, or $9 billion of the $18 billion capital funds which were outstanding on that date.[13] Let us further assume that 50

percent of these hypothetical $9 billion capital notes came due in the four years 1962–65. Could this hypothetical maturity of $4.5 billion capital notes have been met out of the funds flows that actually prevailed in that period? Table 5 gives clues for answering this question.

First of all, the excess of internal funds generation over cash dividends in 1962–65 —$5.9 billion—would have narrowly covered this hypothetical debt maturity. Secondly, substantially more funds than this $4.5 billion hypothetical capital note maturity were allocated by member banks to the "other securities" category. These

[13]National banks have a legal borrowing limit equal to 100 percent of unimpaired capital

stock and 50 percent of unimpaired surplus. See 12 U.S.C., Section 82. Similar limitations exist for state-chartered banks. This limitation applies to total indebtedness of the bank, including straight or convertible debentures, but excludes borrowing from the Federal Reserve Banks or purchase of federal funds.

latter funds would have been available for repaying maturing capital notes.

Three further points on capital note maturities are worthy of mention. First, bank management will ordinarily have ample time in which to prepare for retirement of capital notes, since payments are made on specified due dates. Second, the presence of sinking fund provisions on many of these notes reduces the funds requirements in any year to easily manageable proportions. Finally, management often will have the option of refinancing maturing capital notes provided the position and prospects of the bank and the state of the capital markets permit this to be done on reasonable terms and at reasonable rates.

Repayment of maturing bank capital notes should be easier for commercial banks as the economy moves from prosperity to recession and commercial bank liquidity increases. At such time, appropriate fiscal and monetary policy will increase member bank reserves and the deposit-creating ability of member banks. In such periods individual banks may find that the amount of maturing loans exceeds the amount of loans put on the books.

In summary, the *total* funds flow picture of a commercial bank, especially in the expansion phase of the business cycle, will be an important factor in appraising ability to service principal repayments on bank capital notes. Individual banks may find their funds flow will differ from that of the commercial banking system because of special factors affecting the economy of their service areas. Nevertheless, liquidation of assets can become a prime source of funds for retiring capital notes in addition to internal funds generation represented by net profits and depreciation.

Attention, then, must be paid to the credit quality of bank assets as well as to adequate provision for day-to-day liquidity needs. Emphasis on credit quality focuses on bank loans, for banks do not expose themselves to significant credit risk

in their investment portfolios. Banks will also suffer losses if they must liquidate larger-maturing investments during periods of cyclical expansion accompanied by rising interest rates. An adequate secondary reserve position is required if banks are not to be forced into liquidating larger amounts of longer-maturing obligations in depressed bond markets.

QUALITY OF BANK LOANS

On an aggregative basis bank capital notes very likely should not be seriously exposed to risk of loss because of large-scale loan losses. A recent study of bank loan losses by the Federal Reserve Bank of Boston concluded that ". . . some deterioration in the credit worthiness of bank borrowers has occurred since the 1950's. But relative to pre-war experience bank loans are still of very good quality overall."[14] This study also pointed out that the period 1931–34 were the most serious loss years and that accumulative losses of commercial banks in that period came to $2 billion dollars. These losses compared to total bank capital of $9 billion in 1930.[15] The study concluded that the cause of bank loan losses in the 1930's was not so much actual default in repayment but rather illiquidity of too large a proportion of bank loans and investments relative to deposit withdrawals, especially withdrawals of time deposits.[16] Crosse further points out that nearly 95 percent of the losses taken by banks in the 1930's were absorbed through earnings over a ten-year period.[17]

The information above would lead one to conclude that for banks as a whole, their capital notes would have survived an experience as drastic as the 1930's. However, there is possible doubt whether notes

---

[14]Federal Reserve Bank of Boston, *New England Business Review*, "Bank Loan Losses, Past and Present," May 1966, p. 7.
[15]*Ibid.*, p. 6.
[16]*Ibid.*, p. 6.
[17]Howard D. Crosse, *op. cit.*, p. 66.

of a few banks would have been repaid on schedule had maturity dates occurred during such a period. Such delayed repayment might arise from what Crosse refers to as the primary function of bank capital, i.e.,

". . . to keep the bank open and operating so that time and earnings can absorb losses; to inspire sufficient confidence in the bank on the part of depositors and the supervisor so that it will not be faced with costly liquidation."[18]

It cannot be predicted whether commercial banks as a whole will ever experience a repetition of their experience in the 1930's. What can be stated at this time is that deposit insurance, bank examination procedures and fiscal and monetary policies have been developed to minimize the likelihood of a repetition of widespread bank failures which prevailed in the 1930's. It should be cautioned, however, that these safeguards do not guarantee liquidity and safety of the individual bank for its capital note holders and stockholders.

NET LOSSES ON SALES OF SECURITIES

Net losses on sales of securities by banks are concentrated in periods of business expansion when increasing demands for loanable funds relative to their supply forces interest rates upward and bond

---

[18]*Ibid.*, p. 158. In 1934 many banks having capital notes and preferred stock outstanding and in the hands of the Reconstruction Finance Corporation wished to retire these issues in view of their highly liquid position and to remove the stigma of unsoundness then generally associated with those banks which had these issues outstanding. Cf. David W. Cole, *Senior Securities in the Capital Structures of Commercial Banks,* (Bloomington, Indiana: Indiana University Graduate School of Business Administration, Unpublished Doctoral Dissertation, 1965), p. 7. Cole cites testimony of Mr. Leo T. Crowley, then Chairman of the Federal Deposit Insurance Corporation, before the House Banking and Currency Comittee which pointed up the problem of weakened capital position which such retirements posed even though bank liquidity was adequate after such retirement.

prices downward. These losses are realized when banks are forced to liquidate intermediate and long maturity investments at such times to provide funds for customer loans. Losses also may be taken as part of a plan to take advantage of the special income tax treatment accorded commercial banks on realized security gains and losses.

Table 5 shows net gains from sale of securities equal to $200 million in the 1962–65 period. However, combined net losses on security sales for all member banks were $24 million in 1964 and $2 million in 1965. Related to pre-tax operating earnings of $3.5–$3.6 billion, these are small indeed. (The size of security losses should be somewhat greater in 1966, as banks have accelerated sales of securities to raise funds to meet heavy demands for loans. But such losses should be well within the amount of operating profits.) Of course, individual banks may find it difficult to liquidate long-maturity securities if realized losses should significantly reduce the size of the capital accounts relative to deposits and risk assets.

SUMMARY AND CONCLUSIONS

The case for bank capital notes in general can now be summarized. Their general investment merit resides in the salient fact that commercial banking is an essential industry and is closely regulated in the public interest. Substantial and stable earning power is indicated more accurately by the pre-tax profit margin than by the times interest earned multiple because interest expense on time deposit is an unusually high proportion of gross operating income from commercial banks. Pre-tax profit margins of commercial banks compare favorably with those of electric utility companies which long have had high investor regard. Moreover, the aggregate funds flow of a commercial bank in periods of both tight and easy money should be adequate to discharge maturities of capital notes under all but the most unusual circumstances. The most serious constraint upon timely repayment of capital notes is the effect such repayment might have upon the capital position of the bank and therefore on depositor confidence.

From the point of view of the investor, the following tentative conclusions emerge:

1. A pre-tax profit margin of 20 percent or better after adjustment for estimated tax savings should normally be expected. A bank whose margin is below twenty percent should not thereby be excluded but closer scrutiny of asset liquidity and deposit stability is suggested.

2. Since funds inflows and outflows arising from changes in deposits and assets is important in appraising the ability to service capital notes, it is essential to study carefully the economy of the bank's service area. This study should consider both long-term growth and cyclical stability characteristics.

3. For the great majority of banks, realized losses on loans and securities sales should not pose serious problems for the service of capital notes. Only banks with unusually thin capital positions would seem to be vulnerable. Even here the most likely risk would seem to be delay in payment.

4. Capital notes with sinking fund provisions should ordinarily be preferred. This arises because repayment of notes in periodic installments does not usually cause precipitate declines in aggregate bank capital of the individual bank.

Analysis in this article has argued the case for bank capital notes in general. The discussion in this article has proved clearly that pre-tax profit margins shows more realistically the sizeable and stable earning power of commercial banks. This together with funds inflows from deposit increases and asset liquidations even during periods of severe liquidity pressures

should provide adequate safety for commercial bank capital notes in all but the most unusual of circumstances.

APPENDIX A

Computation of Adjusted Pre-Tax Profit Margins

The objective of this computation was to adjust upward the pre-tax profit margin of 43 commercial banks for the estimated saving in federal income taxes by investment in state and local government obligations. These banks are taken from a list of banks having capital notes outstanding at December 1, 1964.[19] Of the 78 banks listed, sufficiently detailed income account data for 1965 was shown in Moody's 1965 Manual for Banks, Insurance Companies, etc. for only the 43 banks listed in Table 6.

The problem posed for this calculation is that only one bank, Bankers Trust Company of New York, reported separately its 1965 interest income on tax-exempt obligations. All of the other banks reported only the *total* interest income on investments. Consequently, the tax saving had to be estimated for all of the other banks in this study except for Central National Bank of Cleveland. That bank reported its tax saving as a separate item. Consequently, the estimated tax saving had to be calculated by using the procedure described below.

The estimate of tax savings for each bank is based on the following assumptions:

1. An average market yield of 4.15 percent on U. S. government obligations of three-year maturity in 1965 as being a reasonable estimate of the yield on new bank commitments in these obligations.[20]

2. An average market yield of 2.75 per-

---

[19]Stanley Silverberg, "Bank Borrowing: An Analysis of Recent Experience," *The National Banking Review*, December 1964, pp. 232-233.

[20]Author's estimate based on data in Sidney Homer, "1965 Annual Review of the Bond Market," Solomon Brothers & Hutzler, January 1966, p. 11.

TABLE 6
Statistical Data on Pre-Tax Profit Margins
43 Commercial Banks—1965

	Total Resources Dec. 31, 1965 (Million $)	Reported Pre-Tax Operating Profits: Operating Income (percent)	Adjusted Pre-Tax Operating Profits: Adjusted Operating Income (percent)
Bankers Trust Co. of New York	5,176.3	32.3	35.6
Crocker Citizens Nat'l Bank	3,870.4	17.1	20.8
Wells-Fargo Bank	4,061.0	18.4	22.5
United California Bank	3,343.9	12.2	16.2
Franklin Nat'l Bank (L.I.)	1,707.9	17.0	20.2
Union Bank (Los Angeles)	1,280.9	26.2	29.1
Mercantile Trust & Co. (St. Louis)	1,102.6	33.6	38.1
Manufacturers Nat'l Bank (Detroit)	1,511.6	16.3	21.2
First Nat'l Bank of Dallas	1,452.9	29.3	31.6
Bank of California	1,346.8	13.3	17.1
Central Nat'l Bank of Cleveland	1,029.5	22.2	28.3*
Meadowbrook Nat'l Bank (L.I.)	869.1	17.2	23.0
First Nat'l Bank of Atlanta	742.7	26.2	31.2
First Union Nat'l Bk. (Charlotte, N.C.)	595.8	25.3	28.9
Valley National Bank of Phoenix	1,093.1	21.3	26.5
First Western Bank & Trust Co. (L.A.)	780.4	15.5	16.1
Bank of Hawaii	453.3	25.3	28.3
First Nat'l Bank & Trust Co. of Tulsa	490.3	39.3	41.8
First Nat'l Bank of Hawaii	387.0	14.5	17.9
First Nat'l Bank of Miami	557.5	40.7	42.3
Liberty Nat'l Bk. & Tr. Co. (Okla. City)	371.7	30.1	32.8
City Nat'l Bank (Beverly Hills)	297.3	24.4	27.4
Security Nat'l Bank of Long Island	400.7	18.9	26.7
First Nat'l Bank of San Diego	351.0	17.0	24.3
Security Trust Co. of Rochester	298.3	15.5	20.0
Peoples Trust Co. of Bergen County	354.1	15.4	23.0
Exchange Nat'l Bank of Chicago	189.3	10.8	13.6
Central Valley Nat'l Bk. (Oakland, Cal.)	182.6	22.6	26.4
Deposit Guaranty Bank & Trust Co. (Jackson, Mississippi)	338.3	15.1	34.0
First Nat'l Bank of Orlando, Florida	148.7	22.4	26.4
Central Bank & Trust Co. (Denver)	195.4	17.3	22.7
Michigan Bank, N.A. (Detroit)	436.3	15.0	15.6
Bank of Commerce (N.Y.)	159.2	18.1	23.1
Virginia Comm. Corp. (Richmond)	333.7	17.0	20.5
Trenton Trust Co. (N.J.)	127.1	17.3	19.6
First Nat'l Bank of Mansfield (Ohio)	113.2	24.4	28.3
Rockland Nat'l Bank (N.Y.)	105.0	13.8	18.1
Nat'l Bank of Jackson (Michigan)	95.0	26.1	31.3
Bank of Buffalo (N.Y.)	58.9	11.7	14.7
Tinker Nat'l Bank (East Setauket, N.Y.)	62.4	20.7	30.0
First Nat'l Bank of Niles (Michigan)	51.3	18.3	22.2

*As calculated by the bank.

Source: Stanley Silverberg, "Bank Borrowing: An Analysis of Recent Experience," The National Banking Review, December 1964, pp. 232–233.

cent on state and local government obligations of five year maturity in 1965 as being a reasonable estimate of the yield on new bank commitments in these obligations.[21]

3. A 48 percent effective tax rate on incremental bank income, so that the equivalent pretax yield on state and local obligations is 5.2 percent.

4. The distribution of the investment portfolio of the banks between governments and state and local government obligations at December 31, 1965.

The summary calculations for each bank are shown in Table 6. Computations leading to the estimated adjusted pre-tax profit margin for Bankers Trust Company of New York are given below as an example of the procedure employed (dollar figures at December 31, 1965 are in millions).

a. Income based on above assumptions:
   Governments:
   $$\$397 \times 4.15 \text{ percent} = \$16.5$$
   State & Local:
   $$512 \times 2.75 \text{ percent} = \underline{14.1}$$
   $$\$30.6$$

b. Equivalent pre-tax income of computation a.
   Governments:
   $$\$397 \times 4.15 \text{ percent} = \$16.5$$
   State & Local:
   $$512 \times 5.20 \text{ percent} = \underline{26.6}$$
   $$\$43.1$$

c. Actual 1965 security interest income of $24.8 million adjusted upward to estimated pre-tax equivalent.
   $$\$24.8 \times \frac{43.1}{30.6} = \$35.0$$

d. Estimated tax savings:
   $$\$35.0 - \$24.8 = \$10.2$$

e. Adjusted pre-tax profit margin
   $$\frac{\text{Profits}}{\text{Gross Operating Income}}$$
   $$= \frac{\$ \ 63.2 \ (\text{Actual}) + \$10.2 \ (\text{tax saving})}{\$195.5 \ (\text{Actual}) + \$10.2 \ (\text{tax saving})}$$
   $$= \$35.6 \text{ percent}$$

   The adjusted pre-tax profit margin compares with the margin of 32.3 percent based on reported figures.

This bank did report interest income on tax exempt obligations of $13.7 million in 1965. Assuming a 48 percent rate, the tax saving would be $12.5 million versus the $10.2 million estimated above and the adjusted pre-tax profit margin would then be 36.4 percent.

In succeeding calculations, the 35.6 percent figure is used as the estimate for adjusted pre-tax profit margin of commercial banks.

---

[21]Author's estimate based on data in Sidney Homer, "Factors Determining Municipal Bond Yields," Solomon Brothers & Hutzler, July 1966, p. 29.

30. The Use of Convertible Debentures in Commercial Bank Financing*

Eugene F. Brigham and Michael Kawaja

The previous article (by Fichthorn) concentrated on nonconvertible long-term debt of banks. This article analyzes aspects of convertible debt financing. It examines the factors which a bank should take into account in selecting convertibles, the indenture provisions to be considered, and guidelines the bank should follow in establishing these provisions.

In the years since former Comptroller Saxon ruled that subordinated debentures constitute a legitimate source of bank capital, this form of junior debt has become a major factor in commercial bank financing.[1] Until December 1962, when the ruling was issued, debentures had been authorized only in distress situations, and only $21 million were then outstanding. Between December 1962 and June 1966, however, there were 26 public offerings of debentures with a face value of $1,135 million, plus a substantial but unknown amount of direct placements. Eight of the public issues, with a face value of $348 million, were convertible into common stock.

Assuming that a particular bank needs

to increase capital at a faster rate than is possible through retained earnings, it has three primary choices: common or preferred stock, nonconvertible debentures, or convertible debentures. How should it choose between these alternates and, especially, what considerations should lead it to select convertibles? Further, if the decision has been made to use convertibles, what are the important indenture provisions and what rules should the banker follow when setting these provisions? Answering these and other related questions is the purpose of this discussion.

MARKET VALUE OF A CONVERTIBLE DEBENTURE[2]

Like any other marketable security, a convertible debenture's price is determined by investors in the market place, The precise nature of the investor's position can best be considered by references to the hypothetical situation traced out in Figure 1.[3]

---

*From *Bankers Magazine* Autumn, 1967. Reprinted by permission of the publisher, Warren, Gorham & Lamont Inc.

[1]Subordinated capital notes, as well as debentures, were allowed by the ruling. Throughout this paper, both types of instruments are included under the term "debentures." Although Saxon's ruling applied only to national banks, the force of competition between state and federal regulators appears to have stimulated state banking departments to grant permission to the banks under their jurisdictions to similarly use debentures.

[2]Much of the theory and available evidence on convertible debentures applied here to bank convertible debentures are developed more fully in Eugene F. Brigham, "An Analysis of Convertible Debentures: Theory and Some Empirical Evidence," *The Journal of Finance,* XXI, No. 1 (March 1966), 35-54.

[3]The bond's initial market price, M, is $1,000; this is also its par and maturity values. The bond is callable at price, V, which starts at $1,040 and declines linearly to equal par on the maturity date.

By multiplying the market price of the common stock at the time the bond is issued ($45) by the number of shares into which the bond may be converted (20 shares), the original conversion value (C) is found to be $900. Assum-

FIGURE 1
Hypothetical Model of a Convertible Bond

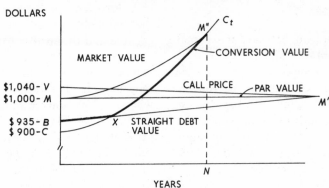

In the illustrative case, as is typically true, the coupon interest rate is below the straight-debt interest rate. This means that the convertible's value as a bond is less than it's par value; in other words, if sold as a straight debt instrument, the bond would sell at a discount. However, the discount diminishes as the bond approaches maturity—the interest component declines and the maturity value begins to dominate. The result is that the straight-debt value of the convertible rises over its life and equals the par value at maturity.

The conversion value and the straight-debt value combine to establish a lower bound for the convertible's market price. Logically, the bond could not sell for less than its value as straight-debt, and if it should fall below the conversion value arbitragers would enter the market, short the stock, and cover their short positions by buying and converting bonds. Arbitrage would continue until the market price of the bond was driven up to its conversion value. Thus, the higher of the two floors—the straight-debt value or the conversion value—dominates. The effective floor is shown by heavy line BXC_t, in Figure 1. The actual market values lies above this BXC_t floor but converges with it over time.

---

ing the common stock grows in value at a constant rate g, the conversion value of the bond will also grow at this same rate. In the example g is 4 percent and the curve CC_t shows the conversion value at each point in time. All of this is expressed by the equation

$$C_t = P_o (1 + g)^t R$$

where:

C_t = conversion value at any time t
P_o = initial price of the common stock = $45 per share
g = expected rate of growth of the stock's price = 4 percent
R = conversion rate, or number of shares received on conversion = 20 shares

In numerical terms, the initial conversion value of the bond is simply $45 x 20, or $900. One year later it is $45(1.04)(20) = $936; after two years it has risen to $973.44; and so on. Had growth turned out to be zero, the conversion value curve (CC_t) would have been a horizontal line; had growth been negative CC_t

would have declined; and had growth been uneven, CC_t would not have been a smooth curve.

In addition to its value in conversion, the bond also pays interest and has a value as an interest-bearing security. At each point in time, the straight-debt value—or the price at which the bond would sell if it did not have the conversion feature—is determined by the following equation.

$$B_t = \sum_{k=1}^{(T-t)} \frac{I}{(1+i)^k} + \frac{M^I}{(1+i)(T-t)}$$

where:

B_t = convertible bond's value as a straight debt instrument at time t
T = original term to maturity, 20 years
i = market rate of interest on equivalent risk, pure debt issues, 4½ percent
I = dollars of interest paid each year, $40 = 4 percent of par value
M^I = bond's redemption value at maturity

WHY ACTUAL MARKET VALUE EXCEEDS THE MARKET VALUE FLOOR

There is a spread between the actual market price (MM'') and the price floor (BXC$_t$) because marginal investors are willing to pay a premium for the conversion option.[4] This premium may be explained by two factors. First, since the bond may be converted into common stock if the company prospers and the stock price rises, the convertible bond commands a premium over its *value as straight debt* (that is, the right of conversion has a positive value). Second, the convertible bond commands a premium over its *conversion value* because, by holding convertibles, an investor is able to reduce his risk exposure. To illustrate, suppose someone buys our bond for $1,000. At the time, it is convertible into 20 shares of stock with a market price of $45, giving a conversion value of $900. If the stock market turns sharply down and the stock price falls to $22.50 per share, a stock investor would suffer a 50 percent loss in value. Had he had a convertible bond, its price would have fallen from $1,000 to the bond value floor (BM' in Figure 1), which is at least $935. Hence, holding the convertible entails less risk than holding common stock; this risk reduction is the reason that convertibles sell at a premium above their own conversion value.

WHY THE MARKET VALUE APPROACHES THE CONVERSION VALUE

Over a period of time, the market value of the convertible rises less rapidly than its conversion value. This means that the market value approaches the conversion value as the conversion value increases.

[4]Marginal investors, often called "the market," are defined as those investors who are just willing to hold the bond at its going price. These investors are, in fact, the ones who actually determine the level of the bond's price.

This fact is caused by three separate factors:

1. First, and probably most important, the bondholders realize that the issue is callable and that if it is called, they have the option of either surrendering for redemption or converting. If the bond is redeemed, holders receive the call price, while if they convert they receive stock at the conversion value. If the market price of the bond is above both of these values, the holder is in danger of a potential loss in wealth in the event of a call. The greater the difference between the market price of the convertible debenture and the higher of the conversion price or the call price, the greater the potential loss. As the potential loss increases, it tends to limit the amount of the premium which holders are willing to pay for convertibles. This potential loss in the event of a call prevents wide spreads between the market price and the market value floor.

2. The second factor is related to the loss protection characteristic of convertibles. Barring changes in the interest rate on the firm's straight debt securities, the potential loss on a convertible is equal to the spread between the market value and the straight debt value. Since this spread increases at high conversion values, the loss potential also increases, causing premium attributable to the loss protection to diminish.

3. The third factor has to do with the relationship between the yield on a convertible and that on the common stock for which it may be exchanged. To make this clear, our illustrative bond originally sold for $1,000 and paid $40 interest annually, so it provided an interest yield of 4 percent. The common stock originally sold for $45; if typical, it probably paid a dividend of about $2.25—about 5 percent. Over time, if the stock price is to grow at the assumed 4 percent rate, it is reasonable to expect a similar increase in the cash dividend—perhaps to $2.75 after five years. Notice what is happening.

Originally, the convertible holder could have converted into common stock and obtained an annual income of $2.25 per share times 20 shares, or $45.00. By holding the convertible, he limited his cash income to $40 but his risk exposure was also lower. Five years later, however, the cash income from the bond is still only $40, while the income from the stock into which the bond could be converted has climbed to $55 ($2.75 x 20 shares). This differential in cash income between the stock and the bond gradually lessens the attractiveness of the convertible and forces its market value down toward the conversion value level.

The combined effects of these three sets of forces—the increasing danger of a call, the bond's declining ability to protect against the risk of a falling stock market, and the erosion of the cash yield on the convertible—will eventually close the gap between the market price of the bond and its conversion value. Very high-priced convertible bonds are found to sell at almost exactly their conversion values.

Data on Convertible Bonds

To gain insight into the corporate planning that lies behind the decision to issue convertibles, as well as to determine the characteristics of convertible bonds themselves, a sample of recent convertible issues was examined. The sample consisted of all convertibles offered to the public by firms listed on a major stock exchange during the period 1961 through 1963; there were 42 such offerings, involving $820 million (a list of the offerings is shown in Table 1.) No commercial banks were included, for banks have issued convertibles only since 1964. Nevertheless, the data obtained from these industrial companies should be of interest to bankers because their convertible debentures must compete with those of other corporations.

Two types of data were obtained on the sample companies. First, quite a bit of information is available from published

TABLE 1

Statistics on the Sample of Convertible Bonds

	Number	Percent
A. Size of Issue In Millions of Dollars:		
2.5– 4.9	3	7
5.0– 9.9	16	37
10.0–19.9	11	26
20.0–29.9	5	12
30.0–39.9	4	9
40.0–60.0	4	9
B. Category:		
Industrial	37	86
Transportation	4	9
Public utility	1	2
Finance	1	2
C. Years to Maturity:		
15	5	12
20	25	58
21	1	2
22	2	5
25	7	16
30	3	7
D. S & P Quality Rating:		
A	3	7
BBB	11	26
BB	20	46
B	9	21
E. Coupon Rate		
3⅛–3½	2	5
3¾–4	4	9
4⅛–4½	17	40
4¾–5	16	37
5⅛–5½	2	5
5¾–6½	2	5
F. Rights Offering:		
Offered to stockholders	23	53
Not offered to stockholders	20	47
G. Conversion Price:		
Price stepped up	8	19
Not stepped up	35	81
H. Sinking Fund Provision:		
Yes	38	88
No	5	12
I. Issues underwritten by number of underwriters:		
1	13	
2	5	
3	2	
5	1	
9	1	

sources—prospectuses, annual reports, and investment advisory services. This material was collected and summarized. The second type of information, however—details on call policy, reasons for issuing the convertibles, the availability of trade-offs between higher conversion prices and lower interest rates, and the like—can only be obtained from the company itself. Accordingly, a detailed questionnaire was prepared and sent to the firms; a surprisingly large 52 percent responded by returning the completed form.[5]

Table 1 summarizes the published data on the 42 issues. They ranged in size from $2.5 million to $62 million, with the majority falling in the $5 to $20 million class. Commercial bank issues, by contrast, ranged between $2.4 million and $266.3 million, with six of the eight being less than $20 million. Maturities of the industrial bonds ran from 15 to 30 years, with 20 and 25 years occuring most often; seven of the eight bank convertibles had 25 year maturities, while one bond matures in 20 years.

Standard and Poor's rated the industrial bonds from A to B, with 67 percent falling below BBB, the lower limit of "investment-grade" securities. Comparable ratings were not available for bank bonds. The fact that the industrial issues were generally rated low *should not* be interpreted as meaning that the firms are basically risky; all but two of the convertible issues were subordinated—generally to all existing and future long- and short-term debt.

About one half of the industrial issues were sold through rights offerings; all eight of the commercial bank convertible debentures were offered to stockholders.[6] Nineteen percent of the industrials employed a stepped-up conversion price, and 88 percent had a sinking fund provision.[7]

---

[5]Interested readers may obtain a copy of the questionnaire on request from the authors.

[6]All national banks and many state banks are required by law to offer pre-emptive subscription rights to their common stockholders if convertible bonds are used.

[7]The typical sinking fund provision does not commence until about ten years after issue and amortizes from 50 to 80 percent of the total amount of the issue.

Of the eight bank convertible issues, none employed a stepped-up conversion price and one had a sinking fund provision. All of the bonds had essentially the same call provisions—they are callable immediately after issue with the call premium starting at the coupon interest rate and declining by ¼ percent per year to par.

Relatively high underwriter concentration was found among the 42 industrial firms; of the 42 sample issues, Lehman Brothers acted as the principle underwriter for nine issues, and Eastman Dillon, Union Securities for five. There was no comparable concentration in the underwriting of bank convertibles.

REASONS FOR USING CONVERTIBLES

A firm sells convertibles for one of two primary reasons: it either wants equity capital and believes that convertibles are an expedient way of selling common stock, or it desires debt but finds that by adding the convertible feature interest costs are reduced substantially. Of the 22 industrials replying to the questionnaire, 73 percent were primarily interested in obtaining equity, while 27 percent used convertibles to sweeten debt issues. The bonds of this latter group generally carried the lower ratings, which was to be expected.[8]

CONVERSION PRICE/INTEREST RATE TRADE-OFFS

To obtain information on the possibility of making trade-offs between coupon rates and conversion prices, the questionnaire included the following question:

At the time of issue, your common stock was selling for approximately $_____; the conversion price was $_____; and the interest rate on the bonds was _____%. What opportunities did you have for making trade-offs between conversion prices and the bond interest rate?

---

[8]The firms in the sample are large. Had the sample been extended to smaller, financially weaker companies, it is likely that a larger percentage would have indicated that convertibles were used to sweeten debt issues.

	Conversion Price	% Rate on Bond
Actual	$_____	_____%
Available*	$_____	_____%
	$_____	_____%

*Underwriter indicated that these alternatives were available.

Two observations on the answers to this question are in order. First, the responses were poor, as only 5 of the 22 responding companies were able to supply the actually offered combinations. The others answered with such statements as "no records at this time," "alternatives discussed, but not actually pinned down," and "not considered." The second observation is that in rights offerings, trade-offs were not thought to be important. As a typical spokesman for a firm selling bonds to stockholders put it: "Not applicable. Ours was a rights offering, and we simply set an interest rate and conversion price that would give the rights a sufficiently high value to ensure exercise." Actually, several combinations of interest rates and conversion prices could have been used to produce this "sufficiently high" rights value, but companies offering the bonds to stockholders were evidently less concerned than those selling directly to the public.

CONVERSION POLICY

It has been pointed out that a firm's policy with regard to forcing conversion by calling the issue is one of the vital determinants of the rate of return to bondholders. To learn something about this factor, the firms were asked about their conversion policy on the questionnaire, and the sample of bonds was examined to see when conversion actually was forced.

The question and the responses to it are shown in Table 2. Almost a quarter of the companies stated that their policy was to force conversion as soon as the conversion value exceeded the call price by about 20 percent. Another 23 percent indicated that they would encourage voluntary conversion by raising dividends.[9]

----
[9]One of these firms returned a schedule showing the way voluntary conversion occurred

The remaining 54 percent either did not plan to force conversion at all or else had no clearly defined policy.

These responses have been borne out reasonably well by actual experience. Of the 43 bonds in the sample, 20 had reached the point where the conversion value exceeded the call price by at least 20 percent. Six of these bonds, or 30 percent, had been called by March 1965.

Pros and Cons of Convertible Bonds as a Source of Bank Capital

Having analyzed the basic features of convertible issues, and particularly the is-

TABLE 2
Conversion Policies

"Which of the following most nearly reflects your company's policy with regard to conversion?"

	No.	%
1. Force conversion by calling as soon as you are "sure" the bonds will actually be converted, not redeemed. (Please indicate by how much conversion value must exceed call price.)*	5	23
2. Encourage conversion by increasing common stock dividends, thus making the yield on common higher than that on bonds.	5	23
3. Have not encouraged conversion at all, but would force conversion prior to selling a new debt issue.	2	9
4. Do not plan to force or encourage conversion at all.	7	31
5. Other. (Please explain.)†	3	14

*Most indicated about 20 percent.
†The three companies checking "other" have no established conversion policy.

in its case. In September 1964, the common dividend was raised by 25 percent. At this point bondholders would receive about 15 percent more income from dividends on conversion than in interest on the bonds. The conversion value was approximately equal to the market value and exceeded the call price by about 30 percent. Between the time of the dividend increase and the record date of the next quarterly dividend, some 50 percent of the bonds were converted voluntarily, and the company indicated that these conversions were continuing as additional bondholders recognized the income differential.

suer's choice between various combinations of conversion prices and coupon interest rates, we are in a position to consider some specific reasons why banks elect to use convertible debentures as a source of capital.

OVERCAPITALIZATION

When a bank raises new capital, it does so on the explicit assumption that deposits will experience continued growth. If the situation changes and this anticipated growth fails to occur, then the bank may find itself in an overcapitalized position and may consequently be earning a subnormal rate of return on capital. In this event, the bank should contract its capital base. If the new capital was raised by selling straight debentures, these bonds can be called and retired, thus bringing the capital structure into alignment. If common stock had been issued, however, retiring it is considerably more difficult.

Now suppose the additional capital had been raised by selling convertible debentures. If the anticipated deposit growth actually occurs, then earnings, dividends, and the price of the common stock will doubtlessly rise too. The increase in the price of the stock will cause the bonds to be converted, thus putting the bank in a position to go to the debenture market for still more capital if more is needed. On the other hand, if growth does not occur, the price of the stock is not likely to rise, the bonds are not likely to be converted, and redundant equity capital is not likely to be raised.

INTEREST RATES AND CONTROL

Convertible debentures invariably bear significantly lower coupon rates than do straight debentures. For example, on the tenth of July, 1964, the Wells Fargo Bank offered a $50 million straight bond issue and a $25.3 million convertible bond issue. Both issues had a maturity of 25 years.

The coupon rate of the straight bond issue was 4½ percent, whereas that on the convertible issue was 3¼ percent. Of course, the lower coupon rate on convertibles does not by itself mean that convertibles are "cheaper" than non-convertibles since a proper appraisal of the cost differences to the issuer of using convertibles or nonconvertibles must also take into account the potential dilution which can result from conversion. However, whatever the long-term cost differences may be, the lower interest payments of convertibles may prove advantageous to the issuing bank, particularly in tight money periods.

In small banks, particularly, working control frequently rests in the hands of a single individual or a small group of stockholders. When control is closely held, using convertible debentures in lieu of common stock may lessen the problem of maintaining this control. There are at least two reasons for this. First, conversion normally does not take place immediately but over time. Convertibles thus offer the controlling group an opportunity to meet immediate capital needs while obtaining the time to acquire firmer control before conversion takes place. Second when the affairs of the bank are going badly, control is generally far more problematic than when the bank is prospering, and conversion normally will not take place unless the bank prospers. Hence, when the affairs of the bank are going badly and the threat of loss of control is greatest, the controlling group is most sheltered from the threat of conversion.

JUDGMENT ABOUT LEVEL OF STOCK PRICES

Whether a bank should raise capital by selling common stock, convertible debentures, or nonconvertible debt should depend in large part upon management's judgment versus that of the market about the "proper level" of share prices.

For example, suppose that a particular bank has established a long run *target* debenture/equity ratio and, based on current projections, decides to raise new capital. Both debt and equity are required if the target debt/equity ratio is to be maintained, but the directors are willing to tolerate short-term deviations on both sides of the target. The necessary equity capital can be raised (1) by selling common stock; (2) by selling debt at present and refunding later with an equity issue (this will cause a temporary deviation from the target debt ratio); or (3) by the sale of convertibles which, when converted, will provide the required equity.

If convertibles are sold, they may be used in either of two ways. The firm can sell both straight and convertible debt now and, thus, have more debt than is called for by the target ratio, with the situation being rectified when conversion occurs. Alternatively, it can sell both common stock and debt to maintain the target debt ratio, but make part of the debt convertible. This issue of convertible debt will provide part of the future equity requirements when it is converted. (The converted debt must, of course, be replaced to maintain the target debt ratio.)

If the bank's management and the "market" are in agreement about the current price of the stock, there is no reason to think that any one of the choices is clearly superior to any other, although the institutional and other factors discussed below may be sufficient to create an advantage for convertibles. If management deems its stock to be undervalued—presumably because it thinks the market is overly pessimistic about the bank's growth prospects or risk, or because the market is simply undervaluing all equities at the particular time—then the best financing decision is to issue debt. Later, when the price of the stock rises, equity can be issued to return to the target debt ratio.

In this situation convertibles are a better choice than common stock, but using them is still not as good as using straight debt. That component of the convertible's return which investors expect to receive from the common stock is presumably undervalued. This means the firm must set the conversion price relatively low, or the coupon rate relatively high, to sell the bonds.

If the stock is considered to be overvalued, exactly the reverse holds true and financing should be with common stock. The required equity capital can be raised at this time by issuing a minimum number of new shares.

INSTITUTIONAL FACTORS

A number of institutional phenomena may serve to make convertibles a cheaper source of bank capital than other alternatives. Among these are the following:

1. Section 5 of the Federal Reserve Act (12 U.S.C. 287) requires a member bank to subscribe to additional Federal Reserve Bank stock when it "increases its capital stock or surplus." The Board of Governors of the Federal Reserve System has ruled that debentures do not constitute "capital stock" or "surplus" for various provisions of the Federal Reserve Act. The legal interpretation given in the 1964 Federal Reserve Bulletin 9 does not refer to convertible debentures, and the Board has not taken a position on the applicability of the act to convertibles specifically. However, it appears reasonable to conclude that, on the basis of section 5 and its legal interpretation, member banks issuing convertible debentures are not required to subscribe to additional Federal Reserve Bank stock until such debentures are converted into capital stock.

2. Convertible debentures may be preferable to time deposits, even when they bear a higher interest rate and even allowing for potential dilution on conversion, because debentures are not subject to legal reserve requirements of FDIC assessments as are time deposits. Also, since the maturity of debentures is known, there is no need to carry secondary reserves against them.

3. The expense of administering convertible debentures is less than that for savings deposits and, in periods when competition for savings is particularly intense, debentures provide an attractive means of raising debt capital since they are not subject to Regulation Q ceilings. (On the other hand, the interest rate on the debentures is fixed and cannot be lowered if the demand for funds falls.)

4. Because interest on convertible bonds is deductible, while dividends paid on common stock are not, convertible bonds may involve less cash outflow than common stocks even when their coupon rate is higher than the dividend rate on common stocks. Of course, the cash-flow advantage of convertibles may be offset by sinking fund payments. However, as noted in the empirical investigation of convertible bond usage discussed earlier, the typical sinking fund provision does not commence for some 10 years after issue, and, in any case, bank convertibles do not generally have a sinking fund provision.

5. A number of institutional investors, e.g., life insurance companies, certain pension funds, etc., are severely restricted in their ability to hold common stocks. The investment officers of many of these institutions feel that it would be desirable to have more equities than regulations permit. Convertible bonds provide these intermediaries with a method of indirectly holding more equities than the law permits.

6. Stock brokers suggest that there exists a class of investors who desire more leverage than is available under current margin requirements. Convertible bonds can typically be bought on a much lower margin than is required on listed common stocks.[10] To the extent that high-leverage investors are important factors in the market, this might increase the supply of funds placed in the convertible market, thus lowering the cost of capital of convertibles *vis-a-vis* either straight debt or common stock.

---

[10]Margin availability on convertibles is somewhat dependent upon general monetary conditions. At the present time (October 1966) many banks are reluctant to make "speculative" loans, preferring to hold back available funds for "productive" lending.

31. New Perspective on the Bank Stock Market[*]

David C. Cates

The marketability of a bank's common stock is a function of many things, the more important being earnings and dividend performance, competitive investment opportunities, and the issuer's administrative policies towards market participants. This article discusses these variables.

In this article, we will discuss the role of annual reports and then examine the market process itself, meaning the sum of research, sales and trading channels by which investors come to buy and sell bank stock.

ANNUAL REPORTS

At a recent seminar on annual report preparation, the author chided an eminent designer for his role in urging bigger type, less text, more photographs and deeply buried footnotes. If designers have their way, we argued, future reports will carry a very brief president's message in bold type announcing:

"See the profits. See the profits grow. Grow, profits, grow."

The designer pondered a long moment and shot back:

"I like it! It has impact!"

ROOM FOR IMPROVEMENT. Fortunately, the trend of bank annual reports is vigorously in the other direction (though if the word "deposits" were substituted for

"profits," the foregoing satire would aptly characterize earlier bank reports). Even so, substantial improvement in annual report disclosure practices is still desirable, in order to achieve the effectiveness that a good report should have.

Certainly there is no other single publication of a company which so concisely —and often involuntarily—conveys a sense of management "style" in coping with business objectives, triumphs and setbacks.

The reason, of course, for this heavy cargo of significance (whether intended or not) is that an annual report is *judged* by the readers as being the company's chief public utterance, and is *compared* by readers against similar reports from many other companies. Thus, regardless of the private niceties of corporate tradition, annual reports willy-nilly enter a competition for attention and opinion which management should do its best to control.

The easiest way to harness this inevitable exposure to wide public view is to stay purposefully abreast of the legitimate expectations of each key segment of the total audience. Customers, correspondents, employees, individual stockholders and the "community" all, of course, like to sense the appeal of an attractive, intelligible report that reaches their capacity for loyalty and respect.

PROFESSIONAL VIEW. The financial analyst is no different, though his specific expectations are far more detailed and the

[*]From *Bankers Monthly*, October, 1969. Reprinted by permission of the publisher.

effects of his judgments far more significant to the company. Whereas the impact of an annual report on a non-financial reader is largely an intangible matter of "image" (which we do not downgrade), to financial people these reports ought to provide the great bulk of material—numbers and text—needed to 1) understand the current posture of the company, 2) chart the history of its growth, 3) most important, compare it against similar companies.

If the disclosure pattern, therefore, of the best reports is clearly tending to include, say, *daily averages* of balance sheet items, management of a given bank should not hesitate to accommodate its own disclosure to the mainstream of professional expectations.

The penalty, moreover, for not recognizing and accepting disclosure trends is that busy analysts have to choose between neglecting the study of a company or else adding to their "homework" burden. Few, of course, will choose the latter unless they feel the investment payoff is correspondingly great.

This pressure on research time is understandably a difficult idea for managements to grasp, since each bank gets deeply involved only with its own report. Yet we cannot emphasize too strongly that a good annual report ought to be designed as a work-organizer and time-saver for analysts whose job is to understand, compare, select and describe companies as quickly as time permits.

ANALYST'S ROLE. So much for the reasonable expectations of financial analysts. What is their influence upon a bank's securities and—as a result—their significance to management? Measured by their ownership of bank stocks, one can probably dismiss the group from serious attention. Measured, however, by their role in research and recommendations leading to transactions by others, analysts probably account for well over half the turnover of big bank stock since 1960.

This is true because stocks—including bank stocks—tend to be *merchandised* to investors rather than privately researched by them. Within this merchandising process, the role of the analyst is to discover, articulate and stand behind the story of a company's value.

To be sure, not all stocks are always attractive to everyone, despite the enthusiasm of dedicated salesmen. A given bank stock—or all banks—may lie in the doldrums for a considerable spell before the intrinsic investment value is recognized. But this natural phenomenon of markets is no justification for primitive and inadequate disclosure. Proper policy during these periods—as utility companies know —is to keep analysts well informed with abundant, attractively packaged information.

Banks, too, should strive to reach and maintain a high level of 1) significant content (measured by current techniques of analyst judgment and comparison), 2) personal continuity with as wide a group of qualified analysts as seems appropriate to reach actual and potential stockholders.

DESIRABLE DATA. Among the elements of "significant content" which we think enhance the report of any bank concerned to win analyst attention, the following examples come to mind:

1. Full detailing of income and expense, reconciliation of undivided profits and reserves, and balance sheet (as specified in Regulation F and the Comptroller's rules for national banks);

2. Average and year-end yields on taxable and tax-free investments (converted, of course, to a fully taxable basis), coupled with a daily average analysis of both segments, average maturity, brief maturity schedule, year-end market value, and a review of pledged assets;

3. Average and year-end yields on loans (preferably by major subcategory), coupled with daily averages and a comment on loan loss experience;

4. Average and year-end effective cost of savings, consumer savings certificates,

negotiable CDs, and borrowed funds, coupled with daily averages;

5. Historical review (covering at least five years) of key balance sheet daily averages, average yields and costs, average maturity, income and expense by principal categories, earnings, a full per share review of earnings, dividends and book value (adjusted for splits and stock dividends), net loan loss, net security gain or loss, and number of branches, employees, number of shares and stockholders.

THE BOTTOM LINE. Our suggestion to include a minimum five-year record of loan and security loss (or profit) illustrates what we mean by the term "significant content," i.e. accommodation to the current techniques of analyst judgment.

Analysts have become broadly aware of the concept that "total operating performance" or the "bottom line" includes these supplementary ingredients as a vital adjunct to "net operating earnings."

Banks that neglect to supply this data in a convenient historical format will thus fall short of analyst expectations. Put another way, a good analyst today wants to know the five-year record in order to adjust stated earnings as closely as possible to the new definition of total performance advocated by many accountants, banks and analysts.

If these supplementary figures are conveniently published by the bank itself, there clearly will be less time spent, less chance of error, and less misunderstanding on the part of the public. If the supplementary figures are not published by the bank, a good analyst will find them anyway, but only if he feels the extra effort is worthwhile.

THE MARKET PROCESS

We are now ready to begin a discussion of the market process itself, having brought a more or less effective annual report to the crowded desk of a workaday analyst. What happens after that? At this point, we should already have divided banks into four broad categories:

1. The small bank whose shares are infrequently traded within a local community by a single dealer or—more likely —by the president and directors;

2. The medium-sized bank (say $100-400 million in resources) whose shares are traded regionally by one or more local dealers;

3. The relatively large regional bank (say $400 million to $1 billion of resources) whose market is chiefly local, but with significant occasional out-of-area ownership by institutions;

4. The giant bank whose share market is dominated by wholesale "Street" firms trading stock 1) direct with institutions and 2) with other dealers reaching the general public as well as smaller institutions.

DIFFERENT MATTER. As for the first group, this writer is not so naive as to insist that snappy 8½ x 11 annuals are always desirable for small banks, unless managements—as many do—find them a valuable tool in sophisticated merchandising and merger programs. Often the simple message "See our deposits grow!" will accomplish everything the local stockholder requires.

For every other bank—wherever an impersonal analyst has a hand in merchandising stock to investors who may not know management—the pressures of security idea competition clearly imply a policy of full-scale disclosure, regardless of size of bank. Conversely, an unwillingness to provide "significant content" exposes a bank to analyst and shareholder neglect, especially if the record itself is not stimulating.

We will turn now to the market characteristics of the three larger bank groups, and attempt to sketch appropriate management policy for the first two.

THE LOCAL DEALER. The medium-sized regional bank stock is marketed almost entirely by one or more local dealers. This means that trading positions—

when necessary to stabilize a market—are carried by firms whose sales outlets are relatively local in scope.

Because of the "position risk," such a firm is reluctant to bid on blocks unless 1) the block acqustion price is unusually low, 2) the bank itself supports key dealers with market information, friendly buying power, and allocation of other types of business, or 3) an active research and sales effort has prepared investors to absorb stock when available.

These inducements to an orderly market are not all of equal value. The first is bound to hurt somebody, the second is somewhat artificial and can be abused, while the last is truly self-sustaining. Management policy should be guided accordingly, with collateral business rewards to those firms who make the research effort.

OUTSIDE INTEREST TOO. The next group of banks faces a very similar market problem, complicated by the occasional intervention of outside institutions and/or dealers. Since the basic market—measured by shareholder activity—will undoubtedly remain a regional one, everything possible should be done by these managements to cultivate good local dealer relations based on dealer performance.

At the same time, the appetite of out-of-area investors should be heartily encouraged in order to build an additional outlet for large (and smaller) blocks of stock. To accomplish this, managements should make a point of knowing and working with qualified, influential analysts (who, by the way, are not always employed by dealer firms) and sending corporate information to them regularly.

Also, those out-of-area dealer firms who express an interest in stock should be given maximum opportunity to bid competitively against local firms. Only in this way, of course, can the outside firm make an attractive offering to its clients and wind up with a fair profit to cover research and sales expense.

NEW BASIS. One of the difficult problems of the bank stock market since early 1965 resulted from a shift in the method of daily newspaper quotations, as furnished by the National Association of Securities Dealers. Prior to 1965, these quotes which appear daily in major national and regional papers—reflected a fairly wide "spread" (say 70–73) based on an arbitrary markup of the bid side. The theory of the markup was to protect one or two middle dealers, give both salesmen a commission incentive, and leave the buyer and seller with the comfortable knowledge that the execution was "at the market."

In actual fact, the *wholesale* quote would not have been 70–73, but rather 70–71. Thus if the buyer and the seller had gone to the same firm on the same day, they could realize the wholesale spread (or better), not the artificial markup spread.

The SEC also observed this, and was responsible for the new national daily quote system inaugurated in early 1965, whereby only the wholesale quotes were henceforth to be reported. The trouble with this change was that the public (having scanned its collective newspaper) expected to get the price benefits which the existing system for trading bank stocks could not really deliver.

Pressed by the public's new awareness of a "good execution," dealer margins shrank, salesmen's commissions were reduced, and bank stocks—many observers feel—began to suffer a prolonged, unintended shrinkage of volume as well as market depth.

REALISTIC? The new system, moreover, exposed some of the inefficiencies of the bank stock market at its "retail" level, that is, the level of *individual* buying and selling.

For illustration, let's use the example of Bank XYZ whose wholesale quote is 70-71. In a typical transaction, Seller A comes to Firm B, which accepts a bid of 70 from Dealer C, who resells to Firm D at 71 for account of Buyer E. If we assume that buyer and seller is each charged roughly an equivalent New York Stock Exchange commission (in order to compensate Firms B and D for handling, research and sales expense), the net sale price is 69½ and the net purchase price is 71¼.

Obviously, the realities of the retail bank stock market are not altogether unlike the old quotation system.

DIRECT ACCESS. For larger institutional investors, however, the established market system has always worked much more effectively, simply because these accounts have direct access to the major dealer firms at net prices. Thus Bank A can sell 200 shares at 70 (or better) and Bank B can buy at 71 (or less).

This efficiency of the institutional market (of which bank stock dealers can be justly proud) should, however, not obscure the fact that the individual investor is in fact less well served than the newspapers suggest he should be.

One reason, therefore, that the public market for bank stocks remains underdeveloped may be this very cumbersomeness of the institutionally oriented trading mechanism when it attempts to motivate individuals with professional research and executions. Too much of this effort is bound to be secondhand, and therefore relatively ineffective.

LISTED BANKS? For the largest group of banks—those whose markets are dominated by wholesale dealer firms—the retail cumbersomeness of the bank stock market mechanism is less apparent when institutions are *buying* stocks, but does appear to take its toll when institutions are net *sellers*. If a more efficient "circulation system" existed, net selling from one investor segment might be more readily absorbed by the net buying of another segment, and vice versa.

This problem—high effectiveness of research and sales at the institutional end of the spectrum, and low effectiveness at the retail end—has led some major banks to consider listing their shares on the New York Stock Exchange. In the opinion of these banks, it would even be worthwhile to accept, if necessary, a temporary setback in institutional marketability in order to achieve a breakthrough to the public investor. Though the objective is certainly a worthy one, several considerations deter these banks from taking action.

First, they worry about the transitional period, that is, whether the specific marketability of their shares will be enhanced or inhibited by a shift to the auction market. Second, they are not at all sure that the benefits of member firm sponsorship will be an "automatic" result of listing their shares. On this point, they are justly skeptical: only when a substantial number of major banks are listed is it likely that member firms will pay the internal overhead costs necessary to upgrade the research and sales status of bank stocks.

LOOK AHEAD. Yet when—and if—this happens, banks can plausibly look forward to a substantial broadening of the shareholder base (the gradual result of more effective research and sales effort by an expanded roster of interested firms). Not only that, but the marketability problems that occasionally arise even under present conditions might diminish under a more centralized and inclusive "circulating system" of bank stocks.

Marketability, in other words, is simply a more or less adequate matching of buyers and sellers, with brains, energy and capital standing between. If the "universe" of buyers and sellers were fully interconnected through one active market, then the conditions would obviously exist for the best possible marketability.

In the writer's opinion, the advantages of listing will gradually outweigh the disadvantages, at least for major banks, though it is impossible to predict when this may begin to happen.

That leaves an important question for somewhat smaller banks: if 10 or 20 very large banks were to list, what would then happen to the markets for other substantial banks whose trading volume might not really justify a listing? Would these bank stocks share in a broadened market appetite for *all* good bank stocks, or would they be relatively neglected as the "over-the-counter" cousins of the listed stocks?

32. Developing Local Markets for Bank Securities*

David C. Cates

Local investors typically own two-thirds or more of a bank's outstanding stock. This article complements the previous one by examining in greater detail the nature of local security markets and managerial guidelines which the issuer should consider in more fully developing these markets.

More and more bank managements are coming to recognize that they need investors at least as much as they need customers. Though the amount of capital banks require is far less than the volume of their deposits, it is also a very costly resource, increasingly scarce, and one which must be made to yield a net return at least 12 times greater than deposits. Any techniques we can develop, therefore, to attract additional capital on favorable terms should greatly ease the planning function of bank managements.

If the strategic objective, then, is to attract capital on favorable terms, the tactical objective must be to build a market for bank securities. This is necessary because markets are not dominated by the issuers of securities, but rather by the merchandisers and consumers of securities. If demand is absent, the securities

go begging and the capital cost skyrockets for the issuer. If demand is strong, the cost to the issuer is reduced. In addition, such a bank can use its high-valued capital base to attract 1) profitable blocks of deposits (through non-dilutive mergers), 2) profitable management (through attractive options), 3) profitable customers (through the momentum of high morale).

The time to start this process, furthermore, is now, well before a specific capital need arises. Markets, like the fairer sex, need to be cultivated, and this takes a long, careful and honest courtship rather than an abrupt snap of the fingers from time to time. Investors and securities people have inertial guidance systems—or established expectational patterns—which learn not to respond to isolated bursts of good news on the eve of merger or financing announcements. They expect, quite understandably, a more regular kind of attention, whose favors occur throughout the year and over many years.

IN PERSPECTIVE. What do we mean by a "market?" Is it something that brokers and dealers do by themselves, like whittling a stick or playing bridge? A surprising number of bankers do seem to believe that markets for their securities arise out of thin air, and turn the grateful dealers

---

*From *Bankers Monthly*, October, 1969. Reprinted by permission of the publisher.

into rich men besides. Or does a "market" depend on a finely-tuned interrelation of several parties, one of which is management itself? Since we can only develop our market-building recommendations by analyzing the roles of participants, let's see who these are, what they want, and the appropriate initiative that bankers can make.

This analysis, furthermore, will be directed primarily at the problem of *local* markets for *local* bank securities, in cities such as Portland (Maine or Oregon) and Springfield (Illinois and Massachusetts). Larger banks—whose securities ordinarily trade nationally—will also profit from any sustained effort to cultivate their local garden of investors.

The reason why larger banks should not concentrate exclusively on their status among Wall Street dealers and analysts is quite simple: influential as this market may be for moving sizable blocks of stock in and out of institutions, it's still just the top of the iceberg.

If local investors—who typically own 65–85 percent of a large regional bank's outstanding shares—are not inclined to place an appropriate value on these shares (reflecting their loyalty and enthusiasm), then the best efforts of Wall Street firms will be no more lasting than if the Swiss Army were to conquer China. After all, parity begins at home. And oughtn't an institution's determination to buy and hold a stock be partly guided—apart from fundamental considerations based on per share performance—by the breadth of its total market? If the effective market is merely other institutions, the structure of demand is weaker and more volatile than if the shares are actively traded locally as well. (In the writer's opinion, the only good reason for large banks to list their shares on the New York Stock Exchange is hopefully to achieve a more broadly-based and efficient market standing among smaller investors, locally and even nationally.)

THE PARTICIPANTS. The "market" for a related group of securities grows out of a three-cornered relationship between investors, company managements and securities firms (including their research, trading, sales and underwriting functions).

Any number can play—the more the better—and they can link up in all kinds of direct and indirect ways. (Let it be said here that a few of these possible linkages are inappropriate, unfair, unethical or downright illegal, and it is vital to identify and avoid these.)

Managements influence the market by their direct link to investors via annual reports, stockholder meetings and the fundamental record of their per share performance. Brokers influence investors by their capacity to perceive a story and stick with it. Managements influence brokers by packaging their performance results in usable form for retailing to investors. Investors themselves influence markets through their shifting groundswells of attitude and appetite, from conservative securities, say, to growth stocks, and back again.

The point is that it takes three to tango: managements, investors, securities people.

INDUSTRY POSITION. What are some of the special characteristics of the banking industry that affect its relation to the securities market?

First of all, banking—if well-managed—is a good industry, offering investors deep and relatively secure roots in the economy of the nation and its localities, as well as a growth pattern of earnings that has regularly exceeded GNP, industrial production, corporate profits and the earnings curve of most utilities.

Second, the management style of the industry is rather rapidly evolving in paths that favor diversification, innovation and profitability, over the dead hand of banking tradition. Securities markets are sensitive to important qualitative shifts of this sort, and should gradually come to recognize the increasingly *proprietary* nature of banking's new services, as against the colorless *commodity* nature of old-style banking.

The entire industry has this year been burdened with a new mandatory requirement to report per share earnings on a "net income" basis ("What's Wrong With The New Accounting?" BANKERS MONTHLY MAGAZINE, September 15, 1969).

There are, however, two benefits that can be seized from this sudden development. The first is the opportunity—virtually forced by necessity on alert managements—to upgrade the over-all quality and scope of bank annual reports and annual meetings, rethink the significant elements in one's earnings history (especially on a per share basis), and explain the new concept of bank performance to brokers and to investors. The planning for this broad-based effort should be undertaken now, before the 1969 reports are written.

More important, the "net income" measure of performance—while harsh and unfair in its treatment of securities gains and losses—is at least a "final number" which requires no arcane and mysterious adjustments downwards. Its acceptability by the man-in-the-street, then, should help to dispel the miasma of distrust through which many people—including brokers—dimly view bank securities.

The acceptability of "net income," finally, should strengthen the death warrant which was issued many years ago against "book value" as a measure of bank stock value. Book value, of course, is only a way of looking backwards, like driving a car with one's eye firmly glued on the rear-view mirror. If the road is straight and the speed slow, you'll probably make it, but neither of these conditions holds true any longer for American banking.

The most important thing we can say about the banking industry in its relation to securities markets is that its capital over-sufficiency has largely vanished. After a long Rip Van Winkle period during which customers, stockholders and em-

ployees waited patiently at the door, managements have awakened to discover that only the borrowers are still knocking. In many parts of the country, the stockholders—and the brokers—have more or less given up.

This disturbing combination of management need for market support and the complacency of market supporters throws much of the initiative back on the bankers. If managements want their share price (that is, the market value of their enterprise) to attain a valuation level which is vital to them in formulating merger and capital policy, they have got to reach out more persuasively to the consumers of their securities. If the industry cannot collectively do this, we face either drastic structural realignment through merger or the beginning of public ownership of financial institutions.

SQUEEZE ON DEALERS. Since we are principally concerned in this article with the solution of a banking problem by means of banker initiative, we will not deal at length with the situation in the securities industry. Suffice it to say that high interest rates and a restrictive credit policy have a far more adverse effect on brokers and dealers than on banks.

This was not always true. In the more profitable yesteryear, brokers could turn an easy living in standard securities and felt no particular pocket book urge to support local securities, however deserving.

If bankers, therefore, can help local brokers develop new profitable business in their securities, this is the time to think out ways to do it. The need is there, on both sides.

THE LOCAL INVESTOR. What can we say about the ultimate consumer of local bank securities? For one thing (leaving aside "insiders" and nearby institutions), he is a small investor. For another he is largely unsophisticated. But he probably knows that the ultimate test of a good investment is what goes up. Moreover, he undoubtedly responds to the credibility of a good management. And he is aware that most securities can be bought or sold with a couple of telephone calls.

If this matrix of local investors believes in its nearby bank(s), the result will be price-to-earnings ratios of 15, 25, 30 times (as can be currently demonstrated here and there in the country). If the local investor doesn't believe, the result is price-to-earnings ratios of 6, 7 or 8 times.

The curious thing about these contrasting valuations is that they do not seem primarily rooted in differences of performance, but rather in differences of attitude.

Some—not all—of these attitude contrasts stem from the positive or negative orientation of management, and not all of these are wise. For example, it borders on shortsighted avarice for bank directors to "make a market" at an artificially low price, hoping thereby to diminish their personal estate tax by passing a presumed ultimate capital gain to the next generation. This is not only unfair to minority stockholders, but is tragically self-defeating in case the bank currently needs equity capital or plans a merger. At the other extreme, it is unwise for managements to promote a high valuation for stock, based on misleading summaries of per share history. To illustrate, it is quite wrong to restate prior years' per share earnings to the *present* number of shares, disregarding the dilutive effects of new stock issued in mergers or cash offerings.

APPROPRIATE POLICY. Having described the three-cornered market relationship between bankers, brokers and investors, let's turn now to a check-list of realistic recommendations for action by managements. These first steps should be initiated by managements, not only because they have the resources to do so, but because securities people usually need leadership and sustained evidence of good faith in order to alter their market habits.

1. Good performance—on a per share basis—is the only bedrock on which better markets can be built. Sows' ears do not make silk purses.

2. Good disclosure—written and spoken —is the only vehicle whereby performance results get translated into investment language. Few banks seem to know how to present (or package) their results for the comprehension of investors and brokers, yet this communication channel is a vital ingredient to an active market. The chief error managements make in this regard is ignorance: many do not appreciate the role of disclosure in financial policy. Their second error is inadequate delegation and supervision: disclosure policy should not be set by public relations or accounting officers alone without executive guidance and review.

3. Good dividend policy—including stock dividends and splits—not only strikes the right balance between payout and retention, but keeps the share price in an attractive range for smaller investors (say $15–$30). In general, a bank with good performance, good disclosure, and an attractive share price will not need to lean as heavily on cash payout for investor support as a bank less progressive.

4. Publicity in local papers should be supplemented by bid-and-asked quotations at least once a week. This is an important way to help brokers and investors believe that bank securities exist.

5. Loan collateral policies which do not discriminate against good local businesses —including banks—provide an incentive to local investors which should help to develop a more active market.

6. Appropriate incentives to brokers and dealers who provide market support will help nourish the market at its inception and produce legitimate extra income as the market develops. What are some of the specific incentives that most banks have available? We have already mentioned disclosure, which—if packaged usably—can save a firm some research overhead. There are three others.

First, local bank stock—when it comes on the market—should be regularly and explicitly directed through the best market. One way to accomplish this is to invite bids beforehand, with or without the right to reject the highest bid. If this market happens to be in New York, the competition will be good for all concerned, and local firms will gradually get the message that management is not interested in sponsoring a tea dance.

Second, commissions arising from general securities transactions—on bank portfolio and for trust accounts—can be channeled to firms who have made an effort to bring buyers and sellers of bank stock together. To be sure, there may not be all that much to go around. When customer-directed commissions and deposit-related commissions are subtracted, the residual is often rather small. But there is no reason why market-making services should be any less rewarded in this way than, say, research services on nationally-traded securities.

Finally, bank securities underwriting offers local firms an opportunity for profitable participation. Membership in this group, if possible, should be based on services rendered, and development of a local market for bank securities should rank as a prime source of merit badges.

If management can make such incentive policies clearly understood, and executes them fairly and impartially, there is no reason why securities firms should not respond. Better yet, an understanding among all the local banks on broad, general ground rules for nourishing a local market ought to make it happen even faster.

DEBT ISSUES. So far, we have confined our discussion to the market for bank stocks. Fortunately, the opportunity to leverage per share earnings means that debt capital will occasionally be issued by good banks. Less fortunately, the market for small private placements of debt instruments is all but nonexistent today. Whether it will ease up in 1970 is a question which finds few optimistic responses.

There is good reason to believe, however, that a well regarded community bank can tailor an issue of straight debentures to appeal to local savings money.

Even though some of this money is apt to come from the bank's own savings deposits, the net cost of local capital (interest rate + amortized cost of sale + allocated interest rate differential on lost savings) will most certainly be less than the most favorable private placement possibility. For example, the writer is convinced that a properly packaged offering carrying the right terms and maturities—can be priced somewhere between Treasuries and triple-A corporate bonds. Once again, the kind of bank that can successfully arrange such a sale will probably have been pursuing many of the policies we have recommended in this article.

33. Are Bank Dividend Policies Too Conservative? *

E. Sherman Adams

It is often said that past modes of behavior are difficult to change. Bank dividend policies would seem to fit this adage—their dividend payout has varied less than nearly any other corporate group. Such consistency is not necessarily wrong, however. This article examines two aspects of bank dividend policy: whether past policy is currently appropriate, and what advantages might result from higher dividends.

After all, there is such a thing as being excessively conservative, even in banking. So we venture to pose the question: Are commercial banks paying out too small a portion of their current earnings in dividends?

This is a question that deserves careful reexamination today by bankers and bank directors. In the judgment of some analysts, a significant liberalization of bank dividend policies might enhance the aggregate market value of outstanding bank shares to the extent of hundreds of millions of dollars.

Some of the points put forward on either side of this question are quite venerable, but others are new. And even the old arguments need to be reappraised in the light of present-day circumstances.

It should be recognized at the outset that bank dividend policies reflect a large element of tradition, which some persons, I suppose, might less respectfully call inertia. In any event, the dividend poli-

cies of most banks do not often change very noticeably. Over the past four years, a representative list of leading banks paid out, on the average, 45 percent of net operating earnings in cash dividends. For the preceding four years, the ratio was 46 percent. For the past 15 years, the ratio has averaged 46 percent. These figures would seem to reflect considerable adherence to traditional payout policies.

This does not mean that these policies are necessarily wrong, of course, but it does suggest that they might be. There may be merit in maintaining some consistency in a bank's payout policy over the years, but only if that policy still makes sense in today's world.

It should be emphasized that this article does not attempt to deal with all of the many factors that a bank must consider in connection with its dividend policy. Instead, attention is focused primarily on just one factor—the effects of payout policy.

No attention is given to the controversial subject of stock dividends, not because the author thinks that stock dividends have no merits, but because, as a practical matter, most banks are not going to use them and consideration of them here might be more confusing than helpful.

We shall examine two main questions:

1. Is the case for conservative bank dividend policies as persuasive as it was years ago?

2. What benefits might accrue if banks

---

*From *Banking,* November, 1967 (copyright 1970 by The American Bankers Association). Reprinted by permission of the publisher.

were to move toward more generous payout policies?

A NEW DEVELOPMENT

On the first of these questions, one
significant new development is that debt
financing by commercial banks has now
become respectable. Previously there were
only two important sources of bank capital: Retained earnings and the sale of
new stock. Of these two alternatives, the
former was by far the more advantageous
from the standpoint of protecting a bank's
earnings per share, and this was always
the clinching argument for accumulating
as much capital as possible from retained
earnings by adhering to a low dividend
payout policy.

Now there is a third source of bank
capital, and one that is even more advantageous, namely, the issuance of capital notes or debentures. To be sure, this
new vehicle is not a panacea. A bank
cannot expand its indebtedness indefinitely. Also, there could be prolonged
periods when market conditions would
make banks reluctant to sell capital notes
—the past year, for example.

It is plain, nevertheless, that over the
years commercial banks will be able to
go considerably further with debt financing than they have to date. So far, less
than 2 percent of all commercial banks
have issued any debt capital, and even
for those that have, the average ratio of
debt as a percentage of capital funds is
less than 25 percent. For the banking
system as a whole, debt issues constitute
only about 6 percent of total capital.

How much higher this percentage will
eventually go, no one can say. Even today, many bankers and bank supervisors
would not be concerned to see debt capital comprise up to one-third or more of
the capital funds of well-managed banks.
And views on this may tend to become
even more lenient as debt financing becomes more prevalent.

Most bankers do not yet think of debt

as being a permanent part of a bank's
capital structure. To be sure, they long
ago abandoned the expectation that governments would retire their debts, and
they are thoroughly accustomed to seeing indebtedness persist on the balance
sheets of their corporate customers. Their
attitude has even softened considerably
toward continuous borrowing by consumers. For that matter, they are quite used
to carrying large debts themselves under
the more appealing name of deposits. But
they have not yet come to regard debt
capital as performing a continuing role
in their capital setup. They still think of
it as something temporary, something to
be retired before too long and presumably replaced with equity capital.

Despite this attitude, they have shown
little reluctance about using debt financing whenever the price is right. The volume of this financing has apparently
abated over the past year or so because
of its increased cost, but when interest
rates subside, it can be expected to expand again.

Moreover, its seems safe to predict that
when banks start retiring their presently
outstanding debt capital, they will replace
it with new. A particular issue of capital
notes may be temporary, obedient to its
sinking fund provisions, but in all probability the existence of debt in bank capital
structures will not be.

It seems clear, therefore, that debt financing will be an important alternative
source of bank capital over the years
ahead. This injects a major new consideration into the formulation of dividend
policy. For most banks, the chief argument for a low payout policy is less compelling than it used to be.

WHAT BENEFITS?

We come now to the second main
question: What benefits might result from
more liberal dividend policies?

Some shareholders would doubtless like
larger dividends simply because they re-

gard increased income as being a fine thing. But from the standpoint of most shareholders, the problem is more complicated than that. It is a question of weighing the comparative benefits that might flow from alternative uses of the bank's earnings: Retention to augment capital or the payment of higher dividends. What payout policies would bring maximum benefits to shareholders not only in terms of income, but also in terms of the market value of their holdings?

The crucial question here is what effect more liberal dividend policies would have on the level of bank stock prices. Indeed, the whole case for such policies rests primarily on the thesis that they would bring about an appreciable improvement in quotations for bank equities.

Market price is a matter of great significance to all bank shareholders, including those who have no intention of selling

their holdings for a long time to come. Whenever a bank has occasion to issue new stock, the price-earnings ratio at which its outstanding shares are quoted is a major determinant of the cost of acquiring new capital and it therefore importantly affects the amount of dilution of per-share earnings that is entailed. Market price is also an important factor in acquisitions, with similar effects on dilution of earnings.

Let's start with the basic fact that the price of almost every stock is influenced to either a greater or lesser degree by its cash dividend rate. At one extreme are some exceptionally high growth-rate stocks, like IBM, Xerox, and Avon Products, whose prices appear to be affected hardly at all by their low payout ratios—though it is noteworthy that even these companies do pay cash dividends. And at the other extreme are stocks that are

FIGURE 1
Parallel Action of Bank and Utility Stocks

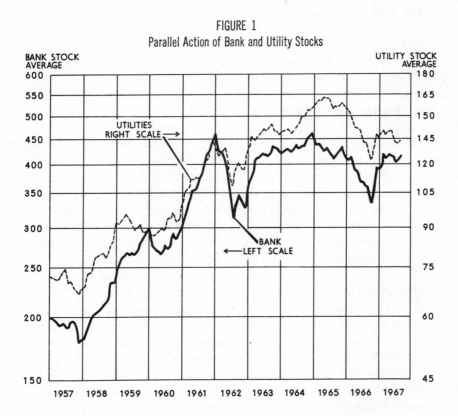

Sources: *Dow-Jones Utility Average; Keefe, Bruyette & Woods Bank Stock Index.*

purchased primarily for income and sell largely "on a yield basis." Most stocks, including the great majority of bank stocks, are somewhere between these extremes.

In days of yore, many large holders of bank stocks had little interest in cash dividends. Indeed, some wealthy investors had no need for additional income and favored low payout policies for tax reasons. From their standpoint, it made sense for a bank to reinvest its earnings directly for the benefit of the stockholders rather than have the Treasury take a big tax bite out of higher dividends. These investors tended to regard book value as a significant indicator of the "intrinsic value" of their bank stocks and preferred to see a rise in book value than a larger dividend.

But wealthy individuals are relatively far less important today as holders of bank stocks. Individuals of more moderate means and institutional investors have become far more important. These investors have little interest in a stock's book value but they are very much interested in dividends and market price. It is the attitude of these investors that determines the average price-earnings ratio of bank stocks as a group.

In short, dividends may weigh considerably more heavily than formerly in the thinking of investors and potential investors in bank stocks. The problem is to evaluate just how important this factor is today and also how much more significant it might become in the future if banks were to liberalize their payout policies.

Good evidence on this is not easy to come by; it has to be dug out. There are of course many different factors that affect the prices both of individual stocks and various categories of stocks. The problem is to isolate the influence of the factor of dividend policy as it now applies, or might apply in the future, to bank stocks as a group.

REVEALING COMPARISON

It is revealing to compare bank stocks with public utility stocks. These two groups differ in a number of important respects, but they are widely regarded by investors as being similar from the standpoint of several fundamental investment characteristics. In general, on the basis of the record, both afford promise of moderate, relatively stable growth in earnings and in dividends over a period of years. The remarkable parallel between the price movements of leading bank and utility stocks over the past decade is shown in Figure 1 (p. 359).

In comparing these two groups, the most striking differences are that banks have a much lower average payout ratio than utilities and they also consistently sell in the market at a lower price-earnings multiple. For example, over the past six years, the average payout ratio of a representative list of leading banks was 45 percent, whereas the average ratio for the stocks comprising Standard & Poor's public utility index was 67 percent. For the same period, the average times-earning multiple at which the bank stocks were quoted was 15.6, whereas the average multiple for the utilities was 20.1.

These facts suggest the possibility, of course, that banks' lower payout ratio might be a major reason for their lower price-earnings multiple. But these few figures alone cannot be regarded as any real evidence that such a causal relationship actually does exist. The correlation between payout ratios and price-earnings ratios may be coincidental. Completely different factors could conceivably be responsible for all of the disparity in the price-earnings multiples.

Several possible factors might be cited. It could be plausibly argued, for example, that for various reasons investors are more confident that utilities will enjoy greater and steadier growth in per-share earn-

FACTORS AFFECTING PRICE–EARNINGS RATIOS
Comparison of the percentage differentials in the dividend payout ratios,
price-earnings ratios, and growth of earnings per share of
representative bank and utility stocks by regions.

	Average payout	Price-earnings ratio	Increase in earnings per share 1961–66
Western region			
A. Utilities (3)	59%	15.0	42%
B. Banks (3)	46%	11.4	30%
C. Differential (A minus B) ..	13	3.6	12
D. Differential (C as % of B) ..	28%	32%	40%
Eastern region			
A. Utilities (4)	74%	15.4	30%
B. Banks (4)	50%	10.9	34%
C. Differential (A minus B) ..	24	4.5	− 4
D. Differential (C as % of B) ..	48%	41%	−12%
All regions			
A. Utilities (19)	65%	17.2	45%
B. Banks (20)	42%	11.8	42%
C. Differential (A minus B) ..	23	5.4	3
D. Differential (C as % of B) ..	55%	46%	7%
Southern region			
A. Utilities (5)	60%	21.6	59%
B. Banks (6)	37%	14.1	59%
C. Differential (A minus B) ..	23	7.5	0
D. Differential (C as % of B) ..	62%	53%	0
Central region			
A. Utilities (7)	68%	15.9	47%
B. Banks (7)	40%	10.6	46%
C. Differential (A minus B) ..	28	5.3	1
D. Differential (C as % of B) ..	70%	50%	2%

Payout ratios are based on 1966 earnings and cash dividend payments.
Price-earnings ratios are based on 1966 earnings and average of high and
low market quotations in 1966.

ings from year to year. Over the past several years, some investors have been concerned about the squeeze on bank profit margins and the decline in bank liquidity. These fears were partly responsible for the poor performance of bank stocks in 1965 and the first nine months of 1966, as shown in the chart comparing bank and utility stocks.

In addition, there are more well-known and actively traded utilities than bank stocks and, as a result, they receive more attention from brokers and analysts and enjoy a broader following among investors. Some investors find the outlook for bank stocks difficult to analyze. There are many utility stocks you could buy for long-term investment almost with your eyes closed, whereas with bank stocks there is a wide assortment of unforeseeable developments that might affect them adversely over the coming years. And many investors are mindful of Murphy's Law; to wit, that if anything can go wrong, it will.

This is no mean array of alleged advantages for the utilities. Do they perhaps account for all or almost all of the disparity in the price-earnings ratios of utilities vs. banks? Or is there room left for dividend payout as a really significant causal factor?

WHAT THE DATA REVEAL

We can get at this question by examining regional data. Both banks and utilities are affected by the economic and population trends in the regions in which they operate and, by comparing companies in the same region, the influence of other factors can be seen more clearly.

Presented here is a summary of pertinent statistics for lists of representative utilities and bank stocks in four broad regions: Eastern, Southern, Central, and Western. The lists of stocks used for this exercise and some of the data relating to them were supplied by David C. Cates, Manager, Bank Stock Department, Loeb, Rhoades & Co. The purpose here is to examine the *percentage differentials* in the payout ratios, price-earnings ratios, and growth in earnings per share of these groups of stocks.

Take the figures for the Western Region. For three representative Western utilities, the average payout ratio in 1966 was 59 percent, and for three leading Western banks, the average ratio was 46 percent. The differential between the two was 13 percentage points. In other words, the payout ratio of the utilities was 28 percent higher than that of the banks. This we refer to as the "percentage differential."

Similarly, the average price-earnings ratio of the utilities was 32 percent higher than that of the banks, and the increase in earnings per share during 1961–66 was 40 percent greater for the utilities than for the banks.

These three percentage differentials of the Western utilities over the Western banks—28 percent, 32 percent, and 10 percent—are all roughly comparable in size. Looking at these figures alone, we cannot say what the causal relationships are. It could be that the higher price-earnings multiple of the utilities reflects their higher payout ratio. But not necessarily. It could be instead that their faster

earnings growth is mainly responsible. Or it could be some of each. By themselves, these three percentage differentials prove nothing.

But look now at the data for the Eastern Region. There the percentage differentials of utilities over banks are higher both for payout ratios and for price-earnings multiples. In this region, however, the banks actually achieved a better average increase in per-share earnings over the past five years than the utilities. In other words, there is good correlation here between payout and price-earnings ratios, but the factor of earnings growth does not correlate at all.

Looking at the Southern and Central Regions, we find the same pattern as in the East. In both the Southern and Central Regions the percentage differentials of utilities over banks are higher than in the East for both payout ratios and price-earnings multiples, but in both of these regions there were almost no differentials in the growth of earnings. Again, payout and price-earnings correlate and earnings growth does not.

The percentage differentials shown in the table are presented graphically in the next chart. Here you can see at a glance the close correlation between dividend payout and price-earnings ratios and the absence of correlation of earnings growth. The correlation between the dividend payout and price-earnings ratios is summarized in simplified form in the chart to the right (Figure 3).

This is simply a plotting of the percentage differentials for these two factors for the four regions and combined. The close correlation of these differentials is indicated by the fact that when they are plotted in this kind of a chart, they are practically in a straight line. The nearness of all the plottings to the so-called "line of regression" indicates how closely correlated these factors are.

In the language of the statisticians, the coefficient of correlation for these differentials is .95, which is a very high degree

FIGURE 2

Factors Affecting Price–Earnings Ratios

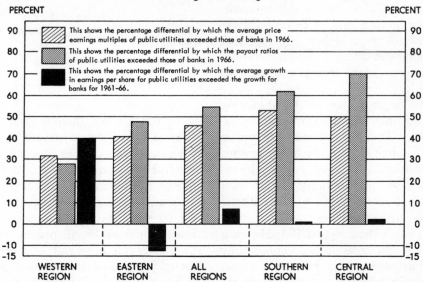

of correlation for factors of this kind. Perfect correlation would be indicated by a coefficient of 1.00, a score rarely encountered in the real world.

OTHER EVIDENCE

Applying the same method, we also computed correlation between the percentage differentials for price-earnings ratios and growth of earnings per share. The coefficient of correlation of these two factors is not just zero; it is actually negative.

As a check on this whole exercise, similar computations for the same lists of utilities and bank stocks were made for an earlier date, using 1965 instead of 1966 figures for earnings, dividends, and market prices and taking 1959–65 rather

FIGURE 3

Close Correlation of Payout and Price–Earnings

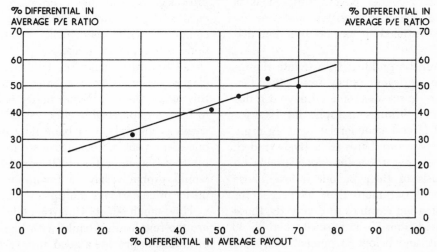

than 1961–66 as the period for measuring the increase in earnings per share. Using these earlier dates, the correlation coefficient for payout and price-earnings ratios was .97, even higher than for 1966, and there was again a negative correlation between price-earnings and earnings growth.

These findings may not be absolutely conclusive, but they are certainly impressive. They lend considerable support to the thesis that one of the main reasons why utilities as a group enjoy substantially higher price-earnings ratios than banks is because of their more liberal dividend payout policies.

The implication is that if banks as a group were to move up to an appreciably higher average payout ratio, this would probably be reflected in a significant enhancement of the market value of outstanding bank stocks. Indeed, one could make a strong case that if banks were to start moving steadily toward higher payout ratios, they would deserve to sell at a considerably higher price-earnings ratio than at present because they have so much room for future dividend increases.

BENEFITS TO ONE BANK

It does not follow, of course, that the stock of any one particular bank would be correspondingly benefited if it alone adopted a higher payout ratio. This is quite a different question and one on which we need to look at different evidence.

Again the problem is to isolate the influence of payout policy from other factors. To do so, we tabulated payout ratios and price-earnings multiples for 1966 for the 50 largest commercial banking organizations whose shares are actively traded. We then put them into four groups on the basis of their payout ratios: Those that paid out more than 55 percent of net operating earnings in dividends, those that paid from 50–55 percent, then 35–49 percent, and below 35 percent. Here are the results:

Payout ratios	Number of banks	Average Ratios	
		Payout	Price/ Earnings
Over 55%	4	61	15.0
50%-55%	11	51	12.2
35%-49%	27	43	11.7
Under 35%	8	31	11.3

As you can see, there is clearly a correlation here between payout ratios and price-earnings multiples. Indeed, the coefficient of correlation for these four groups is .83, which is quite high.

Note, however, that more than half of the 50 banks have payout ratios ranging from 35 percent to 49 percent and that they have all been put into one large group. The reason is that when you look only at these banks within this broad range, you find little correlation between their payout and price-earnings ratios. Specifically, the coefficient of correlation among these banks as a group is only about .30, which indicates some, but rather poor correlation.

In other words, there is no evidence that if an individual bank were to increase its payout ratio from, say, 38 percent to 44 percent, or from 42 percent to 48 percent, the price of its stock would necessarily be affected at all. It might be, of course, but the data indicate that for these banks, other factors—future growth prospects, for example—exert more influence on price-earnings differentials as compared with other banks within the same broad payout range.

On the other hand, the evidence does clearly suggest that if a bank is outside this range, then its payout policy is likely to have an appreciable effect on its price-earnings multiple. If a bank now paying out 45 percent of earnings were to move up to a payout ratio of 60 percent, this would probably have a favorable effect on its price-earnings multiple.

How much effect? Unfortunately, there are too few leading banks with high payout ratios to provide a good answer. Much might depend on how the change is made.

For one thing, investors would undoubtedly be more impressed if they thought the bank intended to adhere to a higher payout policy for a period of years. For example, a bank might announce that it planned, if circumstances permitted, to move steadily in the direction of a 60 percent payout policy over the next five years. This is hardly to be recommended for every bank, of course, but it would not be imprudent for some. For many banks, the announcement of such a policy would create the prospect of an average increase in the dividend rate on the order of 15 percent per year. For investors, such a prospect would be most appealing.

There would be far greater impact, of course, if a considerable number of leading banks were to move simultaneously toward higher payout ratios. Perhaps what is needed is an open conspiracy among bankers to become more generous to shareholders. This might be rather hard to put in motion, admittedly, but it is something to think about.

34. Patterns in Bank Dividend Policy*
James Van Horne and Raymond C. Helwig

The preceding article (by Adams) concerned dividend policies of banking as an industry and relative to public utilities. This article provides intra-industry comparisons. It examines the relative differences in dividend policy between large and small banks, the rationale for the differences, and the possible connection between external financing and dividend policy.

Little is known about the relationship between small- and large-bank dividend policy.[1] What, if any, are the differences that do exist? What are the possible reasons for these differences? Is there any relation between dividend policy and external financing? Analysis of these questions is based on a study of data from two samples of banks.

THE SAMPLES

The small-bank sample was selected from the 181 state banks in Michigan with total deposits of less than $10 million (as of December 31, 1963), which were in continual operation from January 1, 1960 through December 31, 1964.[2] From these banks were excluded 46 that did not reply to the questionnaire and seventeen whose responses did not contain market-price in-

*From Bankers Magazine, Spring, 1967. Reprinted by permission of the publisher, Warren, Gorham & Lamont Inc.

[1]Research dealing with this relationship includes: Eugene M. Lerner and Donald P. Jacobs, "Why We Need a Better Market for Bank Stocks," *Banking* (August and September, 1960), 43-5, 76-7, 128, 130; and Gilbert R. Whitaker, Jr., *The Market for Bank Stocks*, Subcommittee on Domestic Finance, Committee on Banking and Currency, House of Representatives, 88th Cong., 2d Sess., 1964.

[2]This sample was obtained for a broader study that analyzes the market price of small-bank stocks. For additional discussion of the sample, see James Van Horne and Raymond C. Helwig, *The Valuation of Small-Bank Stocks*, Occasional Paper (East Lansing: Bureau of Business and Economic Research, Graduate School of Business Administration, Michigan State University), 1966.

formation, due to the lack of recent sales of stock. The remaining 118 banks constitute the small-bank sample. Deposit size of these banks at December 31, 1964 ranged from under $1 million to approximately $10 million.

The banks are spread throughout the State of Michigan, with no particular clustering evident. Most of the banks in the sample are located in small towns; of the 118 banks, 107 are located in towns of under 5,000 population. The predominantly rural nature of most of these banks is shown by the location of ninety of the 118 outside of Michigan's ten Metropolitan Statistical areas. While there is no reason to believe that dividend policy and market-price behavior of the stocks of the banks in this sample differ greatly from those of many other small country banks throughout the United States, any generalizations based on this sample must be made with care.

The large-bank sample was selected from the 100 largest banks in the United States on December 31, 1964, classified by amount of deposits, as listed in *Moody's Bank and Finance Manual—1965.* From these banks, thirteen were excluded that either were owned by a holding company having other substantial investments or were not in continual operation from January 1, 1960 through December 31, 1964. The remaining 87 banks constitute the sample. Deposit size of these banks at December 31, 1964 ranged from $400 million to $14 billion. Geographically, 33 of the banks are located in the Northeastern part of the United States, 20 in the North Central region, 22 in the South, and 12 in the West.[3] All but three of the 87 banks are located in cities with a 1960 population of 100,000 or more.

---

[3]The regions used are the four major geographical regions of the United States, as defined by the Department of Commerce, Bureau of the Census. For a map showing these regions, see U. S. Bureau of the Census, *Statistical Abstract of the United States: 1965,* 86th ed. (Washington, D.C., 1965), p. xii.

Variables Employed

This study makes use of six variables, all but one of which are ratios.[4] The first variable may be expressed as whether or not a bank engaged in external financing during the 1960–64 sample period. The second variable, market price to book value, is the ratio of 1964 market price per share to book value per share at December 31, 1964. (Market price represents an average of the high and low prices for the year.) The price-earnings ratio, the third variable, is the ratio of 1964 market price per share to average annual earnings per share for the five-year period, 1960–64. For the large-bank sample, earnings represent actual net operating earnings per share. Because operating statements were not available for the small-bank sample, earnings were estimated by adding cash dividends per share to changes in book value per share.[5]

Dividend payout (the fourth variable) is the ratio of average annual cash dividends for the 1960–64 period to average annual earnings for the same period. The next variable, dividends to book value,

---

[4]Information used in calculating the variables for the large-bank sample was obtained from: Frank L. Elliott and William B. Blundin, *A Comparative Analysis of 100 Largest Banks,* 1965 Edition (New York: Paine, Webber, Jackson & Curtis, 1965); *Moody's Bank & Finance Manual,* 1962, 1963, 1965 (New York: Moody's Investors Service, Inc.); *Over-the-Counter and Regional Exchange Stock Reports* (New York: Standard & Poor's Corp., 1965); *Standard Corporation Descriptions* (New York: Standard & Poor's Corp., 1965).

Market-Price Information used in calculating the variables for the small-bank sample was obtained from a questionnaire completed by each bank. Other information for the small-bank sample was obtained from the following sources: statements of conditions, 1959-64, filed with the State of Michigan Banking Department; *Annual Reports of the Commissioner,* 1959-64: State Banking Department, Lansing, Michigan; and *Michigan Bank Directory,* 1960-65 (Nashville: R. L. Polk & Co.).

[5]The State of Michigan Banking Department is prohibited by statute from disclosing operating statements.

is the ratio of 1964 cash dividends per share to book value per share at December 31, 1964. The last variable, dividend yield, is the ratio of 1964 cash dividends per share to 1946 market price per share.[6]

EXTERNAL FINANCING AND DIVIDEND POLICY

A bank is able to build capital through the sale of capital securities or through the retention of earnings. These alternative methods were examined for the two samples of banks. During the 1960–64 period, 36 of the 87 banks in the large-bank sample sold common stock or issued capital notes, contrasting with 16 of the 118 banks in the small-bank sample.[7] Table 1 shows frequency distributions of dividend payout for the two samples of banks. It should be noted that the median ratio of dividend payout for the small-bank sample (32 percent) is considerably lower than the median payout of the large-bank sample (47 percent). Thus, the banks in the small-bank sample tended to retain a greater portion of earnings than did the large banks, and to make relatively less use of external financing during the five-year sample period.

What are possible reasons for this occurrence? One reason could be that small banks have a great deal more difficulty engaging in external financing than do large banks; this difficulty may cause them to rely primarily on earnings retention to build capital. The market for their stock is typically confined to the immediate community and is relatively thin and inactive. Bid and ask quotations for stocks of small banks, unlike those of most large banks, are not published regularly in newspapers.[8] Moreover, knowledge

TABLE 1
Dividend Payout 1960–64
Small- and Large-Bank Samples
(number of banks)

Dividend Payout Ratio (Percent)	Small-Bank Sample (118 Banks)	Large-Bank Sample (87 Banks)
Over 55	5	12
50–55	4	23
45–50	5	18
40–45	19	16
35–40	18	8
30–35	19	7
25–30	11	0
20–25	22	1
Under 20	15	2
Median Dividend Payout	32 percent	47 percent

Source: Questionnaire; Statements of Condition, 1959–64, filed with the State of Michigan Banking Department; *Annual Reports of the Commissioner*, 1959–64; State Banking Department, Lansing, Michigan; *Michigan Bank Directory* (Nashville: R. L. Polk & Co., 1960–65); Frank L. Elliott and William B. Blundin, *A Comparative Analysis of 100 Largest Banks*, 1965 Edition (New York: Paine, Webber, Jackson & Curtis, 1965); *Moody's Bank & Finance Manual*, 1962, 1963, 1965 (New York: Moody's Investors Service, Inc.); *Over-the-Counter and Regional Exchange Stock Reports* (New York: Standard & Poor's Corp., 1965); *Standard Corporation Descriptions* (New York: Standard & Poor's Corp., 1965).

of the investment opportunity is not widespread, and marketability of the typical stock generally is considered to be poor.[9] To sell a new offering of stock, the small bank must find people having money to invest and, equally important, wanting to invest. If dilution of control is a matter of concern, the bank may be confined to a stock offering through rights to existing shareholders. The success of such an offering depends upon whether or not a relatively small number of shareholders want to increase their commitment.[10]

In equity financing, the problem of dilution of book value of stock usually is a far more important consideration for small banks than for large banks. Banks may be hesitant to issue new stock if dilution of book value would result. The ratios of

---

[6]The distributions of data for the five ratio variables were approximately normal; for the ratios involving market price, however, there was a slight skewness to the right, particularly for the small-bank sample.

[7]None of the banks in the small-bank sample issued capital notes during the 1960–64 period.

[8]Whitaker, *op. cit.*, Section 111.

---

[9]Lerner and Jacobs, *op. cit.*, 77, 128.

[10]The median number of shareholders for banks in the small-bank sample was 52.

market price to book value for banks in the two samples are shown in Table 2. As seen in this Table, market price was below book value in only one case for the large banks; in the small-bank sample, the market price was less than book value for over 75 percent of the stocks. The median ratio of market price to book value for the large banks was 166 percent, while that of the small banks was 86 percent. Dilution of book value, therefore, is very much a problem for most of the small banks in the sample. This may explain, in part, the lower dividend payment and less reliance upon external financing compared with that of the large-bank sample.

TABLE 2
Ratio of Market Price to Book Value
Small- and Large-Bank Samples
(number of banks)

Ratio of Market Price to Book Value (Percent)	Small-Bank Sample (118 Banks)	Large-Bank Sample (87 Banks)
Over 300		1
200–300		19
170–200		19
140–170	2	27
120–140	9	19
100–120	13	1
90–100	27	1
80–90	15	
70–80	23	
60–70	14	
50–60	8	
Under 50	7	
Median Ratio of Market Price to Book Value	86 percent	166 percent

Source: Same as Table 1.

Small banks also may be hesitant to sell stock because of relatively low price-earnings ratios. As shown in Table 3, the banks in the small-bank sample had much lower price-earnings multiples than did the large banks. The median price-earnings ratio for the large banks was 17.4, while that of the small banks was 10.9.

Another consideration influencing divi-

TABLE 3
Price-Earnings Ratios
Small- and Large-Bank Samples
(number of banks)

Price-Earnings Ratio	Small-Bank Sample (118 Banks)	Large-Bank Sample (87 Banks)
Over 24	3	7
22–24	2	6
20–22	1	9
18–20	3	15
16–18	3	22
14–16	12	21
12–14	20	7
10–12	26	
8–10	32	
6–8	11	
Under 6	5	
Median Price-Earnings Ratio	10.9	17.4

Source: Same as Table 1.

dend policy is the tax bracket of the bank's shareholders. In the case of large banks, where the stock is widely held, the tax impact of dividends on individuals is unlikely to be known. Therefore, the tax situation of specific shareholders is not likely to have an important influence on dividend policy. However, for most small banks, the tax impact of dividends on the principal shareholders may often be common knowledge. When these shareholders are in similar tax brackets, the tax consideration could be very important in formulating dividend policy.[11] If shareholders are in a comparatively high tax bracket, a policy of relatively high retention may be in order due to the favorable tax treatment of capital gains in comparison with that of dividend income.

The substantial difference in markets for the stock of the large and the small bank, together with the market-price problem, would seem to explain many of the differences in dividend policy and external financing for the two samples of banks. Many—perhaps most—small banks are unable to engage in equity financing success-

---

[11]Lerner and Jacobs, op. cit., 76.

fully and, consequently, must look to earnings retention to build capital. To the extent that principal shareholders in small banks are in relatively high tax brackets, the lower dividend payout for small banks in part may be attributable to this cause.

SMALL-BANK DILEMMA

Small banks which do not pay reasonably attractive dividends probably will refrain from equity financing because the market price of their stock is too low in relation to book value and earnings.[12]

In order to build capital, these banks may have to retain an even greater portion of earnings. This policy may depress further the price of the stock and make equity financing an even less desirable alternative. However, the stocks of those banks that pay generous dividends will probably be high in relation to book value and earnings. As a result, equity financing will be an attractive alternative to earnings retention as a means of building capital. With equity financing, a bank may not feel pressed to build capital through earnings retention; it may be able to increase the dividend. In turn, this action may buoy the price of the stock and enhance future equity financing.

A comparison of the small banks that sold stock with those that did not is consistent with this dilemma. For the 1960–64 period, the median ratio of dividend payout for the sixteen banks that sold stock

was 44 percent, compared with 31 percent for the other 102 banks in the sample. The median ratio of market price to book value of 94 percent and median price-earnings ratio of 12.3 for the banks that sold stock compare with ratios of 82 percent and 10.7, respectively, for the banks that did not sell stock during the 1960–64 period. Due to the size of the sample of banks selling stock, however, caution is necessary in interpreting these results.

CONCLUSIONS BASED ON THE STUDY

Despite the apparent importance of dividends on the market price of a small-bank stock, the small banks in the sample tended to retain a greater proportion of earnings (68 percent) than did the banks in the large-bank sample (53 percent). While the median 1964 dividend yields for the large- and small-bank samples were relatively close—2.8 percent versus 3.2 percent—the median ratio of market price to book value and the price-earnings ratio for the large-bank sample were considerably higher than those for the small banks. To the extent that the market price of a bank stock is determined by dividends, these differences in relative market price can be explained in part by differences in dividend policy.

The main reason for the higher retention rate on the part of small banks may be that earnings retention is the only feasible way to build capital. The narrow geographic market for the stock, poor marketability, and the lack of published quotations plague the small bank in its ability to sell stock. Moreover, the market-price problem, aggravated by low dividend payout, may all but preclude external equity financing as an alternative for building capital.

---

[12]In Van Horne and Helwig, *op. cit.*, relatively strong positive associations were found between the ratios of market price to book value and dividends to book value and also between the price-earnings ratio and dividend-payout ratio. The evidence suggested that dividends were the most important determinant of market price for the small-bank stocks in the sample.

SECTION THREE
Regulation and Allocative Efficiency

Chapter VIII
REGULATORY ASSESSMENT

35. Regulatory Goals for Financial Intermediaries[*]

Thomas G. Gies, Thomas Mayer, and Edward C. Ettin

The legal framework within which financial intermediaries operate is of great importance to the economy. This is due to that framework's influence on the volume and cost of funds made available to various classes of borrowers and the ability of these flows to respond to changing market conditions. This article discusses the goals or objectives that supervisory authorities should consider in deriving and implementing their regulatory policies.

The first goal of financial intermediaries should be to *assist in the efficient allocation of resources* by offering favorable savings outlets and acquiring primary securities.[1] In the American econ-

omy there is a presumption that resources are in most cases efficiently allocated if the market is a guiding force. That is to say, we assume that market forces direct real resources to areas where demand is the greatest as indicated by the price system. This means that goods and services produced will be either those most desired by consumers or those that will best aid in the production of those goods and services most desired by consumers (capital goods). If resources are *efficiently* allocated, these desired goods will be produced at the lowest possible cost.

It follows that financial institutions should not allocate resources to any sector unless so directed by consumer demand. That is to say, financial intermediaries should not initiate production, but instead implement a market demand. In this sense financial intermediaries should be passive. This does not imply that financial intermediaries should be lethargic or non-creative. There is no demand for the new product or innovation until the

---

[*]Reprinted by permission of the authors.

[1]The authors drew freely from the following memoranda and monographs of the Commission on Money and Credit, but are responsible themselves for the ideas presented here: *Criteria for Financial Regulation*, May 12, 1960; Beckhart, B. H., *Criteria of a Well-functioning Financial System*, May 1, 1960; Duesenberry, J. S., *Criteria for Judging the Performance of Capital Markets*, April 10, 1960.

market is aware of it and educated to its use. Financial intermediaries should be creative or dynamic in seeing that the new product and firm gets resources without arbitrarily removing their decision making process from the market. This creativeness is necessary for a dynamic economy.

The goal of regulation is to aid financial intermediaries in furthering an efficient allocation of resources. *The major way regulation can assist this goal is by fostering competition*, since it is presumed competition by financial intermediaries will assist in the efficient allocation of resources. By competition we mean ". . . rivalry on the part of the members of one economic group to secure the patronage of the members of another economic group."[2] Since our concern here is in the "use" side of financial intermediaries and not the "source" side, this statement implies both that deficit units find many institutions "competing" to service their needs and that the financial institutions find many deficit unit's securities from which to choose. If either one group of financial institutions or one group of deficit units find ". . . a state of affairs in which the individual . . . firm is so well entrenched and in command of the situation that he does not have to take into account the offers made by others"[3] we will conclude that the competition does not exist. This means that the number of firms competing is not as important as the number of alternatives for similar services open to both sides of the market. It is not the industry that is important but the market in which they compete.

There are many ways financial regulation can implement and foster competition:

1. *A decision by the saver as between two equally and liquid media for his savings outlet should not determine which*

deficit sectors are serviced. That is, financial asset specialization should not misallocate resources. Portfolio regulations and operating conventions which arbitrarily place limits on which primary securities equally situated financial intermediaries may purchase would be antithetic to this principle. Such procedures reduce alternatives and hence competition.

2. *Government regulation of financial intermediary portfolios should be general in nature rather than specific.* That is, they should set the "rules of the game" rather than predetermine specific financial operations. The latter arbitrarily prevents the financial intermediaries from taking advantage of competitive opportunities. The former determines an environment in which the institution may seek its own adjustment. An economic unit cannot behave competitively when his choices are narrowly limited. For example regulation should be able to limit certain financial intermediaries to creditor claims, but not, say, public utility bonds only.

3. *Regulation should, as far as is practicable, foster the opportunity for wider geographical markets.* Wider geographical markets allow more rivalry and allow more alternatives to be available to all participants, hence improving the allocation of resources. At the same time that wider markets are fostered and local markets are not, regulation should not prevent financial intermediaries from servicing local institutions. Financial institutions often, because of broader information, are able to better serve their local market. But they should not be able to make a "take it or leave it" offer.

4. *Regulation should be identical for identical services.* If two institutions tap not only the same source but in general have the same use of funds, regulations on each should be identical. If not, one institution is facing discriminatory regulation; arbitrary rules rather than the market begins to dominate the allocation of resources.

---

[2]Griffin, C. E. "Needed: A Realistic Antitrust Policy, "*Harvard Business Review,* November-December, 1956, p. 78.

[3]*Ibid.*

5. *The regulations of all states and the Federal Government should generally be uniform for each aspect of operation of the private financial system.* If market forces are to dominate the allocation of resources, the authority of certain geographical areas cannot be different than others. The rules of the game thus becoming established, certain areas begin to have more of one type of financial intermediary than another. Both sides of the market suffer.

6. *Regulations of portfolios should foster flexibility by allowing financial intermediaries to provide various financial services.* Financial intermediaries must be able to adjust quickly to changing credit needs and borrowing techniques in the economy. They must be able to follow their demand geographically (e.g. to the suburbs) and be able to enter any field that is in keeping with the institutional framework (safety, solvency, liquidity, etc.). Such flexibility also allows the filling of credit gaps resulting from innovation and dynamic changes in both the real and financial sectors. Flexibility also implies the competitive elimination of inefficient firms and services as well as the competitive elimination of those financial industry areas no longer needed.

In general, therefore, our desire for efficient allocation of resources by financial intermediaries directs us to be concerned that the regulation of the portfolios of financial intermediaries be consistent with competitive conditions. This is our ideal; our goal. Oftentimes it appears to be a phantom. For example, even cursory examination demonstrates the compartmentalization of financial markets. As Gurley and Shaw suggest,[4] sharecroppers do not issue commercial paper and state treasurers do not buy accounts receivable. This misses the point. The point is: can the sharecropper service his needs efficiently elsewhere, and is there something else the treasurer can buy that fits his needs, there still being a demand for accounts receivable elsewhere. If certain channels are closed to borrowers and lenders, this is not prima facie evidence of lack of competition. That fact *plus* lack of alternative channels is. Competition means the existence of reasonable alternatives.

There are goals other than efficient allocation of resources (narrowly defined) which we expect our financial system, because of its pivotal position, to further. Regulation that furthers the goal of efficient allocation of resources may or may not also further the other economic goals. If they do not, then compromise is necessary. However, it is not an "either or" matter. There are many gradations and shadings between these two goals; and the choice is neither simple nor definite. We can only point out where the two goals conflict and then give our opinion.

These other goals are: (1) growth, (2) stability (price and employment), (3) freedom, and (4) safety (of financial institutions).

In general, competition which furthers the goal of efficient allocation of resources, also furthers the general economic goal of *economic freedom.* By economic freedom we mean freedom to choose types and places of employment and location of business, to own property and especially to manage freely one's financial budget. This last particularly means the right to save freely in any form desired and also to borrow when necessary. No freedom, however, is absolute in an interdependent society. Although sharecroppers cannot sell commercial paper, they also cannot borrow enough to build a four bedroom home. Their freedom to do this is limited by the freedom of lenders to choose their primary securities. Moreover, it is competition that reconciles personal freedom and interdependence in a market economy. We are each dependent on others to live yet the market, by providing

---

[4]Gurley and Shaw, *Money in a Theory of Finance* (Washington, D.C.: The Brookings Institution, 1960).

satisfactory alternatives, provides us with freedom. Simon's dictum is to the point: "A nation that is not willing to submit to the discipline of competition will sooner or later find itself under the discipline of authority."

Regulations that reduce competition, such as control of entry, specific restraints rather than general ones, etc., also reduce freedom. We are plotting a fine line here. If the regulations become general rules of the game and allow parties to make their own adjustment, then freedom is not infringed. Again: no right is absolute.

Efficient allocation of resources, furthered by competition, will also further *economic growth*. Resources allocated to their most efficient uses means that resources are not, in an economic sense, wasted. Quite obviously efficient allocation of resources is the opposite of inefficient allocation of resources and the latter reduces economic growth by wasting resources. However, as already pointed out, above, the desire of consumers may, by efficiently allocating resources to those desires, reduce future economic growth.

The rate of economic growth, however, depends upon the growth rate of the factors of production and of technology. Asset regulation of financial intermediaries affects economic growth primarily through its effects on one of the factors of production, the capital stock. There are several ways it does so. First, it can affect the savings-income ratio by changing the level of income. Asset regulations have some effect on the level of investment and since the productivity of different types of investment differs, asset regulation can, by preventing or limiting failures, limit the severity of depressions, the resulting increased level of income will lead to a greater volume of *saving*. Second, if financial intermediary regulations stimulate certain types of investments compared to other ones, this may affect the volume of investments, and hence the level of income.

In addition to affecting the rate of sav-

ing, asset regulations can also affect the rate of growth more directly by affecting the direction of investment activity. Insofar as the marginal efficiency of the types of investment thus differing exceed the marginal efficiency of the retarded types of investments, income will grow at a different rate. However, one must guard against overestimating the size of this effect, for one should simply compare the marginal efficiency of the assets they would have bought otherwise, because other institutions and households may now buy these assets instead. For example, assume that financial institutions are prohibited from buying an asset with a very high marginal efficiency, surely other surplus units will buy this asset in place of another asset with a low marginal efficiency. Asset regulation of financial intermediaries can therefore affect the marginal efficiency of investments for the whole economy only if they make financial intermediaries buy assets with such a low yield that nobody else is willing to buy them. The stimulation of the mortgage market, particularly the residential mortgage market probably has this effect to some extent.

Finally, asset regulation affects economic growth through its effects on the efficiency of the financial intermediary industry itself. In 1968 the financial intermediary industry accounted for $117.1 billion, or 13.5 percent of GNP,[5] and hence its internal efficiency is important. However, it is probable that asset regulations have relatively little effect on this internal efficiency, since a large part of the work force of the industry is engaged in the deposit rather than the asset side of this business.

One of the reasons for controlling the asset selection of financial intermediaries, is help in obtaining *price stability and full employment*. Regulations can help in

---

[5]*Survey of Current Business*, July, 1969, p. 25.

achieving this goal in several ways. First, they can have an influence on economic stability by affecting the growth rate of financial intermediaries, and according to the Gurley-Shaw theses, the growth of these institutions has an important influence on stability. But this problem is much broader than the question of asset control and since it is discussed in another Staff Paper it will not be taken up here. Instead let us look at some of the more direct ways in which asset control can facilitate economic stabilization. First, by providing for the safety of financial intermediaries it makes these institutions better able to withstand depression and thereby stabilize the expectations of the public. This is clearly the most important effect it can have. More generally, asset regulations can try to have intermediaries maintain the economy's liquidity during recession. For example, by using liberal standards of bank examination during a recession, banks can be encouraged to maintain outstanding loans.

Similarly, asset regulations can try to prevent velocity from increasing during the boom. One way in which financial intermediaries increase velocity during the boom is to sell government securities to holders of idle deposits and to lend the proceeds.[6]

The largest number of regulations of financial intermediaries may be traced to the goal of *safety*, particularly for commercial banks. The reason is historical; past failures of banks, life insurance companies, savings and loan associations, and other financial institutions have made public policy very sensitive to this need. The regulations used to prevent such a contingency deal with regulations about capital and the nature of claims, but mainly with the kinds and the merits of various assets that financial intermediaries may acquire. Ultimately, the claims of

financial intermediaries depend upon the liquidity, marketability, and safety of the primary securities acquired by those institutions.

Safety regulations may seem at first to be quite opposed to the criterion of a competitive economy, allowing each firm to equate marginal cost and price. If so this would raise a serious question about the degree of safety desired. In the long run, asset regulation cannot affect the distribution of credit among various sectors of the economy.[7] To see this, assume an extreme case where each financial intermediary can buy only one specific type of asset. If the demand for credit shifts between the various sectors, the relative profitability of financial intermediaries will change, and the ones serving the sectors with the greatest credit demand will grow relative to other ones. The net result, in the long run equilibrium, is therefore the same as if financial intermediaries were free to buy assets of various sectors.

But in the short run there is likely to be a difference between such a "tied" system and one where intermediaries are given more freedom to select their assets. The reason for this is that in a free system, officers of financial intermediaries can shift freely between different uses as soon as they perceive differences in yields, whereas in a "tied" system, depositors have to shift funds between institutions. Since officers of financial institutions are specialists, they are likely to notice and react to differences in yields much sooner than depositors. However to the extent that financial institutions develop operating conventions which are hard to change, their reaction time will be lengthened and may at times be not much shorter than those of households. But, in any case, a free system cannot take much longer to

[6]Smith, W., "On the Effectiveness of Monetary Policy," *American Economic Review*, September, 1956.

[7]This assumes that new financial institutions are allowed freely and are allowed to select the assets in which they want to specialize and are allowed to develop.

react than a tied system. To see this, assume that a financial manager in a free system were to be slower to adjust than households. In this case, households would shift from one type of financial institution to another before portfolio managers shift their assets, and in this limiting case, both systems would be equally fast, but in the presumably more likely case where portfolio managers react faster than depositors, a free system would be more flexible.

Another way of showing that regulation does not *necessarily* conflict with the competitive goal is the following: What regulation does is to abolish one product— deposits in uninhibited intermediaries— and create another one—deposits in regulated intermediaries instead. One cannot tell *a priori* whether this increases or decreases household's choice.[8]

But the fact that some regulation of the safety of financial intermediaries can be justified does not imply that the present extent of regulation is an optimal one. It may well be that our financial intermediaries are at present too safe. The reason for this is that safety is not a free good, but has the opportunity cost of lower earnings for the financial institution. Let us look at this in the context of an optimum financial system. In such an ideal system entrepreneurs would not be prevented from assuming risky ventures—all risks could be financed at some risk premium or other. Similarly, households could allocate their assets among instruments of different risk, so that the household's marginal rate of transformation between risk and yield would equal the entrepreneur's marginal rate of substitution between risk and income.

Although we may hear many discussions of the difficulty of financing risky ventures (e.g. the complaints about the lack of equity capital), allowing households a choice among instruments with different degrees of risk is also important, for households may have deeply felt risk references. Indeed, Milton Friedman has argued that it is possible that much of the difference of incomes amongst households can be explained by differences in risk preferences.[9] An important function of the financial systems consists therefore in providing households with assets having different risk coefficients. One way in which a financial system can allow households to reach their preferred risk position is to provide a large number of financial instruments with different degrees of risk —thus allowing each household and asset having the degree of risk it wants.

But a large number of risk differentiated assets is not a necessary condition— if the financial system provides two or more assets with extreme risk coefficients, then households can hold mixed portfolios of the two assets which gives them the risk exposure they desire. To what extent is our desire to regulate the safety of financial intermediaries consistent with this criterion of allowing the consumer to choose his optimum risk position? At the one extreme, it provides almost absolutely safe assets in government insured deposits, and at the other extreme, it provided penny uranium stocks. Since the function of most financial intermediaries in this system is to furnish assets at or very close to the safety end of this spectrum, it may seem that there is no conflict between having stringent regulations

---

[8]This argument seems open to an objection, for could it not be extended to show that regulating all products may be consistent with competition? The answer to this is, that, on a very abstract level, regulation of all types of commodities *may* be consistent within competition. However, for most commodities, firms are able to offer a very close substitute for a governmentally regulated commodity, if consumers desire it, and hence by suppressing an unregulated commodity and offering a regulated one in its stead, the government is probably putting households on a lower difference curve. But, for depositors in financial intermediaries the private market is not able to offer a commodity very similar to the regulated ones, for the ultimate safety of financial deposits can be guaranteed only by the money issuing authorities.

[9]Friedman, M., "Choice, Chance and the Personal Distribution of Income," *Journal of Political Economy*, August 1953, pp. 270–290.

for those intermediaries and allowing households to select the optimum risk co-efficient for their total asset portfolios.

But this optimistic conclusion represents too facile a view, for due to lack of knowledge and sufficient capital for diversification, stock purchases are not an easily available alternative for a large segment of the population.[10] Thus, the existence of assets with extreme risk differentials is not sufficient to provide the possibility of portfolio balance, and we therefore have a "risk gap" in the economy.

One may therefore question our present policy of requiring all our financial intermediaries to be extremely safe. In particular, one may become dubious about our apparent tendency to make the degree of safety of various intermediaries homogenous by such devices as government insurance of savings and loan shares, for example.

It may be still argued that differences in the degree of risk among financial intermediaries are undesirable because of consumer ignorance. This argument asserts that households are too ignorant to be able to evaluate risk differentials among financial intermediaries. However, this argument is open to the objection that such a policy of preventing risk differentials among financial intermediaries drives into the stock market a number of households who, in terms of this argument, should not be there. Hence, even aside from the philosophical question, whether people should be prevented from taking risks, it is by no means clear that the damage done by consumer ignorance is reduced by allowing a "risk gap." Hence the case for imposing rigid risk restrictions on all or most financial intermediaries is much weaker than the case for imposing them on only one or a few intermediaries.[11]

In addition to the creation of a risk gap, safety regulations interfere with competitive resource allocation in still another way. It limits the failure rate of financial intermediaries quite sharply and we generally rely on failures to weed out inefficient firms. But again, asset regulation does not counteract the competitive process as much as might appear at first. The main way in which it interferes with the weeding-out process is that it inhibits the punishment of firms taking excessive risk, for it prevents them from indulging in such excessive risks. But since the firms *cannot* take these risks, the fact that they want to do so cannot do any significant damage, and hence there is no reason why these firms should be eliminated.[12] There is, however, one important qualification here. By limiting risk taking, asset regulations restricts the Schumpeterian firm in its attempt to drive its rivals out of business, and hence slows up the "weeding-out" process.

But given the fact that asset regulation severely limits bankruptcies among finan-

---

the public treating all financial intermediaries as being homogenous. To be sure, the reason why savings and loan associations pay a higher rate for funds than do banks, may be that the public is concerned about liquidity rather than about safety. But even so, it does show that the public is capable of discrimination between financial institutions. However, if the differential is due merely to unfamiliarity with savings and loan associations, then the differential would prove little about the public's ability to discriminate. Moreover, it must be admitted that the differential can allow us only to make inference about the marginal saver—there may well be many intramarginal people who treat most assets as being equally safe.

[12]The propensity to take *excessive* risks may well be correlated with other types of inefficiency. If so, by preventing the elimination of firms which should fail, it may well happen that the taking of excessive risks result in failure faster than other types of inefficiency, and hence asset regulation may keep such firms alive too long. But this qualification is itself subject to a qualification. Failure of financial intermediaries because of excessive risk, rather than because of other forms of inefficiency, is more likely to occur during a recession than at any other time. But, at that time, they are more prone to cause damage—hence spreading failure out more evenly over the cycle is highly desirable.

---

[10]Moreover, the possibility of buying stocks does little for those people who feel that the stock market is currently too high.

[11]The fact that savings and loan associations pay a higher rate to all savers than do other institutions shows that there is little danger of

cial intermediaries, how are inefficient ones eliminated? The answer is that in the relevant sense, a firm may be eliminated without disappearing as a formal entity. If a firm is inefficient and earns below average rate of return, then there will be a tendency for its management to be replaced. And if the firm has a new management which follows different policies, then for purposes of economic analysis we must treat it as a new firm.

Leaving aside the question whether all or most financial intermediaries should have to meet similar safety standards, let us look at some of the criteria for safety regulations.

The main thing we want safety standards to do—apart from ensuring safety—is to interfere as little as possible with portfolio choices desired by financial intermediaries, for as an "operating convention" we can assume that these choices tend toward an optimal allocation of resources. Hence one should beware of attaching the safety label to proposals for supporting the market for particular assets such as government securities or mortgages.

Another reason often used for controlling the asset choice of the financial intermediaries is the desire to *stimulate home ownership*. But for several reasons asset regulation of financial intermediaries is an inefficient way of doing this. First, insofar as the costs of home ownership are reduced this way it provides a subsidy not only for the marginal buyer who is bought into the market by this subsidy, but also for the intra-marginal buyer who would have bought a home even without this subsidy. Second, there is grave doubt whether asset regulations really stimulate mortgage lending to as great an extent as may appear at first. To be sure, by limiting the alternatives available to savings and loan associations and savings banks, these institutions are made to place a larger proportion of their funds into mortgages. But the total volume of their mortgage lending depends

not only on the proportion of their funds they place into mortgages, but also on the volume of their funds. And the volume of their deposits is a function of the rate of return on their assets, so that ultimately the amount they lend on mortgages depends upon the rate of return on mortgages. To illustrate this point, assume an extreme case where, say, savings banks are forced to invest all of their funds in securities yielding 1 percent interest. The net effect of this would be the disappearance of savings banks, and not the sale of a large number of such securities. In other words, financial intermediaries are just as the name implies, intermediaries—and in the long run it is the final lender, rather than the intermediary who determines the uses of funds. To be sure one could argue that with interest rates on commercial banks time deposits held down by the Federal Reserve and with both savings banks and savings and loan associations controlled in the direction of mortgages, the average depositor would have few alternative places to put his funds and hence would have little choice but to let his funds go in the mortgage market. But even so, the consumer has some alternatives open to him—he can keep his funds in a demand deposit for example, thus surrendering yield for greater convenience. Moreover, had it not been for the profitability of the mortgage market in the post-war period, other financial intermediaries not oriented towards the mortgage market might have arisen.

The final major goal of regulation one hears of is keeping local capital at home. Whatever one may think of the ultimate value judgments underlying this goal, it is a significant factor in the minds of legislators and therefore worth discussing. In general, regulating the assets of certain financial intermediaries is not a very powerful method of preventing the migration of capital. For example, if we prevent savings and loan associations from making mortgage loans outside the district, the resulting decline in local mortgage rates will cause national lenders, such as insurance companies, to cut back on their mortgages in this area. But regional differences in mortgage rates suggest that shifts by national lenders are not sufficient to offset completely the

effect of local conditions on the credit market, and hence that regulations may succeed in increasing an area's capital stock to some extent. In general, the criteria for such regulations are the same as those for the policies to stimulate mortgage lending discussed above.

36. Stimulating Bank Competition through Regulatory Action [*]

Paul M. Horvitz[†]

The previous article (by Gies, Mayer and Ettin) provided general guidelines for regulators to follow in maximizing the economic contribution of financial intermediaries. The common element in these guidelines is the fostering of competition. This article treats specific actions in the areas of banking structure, pricing, bank portfolios and services which the various supervisory agencies can take to stimulate interbank and non-bank competition.

In recent years there have been many proposals for legislation to stimulate competition among financial institutions. There have been extensive legislative proposals made by the Commission on Money and Credit, by the President's Committee on Financial Institutions, and by the Advisory Committee to the Comptroller of the Currency.[1] In a recent article in this journal Almarin Phillips advanced several proposals for legislation to stimulate banking competition.[2] These and other studies have led to the introduction of a large number of bills in Congress relating to banking.[3]

Very few of these bills, and none of the significant ones, have been enacted into law. As our past history has demonstrated, it is very difficult to get significant legislation pertaining to financial institutions through Congress in the absence of a financial crisis. Because the prospects for legislative action in the near future are not very great, it is worthwhile to investigate the possibilities for stimulating competition among financial institutions

[*]From *Journal of Finance*, March, 1965. Reprinted by permission of the publisher (the American Finance Association) and the author.

[†]The author was Senior Economist, Office of the Comptroller of the Currency at the time this article was prepared. He is now Director of Research, F.D.I.C. The views expressed in this paper are those of the author. He is grateful to Weldon Welfling, Benjamin Klebaner, and his colleagues in the Office of the Comptroller of the Currency for many helpful comments.

[1]*Money and Credit.* Report of the Commission on Money and Credit (Englewood Cliffs, N.J.: Prentice-Hall, Inc., 1961); *Report of the Committee on Financial Institutions* (Washington: U.S. G.P.O., 1963); *National Banks and the Future,* Report of the Advisory Committee on Banking to the Comptroller of the Currency (Washington: U.S. G.P.O., 1962).
[2]"Competition, Confusion, and Commercial Banking," *Journal of Finance,* March 1964.
[3]For a list of the bills pending before Congress in mid-1964, see *American Banker,* June 22, 1964, p. 7.

through action of the regulatory authorities. The purpose of this paper is to consider some of the actions that have been taken and which could be taken by the various supervisory agencies (without new legislation) to stimulate competition among commercial banks, and between commercial banks and other financial institutions.

I. BANKING STRUCTURE

Probably the most important area for regulatory action by the banking supervisory agencies lies in the field of bank chartering, branching, and bank mergers. An increase in entry by new banks is clearly one of the most effective ways of stimulating competition in banking.[4] In recent years there has been some discussion of the desirability of easing entry into banking; these discussions have even gone to the extent of considering "free banking," a subject which had been thought dead for many years.[5]

1. CHARTERING. The major regulatory barrier to new entry is heavy reliance on what Alhadeff calls "the need doctrine." Under present procedures, a new bank is chartered only if the community "needs" a new bank. The major reason for rejection of applications for new entry by national banks has been "insufficient need."[6] There is, of course, no clear criterion of what constitutes sufficient need. When a charter application is rejected on grounds of "insufficient need" or "unfavorable earnings

prospects," the chartering authorities are in effect substituting their judgment for that of the applicants. A considerable easing of entry would result from a decision of the chartering authorities to refrain from overruling the judgment of the people risking their capital on the new bank.

In many cases "insufficient need" really means that there is insufficient demand to support comfortably the existing banks plus a new bank. This decision fundamentally involves the degree of risk of bank failure we are willing to tolerate to gain a more competitive banking structure, since it is likely that freer entry and more competition in banking would lead to more bank failures. Attitudes on this issue vary. There are those who hold that bank failures are disastrous and we should at all costs keep the number of failures as close to zero as possible. This approach can be found in statements by state banking supervisors to the Joint Economic Committee in 1952. For example, the Oregon supervisor stated that:[7]

I do not believe that . . . I should approve a second bank . . . where it seems evident that the existing bank would be weakened by the loss of a portion of the existing business.

Along the same lines, the California supervisor argued that "competition is not a reasonable public necessity in the case of banking,"[8] and the Connecticut supervisor stated that "[s]ound and ethical competition is . . . a healthy thing but, of course, not to the extent of hazard to existing independent banking institutions."[9] Most other state banking supervisors made similar responses.

However, it is by no means clear that bank failures are necessarily the disaster they are commonly considered to be. The failure of the textile mill in the one-mill

---

[4]Phillips argues that "[t]he most important single policy [to improve performance] would be to permit freer entry." *Op. cit.*, p. 44.

[5]See, for example, David Alhadeff, "A Reconsideration of Restrictions on Bank Entry," *Quarterly Journal of Economics*, May 1963; Donald P. Jacobs, "The Framework of Commercial Bank Regulation: An Appraisal," *The National Banking Review*, March 1964; and David C. Motter and Deane Carson "Bank Entry and the Public Interest: A Case Study," *National Banking Review*, June 1964.

[6]See Bernard Shull and Paul Horvitz, "Branch Banking and the Structure of Competition," *National Banking Review*, March 1964, Tables 4 and 5.

[7]Joint Committee on the Economic Report, *Monetary Policy and the Management of the Public Debt*, 82d Cong., 2d Sess. 1952, p. 994.
[8]*Ibid.*, p. 995.
[9]*Ibid.*, p. 990.

New England town is almost certainly a greater community disaster than the failure of the local bank in a one-bank town. Of course, an epidemic of bank failures such as we have experienced in the past is to be avoided, but with the existence of federal deposit insurance a few bank failures need not lead to disaster to any community or to a wave of bank runs or failures. Much concern has been expressed over the failure of five banks in the first eight months of 1964, although losses to depositors were small and in no sense had a calamitous effect on the local economy. In contrast to the five bank failures out of over 13,000 banks in operation, we might note that during this same period business failures were at an annual rate of about 55 per 10,000 concerns. Obviously bank failures are not desirable, but failures may be symptomatic of vigorous competition, and vigorous competition *is* desirable.

In addition to the need criterion, another regulatory restriction on entry concerns management of the proposed bank. "Unsatisfactory management" has been an important reason for rejection of applications for new national bank charters. Chartering authorities put heavy weight on the background and character of the proposed bank's management and directors. There is no information available to indicate the basis on which the authorities separate the "good guys" from the "bad guys." It is not impossible that those charter applicants whose backgrounds and experience indicate a tendency toward vigorous competition and price cutting may be classified with the "bad guys."[10]

2. BRANCHING. Competition can also be stimulated by new entry through branching. There has been an increase in branching activity where it is authorized

by law in recent years. Again it is important that applications for new branches be evaluated on their merits and not on the basis of any sort of territorial or numerical allocations among the supervisory agencies. In this area, also, there have been claims of a breakdown in coordination between federal and state regulatory agencies. Part of this coordination involves the concept of priority. As Llewellyn Brown, Mississippi State Comptroller has put it: "There has always been an informal understanding between the supervisors and the Comptroller that in competitive application situations, and all other factors being equal, priority would be given to the application filed first."[11] In practice, the policy of "priority" meant that once a bank filed an application for a branch in a particular community, it could rest assured that no competing bank could establish a branch in that community first. There was then no hurry to provide the additional branch facilities applied for.

Recent hearings before the House Banking and Currency Committee provided an excellent example of this practice:[12]

MR. BROWN. Canton, Miss. is a small agricultural town of 9,700 people located in the center of my State. There are two banks there, the Canton Exchange Bank, a State bank, and the First National Bank.

On April 16, 1962, I received a letter from Mr. J. D. Gwin, the chief national bank examiner of the Sixth Federal Reserve District, indicating the receipt of an application from the First National Bank to establish a branch in the neighboring community of Ridgeland. . . .

. . . I replied by stating that the Canton Exchange Bank had an application on file to open a branch in Ridgeland and that I was in the process of approving that application. I might state that the Canton Exchange Bank application had been on file since August of

---

[10]Reuben Kessel has discussed the way in which restrictions on entry into medicine operate to discourage or discriminate against those who may become price-cutting doctors. See his "Price Discrimination in Medicine," *The Journal of Law and Economics*, October 1958, esp. pp. 46–50.

[11]Llewellyn Brown, State Comptroller, Mississippi, *Conflict of Federal and State Banking Laws*, Hearings Before the Committee on Banking and Currency, House of Representatives, 88th Congress, First Session, 1963, p. 200.

[12]*Ibid.*, pp. 199, 200, 234.

1961 and that we had been discussing the matter for some time before that. Frankly, I thought my letter would end the matter. . . .

. . . The next thing I knew about this matter was informal advice from the Canton Exchange Bank that the application of the First National Bank had been granted. The application of the Canton Exchange Bank had already been granted by me. The result, therefore, is two branches in a location which, in my view, can only support one branch. . . .

MR. ST. GERMAIN. You cite the Canton Exchange Bank, that an application had been filed since August of 1961. Is it not a fact that this particular one was pending since 1957?

MR. BROWN. True, sir, I didn't think you would be interested in going back too far. . . .

It appears that in this case the state supervisor had a branch application since 1957. No action was taken on the application until a branch of a national bank in the community became a possibility. Collusive arrangements among the supervisors to bar entry are just as serious as collusive practices among the banks and should not be allowed to continue even if masked as "coordination" or "cooperation."

New branches can be authorized under existing interpretations of branching laws in some states and also by reconsidering the restrictions on branching which exist in others. Federal law restricts national bank branches in any state to the same geographic limitations which apply to state banks under the laws of that state. Many of these state laws are not clear as to the geographical limitations on branching privileges of state banks. Previous policy of the Office of the Comptroller of the Currency seems to have been that branches would not be approved for national banks unless the state law was clearcut in authorizing branches in certain areas. Present policy seems to be that branches will be approved for national banks where, under a reasonable interpretation of the state law, it is not forbidden.

An example may be the Michigan law which does not allow a bank to establish a branch in any "village" in which a bank is already operating. The law does not define "village." This leaves to the chartering authority the decision as to whether a proposed branch will be located in the same village as an existing bank. Another example of a state law subject to diverse interpretation is that of Virginia. Virginia allows branching statewide if and only if the branch is acquired by merger. The question has been raised as to whether such procedural restrictions bind the Comptroller in his decisions or whether he is bound only by the *geographical* limitations of state law.

Obviously, a policy of making decisions in such cases can and has led to some litigation of disputed interpretations of the law.[13] This seems to be perfectly appropriate under our judicial system. Differences of opinion as to interpretation of law should be settled in the courts, rather than through the decision of a regulatory authority to avoid controversy and lawsuits by adopting an overly restrictive policy on approval of new branches.

3. MERGERS. Probably the most important decisions of regulatory authorities which affect competition in banking are those with respect to bank mergers. Under the Bank Merger Act of 1960, a merger resulting in an insured bank must be approved in advance by either the Comptroller of the Currency, the Federal Reserve Board, or the FDIC, depending on whether the resulting bank is a national, state member, or non-member insured

---

[13]Among the cases which have led to litigation are: *Manufacturers National Bank of Detroit v. James J. Saxon and Community National Bank of Pontiac*, Civil Action No. 25172 (D.C. E.D. Mich.); *W. M. Jackson v. First National Bank of Valdosta*, Civil Action No. 647 (D.C. M.D. Ga.); *Manufacturers National Bank of Detroit v. James J. Saxon and Michigan Bank, N. A.*, Civil Action No. 2460 (D.C. E.D. Mich.); *North Madison Bank v. National Bank of Madison, Indiana, and James J. Saxon*, Civil Action No. NA 63–C–76 (D.C. S.D. Ind. 1963). For a summary of the issues in pending cases, see each issue of *The National Banking Review*.

bank. Of course, not all bank mergers are undesirable. By most standards there are too many small, inefficient banks operating in the United States. It is clear that whatever the general policy on bank mergers may be, over the long run the tendency is going to be toward reduction in the number of these small banks.[14] The Bank Merger Act requires that the appropriate regulatory agency weigh the impact of the merger on competition along with the so-called banking factors (financial history of the banks, adequacy of capital, character of management, etc.). Many economists and some lawmakers have complained that the regulatory agencies do not give sufficient weight to the competitive factor.

It is not easy to determine how much weight is given to the competition factor by the regulatory authorities in making merger decisions. George Hull and Charles Phillips have attempted to make such a determination by careful analysis of published merger decisions.[15] Hall and Phillips recognized the limitations of their approach, but came to the general conclusion that competition as defined by economists is not the most important consideration:

The Federal banking authorities share a common approach to their duties under the Bank Merger Act of 1960. . . . Great stress is placed on the advantages to customers from the creation of larger banking organizations. . . . All three regard mergers as justified to neutralize the power of large banks. Conversely they all regard the existence of other large banks as protection against the

misuse of market power stemming from a merger.

. . . Increases in concentration as a result of a merger are regarded as a necessary price to pay to increase the availability of local banking services.

Part of the explanation for this may lie in the tendency within the supervisory agencies to have preliminary investigation of merger applications made by personnel connected with the bank examination function. Because of the close association of these people in their daily work with problems of bank safety, they may tend to give heavy emphasis to the strengthening aspects of bank mergers. Examiners may sincerely view the strengthening of the bank that results from a bank merger as increasing its ability to compete, and hence they may regard virtually all mergers as strengthening competition.

It had been true until quite recently at all three federal regulatory agencies that the merger application proceeded through bank examination and legal channels exclusively. Now, at the Federal Reserve and the Office of the Comptroller of the Currency, economists are involved at some stage in reviewing merger applications. These procedures, however, do not seem to have had much effect on decisions. It is rather the activities of the Justice Department which may lead to more weight being given to competitive factors in future merger decisions.

The emergence of the Justice Department as an important factor in bank mergers deserves some comment. The Bank Merger Act allows other factors to be taken into consideration in addition to the effect of competition and, of course, many mergers are justifiable and desirable on consideration of these banking factors.[16]

---

[14]In fact, as Phillips has pointed out, a policy of freer entry coupled with the Federal Reserve restriction of the aggregate amount of bank credit would lead to a reduction in the average size of banks in the absence of exit by some banks. If there are economies of scale in banking, merger is a relatively painless way of eliminating firms too small to be efficient. Phillips, *op. cit.*, p. 41.

[15]George R. Hall and Charles F. Phillips, Jr., *Bank Mergers and the Regulatory Agencies* (Washington: Board of Governors of the Federal Reserve System, 1964).

[16]A bank may have management problems that can best be solved by merger. Merger may be the best solution for banks in a declining community. Some mergers that reduce competition may be desirable to provide larger banking units in areas in which *de novo* branching is prohibited.

It was inevitable, however, that the Justice Department would seek influence and control over bank merger decisions because, in terms of anti-trust concepts, the regulatory authorities in the past have not given sufficient stress to competitive factors. Judging from the comments on the Philadelphia merger decision, it appears that most academic economists favor applying the anti-trust laws to banking.[17] Probably there would be less support among economists for applying the anti-trust laws to banking if, for example, Governor Robertson had been the sole decision-maker in bank merger cases—that is, if the decision-makers under the Bank Merger Act were more antagonistic to merger proposals.[18]

II. PRICE COMPETITION

1. REGULATION Q. Apart from matters of banking structure, the regulatory authorities can also play a significant role in promoting or allowing more price competition among banks. One of the most serious limitations on the ability of commercial banks to compete on a price basis with one another and with other financial institutions is the Federal Reserve Board's Regulation Q, which limits the rate of interest which may be paid by member banks on time deposits. The FDIC has a similar regulation applying to insured non-member banks. The best thing that could be done with Regulation Q is simply to eliminate it. Banks should be allowed to compete for time deposits on a price basis, with the efficient banks paying higher rates and perhaps with some of the less efficient banks falling by the wayside.

Short of abolishing Regulation Q, the next best solution would be to put Regu-lation Q on a stand-by basis. This proposal has been made by the Commission on Money and Credit, the President's Committee on Financial Institutions, and the Comptroller's Advisory Committee. Supporters of the proposal feel that the Federal Reserve should have the power to impose ceilings paid on time deposits if it should become necessary, but they have not yet been able to spell out the circumstances under which it would be desirable to impose such ceilings.

Legislation is required either to eliminate Regulation Q or to put it on a stand-by basis, but even if no basic legislative change is made it is still possible to secure the desired result simply by raising the present ceiling to a point where it becomes inoperative. That is, with the ceiling now set at 4 percent some banks are precluded from competing on a price basis for time deposits. If the ceiling were raised to, say, 6 percent, there would be no banks which would be limited as to the interest they could pay by the ceiling.

The principal justification for Regulation Q is the fear that competition for time deposits on a rate basis may lead banks to "reach" for unsound assets and thereby lead to a wave of bank failures.[19] It is frequently alleged that this occurred during the 1920's. There is, however, no evidence to support this. In fact, rates paid on time deposits by member banks *declined* during the 1920's.[20] Furthermore, as Anderson has pointed out, commercial banks maintained their holdings of U.S. government securities at 10 percent of total earning assets from 1920 to 1929.[21] This indicates

---

[17]See "Competition, Confusion and Commercial Banking," p. 45.

[18]Governor Robertson dissented from the Board of Governors majority on 21 of the 46 mergers approved by the Board from January, 1963 to December, 1964. He was absent and did not vote in five of these approvals.

[19]There is one other important justification for Regulation Q. The ceiling probably increases bank earnings over what they would be in the absence of the ceiling. The majority of bankers probably are in favor of retaining Regulation Q, and both the Federal Reserve and Congress seem to give weight to the views of the banks in such matters.

[20]See Paul S. Anderson, "A Note on Time Deposit Theory and Practice," *The National Banking Review*, March 1964, pp. 388–9.

[21]*Ibid.*

an attempt on the part of banks to maintain the proportion of high quality assets in their portfolios.

There is not adequate data to answer the questions raised about the tendency of banks under competitive pressure during the 1920's to reach for unsound assets. Alhadeff has concluded that fears of deterioration in the quality of bank assets in response to increased competition are exaggerated.[22]

One other aspect of Regulation Q should be mentioned. Under the definitions promulgated by the Federal Reserve Board under Regulation Q, corporations cannot hold savings deposits. This means that commercial banks cannot compete with one another and with savings and loan associations for this segment of time deposit business (except through the somewhat clumsy device of certificates of deposit). This is an important part of the market, not only because of its size but also because corporate savings depositors would probably be the most interest-sensitive segment of the market. If banks had to consider this group in their pricing decisions, the whole time deposit business could become more competitive. Again this is a step that can be taken by administrative ruling rather than requiring legislation.

In view of the failure of the Federal Reserve to loose the bind of Regulation Q, it is not surprising that various means of legally evading the regulation have been devised. The sale of commercial paper by commercial banks is a promising development of this sort.

2. SERVICE CHARGES. Another area in which price competition could be stimulated is in the area of service charges on checking accounts. Until recently many local clearing houses had apparently set service charges on checking accounts to be charged by their members. Recent action by the Justice Department and the banking regulatory agencies, culminating in the conviction on price fixing charges of several banks in Minnesota, has greatly reduced this overt setting of prices. It is still not clear, however, whether collusion in the setting of service charges has been completely eliminated or simply driven underground. National Bank Examiners have been instructed to examine the service charge structure of national banks to determine that charges are established independently. While there are difficulties in making such a determination, the banks have learned that such practices are not acceptable banking procedure. There may still be collusive arrangements among banks in which clearing houses play a prominent role. Business hours are one possible example.

Obviously, all conspiracies to fix prices can and should be eliminated. Apart from actual conspiracy, however, tacit collusion is still a problem. Professor Phillips has argued that tacit collusion is a more serious problem in banking than in most other industries. This is due not only to the small number of competing banks in most market areas, but also to the existence of a structure of public regulation that "has the express purpose . . . of producing essentially non-competitive results." Phillips notes that:[23]

Without formal agreement and without direct communication concerning prices to be charged and market areas and customers to be served, tacit understandings quite similar to those which would be achieved by overt agreement are apt to arise. In the case of banks the tacit understandings . . . are abetted by public regulation and supervision which helps to assure that no individual bank will behave in a way which would have a strong competitive impact on others.

While there is no obvious solution to this problem, it may be that an atmosphere

---

[22]"A Reconsideration of Restrictions on Bank Entry," pp. 256–260. See also George Benston, "Interest Payments on Demand Deposits and Bank Investment Behaviour," *Journal of Political Economy*, October 1964.

[23]"Competition, Confusion and Commercial Banking," p. 39.

of public regulation designed to stimulate rather than to inhibit aggressive competition will have some beneficial effects.

III. BANK PORTFOLIOS AND SERVICES

1. BANK EXAMINATION. Some stimulus to competition in banking can be achieved through revision of bank examination procedures. All insured commercial banks are examined by one of the Federal supervisory agencies. Traditionally the examiners have put great stress on safety and conservatism, and the highest compliment paid by an examiner was that management is "ultraconservative." A former Comptroller of the Currency has pointed out: "Bank examination exercises a considerable influence on lending policies . . . through its insistence upon sound standards."[24]

The examiners criticize unsound or risky loans and investments but rarely criticize a bank for not vigorously competing for business or for not adequately serving local needs.[25] While there probably has been some change in this attitude in recent years, there is room for further change. If banks could be encouraged to seek more lending opportunities, competition would be increased in the loan markets. If, for example, all banks were to attempt to increase their loan/deposit ratio by, say, 3 percentage points, there would be a considerable increase in the supply of funds available for loans and thus considerable competitive pressure on

loan rates. This does not mean that bankers should be encouraged to make unwise loans or that bankers should be encouraged to have a higher loan/deposit ratio than they consider prudent. The fact is, however, that there are some banks that restrain their lending activity not because they think further lending would be imprudent but because of a desire to avoid possible criticism by the bank examiners.[26]

The only detailed analysis of bank examination procedures and policies that has been published in recent years is the study by Donald Jacobs for The House Banking and Currency Committee.[27] Jacobs concluded that "[t]here is no doubt that bank examiners have an impact on bank loan and investment practices."[28] At times, moreover, this impact is an undesirable one. Jacobs places some of the blame for the curtailment of bank lending and the maintenance of large excess reserves during the 1930's on the bank examiners. He finds that the data on the 1930's:[29]

. . . suggest that the sharp decline in bank lending during that period was intensified by the activities of bank examiners . . . The maintenance of excess reserves that appeared during the 1930's can be explained, in part, as normal portfolio strategy by the banks. Their depleted capital position and the examiner's insistence that they were maintaining an overly high risk exposure in

---

[24]Statement of Preston Delano to Joint Committee on the Economic Report, *Monetary Policy and The Management of The Public Debt,* 82d Cong., 2d Sess. 1952, p. 936.

[25]"Examiners are not especially interested in the justification of given loans from the standpoint of public welfare . . . but rather in the probabilities of their being repaid at maturity so that depositors will not be endangered by losses." Raymond Kent, *Money and Banking,* 4th ed (New York, 1961). p. 292. Note also the position of the FDIC on bank holdings of securities: "Banks are encouraged to limit their commitments to high grade bonds of short to medium term maturity." FDIC *Annual Report,* 1956, p. 5.

[26]As Comptroller Delano noted: "Officers and directors . . . know that by adhering to high standards, their bank will avoid criticism." *loc. cit.* An example of the possibility of affecting bank investment policy by examination procedures is the treatment of the regulatory authorities of paper losses on securities. Examiners must evaluate the capital position of a bank under examination. In calculating capital of the bank, however, paper losses on high-quality bonds are not deducted. If it were not for this policy, banks would be very reluctant to purchase long-term bonds.

[27]"The Impact of Examination Practices upon Commercial Bank Lending Policies," Subcommittee on Domestic Finance, Committee on Banking and Currency, House of Representatives, 88th Cong., 2d Sess. 1964.

[28]*Ibid.,* p. 1.

[29]*Ibid.,* pp. 2, 33.

their loan portfolios dictated a reduction in risk, and this could be achieved primarily through shifts in their portfolios to assets classified as less risky.

It is interesting to note that even at the present time Jacobs feels that "The bank examination process . . . tends to influence bank portfolio management toward maintaining a smaller ratio of loans to assets."[30]

The traditional role of the bank examiner has been that of protecting depositors. Perhaps we should give more stress to assuring that adequate credit will be made available to potential borrowers, and that examination standards themselves will not result in an undesirable reduction in the volume of bank assets. At least the examination procedure should not discourage the proper assumption of risk by commercial banks. The very low losses on loans incurred by banks in the post-war years (despite recent expressions of concern about the "quality of credit") raise the question of whether the banks are assuming the risks they properly should.

2. PERMISSIBLE LOANS AND INVESTMENTS. Another means of increasing competition in the financial field is to lower some of the barriers that prevent or inhibit competition between banks and other financial institutions. The Comptroller of the Currency has in recent months issued certain rulings allowing national banks broader scope for their financial activities. National banks are now allowed to do direct lease financing. There is, of course, very little economic difference between direct leasing and making lons secured by equipment. Since there may be some advantages to users of the equipment to leasing rather than borrowing and purchasing equipment outright, this ruling increases the number of alternative suppliers available to the firm seeking to lease equipment.[31] That this increase in compe-

tition has been and will be effective is demonstrated by the strong opposition to this ruling by the leasing companies.[32]

Other recent rulings have liberalized the basis on which national banks can make loans secured by real estate. Again, this will increase competition in the mortgage lending field between commercial banks and savings and loan associations. As is to be expected, the latter have voiced considerable objection to such rulings.

National banks may now underwrite, in certain cases, securities which heretofore had been classified as revenue bonds and hence were not eligible for underwriting by national banks. This measure significantly increases competition in the municipal underwriting field. The increased competition in municipal bond underwriting has had measurable effects on the prices of bonds declared eligible for underwriting by national banks. For example, following a ruling that bonds of various Georgia State Authorities could be underwritten and dealt in by national banks, there was an immediate increase in the market price of all such bonds. An issue of Georgia Highway Authority bonds which was selling at a yield of 3.30 percent on the Friday before the ruling was yielding 3.15 percent by the following Friday. The advantages of this increased competition to state and local governments, and hence to the general public, is clear despite the opposition of the investment banking industry.

The revenue bond underwriting case is an excellent example of the difficulties involved in stimulating competition through legislation. A bill introduced in Congress to do approximately the same thing as the Comptroller's ruling has run into strong opposition from the Investment Bankers

---

[30]*Ibid.*

[31]See Eugene F. Brigham, "The Impact of Commercial Bank Entry on Market Conditions in the Equipment Leasing Industry," *The National Banking Review,* September 1964.

[32]For an example of this opposition, see Alvin Zises, "Equipment Leasing By Banks: Problems and Solutions," *The Banker's Magazine,* Winter 1964. Mr. Zises is president of Bankers Leasing Corporation.

Association and its passage is by no means certain.

The basic argument of the leasing companies, investment bankers and savings and loan associations in these matters is that they have developed techniques, and invested in the business involved, because of the limitations on commercial bank participation in the field. They argue that removal of the barriers on commercial banks is a change in the rules of the game and is unfair to them.

Their protests at new competition from an unexpected quarter are not unexpected and not entirely unjustified. In general, however, in a free economy no group should be able to stake a claim on any particular type of financing business and expect the government to respect that claim. Changes in the rules of the game are part of the game. The investment bankers have no claim to freedom from commercial bank competition in the municipal underwriting field, the leasing companies have no claim on sole possession of the leasing field, and the savings and loan associations must be prepared to meet increased competition from commercial banks.[33]

Most of the regulatory actions discussed in this paper involve reducing restrictions on commercial bank operations. The question is frequently raised as to whether allowing banks to engage in "risky" activities (leasing, revenue bond underwriting, etc.) or to compete more freely on a price basis, may lead to serious danger of widespread bank failures. That is, if we substitute reliance on bankers' judgment and the free market for regulation, will profit-maximizing behavior lead to greater risk-taking than is socially desirable?[34]

There is reason to believe that the traditional conservatism of most bankers would tend to restrain excessive risk-taking even in the absence of regulation. Alhadeff has pointed out that in "many institutions, regulatory restrictions merely reinforce actions which operating conventions would dictate in the absence of those regulations."[35]

Apart from traditional conservatism or adherence to cautious operating conventions, there are other restraints on the desire of bankers to take risks. Bank stockholders are not anxious to lose their investment even though depositors would share the loss. But the market provides a still more important restraint. Banks must attract deposits in order to earn profits and large depositors, who are *not* protected by deposit insurance, will evaluate the riskiness of banks before making a decision among alternatives. Part of the competition for large deposits involves competition in safety. A bank which goes too far in the direction of risky assets will tend to lose deposits, and thus purely in the interest of profit maximization a bank will find it desirable to avoid undue risk-taking. As long as this incentive to conservatism exists, it is unnecessary to require excessive conservatism through regulation.[36]

---

[33]Of course, commercial bankers have often taken the other side of this argument in opposing extension of the powers of other institutions, mainly savings and loan associations. Certainly a beneficial effect on competition would result if savings and loans were allowed to make consumer installment loans. There are complications here, however. Savings and loans have been given considerable tax benefits as part of a public policy to encourage home ownership. Even assuming that there is some logic to this policy, there would be no justification for continuing the special tax treatment of savings and loans if they became general purpose lenders.

[34]It is important to note why this is a problem in banking but not in other industries. If a manufacturer takes too great a risk and fails, the loss is suffered, for the most part, by stockholders. When a bank fails, a large part of the loss is borne by depositors. Thus risk-taking bank stockholders reap all of the gain if the risk is successful, but share the loss with depositors if they are unsuccessful. Thus the incentive to excessive risk-taking by banks.

[35]David A. Alhadeff, "The Commission on Money and Credit's Research Studies," *Journal of Finance*, September 1964, p. 524.

[36]The strength of this incentive rests upon the importance to the bank of depositors whose accounts are not insured. If deposits were insured in full, as has frequently been proposed, this incentive would be eliminated. This effect

IV. CONCLUSIONS

Most of the measures discussed above involve freeing banks from regulations which restrain their activities. I have argued that many of these are unnecessary, and in many cases administrative decisions or changes in emphasis by various

federal and state supervisory agencies can improve the level of competition in banking.

Actions taken by the banking regulatory authorities cannot, of course, make banking a perfectly competitive industry. There is certainly a need for legislation to improve competition in the financial field.[37] Nevertheless, it is important to realize that even within our present statutory framework it is possible to make some improvements in banking competition through administrative action by the regulatory authorities.

---

should be considered in evaluating such proposals.

The strength of this effect also depends upon the ability of large depositors to obtain adequate information to evaluate the financial position of banks. This is made difficult by the failure of many banks to publish sufficient relevant data. Data on valuation reserves is the most significant such omission. The regulatory agencies should require disclosure of valuation reserves, in connection with the regular publication of the report of condition, as was done by the Comptroller in September 1963 but not subsequently.

---

[37]Legislation is necessary, for example, to obtain the full competitive benefits of branch banking. Also, since many of the restrictions on bank operations are part of the law, legislation is required to eliminate them.

Chapter IX
BANK COMPETITION AND ANTITRUST

37. Competition in Banking: The Issues°
Federal Reserve Bank of Chicago

The effect of competition upon the performance of commercial banks has received increasing attention in recent years. Since the number and types of banks and other financial institutions in a market area are assumed to have an important effect on competition, much attention has focused on the possible interrelationships between market structure, competition and performance. This article examines the rationale for bank regulation, the need for interbank competition, changes in the nature of this competition, and the prevalent uncertainty as to appropriate public policy towards interbank competition. The last point is particularly important and will be treated in greater detail in a following article by Andrew Brimmer.

In an economy characterized by private property and production for profit, competition among buyers and sellers has long been considered a prime prerequisite of economic efficiency—efficiency in this context being construed to include both the maximizing of output for any given

°From *Business Conditions*, January, 1967. Reprinted by permission of the publisher, the Federal Reserve Bank of Chicago.

resource used and the allocation of resources among all possible uses such that total production is maximized.

So strong has been the American belief in impersonal market forces to set prices and guide production, as opposed to joint decisions among producers or the decrees of government boards, that our country early put on the books the strictest and most comprehensive antitrust legislation in the world. The basic statutes are the Sherman Act of 1890 and the Clayton and Federal Trade Commission Acts of 1914.

To be sure, it has long been recognized that the technologies of some industries preclude primary reliance upon competition to guide investment, production and pricing. In these so-called "natural monopolies," such as the production and distribution of electric power and other "public utilities," the discipline of the marketplace has been replaced by the deliberations of public regulatory agencies.

Still other industries, although not considered natural monopolies, have been acknowledged as greatly affecting the public interest. Because the failure or other malfunctioning of an individual establishment in these industries has been deemed to have adverse effects on the economy over and beyond the injury accruing to the firm's stockholders, public regulation has been imposed in order to assure that certain minimal operating and fiduciary standards are met. Of the industries accorded such treatment, commercial banking is both the most prominent and the most heavily regulated.

WHY BANKS ARE REGULATED

Demand deposits of commercial banks provide the primary means of payment and are the major component of the money supply. Furthermore, banks, while presumed by the public to be safe depositories, typically have liabilities that are very large in proportion to their capital and consequently could provide an attractive temptation to gambling by reckless entrepreneurs. These facts alone would suggest the desirability of regulation to assure the liquidity and solvency of commercial banks.

In addition, historical experience provides dramatic, if superficial, evidence for the view that permitting banks to engage in unrestrained competition may lead to disastrous results. The evils of the past —specifically, the chaos and instability that attended the era of "free banking" between 1837 and 1863, the large numbers of bank failures in the 1920s and the banking collapse and economic depression of the early 1930s—have sufficed to convince most people that some measure of Government intervention is not only desirable but an absolute necessity.

The Federal and state governments have responded to this apparent need by constructing over the years a highly detailed and extensive system of commercial bank regulation that includes specific lending and borrowing restrictions, usury laws, ceilings on rates that banks may pay on time deposits, the prohibition of interest on demand deposits, capital and management requirements for the establishment of new banks, geographical restrictions on branching, requirements for periodic publication of statements of condition and examinations by public officials.

WHY COMPETITION IN BANKING?

Since official regulation imposes numerous limitations on the activities of banks, vigorous competition among banks may appear both superfluous and inconsistent. After all, one may ask, is not the public's interest in having quality services provided at reasonable prices protected in banking through public regulation, as it supposedly is in the case of electric utilities and transportation? The answer, clearly, is in the negative.

Although commercial banks are subject to a great number of specific regulations limiting the scope of their activities, a broad range of discretion still remains open to them. As far as their lending and investment activities are concerned, banks retain the prerogative of emphasizing particular kinds of loans (for example, business, consumer, agriculture and mortgage loans) and of setting prices for these loans at whatever levels they choose, subject only to the ceilings on some types of loans established by state usury laws. Thus, there is ample room for the play of competitive forces to establish the actual levels of charges.

The scope for nonprice competition in banking is even wider. The services provided in conjunction with the bank's lending and deposit business provide a variety of opportunities for nonprice maneuvers designed to win new customers and retain old ones. It is the incomplete nature of regulation which, while imposing definite constraints on each bank's choice of alternative policies, nevertheless permits a wide latitude for the exercise of individual discretion that makes possible a meaningful role for competition in banking. This is the consideration that lay behind the Supreme Court's dictum in *U. S. vs. Philadelphia National Bank* that the regulated character of banking "makes the play of competition not less important but more so."

CHANGING VIEWS ON COMPETITION

Interest in banking competition has intensified in recent years. After virtually ignoring the commercial banking industry for many years, the Justice Department brought suit in the late 1950s in a number of cases involving clearinghouse agreements to set uniform service charges. In more recent years, despite a long and widely held belief to the contrary, the courts have ruled that the antitrust laws apply to acquisitions and mergers in banking as well as in other areas.

It may appear rather anomalous that the Federal Government, having established a superstructure of regulation designed at least in part for the purpose of limiting competition in banking, now undertakes to restrict banks' actions which might tend to reduce competition. The issue is further confused by the fact that the Office of the Comptroller of the Currency and the Department of Justice— two agencies of the Federal Government —have been on occasion cast in the roles of opposing parties in recent bank merger cases. It would be inaccurate to portray these events as reflecting merely a jurisdictional dispute between Federal agencies. Instead there appears to be a growing conviction on the part of public officials and bankers alike that a reevaluation and revision of policy may now be in order— though there is little agreement on specific issues.

Until recently students of banking were generally agreed that competition was not only less essential in banking than in most other industries but in many circumstances inherently destructive. However, new evidence and reexamination of old arguments now suggest that competition in banking may not have been the culprit it has been painted to be in bringing about the financial crises of earlier days. The banking troubles of the era before 1863 are now considered to have been more the result of the absence of a uniform national currency than of excessive competition or the lack of detailed controls over banking. This deficiency was remedied by the passage of the National Banking Act of 1863, which substituted national bank notes for the bewildering variety of state bank issues then in circulation.

Similarly, the periodic epidemics of bank failures of the late nineteenth and early twentieth centuries, as well as the striking and unprecedented attrition of banks in the decade following World War I, appear to have had their roots more in cyclical factors and secular changes in transportation and agriculture than in any inherent tendency toward destructive competition in banking. Even the banking debacle of the early 1930s is no longer uncritically viewed as the inevitable result of imprudent banking practices attributable largely to excessive competition for deposits. On the contrary, all of these instances of injury to the banking system —and in most cases, to the economy as well—are now generally agreed to have had their major cause in developments much broader than local competition and often far removed from the sphere of individual bank management.

Today, there exist numerous safeguards against any widespread and self-reinforcing epidemic of bank failures. To the extent that violent cyclical fluctuations in aggregate economic activity may have been responsible for the waves of bank failures in the past, the announced readiness of the Federal Government and the Federal Reserve System to take whatever fiscal and monetary measures are required to maintain a high and growing level of income and employment serves as protection against similar future disturbances.

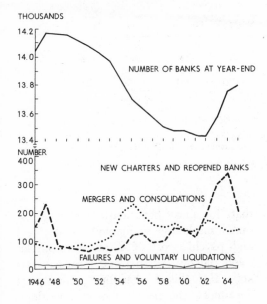

FIGURE 1

Number of Commercial Banks Rises in Recent Years
Following Many Years of Decline

a major contributing cause to the rapid
and continuing growth of such nonbank
financial intermediaries as savings and
loan associations, a growth that has
brought with it increased interindustry
competition.

Similarly, the attempt to relieve effects
of unduly severe competition among
banks by prohibiting them from paying
interest on demand deposits has been
only partially successful at best. Far from
eliminating competition, the prohibition
simply caused banks to substitute less
overt but nonetheless vigorous nonprice
rivalry for the rate competition that previously existed. In effect, "interest" on
demand deposits continues to be paid
through an earnings credit offset to deposit service charges and numerous "free"
services, all dependent largely on the size
of the average balance and the number
of transactions associated with each account. On the other hand, the depositor
has been deprived of the option of being
paid in cash.

CHANGES IN NUMBER OF BANKS

While much of the recent interest in
competition in banking has been focused
on the system of bank regulation as presently constituted, expressions of concern
have also been voiced concerning the
merging and branching activities of the
banks themselves. Despite virtually un-
interrupted prosperity and population
growth in the postwar period, the decline in the number of commercial banks
in the United States that began in the
1920s continued until very recently.

After a small immediate postwar rise
from 14,011 in 1945 to 14,181 in 1947,
the number declined steadily, reaching a
low of 13,427 at the end of 1962. Since
then the number of banks has increased
slightly to 13,784 in November 1966. The
net decrease of 227 banks since World
War II—an average of about 10 a year—
is small compared to the rate that prevailed through the generally prosperous

To the extent that bank failures were the
result of "runs" on banks occasioned by
general fears on the part of the public
of the inability by banks to redeem their
deposits for currency, Federal Deposit
Insurance and the readiness of the Federal Reserve to act as the lender of last
resort appear to afford a sufficient remedy. Although the evidence is not un-
equivocal on each of these points—and
even though all are agreed that supervision remains a necessary means for
promoting good bank management and
ensuring the safety of depositor's funds—
there seems little doubt that competition
can safely play a more important role in
banking than has until recently been
deemed prudent.

One piece of evidence for this conclusion is the fact that regulation frequently
has been unsuccessful in suppressing competition even where it has undertaken to
do so. For example, the attempt to reduce
interbank competition by erecting strict
legal barriers to entry has been at least

Change in Number of Banks and Branches by Type of Branch Statute

State Classification†	Change,* 1946–64					
	Banks		Branches		Banking offices	
	Number	Percent	Number	Percent	Number	Percent
Branch banking						
Statewide	−323	−23	3,922	24	3,599	118
Limited	−979	−15	6,097	290	5,118	60
Unit banking	1,018	17	338‡	148‡	1,356	21
Total	−284	−2	10,357	260	10,073	56

*Increased number of branches more than offsets decline in number of banks.
†Includes 50 states and District of Columbia.
‡Includes offices that do not offer a full line of banking services. In addition, a few full service branches that were established before legal prohibitions of branching or after removal of such prohibitions are included.
Source: U. S., Comptroller of the Currency, *Annual Report 1964* (Washington, 1965).

1920s when the average net annual attrition exceeded 700. However, in contrast to the earlier period when a significant part of the attrition resulted from bank failures and voluntary liquidations, virtually all the recent decline has been the result of mergers and acquisitions that have absorbed formerly independent banks.

NUMBERS AND COMPETITION

To many observers this decrease in the number of banks provides evidence that the availability of alternative sources of supply of banking services, and hence the vigor of competition, is undergoing a decline. This conclusion is based on the theory that the chances of collusion are less and the likelihood of independent rivalry greater when sellers are many than when they are few.

However, in evaluating the effect of the decline in the number of banks, it must be noted that all of the more than 13,000 banks in the United States do not compete in a single, nationwide market. A relatively few giant banks do operate in what is loosely referred to as the "national banking market"—the market for the loans and deposits of the largest corporations that have banking connections throughout the country.

But it is a widely acknowledged fact

that, for most bank customers, the national market is segmented by the real and psychic cost of distance into relatively narrow regional and local submarkets. For this less mobile majority of customers, the most relevant consideration is the number of independent banks within the confined area in which their reputations are known and in which they find it practicable to seek accommodation. This number of banks, however, is not deducible from a knowledge of how many banks there are in some broader area, such as the state.

Although states which permit branch banking have experienced deep declines in the number of banks, it does not necessarily follow that significantly fewer different banks are represented in individual communities in these states than in those that prohibit branch banking. This apparent contradiction is explained by the great expansion in the number of branch offices during the past several decades. Similarly, even when mergers have decreased the total number of banks in the country and the number of alternatives available to customers in particular local markets, they may have added to the number of effective competitors in the markets serving large- and medium-sized corporate customers by permitting the merging banks to attain the minimum size required to operate in these markets.

CONCENTRATION IN BANKING

Concomitant with the decline in the number of banks, the average size of bank and the percentage of banking resources concentrated in the hands of a relatively few large banks have increased in many broad areas of the country. Concentration in this sense is often considered to have a potentially adverse effect on competition because, however large the total number of banks in a market, if one or a few of them control most of the total supply, they will be able to influence prices strongly.

Available data on concentration of deposits in major metropolitan areas indicate that concentration levels were generally higher in the early 1960s than a decade earlier. On the other hand, they appear to have been lower than in the prewar year of 1939. It is necessary, however, to take account of important interarea differences. For the period 1960–64 increases in concentration have been typical in metropolitan areas in states where statewide branching is prevalent (see accompanying table). In metropolitan areas where restricted branch banking is the rule, increases and decreases were about equally frequent. Decreases predominated in these areas where unit banking was the most common form of bank organization.

Some would interpret these figures as demonstrating that unit banking is more conducive to competition than branch banking. However, inasmuch as concentration and changes in concentration have significance for competition only in relation to specific product markets and particular groups of customers, such a conclusion follows only if certain conditions are satisfied. Among these is the rather crucial assumption that metropolitan areas serve equally well as approximations to local banking markets under both branch and unit banking. To the extent that locational convenience serves to restrict the practicable range of alternatives of some

Deposit Concentration in Metropolitan
Areas by Type of Branch Statute

SMSAs including reserve cities[*]	Percent of total deposits held by three largest banks		
	1960	1962	1964
Statewide Branch Banking:			
Baltimore	59	73	72
Los Angeles	78	75	71
Portland, Ore.	87	90	89
San Francisco	60	79	77
Seattle	68	72	72
Limited Branch Banking:			
Atlanta	72	75	74
Birmingham	93	93	97
Boston	79	83	83
Buffalo	77	93	95
Cincinnati	82	84	84
Cleveland	78	77	76
Columbus	88	87	93
Detroit	78	76	74
Indianapolis	97	96	96
Louisville	68	76	76
Memphis	93	93	93
Nashville	89	92	93
New Orleans	85	80	79
New York	49	53	54
Philadelphia	64	62	64
Pittsburgh	82	83	81
Richmond	80	78	73
Toledo	90	88	88
Washington, D. C.	74	75	73
Unit Banking:			
Chicago	48	53	52
Dallas	80	79	76
Denver	69	68	68
Fort Worth	77	76	73
Houston	60	59	64
Jacksonville	79	75	72
Kansas City, Mo.	63	61	58
Miami	41	43	40
Milwaukee	68	67	66
Minneapolis	60	62	60
Oklahoma City	70	72	71
Omaha	82	80	79
St. Louis	52	50	48
San Antonio	67	64	62
Tulsa	81	79	76

Note: Metropolitan areas in statewide branch banking states show greatest increases in concentrations.

[*]Metropolitan areas of Reserve Cities having populations in excess of 400,000 as of April 1, 1960.

Source: Federal Deposit Insurance Corporation, *Annual Reports*.

customers to an area smaller than the whole metropolitan area, concentration in unit banking areas is understated by the measure used here. A more important qualification is that competition has not been shown to depend in any simple and reliable way on the degree of concentration in bank markets.

PUBLIC POLICY TOWARD BANK MERGERS

In deciding whether to approve or disapprove a particular application to merge, the appropriate regulatory agency must arrive at a judgment concerning the probable effect of the merger on the public interest. The fundamental questions that must be answered include the justification of the consolidation in terms of economies of scale or the ability of a larger bank to render better, cheaper and more complete banking services and its effect, via changes in the number and size distribution of banks, on the competitive relations among the remaining firms. It is over answers to these questions that much of the interagency conflict has arisen.

For example, advantages in the form of lower operating costs have often been advanced as a major factor in bank mergers. Yet, available empirical studies tend to indicate that such economies may be quite modest—at least when the differences in output mix between large and small banks are taken into consideration, as they must be.

A second argument in support of mergers emphasizes the ability of a bank with greater resources to hire better management and to utilize more fully the services of a large number of specialists. This argument appears to have fairly general validity as indicated by both casual observation and a number of recent studies. Large banks generally do offer a broader variety of services than is obtainable at small banks in the same locality. But whether this constitutes a net advantage is not immediately obvious. It must be determined first whether a decrease in the number of alternative sources of banking services is adequately compensated by the availability of a number of special, but infrequently utilized, services that only large banks can supply.

BRANCH BANKING

Any discussion of the relative merits of large and small banks must include consideration of the advantages and disadvantages of branch banking. One of the major advantages claimed for branching is that it is often the quickest way a bank can grow to large size. Also, since the full resources and facilities of the bank can be made available to the customers of each branch, branch banking provides a means of bringing a fuller range of banking services and larger lending capacity to individual communities.

The still unresolved issue of branch banking underlies one of the oldest and most vitriolic controversies in American banking. It involves questions both political and economic in character. Without evaluating the merits of the arguments, it may be noted that the unit-branch issue is an inseparable part of the larger public debate over competition in banking reviewed above.

The precise relationship between branch banking and banking competition is a matter of dispute. A number of economists, bankers and public officials maintain that branching is an essentially procompetitive form of banking that facilitates the penetration of additional banking markets and brings to bear the force of potential competition in even the smallest and most isolated communities. Other students of banking hold that branching is a monopolistic device whose prime purpose is to eliminate competition. Which characterization is the more accurate may depend as much on what one understands by competition as on the objectively determinable facts of the case.

It is hardly open to serious doubt, for example, that some portion of the criticism of branch banking is of a protectionist nature, more concerned with preserving locally owned unit banks than with fostering vigorous interbank rivalry. Independent bankers frequently feel themselves threatened by the presence of a nearby office of a large branch bank.

On the other hand, it is not always easy to distinguish in practice between the protection of competitors and the preservation of competition. On reason is related to the difference between the incentives required to induce merger and those required to induce *de novo* establishment of a new bank or branch. It appears easier for two existing banks to come to terms on a merger agreement which has as one of its "fringe benefits" the elimination of competition than it is for a potential entrant into the banking field to obtain financing and run the regulatory gauntlet required to obtain a charter for a new bank. As was indicated above, it is in those areas where the possibility of operating an acquired bank as a branch maximizes the incentive to merge that the disappearance of banks and the concentration of banking have proceeded most rapidly. This pronounced assymmetry between merger and entry is the primary reason why branching via merger, which *ipso facto* involves the elimination of an independent source of supply, may have adverse and irreversible effects on competition. It is also one of the considerations that prompted Congress in 1950 to strengthen the Clayton Act and to pass the Bank Merger Acts of 1960 and 1966.

It might still be maintained, on the other hand, that *de novo* branching could have nothing but beneficial effects on competition. Its immediate effect is always to introduce a new competitive force into a banking market or submarket. When, for example, a branch bank sees a potentially profitable location for a banking office and opens a branch there —perhaps years in advance of the time when it would have been profitable to organize a new unit bank—it clearly bene-fits the community to have banking facilities where none existed before or would otherwise have existed for a considerable period of time. Whether this is a net gain in the long term depends on the potential benefit to the local populace of having an independent source of supply of banking services when it would become feasible to open a new unit bank.

Where banks find it easy to establish branches within a local banking market they may—and often do—anticipate profitable locations and saturate entire areas with branches, thereby largely foreclosing future entry by competitors. In this they may be inadvertently aided and abetted by the regulatory agencies which, though reluctant to grant a new charter that could conceivably result in "overbanking," are usually willing to rely on the applicant's judgment regarding the prospective profitability of a new branch.

At a theoretical level a good case can be made for removing all geographic restrictions on branching, while simultaneously discouraging concentration in particular local banking markets. However, this would require a uniform national policy with respect to branching and the chartering of new banks, a development not now on the horizon. Legislation regarding branching traditionally has been left to the states. Nevertheless, the competitive environment created by state branching restrictions is clearly one of the many factors that must be taken into account in Federal Agency decisions governing mergers.

CONCLUSION

There exists a great deal of uncertainty at the present time as to the proper public policy toward competition in banking. Ideally, policy should undertake to foster a degree of interbank rivalry that assures that consumers will be provided bank services of high quality at minimum cost, without sacrificing the private and public benefits of large-scale production or the regulatory aim of ensuring the liquidity and solvency of the banking system. The extent to which these goals can be realized simultaneously and even the direction in which policy should move to approach them as closely as possible is still imperfectly understood.

38. Market Structure, Public Convenience, and the Regulation of Bank Mergers [*]

Andrew F. Brimmer[†]

Bank competition has nearly always been a controversial topic. The breadth of current interest is reflected in recent changes in Federal law pertaining to bank mergers and holding company acquisitions, and in recent judicial decisions attempting to clarify the relation between anti-trust legislation and banking. The previous article concerning the issues in banking competition alluded to the uncertainty of supervisory agencies regarding suitable public policy towards interbank competition. This article discusses that point further. Examined are the observable differences in the pattern of merger decisions made by the supervisory agencies, and the degree of importance assigned to future or potential competition and regional economic growth as factors in regulatory decisions.

The Bank Merger Act, originally enacted in 1960, and the Bank Holding Company Act, enacted in May 1956, were both amended in 1966. Principal among the amendments to each of the statutes was a change in the statement of circumstantial factors the Board is required to consider under the Bank Holding Company Act, and which the appropriate Federal supervisory authority (Board, Comptroller of the Currency, or Federal Deposit Insurance Corporation—depending on the charter status of the continuing institution), must consider under the Bank Merger Act. . . .

Thus, with respect to either a proposed bank merger where the resulting bank is to be a State member bank, or a bank holding company acquisition, the Board may not approve any proposal that would result in a monopoly or that would be in furtherance of any combination or conspiracy to monopolize or to attempt to monopolize the business of banking in any part of the United States. Nor may the Board approve any proposed merger or holding company acquisition the effect of which, in any section of the country, may be substantially to lessen competition *unless* the Board finds that the anticompetitive effects of the proposed transaction are *clearly outweighed* in the public interest by the probable effect of the transaction in meeting the convenience and needs of the community to be served.

. . . .

It is in this legal framework that the assessment of bank mergers and bank holding company proposals must be made.

[*]From *The Banking Law Journal*, September 1969. Reprinted by permission of the publisher, Warren, Gorham & Lamont Inc.

[†]Member, Board of Governors of the Federal Reserve System.

In approaching this task, I have attempted to answer the following questions:

1. To what extent, if any, can one observe significant differences in the pattern of merger decisions by the Federal Reserve Board, the Comptroller of the Currency and the Federal Deposit Insurance Corporation?

2. In deciding proposed bank mergers or bank holding company acquisitions, what weight, if any, should be given to possibilities of future, or potential, competition?

3. Should the rate of economic growth in an area influence the policies of the regulatory agencies?

In answering these questions, I have reached the following conclusions:

1. The Comptroller of the Currency and the FDIC apparently approve a much higher proportion of merger applications than does the Federal Reserve Board. These divergencies in denial rates seem to reflect differences in policies among the agencies rather than differences in the seriousness of anticompetitive effects involved in the kinds of cases handled.

2. Potential competition should be assigned considerable weight in merger cases. However, the Federal Reserve Board seems to follow this practice to a far greater extent than does either of the other two agencies.

3. A more permissive approach toward mergers in growth areas is not warranted as a general proposition. However, there may be some cases in which the effect of mergers on competition in such areas is offset by the advantage to the community in convenience and needs.

THE PATTERN OF DECISIONS IN BANK MERGERS AND ACQUISITIONS, 1966–1968

. . . As one would expect, in view of wide differences in State laws governing multiple-office banking, merger and holding company activity is not evenly distributed throughout the United States.

Over the period, more than 80 percent of the applications received came from seven Federal Reserve Districts: New York, Philadelphia, Cleveland, Richmond, Chicago, and Minneapolis. The Richmond district alone accounted for close to 20 percent of the applications. By and large, each of these Districts include one or more states in which multiple-office banking is prevalent. On the other hand, there has been less activity in the St. Louis, Kansas City and Dallas Districts, principally because of State restrictions on multiple-office banking.

Over this period, there were 427 decisions by the three banking agencies. There were 409 approvals and 18 denials. While the Board accounted for about one-quarter of the decisions, it also accounted for two-thirds of the denials. The FDIC and the Comptroller each had three denials; the Board had 12. The denial rate at the Board has been close to 11 percent (with about the same rate for mergers, holding company formations and acquisitions). The denial rate at the FDIC has been less than 3 percent and at the Comptroller of the Currency, less than 2 percent. These data strongly suggest that there are significant differences among the agencies with respect to the way each handles its cases, and these differences in approach may have a strong bearing on whether the cases are likely to be approved or denied.[1]

Either the policies of the Board differ from those of the other banking agencies, or the kinds of cases handled by the Board involve more serious anticompetitive effects. While the latter possibility may account in part for the difference between the denial rate at the Board and

―――――――
[1] For the technicians who may be interested, the relationships appearing in the pattern of merger decisions were tested statistically. Cross classifying Board and "other agency" decisions by "approvals" and "denials" permitted a nonparametric contingency test which yielded a chi square value of 13.7. This value is significant at better than the 1 per cent level and supports the hypothesis indicated above.

the FDIC, it hardly seems likely to account for the difference between the Board and the Comptroller.

If, in fact, the denial rates at the Board and at other agencies reflect a difference in policy, this might be reflected in the way the Board's advisory opinions on competitive effects on merger cases are received. Over the period covered, the Board issued 121 advisory opinions to the FDIC and 204 to the Comptroller of the Currency—325 in all. In 94, or close to 30 percent of these reports, the Board indicated that the competitive effects of the proposed merger would be serious. (As might be expected, given the small size of the typical insured nonmember bank, the proportion submitted to the FDIC deemed serious was lower—about 22 percent—than the proportion submitted to the Comptroller—about 33 percent.)

An indication to another agency that the anticompetitive effect of a merger is serious does not necessarily mean that the Board itself would have denied the application. Serious anticompetitive effects could be offset, or "clearly outweighed" by the convenience and needs of the community. This would, however, have had to be the situation in a little less than two-thirds of the 94 cases in which a serious effect was indicated in order to bring the denial rate down to the Board's own 11 percent.

In fact, however, the other two banking agencies issued denials in only three of the 94 cases in which the Board found a serious anticompetitive effect. The three other denials issued by the FDIC and the Comptroller were in cases in which the Board did not find a serious anticompetitive effect. There does not appear to be a significant relationship between the finding of a serious anticompetitive effect by the Board and the decision by the other banking agencies.[2]

In my opinion, the pattern of merger decisions examined here is strong documentation of differences in the approach taken by the three supervisory agencies in carrying out their responsibilities under the bank merger statute. Since each agency must determine for itself how well it is meeting the requirements of the Bank Merger Act, I clearly cannot—and would not want to—judge the performance of the other agencies. With respect to the Federal Reserve Board, I obviously believe that we are performing reasonably well.

THE ROLE OF POTENTIAL COMPETITION

While one can describe statistically the differences in the pattern of merger decisions by the Federal bank supervisory agencies, it is far more difficult to explain those differences. Whatever the basis for the differences among the supervisory agencies, it appears to be reflected in their attitudes toward potential competition—that is, the extent to which weight is given to possibilities of future competition in a proposed bank merger or holding company acquisition.

Although it is not clear just how much importance the Comptroller and the FDIC assign to potential competition in deciding cases before them, one does get the impression that the weight they accord this factor is quite small. In contrast, the Federal Reserve Board places considerable emphasis on potential competition in the determination of both bank merger and bank holding company applications.

I believe it to be clearly established that the effect of the 1966 amendments to the Bank Merger and Bank Holding Company Acts was to impose on the responsible supervisory agencies a scheme for appraising and determining competitive consequences that, in major respects, is utilized generally in the Government's enforcement of Section 7 of the Clayton

---

[2]Cross classifying Board findings of serious and nonserious anticompetitive effects, in advisory opinions by "approvals" and "denials" by other agencies permitted a nonparametric contingency test which yielded a chi square of .48, which cannot be taken as significant.

Act as amended in 1950. Most relevant to this discussion is the question: Does a determination of whether the effect of a proposed merger or holding company acquisition "may be substantially to lessen competition" encompass situations involving "potential competition?"

The concept of "potential competition," treated herein, does not automatically encompass—nor absolutely exclude—the related concepts of "potential injury to competitors" and "ease of market entry." Both of these concepts are properly the subject of inquiry in competitive analysis, but are not necessarily related to a determination of the likelihood that parties to a merger or holding company proposal will become active competitors.

Effective, workable competition in a given market exists when buyers of products or services are offered purchasing alternatives sufficiently real to provide these buyers with the opportunity to change from one seller to another, with the possibility of such change influencing sellers to seek improvements in the quality and price of the products and services which they offer. However, particularly in a market in which actual competition is in some manner deficient, sellers may be influenced as much by the realization that a low level of quality or a high price level may attract more competent or efficient entrants from the periphery of the market as they are by the threat posed by existing competitors. Effective competition in such markets, therefore, requires the preservation of the threat of potential competition.[3] Admittedly, to deal with "the preservation of the threat of potential competition" is, on its face, conjectural. But Congressional concern over *probabilities*, not certainties, was the precise reason for the Celler-Kefauver Amendment (1950) to Section 7 of the Clayton Act.[4]

. . . .

The doctrine of potential competition, while not relied upon by the courts as a decisive consideration in a court contest involving alleged anticompetitive consequences of a proposed bank merger or holding company acquisition, has been considered and rejected, not as being *per se* inapplicable, but as being inapplicable in view of the facts of record.[5] Preclusion of entry into a defined banking market by a substantial potential competitor through consummation of a merger involving the potential entrant, and the question of whether such result violates Section 7 of the Clayton Act, and should have been denied under the Bank Merger Act, are issues recently (9/10/68) placed before a Federal District Court by the U.S. Department of Justice, following the Board's approval of merger proposals involving Girard Trust Bank and Doylestown National Bank (Doylestown, Pa.) and The Fidelity Bank & Doylestown Trust Co. (Doylestown, Pa.). The Board, in its 6-1 decision in those cases which were considered together, took into account the possible impact of potential competition. While five members of the majority ruled that the net effect of the proposed mergers on competition would not be adverse, I felt that the overall competitive effect would be no more than slightly adverse. Nevertheless, I, too, felt the applications should be approved.

The complaints filed by the Department of Justice in each case assert numerous violations of Section 7 of the Clayton Act, the majority of which relate to asserted elimination of *potential competition* in commercial banking between and among the banks involved in the two mergers, and a general allegation of violation premised on the contributory effect of the two mergers on the continuing trend toward reduction in potential bank competitors in the Philadelphia area. We can safely assume, I believe, that the

---

[3]Wilcox, Competition and Monopoly in American Industry, Temporary National Economic Committee Monograph No. 21 (1940), p. 7.

[4]United States v. Philadelphia National Bank, 374 U.S. 321 (1963); Brown Shoe Co. v. United States, 370 U.S. 294 (1962).

[5]United States v. Crocker-Anglo National Bank, 223 F. Supp. 849, 856-7 (N.D. Cal. 1963).

Department of Justice currently takes the position that potential competition is a major factor for consideration in determining the legality of a proposed bank merger; and that proven miscalculation or disregard of a merger's effect on potential competition can require remand to an agency or reversal of agency action.

Not less import is attributed by the Board to the factor of potential competition in its consideration of Bank Holding Company Act applications. In the Board's denial action (April 1967, Fed. Res. Bull. 763) on the application of Allied Bankshares Corp., Norfolk, Virginia, to form a bank holding company through ownership of the Virginia National Bank, Norfolk, and The Central National Bank of Richmond, existing competition between the banks was found to be insignificant, and the effect of its elimination of minimal consequence. However, the likelihood that substantial potential competition between the banks would be precluded by their affiliation was stated to weigh heavily in the Board's decision. In May 1967, one month following the Allied denial, the Board, by unanimous vote, denied a proposal by BT New York Corporation to acquire Liberty National Bank and Trust Company, Buffalo (50 Fed. Res. Bull. 769). As in the *Allied* case, the Board concluded that existing competition between and among the banks involved in the proposal was sufficiently negligible that it posed no bar to approval. However, the proposal's probable effect on *potential* competition was found to present a severely adverse consideration. Rejecting applicant's assertion that consummation of the proposal would promote deconcentration in the heavily concentrated Buffalo area—through Liberty National's anticipated greater ability to compete with its two larger rivals—the Board concluded that Liberty Bank was presently capable of offering to customers in its market area, both large and small, an alternative source of essential banking services. Noting that

legal and economic barriers to new entry into the Buffalo market area were already high, the Board expressed its concern that there be preserved whatever incentive might exist for entry by potential competitors having the resources and capacity to surmount existing barriers. Based on the financial and management resources of BT New York Corporation, the Board found that the applicant was a potential competitor in the Buffalo market, whose greater participation in the market was not dependent on consummation of the proposed acquisition, and that the entry of such a sizable organization by that means would simply raise the entry barriers for others without increasing the banking alternatives already available to the public. Further, it was concluded that Liberty Bank, through a less anticompetitive affiliation, could offer meaningful competition to the applicant and other banking organizations in the upstate banking markets.

. . . .

MERGER POLICY AND ECONOMIC GROWTH

Should the rate of economic growth in an area influence the policies of the regulatory agencies toward proposed acquisitions? It apparently has been argued that competition tends to be more intense in a rapidly growing area than in an non-growing area; therefore, the regulatory agencies can afford to pursue a more permissive approach toward acquisitions.

There is nothing in current law or in recent court decisions that would suggest that rapid economic growth is taken by the Supreme Court as a relevant competitive consideration offsetting, let us say, the effect of a merger on concentration in an area. Nor has the Court suggested that the growth of an area, past or prospective, constitutes a justification for a merger that would otherwise be illegal—as might be the case if it were found that mergers in growing areas contributed substantially to the convenience and needs of the community. However, the bank regulatory agencies deal with large numbers of proposals that merit a full scale economic review, many of which are, in all likelihood, not violations of the antitrust laws as currently interpreted. In such cases, there is no necessary reason to adopt exactly the same presumptions as have been applied in antitrust cases by the courts. Moreover, the substantive question would, in any event, remain and it does warrant consideration.

The view that the regulatory agencies need not be as restrictive in preventing mergers in a rapidly growing area as in a slow-growing or stagnant area is presumably based on the belief that economic growth would, in and of itself, intensify competition and would tend to offset high levels of concentration. There are several intuitively appealing reasons why this might be the case. If the economy of an area is growing, there may be a stimulus toward more intensive competition as the aggressive competitors in the area attempt to obtain new customers and also to secure the old ones whose accounts become more valuable. Moreover, marginal banks that might otherwise offer little in the way of effective competition, either because of their small size or limited management, would have an opportunity to grow with their area and to become more vigorous competitors. Finally, in a growing area, there is likely to be room for new entry, either by branching or new charter. Banks in other areas and other entrepreneurs will see an opportunity for profit. Bank supervisors should see a "need" for new facilities.

The above arguments may seem persuasive to many in the banking community. However, the regulatory agencies should not accept them easily. It is by no means obvious that the prospects of obtaining new business will stimulate banks to more effective competition. This would seem to depend on the extent to which banks find it profitable to compete. In a highly concentrated market, it may still be more profitable to follow customary rather than competitive patterns of behavior. Indeed, evidence from the experience of other industries suggest that competition frequently becomes intense, not when conditions are prosperous, but when they are depressed and there is pressure on earnings. I would suggest that we simply do not have enough evidence to state with assurance the effect of the rate of economic growth and changes in the rate of growth on the competitive behavior of banks.

On the other hand, there probably is enough evidence to state that economic growth can, at times, convert a marginal competitor to a larger and more effective competitor. Much would depend on the attitude of management. But, at the same time, such banks may also be very attractive merger partners for larger banks. If a permissive policy is adopted, it is difficult to see how this source of increased competition would be realized.

There should, nevertheless, be room for new banking facilities in a rapidly growing area whereas there might not be room in a slowly growing area. But whether or not the new growth is accommodated by "inside" banks on the one hand, or "outside" banks and new charters on the other, depends in part on the attitude of bank supervisors who regulate branching and new charters, and also in part on the aggressiveness of the larger banks already in the area. If the large and aggressive "inside" banks are permitted to acquire the most favorable office sites through de novo branching or merger, particularly with financially marginal institutions—and they have some real advantages in finding them—the entry of new organizations may be quite limited. The establishment of new branches, and mergers with marginal institutions may make it more difficult for new entrants to become established in the fringe areas. In the long run, the effect would be to maintain the same or even higher levels of concentration.

There appears to be, however, an inverse relationship between concentration and growth. Slow growing areas often have higher concentration ratios than rapidly growing areas. This is understandable. Regulatory policy, which in part is aimed at protecting existing banks from excessive competition, tends to be restrictive toward new entry in stagnant areas and perhaps somewhat more permissive towards mergers. The observed inverse relationship between economic growth and banking concentration has, it should be noted, taken place within a framework of bank supervision that has not been permissive toward mergers in rapidly growing areas.

. . . .

If it is not reasonable, in evaluating the competitive effects of mergers, to rely on economic growth in banking as an offset to higher concentration, it does seem reasonable to conclude that merger policy should be viewed as a complement to economic growth in highly concentrated markets. In an unregulated industry, economic growth and the prospect of high return would tend to attract new capital; and if entry barriers are not too high, this should result in an intensification of competition. In a regulated industry like banking, where barriers to entry and concentration are high in part because of regulation, economic growth should be given the opportunity to produce the degree of competition more prosperous conditions

make possible. This means, by and large, permitting new entry to meet rising demands for banking services and also permitting marginal banks to emerge as effective competitors. It is in the slow growth areas that marginal banks are not likely to emerge as effective competitors, and new entry may also be unlikely whatever regulatory policy.

While a more lenient policy toward mergers in growth areas on competitive grounds seems unwarranted as a general proposition, there may, nevertheless, be some justification for such a policy on grounds of convenience and needs. A growing area develops large demands for bank credit. Small local banks may not be able to meet such demands, because of the volume of their resources, their loan limit or simply their customary ways of doing business. It is quite conceivable that, in some cases, mergers in growing areas would involve benefits to the community that offset any anticompetitive impact. This would be particularly true in the absence of banks suitable in size and approach to meet the demands for banking services generated by growth. But just as in the analysis of competition, generalization is difficult, and a careful study of the likely benefits in each case would be required.

It may be concluded that an easier policy toward mergers in growth areas is not warranted as a general proposition. There may, however, be some cases in which the effect of mergers on competition in such areas is offset by the advantages to the community in convenience and needs.